Wallace Li

❖

A LIBRARY OF PROTESTANT THOUGHT

❖

ELIZABETHAN

PURITANISM

Edited by

LEONARD J. TRINTERUD

New York

OXFORD UNIVERSITY PRESS

1971

To Betty

A Library of Protestant Thought

A LIBRARY OF PROTESTANT THOUGHT is a collection of writings intended to illumine and interpret the history of the Christian faith in its Protestant expression. It is as variegated in its literary forms and theological positions as is the movement it mirrors. Tracts, letters, sermons, monographs, and other types of literature comprising the heritage of Protestant thought find a place in this series. Works that were originally composed in English, whether in Great Britain or in the New World, and works that were originally written in other languages, many of them not previously translated into English, are included. But it is neither necessary nor desirable that every segment of Protestant theology, piety, and ethics receive equal space. The trite theology, the conventional piety, and the platitudinous ethics always bulk larger in any tradition, also in the Protestantism of the past four centuries, than does the creative output of the religious spirit. The latter is our primary interest in this Library. While we have not felt obligated to grant them equal attention, we have included works that are typical of the more commonplace literature of the Protestant tradition. On the other hand, some works which logically belong in this series have not been included because they are readily available elsewhere.

In keeping with the fundamental purpose of this Library, the voices of Protestantism are allowed to speak for themselves, with only as much introduction, commentary, and exposition as will in fact allow them to do so. Wherever feasible, documents are reproduced in their entirety. A few representative selections have been preferred to more numerous but shorter passages, for the Library tries to depict the structure of thought rather than the genetic development of a man or a movement. Nevertheless, the variety of Protestant forms precludes a uniform treatment throughout. Our aim has been to be representative rather than exhaustive and to employ the best available tools of critical historical scholarship. Despite its ambitious scope, A Library of Protestant Thought is not an encyclopedia of Protestantism. It is a series of volumes from which not only clergymen and theologians, but students of philosophy, history, literature, political science and other disciplines can gain a more balanced view of how the Protestant mind has thought and spoken since the Reformation.

The Board is grateful to the Hazen Foundation for an initial grant enabling it to begin its work; to the Sealantic Fund, Inc., for a grant making possible Board meetings, consultations, and editorial assistance in the preparation of specific volumes; and to the Oxford University Press for undertaking the publication of the Library.

THE EDITORIAL BOARD

Preface

A COLLECTION OF DOCUMENTS can never be a complete history of the people and times from which they sprang. Yet if the documents have been selected with adequate care they can be wonder-working mirrors of those times and people. Still the reader will be left unsatisfied. And that also is the function of such a volume. It should serve as an invitation to further study.

Few areas of Christian history have drawn more varied scholarly attention than the Puritan movement. At times it seems as though only the zoologists have not studied the Puritans. Economists, psychologists, political scientists, astronomers; historians of art, literature, music, drama and natural science; philosophers, theologians and hagiographers have rumbled and grumbled over the history of the Puritans. And that is the abiding fascination of the field of Puritan studies. Wherever one turns, the vistas in it widen and deepen. Not many fields of history provide a like opportunity for studying the role of Christianity within a culture.

The debts an editor accumulates while preparing a volume such as this are great, and cannot be repaid. I must, however, express my thanks to a few of those persons who have aided me in special ways. Louis B. Wright, William Haller, and Dorothy Mason of the Folger Shakespeare Library in Washington, D.C., made possible, and even more, made enjoyable, several extended periods of study in that unique institution. My former colleague Calvin H. Schmitt, Librarian of the McGaw Memorial Library, McCormick Theological Seminary in Chicago, provided me with an almost unending succession of books, microfilms and photographic copies of every sort. David Green and his staff at the library of San Francisco Theological Seminary have gone the second mile in my behalf on numerous occasions. The Huntington Library of San Marino, California has provided me in recent years with an ideal place for summer study.

Several colleagues have made of my manuscript a much better book. Patrick Collinson of the University of London, Winthrop S. Hudson of

Colgate-Rochester Theological Seminary, and George L. Mosse of the University of Wisconsin, who were my advisory committee, read the manuscript with care, made invaluable comments upon it, and enabled me to clarify and improve it in many ways. My late colleague Joseph Haroutunian, of the University of Chicago, read a part of the manuscript and gave me the benefit of his unrivalled acquaintance with the devious ways of theology.

Although the title page fails to disclose the fact, this volume has had two editors rather than one. My wife transcribed the first draft of the manuscript, working from the Black Letter type, sixteenth-century spelling, and wondrous punctuation of the original publications. She has also carried the burden of checking the several drafts through which a large part of this volume has passed.

Mrs. Glen Egnew prepared the greater share of the final typescript with her usual competence, aided by Mrs. Robert Jones and Mrs. Virginia Reed. To each of them, as well as to Miss Amy Clampitt, copy editor for A Library of Protestant Thought, I am most grateful.

L.J.T.

Abbreviations

Corpus Reform. *Corpus Reformatorum,* edited by C. G. Bretschneider and H. E. Bindseil (87 vols., Brunswick, 1843–1900. Vols. 1–18 published at Halle).

D.N.B. *Dictionary of National Biography,* edited by Leslie Stephen and Sidney Lee (63 vols., London, 1885–1900).

Original Letters *Original Letters Relative to the English Reformation 1531–58 . . . ,* edited by Hastings Robinson (Cambridge, 1846–7; Parker Society).

S.T.C. *A Short-Title Catalogue of Books Printed in England, Scotland, and Ireland, and of English Books Printed Abroad, 1475–1640,* edited by Alfred W. Pollard, Gilbert R. Redgrave *et al.* (London, 1926).

Zurich Letters *The Zurich Letters, Comprising the Correspondence of Several English Bishops and Others During the Early Part of the Reign of Queen Elizabeth,* translated and edited by Hastings Robinson (Cambridge, 1842–5; Parker Society).

Table of Contents

xiii

❖

ELIZABETHAN PURITANISM

❖

General Introduction

THERE WAS SOMETHING odd about the English Puritans. On that, everyone seems to have been in agreement for the last four hundred years. But possibly the oddest thing about them is that, since the name first emerged in Elizabethan England around 1565, there has not been any agreement about who were Puritans or what was Puritanism. The name originated as a term of abuse in the religious propaganda of the period, and from the beginning it was applied to all sorts of people for all sorts of reasons. Throughout the sixteenth century it was used more often as a scornful adjective than as a substantive noun, and was rejected as slanderous in whatever quarter it was applied. But when it came to a definition of what was meant by Puritanism, there was no such unanimity.

The term "Puritan" appeared in England as a new twist in a line of propaganda that was nearly a century old. The pre-Reformation Christian Humanist movement was an attempt by Catholics all over Europe to reform their church according to the example of the churches of the New Testament and the early fathers. Quite in keeping with the Renaissance notion of "returning to the sources," with the Neo-Platonic idea that all things mundane tend toward decline and corruption, and with much of Catholic piety through the centuries, was the idealization by these Christian Humanists of the simplicity, devotion and purity of the primitive Christians. Prior to the Protestant Reformation, these Catholic reformers produced an arsenal of emotionally loaded terms: "abuse," "corruption," "pollution," "contamination," "vices," "degenerate," "regenerate," "reborn," "renovate," "purge," and many more. Implicit in most of these terms was the Christian Humanist view of reform as a "purging from defilement," a "rebirth from a foul and fleshly life to a spiritual life," by returning to the purity and simplicity of the primitive church.[1]

1. See Lewis Spitz, *The Religious Renaissance of the German Humanists* (Cambridge, Mass., 1963). See also Erasmus, *Paraphrases on the New Testament*, English translation (2 vols., 1551–2; *S.T.C.*, 2866), Mark, fol. cxiii–cxv, clxxxi, clxxxvi; Luke, fol. cccliii; John, fol. ccccciiii, ccccxxviii, cccccii; Galatians, fol. cvi *et passim;* Erasmus, *De Puritate Ecclesia, Opera Omnia*, edited by J. Clericus (Leyden, 1703–6), V, 291 f. On the pervasiveness of these views, see also M. Bataillon, *Erasme et l'Es-*

3

Most of the Protestant reformers criticized as inadequate the understandings of sin and grace that underlay the Christian Humanist view of reform. But they accepted, continued and expanded the belief that the standard of Christianity was the purity of the primitive church,[2] and that the medieval era had been one of decay and degeneration. The Protestant reformers continued to employ the same emotional symbols that had grown up in the Christian Humanist literature. At times these were carefully redefined, but very often such expressions as "foul," "rotten," "superstition" and "abuse" were used simply as propaganda terms to elicit a predictable emotional response from the people.

Among the most widely used of these emotional symbols were the Latin terms for "pure," "purity" and "purify." Their very use was an indictment of the Catholic church as "foul" and "corrupt." Moreover, this notion of "pure" refuted the charge that the Protestants were "innovators." Instead, their aim was merely a cleansing of the church. "Pure" carried with its use the culturally respectable idea of "returning to the sources," to the true, original, primitive church — away from the pollutions of the papacy, the monks, and the "accretions to the pure gospel." The terms "pure," "purify" and "purity" were in common use among the German and Swiss reformers — Melanchthon, Bucer, Martyr, Bullinger and Calvin, and many others.[3] They were also prominent in England during the propaganda campaign by Henry VIII against the papacy, a campaign conducted largely by Christian Humanists.[4]

During the early years of the Protestant Reformation these terms associated with "pure" seldom became controversial among the major Protestant leaders. The reformers of southern Germany and Switzerland followed more fully than the Lutherans the attempt at practical reform

---

pagne (Paris, 1937), 153 f; Alfons Auer, *Die vollkommene Frömmigkeit des Christen . . . Erasmus . . .* (Düsseldorf, 1954), 152–8, 172–9, 206–7; Hans Treinen, *Studien zur . . . Gemeinschaft bei Erasmus . . .* (Saarlouis, 1955), 67 f, 92–108; N. K. Andersen, *Confessio Hafniensis* (Copenhagen, 1954); and Berndt Moeller, "Die deutschen Humanisten und die Anfänge der Reformation," *Zeitschrift für Kirchengeschichte*, LXX (1959), 46–61.

2. See especially Peter Fraenkel, *Testimonia Patrum, the Function of the Patristic Argument in the Theology of Philip Melanchthon* (Geneva, 1961).

3. Note this terminology in letters written home to England by various reformers, as collected in G. C. Gorham, *Gleanings . . . during the Period of the Reformation in England . . . 1533–88* (London, 1857), 36, 55–71, 114–18, 132, 188, 216, 226, 232, 277–80, 338, 387–9, 406, 408, 410, 415.

4. J. K. McConica, *English Humanists and Reformation Politics under Henry VIII and Edward VI* (Oxford, 1965).

first advocated by the Christian Humanists.[5] Such reform attempts extended the usage of the terms associated with purification. It was not, however, until the German Interim (1547–55) that these terms became controversial among Protestants. The emperor Charles V commanded the German Lutherans to resume the use of many discontinued Catholic vestments, rites, ceremonies and controls, although he allowed them to retain certain Protestant doctrines, such as that of justification by faith. Some Lutherans led by Melanchthon (Luther himself had died in 1546) sought to ease the agony of the Interim by arguing that so long as "pure doctrine" could be preached, such things as vestments, rites, ceremonies, bishops and other "external matters" were *adiaphora*, i.e., things indifferent. Other Lutherans fought vigorously against the Interim until the order was finally lifted in 1555. The reformers in Strassburg and in Switzerland similarly opposed the Interim. Among these opponents the assertion was commonly made that purity of doctrine had no significance except as a means to actual or practical reform. During the Interim controversy, and afterward as well, the term "purer churches" was in constant use to designate those churches arguing that purity of doctrine was inadequate if it did not lead to the thorough practical reforms instituted by the "best reformed" (i.e., most fully reformed) churches.[6]

During the reign of Edward VI (1547–53) this same controversy was brought into England by such refugees from the German Interim struggle as Bucer, Martyr, Lasco and Fagius, and by such returning English exiles as Hooper, Turner and Coverdale. The notion of the pure primitive church, and the conviction that purity of reform must extend to practice as well as to doctrine, were common in the writings of Cranmer, Ridley, Coxe and other Edwardine leaders. Bucer and Martyr frequently expressed both ideas freely in the works they wrote in England. So did the martyrs and the exiles when Mary restored Catholicism to England. In Frankfort, Strassburg and Basel, the colonies of exiles were now torn by conflict over the terms "pure," "purity" and "purify." In the heresy trials

5. W. Köhler, *Zürcher Ehegericht und Genfer Konsistorium* (2 vols., Leipzig, 1932, 1942).

6. Bullinger to Utenhoven, in Gorham, *Gleanings*, 410. Musculus to Bullinger, in *Original Letters Relative to the English Reformation* (Cambridge, 1846–7), I, 337. R. Gualter and H. Bullinger, *Newes concerning the general councell holden at Trydent* (1549; S.T.C., 24266), fol. 24–5, 45. John Calvin, *Tracts and Treatises*, English translation by H. Beveridge, (London, 1958), III, 189–239, 360–411. Letter to Melanchthon on the Interim, *Corpus Reform.*, *J. Calvini Opera*, (Brunsvigae, 1874), XIII, 593 f.

during Mary's reign, Protestants from Bishop Ridley on down to obscure lay people denounced the vestments as the "filthy rags and ceremonies of Antichrist." [7]

Bishop Jewel, in his "challenge sermon" against the Catholics of November 1559, and again in his *Apology* of 1562, asserted that England was reforming the church according to the pure pattern of the primitive church. This theme was common in Parker's letters and in the works of such older reformers as Becon.[8] Jewel's Catholic opponents attacked this professed recovery of "the pure and unspotted age of the primitive church." They derided the "Lutherans, Zwinglians and Calvinists," their "lies and . . . promises to bring all men to the faith and pureness of the primitive church," and "our new primitive Church of England where the gospel is hottest." [9] These Catholics pointed out, among other things, that there had been no royal supreme head in the primitive church. Christ's church had indeed begun "clean and unspotted" (a reference to Ephesians 5:27), and had continued in "pure and unspotted doctrine" since the beginning. "These protestants . . . so few, so wild, so out of order, and such upstarts," they asserted, were not reforming the church according to its primitive pattern. Rather, like the ancient Donatists they were bringing in novelty, schism and heresy under the guise of reform. They were "right protestant, and of the purest sort." [10]

During these Catholic-Protestant debates over the pure primitive

7. Thomas Cranmer, *Writings and Disputations* . . . (Cambridge, 1847; Parker Society), 97, 354, 366–8, 378, 429–30. Nicholas Ridley, *Works* . . . (Cambridge, 1841; Parker Society), 130, 392. John Bradford, *Writings* . . . (Cambridge, 1849–52; Parker Society), I, 127, 202, 458, 471. *Original Letters*, I, 122, 131–4, 156; II, 769. *A Brief Discourse of the Troubles at Frankfort, 1554-1558 A.D.* (1574; reprint edited by E. Arber, London, 1908), 51, 54, 64, 74, 78. M. Coverdale, ed., *Certain . . . letters of such . . . as gave their lives* . . . (1564; S.T.C., 5886), 42, 55, 216, 346–7, 363, 523. John Foxe, *Actes and monuments* . . . (1563; S.T.C., 11222), fol. 6, 7, 404–7, 883, 1023, 1039–40; also, the condemnation by John Aylmer of the "adiaphorists," i.e., those who obeyed the Interim in Germany, *An harborowe for faithfull and trewe subjects* . . . (1559; S.T.C., 1005), dedicatory epistle, and fol. Hi verso.

8. Matthew Parker, *Correspondence* . . . (Cambridge, 1853; Parker Society), 175, 216, 266.

9. Thomas Dorman, *A proufe of certayne articles . . . denied by M. Juell* (1564; S.T.C., 7062), fol. 80b. Thomas Harding, *A confutation of . . . An apologie for the church of England* (1565; S.T.C., 12762), fol. 259a. Harding, *A reioindre to M. Jewels replie* . . . (1566; S.T.C., 12760), fol. 245 recto. John Jewel, *An apologie of private Masse . . . with an answer* [by T. Cooper] (1562; S.T.C., 14615), fol. 7b.

10. Thomas Stapleton, *A Fortresse of the faith* (1565; S.T.C., 23232), fol. 34 recto, 40 recto, 41 recto, 62 verso.

church, the English Protestants themselves fell into disagreement over what reforms were called for in the English church. The controversy that ensued among the English Protestants over vestments, ceremonies and church ornaments brought numerous ironic comments from Catholic controversialists, who asserted that the hollowness of their pretence to be following the pattern of the pure primitive church was being revealed. The first printed use of the term "Puritan" seems to have occurred in these Catholic attacks on the official Anglican policy statements. In an attack on Jewel, Nowell and the Protestant claims for the primitive church in general, Thomas Stapleton, a Catholic, referred almost in passing to "the Puritans" and the vestment controversy. The censor's date on his book, which abounded with epithets and maledictions, was June 23, 1565.[11]

The following year the term "Puritan" appeared in another Catholic polemic, whose author was John Martial, a don at Oxford during the reigns of Edward and Mary, and now an exile in Brussels. The outcry of the Protestant leaders — notably Parker, Coxe and Jewel — against Elizabeth's retention of the crucifix on her chapel altar, despite the royal injunction in 1560 that crucifixes were to be removed from all churches, had been vigorous, and in 1564 Martial had capitalized on the issue in a *Treatise of the Cross*. There had been an answer by James Calfhill of Oxford in 1565. Martial's reply, passed by the Catholic censor at Brussels on June 12, 1566, brought up the controversy over the vestments, whose use Calfhill had once opposed. "May not some hot puritans of the new clergy be dispensed with," Martial inquired, "for wearing of a long gown, square cap, and satin tippet, unless all be dispensed withal? I think you will gladly subscribe to these: and if they be lawful, why may not the cross of Christ be honored, worshipped and esteemed, unless all other means and instruments heretofore wrought be esteemed [to be merely] of us?" In another passage, Martial used the phrase, "a plain puritan, and notorious protestant."[12] Two years later, Thomas Harding's *Detection*, directed against Jewel, used the terms "Puritan" and "unspotted brethren," and referred contemptuously to a certain "Browne." Other accounts, by the Spanish ambassador, De Silva, and by John Stowe (1568), mention secret, underground, separatist sects in London that had been referred to con-

11. Stapleton, *Fortresse . . .* , fol. 134 verso. See also the long list of epithets used in John Martial, *A treatyse of the crosse* (1564; S.T.C., 17496).

12. Martial, *A replie to M. Calfhills blasphemovs answer . . .* (1566; S.T.C., 17497), fol. 185, 80 recto.

temptuously by the English authorities themselves as "unspotted brethren," "Puritans" and "Brownings," among other epithets.[13] Thomas Cartwright's later assertion that the name Puritan had first been invented by
the Catholics, and adopted from them by the English bishops, was therefore plausible.[14]

By sheer chance, then, the name "Puritan" seems to have achieved currency as one among the many employed by Catholic opponents of the
new official English religion to express their contempt for the English
claim to be restoring the purity and simplicity of the primitive church,
while their own ranks were torn apart by controversy over vestments and
the prerogatives of the royal head. The name became fixed in the polemics of the era when Martial, by calling Calfhill a Puritan, mocked Jewel's
learned defense of Anglicanism as the restoration of the pure primitive
church. At this stage (1565–6) the name had no more status than many
other epithets which have long since disappeared. However, because of
the background of controversy behind the terms "pure," "purity" and
"purify," once "Puritan" had been coined it came quickly into use.

It is significant that Parker and the officials who enforced the wearing
of the vestments did not attach the name of Puritan to those who refused
to wear them, but confined themselves to "good sprights," "silly recusants," "precise men," and other contemptuous phrases. Parker used "mediocrity" in describing his own position. Not until 1572 (after the Admonition controversy) did Parker and his colleagues begin to use the term
"Puritan" for their critics, and even then they also continued to use the
earlier adjective "precise."[15] Catholic controversialists went on belabor-
ing the term "Puritan" for the rest of the century, often as an equivalent
of "Protestant," or as the equivalent of what Protestantism would be if its
English advocates were not too cowardly and ambitious to be consistent.
At other times they set Puritan against Anglican in an effort to discredit
the entire Elizabethan establishment. In due time "mediocrity" (what
Jewel called "leaden mediocrity") became sanctified as the *via media*, and
"Puritan" became a term of limitless application for all who opposed the

13. Harding, *A detection of . . . errours . . . by M. Jewell* (1568; S.T.C., 12763),
fol. 332 recto; Albert Peel, *The First Congregational Churches . . . , 1567–81* (Cambridge, 1920), 20–21.

14. Thomas Cartwright, *A replye to an answere . . . of . . . Whitegift* (1574;
S.T.C., 4711), 172. The Browne referred to by Harding is almost certainly the John
Browne mentioned below as a possible compiler of the *Fortress of Fathers.*

15. Matthew Parker, *Correspondence,* 272, 278, 284, 377, 398, 408, 429, 439, 450,
et passim. Other writers used much the same terminology.

status quo. By the 1590s "Puritan" was being used by the dominant group in English society as an emotional symbol for things as various as sedition, foreign influence, hypocrisy, usury, social rank, popular unrest, rigidity and singularity. Like the terms "popery" and "Jew," the term "Puritan" was now firmly established in the language as an emotionally loaded word far removed from the historical situation that had given rise to the name. Against such a background, the historian who attempts to establish precisely who "the Puritans" were, or to make a catalog of their specific characteristics, cannot but meet with difficulty.

Defined as simply as possible, Puritanism was the Protestant form of dissatisfaction with the required official religion of England under Elizabeth. Like the Catholic discontent, it varied in area of concern and in intensity. At the beginning of the new religious regime, early in 1559, the overwhelming majority of Englishmen, laymen as well as clergy, were at least nominally Roman Catholic; certainly they were not Protestant. By the close of the same year all but one or two per cent of these had made the legally required submission to the compromise Elizabethan religious policy. This submission, however, was often reluctant and without conviction. In early 1559 the convinced Protestants were a tiny minority in England—perhaps amounting to no more than five per cent of the clergy, and to an even smaller proportion among the laity. By the end of 1559 they too had submitted to the new form of the established religion, but likewise reluctantly and with misgivings. No significant group had accepted the new religious policy with enthusiasm. Thus by 1559-60, although in theory the nation had acquired religious uniformity, there was active dissatisfaction both among former Catholics, who sought to retain or regain some part of their religious heritage, and among radical Protestants, who wanted further religious changes. The official leadership itself included both uneasy former Catholics and restless radical Protestants, along with perplexed defenders of the establishment. All three parties passed through several major phases in the course of Elizabeth's reign.

By the mid-1570s various wings or parties had begun to emerge among the Protestant religious radicals in England. Officialdom was by then indiscriminately applying the contemptuous term "Puritan" to all of them. No neatly systematic classification of the opinions and activities of these radicals is possible. But a roughly comprehensive typology can be established, out of which three wings or parties are distinguishable by the mid-1570s: the original anti-vestment party; the passive-resistance party; and the Presbyterian party.

Although there was agreement among the members of Groups I and II that to resist divinely instituted authority was a sin, they differed in their ultimate hopes. The members of Groups II and III had much in common in the area of goals. Their disagreement was over timing and tactics in the effort to bring about reform. Serious clashes broke out at times between the members of Groups I and III, whose differences were great. Nevertheless, the three parties had enough in common to make them all discontented with the established order, and to make them all Puritans in the eyes of the authorities on most occasions. (It must be reiterated that any attempt at consistent and coherent classification must eventually break down, defeated by the constantly changing character of what was essentially a protest movement. Professor Patrick Collinson is certainly right in saying that the circumstances in which a given Puritan preacher found himself often had much to do with the manner in which he expressed his protest. Under a friendly bishop a man might have held a position identifiable with Group I or II, whereas under Archbishop Whitgift the same man might easily have become an aggressive Presbyterian.)

GROUP I: THE ORIGINAL, ANTI-VESTMENT PARTY

Although it seems not at first to have been officially labelled "Puritan," the party organized in the 1560s against the wearing of clerical vestments turned out to have been the opening phase of the Puritan movement. This wing of Puritanism has been discussed by historians under a variety of names, such as "original Puritans," "vestment Puritans," "episcopal Puritans" and "conforming Puritans" — all of which suggest that after a brief conflict in the 1560s the great majority of these Puritans chose to remain within the unchanged official church, and were responsible for little further controversy.

Those who had raised the controversy against the vestments in the 1560s were in general older men, who had served in the Edwardine church or had been Marian exiles, or at any rate looked to that era for guidance and inspiration. By the mid-1570s a majority, though not all, of the survivors among these men were persuaded that it was wicked to rebel against the Queen, and that "worse" men would replace them if they gave up the ministry because of the vestment controversy. They desired no structural changes in the church, nor did they look to the Continent for guidance. The experiences of those who had once been Marian exiles were now far behind them. Of this group Laurence Humphrey, Robert Crowley, John Foxe, John Philpot and bishops Parkhurst and Pilkington were typical. Their dislike of official policy was well known. But they made the minimal conformity, accepted the church structure as it was established, and worked for reform through preaching and teaching, while urging obedience to authority upon their followers. In general, their outlook was distinctly passive. This stance proved persuasive to many Englishmen, and by the close of Elizabeth's reign it was so typical of grass-roots Protestantism in England that "Puritan" has often been used interchangeably with pre-Laudian Anglicanism, and has been applied to men as different as Archbishop George Abbot and Edmund Spenser. In this volume, however, the views of this group are not documented past the decade of the 1570s, because thereafter those who refused to move into Group II or Group III became less and less self-consciously a wing of the Puritan opposition. Rather, they became more and more a wing of the established church. Yet in many respects their attitudes remained "Puritan."

From among the many available documents for the study of this original radical Protestant group of the 1560s, three have been selected:

The Prologue by John Gough to an abridged edition of Erasmus' *Enchiridion* (1561).

Two prefaces from the *Acts and Monuments* of John Foxe (1563, 1570).

The Fortress of Fathers, by "J. B." (1566).

These documents, in some ways very different, reflect most of the major facets of the original radical Protestant opposition to the Elizabethan Settlement. They also indicate the junctures or nodes from which divergences would soon spring to prevent Puritanism from becoming a cohesive movement with a single set of acknowledged leaders and clear-cut policies.

GROUP II: THE PASSIVE-RESISTANCE PARTY

This group represents the majority of Puritans during the reign of Elizabeth. It is best known for its famous preachers — men such as Edward Dering (1540?–76), Richard Greenham (1535–94), William Perkins (1558–1602), and John Preston (1587–1628). They shared with those typical of Group I a dislike of vestments, ceremonies, "popery," etc. But they did not agree with the older men of that group that the basic structure of the church was satisfactory, or that the reforms they desired could be achieved by proper use of its existing structure. Most of them were in sympathy with proposals then current for eliminating the hierarchical structure of the church, and for either modifying or abolishing the episcopate and the ecclesiastical court system.

These men, however, refused to accept the aggressive role of the activist "Presbyterians" who formed Group III. They were in effect "passive resisters." Through the popular preaching and intensive pastoral work to which they devoted their chief efforts, they hoped to build up a sufficient following among laymen to compel the authorities to make the changes they believed were necessary. Along with the "Presbyterian" group, they looked to Parliament rather than the Crown to put those changes into effect. In their terminology, this was "tarrying until the Lord moved the heart of the magistrate."

Those Puritans who adopted the tactics of passive resistance to the official religion of Elizabethan England have drawn much attention and widely divergent evaluations from historians. They have perhaps most often been dealt with as representing "standard" or "normative" Puritanism, and constituting the main branch of the movement. But some historians have regarded these men as half-way Puritans, as not Puritans at all, or as proto-Separatists who were thus the forerunners of the "real" Puritans — i.e., the Independents and the Separatists. Their choosing the route of passive resistance meant that in some manner they usually retained a place in the official church, that they sublimated their opposition in various ways, and that they avoided at all cost any overt moves that might involve them in rebellion or schism. Were they not, therefore, merely Anglicans? To that question the standard response has been to emphasize that these men were truly a resistance movement. For the same reason, some historians have also been over-quick to find these men secret conspirators and seditious, or inconsistent and cowardly.

The writings of these men were regarded by Puritans of the following century as being among the most generally approved and standard works. They were almost all learned, able preachers and academics who through intermarriage and other personal ties formed a "spiritual brotherhood" extending over most of southeastern England. They had the aid of numerous patrons and supporters in the Privy Council, among London lay leaders, and from the country nobles and gentry. An attitude of passive resistance made it possible for such persons to defend them with relative impunity.

Because of this same passive resistance, and because these men subli- mated their opposition in a variety of ways, the Puritanism they represent is not easy to define. The following documents have been selected to show something of the range of opinion that existed within this wing:

A sermon preached before the Queen (1570), and a letter to Mrs. Barret (c. 1572), by Edward Dering.

A speech in the House of Commons, 8 February 1576, and ten questions presented to the House of Commons, 1 March 1587, by Peter Went- worth.

The Order of the Prophecy at Norwich (1575).

Three prefaces to the Geneva Bible (1560, 1576).

Over four centuries scarcely a scholar has failed to classify these docu- ments as Puritan, although scholarly judgment upon them has ranged all the way from wrath, through cynical scorn and kindly indulgence, to lavish praise. So, whatever Puritanism was, these documents would seem to have been a part of it.

GROUP III: THE PRESBYTERIAN PARTY

The third and most radical wing or party, whose members were later known as the "Presbyterian" Puritans, emerged between 1570 and 1572. Its original young leaders included Thomas Cartwright, William Fulke, John Field and Thomas Wilcox, all of whom had entered the ministry under Elizabeth. They differed from the earliest group of Puritans in sev- eral ways. For these new men, the disputes over vestments, rites and other "abuses" were merely symptoms of more fundamental problems. They demanded far-reaching structural changes in the church, in its administra- tion and finances, and in the relation between church and state, as well as in doctrine and liturgy. Although none of its earliest spokesmen had been abroad before 1572, the members of this wing were international in their orientation. From time to time they invoked the name of Calvin (dead since 1564), but chiefly they had their eyes on the "Calvinistic" Hugue- nots and the Protestants of the Palatinate and the Netherlands, as well as Scotland. Like the Huguenots, the Dutch Calvinists and the party of Knox in Scotland, these men were activists who considered it their duty to work aggressively for reforms, and who believed that their endeavors could force the civil authorities to act. Usually, though not always, they were advocates of a greater role for Parliament in church affairs.

A few of the men who first opposed the vestments, such as Gilby,

Whittingham, Sampson and Browne, were associated to some degree with this Presbyterian wing. So, in certain ventures, were Dering, Perkins, Greenham and Preston, among others. Moreover, the grievances, the concern for preaching, the personal ties and the lay followings that all three wings had in common often overshadowed the differences among them. But whenever a serious issue arose, the Presbyterians' activist demand for far-reaching structural change would be either resisted or evaded by the more passive Groups I and II. Most of the time, in the eyes of the authorities the members of all three wings were lumped together as "wretched Puritans." Occasionally, the first two wings, with their passive orientation, were identified as dutiful subjects of her Majesty who realized that their grievances were confined to "matters indifferent," and were used by officialdom as examples for the Presbyterians.

The "Presbyterian" wing of the Puritan movement has been so called because of its attempt to make sweeping changes in the structure, functioning, financing and worship of the church along lines usually described as Presbyterian. It developed an organization, with centers in many parts of southeastern England; it attempted to draft constitutional documents for itself; it engaged in extensive controversial propaganda; and it had both the participation and support of a significant number of laymen. For all these reasons, it has been much studied. Because of its international outlook, this wing of Puritanism sought to establish ties with the Calvinistic churches of Scotland, France, the Netherlands, Germany and Switzerland, and its basic theories were worked out far more fully than those of the two less aggressive wings of Puritanism, upon whom the Continental influences were far less strong. The attention of many historians has also been drawn to the Presbyterian party because it was connected (just how is still being debated) with the Puritan Revolution of the seventeenth century and the later Presbyterian church in England. It is not without reason, therefore, that some historians have regarded this wing of Puritanism as the only one, before the emergence of the "Separatist Puritans," with any ideas or program that made it significantly different from Anglicanism. What is often overlooked, however, is that in Elizabethan England neither "episcopal" or "presbyterian" had those infallibly stable definitions and connotations which function as controlling assumptions in many historical studies.

The selections presented for this wing of the Puritan movement are longer than those in Parts One and Two. This is not, however, to imply that they mark the advent of "true Puritanism." Rather, these four documents show how, after a period of active debate and some organized effort, the implications of certain basic Puritan ideas had begun to work out: they had produced dismay in some who had once thought they were Puritans; they had aroused some hitherto sluggish defenders of the official church; and they had brought some enthusiasts to the edge of rebellion, only to recoil in confusion over their own ideas. The selections also show how, by the middle of Elizabeth's reign, certain theological ideas had begun to develop which gave this wing of Puritanism a character somewhat different from that of earlier forms of Puritan thought.

The documents presented here for study are:

A Brief and Plain Declaration . . . (1584), by William Fulke.

Lectures . . . upon the Twentieth Chapter of Exodus . . . (1577), by John Knewstub.

The answer of Eusebius Paget before the Ecclesiastical Commissioners (1584).

A Brief Treatise of Oaths Exacted by Ordinaries and Ecclesiastical Judges (1600), by James Morice.

Such a classification of Elizabethan Puritanism into three groups or wings may serve to explain how throughout the forty years of Elizabeth's reign there was a clearly discernible Puritan movement in which there was substantial agreement on many grievances and some desired reforms. But common action was ruled out by differences on the underlying cause of those grievances and the means of rectifying them. Out of the frustration experienced by all three wings, all committed to the same ideal of a national church which, with the aid of the civil authority, would enforce the true religion, a fourth Puritan group began to emerge, late in the reign of Elizabeth. It consisted of men committed to the view that the Puritan ideals in religion could be achieved only in small gathered or covenanted groups, either within or outside of the national church. Even these early "Separatists," however, were largely in agreement with the general Puritan outlook, especially in preaching and piety. Theologically, the differences among these four Puritan wings were over the relation between nature and grace, between reason and revelation, between law and gospel, and between the meanings of history and of eschatology; or, to put it more simply, how man's role was to be understood in light of the belief that all definitive events in the world were the acts of God. In short, how was a religious reformer to function in such a world?

Instead, then, of an abstract definition, this volume is based on a historical approach to Elizabethan Puritanism. The documents it offers for study were written during the reign of Elizabeth I by men who were called Puritans, and who were active defenders of positions representative of the three major groups denounced as Puritan. (The Separatists are to be discussed in another volume in this series.) As these documents and others referred to in the editor's comments make very plain, there can be no simple definition of that Puritanism which was so fiercely opposed by Elizabeth and her ecclesiastical lieutenants during forty long years. Protean the Puritan movement was. But, as the officials complained repeatedly, Puritanism was present everywhere in England, and it was as versatile as it was unrelenting in its opposition to the royalist-episcopal policies.

In choosing the documents that follow, I have aimed to show chronologically the developing and complex character of that religious outlook in England which was denounced as Puritan.

There can be no denying that when, out of the welter of Elizabethan Puritan literature, published and unpublished, an editor selects seven small books, a speech, a letter, and several official minutes, he is assuming — not to speak of presuming — a good deal. What those assumptions add up to is his own view of the course taken by English Protestantism during the reign of Elizabeth I. These documents can, of course, be approached in their own right, or indeed in defiance of that view. Nevertheless, it is hoped the essays that precede each of the documents may afford the reader some initial orientation to the field of Puritan studies.

PART ONE

❖

The Original, Anti-vestment Party

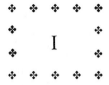

I

JOHN GOUGH

Prologue to an Abridged Edition
of Erasmus' Enchiridion

Editor's Introduction

What, after religion had been newly "established" in 1559, did Englishmen think it was? One interesting answer is found in the Prologue John Gough wrote for an anonymous abridgment of Erasmus' *Enchiridion*, published in 1561. It is also a good example of the outlook that gave rise to the "vestment controversy."

John Gough was the son of a bookseller of the same name who was active in London *c.* 1526–43. The elder Gough died *c.* 1556, after having been in trouble several times for publishing and selling heretical books.[1] The younger Gough was ordained deacon by Bishop Grindal on January 14, 1560.[2] He seems not to have been a Marian exile, and apparently was not a university graduate. On November 15, 1560, he was presented to the traditionally radical parish of St. Peters in Cornhill, London, by the Mayor, Aldermen and Commonalty of London. Thereafter he was frequently associated with the more advanced reformers, such as Robert Crowley (once a printer and seller of radical religious books, then a preacher, then a Marian exile, and, after his return to England, archdeacon of Hereford and pastor of a London church). Gough, along with Crowley, was also one of the Saint Antholin Lecturers in London, a popularly supported team of vigorous preachers of practical reform.[3]

1. On John Gough, Sr., see E. G. Duff, *A Century of the English Book Trade* (London, 1905), which gives the year of his death as 1543, whereas *D.N.B.* gives it as 1556.
2. J. Strype, *History of the Life and Acts of . . . Edmund Grindal . . .* (Oxford, 1821), 53.
3. *The Diary of Henry Machyn . . .* (1550–63), edited by J. G. Nichols (London, 1848; Camden Society), XLII, 269, 285, 387 n. By error Nichols identified

From the time of his ordination, Gough was associated with the middle-class merchants, artisans and popular preachers who were uneasy about the state of religion under the Elizabethan Settlement. On March 20, 1565, he was one of twenty ministers who sought vainly for some amicable compromise with the Ecclesiastical Commissioners over the wearing of vestments. Included in the group were three of the archdeacons of London — John Mullins, Thomas Cole and James Calfhill — together with Alexander Nowel, the dean of St. Paul's, Miles Coverdale, Crowley, John Foxe, Laurence Humphrey, Thomas Lever, Thomas Sampson, William Whittingham and Percival Wiburn. A year later, on March 26, 1566, Gough, with thirty-six others, was suspended from his benefice for nonconformity in the wearing of clerical vestments. In June he was sent into the diocese of Winchester, where he was kept under house arrest, in care of Bishop Robert Horne. Only Gough, Crowley and John Philpot received equally severe treatment. They, along with John Barthlet, were regarded as the leaders of the non-conformist party in London.[4] After the Parliament of 1571, in which religious issues were vigorously debated, Gough was among the ten prominent Puritan leaders brought before the Ecclesiastical Commission in a futile effort to reduce them to conformity.[5] Gough was then unemployed, although his controversy with John Fecknam, published in 1570, indicates that he was preaching occasionally in London. After 1571 he drops from sight.

Gough was responsible for two publications. The first, *A Godly Book Wherein is Contained Certain Fruitful, Godly, and Necessary Rules, to be Exercised and Put in Practice by All Christ's Soldiers Living in the Camp of this World* (1561; S.T.C., 12132), was the abridgment of Erasmus' *Enchiridion* to which he contributed a prologue. The second was *The Answer of John Gough to Master Fecknam's Objections Against His Sermon Lately Preached in the Tower* (1570; S.T.C., 12131).

Gough says in his prologue that he found this "godly boke" in manuscript, without any indication of its title or authorship, and that these re-

---

Gough with another of that name (a fairly common one in Tudor records) beneficed at Braintree in Essex. See also Isabel M. Calder, "The St. Antholin Lectures," *Church Quarterly Review*, CLX (1959), 49–70.

4. P. Collinson, *The Elizabethan Puritan Movement* (London, 1967), 74–7, 82, 93.

5. The men were Goodman, Lever, Sampson, John Walker, Wiburn, Gough, Edward Dering, Whittingham, John Field and Robert Johnson. See M. M. Knappen, *Tudor Puritanism* (Chicago, 1939), 230.

main unknown to him. Inasmuch as his father had published at least one of Erasmus' works, *Sileni Alcibiadis* (n.d.; *S.T.C.*, 10507), and was closely associated with others in the selling and circulating of such books, the manuscript probably came to him through his family or its associates. There would have been little reason for Gough to conceal the author's identity if he had known it. Associates of his such as Coverdale, Calfhill and Foxe were admirers of Erasmus, and the *Paraphrases on the New Testament* by Erasmus were required to be set up openly in all the churches at the time.

This abridged version of the *Enchiridion* depends in no way on the abridgment made by Coverdale (1545; *S.T.C.*, 10488). Whoever prepared Gough's abridgment had done it from the Latin rather than from the complete English translation that first appeared in 1533, and that had been reprinted at least seven times by 1550. The abridgment found by Gough had been well done and was in no way tendentious. It remained an Erasmian, Christian Humanist expression of the "philosophy of Christ," the "simple faith." Passages emphasizing the Erasmianism that angered Luther remained essentially Erasmian.[6] Some of the more strident critiques of the clergy had been toned down,[7] but Erasmus' great concern for "purity" appears in several contexts throughout the abridgment.[8] The numerous marginal notes, presumably by Gough, are based largely on the text itself, and emphasize practical religion rather than theology.

The entire thrust of Gough's prologue is the Christian Humanist concern for earnest, practical godliness following the rule of the Scripture. As in Erasmus' *Enchiridion* itself, the Christian life is seen as a struggle against impurity, vice, superstition and external religion. The godly, he declared, had always been a remnant, subject to persecution. The "dirty dregs," "dirty traditions," "foolish ceremonies," superstitious popular piety, monastic observances, worship of saints and the like, belonged to England's Catholic past, a time of darkness that the true gospel had now begun to dispel. Gough naively assumed that his readers would know

6. *Cf.* the great emphasis on the rewards of godliness, fol. Av verso, vi recto, Bii verso, iii recto, Ciii, Dviii, Evi, viii verso, Gi recto, iv verso. On the "rule of Christ only," see Hv recto; on "simplicity," Ivi; on "desire for heavenly things," Mii verso.

7. For instance, the passage on fol. Lii verso is much abridged, as is the section on ceremonies, Gviii verso–Hi recto.

8. *Cf.* fol. Biii recto, vii, Ci verso, Eviii recto, Gv verso, vi verso, Liiii recto, *et passim.*

what true godliness was, that the nation was officially committed to that godliness, and that the problem before England now was the practical one of turning to God. Three years later, the tiny Protestant minority within the Church of England was itself torn asunder by internal differences that neither the new English bishops nor men like Gough had foreseen. These differences were over the direction the Church of England as now established ought to take in its attempt to win the people, and they gave rise in their turn to the so-called "vestiarian controversy" of the 1560s.

Since the sixteenth century, this clash of opinion has often been interpreted as a native English rejection of foreign ideologies imported into England by the returning Marian exiles, notably those from Switzerland, and in particular from Geneva. This interpretation, common though it still is, derives from a superficial reading of both Continental and English history, and must be qualified if not entirely reformulated. The vestment controversy was rooted far more deeply in the English past than in Geneva or in Zurich. It was this fact, as patent to Archbishop Parker as it was to the arch-Puritans Gough and Crowley, that made the controversy so hopelessly muddled for all concerned.

Between 1559 and 1561, the percentage of Englishmen, both laymen and clergy, who could be called "Protestant" in terms of current German or Swiss theology was extremely small. Moreover, the overwhelming majority of Englishmen knew very little about Lutheranism, Zwinglianism, Calvinism, or any other form of Continental "heresy." And they were opposed to what they did know about these heresies. They wished to remain nominal Catholics, even though many included the papacy in their hatred of things foreign. How, then, was the new Elizabethan church to deal with such Englishmen? By 1560 Parliament and the Royal Visitation had made it plain that "the Elizabethan Settlement" was not to become the springboard for a resolute protestantizing of the nation.

In the fearful controversies that created deepening divisions within Continental Lutheranism between 1558 and 1580, Englishmen saw little to emulate. The frequent comment among them was indeed that the controversies over the sacraments and the Interim which had torn Germany to pieces must be avoided at all costs. English Protestants who understood German theology were aware, moreover, that although Lutherans might war among themselves concerning certain doctrines, they were united in condemning as heretical the church reforms carried out in England under Henry and Edward, and likewise all that had been done by the martyrs under "Bloody Mary." The Lutherans were united as well in condemning the churches of those Continental Protestants who had befriended the Marian exiles.

Those few Englishmen who during the years from 1559 to 1561 were in some measure disposed to follow the lead of the Reformed churches of the Continent, were not of one mind in either theology or churchmanship. They had not all been exiles under Mary, and those who had been, had spent the years of exile among various kinds of Reformed churches and had also reacted in different ways to their Continental experiences. Moreover, as churchmen belonging to a minority group they had no sense of a common program, and no acknowledged leader or spokesman. Also, those former exiles who had developed the closest personal ties with leaders of the Reformed churches on the Continent — namely, those who had been in Zurich — very quickly moved into high offices in the Elizabethan establishment. The English government was resolutely opposed to any ideological or theological approach to church affairs. Consequently, no matter how much a bishop like Jewel, Parkhurst or Pilkington might prefer the ways of Zurich, he could not become a religious and theological leader such as Bullinger or Gualter of Zurich. The civil authorities did encourage these men to become, like Jewel, stalwarts against Rome. But the civil policy effectively prevented these men, whose adherence to the ways of Zurich was deep and well-informed, quite aside from personal ties, from developing through the pulpit, the school, the university and the printing press, a thorough, comprehensive, ideologically grounded reform of church and society, such as had taken place at Zurich. The "English Zurchers" became *ex officio* the administrators of a deliberately non-ideological national religious establishment based on compromise.

The leadership in this ideological battle — the battle for the English mind — passed almost at once to self-appointed, uncontrolled city pastors, to free-lance writers (laymen as well as clergy), and to independent printers; in short, to the popular pulpit and press. As under Henry and again under Edward, no attempt to reach the popular mind was made by official spokesmen, but only by those self-appointed groups with whom officialdom often found itself at cross-purposes. Among the ringleaders of this popular propaganda campaign in the years from 1559 to 1561 were John Gough, Crowley, Coverdale, Becon, Lever and others who had been active even in the time of Henry. The movement included men who had been underground Protestants in Mary's reign, as well as former exiles.

The most active of the latter, however, had not been at Zurich (few of those who had settled at Geneva returned until late in 1559, and some not until mid-1560) but were the intensely English refugees who had settled at Frankfort, Strassburg and Basel — cities in which the local clergy had been hostile or indifferent toward the English, and where the struggle over the Interim had been acute.

The appeal made by these popular preachers and publicists had been very English, and at first it operated within the limits of the new establishment. They urged a popular, practical, biblicistic religion, based not upon Continental patterns but on the tradition of reform they had advocated under Henry and Edward. The death of Edward was only six years in the past, and Henry had died only six years before Edward. Beginning in 1559, these self-appointed propagandists produced a steady stream of works by and concerning Bradford, Careless, Cranmer, Hooper, Hutchinson, Latimer, Philpot, Ridley, Rogers and Tyndale. Many of those who had already been active even during Henry's reign — including Bale, Becon, Coverdale, Crowley and Veron — reissued their old works (often with little revision) and produced new ones. The Paraphrases of Erasmus on the New Testament, in their oddly composite English version, lent themselves perfectly to this conception of practical reform. John Foxe's martyrology, begun during the Marian exile and destined to pass through many later editions, blended into one English religion the memory of Bilney, Latimer, Tyndale, Lambert, Barnes, Cranmer, Hooper, Ridley and many more who had differed over theology while they were alive. Foxe's vigorous defense of Erasmus and his Paraphrases was fully in keeping with this attempt to restore the true faith of England. John Gough's earnest espousal of practical reform, and the theology of Erasmus, was just about what was called for by the Elizabethan Settlement. But the Parliament and Convocation of 1563 would soon bring many Englishmen face to face with the stern realization that whereas practical reform meant reform in practice, reform was just as contrary to the policy of the Crown as an ideology would have been. It was then that Gough and most of his fellow advocates of a popular, practical reform based on a rather loosely construed theology, turned rebel against the Elizabethan Settlement.

The text of Gough's prologue has been taken, by permission, from the unique perfect copy in the Henry E. Huntington Library. The *S.T.C.* lists a copy of the prologue only at the Bodleian Library, Oxford. Apparently the work was never reprinted.

Gough's biblical quotations are taken mostly from the Great Bible of

1540; some are from Tyndale's New Testament of 1535, and a few seem to be his own translations from the Vulgate or quotations from memory.

❖ ❖ ❖ ❖

A Godly Book

wherein is contained certain fruitful, godly and necessary rules to be exercised and put in practice by all Christ's soldiers living in the camp of this world

[1561]

CUM PRIVILEGIO AD IMPRIMENDUM SOLUM

John Gough, Pastor to the Parish of Saint Peter's in Cornhill of London, to the Christian Reader.

Grace, mercy, and peace from God the Father, and from our Lord Jesus Christ his Son, be with thee, good Christian reader, and with all those that love the Lord unfeignedly. Amen. Calling to remembrance the saying of Jesus the son of Sirach in Ecclesiasticus 20:30, "Wisdom that is hid and treasure that is hoarded up, what profit is in them both?" [I] thought it no less than my bounden duty (after I had perused this work) to do my endeavor that the same might be put in print, whereby others might be partakers with me therein. For after I had read the same, and finding therein so heavenly doctrine, so consonant and agreeing with God's book, and so meet for the use of all estates and sorts of people (being Christians), [I] thought I should do injury to God and wrong to my Christian brethren if I should any longer detain the same from them. And as I know not the author thereof, no more found I any title or name given unto the book, but for that the author took (as it were for his theme) the beginning of the seventh chapter of Job, where he saith, "the life of man is a warfare upon the earth and his days like the days of an hired servant." Whereupon he hath most livelily set before our eyes as well how we are incessantly assaulted and assailed by the continual flattering promises of the world, the carnal allurements and enticements of our domestic enemy, the flesh, and crafty temptations and provocations of our old enemy the devil (which three fierce and cruel enemies never cease day nor night to invade us and what they can to provoke us, to fall from God) as also our duties both in the resistance of sin and of cleaving to our captain and head, Christ, and also by certain rules instructing us, as it were with a certain armor and weapon, both how to bear of the sudden invasions of those our enemies, and also to repulse them when they shall assail us.

Wherefore that the name of the book might agree with the work, I thought it good to attribute to the same such a name as the work desired: (that is to say) "Godly and necessary rules to be exercised and put in practice by all Christ's soldiers living in the camp of this world." And in the diligent reading of this work and digesting of the same, thou shalt well perceive (dear reader) that the life of a very Christian (of what estate or degree soever he be) to exceed and far pass the counterfeit lives of cloyning cloisterers, of mumming monks, fond friars, or of hypocritical hermits, and that we need not run to seek a straight life among the Charterhouse monks for the perfection of a Christian life. But as the same is most perfectly set forth in God's book (I mean the sacred Scriptures), so it is to be followed of all Christians (if we will be Christians indeed).

For it is not the name of a Christian that maketh us Christians before God, unless we have also the deeds of Christians, as Christ saith in Matthew 7:21, "Not whosoever saith unto me Lord, Lord, shall enter into the kingdom of heaven, but he that doeth the will of my father." And in Luke 6:46 he saith, "Why call ye me master and Lord, and do not that I bid ye?" And Saint John saith, 1 John 2:4, "He that saith I know him, and keepeth not his commandments is a liar, and the truth is not in him." So that as the name of a Jew maketh not a Jew (Romans 2:17), no more doth the name of a Christian make a Christian except we also show forth the works of a Christian. That our Christian lives might shine in purity, in cleanness, in sobriety, in patience, in charity, in long suffering, that the enemies of the gospel, seeing our godly conversation, might be won by the same to the gospel. As Christ saith in Matthew 5:16, "Let your light so shine before men that they, seeing your good works, may glorify your Father which is in heaven." And that they have no cause justly to report evil of us, following the counsel of Seneca in his book *De Moribus*, where he hath this pithy saying: "Have peace with all men, but be at defiance with sin." [1] (God grant that this heathen philosopher rise not at the Judgment to condemn a number of us Christians for our negligence.) [2]

---

1. [ED.] Martin, Bishop of Braga, *A fruteful work of L. A. Seneca called the Myrrour or glasse of maners* (1547; S.T.C., 17502), fol. Biv recto.

2. [ED.] *Cf.* Erasmus, "Saint Socrates, pray for us," in "The Godly Feast," *The Colloquies of Erasmus*, translated by Craig R. Thompson (Chicago, 1965), 68.

So that now, I hope, it is apparent to all eyes that will not willfully be blind, that it is the duty of all Christians to live so straitly in this world, and so earnestly to wrestle against vice and sin, as the weakness of our flesh shall or can bear in our minds detesting and abhorring sin, and from the bottom of our hearts to wish that we could not sin. For it is our part to wrestle against the same, and therein hath the Holy Ghost by his elect vessel, Saint Paul, comforted us, saying in 1 Corinthians 10:13, "God is faithful which shall not suffer you to be tempted above your strength, but shall in the midst of temptation make a way that ye may be able to bear it." And what we are not able to do, by reason of our weakness, that hath Christ fulfilled for us, as the same apostle saith also in Romans 8:3, "For what the law could not do inasmuch as it was weak because of the flesh, that performed God, and sent his Son in the similitude of sinful flesh . . ." And in the beginning of the same chapter he saith, "There is then now no damnation to them that are grafted in Christ Jesus." What? To do what they list, and to run carelessly headlong into sin? Nay, he addeth: "Which walk not after the flesh but after the Spirit." As God himself saith in Leviticus 15 [? 20:26], "Be ye holy for I am holy." So that the life of every true Christian ought to be such as no man worthily can rebuke, which thing is most plentifully, and at the full, set forth in this godly work.

And this I write only to stop the mouths of such as slanderously report and say that these new preachers (for so it pleaseth them to term such as most sincerely preach God's truth) would have no good works, but preach liberty, liberty. Who (indeed) mean nothing less. But because they seek to pluck them from their fond trust in their vain meritorious works taught them by the papists (thereby making Christ but half a savior) and set forth the perfection of a true faith which is most plainly taught us, in Luke 17:10, by Christ himself, by the parable of the servant coming from the plough, which parable he concludeth with this saying: "So ye also, when ye have done all that are commanded you, say we are unprofitable servants, we have done that which was our duty to do." And therefore saith Saint Paul in Ephesians 2:8,9, "For by grace are ye saved, through faith, and that not of yourselves. For it is the gift of God, and not of works, lest any man should boast." And because, that we should not mistake Saint Paul and think that the opinion of faith were enough, and therefore we might be idle and live carelessly, without desire or regard of virtue, he immediately addeth, saying: "For we are his workmanship," saith he, "created in Christ Jesus unto good works, which God hath prepared, that we should walk in them." So that it is most manifest what impudent and unshamefaced liars and slanderers the papists and their adherents are upon God's preachers and his ministers, for neither they nor none other at any time, heard any other doctrine out of any of those preachers' mouths (whom it hath pleased them to call new preachers) but they and their doctrine (I mean the papists) may be called this day's baking in comparison of the antiquity of the doctrine which is taught by those new fellows, than this that I have above written. Which indeed most abundantly and plentifully is set forth in this little book, both godlily and learnedly.

Whereby it may well be perceived that though the time of darkness hath been much in the world, by reason the same hath been so obfuscated and overwhelmed with the dirty traditions of wicked men that the light and purity of God's gospel could not shine; yet was it not hidden from all men. But at all times and in all ages there ever have been some that saw and knew the truth, and left the same in writing to their posterity, as appeareth by this little work which came to my hands written [i.e., in manuscript]. And when I had read the same, considering the antiquity thereof, I remembered the answer of God made to Elijah the Prophet, 1 Kings 19:18, "I have left me," saith God, "7,000 men in Israel whose knees never bowed before Baal nor kissed him with his mouth." So that God always as appeareth (though they be not taken of the worldlings) hath his church and people in the world, though (indeed) they be very few and so have always been (in respect of the contrary part) and oftentimes exercised under the cross and afflicted by the world.

For if we should consider the estate and condition of God's church from the beginning of the world, even until our time, we shall perceive the same, always to be very few in comparison of the residue of the world and that for the most part afflicted. For anon after that Adam and Eve were cast out of paradise, Genesis 3, did not wicked Cain kill just Abel? Genesis 4. And after, as the world increased, so did wickedness abound and sin waxed rife and God so put in oblivion, that, 1556 years after the creation of the world (in the which the deluge or universal flood came whereby all the world was drowned) there was no more found God's people, and God's church, in all the world, but eight persons, that is to say, Noah, his wife, his three sons, and their wives which were saved and escaped the flood, as appeareth in Genesis 7. And after the flood was passed and Noah and his household came out of the ark, the world being divided among his three sons, Shem, Ham and Japheth, and that the people began eftsoons [i.e., soon after] to multiply and increase, the world was so foregrown in wickedness that there was none found that truly worshipped God but Terah, Abraham's father, and his household, as may appear to the diligent reader from the ninth to the twelfth of Genesis. And after the death of Terah, God called Abraham from among the Chaldeans lest he should have him plucked from the true worshipping of God to idolatry which then was rife among the Chaldeans, and flowed also over all the world. Abraham obeyed God's calling, took with him his wife Sarah and all his household, and Lot his brother's son, and so departed from Haran where Abraham's father died, into the land of Canaan, which afterward his posterity enjoyed (after much tribulation) as from the twelfth of Genesis, and also the five books of Moses and Joshua, is plainly set forth and at large described.

And so to see the whole course of the Bible, from Abraham's coming from among the Chaldeans, unto Moses' departure out of Egypt with the people of Israel, his rule of them in the wilderness, what travail and rebellion he had amongst them, and so to Joshua who was their guide to the promised land (in whose time the true and pure religion of God flourished amongst them), and from Joshua's time the manner of the governance of their commonwealth under judges, and from judges unto kings, and from kings unto priests, after the captivity of Babylon, even until Christ's time; and it shall be well perceived that even among the Jews, being God's peculiar people (all the world besides, being altogether given to idolatry and knowing not God), that God's people were always the least in number, and the true worshipping of God was in very few. And that always the greater sort, and more in number were such, as following their own dreams and inventions, forsook the true worshipping of God and with most cruelty put to death the professors thereof, and slew the prophets which told them God's will and rebuked their sins and idolatry, as in the sacred Scriptures is most plentifully described. As for example, of six hundred thousand which came out of Egypt under Moses, there entered but two, namely Joshua and Caleb, into the land of promise. And when that Moses (by the commandment of God), sent forth twelve of the people of Israel (out of each tribe one) to view the promised land, after they had been out forty days and returned, of the twelve which were sent two persons only (that is to say, Joshua and Caleb) told the truth, and ten of the twelve were liars and persuaded the people from going into the land which God had promised. Yea and such hurly-burly was amongst them, that not only Moses and Aaron, but also Joshua and Caleb, the true messengers, were like to be stoned, and [the people] would have made themselves captains, and so have returned back into Egypt. What plague followed them? Read the place, Numbers 13. Not one of them entered the land (no more any rebellers against God's truth and his true preachers which are signified by Joshua and Caleb shall enter into our promised land, which is the kingdom of heaven, purchased by the precious death and bloodshedding of the immaculate lamb, Jesus Christ, our only savior and advocate). Again was not Micaias the prophet of God against 400 false prophets of Baal which promised Ahab victory in his affairs? But Micaias told him of his destruction. Was not here 400 against one? Read the place, 1 Kings 22:8–38, and you shall see manifestly the bragging lies of the false prophets against the simple true tale of Micaias, the prophet of God.

And not only thus in the Old Testament, but also Christ himself witnesseth the same in the New Testament, saying in Matthew 7:14, "Strait is the gate and narrow is the way which leadeth unto life, and few there be that find it." And in Matthew 20:16, "Many are called, but few are chosen." And Christ calleth them his little flock, saying in Luke 12:32, "Fear not, little flock, for it is your Father's pleasure to give you a kingdom." And Saint Paul in Romans 10:16 saith, "But all have not obeyed the gospel." And in 2 Thessalonians 3:2 he saith, "For all men have not faith." And therefore when Esdras asked the angel whether many or few should be saved, he made him this answer: "The Most Highest hath made this world for many, and the world to come for few" (4 Esdras 8:1).

Thus much have I written to answer such as have this reason in their mouths, will God suffer so many to perish and to be led blind so many hundred years? What shall I speak of hundreds of years? Was not the world from the beginning thereof until after Christ's ascension (setting the Jews apart, which were but a handful in comparison of the whole world besides) altogether not only without the knowledge of God, but also worshipped devils and creatures, every man after his own fantasy, some the sun, some the moon, some the stars, some the fire, and some the similitude of beasts, and some of men. And as they received benefits of men, so after their deaths, they worshipped them for gods. As [i.e., for example] because Bacchus first found amongst them the means to make wine; therefore after his death they made him a god (if creatures may make gods as the pope may saints) and called him the god of wine. Mars first found out armor and weapon. When he was dead they made him a god and called him the god of war. Ceres, a woman, she first found the means to plow the ground and to sow corn, and so to make bread (where before they ate acorns). And when she was dead they made her a goddess, and called her the goddess of corn. And so of others, as they received benefits by them when they lived, so gave they the names of gods unto them after their deaths, and gave them godly honors. As Neptune was the god of the mariners for the sea, Pan was the god of the wood, Apollo was the god of wisdom, Juno was the goddess for women that were with child or in travail. So that they had for everything a sundry god, whose images they worshipped. And their blindness ran so far that they worshipped devils which were in images and spoke and gave them answers, as the image of Apollo in the isle of Delos. Yea, they killed their own children and offered them up to their images.

This wickedness and detestable idolatry endured, I say, until after Christ's ascension (which was the space of four thousand years or thereabouts), until Saint Paul and other apostles preached the gospel over all the world. So that we must not take hold of our faith by continuance of years, neither prescription of time maketh the thing good if it be contrary to God's sacred Scriptures, have it never so fair a show. And now ye see how far those fond reasons of worldly wisdom are from God, and how quite they are overthrown.

And I pray you, how far dissented our Christianity from their gentility? They had for everything a sundry god. We had for everything a sundry saint. We had Saint Uncumber for ill husbands, Saint Job for the pox, Saint Roch for the plague, Saint Barbara for thunder, Saint Sithe for our keys, Saint Anthony for our pigs, Saint Loye for our horse, Saint Agatha for the toothache, Saint Leonard was good master to thieves, our Lady for women with child, and a number of such abominable and stinking idolatries. Yea, and because we would be nothing inferior unto them, we would have for their drunken Bacchus a drunken Martin.[3] So that we had nothing but the names of Christians, for in our rites and ceremonies we were altogether heathenish. They had for everything a god; we had

3. [ED.] On the cult of these saints in England see Thomas Becon, *The Pathway to Prayer*, in *Works* (Cambridge, 1844; Parker Society), II, 139; John Bale, *Image of Both Churches*, in *Select Works* . . . (Cambridge, 1849; Parker Society), 348, 498; Roger Hutchinson, *Image of God*, in *Works* . . . (Cambridge, 1842; Parker Society), 171 f; John Jewel, *Works* . . . (Cambridge, 1845–50; Parker Society), II, 922; Thomas Rogers, *Faith, Doctrine and Religion Professed in England* (Cambridge, 1854; Parker Society), 226–8.

for everything a patron. They worshipped images; so did we. Their images spoke; ours were not dumb, and the craft of the devil oftentimes working blasphemous miracles by them.[4]

But now methinketh I hear some say, "Sir, it was then a merry world and all things were then plenty. But since this new gospelling came up, all things have been very dear and scarce, and we have had a very hard world."[5] Forsooth herein ye are the right children of your forefathers the idolatrous Jews. For even the same answer made they to Jeremiah the prophet when he had rebuked them for their idolatry in the forty-four[th] chapter of his prophecy, saying: "We will not hear the word which thou hast spoken unto us in the name of the Lord, but we will do whatsoever goeth out of our own mouths, that we may sacrifice to the queen of heaven, and bake cakes unto her as we ourselves, our forefathers, our kings and princes have done, in the cities of Judah and in the streets of Jerusalem, and had our bellies full of bread. And then went it well with us and saw no misfortune" [Jer. 44:16–17]. And why would they not hear the prophet speaking unto them? It followeth: "But since we left to do sacrifice to the queen of heaven, we have had scarceness of all things, and are consumed with the sword and hunger."

The gospel is not the cause of the wickedness that now reigneth in the world (far be it from every Christian heart to think so unreverently of that most precious jewel, the word of God) but our own sins and wickedness, our exceeding pride, our bottomless covetousness, our abominable whoredom, our terrible swearing, our wicked blasphemy, our neglecting of God's gospel, our despising of his true prophets and preachers. My pen is not able to write and describe the exceeding wickedness which now reigneth and floweth in England (God for his mercy amend it, and grant us hearty repentance for the same). For the devil now so rageth, for that he seeth his kingdom and his eldest son (Antichrist of Rome) like to be overthrown. Therefore I say, he now rageth according to the saying of Saint Peter in 1 Peter 5:8, "For your adversary the devil walketh about like a roaring lion, seeking whom he may devour." And for that he seeth his dominion and power to be now at the point of overthrowing because the last day is at hand after the which time he shall never more trouble God's people, and therefore whilst he may, he bestirreth him and

4. [ED.] On the official campaign against shrines and images in 1538, see A. G. Chester, *Hugh Latimer, Apostle to the English* (Philadelphia, 1954), chap. 18; also Philip Hughes, *The Reformation in England* (London, 1951), I, 360 f.

5. [ED.] That the Reformation had brought hardship to the lower classes was a common charge under Henry and Edward.

soweth his wicked seed amongst men with all his diligence, he leaveth no corner unsought, no ground untried, nor heart unproved. And therefore (I say) it is no marvel that the world is wicked.

But as I said before, so say I again, God grant us better hearts and more fervent zeal both to repent our former lives, amending the same, and also to embrace with most willing minds his holy gospel and the true preachers thereof, lest that be verified upon us which is spoken by the wisdom of God, in the Proverbs of Solomon 1:24, saying, "For I have called," saith the wisdom of God, "and ye refused it, I have stretched out my hand and no man regarded it, but all my counsels have ye despised and set my corrections at naught." Have not we played even the same parts? How abundantly hath God set forth his truth amongst us! How freely and sincerely is it continually preached amongst us! But what carnal gospeller amendeth his life? What papist believeth his truth? Or what heretic repenteth his error? Do not we all (whilst every man looketh on at others' faults, no man amending his own) continue still in our wickedness and errors? What will come of it? Hark what the wisdom of God saith, even in the next words following. "Therefore shall I also laugh in your destruction, and mock you when that thing that you fear cometh upon you. When sudden misery shall come upon you and destruction shall suddenly oppress you as a storm, when trouble and heaviness cometh upon you, then shall they call upon me, but I will not hear. They shall seek me early, but they shall not find me." Can we therefore, seeing we thus stubbornly resist God's truth, disobey his gospel, repent not our evils, nor amend or reform our lives, look for any other at his most righteous hand but worthy punishment and utter destruction, unless we repent? I therefore (in the bowels of our Lord Jesus Christ) most earnestly desire all such as love God's truth, desire the preferment of his glory, and do long after the perfection of his most holy and sincere religion and the flourishing thereof, with the utter overthrow of Antichrist, and all his dirty dregs and sink of devilish dreams and filthy ceremonies, as many (I say) as wish the continual health, prosperity and long life of our most worthy and gracious sovereign lady Queen Elizabeth (whom God long preserve amongst us), earnestly and with speed to repent their former deeds and become new men, both in life and word, that God may bless us, and increase that his goodness towards us which he hath begun, that his enemies seeing our just conversation may be won unto God, and that we may be one flock as there is one true shepherd. And this shall we be, if gospellers would follow the good lessons they read in God's holy gospel, and if such as do cleave to prescription of time and number of people would relinquish the fond reasons of carnal wisdom, and cleave unto God's truth, wherein is contained the wisdom of God, and in which also is largely and sufficiently set forth, both how God would have us to honor him and also what offendeth him.

Alack, why should this term of forefathers so much stick in our hearts, and so stubbornly cause us to resist the manifest truth of God's most sacred Scriptures? And as I have somewhat said before to stop the mouths of such as cleaved to number of years and multitudes of people, so I think it good to write somewhat also of forefathers, to answer those fond people which have these reasons in their mouths, "We will do as our forefathers have done." And, "What, I pray you," say they, "are we wiser than they? Were there not as great learned men, as wise men, as good men in times past as now?" And, "Why then should we not credit them, and do as they did?" I pray you let me also ask you this question, if the apostles should have made Christ that answer when he called them, if the Romans, Corinthians, Thessalonians, Ephesians, Galatians, and all the whole world besides, should have made the apostles and God's messengers that answer (which they might more justly have done, if either continuance of years might have served, for they had been nozzled in their gentility above four thousand years, or else if worldly wise and learned heads, for they had within that space risen amongst them Plato, Aristotle, Seneca and a number of other wise, witty and learned philosophers) when they preached Christ unto them — O Lord, when should the apostles or we have come to the knowledge of Christ? So that now ye see how strong a foundation you stand on which will needs stick to forefathers, that is so soon overthrown and blown up, even from the foundation.

But because I will not follow the steps of your forefathers (which ground themselves altogether upon human reason, without God's word) I will also allege some Scriptures against you. So that if you may by any means be plucked from Antichrist (the pope, I mean, and all popishness) I will do my best, both now and at all times (God willing) to the uttermost of my power, according to the small talent which God hath lent me, and yet herein nothing but my duty. And as Saint Paul said to the Corinthians [2 Cor. 12:14], "I seek not yours, but you." So (I take God to record) do I write this only because I would (what in me lay) keep you from our enemy the devil, and to bring you to God. Well, harken what God himself saith in Leviticus 18:30, "Do not ye as they which were before you, and be ye not defiled in them. I am the Lord your God, keep my commandments." And in Amos the prophet [2:14], he saith, "Thus saith the Lord, for three and four wickednesses of Judah I will not spare him; because he hath cast aside the law of the Lord and not kept his commandments, for their idols have deceived them, after whom their forefathers went." And therefore saith God in Deuteronomy 12:32, "Whatsoever that I command you, that take heed ye do, only unto the Lord, and put thou nothing thereto nor take ought therefrom." And therefore saith Solomon in Proverbs 30:5, "The word of God is a fiery shield unto all them that put their trust in him; put thou nothing unto his words lest he reprove thee, and thou be found a liar."

So that now we see that this reason of forefathers is clean overthrown, and nothing left unto us to follow but the sacred Scriptures. If this will not avail nor profit such as have that fond and vain toy in their heads, I know not what to say unto them. But I may well allege the saying of Hosea the prophet [8:12] against them, "Though I show them my law never so much, they account it but strange doctrine." Indeed such is the blindness of the world and of man's nature that they cannot see the verity without the special gift of God, which is bound neither to doctor's hood nor yet to bishop's miter. For the Holy Ghost saith in the Book of Wisdom 1:4, "Wisdom shall not enter into a forward soul, nor dwell in the body that is subdued unto sin." And therefore he saith a little before in the same chapter [v. 2], "For he will be found of them that tempt him not, and appear to them that put their trust in him." And therefore saith God by the prophet Isaiah (Is. 66:2), "Upon whom shall my Spirit rest but upon the humble and contrite spirit, and such a one as standeth in awe of my words." With whom agreeth Saint Peter (2 Pet. 1:5), saying, "And hereunto give all diligence, in your faith minister virtue, in virtue, knowledge . . ." And then he concludeth, saying, "If these things be with you and be plenteous, they will make you that ye neither shall be idle nor unfruitful in the knowledge of our Lord Jesus Christ. But he that hath not these things, he is blind, groping the way with his hand, [and] hath forgotten himself to have been purged from his old sins." And hereunto agreeth Saint Paul in the first chapter of the first Epistle to the Corinthians, read the place. So that where those virtues be, there doth God indeed open his secrets by his Holy Spirit.

I write not this that I mean thereby to discourage any from learning. But rather I exhort all men to set their children thereunto, and especially to the universities, whereby good literature may be maintained in the youth which are the seed of the commonwealth of this realm, and God's

truth sincerely preached.[6] But I only inveigh against those papists which
say that such learned men as maintain their errors are learned. They are
bishops. They have studied the Scriptures, so many years and so many
years. And how can it be but that these must needs understand the Scriptures? Yea, and some say it is not possible for any man to understand the
Scriptures unless he were a graduate of the university. But whether this
impossibility be true or no, both the Scriptures above recited, and also experience in these our days (thanks be to God) doth prove the contrary.
For that there be divers which never came in the universities, yea, and
some such as have no more but their mother's tongue do understand the
Scriptures, and [are] able to teach good and sound doctrine.

But how those men understand the Scriptures (which brag so much of
their doctrine and continuance of their study) by their doctrine is apparent. For seek they aught in all their preachings and doings other than
their own praisings and establishment of their own traditions, yea, and extolling and preferring the same above God's commandments? As when
papistry reigned, how little was the terrible swearing and tearing of God
spoken against, how was whoredom winked at, which are utterly against
God's commandments and by God's law punished by death. But yet so
little regarded with them, that rather it was winked at than spoken
against. If a man had sworn never so great an oath in tearing of God, ye
should have had that mark (the pope's shavelings I mean) sit by and say
never a word. But if one had sworn by their stinking and idolatrous mass,
by and by Sir John would have been busy for so misusing his occupation.

Again, if one of their vowed priests (repenting his errors and minding
to live in God's laws) had chanced to have married a wife (leaving the
taking of other men's wives and daughters forsaking their liberty. *Si non
caste, tamen caute* [If not chastely, nevertheless cautiously]).[7] Or if a
man had chanced to eat a piece of rusty [i.e., moldy] bacon for lack of
other meats (though perchance Master Parson had fed himself and well
filled his belly with pike, carp, tench, and such small fish, and perchance
with a piece of a custard and tart and such hard and unsavory meats)

6. [ED.] "Good literature" was a favorite theme of Erasmus.
7. [ED.] The origin of this widely quoted phrase is unknown. Its earliest use
seems to have been at a time of bitter opposition to the newly instituted prohibitions
against clerical marriage, during the eleventh century, in the archdiocese of Hamburg-
Bremen. See Adam of Bremen, *History of the Archbishops of Hamburg-Bremen*,
edited with a translation by F. J. Tschan (New York, 1959; Records of Civilization),
139 n, citing Archbishop Adalbert, 1043–72; and H. C. Lea, *History of Sacerdotal
Celibacy in the Christian Church* (New York, 3rd rev. ed., 1907), I, 211, citing
Albert the Magnificent, eleventh-century Archbishop of Hamburg.

upon a Friday or upon any other their forbidden days (1 Timothy 4:1-5), if this gear had come to their knowledge would they have winked at it, or looked through the fingers, trow ye? [8] As they did at whoredom, swearing, and such like offences? No, I warrant you. Marry! Out on him! Heretic! Fie upon him! He is not worthy to live! To the fire with the heretic knave! So straitly looked they to their dirty dreams, preferring and extolling the same (as much as in them lay) before God's commandments. So preposterous was and is their judgment.

God said to Moses, Exodus 3:5 (at such time as he sat keeping his sheep in Midian, when he saw the bush burn and as he was going towards it), "Come not hither," saith he, put thy shoes off thy feet, for the place wherein thou standest is holy ground." Hear, saith God, the place is holy, put off thy shoes. The chalice is holy (say they), put on thy gloves; put off, saith God, put on, say the papists. God esteemed Moses' bare flesh better than his leather shoes. The papists esteem a sheepskin above the flesh of man, redeemed with the death and blood of Christ. For if thy gloves were on, the matter was well enough, were the thing never so holy. But if he happened to touch the same with his bare hand, Marry! Fie! What a sin was it! It was marvel if his hand had not rotted off for it. If this judgment be not preposterous and extolling their own traditions above God's commandments, what is preposterous? [9]

What is or can be more plainly against the manifest truth? Yet all is done with a godly show to the eyes of worldlings, with golden copes, golden crosses, silver censers, frankincense burning before their idols, with many other gay goodly things. Surely the saying of Christ in Matthew 15:7-9 might well be verified upon them, where he saith, "Ye hypocrites, rightly did Isaiah prophesy of you saying, 'This people draw nigh me with their mouths and honor me with their lips, but their heart is far from me, teaching the doctrine and precepts of men.'" Therefore Saint Paul willeth (as many as be desirous to be very Christians) by most manifest words, to eschew and fly from such doctrine as is so infected with superfluous ceremonies, without the word of God, saying in his Epistle to the Colossians 2:20-23, "If ye be dead with Christ from the ordinances of the world, why as though ye [yet] lived in the world are ye led with

8. [ED.] On fasting see Erasmus, "A Fish Diet," *Colloquies* (1965), 312–57; and Erasmus, *An Epystell unto Christofer bysshop of Basyle concernyng the forbedinge of eatynge of flesshe* (?1530; *S.T.C.*, 10489).

9. [ED.] Gloves could be worn by a bishop while celebrating mass, or by certain persons while handling relics. Gough's reference either mingles these two uses, or else reflects local customs that did so.

traditions? 'Touch not, taste not, handle not,' which all perish through the very abuse after the commandments and doctrines of men. Which things outwardly have the similitude of wisdom, by superstition and humbleness of mind, and by hurting of the body, and in that they do the flesh no worship to the need thereof." Thus doth Saint Paul by most evident words pluck us from the superstitious rites of the papists, whose religion (indeed) is altogether in outward show and worldly pomp.[10] And therefore the apostle, preventing the question which might be asked him by some worldly wise man, which would say: "Why, sir, what manner of life would you have us to lead? After what sort would you have us Christians to do and use?" He answereth even in the beginning of the next chapter of the same Epistle (Col. 3:1–3), saying, "If ye be then risen again with Christ, seek those things which are above, where Christ sitteth on the right hand of God. Set your affections on heavenly things and not of [i.e., on] earthly things, for ye are dead and your life is hid with Christ in God." Thus is it evident that the right life of a Christian consisteth not either in multitude of people, prescription of time, forefathers, nor outward ceremonies, but only in virtuousness of life, leaving our own dreams and inventions, and in following the sacred and holy Scriptures, setting the same always before our eyes as our only lodestar to follow, and touchstone to try all doctrine by. For whatsoever is not contained in God's book (I mean the Holy Bible) no Christian is bound of necessity to do. Neither (as I said before) need we to run into any cloister to seek a perfect life, seeing it is the duty of all Christians (of what estate or degree soever he be) to live in the fear of God, and in such sort as in this godly work following is most livelily and Christianly set forth. So that in that matter I shall not need anything to entreat of.

Thus seeking to end my prologue lest I be too tedious, I send thee (good reader) to this book. Praying God of his mercy so to open our hearts to receive his truth and follow the same in our living, that he may (seeing our repentance) pour his blessing upon us, that his true and sin-

10. [ED.] "Yea, if I had leisure I could make you perceive and understand that every greatest decay and mischief of the Christian commonwealth hath sprung out and had their beginning of ceremonies. . . . At the leastwise for this cause: lest of this spark kindled a greater fire might grow, and more hatred against the clergy (which is too great and overmuch already). It doth displease me whatsoever thing pertaineth to sedition and strife. But yet if no man should resist and withstand such manner [of] ceremonies always increasing and waxing more and more, the liberty of the gospel should be destroyed forever . . ." Erasmus, *An Epystell unto Christofer*, fol. Pii–iii (spellings modernized). This connection of ceremonies with hatred of the clergy was a matter of constant concern to Erasmus.

cere religion now beginning (as it were) to spring up (but wonderfully hindered in the growing thereof by God's enemies, the papists and carnal gospellers, who have the gospel in their mouths but not in their conversations) that it may come to a perfect ripeness, that God may be glorified in this world by our Christianly conversation. And that we (after this transitory life once finished) may continually praise him, in the heavenly habitation with his holy angels world without end, by the merits, death and passion of the immaculate lamb, our only lord and savior Jesus Christ: to whom with the Father and the Holy Ghost be all honor, praise and glory now and evermore, world without end. Amen.

God preserve the Queen.

Farewell in the Lord.

J. G.

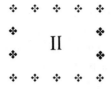

II

JOHN FOXE

Two Prefaces from Acts and Monuments

Editor's Introduction

John Foxe (1517–87) was educated at Oxford (1534–45), where he formed lifelong friendships with Robert Crowley and Alexander Nowel.[1] Very early he came under the influence of Hugh Latimer, "the first apostle of England," and like-minded reformers during the reign of Henry VIII. With them Foxe endured Henry's Catholic reaction of 1539–47, and welcomed joyously the Protestant triumphs under Edward VI (1547–53). His role during the reign of Edward was modest. Ordained a deacon in 1550, he served as tutor in the household of the Duke of Norfolk. His associates were such adherents to the Latimer school as John Bale, Crowley, Nowel, the Duchess of Suffolk, John Rogers and John Hooper. His first three publications (1547–8) were translations of sermons by Martin Luther, Johannes Oecolampadius and Urbanus Rhegius.[2] Like Miles Coverdale, Foxe combined an accurate knowledge of Lutheran, Zwinglian and Calvinistic theology and affairs with a strong admiration for Erasmus and a belief in his essential orthodoxy.

Upon the death of King Edward, Foxe fled abroad, stopping along the way to visit Erasmus' birthplace in the Lowlands. He then paid a visit to Erasmus' favorite printer, Froben, at Basel, in order to learn more of the great Christian Humanist. He visited several colonies of English exiles before settling down with Bale and Humphrey at Basel. He had taken part in the conflicts at the Frankfort colony; he had a certain sympathy for

---

1. On Foxe's life see J. F. Mozley, *John Foxe and His Book* (London, 1940); also William Haller, *Foxe's "Book of Martyrs" and the Elect Nation* (London, 1963).
2. *S.T.C.*, 16983 (dated incorrectly); 18787; 20847 (dated incorrectly).

the Knoxians, and deplored the excesses of the Coxe party, although he identified himself with neither. At Basel Foxe, along with other English exiles, worked as a proof-correcter for local printers. His interest in printing recommended him to the exiles, and as a propagandist and translator he was soon in correspondence with members of all the exile colonies. Even though his sympathies were with the more radical Protestants, his activities were with the Cranmer, Ridley, Latimer group—the core of officialdom under Edward. It was in the interests of the Edwardine Reformation, and of English Christianity as interpreted for him by Bale especially, that he published in Latin at Strassburg (1554), and at Basel (1559), brief versions of what was later to appear in England as his *Acts and Monuments*.[3]

Foxe returned to England in October 1559, after the Elizabethan Settlement had been enacted into law. Almost at once, with Coverdale, Bale, Becon and others, he began publishing and reissuing the works, and commemorating the deeds, of the Protestant martyrs under Mary. This led in time to the publication as well of much material dating to the reign of Edward, and to the early reformers under Henry. In 1563 (while Parliament and Convocation were still in session) Foxe issued the first English edition of his *Acts and Monuments* (popularly known as "Foxe's Book of Martyrs"), a large folio volume of nearly 1800 pages with more than fifty woodcuts. The book created a sensation; it was enthusiastically praised by Protestants and severely criticized by Catholics. So great was its success that in 1570 Foxe issued a second edition, consisting of two volumes, containing a text nearly twice as long as the first and illustrated with about 150 woodcuts. In 1576 and 1583 Foxe reissued this version with minor additions. The work had an influence on the English mind second only to that of the English Bible.

What this literature by and about the reformers, heroes and martyrs under Henry, Edward and Mary did was to set a pattern for "English" Christianity so persuasive that it came to be accepted even by many who did not altogether like it. In all this outpouring of books, Foxe's writings were the most voluminous. The point of view he set forth, however, was not new; in fact, it was shared by most English Protestants. Elizabeth herself had outlined it in a letter to the English Catholic bishops while Foxe

3. Edmund Grindal, *Remains* . . . (Cambridge, 1843; Parker Society), 219–40; John Foxe, *Commentarii rerum in ecclesia gestarum . . . a Wiclevi temporibus . . . descriptio* . . . (Strassburg, 1554); and *Rerum in ecclesia gestarum . . . digesti per Regna et nationis Commentarii* (Basel, 1559).

was still at Basel.[4] In Foxe's work the theme of the pure primitive church was treated with great elaboration. Christianity, so the story went, had been brought to England by Joseph of Arimathea and others directly associated with the original twelve apostles. Out of this pristine pure Christianity the Roman emperor Constantine (born of a Christian "emperor" whose body lay buried at York) had gone forth "as a second Moses" to save the ancient church from pagan persecution and to restore its faith and its Bible at the Council of Nicaea. Later the Roman papacy had gained control of the English church, had debauched it, and had become a plague on the English rulers and people. But at all times in the English church some people had been found faithful. Among them was John Wycliffe, "who begat John Hus who begat Martin Luther." Another forerunner of Luther was the great Erasmus, who had compiled his famous Greek New Testament in England, and had taught Greek to early reformers at Cambridge. All through the tumultuous sixteenth century, godly men of action, kings, officials, ordinary laymen and earnest preachers had labored to purge England of the dregs of Rome and Antichrist. What the English exiles during Mary's reign had found abroad was a faith much like their own. The Germans and Swiss had been kind to the persecuted English, but the English had now returned home, to restore once again what Joseph of Arimathea had begun in their land during Paul's own lifetime, while Germany and Switzerland were still pagan wildernesses. (John Jewel thought it probable that Paul had first converted England to Christianity.[5])

In all of this literature, most of which proved popular and much of which was several times reprinted, godliness rather than scholastic learning, preaching and teaching the Bible rather than academic theology, were emphasized. The great churchmen were preachers, and this was their chief glory. The great ecclesiastics — popes, cardinals, prelates, monks and bureaucrats — had been the principal source of evil all through the centuries, the cause of far more evil than the wicked kings, nobles or any other men. Piety and morality were everywhere set against ceremonies, rites, vestments and trumpery. Lay people had played a great and noble role all through Christian history, and the true preachers had always recognized this fact.

4. Text in John Strype, *Annals of the Reformation* . . . (Oxford, 1824), I, 1, 218–19.

5. John Jewel, *Works* . . . (4 vols., Cambridge, 1845–50; Parker Society), I, 278 f, 305 f; III, 128 f, 163 f.

Against such a background it is not surprising that Foxe and his friends Crowley, Nowel, Coverdale, Becon and Humphrey, among many others, should have refused at first to comply with the terms of the Elizabethan Settlement. Having to wear the vestments galled them especially. In the primitive church such things had been unheard of. They were the sign of Roman priests. Erasmus had ridiculed them, the best of the reformed churches had gotten rid of them, and the Lutheran opponents of the Interim had refused to go back to them. The Marian martyrs (even Bishop Ridley, who had once forced the vestments upon Hooper) had all condemned the Roman clerical garb.

Nevertheless, by 1570 "Englishness" had triumphed, and most of those who opposed the vestments had concluded that it was better to labor for the Lord in the hated garb than leave the English to the mercies of either Roman or Lutheran priests (whom they thought of as the only alternatives). Foxe refused throughout his life to accept any office that required him to wear the vestments or to subscribe to the objectionable terms of the official church. Yet, as even Queen Elizabeth and Archbishop John Whitgift had to admit, few men had done more to aid the English church. Parker's Canons of 1571 ordered all bishops, deans and other ecclesiastical dignitaries, and all archdeacons, to set up for public use the massive two-volume 1570 edition of Foxe's book in their houses or halls.[6] Indeed, throughout the Tudor-Stuart era not only Foxe, Crowley, Nowel, Coverdale, Bale, Becon, Humphrey, Latimer, Cranmer and Ridley, but even Tyndale, Frith and Barnes (whose works Foxe first collected and published) were repeatedly marshalled to prove the correctness now of Puritanism, now of anti-Puritanism. The same literature could be used for either purpose, depending on how "Puritan" was defined.

Two prefaces by Foxe cannot represent the whole range of his thinking. The address to the Catholics makes several points. The first is that persecution for religion is always wrong and self-defeating, because it is based upon the human will to power — which Foxe saw as the essence of Roman papalism and clericalism. The heresy laws and trials, the wicked *ex officio* oath, the cruel punishments, all depended on the partisan learning of the clergy as enshrined in their dogma and canon law. The whole of this "law of man" was built on the special claims of the clergy, as symbolized by the vestments, ceremonies and trumpery with which they had

6. *A booke of certaine canons, concernynge some parte of the discipline of the Churche of England* (1571; *S.T.C.*, 10063), fol. Aiii verso, iiii verso, v recto.

surrounded themselves. Now, so evident had the folly of all this become, and so clear was the historical evidence for its falsity, that these very garments and ceremonies mocked the priests in the eyes of informed people. Nevertheless, persecution was still wrong. Therefore the Roman clergy ought to repent, so that ". . . you and we may agree and consent together in one religion and truth in Christ Jesus our Lord . . ."

Foxe's preface setting forth his theory of history shows once again the problem of defining Puritanism. The function of history, according to Foxe, was to give meaning, or to enable people to find the meaning of human life under God. This providential interpretation of history, as set forth by Foxe, encompassed a number of conflicting beliefs, each of which was part of Elizabethan thought. One such belief was that the first is the truest, and that by this test truth was to be discerned as opposed to decay and alteration, and antiquity as opposed to novelty. This world had always had two churches, God's true church and the devil's chapel nearby. The true church had seldom been visible, and had usually been small and under persecution, discernible only to those who were its members. The false church had usually been visible, powerful, pompous, wealthy, cruel and persecuting — a clerical church. Only occasionally, when godly rulers had aided it, had the true church been relieved of suffering and hardship. The clerical false church had charged the true persecuted church with heresy. But through the ages a long list of men had witnessed to the truth. And the gospel preached in England in the fourteenth and fifteenth centuries by Wycliffe and his followers was the same as that preached in England in 1570. The true faith had not begun with Luther and Zwingli. The martyrs under Queen Mary were not less than those of the first centuries. The return of Christ was near; strife among Christians was wrong. Only God could set things right; man could not.

If the reader had followed Foxe's view that godly monarchs were those who had always given the church its best days, from Moses through David, from Constantine down to Elizabeth, then logically he ought not to have been in rebellion against the godly ruler. But that would have meant that he should conform to the Elizabethan establishment! If the true church was not the glorious, wealthy, persecuting establishment, but the poor, despised, suffering body whose members the proud clerics cursed as heretics according to their man-made dogmas, laws, and ceremonies, then the contemptible little separatist groups in London must be the true church, as they told Parker and Grindal, for they had been faithful under Mary at great cost while Parker hid and Grindal fled. All this notwithstanding, Foxe did not approve of separatist sects. And so throughout his massive and supposedly unanswerable work, the reader could find proof positive for contrary opinions about the Elizabethan compromise in religion. Foxe himself drew the conclusion of Erasmus, and the conclusion the Elizabethan Settlement had called for, namely, that there was a distinction between the religion of the spirit (the invisible church) and the external religion supported by the state for the welfare of the nation (the visible church). By 1572 he had decisively rejected the activist position of the Presbyterian "Admonition." Only God and the monarch could be activists. Then was Foxe a Puritan? All the way down to John Bunyan's time, "Puritans" of every complexion supposed that Foxe had been a defender of their position. But the pious "royalism" that appears throughout the book also made Foxe's massive martyrology a standard defense of "the royal supremacy in matters ecclesiastical."

The text of the two prefaces by Foxe that follow is from the Cattley-Townsend edition of 1843, corrected from the original editions of 1563 and 1570. Foxe's annotations have been dispensed with, since the concern here is not with his work as a historian but with his ideas. On Foxe as a historian, see the works by J. F. Mozley and William Haller cited above.

Foxe's biblical quotations were evidently his own translations.

❖ ❖ ❖ ❖

To the Persecutors of God's Truth, Commonly Called Papists, Another Preface of the Author

[1563]

If any other had had the doing and handling of this so tragical an history, and had seen the mad rage of this your furious cruelty in spilling the blood of such an innumerable sort of Christ's holy saints and servants, as in the volume of this history may appear by you, O ye papists (give me leave by that name to call you), I know what he would have done therein; what vehemency of writing, what sharpness of speech and words, what roughness of style in terming and calling you he would have used, what exclamations he would have made against you, how little he would have spared you. So I likewise, if I had been disposed to follow the order and example of their doing — what I might have done herein let your own conjectures give you to understand, by that which you have deserved. And if you think you have not deserved so to be entreated as I have said and worse than I have done, then see and behold, I beseech you, here in this story the pitiful slaughter of your butchery! Behold your own handiwork! Consider the number, almost out of number, of so many silly [i.e., defenseless] and simple lambs of Christ whose blood you have sought and sucked, whose lives you have vexed, whose bodies you have slain, racked, and tormented. Some also you have cast on dunghills to be devoured of fowls and dogs, without mercy, without measure, without all sense of humanity! See, I say, and behold here present before your eyes the heaps of slain bodies of so many men and women, both old, young, children, infants, newborn, married, unmarried, wives, widows, maids, blind men, lame men, whole men; of all sorts, of all ages, of all degrees; lords, knights, gentlemen, lawyers, merchants, archbishops, bishops, priests, ministers, deacons, laymen, artificers, yea, whole households and whole kindreds together; father, mother and daughter, grandmother, mother, aunt and child, etc.; whose wounds yet bleeding before the face of God cry vengeance! For whom have you spared; what country could escape your hands? See therefore, I say, read, and behold your acts and facts; and when you have seen, then judge what you have deserved. And if ye find that I have tempered myself with much more moderation for mine own part (but that I have in some places inserted certain of other men's works) than either the cause of the martyrs or your iniquity hath required, then accept my goodwill in the Lord which here I thought to signify unto you in the beginning of this preface, not to flatter or seek for your acceptation (which I care not greatly for), but only as tendering the conversion of your souls, if perhaps I may do you any good. Wherefore, as one that wisheth well unto you in the Lord, I exhort you that with patience you would read and peruse the history of these your own acts and doings, being no more ashamed to read them now than you were then to do them; to the intent that when you shall now the better revise what your doings have been, the more you may blush and detest the same.

Peter, preaching to the Jews and Pharisees after they had crucified Christ, cried to them: *"Delictorum poenitentiam agite* ["Repent of your sins"; *cf.* Acts 2:38], and turned three thousand at one sermon. So the said Peter saith and writeth still to you, and we with Peter exhort you: "Repent your mischiefs; be confounded in your doings; and come at length to some confession of your miserable iniquity." First, you see now your doings, so wicked, cannot be hid; your cruelty is come to light, your murders be evident, your pretty practices, your subtle sleights [of hand], your secret conspiracies, your filthy lives are seen, and stink before the face both of God and man. Yea, what have you ever done so in secret and in corners but the Lord hath found it out and brought it to light? You hold, maintain and defend that ministers ought and may live sole, without matrimony. What filthiness and murdering of infants followed thereupon! Your ear-confessions can say something, but God knoweth more; and yet the world knoweth so much that I need not here to stand upon any particular examples of cardinals, doctors and others taken in manifest whoredom at London, at Oxford, at Cambridge, at Chester and other places more.

But to pass over this stinking Camarine [1] of your unmaidenly lives I return again to your murders and slaughters which you may here in this volume not only see, but also number them if you please. God so hath displayed and detected them that now all the world may read them. As I have said, God, I assure you, hath detected them who hath so marvellously wrought such help and success in setting forth the same that I dare assure you it is not without the will of him that these your murders should be opened and come to light. And what if they were not opened nor made to the world notorious, but secret only, betwixt God and your conscience? Yet what cause have you to repent and to be confounded, now the world also seeth them, hateth and abhorreth you for the same! What will you say, what will you or can you allege? How will you answer to the high Judge to come, or whither will you fly from his judgment when he shall come? Think you blood will not require blood again? Did you ever see any murder which came not out and was at length repaid? Let the example of the French Guise [2] work in your English hearts and mark you well his end. If Christ in his gospel, which cannot lie, doth [threaten a millstone to such as do but hurt the least of his believers, in what a dangerous case] stand you which have smoked and fired so many his worthy preachers and learned ministers! And what if the Lord should render to you double again for that which ye have done to them! — Where should you then be come? And hath he not promised in his word so to do? And think you that that Judge doth sleep or that his coming day will not come? And how will you then be able to stand in his sight when he shall appear? With what face shall ye look upon the Lord whose servants ye have slain? Or with what hearts will you be able to behold

1. [ED.] Legendary swamp from which a plague spread after it was drained.
2. [ED.] Francis, Duke of Guise, who took part in the slaughter of Huguenots in March 1562.

the bright faces of them upon whom you have set so proudly here, condemning them to consuming fire? In that day when you shall be charged with the blood of so many martyrs, what will ye, or can you say? How think ye to excuse yourselves? Or what can you for yourselves allege? Will ye deny to have murdered them? This book will testify and denounce against you; which if you cannot deny now to be true, then look how you will answer to it in that counting day.

Peradventure you will excuse yourselves and say that you did but the law; and if the law did pass upon them you could not do with all [i.e., you were not primarily responsible]. But here will I ask, what law do you mean? The law of God or the law of man? If ye mean the law of God, where do you find in all the law of God to put them to death which, holding the articles of the creed, never blasphemed his name but glorified it, both in life and in their death? If you answer by the law of man, I know the law (*ex officio* [3] or rather *ex homicidio* [of murder]) which you mean and follow. But who brought that law in first, in the time of King Henry IV,[4] but you? Who revived the same again in Queen Mary's days but you? Further, who kept them in prison before the law, till by the law you had made a rope to hang them withal? [5] And think you by charging the law to discharge yourselves? But you will use here some translation of the fact perchance; alleging that you burnt them not, but only committed them to the secular power by whom, you will say, they were burnt, and not by you. It will be hard to play the sophister before the Lord. For so it may be said to you again, that the fire burned them and not the secular power. But I pray you, who put them in? But they were heretics, you will say, and Lutherans, and therefore we burnt them thinking thereby to do God good service, etc. Of such service-doers Christ spake before, saying that such should come who, putting his servants to death should think to do good service to God [*cf.* Jn. 16:2]. And forsomuch as under the pretence of heresy you put them to death; concerning that matter there is, and hath been, enough said to you by learning — if either learned books or learned sermons could move you. But to this none answereth you better than the martyrs themselves, which in this book do tell you that in the same which you call heresy, they serve the living God. And how do you then serve the living God in put-

3. [ED.] See below, editor's introduction to James Morice, *Brief Treatise of Oaths* . . .

4. [ED.] 2 Henry IV, cap. 15 (in 1401), decreed burning at the stake for heretics.

5. [ED.] Cranmer and others were held in prison until after England had been reconciled to the papacy and the anti-heresy laws had been restored.

ting them to death, whom they in the death do serve so heartily and so heavenly as in this book here doth well appear? And because you charge them so much with heresy, this would I know, by what learning do you define your heresy, by the Scripture or by your canon law? I know what you will answer: but whatsoever you say, your own acts and deeds will well prove the contrary. For what Scripture can save him whom your law condemneth? What heresy was there in speaking against transubstantiation before Innocent III did so enact it in his canon, A.D. 1215? [6] What man was ever counted for an heretic which, worshipping Christ in heaven, did not worship him in the priest's hands, before Honorius III in his canon did cause the sacrament to be elevated and adored upon the altar? "Faith only justifying," in Saint Paul's time and in the beginning church, was no heresy before of late days the Romish canons have made it heresy!

Likewise, if it be heresy not to acknowledge the pope as supreme head of the church, then Saint Paul was a heretic and a stark Lutheran, which, having the Scriptures, yet never attributed that to the pope nor to Peter himself to be supreme head of the church. So were all the other fathers of the primitive church heretics also, which never knew any such supremacy in the pope before Boniface I called himself "universal bishop" six hundred years after Christ. After like sort and manner, if receiving in both kinds and having the Scripture in a popular tongue, be a matter worthy of burning, then were all the apostles and martyrs of the first church worthy to be burned, and the Corinthians ill instructed of Saint Paul, having both *panem* [bread] and *calicem Domini* [the cup of the Lord]. Either condemn Saint Paul and them with these, or else let these be quit with the other. The same I may infer of purgatory, the setting up of images, going on pilgrimage and such like, etc. [And] but that I am wearied to see your miserable folly, I might here argue with you. For if your heresy (as you call it) be a sin with you so heinous that it deserveth burning, then would I know how can that be a sin now which was a virtue once? In the time of the old law it was a virtue among the Jews to have no image in the temple. Also Hezekiah, Josiah, with divers other good kings more, were commended for abolishing the same. And have we not the same commandment still? And how cometh it now to be a vice which was a virtue then? Likewise in the new law, both Paul and Barnabas would have torn their garments for doing that for the not doing whereof you burn your brethren now. You see, therefore, how your her-

6. [ED.] Fourth Lateran Council, 1215.

esy standeth not by God's word, for which you burn God's people, but only by your own laws and canons, made by men. Wherefore if these your laws and canons (without the which the church once did stand and flourish) be now of such force that the breach thereof must needs be death, better it were either they were never made or that now they were abolished; seeing both the church may well be without them, and that God's people in no case can well live with them, but be burned for them.

And now, as I have hitherto collected and recited almost all your excuses and reasons that you can bring and allege for yourselves (and yet you see they will not serve you), so I exhort you to turn to that which only may and will serve; that is to the blood of "the Lamb of God, which taketh away the sins of the world." Wash your bloody hands with the tears of plentiful repentance; and though you cannot call back again the lives of those whom you have slain, yet call yourselves back again from the way of iniquity and from the path of destruction which you were going to! Consider how long now you have spurned and kicked against the Lord and his truth, and yet you see nothing hath prevailed. What have you but "kicked against the pricks"? If killing and slaying could help your cause, you see what an infinite sort you have put to death; the number of whom, although it doth exceed man's searching, yet Paulus Vergerius in his book against the Pope's Catalogue, taking a view thereof, doth account them to the number of a hundred thousand persons slain in Christendom of you whom he there calleth "papists") in the cause of Christ's gospel within this forty or a hundred years; [7] besides them in Queen Mary's time here in England, and besides them within these two years slain in France by the [Duke of] Guise, which as you know cometh to no small sum.[8] And yet for all this horrible slaughter and your so many fought fields against the poor saints, what is your cause the better? What have you thereby got or won but shame, hatred, contempt, infamy, execration, and to be abhorred of all good men; as may appear not only by your habit and garment, the form and wearing whereof it shameth and abhorreth men now, as you see, to be brought unto; but also, the title and name of your profession? For though ye profess popery inwardly in your hearts, yet which of you all now is not ashamed to be called a papist, and would be angry with me if I should write to you under the name of papists? You see, therefore, how little you have won.

7. [ED.] Since the condemnation of Luther, or since the campaign against the Lollards.

8. [ED.] See note 2, above; also Pietro Paolo Vergerio, *Postremus catalogus haereticorum Romae conflatus* (Pfortzheim, 1560; no copy located).

Let us compare now your winnings and losses together. And as you have gained but a little, so let us see what great things you have lost; which first have spilt your own cause, the quiet of your conscience — which I dare say shaketh within you. Ye have lost the favor both of God and man, the safety of your souls, and almost the kingdom of the Lord except you take the better heed. What think you then by these your proceedings, to win any more hereafter which have lost so much already? Do not the very ashes of the martyrs which you have slain rise up still against you in greater armies? Seeing therefore the Lord doth and must prevail, be counselled and exhorted in the Lord; leave off your resisting and yield to the truth which your own boiling consciences, I am sure, doth [sic] inwardly witness and testify, if for your own willful standing upon your credit and reputation (as ye think) ye would come to the confession of the same. And what reputation is this of credit, to be found constant in error against the truth, in Antichrist against Christ, in your own destruction against saving of your souls? Briefly and to be short, if my counsel may be heard, better it were for you in time to give over while it is thankworthy, than at length to be drawn, by compulsion of time, will ye, nill ye, to give over your cause, losing both thanks and your cause also. For see you not daily more and more the contrary part (the Lord's arm going with them) to grow so strong against you that not only there is no hope, but no possibility for your obstinate error to stand against so manifest truth? First, learning, and all best wits, for the most part repugn against you. Most nations and kingdoms have forsaken you, as Germany, Poland, Bohemia, Denmark, Swabia, Dalmatia, Croatia, Epirus and a great part of Greece; England, Ireland, Scotland and France, God be glorified, well favorably cometh on, you see, and other more be like to follow; so that if things come handsomely forward as they begin and are like to do, the pope is like to pay home again shortly his feathers that he hath so long time borrowed. Moreover, universities and schools in all quarters to be set up against you, and youth so trained in the same that you shall never be able to match them.

To conclude, in countries, kingdoms, cities, towns and churches reformed, your errors and superstitious vanities be so blotted out within the space of these forty years in the hearts of men, that their children and youth, being so long nouseled [i.e., nourished] in the sound doctrine of Christ, like as they never heard of your ridiculous trumpery, so will they never be brought to the same. And if nothing else will deface you, yet printing only will subvert your doings, do what ye can, which the Lord only hath set up for your desolation. Wherefore forsake your cause and your false hopes, and save yourselves. And take me not your enemy in telling you truth, but rather your friend in giving you good counsel — if you will follow good counsel given. Return therefore and reform yourselves; repent your murders, cease your persecutions, strive not against the Lord; but rather bewail your iniquities which, though they be great, and greater than you are aware, yet they are not so great but Christ is greater, if ye repent betimes. Ye see here, I trust, good counsel given; God grant it may as well fructify in you, as on my part it hath proceeded of an open and tender heart, wishing you well to do, as I pray God ye may, so that you and we may agree and consent together in one religion and truth in Christ Jesus our Lord, to whom be praise forever. Amen.

To the True and Faithful Congregation of Christ's Universal Church,

With all and singular the members thereof, wheresoever congregated or dispersed through the Realm of England; a Protestation or Petition of the author, wishing to the same abundance of all peace and tranquillity, with the speedy coming of Christ the spouse, to make an end of all mortal misery.

[1570]

Solomon, the peaceable prince of Israel, as we read in the first book of Kings, after he had finished the building of the Lord's temple (which he had seven years in hand), made his petition to the Lord for all that should pray in the said temple or turn their face toward it; and his request was granted, the Lord answering him, as we read in the said book: "I have heard," saith he, "thy prayer, and have sanctified this place . . ." (*cf.* 1 Kings 9:3). Albeit the infinite majesty of God is not to be compassed in any material walls, yet it so pleased his goodness to respect this prayer of the king, that not only he promised to hear them which there prayed, but also replenished the same with his own glory. For so we read again in the book aforesaid, "*Et non poterant ministrare propter nebulam, quia replevit gloria Domini domum Domini* [And they were not able to minister because of the cloud, because the glory of the Lord had filled the house of the Lord." *Cf.* 1 Kings 8:11.]

Upon the like trust in God's gracious goodness if I, sinful wretch, not comparing with the building of that temple but following the zeal of the builder, might either be so bold to ask or so happy to speed after my seven years' travail [it was now 1570] about this Ecclesiastical History, most humbly would I crave of almighty God to bestow his blessings upon the same; that as the prayers of them which prayed in the outward temple were heard, so all true disposed minds which shall resort to the reading of this present history, containing the acts of God's holy martyrs and monuments of his church, may, by example of their life, faith and doctrine, receive some such spiritual fruit to their souls, through the operation of his grace, that it may be to the advancement of his glory and profit of his church, through Christ Jesus our Lord. Amen.

But, as it happened in that temple of Solomon that all which came thither came not to pray, but many to prate, some to gaze and see news, others to talk and walk, some to buy and sell, some to carp and find fault and, finally, some also at the last to destroy and pluck down, as they did indeed — for what is in this world so strong but it will be impugned, what so perfect but it will be abused, so true that will not be contraried, or so circumspectly done wherein wrangling Theon [9] will not set in his tooth? — even so neither do I look for any other in this present history but that, amongst many well-disposed readers, some wasp's nest or other will be stirred up to buzz about mine ears. Such a dangerous thing it is nowadays to write or do any good, but either by flattering a man must offend the godly, or by true speaking procure hatred with the wicked. Of such stinging wasps and buzzing drones I had sufficient trial in my former edition before [1563]; who if they had found in my book any just cause to carp, or upon any true zeal of truth had proceeded against the untruths of my story and had brought just proofs for the same, I could have right well abided it. For God forbid but that faults, wheresoever they be, should be detected and accused. And therefore accusers in a commonwealth, after my mind, do serve to no small stead.

But then such accusers must beware they play not the dog of whom Cicero in his Oration speaketh, which being set in the Capitol to fray away thieves by night, left the thieves and fell to bark at true men walking in the day.[10] Where true faults be, there to bay and bark is not amiss; but to carp where no cause is, to spy in others' straws, and to leap over their own blocks, to swallow camels and to strain gnats, to oppress truth with lies and to set up lies for truth, to blaspheme the dear martyrs of Christ, and to canonize for saints [those] whom Scripture would scarce allow for good subjects — that is intolerable. Such barking curs, if they

9. [ED.] One of Horace's characters, a slanderer.
10. Cicero. [ED.] *Pro Sex. Roscio Amerino Oratio,* cap. xx.

were well served, would be made a while to stoop. But with these brawling spirits I intend not at this time much to wrestle.

Wherefore to leave them a while, till further leisure serve me to attend
upon them, thus much I thought in the mean season by way of protestation or petition to write unto you both in general and particular, the true
members and faithful congregation of Christ's church, wheresoever either
congregated together, or dispersed through the whole realm of England;
that forsomuch as all the seeking of these adversaries is to do what they
can, by discrediting of this history with slanders and sinister surmises,
how to withdraw the readers from it, this therefore shall be, in few
words, to premonish and desire of all and singular of you (all well-
minded lovers and partakers of Christ's gospel) not to suffer yourselves to
be deceived with the big brags and hyperbolical speeches of those slan-
dering tongues, whatsoever they have or shall hereafter exclaim against
the same, but indifferently staying your judgment till truth be tried, you
will first peruse and then refuse; measuring the untruths of this history
not by the scoring up of their hundreds and thousands of lies which they
give out, but wisely weighing the purpose of their doings according as
you find; and so to judge of the matter.

To read my books I allure neither one nor other. Every man as he
seeth cause so [let him] like as he list. If any shall think his labor too
much in reading this story, his choice is free either to read this or any
other which he more mindeth. But if the fruit thereof shall recompense
the reader's travail, then would I wish no man so light-eared [as] to be
carried away for any sinister clamor of adversaries, who many times deprave good doings not for the faults they find, but therefore find faults
because they would deprave. As for me and my history, as my will was
to profit all and displease none, so if skill in any part wanted to will, yet
hath my purpose been simple; and certes [i.e., certainly] the cause no less
urgent also which moved me to take this enterprise in hand.

For, first, to see the simple flock of Christ, especially the unlearned
sort, so miserably abused, and all for ignorance of history, not knowing
the course of times and true descent of the church, it pitied me that [this]
part of diligence [had] so long been unsupplied in this my-country [11]
church of England. Again, considering the multitude of chronicles and
storywriters, both in England and out of England, of whom the most part
have been either monks or clients to the See of Rome, it grieved me to

---

11. [ED.] Foxe uses "my-country" (native to me) and "other-country" (alien to
me) as adjectives.

behold how partially they handled their stories. Whose painful travail albeit I cannot but commend in committing divers things to writing not unfruitful to be known nor unpleasant to be read; yet it lamented me to see in their monuments the principal points which chiefly concerned the state of Christ's church and were most necessary of all Christian people to be known, either altogether pretermitted, or if any mention thereof were inserted, yet were all things drawn to the honor specially of the church of Rome or else to the favor of their own sect of religion. Whereby the vulgar sort, hearing and reading in their writings no other church mentioned or magnified but only that church which here flourished in this world in riches and jollity, were drawn also to the same persuasion, to think no other church to have stood in all the earth but only the church of Rome.

In the number of this sort of writers, besides our monks of England (for every monastery almost had his chronicler) I might also recite both Italian and other-country authors, as Platina, Sabellicus, Nauclerus, Martin, Antoninus, Vincentius, Onuphrius, Laziarde, George Lily, Polydore Virgil,[12] with many more who, taking upon them to intermeddle with matters of the church, although in part they express some truth in matters concerning the bishops and See of Rome, yet in suppressing another part, they play with us, as Ananias and Sapphira did with their money, or as Apelles did in Pliny, who painting the one half of Venus coming out of the sea, left the other half imperfect. So these writers, while they show us one half of the bishop of Rome, the other half of him they leave imperfect and utterly untold. For as they paint him out, on the one part, glistering in wealth and glory, in showing what succession the popes had from the chair of Saint Peter, when they first began and how long they sat, what churches and what famous buildings they erected, how far their possessions reached, what laws they made, what councils they called, what honor they received of kings and emperors, what princes and countries they brought under their authority, with other like stratagems of great pomp and royalty; so, on the other side, what vices these popes brought with them to their seat, what abominations they practiced, what superstition they maintained, what idolatry they procured, what wicked doctrine they defended contrary to the express word of God, [in]to what heresies they fell, into what division of sects they cut the unity of Christian religion, how some practiced by simony, some by necromancy and

12. [ED.] These writers are identified and referred to frequently by Foxe, especially in his first volume.

sorcery, some by poisoning, some indenting with the devil to come by their papacy, what hypocrisy was in their lives, what corruption in their doctrine, what wars they raised, what bloodshed they caused, what treachery they traversed against their lords and emperors, imprisoning some, betraying some to the Templars and Saracens, in bringing others under their feet, also in beheading some (as they did with Frederic and Conradine, the heirs and offspring of the house of Frederic Barbarossa, in the year 1268);[13] furthermore, how mightily Almighty God hath stood against them, how their wars never prospered against the Turk, how the judgments of the godly-learned from time to time have ever repugned against their errors, etc. — of these and a thousand other more, not one word hath been touched, but all kept as under *benedicite* [speak well] in auricular confession.

When I considered this partial dealing and corrupt handling of histories, I thought with myself nothing more lacking in the church than a full and a complete history which being faithfully collected out of all our monastical writers and written monuments should contain neither every vain-written fable (for that would be too much), nor yet leave out anything necessary, for that would be too little; but with a moderate discretion, taking the best of every one, should both ease the labor of the reader from turning over such a number of writers, and also should open the plain truth of times lying long hid in obscure darkness of antiquity: whereby all studious readers, beholding as in a glass the state, course and alteration of religion, decay of doctrine, and the controversies of the church, might discern the better between antiquity and novelty. For if the things which be first, after the rule of Tertullian,[14] are to be preferred before those that be later, then is the reading of histories much necessary in the church to know what went before and what followed after; and therefore not without cause *historia*, in old authors, is called the Witness of Times, the Light of Verity, the Life of Memory, Teacher of Life and Shower of Antiquity, etc., without the knowledge whereof man's life is blind and soon may fall into any kind of error; as by manifest experience we have to see in these desolate later times of the church, when the bishops of Rome under color of antiquity have turned truth into heresy, and brought such new-found devices of strange doctrine and

13. [ED.] John Foxe, *Acts and Monuments* . . . , II, 455–509; IV, 143–4.
14. [ED.] "That which was first is the truest"; *De praescriptiones haereticorum,* 31:3.

religion as in the former age of the church were never heard of before, and all through ignorance of times and for lack of true history.

For to say the truth, if times had been well searched, or if they which wrote histories had, without partiality, gone upright between God and Baal, halting on neither side, it might well have been found the most part of all this catholic corruption intruded into the church by the bishops of Rome, as transubstantiation, elevation and adoration of the sacrament, auricular confession, forced vows of priests not to marry, veneration of images, private and satisfactory masses, the order of Gregory's mass now used, the usurped authority and *summa potestas* [supreme power] of the See of Rome, with all the rout of their ceremonies and weeds of superstition overgrowing now the church; all these, I say, to be new-nothings lately coined in the mint of Rome without any stamp of antiquity, as by reading of this present history shall sufficiently, I trust, appear. Which history therefore I have here taken in hand, that as other storywriters heretofore have employed their travail to magnify the church of Rome, so in this history might appear to all Christian readers the image of both churches,[15] as well of the one as of the other; especially of the poor oppressed and persecuted church of Christ. Which persecuted church, though it hath been of long season trodden under foot by enemies, neglected in the world, nor regarded in histories, and almost scarce visible or known to worldly eyes, yet hath it been the true church only of God, wherein he hath mightily wrought hitherto in preserving the same in all extreme distresses, continually stirring up from time to time faithful ministers by whom always have been kept some sparks of his true doctrine and religion.

Now forasmuch as the true church of God goeth not lightly [i.e., commonly], alone, but is accompanied with some other church or chapel of the devil to deface and malign the same, necessary it is therefore the difference between them to be seen, and the descent of the right church to be described from the apostles' time: which hitherto in most part of histories hath been lacking, partly for fear, that men durst not, partly for ignorance, that men could not, discern rightly between the one and the other. Who, beholding the church of Rome to be so visible and glorious in the eyes of all the world, so shining in outward beauty, to bear such a port, to carry such a train and multitude, and to stand in such high au-

15. [ED.] A favorite theme of the sixteenth-century polemics. Several books used the title.

thority, supposed the same to be the only right catholic mother. The other, because it was not so visibly known in the world, they thought therefore it could not be the true church of Christ. Wherein they were far deceived: for although the right church of God be not so invisible in the world that none can see it, yet neither is it so visible again that every worldly eye may perceive it. For like as is the nature of truth, so is the proper condition of the true church, that commonly none seeth it but such only as be the members and partakers thereof. And therefore they which require that God's holy church should be evident and visible to the whole world, seem to define the great synagogue of the world rather than the true spiritual church of God.

In Christ's time who would have thought but [that] the congregation and councils of the Pharisees had been the right church? And yet had Christ another church in earth besides that; which, albeit it was not so manifest in the sight of the world, yet was it the only true church in the sight of God. Of this church meant Christ, speaking of the temple which he would raise again the third day; and yet after that the Lord was risen, he showed not himself to the world but only to his elect, which were but few. The same church, after that, increased and multiplied mightily among the Jews; yet had not the Jews eyes to see God's church, but did persecute it till at length all their whole nation was destroyed.

After the Jews, then came the heathen emperors of Rome, who having the whole power of the world in their hands did what the world could do to extinguish the name and church of Christ. Whose violence continued the space of three hundred years. All which while the true church of Christ was not greatly in sight of the world but rather was abhorred everywhere, and yet notwithstanding the same small silly [i.e., feeble] flock so despised in the world, the Lord highly regarded and mightily preserved. For although many then of the Christians did suffer death, yet was their death neither loss to them nor detriment to the church; but the more they suffered, the more of their blood increased.

In the time of these emperors God raised up then in this realm of Britain divers worthy preachers and witnesses, as Elvanus, Meduinus, Meltivianus, Amphibolus, Albanus, Aaron, Julius and other more: [16] in whose time the doctrine of faith, without men's traditions, was sincerely preached. After their death and martyrdom it pleased the Lord to provide a general quietness to his church, whereby the number of his flock began more to increase.

16. [ED.] Foxe, *A. & M.*, I, 257, 231, 327.

In this age then followed here in the said land of Britain, Fastidius, Ninianus, Patricius, Bacchiarius, Dubricius, Congellus, Kentigernus, Helmotus, David, Daniel, Sampson, Elvodugus, Asaphus, Gildas, Henlanus, Elbodus, Dinothus, Samuel, Nivius and a great sort more which governed the church of Britain by Christian doctrine a long season; [17] albeit the civil governors for the time were then dissolute and careless (as Gildas very sharply doth lay to their charge), and so at length were subdued by the Saxons.

All this while, about the space of four hundred years, religion remained in Britain uncorrupt, and the word of Christ truly preached, till, about the coming of Augustine and of his companions from Rome [A.D. 597], many of the said Britain-preachers [18] were slain by the Saxons. After that began [the] Christian faith to enter and spring among the Saxons after a certain Romish sort, yet notwithstanding somewhat more tolerable than were the times which after followed, through the diligent industry of some godly teachers which then lived amongst them — as Aidan, Finian, Colman archbishop of York, Bede, John of Beverly, Alcuin, Noetus, Hucharius, Serlo, Achardus, Ealtedus, Alexander, Neckham, Negellus, Fenallus, Aelfricus, Sygeferthus and such other — [19] who, though they erred in some few things, yet neither [are] so grossly nor so greatly to be complained of in respect of the abuses that followed. For as yet, all this while the error of transubstantiation and elevation, with auricular confession, was not crept in for a public doctrine in Christ's church as, by their own Saxon sermon made by Aelfric and set out in the volume of this present history,[20] may appear. During the which meantime, although the bishops of Rome were had here in some reverence with the clergy, yet had they nothing as yet to do in setting laws touching matters of the church of England: but that only appertained to the kings and governors of the land, as is in this story to be seen, page 922.

And thus the church of Rome, albeit it began then to decline apace from God, yet during all this while it remained hitherto in some reasonable order, till at length after that the said bishops began to shoot up in the world through the liberality of good princes, and especially of Matilda, a noble duchess of Italy, who at her death made the pope heir of all her lands and endued his see with great revenues. Then riches begat ambition, ambition destroyed religion, so that all came to ruin. Out of this corruption sprang forth here in England, as did in other places more, another

17. [ED.] Foxe, *A. & M.*, I, 313 f.   18. [ED.] Foxe, *A. & M.*, I, 314-25.
19. [ED.] Foxe, *A. & M.*, I, 325, 350 f.   20. [ED.] Foxe, *A. & M.*, V, 275-90.

Romish kind of monkery worse than the other before, being much more drowned in superstition and ceremonies, which was about the year of our Lord 980. Of this swarm was Egbert, Agilbert, Egwin, Boniface, Wilfrid, Agatho, James, Romain, Cedda, Dunstan, Oswald, Ethelwold, Athelwin (duke of East-Angles), Lanfranc, Anselm and such others.[21]

And yet in this time also, through God's providence, the church lacked not some of better knowledge and judgment to weigh with the darkness of those days. For although King Edgar, with Edward his base son, being seduced by Dunstan, Oswald and other monkish clerks, was then a great author and fautor [i.e., favorer] of much superstition, erecting as many monasteries as were Sundays in the year, yet notwithstanding, this continued not long. For, eftsoons after the death of Edgar, came King Ethelred and Queen Alfrida his mother, with Alferus duke of Merceland, and other peers and nobles of the realm who displaced the monks again and restored the married priests to their old possessions and livings. Moreover, after that followed also the Danes, which overthrew those monkish foundations as fast as King Edgar had set them up before.[22]

And thus hitherto stood the condition of the true church of Christ, albeit not without some repugnance and difficulty, yet in some mean state of the truth and verity, till the time of Pope Hildebrand, called Gregory VII, which was near about the year 1080, and of Pope Innocent III in the year 1215: by whom all together was turned upside down, all order broken, discipline dissolved, true doctrine defaced, Christian faith extinguished; instead whereof was set up preaching of men's decrees, dreams and idle traditions. And whereas before, truth was free to be disputed amongst learned men, now liberty was turned into law, argument into authority. Whatsoever the bishop of Rome denounced, that stood for an oracle of all men to be received without opposition or contradiction; whatsoever was contrary, *ipso facto* it was heresy, to be punished with faggot and flaming fire. Then began the sincere faith of this English church, which held out so long, to quail. Then was the clear sunshine of God's word overshadowed with mists and darkness, appearing like sackcloth to the people, which neither could understand what they read nor yet [were] permitted to read that they could understand. In these miserable days, as the true visible church began now to shrink and keep in for fear, so up start[ed] a new sort of players to furnish the stage — as school-doctors, canonists and four orders of friars, besides other monastical sects and

21. [ED.] Foxe, *A. & M.*, II, 103.   22. [ED.] Foxe, *A. & M.*, II, 18 ff.

fraternities of infinite variety, which ever since have kept such a stir in the church that none for them almost durst rout, neither Caesar, king nor subject. What they defined stood; what they approved was catholic; what they condemned was heresy; whomsoever they accused none almost could save.[23] And thus have these hitherto continued, or reigned rather, in the church the space now of four hundred years and odd. During which space the true church of Christ, although it durst not openly appear in the face of the world, [was] oppressed by tyranny; yet neither was it so invisible or unknown, but, by the providence of the Lord, some remnant always remained from time to time which not only showed secret good affection to sincere doctrine, but also stood in open defense of truth against the disordered church of Rome.

In which catalogue first, to pretermit Bertram and Berengarius, who were before Pope Innocent III, a learned multitude of sufficient witnesses here might be produced, whose names neither are obscure nor doctrine unknown — as Joachim abbot of Calabria, and Almeric, a learned bishop who was judged a heretic for holding against images in the time of the said Innocent. Besides the martyrs of Alsace of whom we read a hundred to be burned by the said Innocent in one day, as writeth Ulric Mutius. Add likewise to these [the] Waldenses or Albigenses which to a great number segregated themselves from the church of Rome. To this number also belonged Reymund, Earl of Thoulouse, Marsilius Patavinus [of Padua], Gulielmus de Sancto Amore, Simon Tornacensis, Arnoldus de Nova Villa, Johannes Semeca, besides divers other preachers in Swabia standing against the pope, A.D. 1240; *ex chron.* Laurentius Anglicus, a master of Paris, A.D. 1260; Petrus Johannes, a minorite who was burned after his death, A.D. 1290; Robertus Gallus, a Dominican friar, A.D. 1292; Robert Grosthead [Grosseteste], Bishop of Lincoln, who was called *Malleus Romanorum* [hammer against the Romans], A.D. 1250; Lord Peter of Cugnières, A.D. 1329. To these we may add, moreover, Gulielmus Ockam, Bonagratia Bergomensis, Luitpoldus, Andreas Laudensis, Ulric Hangenor, treasurer to the emperor, Johannes de Ganduno, A.D. 1330, mentioned in the Extravagants, Andreas de Castro, Buridianus, Euda, Duke of Burgundy, who counselled the French king not to receive the new-found constitutions and Extravagants of the pope into his realm; Dantes Aligerius, an Italian who wrote against the pope, monks and friars and against the donation of Constantine, A.D. 1330; Taulerus, a German preacher,

23. [ED.] The crusade against heresy launched at the Fourth Lateran Council, 1215.

Conradus Hager, imprisoned for preaching against the mass, A.D. 1339, the author of the book called *Poenitentiarius Asini* [Penitential of Asses], compiled about the year 1343; Michael Cesenas, a grey friar; Petrus de Corbaria, with Johannes de Poliaco mentioned in the Extravagants and condemned by the pope; Johannes de Castilione with Franciscus de Arcatara, who were burned about the year of our Lord 1322; Johannes Rochtaylada otherwise called Haybalus, with another friar martyred about the year 1346; Franciscus Petrarcha who called Rome the whore of Babylon, etc., A.D. 1350; Gregorius Ariminensis, A.D. 1350; Joannes de Rupe Scissa, imprisoned for certain prophecies against the pope, A.D. 1340; Gerhardus Ridder, who also wrote against monks and friars a book called *Lacrymae Ecclesiae* [Tears of the Church], A.D. 1350; Godfridus de Fontanis, Gulielmus de Landuno, Joannes Monachus Cardinalis, Armachanus, Nicolaus Orem, preacher, A.D. 1364; Militzius, a Bohemian, who then preached that Antichrist was come and was excommunicated for the same, A.D. 1366; Jacobus Misnensis, Matthias Parisiensis, a Bohemian born and a writer against the pope, A.D. 1370; Joannes Montziger, rector of the University of Ulm, A.D. 1384; Nilus, Archbishop of Thessalonica, Henricus de Iota, Henricus de Hassia, etc.[24]

I do but recite the principal writers and preachers in those days. How many thousands there were which never bowed their knees to Baal, that is known to God alone. Of whom we find in the writings of one Bruschius, that thirty-six citizens of Mentz were burned, A.D. 1390, who, following the doctrine of the Waldenses, affirmed the pope to be the great Antichrist. Also Massaeus recordeth of one hundred and forty which, in the province of Narbonne, were put to the fire for not receiving the decretals of Rome; besides them that suffered at Paris to the number of twenty-four at one time, A.D. 1210; and the next year after there were four hundred burnt under the name of heretics; besides also a certain good heremite [i.e., hermit], an Englishman, of whom mention is made in John Bacon (*Dist.* 2, *Quaest.* 3), who was committed for disputing in Paul's church against certain sacraments of the church of Rome, A.D. 1306.[25]

To descend now somewhat lower in drawing out the descent of the church. What a multitude here cometh of faithful witnesses in the time of John Wickliff, as Ocliff, Wickliff (A.D. 1379), William Thorp, White, Purvey, Pateshul, Pain, Gower, Chaucer, Gascoin, William Swinderby,

24. [ED.] Foxe, *A. & M.*, II, 319 — III, 220.
25. [ED.] Not elsewhere mentioned by Foxe.

Walter Brute, Roger Dexter, William Sautry about the year 1401; John
Badby, A.D. 1410; Nicholas Tailer, Richard Wagstaff, Michael Scrivener,
William Smith, John Henry, William Parchmenar, Roger Goldsmith
(with an anchoress called Matilda, in the city of Leicester), Lord Cob-
ham, Sir Roger Acton (knight), John Beverley (preacher), John Huss,
Jerome of Prague (a schoolmaster), with a number of faithful Bohemians
and Thaborites not to be told; with whom I might also adjoin Laurentius
Valla and Joannes Picus (the learned Earl of Mirandula). But what do I
stand upon recital of names, which almost are infinite? [26]

Wherefore, if any be so far beguiled in his opinion [as] to think the
doctrine of the church of Rome as it now standeth to be of such antiquity, and that the same was never impugned before the time of Luther
and Zwingli now of late, let him read these histories. Or if he think the
said history not to be of sufficient credit to alter his persuasion, let him
peruse the acts and statutes of parliaments passed in this realm of ancient
time, and therein consider and confer the course of times; where he may
find and read in the year of our Lord 1382 of a great number (which
there be called evil persons) going about from town to town in frieze
gowns, preaching unto the people, etc. Which preachers, although the
words of the statute do term there to be dissembling persons, preaching
divers sermons containing heresies and notorious errors to the emblemish-
ment of Christian faith and of holy church, etc., as the words do there
pretend; yet notwithstanding, every true Christian reader may conceive
of those preachers to teach no other doctrine than now they hear their
own preachers in pulpits preach against the bishop of Rome and the corrupt heresies of his church.[27]

Furthermore, he shall find likewise in the statutes, in the year of our
Lord 1401, another like company of good preachers and faithful defenders of true doctrine against blind heresy and error.[28] Whom, albeit the
words of the statute there, through corruption of that time, do falsely
term to be false and perverse preachers, under dissembled holiness, teaching in those days openly and privily new doctrines and heretical opinions
contrary to the faith and determination of holy church, etc., yet notwithstanding whosoever readeth histories and conferreth the order and descent
of times shall understand these to be no false teachers but faithful witnesses of the truth; not teaching any new doctrines contrary to the determination of holy church, but rather shall find that church to be unholy

26. [ED.] Foxe, *A.* & *M.*, II, 790 — III, 708.   27. [ED.] Foxe, *A.* & *M.*, III, 37-9.
28. [ED.] 2 Hen. IV, cap. 15; see note 4, above.

which they preached against; teaching rather itself heretical opinions, contrary both to antiquity and verity of Christ's true catholic church.

Of the like number also, or greater, of like true faithful favorers and followers of God's holy word, we find in the year of our Lord 1422, specified in a letter sent from Henry Chichesley, Archbishop of Canterbury, to Pope Martin V, in the fifth year of his popedom, where mention is made of so many here in England infected (as he said) with the heresies of Wickliff and Huss that without force of an army they could not be suppressed, etc. Whereupon the pope sent two cardinals to the archbishop, to cause a tenth to be gathered of all spiritual and religious men, and the money to be laid in the chamber apostolic; and if that were not sufficient, the residue to be made up of chalices, candlesticks and other implements of the church,[29] etc.

What shall need then any more witness to prove this matter, when you see, so many years ago, whole armies and multitudes thus standing against the pope, who though they be termed here for heretics and schismatics, yet in that which they call heresy served they the living Lord within the ark of his true spiritual and visible church?

And where is then the frivolous brag of the papists which make so much of their painted sheath; and would needs bear us down, that this government of the church of Rome which now is, hath been of such an old standing, time out of mind, even from the primitive antiquity; and that never was any other church demonstrable here in earth for men to follow, besides the said only catholic mother church of Rome, whenas we have sufficiently proved before, by the continual descent of the church till this present time, that the said church, after the doctrine which is now reformed, is no new-begun matter but even the old continued church by the providence and promise of Christ still standing; which, albeit it hath been of late years repressed by the tyranny of Roman bishops more than before, yet notwithstanding it was never so oppressed that God hath ever maintained in it the truth of his gospel, against heresies and errors of the church of Rome, as, in this history more at full is to be seen.

Let us now proceed further as we began, deducing this descent of the church unto the year 1501. In which year the Lord began to show in the parts of Germany wonderful tokens and bloody marks of his passion; as the bloody cross, his nails, spear, and crown of thorns, which fell from heaven upon the garments and caps of men and rocks of women, as you may further read in this book, page 969. By the which tokens Almighty

29. [ED.]? Foxe, *A. & M.*, III, 567; 847, note 2.

God, no doubt, presignified what grievous afflictions and bloody persecutions should then begin to ensue upon his church for his gospel's sake, according as in this history is described; wherein is to be seen what Christian blood hath been spilt, what persecutions raised, what tyranny exercised, what torments devised, what treachery used against the poor flock and church of Christ; in such sort as since Christ's time greater hath not been seen.

And now by revolution of years we are come from that time of 1501 to the year now present, 1570.[30] In which the whole seventy years of the Babylonish captivity draweth now well to an end if we count from the first appearing of these bloody marks above mentioned.[31] Or if we reckon from the beginning of Luther and his persecution, then lacketh yet sixteen years. Now what the Lord will do with this wicked world, or what rest he will give to his church after these long sorrows — he is our Father in heaven, his will be done in earth as seemeth best to his divine Majesty.

In the meantime let us, for our parts, with all patient obedience wait upon his gracious leisure, and glorify his holy name, and edify one another with all humility. And if there cannot be an end of our disputing and contending one against another, yet let there be a moderation in our affections. And forsomuch as it is the good will of our God, that Satan thus should be let loose among us for a short time; yet let us strive in the meanwhile what we can to amend the malice of the time with mutual humanity. They that be in error, let them not disdain to learn. They which have greater talents of knowledge committed [to them, let them] instruct in simplicity them that be simple. No man liveth in that commonwealth where nothing is amiss; but yet because God hath so placed us Englishmen here in one commonwealth, also in one church, as in one ship together, let us not mangle or divide the ship, which being divided, perisheth; but every man serve in his order with diligence wherein he is called — they that sit at the helm keep well the point of the needle to know how the ship goeth and whither it should; whatsoever weather betideth, the needle, well touched with the stone of God's word, will never fail. Such as labor at the oars start for no tempest but do what they can to keep from the rocks. Likewise they which be in inferior rooms, take heed they

30. [ED.] The year of the second English edition.
31. [ED.] On Foxe's chronological scheme, see William Haller, Foxe's "Book of Martyrs" and the Elect Nation (London, 1963), chap. v, especially 157, 171; Foxe, A. & M., I, 87 f, 290 f, 388 f.

move no sedition nor disturbance against the rowers and mariners.[32] No storm so dangerous to a ship on the sea as is discord and disorder in a weal public. What countries and nations, what kingdoms and empires, what cities, towns and houses discord hath dissolved, in stories is manifest; I need not spend time in rehearsing examples.

The Lord of peace, who hath power both of land and sea, reach forth his merciful hand to help them up that sink, to keep them up that stand, to still these winds and surging seas of discord and contention amongst us; that we, professing one Christ, may, in one unity of doctrine, gather ourselves into one ark of the true church together; where we, continuing steadfast in faith, may at the last luckily be conducted to the joyful port of our desired landing-place by his heavenly grace. To whom, both in heaven and in earth, be all power and glory, with his Father and the Holy Spirit, for ever. Amen.

32. [ED.] ? An admonition to the more radical Puritans?

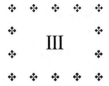

The Fortress of Fathers

Editor's Introduction

Within five years after John Gough made his plea for a reformation based on the earnest following of Erasmus' godly rules for living, the English Protestant party, although still a small minority movement within the English church, was so divided that for centuries afterward English Protestantism was to remain a group of separated if not hostile camps. It may be debated whether the "vestiarian controversy" began this rift or merely uncovered it. But there can be no doubt that that controversy, which came to a climax in 1566, to a large extent set the future character of English Protestantism. Among the several "Puritan" documents that came out of the vestment controversy in 1566, the anonymous *Fortress of Fathers* reflects more accurately than any other the many facets of the debate. It also does much to explain why, after the particular furor of the vestment controversy had subsided in some measure, the conflict did not end, but deepened and became more widespread. By the time the *Fortress* was published, it was becoming evident that the clerical vestments symbolized rather than constituted the issues of the controversy.

The English authorities were in a very difficult situation as Elizabeth's reign began. A national church, plagued by many long-standing problems, had to be administered as a Protestant establishment staffed by a clergy of whom the vast majority had been Roman Catholic and would have preferred to remain so. The incoming Protestant clerics, a tiny fraction (perhaps five per cent) of the total, were at best an unpredictable element. No one doubted, however, that tension between the two clerical groups would be severe. The politicians, all laymen, gambled on the supposition that status would be of more concern than doctrine to the Catholic clergy, most of whom under Edward, scarcely six years earlier, had been Protestant by compulsion, and had been Catholic under Henry a few years before that. Accordingly, the Settlement had allowed the old clergy to retain most of their status symbols, attire, insignia, recognitions, privileges and incomes. The returning and newly ordained Protestant clerics were required to accept and use these same symbols as an expression of unity within the church. Compelling these men to identify themselves thus with the former Marian clerics, it was believed, would prevent a polarization of the Elizabethan clergy into two parties, "turn-coats" and "Protestants." This was the meaning of the Elizabethan "uniformity." [1]

The earliest leaders of the opposition to this policy were exiles newly returned from Zurich, Frankfort and Strassburg, where they had learned much about the Interim controversy over vestments, rites and the episcopate. Most of these men also had been active in the Edwardine church at a time of severe controversy over vestments and ceremonies. During the Marian exile the colony at Frankfort had been torn by strife over vestments, rites and ministerial authority. The dissension had spilled over into all the other exile colonies. The governmental policy on vestments was therefore a cause of dismay to the returning exiles. Being forced to identify themselves with "Queen Mary's clergy," as Parker called them, seemed in effect to merge them into one body defined now in Catholic terms.[2] Opposition to the vestments was in fact opposition to the basis on which the Marian clergy were being carried over. The early opponents of the vestments were demanding that the Marian clergy be forced into an identification with themselves by the acceptance of a distinctively Protestant vesture. The civil authorities dared not accede to these demands. Toleration — whether for Catholics, for Protestants, or for Tudor monarchs — was not a virtue in the sixteenth century. But in England it became a hard and disagreeable necessity, even though more than three centuries were to pass before Englishmen would confess verbally what they had long since found themselves obliged to accept.

The shock that quickly led to the vestment controversy came with the Parliament of 1563 and the accompanying Convocation of the clergy. Whereas in 1559 there had been numerous Catholics in Parliament, and

1. On the Settlement see especially John Neale, "The Elizabethan Acts of Supremacy and Uniformity," *Eng. Hist. Rev.*, LXV (1950), 304–32; Neale, *Elizabeth I and Her Parliaments, 1559–81* (London, 1953); W. T. MacCaffery, "Elizabethan Politics, the First Decade, 1558–68," *Past and Present*, XXIV (April 1963), 25–42.

2. *A brieff discours off the troubles begonne at Franckford, A.D. 1554* (1574; S.T.C., 25442; reprint edited by E. Arber, 1908); Patrick Collinson, "The authorship of *A brieff discours* . . . ," *Jrl. Eccles. Hist.*, IX (October 1958), 188–208; Collinson, ed., *The Letters of Thomas Wood, Puritan, 1566–77* (London, 1960); C. H. Garrett, *The Marian Exiles* (Cambridge, 1938); *Zurich Letters*, I, 131–4, 156, *et passim*. See also John Strype, *Ecclesiastical Memorials . . . Henry VIII, Edward VI, and Mary I . . .* (Oxford, 1820–2), III, II, 313–15; Parker, *Correspondence*, 157.

Convocation had been exclusively Catholic, now in 1563 the entire kingdom was professedly Protestant. Many Englishmen, lay and clerical, expected further reforms as Parliament met. Various proposals had been made in advance, and still others were presented after the Convocation had assembled.[3] The House of Bishops drew up the Thirty-Nine Articles of Religion, based upon the Forty-Two Articles of Edward's reign, and required the Lower House of Convocation to sign them. Parliamentary sanction for these Articles was not given, however, until 1571.

The Lower House turned its attention to a reform of liturgy, ceremonies, church administration, finances, and lay and clerical discipline. Some major changes were advocated, but only on one very modest proposal was a vote taken. This proposal, in six articles, was to abrogate all holy days except Sundays and the "principal feasts of Christ"; to require the minister to face the people as he read the service; to permit but not require the omission of the sign of the cross on the child's forehead in baptism; to allow each bishop his own discretion in requiring the communicant to kneel for the reception of the sacrament; to permit the wearing of the surplice or some other "comely garment or habit" by the minister during the service; and to remove organs from the churches. None of these articles was either new or the result of foreign influence, least of all Genevan influences. The first and sixth, those limiting holy days and doing away with the organ, dated back to the pre-Reformation Christian Humanists. Later, under Edward VI, Bishop Ridley had been very active in doing away with organs. The second article, requiring the minister to face the people, indicated the non-sacerdotal character of his office. The three permissive articles, on the sign of the cross, kneeling and vestments, amounted to no more than a tolerance of scruples. There was much debate on all six articles, but especially on the fourth, the old question of kneeling, which — along with that of vestments — had been a subject of controversy during the reign of Edward.

When the vote was taken the proposal passed by 43 to 35, out of a total of 144 seats. But finally, once the 39 proxy votes cast for absentees had been tallied, it was defeated, 58 to 59. Twenty-seven men, for reasons that are not recorded, had abstained from voting. Of the 35 who voted

3. Strype, *Annals*, I, 1, 470–538; J. C. Barry, "The Convocation of 1563," *History Today*, XIII (1963), 490–501. E. Cardwell, *Synodalia, A Collection . . . Convocations . . . 1547 . . . 1717* (Oxford, 1842), II, 495–527, gives some slightly different figures for these votes. The best account is by A. J. Carlson, "The Puritans and the Convocation of 1563," in Theodore K. Raab and Jerrold E. Seigel, eds., *Action and Conviction in Early Modern Europe* (Princeton, 1969), 133–53.

"Nay," and who controlled 24 proxies, only one had been an exile. He had spent three years in France, studying law, it seems, and was now a chaplain to Parker. At least 21 of the 35 had held office under Mary. Of the 43 who voted for the proposal, and who controlled 15 proxies, 22 had been exiles; 21 others (who controlled 10 proxies) had not. Of the 22 former exiles, only 4 were of the Geneva party. Of the others, all but one (who came from Aarau) had been at either Frankfort or Strassburg. None of the Zurich party were recorded in the voting. It is noteworthy that in the fourth year of Elizabeth's reign, the Lower House of Convocation was firmly in the hands of the non-exiles, who controlled 89 votes, whereas former exiles controlled only 28. The 27 non-voting men came from every kind of background — exiles, Marian carryovers, and former secret Protestants. Carryovers from Mary's reign were firmly entrenched all through the church bureaucracy.

Just where the bishops stood concerning this attempt by the Lower House to reform the church is not clear. Parker expressed irritation over the debates, and two other bishops made vague general statements; no other records survive.[4] Everyone knew, of course, that even if the proposals had passed in the Lower House they would not become law without approval by the House of Bishops, the two Houses of Parliament, and the Queen. However, the failure of these very mild proposals for change and toleration produced a militant reaction among many Englishmen, both laymen and clergy. It was one thing, in 1559, to have accepted the Elizabethan Settlement as a means of initiating reform. But things were not the same once it began to appear that no further changes could be made, and that there would be no toleration of conscientious scruples. For those who opposed reform, there had now been an opportunity to assess the strength (or the weakness) of the radical party. Within a few months both sides had gone into action. The most notable consequence of the contest in the Convocation of 1563 was that henceforth the battle for further church reform would be fought out in Parliament, rather than in Convocation. The church officials not only lost the chance to have the church reform itself; they also lost the capacity to develop a leadership, a policy, or a sense of purpose in any way comparable to what had been achieved on the Continent among Lutherans, Calvinists or Catholics. For Parliament, especially Commons, becoming the battleground of church reform meant a vast change in the way it understood its own role in the national life.

4. Parker, *Correspondence*, 173; Jewel, *Works*, IV, 1259–61; *Zurich Letters*, I, 54–60; II, 124–35.

More than one revolution has grown out of an irritation, leading to the discovery of more serious grievances, and has finally exploded into violence because of an evil become intolerable. Once the reform party had become persuaded that the church bureaucracy was opposed to further change, a religious discontent that had many causes began to simmer around the issue of the vestments. This issue had been the concern of only one of the six proposals defeated in 1563. The unreformed church courts, the financial chaos of the church, the demoralization of many older priests, the doctrinal confusion, the lack of pastoral concern, were among the problems that had been bypassed by the critics as well as by the defenders of the Elizabethan Settlement.

Several things are to be noted in order to understand why, in the face of such major evils, a controversy should have raged over the wearing of vestments. The Queen, her Privy Councillors, and the power-holders of the nation had so large a stake in the church's corrupt finances that no one had yet dared to raise the issue in public. The state of the ecclesiastical courts not only angered the radicals; it also defied the efforts of Archbishop Parker, and of Whitgift after him. No simple fiat could have restored the morale or the zeal of those priests who over a period of twenty-five years (1534–59) had passed through the successive changes of religion commanded by the civil government. Besides, most of the lower clergy were desperately poor. The Queen resolutely opposed any clear statement of doctrine or of canon law. She and her counsellors believed that the pastoral needs of the people could best be met by keeping them under control. Popular resentments could be drained off in violent polemics against a foreign pope, against Catholic enemies abroad, and against a "disloyal" (and dispossessed) Catholic clergy. The function of the liturgy was to channel the attention of worshippers into ceremonial observances; often repeated homilies on harmless, traditional and outmoded themes would lull them into passivity. A defensive episcopate, with neither cohesion nor any sense of religious leadership, were to act merely as repressive agents for the civil authority.

Although, on the one hand, there was much dislike of the vestments even among the bishops, and on the other, as early as 1561, the Queen was reported to be impatient with the bishops and clergy who refused to wear the vestments,[5] the controversy that broke out was directly related to the politics of the Court. It would appear, in fact, to have been deliberately launched, and to have been the latest move in a struggle for power between the rival parties of Cecil and Leicester. Of the two, Robert Dud-

5. Parker, *Correspondence*, 156 f

ley (who became Earl of Leicester in 1564) as the suitor and lover of the Queen, was now the most influential member of the Privy Council. William Cecil, its Secretary as well as the most competent administrator among its members, was now desperately insecure in that post. The lifelong duel between the two men went on behind a façade of correctness, and by 1564 both were fighting for ultimate stakes. Cecil had been implicated in John Hales' scheme to designate the Suffolk (Grey) family as successors to the throne if Elizabeth should die childless. It was with the greatest difficulty that he managed to avoid being ruined. Moreover, he was regarded by Leicester as one of those responsible for the proposal, aired that summer, to give Leicester to Mary Queen of Scots as a husband — which Leicester saw as a plot to get him out of English politics. Since Mary was the most obvious claimant to the English throne after Elizabeth, the scheme had a certain plausibility. But Leicester wished to marry Elizabeth — a development that promised little for the party of Cecil.[6]

It was in the midst of these intrigues that Cecil and Parker launched the controversy over the vestments. The legendary picture of a ceremony-loving queen forcing a hapless, pacific archbishop into a battle he had no taste for does not accord with the facts: namely, that Cecil (with Parker as his front man), using Elizabeth's known predilections and the political situation behind the religious settlement, sought to drive a wedge between Leicester and the Queen. Leicester had little religion and few scruples. But he was a party politician, one who worked through others to gain his own ends, and who thus had in some measure to serve theirs. If the Queen could be maneuvered into condemning the radicals outright, Leicester would be confronted by a dilemma. If he supported the Queen, he would lose the influence he had carefully built up with the anticlerical and radical Protestants among the nobility, the clergy, and certain powerful laymen in London. If he continued to protect the radical clerics, he would have to turn against the Queen. Either way, both Cecil and Parker had much to gain, especially if Leicester could not after all be married off to the Scottish queen.[7]

6. On the conflict between Cecil and Leicester at this time, see Conyers Read, *Mr. Secretary Cecil and Queen Elizabeth* (London, 1961), 201, 252-6, 278-87, 315, 329-37, 351, *et passim*. The conflict went on until Leicester's death in 1588.

7. Concerning the hostility between Leicester and Parker, the latter's dependence on Cecil, and the reactions of Parker and Cecil to Leicester's support of the radicals, see Read, *Mr. Secretary Cecil* (note 6, above); V. J. K. Brook, *The Life of Archbishop Parker* (Oxford, 1962), 162, 169-70, 178, 301, 315, 335 f, 344, *et passim*;

Parker began, in December 1564, by attacking the two most prominent radicals, Laurence Humphrey and Thomas Sampson of Oxford University. (Leicester was Chancellor of Oxford, and Cecil held the same post at Cambridge.) At a conference Humphrey and Sampson agreed to a statement drawn up jointly by Parker, several bishops, and themselves — namely, that in a church that confessed pure doctrine, where preaching flourished, and where Antichrist was publicly repudiated, ministers might wear distinctive dress when commanded by the civil magistrate, provided it was made clear that no idea of religious necessity had dictated it. Humphrey and Sampson, however, understood the statement to mean that pure doctrine, lively preaching, and public repudiation of Antichrist (none of which, they believed, characterized the English church at the time) would forestall any popular misunderstanding of the continued use of the old Roman Catholic vestments. Accordingly, they offered a double compromise: they would agree to the statement as one of general policy, and they would agree not to preach or work against any clerics who wore the vestments. But they asked, given the situation then prevailing, to be allowed to continue in the ministry without the wearing of the vestments, on the grounds of conscientious scruple. Parker refused this compromise, insisting that the statement agreed upon compelled the men to wear the vestments.[8]

Owing to Leicester's influence, Parker's effort was nullified. From his bitterness over the outcome it is evident that in this matter he had not merely yielded to pressure by the Queen. In their next move, on January 25, Cecil and Parker secured Elizabeth's approval of a letter they had drawn up, ordering immediate and total conformity by all the clergy. But Elizabeth would neither sign the letter nor acknowledge it publicly, and the Privy Council consequently refused to sanction it either. In addition, the legality of the plan they had devised to implement the Queen's letter was questioned. In June 1565 came the news that Mary Queen of Scots was to marry Lord Darnley, an English Catholic (and like her a claimant to the English throne). In the crisis that ensued, the Privy Council re-examined many of its domestic policies. Among other things, its members concluded that religious truth and civil policy were joined together, and

---

also John Strype, *The Life and Acts of Matthew Parker* . . . (Oxford, 1821), I, 308 f, 314, 326-8, 437; II, 191, 273; III, 76-84, *et passim;* and Eleanor Rosenberg, *Leicester, Patron of Letters* (New York, 1955), chap. VI. In the last letter he ever wrote (April 11, 1575), Parker referred to this continuing hostility.

8. Strype, *Parker*, I, 329-33, 344; III, 95-7; Jewel, *Works*, IV, 1265; Parker, *Correspondence*, 223-30, 233-5, 240.

that these now required that relief should be given at once to those who opposed the clerical vestments. Accordingly, the way must be paved for a change of policy at the next Parliament. Renewed fears of the Catholic threat caused radical Protestants to appear as much more reliable defenders of the public weal than "half-hearted" ones were. There was little doubt that Parliament would favor the radicals. In that same month of June 1565, Humphrey and Sampson, who had been removed from office and confined in some manner, were released. Humphrey returned to his post at Oxford; Sampson, who could not, was made master of a hospital in Leicester.[9]

For the next nine months Parker was in despair. Cecil had launched this scheme, he lamented, but now he refused to back it openly. In Edward's time, Parker expostulated, the entire Privy Council had backed the bishops against John Hooper's refusal of the vestments. Now Parker stood alone, with the imperious letter he and Cecil had drafted, and which he was now helpless to enforce, hanging over his head. It was now Parker, not Leicester, who had been caught in a dilemma. Cecil, he wrote, and equally the Queen, could not stand by and allow royal authority thus to be flouted.[10] Cecil, whose personal religion may have been somewhat shallow, was totally committed to Protestantism as the religion of England. Yet he was at bottom anticlerical and a politician. Until his death in 1598 he opposed every move that might have increased the constitutional authority of the bishops over the laity. Throughout Elizabeth's reign, however, when the issue at stake was the authority of the episcopate over clergymen, Cecil was often ambivalent, to the dismay of bishops and of dissident clerics alike. He might support a bishop to preserve law and order, but he might equally well befriend a very troublesome preacher to cut down a lordly prelate. In late 1565 and early 1566, he would not risk his career to save Parker.[11]

After consulting with lawyers, Parker drew up a plan, evidently with the help of the Ecclesiastical Commission, that appeared immune to challenge in the courts of common law. Apparently acting in the name of the Commission, he planned to summon all the clergy of London to Lambeth for a showdown on March 26, 1566. To lend an appearance of legality and give force to the proceedings, he invited Cecil and his two

9. Read, *Cecil*, 315, 322–4; Parker, *Correspondence*, 243–5. See also Bishop Horne to R. Gualter, July 17, 1565, *Zurich Letters*, I, 143, in which opposition to a parliamentary change of policy on vestments is laid to "the papists"!

10. Parker, *Correspondence*, 245–6, 262–4.

11. Note the manner in which he handled the Hales affair; Read, *Cecil*, 283.

closest supporters on the Privy Council to attend also. They did not accept. Three of the five bishops on the Commission — Bullingham, Coxe and Horne — likewise stayed away. Coxe, however, was a supporter of the move. Parker, Grindal and Gabriel Goodman (a Marian carryover, who was dean of Westminster and chaplain to Cecil) were the only prominent clerics present.

The assembled parish clergy were confronted with three demands: total conformity in the wearing of vestments, unqualified use of the prayer book, and acceptance of the Articles of Religion drawn up at the Convocation of 1563. No debate was tolerated; the participants were compelled to subscribe in writing "Yes" or "No." Parker reported to Cecil that 61 wrote "Yes" and 37 "No." Among the latter, he said, were some of the best of the London clergy. Those who wrote "No" were forbidden to preach or minister, and their livings were sequestered. If after three months they had not given affirmative answers, they were to be excluded permanently from the ministry. Parker expected that most of them would shortly give up. This showdown took place just before Easter, with the result that many churches were without pastors or services on that holiday. In the reaction that followed the suspensions, Parker and the Ecclesiastical Commissioners were obliged to shoulder the entire responsibility. Parker was soon so embittered that he wished all these "silly recusants were out of the ministry." Most of the other bishops avoided taking a position; some openly opposed Parker and his policy.

Following this showdown with the parish clergy of London, Parker issued what were known as the Advertisements, a series of episcopal orders that adroitly hinted at royal authority while taking care to make no legal claim thereto. The Advertisements were at best extra-legal if not illegal. But because they purported to emanate from the Queen, any open challenge to their legality would have forced the Queen to act in their defense. Consequently, for legal reasons the more astute opponents held back, for practical reasons the more timorous did the same, and Parker succeeded in his bluff. The Advertisements had been ordered, it was said, for the sake not of religion but merely of decency and order. They dealt at great length with the vestments required, gave orders concerning a number of rites and ceremonies that had been in dispute, cancelled all preaching licenses issued before March 1, 1564, forbade criticism of the established religion, and set up procedures (including a nine-point subscription formula) for securing the adherence of every cleric in the kingdom to the new regulations. The controversy over the vestments was now irretrievably launched, and the radicals found themselves at a great disadvantage. There is no evidence that any other bishop — not even Coxe or Guest, both of whom had aided Parker in the move — took action in his own diocese at the time. Coxe wrote that if London could once be forced to conform, then the rest of the nation would fall into line. So the policy was to wait and see what happened in London.[12]

The radicals now took their case, by way of irregular preaching and the underground press, directly to the people of London. In so doing they had soon given to Protestantism in England a character that would forever after distinguish it from Protestantism on the Continent. Although there was a very significant popular religious literature on the Continent, it was developed and controlled by the leadership of the established Protestant churches as a part of their official activity. In England the leadership of the official church was defensive, authoritarian, repressive, and unconcerned with developing a popular literature. Such literature as did appear thus came in large measure from Protestant critics of the establishment, and was designed by them to promote criticism of the established religion and of the power behind it.

At some time in April 1566, the first published criticism of Parker's moves to compel vestments appeared. Elizabeth took the position that to make an answer to these books would only breed "contention." Parker argued vigorously that there must be an answer, and he finally prevailed.[13] Here again it was Parker, not Cecil or the Queen, who took the lead. Traditional accounts placing all the responsibility on the Queen are as dubious as the later Puritan tactic of exonerating her and blaming only the wicked bishops. The Queen, the parties of Cecil and Leicester, Parker and the Ecclesiastical Commission, a faction in Parliament, and the radical preachers all saw in the vestment controversy either a menace or an opportunity that could not be ignored. To ascribe it solely to the Queen's reputed love of ritual, or to a coldness in the Puritans toward aesthetic considerations, is to misconstrue altogether what it meant to the several parties to the dispute.

The exact sequence of some twenty documents that were issued during the controversy cannot now be readily determined. All but three (which came out years afterward) seem to have appeared between April 1566 and the opening on September 13, 1566 of the Parliament into which the

12. Parker, *Correspondence*, 267–74, 280–84; R. W. Dixon, *History of the Church of England* . . . (Oxford, 1878–1902), VI, 90–101.

13. Parker, *Correspondence*, 284.

Privy Council had agreed to introduce a bill amending the vestment requirements. There are also baffling overlappings, borrowings and connections among these documents that make their exact sequence a puzzle.

If a letter from Coxe to Parker, written May 3 and mentioning a recent publication by Parker, does refer to the vestment controversy, the first books in this controversy must have appeared in late April.[14] These were *The Voice of God . . . a Ballet . . .* (now lost) and *A Brief Discourse Against the Outward Apparel and Ministering Garments of the Popish Church . . .*, known also as *The Unfolding of the Popish Attire* or as *A Declaration of the Doings of Those Ministers . . . of London . . .* (usually attributed to Crowley and others; S.T.C., 6078). Appended to some copies of this work are two letters which may or may not originally have been published with it. The letters, which reappeared in various forms in other, later publications, were anonymous and without addressees. One was from Anthony Gilby to Coverdale, Turner, Whittingham, Sampson, Humphrey, Lever, Crowley "and others." The second was from Bishop James Pilkington of Durham to Leicester (written October 25, 1564, and asking his aid on behalf of the radicals) with the salutation and closing altered to conceal author and addressee. The official answer to the *Brief Discourse*, usually attributed to Parker, was *A Brief Examination for the Time of a Certain Declaration* (S.T.C., 10387), which (assuming that Coxe's letter noted above does refer to this item) had appeared as early as May 3. Walter Haddon wrote from Bruges on May 27 about Crowley's book. Parker sent him his *Brief Examination* on June 6. On that same date John Abel referred to both books in a letter to Bullinger, and added that the printers of Crowley's book had been imprisoned and the copies destroyed.[15] However, the book was soon reprinted secretly, with the date 1566.

Crowley's *Brief Discourse* had cited Bucer, Martyr, Ridley and Jewel in support of the radicals. Parker had challenged each of these citations, and had appended to his *Brief Examination* letters of Cranmer, Bucer, Hooper, Martyr and Lasco concerning Hooper's fight against the vestments in 1550. The letters of Bucer and Martyr were the same ones that had been used in March 1565 in an effort to convince Humphrey and Sampson. The Bucer letter had been tampered with, a long section oppos-

14. Parker, *Correspondence*, 281.

15. *Zurich Letters*, II, 119-20; *A Transcript of the Registers of the Company of Stationers of London, 1554-1640*, edited by E. Arber (London, 1875-94), I, 307, 314, 316.

ing Parker's position having been deleted. Parker had claimed the support also of a number of authors and books from the Continent. It may be that two slightly different editions of Parker's book were published.

The radicals answered by reprinting and refuting Parker's *Brief Examination*, paragraph by paragraph, in *An Answer for the Time to the Examination . . . (S.T.C.,* 10388). Because the radicals did not have access to the manuscripts, they could not detect the tampering with Bucer's letter. But they did contest Parker's other citations.

Each side also resorted to certain "supporting documents," whose exact sequence, once again, is not wholly clear. The radicals issued a lengthy passage from Bucer's commentary on Matthew dealing with the verse (18:7), "Woe unto the world because of offences," a passage over which there had been controversy since Crowley's first reference to it in the *Brief Discourse.* They appended a section, "Answers to Objections," in which the controversy over vestments in Edward's day was related to the current one, and the issue of disobedience to the civil magistrate was resolved by urging "no rebellion" but passive acceptance of any legal penalty (see *S.T.C.,* 3964). Two anonymous letters are appended to some copies of this document, one urging steadfastness and the other giving reasons why the vestments should not be used. The radicals issued also a new edition of William Turner's well-known "fox-wolf" attack upon Bishop Stephen Gardiner, which had appeared twice in 1543 and had been revised again in 1545, and also in 1554 during Mary's reign (*S.T.C.,* 24353-7). The work carried also Gilby's letter to Turner, Coverdale and others, again without the names of authors or addressees. The intent, of course, was to point to the parallels between the lordly, persecuting prelate Gardiner (notorious among all English Protestants) and the bishops of 1566.

The letters now found appended to the several radical documents noted above are always in separate foliations, thus raising the question of whether they were parts of the original documents or were bound with them later. Separate copies of these same letters, as well as of two others, are to be found in some libraries,[16] and they seem to have passed through various editions and revisions (see *S.T.C.,* 10389-91). Parker wrote bitterly on one occasion about certain letters and books that had been in circulation for two or three years. These letters do not refer specifically to any incidents, and could have been issued at any time after October 1564,

16. The copies at the Bodleian and Folger libraries and the British Museum had perhaps been bound up differently by previous owners.

when Parker first moved against Humphrey and Sampson. Thus the Turner reprint also could have appeared before 1566.

Ever since their return from exile, some of the English had carried on a correspondence with Bullinger, Martyr, Gualter and other leaders of the Zurich church. Because the English had been neither associated with nor accepted by the official clergy at Frankfort, Strassburg and Basel, they had no continuing ties with those cities. In Geneva the English had been well received, but the followers of Calvin there at the time were engaged in a life-and-death struggle to survive, which kept them far too occupied to give much personal attention to the English. Beza moved to Geneva only in October 1558, and was at once so deeply involved in the political concerns of the party of Calvin on the Continent that he had little time for the English. Moreover, because of the Knox and Goodman tracts on politics, the Genevan exiles had found no very warm welcome on their return to England. After the deaths of Martyr in 1562 and Calvin in 1564, the returned English exiles looked to Zurich as the one place where they had found friendship and inspiration.

As the vestment controversy developed, therefore, returned exiles from Strassburg, Frankfort, Basel and Zurich had written to Bullinger and his colleagues for advice. The Zurich church was, of course, thoroughly "Zwinglian" on all liturgical and ecclesiastical matters. The old clerical vestments were utterly forbidden, as were all the old rites and ceremonies. Moreover, during the Interim controversy in Germany, and all the while the English exiles were in Zurich, the Zurcher ministers had been vigorously opposed to any compromise on the vestments, rites and ceremonies that were then in controversy. Consequently, in 1558-9 and the early 1560s, the Zurich ministers advised their English correspondents to labor to bring the English church to primitive purity and simplicity, especially in the matter of clerical vestments. Once the issue of obedience to the civil magistrate had been raised, however, the Zurchers were in a quandary. During the Interim controversy the Zurich magistrates had disciplined their ministers for impinging on the right of the magistrate to decide definitively on all externals in the church. When in 1560 the civil magistrates at Heidelberg by their own act had altered the official church from Lutheran to Reformed — and had tolerated no debate by ministers — the Zurich ministers had applauded. So on May 1, 1566 Bullinger declared to Humphrey and Sampson that "if the consent of the clergy [had] always to be waited for by the sovereign," the Old Testament kings could probably never have reformed ancient Israel. Bullinger might have extended the observation to the reform of Protestant Europe, but he did not. He merely went on to say both "Yes" and "No" to the returned exiles who sought his advice.[17]

The difficulty was that the English situation was not at all like that of Zurich or Heidelberg. In England the magistrate was opposed to the purity and simplicity of the primitive church as practiced in Zurich. So, in one letter to England the Zurchers would be urging Zwinglian purity and simplicity, and in another the good old Zurich relationship between church and state. At length, on May 1, 1566, Bullinger and Gualter wrote Humphrey and Sampson a long letter which — except for a few minor Zurich-saving caveats — went all the way toward justifying not only the English civil authorities and the English bishops, but even, at some length, the wearing of the vestments. Not that the Zurich ministers themselves would ever have done so in their own city. At the time, in the primitive simplicity of Zurich even congregational singing of hymns was forbidden. To clinch the matter, and without informing Humphrey and Sampson, Bullinger sent a copy of this letter to Bishops Horne, Grindal and Parkhurst.[18] By early June it had been received with joy by the bishops. Almost at once, to the dismay of the radicals, Grindal had the letter published in English and in Latin (S.T.C., 4063, 4, 75). It was followed by another publication entitled *Whether it Be Mortal Sin to Transgress Civil Laws . . .* (S.T.C., 22572), to which the conclusion was heartily given in the affirmative. The book had neither preface nor comment, and listed no author. It contained passages from Melanchthon's *Epitome of Moral Philosophy* and from his commentary on Romans, verse 13:1: "Let every soul be subject unto the higher powers." Then came Bullinger's letter to the bishops, followed by the Bullinger-Gualter letter to Humphrey and Sampson, then the five letters from the Hooper controversy that had been appended to Parker's *Brief Examination*. At about this same time, on June 29, the Privy Council laid down exceedingly severe penalties for unlicensed publication.[19] Criticism of the establishment was not to be tolerated.

William Turner, who had known the Zurcher leaders since his sojourn there after Henry's Six Articles were handed down in 1539, wrote to ask Bullinger whether he had turned into a Melanchthon (for during the In-

17. See the *Zurich Letters* from the years 1559–68, especially I, 354.
18. *Zurich Letters*, I, 345–62.
19. *Transcript of the Registers of . . . Stationers . . .* , I, 322.

terim, according to the Zurchers at the time, the latter had vacillated shamefully). Turner pointed out that the Bullinger-Gualter letter conflicted with the printed works of both men, and urged them in some manner to repair their credit. Humphrey and Sampson also expostulated with the Zurchers for having secretly dispatched their letter to the bishops.[20] The radicals now issued a pamphlet made up of selections from Bullinger's most famous book, the *Decades*, fifty sermons dedicated in part to Edward VI and in part to Henry Grey, Marquis of Dorset. Grey was the father of Queen Jane, the heroine of the Marian exiles and martyrs. The radicals compiled, out of Bullinger's dedication to Grey and the portion of the *Decades* dedicated to him, a book entitled *The Judgment of . . . Bullinger . . . in Certain Matters of Religion Being in Controversy in Many Countries . . .* (S.T.C., 4065). The *Decades*, having originated in Zurich, set forth vigorously the Zurich simplicities. And because Bullinger was at the time deeply exercised over the German Interim, he had also said as much as he dared against the actions of wicked magistrates. Its wholly fortuitous connection with Jane Grey gave the tract an added bite in the England of 1566.

The last printed document to emerge from the vestment controversy of 1566 seems to have been *The Fortress of Fathers* (S.T.C., 1040). Its place in the sequence is indicated by the extensive detail with which almost every argument or controverted "authority" cited in the other documents is presented. The document shows, as do all the others, the background of the vestment controversy in the church under Edward and in the colonies of Marian exiles at Frankfort, Strassburg and Zurich, as well as in the controversy in those places over the German Interim. The Genevan influence in the conflict was insignificant. The anticlerical and anti-ceremonial attitudes of the Christian Humanists and of Erasmus in particular, on the other hand, were clearly reflected. The long quotations from Bucer and Martyr were not merely old hat. Most of that material had been produced in England or while the English were with Martyr in exile. The passage from Melanchthon was an answer to *Whether it Be Mortal Sin . . .* ; Gualter and Bullinger were quoted once again to show how their recent letters were confuted by their own earlier statements. The long letter of Lasco harked back to the church under Edward. The quotations from Epinus and Flacius were part of the Interim controversy; several of these came from works regarded as standard by the English

20. *Zurich Letters*, II, 124–6; 121–4, 133, 136–44; I, 157–70.

bishops — in short, they were anything but *ex parte* pronouncements elic-
ited for a purpose — although they were made to serve one in the *Fortress*. It is noteworthy that almost every selection evokes a charge of
"tyranny." The compiler of the *Fortress* came close to sanctioning some
kind of resistance to the magistrate, as Bucer and Fagius had done at
Strassburg in 1548.[21]

The compiler of the *Fortress* identified himself only as "J.B." The
book seems to have been published after June 29, 1566, when the Privy
Council laid down severe censorship regulations in order to prevent criticism in print of current ecclesiastical policy. That "J.B." was never apprehended may argue that the initials were fictitious. They have been
plausibly identified as those of John Barthlet, a vigorous participant in the
vestment controversy. But in the same year, 1566, Barthlet issued a licit
anti-Catholic work, *Pedigree of Heretics* (S.T.C., 1534), and when Barthlet's English, and his translations from the Latin, are compared with
those in the *Fortress*, it becomes difficult to suppose that he was the author of both books. Moreover, Barthlet had not been a Marian exile, nor
had he been active in the church under Edward.

A more likely "J.B." (assuming that the initials were genuine) would
have been John Browne, a Marian exile and chaplain to that outspoken
champion of Protestantism and Puritanism, the Duchess of Suffolk.
Browne was deeply involved in the vestment controversy, and continued
active in the Puritan movement as late as 1573. A John Browne (or
Brome) had been at Frankfort and Strassburg during the exile, and had a
part of some consequence in the struggles within those colonies. At
Frankfort he joined with those who opposed the attempt of the Geneva
colony to establish a common front of all the exiles before they returned
to England. The compiler of the *Fortress* drew his support and his documents from the Edwardine church, the Strassburg and Zurich reformers,
the German Interim controversy, and Erasmus. The Genevan reformers
were nowhere mentioned. Also, the compiler had access to a letter from
John à Lasco to King Edward VI that is otherwise unknown. Lasco was
for a time with the exiles at Frankfort, and also was associated with the
Suffolk party in exile, as John Browne (or Brome) was. If John Browne
the chaplain to the Duchess of Suffolk in the 1560s and '70s was the same

---

21. On the resistance to the magistrate over the Interim, vestments, etc., by Bucer,
Martyr, Fagius and others, see J. Adam, *Evangelische Kirchengeschichte der Stadt
Strassburg* (Strassburg, 1922), 266–76; also Werner Bellardi, *Die Geschichte der
"Christlichen Gemeinschaft" in Strassburg, 1546–50* (Leipzig, 1934), 25–67.

man as the exile at Frankfort, he would have had much the same kind of background as is apparent in the *Fortress*.[22] It is more likely, however, that the initials of "J.B." were fictitious.

An earlier author who used the same initials to conceal himself issued *A Brief and Plain Declaration* . . . , and a revision of the same, in 1547 (*S.T.C.*, 1035, 6, and 14539–40, 40ª). The English of this item is quite different from that of the *Fortress*. Thus, even though the earlier "J.B." was also a critic of the established religion and could easily have been active in 1566, he could hardly have been the compiler of the *Fortress*.

There were rumors in 1566 that some of the antivestment tracts were of composite authorship, and there is evidence that all were hastily put together. These facts, plus the exigencies of secret printing, may account for the very bad style of this document. On the other hand, long, involved sentences were standard in the Latin originals from which "J.B." worked, and a hasty secret translation would have given little time for smoothing them out.

The text of the *Fortress* that follows is taken, by permission, from a copy in the possession of the Folger Shakespeare Library. There seem to have been no reprintings of the work.

A very few transpositions of phrases, and some changes in punctuation, have been made by the editor of this present volume. But these alterations have been held to a minimum. "J.B.'s" second table of contents has been eliminated, and the headings of his texts have been moved to the footnotes. "J.B." used a number of marginal notes to point up his selected texts. These notes have been eliminated except where they contain ideas not set forth in the texts themselves.

❖   ❖   ❖   ❖

The Fortress of Fathers

earnestly defending the purity of religion and ceremonies by the true exposition of certain places of Scripture against such as would bring in an abuse of idol stuff, and of things indifferent, and do appoint the authority of princes and prelates larger than the truth is. Translated out of Latin into English for their sakes that understand no Latin by

J. B.

22. Albert Peel, *The First Congregational Churches* . . . , *1567–81* (Cambridge, 1920), 22–6, 31–3; also Peel, ed., *The Seconde Parte of a Register* . . . (Cambridge, 1915), I, No. 34–5; and Garrett, *Marian Exiles*, 98.

Acts 9:4–6

"Saul, Saul, why persecutest thou me? What art thou, Lord? I am Jesus whom thou persecutest. It is hard for thee to kick against the pricks . . .

"Go into the city and it shall be told thee what thou shalt do."

M. D. LXVI

The Names of the Fathers in This Fortress

1. Saint Ambrose, Bishop of Milan
2. Theophilact, Archbishop of Bulgaria [i.e., Achrida]
3. Erasmus of Rotterdam, the Pearl of this Age
4. Martin Bucer, sometime Reader of the Divinity Lecture in Cambridge
5. Peter Martyr, sometime Reader of the Divinity Lecture in Oxford
6. John Epinus, Superintendent of Hamburg
7. Matthias Flacius Illyricus
8. Philip Melanchthon
9. John à Lasco, Baron of Poland, and Superintendent of All the Strangers' Church in England
10. Henry Bullinger
11. Wolfgang Musculus, Reader of Divinity in Bern
12. Rodolph Gualter

To all such as unfeignedly hate (in the zeal of a godly love) all monuments and remnants of idolatry. The translator wisheth perseverance unto the end, through Christ Jesus.

This hath always been the practice and policy of the Fiend, to trouble the congregations of Christ (that have received some strength in doctrine) with the questions of ceremonies, of things indifferent and dominion [i.e., authority] as a means whereby he often doth assuredly prevail, whilst that the brethren, only regarding the direct doctrine of faith, do little attend that these things in their use touch and concern oftentimes the first table [of the Decalogue], but always the second, and so in regard of the second also the first.[1] As in Corinth it did appear in Paul's time and

1. [ED.] A reference to the German Interim. The next paragraphs contain several allusions to earlier pamphlets in the vestment controversy; e.g., "Common alarm," "Ministers of London," "strengthen . . . and restore . . . the fallen," are captions from earlier titles. Also the debate over the Bullinger-Gualter letters is noted.

since in divers ages. By practicing of which device he [i.e., the Fiend], thinketh now (unless God help us) to overthrow the work of God begun amongst us in England. Against which danger it behooveth all men, as in a common alarm, to put forth himself [themselves] to serve.

But forasmuch as it hath hitherto been reported that this is but a particular combat against the ministers of London, I have here translated into our English speech the judgments of certain fathers being on those ministers' side, to this intent that both truth of religion, reverence of these fathers, or else shame, might prevent [i.e., forestall] the enemy, by causing the lording bishops to cease and [to] retire their folly, and also may strengthen such as stand, and restore those that are fallen through their devices.

And to the fuller accomplishing hereof I have pointed out where and on whose side those reverend fathers Masters Bullinger and Gualter are and stand. Whose letters they have unjustly abused as having obtained them [when] the plain case and truth of the deformed estate of the church of England [had] not [been] opened truly to them. As ere it be long you shall dear Christians (I hope) understand by their writings, if they cease not to abuse their first. Thus thirsting your health in Christ, I humbly crave your prayers to God that by his Spirit he will guide me to know his will and to perform the same through Christ. The Lord Jesus keep you and bless you all. Amen.

Certain conclusions, partly held and defended by [the] good doctors' sentences contained in this book, and partly to be defended by the translator (if the same be not sufficiently defended by the doctors mentioned in this book) against all that will write against them.

The king, prince or other supreme magistrate hath power and authority to exercise his sword and to punish with it all the bishops, elders and clerks [i.e., clergy] of his realm or country, if they be offenders and breakers of God's law, either with imprisonment or deprivation, or with death, or any such like punishment according to the greatness of the offence that is committed.

If the bishops or elders either do not their duties in preaching, or preach false doctrine and commit faults worthy deprivation, he may command the clergy that is neither infected with false doctrine nor idolatry, neither defiled with any notable crime of evil life, to examine the faulty bishops and their doctrine, and if they deserve it suspend them, deprive them, or to make them recant.

The lordship of bishops now exercised over both the rest of the clergy and over the lay people hath no ground in the word of God.

Christ only is the head of his mystical body which is the church, as the prince or chief magistrate is the head of the politic body of his realm and country.

The supreme magistrate is bound to obey the word of God preached by Christ's messengers, and he is also subject to the discipline of the church.

Neither the prince nor any prelate hath any authority by the word of God to make any ecclesiastical law or rite to bind men's consciences in pain of deadly sin to keep them.

Princes have authority so to reform the church that they reform it not after any doctrine or traditions of their own making or any other man's making. But only according to the written word of God, and then shall they bring none of their policies into the church be they never so gorgeous and goodly to look to.

As the Jews were greatly to be commended which offered their bare necks to be cut off with the soldiers' swords rather than they would contrary to their law and liberty suffer the Emperor's image to be brought into their temple. So the pastors of Christ's flock are greatly to be commended that had lever [i.e., rather] lose their goods and lives than suffer any men's politic rites and traditions to be brought into Christ's church, whereby either the whole church, and especially the ministers, should be brought into any bondage, or the word of God should be hindered thereby, and man should be made as it were a god, or take unto him the honor of God.

The exposition of certain parts of Scripture according to the minds of the chief doctors that in our time were in reformed churches, and also of some old doctors wherein thou shalt see the true doctrine of indifferent things, of garments, and of the authority that princes and prelates have to set out rites and ceremonies.

1. Saint Ambrose, Bishop of Milan

"Ye are bought with a price, be ye not made the bondmen of men." It is true, because we are bought with so dear a price, that we could not have been bought again of any but only of Christ, who is rich in all things. Therefore he that is bought with a price ought more to serve, or to do his duty in the office of a bondman, that he may after a manner make recompense to his buyer. Therefore those that are bought of God (that is, of Christ) ought not to be bondmen of men. But such are bondmen of men that subdue themselves or obey men's superstitions.[2]

2. THEOPHILACT, ARCHBISHOP OF BULGARIA

The apostle reasoneth not these matters only to slaves or bondmen, but he speaketh them to those that are free. Or he rather doth instruct all sorts, yea the Christians themselves, that they do not anything for man's sake or pleasure, and that they do not execute or fulfill those commandments of men which are naught. For that were to serve men, even by such as are ransomed for a price. (And a little after, he having spoken of this worldly and spiritual bondage, writeth thus:) Therefore the apostle hath provided very well in both cases (to wit) first, lest under the pretence of God's service servants should depart from their masters in whose power their bodies are. Secondly, lest they should fall from God whenas [i.e., whensoever] they will serve their bodily masters further than becometh, or that they ought to do.[3]

3. ERASMUS OF ROTTERDAM

3A. "Neither shall ye be as exercisers of lordship against the people or parishes." For he understandeth by this word *cleros*, not deacons or elders, but the flock which fell to every man by chance to be governed, lest any man should judge that bishops were forbidden to exercise any lordship over clerks but that it was granted them to be lords over others. And here he calleth elders bishops, for as yet there was not so huge a number of priests. But as many elders as there were, so many bishops there were. This commandment of the prince of the apostles should have been written in golden letters and set up in all palaces of the bishops. "Feed," saith he, "the flock, oppress it not, pill[age] it not, and do this not unwillingly, but of a sincere desire and mind as fathers, neither for filthy lucre's sake," as though he had seen before that thereupon should rise a plague or pes-

2. Ambrose upon 1 Corinthians 7:23. [ED.] J. P. Migne, *Patrilogiae . . . Series Latina* (Paris, 1878–90), 17, col. 233.

3. Theophilact upon 1 Corinthians 7:23. [ED.] Migne, *Patrilogiae . . . Series Graeca* (Paris, 1857–66), 124, col. 647–50.

tilence to the church. To conclude, not playing lords after the manner of kings, but feed with example and overcome with good deeds. Nowadays the common sort of bishops heareth nothing of their learned flatterers but lordships, dominions, swords, keys and powers. Whereupon riseth in some of them more pompous pride than some kings use, and more cruelness than some tyrants occupy.[4]

3B. Surely Saint Peter in the Acts of the Apostles doth openly call the law of Moses (which was laid for a time upon the rebellious people of the Jews) a hard and a heavy burden, which neither we nor our fathers were able to bear, neither can any man doubt but that it is truth which the truth hath pronounced. The yoke of Christ is in very deed pleasant, and his burden is light, so [i.e., provided] that no men's traditions be laid upon men's shoulders beside, or more than, that thing which he hath already appointed. And he hath commanded nothing else but that one should love another. And there is nothing so bitter but that charity will season and make it sweet. Whatsoever is according to nature it may easily be born. But there is nothing that agreeth more with man's nature than Christ's philosophy which goeth about to do no other thing almost than to restore our nature (that is fallen) to her innocency and sincerity again. But even as the ordinances of men did make heavy the law, being by itself grievous enough for the Jews, even so must we diligently take heed that the additions, ordinances and doctrines of men make not the law of Christ (which of itself is pleasant and light) heavy and hard to bear. Which ordinances so at the first crept in as though they were small, and ought not to be cared for or regarded, or else, they being commended with the show of godliness be gladly received of them that are more simple than foresighted. Those that are once received by piecemeal, do grow and increase unto a huge quantity, and do press down and overthrow men, whether they will or no, either by the help of custom (whose violence is a certain tyranny) or else by the authority of princes, which hold stiffly it that is rashly received, abusing it for their profit and gains. [. . .] There are some that knit together either a cold syllogism of a piece of Scripture, which they do not understand, or else make an article of faith of a man's ordinance, and of such men [i.e., by such criteria] are we judged to be Christians or no Christians, which appertain nothing at all to Christian religion. [. . .] What availeth it to speak of the burden of man's institutions, whenas many years ago Saint Augustine in a certain epistle to Jan-

4. Desiderius Erasmus upon 1 Peter 5:3. [ED.] *Opera Omnia*, edited by J. Clericus (Leyden, 1703–6), VI, col. 1055.

uarius, he is angry and bewaileth the estate of Christ's church so to be burdened that the condition of the Jews was almost more tolerable than the condition of the Christians. [. . .] What if he saw the free people of Christ snared with so many laws and ceremonies, and not only oppressed with a single tyranny of profane princes, but also of bishops, cardinals, popes and most of all of their servants, who (being disguised with the visure [i.e., mask] of religion) go busily about the business of their bellies. [. . .] The Jews had no certain kind of apparel forbidden them more than that which was made of flax and wool [mixed] together. How many constitutions are there made now for apparel [Latin, *de cultu*]. And what superstition is there in garments, and in colors of the same, at this present time.[5]

3C. Some wrest this place so far as [though] men ought to obey all manner of things whatsoever the bishops, presidents or rulers command, although they be ungodly, and that for their authority's sake.[6] Whenas Christ did speak only of them which did teach rightly the law of Moses, and not of such as did snare men with their ordinances and constitutions. Now peradventure, after the same manner a bishop might be heard which preacheth truly the gospel, although he live but a little according to the same. But who can abide that they should occupy an open tyranny against Christ's doctrine, and make laws for their own advantage, measuring all things according to their gain and glorious majesties? They that snare the people with rites and ordinances devised for their profit, and to fulfill their tyranny, do not sit in the chair of the gospel, but in the chair of Simon Magus and Caiaphas.[7]

4. MARTIN BUCER

Amongst the members of this church there is none in all the earth that is the head thereof. But the church hath Christ head thereof in heaven. The princes indeed, and the magistrates of all places may be called heads, but not in the ecclesiastical body, but in the politic body and in the politic government. [. . .] Christ by himself is governor of the church. Yet notwithstanding he useth the service of angels and of men, and yet for all

5. Erasmus upon Matthew 11:29–30. [ED.] *Opera*, VI, col. 63d–64c. This selection is from Erasmus' comment on *Jugum meum*, an attack upon clerical ceremonies notorious all over Europe.

6. Such bishops we have some nowadays in England.

7. Erasmus upon Matthew 23:1–2. [ED.] *Opera*, VI, col. 117e.

that he is always present with his church. [. . .] Seeing that the church hath Christ her head, he surely as a good shepherd, with his word gathereth together his sheep that go astray, and he cometh to open [i.e., reveal] his Father to his sheep, and to draw all things to him, to open their minds that they by true faith may understand the gospel, by the which faith he justifieth them. This faith is mighty in working through charity, which charity seeketh not her own. Wherefore there is a wonderful unity and joining together of the members as it was said in the primitive church, "They had one soul and one heart in the Lord" [Acts 4:32]. Furthermore, forasmuch as Christ is the ruler and governeth it in all things (as Paul beareth witness hereafter in the fifth chapter monisheth [i.e., admonishing] women that they should be subject or obedient unto their husbands as the church is unto Christ [Eph. 5:22–4]), he purgeth it, or maketh it clean, with his blood. Although he use in it divers ministries or services, yet is he the chief governor, the first, and the most strong and mighty. [. . .]

Wherein standeth or consisteth the unity of the church? Not in garments, not in ceremonies, as thou shalt see hereafter in the fourth chapter in these words, "Endeavoring or laboring to keep the unity of spirit in the bond of peace . . ." [Eph. 4:3]. Therefore the unity of the church standeth in the unity of the spirit, of charity, of the word of God, of Christ, of the sacraments, and in the communion of gifts, that we may consent in one, that we may agree in one thing, that we may speak one thing, that no man shall rule himself, but give himself to be ruled unto Christ and the Spirit, that we should consent with the will of our heavenly Father, that we should allow altogether the same things and reprove also the same. For by the Spirit (in the same place) he doth understand the inward power of the Spirit, from whence come all our counsels and doings, which in all things ought to be the same, and like it that is of God opened unto us in the word. There is one word, one Scripture, one baptism, and one death of Christ, one Father, one religion, and one charity, one sacrament of thanksgiving, and one laying on of hands, and one discipline, and one consent of the ministers and of those by the which these are ministered. To conclude, all things that are ordained to the building or profit of the church, we must have all those as one thing. But whatsoever is not declared in the word: there is no necessary unity in that, but rather liberty, etc. [. . .]

To the building of godliness, all things ought to be done in the church. And it is commanded that the rulers of the churches should teach those things that Christ hath commanded. Wherefore they ought not to make themselves tyrants in exacting or requiring of men's consciences that which Christ never commanded.[8]

4B. "An offence is whatsoever we say or do by any means, which riseth not of sound or perfect faith, and is not ordered of sincere and true love, promoting God's glory and our neighbor's salvation."

After that this doctor hath spoken of offences generally and showed them not to beseem Christians, and hath also particularly amplified the matter in deeds of themselves not evil but done contrary to charity with abuse of Christian liberty, as Romans 14, 1 Corinthians 8 (this note first given that Saint Paul often with some force repeateth this name "a brother"), he concludeth that this is the scope and drift of all: so to order and do all things that they may make to the edifying of our brethren. So shall it fall out that sometimes liberty is to be used, sometimes not. For whenas words are to be confirmed with deeds, then must (saith he) the liberty that is preached needs be confirmed with examples. This he setteth out with the examples of Peter, etc., at Antioch (Galatians 2), commending his using of Christian liberty in meats, and discommending his dissimulation, and also of Paul in not circumcising of Titus (Galatians 2) wherein he noteth thus:

1. First, if in this slippery place Peter caught a fall, who is it that ought not to be careful herein and to take heed.

2 . Secondly, in reproving of Peter's dissimulation, he saith, to conclude, for that we must always press [on] to perfection and fullness of faith, greater respect was surely to be had to the Gentiles which had already received Christ plainly (*plane*) than to them which did lewdly stick yet to the ceremonies of the world (*elementis mundi*), who in conclusion by long bearing with, might be the more confirmed in their error.

3. Thirdly, we must further consider whether they be true or false brethren which go about to infringe or weaken Christian liberty. For we must regard only the true brethren to bear with them herein.

These things premised after this manner, he applieth the whole doctrine of offences, by the example of outward things and ceremonies, to our time and state of religion in these words:

"As in our time if a man would still dissimulate or hide the liberty of outward things (which the visured [i.e., masked] churchmen by subtlety

8. Martin Bucer upon Ephesians 1:22. [ED.] *Praelectiones . . . Ephesios . . . habitae Cantabrigiae in Anglia, Anno MDL et LI* (Basel, 1562), fol. 36f, 37b, 39c, 40f; Bucer's lectures while professor at Cambridge, published posthumously, edited by I. Tremellius. The book was dedicated to a relative of Queen Catherine Parr, Sir Nicholas Throckmorton, who was prominent under Edward VI, an exile under Mary, and a career diplomat under Elizabeth.

and tyranny have taken from Christian people for the obstinate enemies of the gospel's sake, who do abhor and blaspheme all that doth come from us, seeing they abhor and blaspheme Christ and the gospel itself) it [i.e., the dissimulation] should not only not amend those [i.e., the enemies] but rather should more confirm them in evil, and very much offend such which have received Christ, whilst the minister preacheth unto them truth utterly void of examples. For they are many which hardly can be persuaded that we have all things in Christ whilst men's inventions are had in such price and estimation. Out of question great fault is herein nowadays committed, and that not of the rude and common sort of people, but of the head Protestants and chief gospellers.* I confess indeed that although all the ordinances against the liberty of outward things were of Antichrist's bringing in (as is difference of persons, meats, days, places and infinite such other things), yet for [all] that, the common people were born in hand [i.e., were told] that they all were commandments of the church guided by God's Spirit. And so [these ordinances were] generally received of men as things proceeding from God's will and appointment. That therefore we should use the liberty (purchased unto us by Christ) circumspectly and warily, even nowadays, and with Paul many times "circumcise Timothy," (that is to say) for our parts, use well some ceremonies which other men abuse, so as [i.e., provided that] it were seeking occasion to preach Christ sincerely and purely. Although indeed these devices of men can by no means be compared to circumcision and such like orders of God.*

But what is the common practice? Many fearing forsooth the offence of the cross, and in vain going about to please both men and God, after long preaching of the word, when words and talk require now example and deeds (pretending other men's infirmities when indeed they are therein let [i.e., hindered] with their own weakness) both themselves become yet slaves to men's traditions, and cause other men also to be the like. Oh, say they, nothing is to be attempted rashly. These things have continued many years. They cannot be put away suddenly. Regard must be had to the weak. With hasty speed we should not plant the gospel, but overthrow it.

I would wish these men first considered what that sentence meaneth, "The kingdom of heaven suffereth violence and the violent catch it unto them" (Mt. 11:12). Then that these things are not hasted rashly but then [i.e., except] when they are changed [with] Christ not yet being once commended, and [that] without faith. And [they are] not [rashly hasted]

* See note 10, below.

when Christ is already preached and the net of the gospel so long cast forth that it hath in a manner taken as much as may be taken in that circuit or compass of sea, and now there remaineth nothing else but to confirm and bring credit to words by example in doings. Surely the case thus standing, words also, wherein men have put their confidences more than in Christ, are to be forsaken. And men must remember that there can be no fellowship had between Christ and Antichrist.

Again it is a thing very absurd and foolish that, because that falsehood hath by little and little, and of long time, crept in and grown, therefore to go about to prescribe long time also to receive the truth in Christ. Otherwise should Christ no more be esteemed of us than Antichrist. Certainly if we shall not receive Christ so soon as we know him, we shall never enjoy him. Moses, Samuel, Elijah, Hezekiah, Josiah dealt not after this sort. But as soon as they had restored the knowledge of the law to the people, by and by they abolished, and at once, all abominations, and restored the ceremonies of God.

Wherefore it is nothing worth that they say, who always brag that there are greater things to be urged than reformation, or amendment of ceremonies, [and] so become patrons to Antichrist's relics. As for ceremonies, they are cognizances or testimonies of our religion. And therefore we also begin our religion with the ceremony of baptism. And if any be to be received again by means of his repentance, after that he is excommunicated for his wickedness, he is straight[way] reconciled to the church by the sacrament of the supper. Wherefore they must needs be weak in the faith of Christ which defer the removing of Antichrist's ceremonies. And newness of life will surely very lately appear in them, if ever it appear at all. And indeed we see at this day cold and slack proceeding in Christian religion and profession, in those places where Antichrist's ceremonies be born withal; and all things much more lively and effectual where they be abolished and done away. For if they stay [their removal] at any time, this only is the cause: that the word of God either is not thoroughly credited, or not esteemed accordingly. For howsoever those that suppose themselves to be strong in faith use not these things, where, I pray you, is there zeal for Christ's glory or their brethren, whereas they still use them, so no doubt they do it of weakness of faith.

Certainly as there is no agreement at all between Christ and Belial, so sincere and unfeigned Christians can by no means abide any of Antichrist's trumpery. Although with this their zeal they [i.e., the sincere Christians] endeavor themselves to purge the church here, as the glory of Christ may thereby chiefly be advanced, yet to the weaker sort they will have such respect as to do nothing rashly, or out of season. But [they] will teach the weak with gentleness to wax stronger in knowledge. Yet will they do their endeavor, with examples, to bring them forward, not regarding the blindness of a few who are too much addicted to Antichrist's ceremonies, and perhaps no true and unfeigned brethren. Offending there whilst very many other weak ones [who] continually think thus with themselves: "If these things were so evil they should surely be abolished. If either [i.e., on the other hand] they were so good, all men (especially that reckon themselves Christians) would indeed receive and embrace them." These men surely, if they be elect shall at the length be confirmed, although all the world offend them and no man edify them. But woe in the meantime unto them by whom they are offended. Wherefore as soon as true godliness hath been preached and professed of many, Antichrist's ceremonies and rites must by and by be abrogated. Neither must delay be made till godliness be in all points grown up to perfection, else should that trash never be abolished and removed.

These mild and too, too moderate and sober Christians, who can bear all antichristian things, in very deed [are] like unto them at Corinth, who knowing that an idol was nothing did eat things offered unto idols and boasted (as these our men do), "In outward matters we are free; what is that to me that another abuseth these things naughtily? I will use them well." For as those weakened the faith of many, both in that they less abhorred idols through their example, and also in that they for the most part communicated with them against their consciences, so no doubt do these our lukewarm gospellers nowadays. They know right well that all Antichrist's ceremonies (that is to say, all such [as] have been brought in without God's word) are not worth a rush. And because they are outward things wherein we have liberty, they will use them as freely forsooth, not weighing that many things are lawful which are not expedient, and that our liberty must either serve those whom they in the meantime offend, or [else] obscure the glory of Christ. For they confirm those in their error which as yet know not that these things are free and at liberty. As for the defenders thereof, the professed enemies of Christ, they make them glad and bold, and finally they weaken the feeble's faith which had forsaken and cast them [i.e., the ceremonies] away.[9]

Thus on God's name they provide fairly [i.e., in fair words only] for the weak ones! Yea rather they serve herein their own bellies, in that they study to gratify either Christ's enemies or else backsliders. For no man other than these will earnestly contend for superstitious ceremonies. This

9. They shut Christ out of doors that bear with ceremonies.

is their modesty or bearing, wherewith they are so far from helping the gospel, or increasing it, that by little they displace it. Surely we have to thank these men that at this day all [i.e., every] thing is gone backward and turned upside down in many places where the gospel hath been long time preached. Whereas no example can be brought of like alteration in those places where, Christ being earnestly and purely preached, [the] ceremonies also [have] been reformed according to the rule of his word. For as for those things which have disorderedly or confusedly happened, Christ either not at all or not sincerely preached, they appertaining nothing to us.

Forasmuch therefore as Christ so sore detesteth offences, and crieth, "Woe unto the world by means of offences, woe unto the man by whom offence cometh," we must with all diligence take heed both in these and other things that we be offensive to no man, but especially to the little ones (those I mean not that are such in age only, but in faith and understanding also). The perfect knowledge of God and Christ is life everlasting. Whatsoever therefore may by any means either hinder or obscure it, let it neither be spoken nor yet done of us. But to the uttermost of our powers, let us remove those things away. Then let us provoke them [i.e., men], both by exhortations and examples, that men will express those things in their life, giving no place herein either to our own affections or other men's, seeing that it is better to be drowned in the sea than to give offence . . .[10]

5. PETER MARTYR VERMIGLI

5A. If, as we have concluded, they are to be reproved that render evil for evil, and it is the office of Christian men to show the office of charity

---

10. Bucer upon Matthew 18:7. [ED.] *Enarrationes perpetuae in sacra quatuor evangelia* . . . (Strassburg, 1530), fol. 146b, c, d, 147a, b–d. This passage on "Woe . . . because of offences" had been cited in Crowley's first attack on the vestment requirements. Parker had accused him of misrepresenting Bucer, and had quoted against Crowley the brief section marked here by asterisks. Crowley's reply, *An answer for the tyme* . . . (S.T.C., 10388), had again gone over the passage. Someone then issued *The mind . . . Bucer upon . . . "Woe . . . because of offences . . ."* (Emden, 1566; S.T.C., 3964), giving the entire passage together with other documents, one of which states (fol. Bii) ". . . that in number both of doctors and sentences we shall be nothing inferior to them [i.e., the bishops]. In the meantime this may suffice . . ." From this comment it is clear that the publication of the *Fortress* came after the pamphlets just cited. The *Fortress* goes on to reprint the entire passage as part of its corpus of proofs.

unto them that have deserved evil of us, they are doubtless greatly to be reproved which for good deeds restore evil deeds, and show not unto men that have been friendly unto them (as the magistrates be) honor and obedience. Because the apostle is about to entreat diligently and largely of this matter, that we may understand the better what his meaning is, we will define what is a magistrate. A magistrate is a chosen person, and that of God, that he should defend the laws and peace, and repress and hold down vices and all things that are evil, with punishments and his sword. The efficient cause is God. The end is the keeping of the laws and of peace, and driving away of vices and all hurtful things, and the increase of virtues. The formal cause is the order that he appointeth by the providence of God in matters that appertain unto men or in worldly matters. The material cause is a man or a person, for whosoever is chosen to be a magistrate, he is one chosen out of men. The right way and compendious manner of teaching is almost general. First it is ordained that all men shall be under the power of the magistrate. And afterward that is proved, of the cause efficient, that all such powers are of God. And after, it is proved by the contrary, that they that despise the chief ruler are enemies to God, and that to their harm. And furthermore the same thing is proved by the end, or final cause, that the ruler is made for our great profit and commodity. [. . .]

But these ecclesiastical papists will say that the kings themselves, and the common powers, have given over of their own right and have willed that clerks should be exempted. But we ought not to look what princes have done in these matters, but what they ought to have done. For it lieth not in their power to put down the laws of God. Wherefore if this godly commandment of Paul will that every soul should be subject to the higher power, in any case men must needs obey it. For those things that God hath ordained and decreed cannot be called back again by man's authority. Howbeit these words are to be restrained and drawn together, that we may understand that we are subject unto the magistrate no further than belongeth unto his vocation and office. But if he would go beyond those bounds, and command anything that is contrary to godliness or the law of God, we ought rather to obey God than men. [. . .]

The matter now will not suffer us to cover with silence how that Boniface [VIII], in his *extravagant* [i.e., papal bull] which beginneth *"Unam sanctam,"* abuseth the words of the apostle to confirm his pride. For hereupon he would prove that those things that are of God, have some orders amongst themselves, that their dignities may be known one from another, being distinct and separated by certain degrees, and that thereupon it followeth that the powers that are of God are not all alike, and that is the higher power which is exercised or occupied about the worthier matter, and because the ecclesiastical power is occupied in spiritual matters and the civil in bodily matters, therefore it followeth, saith he, that the ecclesiastical power is highest and ought not to be subject unto the civil magistrate. For the pope, saith he, hath jurisdiction over all princes, because Christ did say, "Whatsoever thou shalt bind on earth shall be bound in heaven . . ." [Mt. 16:19]. And to make the matter more plain, he allegeth out of Jeremiah these words, "Behold, I have ordained thee above kings and nations, that thou shouldest pull in pieces and destroy, and that thou shouldest build and plant" [Jer. 1:10].

But as these arguments are full of pride and swelling, so are they most full of vanity. For first to begin withal, Paul doth not speak here [Rom. 13:1] of the degrees of powers distincted or dissevered amongst themselves. For he only saith thus, that all powers whatsoever they be, are ordained of God, and I do not deny but the ecclesiastical power, or the power that ecclesiastical persons have, is in spiritual matters. For it is occupied in the ministry of the word of God. And therefore we grant that that power is the greatest because the word of God ought to command and rule all men. But this power maketh men to bring to subjection all understanding, and to bring down or destroy the highness of all men's reasons. Let these excellent great lords do these things: let them preach the word of God, and let them leave their inventions of men, and then if there be any that will not hear them, we do not doubt but that they condemn them justly, whether they be princes, kings, monarchs or emperors. Yet for all that, it shall not follow that they are not subject unto the politic power in things pertaining to this bodily life, and to possessions and lands, houses and manors. Nay, rather (as concerning the prince's office), they ought to be subject to a godly and religious magistrate, not because we think that the word of God or sacraments ought to be subject or subdued to man's laws, but that it is the office of a magistrate to punish or displace church ministers if they behave themselves ill in their office, or juggle with the truth, or deface it, or do falsely minister the sacraments. Let them bind and loose (that is to say) by the word and preaching, let them declare who be bound and who be loosed. Yet for all this, they ought not to exempt themselves from the civil magistrate. For even as a king, though he excel in his excellent dignity, is bound to obey the word pronounced by the ministers of the church, even so an ecclesiastical man, although he be set in an excellent place and office, is not exempted or discharged from the obedience or subjection of the magistrate. [. . .]

Even as he is the officer of God unto thy good and profit if thou do well, even so is he the officer of God unto wrath (that is to say), to revenge and punish, if that thou behave thyself naughtily. Neither ought he, to whom the sword is committed, to be ignorant that he is the keeper not only of the latter but also of the former table [i.e., of God's law]. Wherefore he ought diligently to take heed that religion be ministered out of the word of God. And let him not think, as many princes nowadays bear themselves in hand, that that charge appertaineth nothing unto them. For they will indeed deal out benefices and bishoprics to whomsoever they list. But they care not whether they whom they have promoted to such dignities to their duties or no.[11]

5B. There are other bondages of men which ought also to be eschewed. That for the getting and purchasing of riches we should not be parasites, flatterers or men-pleasers. Or we should not be too much afraid, and for these causes should be turned to idol service and evil kinds of worshipping. They are grieved with this kind of bondage which obey the naughty will of their ungodly masters or lords, and set more by them than by God. It appeareth by these things that the Corinthians came to this opinion, that such as came to Christ should change and overturn all things. And with this kind of foolishness are the religious men nowadays sick, which will have their garments, their manners, and the outward condition of their life new, insomuch as they must change their old names also wherewith they were named before.[12] But Paul denieth that we should do so, and he doth determine that those are to be held that are not contrary unto the word of God.[13]

11. Peter Martyr Vermigli upon Romans 13:1. [ED.] *In epistolam S. Pauli ad Romanos commentarii* (Basel, 1558). These were the lectures Martyr had given as a professor at Oxford in 1551-2. They were prepared for the press at Strassburg and Zurich while the Marian exiles were attending Martyr's lectures in those cities. He dedicated the publication to one of the exiles, Sir Anthony Cooke, who had been tutor to Edward VI, and who in 1566 was to be a Privy Councillor under Elizabeth. In their pamphlets Parker and Crowley had argued over Martyr's comments on Romans 13:1. "J.B." now gives the text *in extenso*. In the subsequent English translation of the entire work (1568; *S.T.C.*, 24672), the passages occur on fol. 426b, 427a, b, 428b, 431a.

12. [ED.] "New garments," "new names" — i.e., the apparel and names assumed upon entrance to the monastic order.

13. Martyr upon 1 Corinthians 7:23. [ED.] *In selectissimam Pauli priorem ad Corinthios epistolam* (Zurich, 1551). Fol. 98a (of 1572 ed.). These were Martyr's

5C. Surely the state of Christendom was never in worse case than since the bishops [. . .] did usurp and take unto them the sword. For every man doth see that these two offices (that is), the temporal and ecclesiastical, do so hinder one another that he that occupieth the one cannot exercise the other. For there is not any man that can be found so prompt and diligent that he is able to execute either of both of them rightly and in order.[14]

5D. Moreover the bishop of Rome did boast that he was made head of the church, which thing cannot in any wise appertain unto any man. For both moving, and the five wits called senses, flow down from the head through the sinews into the members, as Paul doth very truly teach in his epistles both to the Ephesians [4:15–16] and Colossians [1:18]. But there is no man that is able to perform that as of himself, by joints and to-settings, to quicken the members of the church with the Spirit of God. It belongeth only unto Christ to deal out unto his members spiritual motions, the [en]lightening of the mind, and everlasting life. Indeed, kings and magistrates may be called the heads of the people because the civil government is exercised by them, and we may look to have from them good laws and civil motions. But in the church, it is not entreated of the civil life, but of the spiritual and everlasting, which we cannot look for of any but only of God. Neither is there any mortal man that can quicken the members of the church. I do judge that the kings and magistrates that are godly, ought to be set or counted in the church in the foremost or highest place or dignity, and that it belongeth to their office, if that religion be evil handled, to correct the defaults. For they bear the sword for that end that they may defend the honor of God. But they cannot be the heads of the churches. Paul, to the Romans and Corinthians (where he maketh comparisons between the members of the church), maketh some of them to be eyes, some to be nostrils, ears, hand[s] and feet [Rom. 12:4–8; 1 Cor. 12:14–26]. But he vouchsafeth not to deck any member with the dignity of the head. And yet the same Paul, writing to the Ephesians, saith of Christ that God gave him to be head of the body of the

---

first lectures at Oxford, in 1550–51. They were transcribed for publication by John Cheke and Richard Coxe (who were both to be exiles under Mary; Coxe was bishop of Ely in 1566). Martyr's series on 1 Corinthians 7 had occasioned a major dispute at the university. Crowley had cited Martyr in his *Brief Discourse,* and Parker had replied, "No writer of these days is more evidently against you." Crowley's *Answer* continued the debate, and the *Fortress* reprinted the passage in question.

14. Martyr upon Romans 13:1. [ED.] See note 11, above; English translation, fol. 429a.

church [Eph. 1:22–3]. Therefore let the papists show where it is said in Holy Scripture that there was another head given unto the church besides Christ. If they can do that, let them have the victory. But I am sure they are never able to do it. For if such a head should be given to it, then the church should be a monster with two heads.[15]

5E. Jehu brought to pass that the temple of Baal should be overthrown, so that it should not be any more occupied as it was before. Wherefore many thought that it was not well done that Christians (after that they had embraced the gospel of the son of God) should yet still keep undestroyed the instruments of the pope after a manner. And they do much better promote godliness which did bring to pass that all images, standing images and others, and that all ornaments of the pope's device, should be utterly destroyed at once. For, as we read in the ecclesiastical histories, when Constantine the Great became a Christian man he commanded that the idols' temples should be shut up. But because they remained so unput down, it was an easy matter for Julian the Apostate, who came after, to open them again and to bring in the idols of the old superstition to be worshipped in the same places. The which thing the noble Prince Theodosius perceiving, commanded them so to be put down that they should no more be restored again. After this manner did Jehu, because the idols should not be restored again.[16]

6. JOHN EPINUS

The devil could not have found or devised anything more crafty or subtle to destroy the true worshipping of God and to overthrow the true church of Christ, than the changing and bringing in of things called "indifferent." He hath profited more therewith than if he should have gone

15. Martyr upon Judges 8. [ED.] *In librum Judicum commentarii* (Zurich, 1561). These lectures were delivered at the University of Strassburg, 1554–6, and transcribed by John Jewel, Peter Martyr's most faithful English follower, who was bishop of Salisbury in 1566. This passage had also been debated by Parker and Crowley. "J.B." chose to translate from the Latin rather than cite from the English translation, dedicated to Leicester by the printer (1564; *S.T.C.*, 24670), where the passage occurs on fol. 148b–f.

16. Martyr upon 2 Kings 10. [ED.] *Melachim, id est regum libri duo posteriores cum commentariis*, edited by J. Wolf (Zurich, 1566), fol. 275b (of 1571 ed.). On these lectures, published posthumously, see Coxe to Martyr, August 5, 1562, *Zurich Letters*, I, 112. Though issued only in 1566, they had figured in the debate between Parker and Crowley.

about with cruelness and tyranny. For there is such strength in this poison of indifferent things, that it can make men that were before in other matters talkative, and most fullest of words, utterly dumb and speechless, and other, that were eloquent, to be now stutterers, and some that were honestly and rightly brought up, to be doubtful and wavering, some that were shepherds to become wolves, and some that were Christians to be epicures, that is to say, godless and of no religion, and only giving themselves and studying to get and hold the commodities and riches of this world. That transformation and change that is written by Homer to have been wrought by sorcerous charms and cups of the famous witch Circe, is nothing to be compared to this new change which is brought to pass by the sorcery of things indifferent. [. . .]

This is the best counsel of all, that godly doctors and teachers of the church join their minds together, their studies, their labors, prayers, and their confession, that they may defend the doctrine and learning of Christ, and true worshippings of their churches, with one consent with the sword of God's word and the bearing of Christ's cross. The prophets and apostles, following this counsel, overcame the whole world, and did purge and scour the church from ungodliness and idolatry. There cannot be any better counsel found than God himself hath given. It belongeth to us to do our duty, and to commit (with our prayers) unto the Lord the success and prosperous end of the matter.[17]

7. MATTHIAS FLACIUS ILLYRICUS

First, forasmuch as I intend to write of things indifferent, as they are named, and some are so indeed, it is best to tell what this word indifferent meaneth. Indifferent is called in the Greek *adiaphoron* and in Latin *indifferens* and in Dutch [i.e., German] *eine mittelding*. And it signifieth a thing whereof is made no matter, whether a man keep it or do not keep it, or whether it be handled after this manner or that manner. There are in the church certain things which are indifferent. And that there is such in the church of God it may easily be proved by Paul, as in the former

17. Johannes Epinus, in Matthias Flacius Illyricus, *Liber de Veris et falsis adiaphoris . . . epistola . . . Epini . . .* [ED.] (Magdeburg, 1549), in *Omnia Latina scripta Matthiae Flacii Illyrici, hactenus sparsim contra Adiaphoricas . . . Omnia correcta et aucta*, n.p., n.d. (1550), fol. R5 recto, R7 verso. Epinus (also Aepinus) served in London from June 1534 to January 1535 as Ambassador from North German cities, and was known to many early English reformers.

[epistle] to the Corinthians the seventh, eighth, tenth and fourteenth chapters, also to the Romans in the fourteenth chapter may appear. Of which sort are: to live married or unmarried, so that it be done in chastity; to eat meats or to abstain therefrom; to keep days or not to keep days, without superstition; to take wages of them to whom a man preacheth to, or to take none at all; to use a prescribed manner of teaching in the temple, to hear or to sing. [. . .]

If any man would call back again and restore the garments or vestments of ethnic or popish sacrifices, and bring them into the churches after the use of them were once put down, he should do contrary to that which is seemly and comely. [. . .]

It lieth not in the power of any man to ordain any worshippings of God without the commandment of God. [. . .]

All things that are indifferent, are so far indifferent as they serve for the glory of God and the profit of the church. But if they pass beyond those bonds, [i.e., bounds] they are not indifferent, but are ungodliness and abominations, and by all means of all men to be eschewed. [. . .]

Whatsoever Antichrist doth, the same he doth for the devil's sake whose vicar he is, and of whom he is stirred up to play his part. And whatsoever unchristian princes do in religion, they do it for Antichrist's sake and his seat's sake, as the letters of the pope unto the bishops, and the bishops' letters sent to popish princes and to divers churches, bear witness. And further, whatsoever the popish princes and unchristian courts do in these matters and changes, they do it for the pleasure and favor of the supreme governors. Also, whatsoever the old divines do in these matters, they do it to gratify the court and the inferior princes. At the last, whatsoever the younger divines do, either to set forth or not to hinder this mischief of indifferent matters, they do it for the pleasure of their old masters. Wherefore, from the first to the last, they serve all Antichrist and the devil, and commit whoredom with the great whore and drink of her cup, as it is prophesied in the Apocalypse (not without a cause) of the last times. [. . .]

We need not to care for that which some do ofttime rehearse, that the church hath always been in some bondage, for although it hath been always in politic bondage, yet she never did temper herself or fashion her to the religion of ungodly men, neither would God that she should be subdued unto any spiritual bondage, but rather that she should steadfastly defend her liberty and not to be made the bondwoman of men, seeing that she is redeemed with the precious blood of Christ. Wherefore, seeing that these rites are thrust upon the church whether she will or no, and that of the greatest and most openly known enemies of Christ ([parenthesis by J.B.] that is of the pope and both of learned and lay papists) it is not lawful by any means to receive them, neither are they things indifferent, but the wicked commandment of Antichrist and Antiochus.[. . .] [The German and Latin versions differ slightly here.]

Our "indifferentiaries" that are of stouter stomachs, would not be so nice and of a straight conscience that they dare not defy the gold of the golden calf, but that they would [i.e., if they did not] desire some fat part of it to be given unto them. [. . .]

Those things that have been offered in idol service or served idolatry, they are idolatrous and cannot serve God, and he would that such should be cast away. The brazen serpent was ordained of God, and that by Moses the servant of God and his great prophet. But after it served idolatry, it was no more God's serpent or Moses' serpent, but the serpent of idolaters and the devil's serpent. And Hezekiah, who broke it, is praised for that deed. [. . .] [18]

Even as we defy and abhor the garments or coat of a thief, of a murderer, of a hangman, or of a common whore, though the garment itself be innocent and hath done no harm, neither will any honest man do so much as gladly touch it, so, all they that are godly indeed defy such popish trifles with all their hearts, because that they have served in the popedom, and [have] been occupied with abuses and wickedness, and have served the sacrificers that were polluted and defiled with idolatry. [. . .]

Augustine saith that faith is in great jeopardy when it is amongst a great number of ceremonies. [. . .]

[J.B.] This is most true in all things, that the man that is occupied about many things doth not sufficiently take heed to every one of them. And therefore it is truly said,

> They that in the fire many irons hold
> Must needs have some of them right cold.

So the people being charged to keep all the commandments of God and his ordinances, and more straitly commanded to keep more ordinances of men than God's commandments, must needs coldly keep some of the commandments of God [end J.B.].

If that the indifferentiaries go forward to reform the church of Christ as they [Latin, "at Torgau"] have begun, and will set in the place of

18. What then to surplices?

godly and learned preachers, whom they have put away, fools and
courtly flatterers, shortly we shall have no godly preachers at all. [. . .]

Where there is a heavy bondage in ceremonies and in the worshipping
of God, there cannot the glad liberty of Christ be. [. . .]

Ceremonies are the chief sinews or strength of the popedom. And the
greatest posts and stays of religion stand therein among the papists. When
the indifferentiaries propound and offer unto the ministers (that do not
gladly receive any popish thing) the queer coat called in Dutch [i.e.,
German] *chorrok* ([J.B. paraphrases the three lines that follow] which
we call commonly in English a surplice) and they will not receive it, then
the traditioners make exclamation, saying, "What a small matter is it to
wear a surplice, or a whitecoat above a black." [The text from Flacius is
resumed.] But indeed, if they can get them once in these coats they will
afterward deliver them to the Romans that they may buffet them, as the
old Romans did handle Christ when they buffeted him, having the white
coat upon him which they put on against his will. [. . .]

What other thing goeth the devil about, with all his thousand crafts
and subtleties, but to confirm the wicked in their wickedness and to give
them occasion to triumph over the true church, and over Christ himself,
and to blaspheme the holy name of the Lord; and of the contrary part, to
discourage and make sad the Holy Ghost in godly man, and to make
them faint in godliness, and at length also to doubt of the whole doctrine
of the true church. What thing can more make afraid and make faint soldiers, than to see their captains quake and tremble for fear? Caesar [Latin
"Chabriae ducis," German "Hauptmann Chabrias"] said that he had lever
[i.e., rather] fight with an host of lions that had a hart for their captain,
than with an host of harts whose captain were a lion. [. . .]

If any man should speak thus to another, and say, "Thou hast stolen
from me an hundred crowns. I require of thee that thou restore me them
again quietly lest I be compelled to use against thee some more violent
remedies"; and if this man accused of theft should first pay him ten
crowns in part of payment, and afterward twenty crowns, should not he
make himself guilty of theft and thereby be bound in pain of hanging to
pay the whole sum of money that is required of him? And should not he
show himself as ready to pay the rest as these two portions, of whatsoever purpose or intent he should do so? I suppose so indeed. Even so,
when we are accused of the corruption and marring of the whole religion
of Christ and are commanded to restore it to the old estate again, and we
begin to restore it in such things as seem most commonly before men's

eyes (as are outward rites and ceremonies), do not we seem to condemn our own selves? May not we be thought to deny our own religion, howsoever beauteous dreams we feign in our thoughts? [. . .]

It was an indifferent thing for Christ to wash his hands. Yea, it had a civil and a natural cause. For it is good manners and civility to come to the table rather with washed hands than with foul hands. Besides that, after the doctrine of the physicians of Salerno, it is wholesome for the eyes to wash the hands oft. Yet not withstanding all these, Christ would not wash his hands with the Pharisees because he would overthrow their traditions and would not seem by his washing to confirm and allow their traditions. [. . .]

It is not the point of a good Christian, and as little the office of a good divine, to believe that by angering of God and by assuaging of man's wrath that we shall come to any perfect peace. For tyrants are only as it were certain rods in God's hand, as God witnesseth himself in Isaiah the prophet [? Is. 7:17–20]. Wherefore the hand should rather be pacified and assuaged from wrath than the rod. But if it were possible to pacify and please the rod, that it should not beat us against the will of the hand, then were it to be feared that the hand should cast the rod away, and take a betell [?] or a maul and break us all as small as powder. [. . .]

Luther did truly name wicked wisdom to be the fair whore of the devil. [. . .]

The apostles had lever [i.e., rather] that their schools should be broken up than in any part to give place unto the ungodly or to confirm or allow their traditions. [. . .]

What boldness is this, that men dare give unto God's enemies any part of the treasures of the church which the Son of God hath given unto it. [. . .]

It belongeth not to any one man, neither to a few men, to ordain such ceremonies or rites as are above named, (to wit) such as neither promote the glory of God nor profit his church, but have only a vain show of holiness or seemliness and do no other good, and that without the consent of the church or congregation. Much less ought any man to make such quite contrary to the mind and will of the church or of the assembly of God's people. For all things belong unto the church, and the ministers are teachers of it and not lords, as Saint Paul saith, and they are given to the church of Christ. Therefore all they offend grievously *videlicet papa cum suis* [like the pope and his followers], whether that they are bishops or other men, which without the consent of the church or against the consent of the church, with an intolerable licentious usurping liberty, dare ordain anything in the church of Christ, yea although it be not ungodly. [. . .]

As they that put on the crown of thorn upon Christ's head to mock him gave him no honor (although they seemed to make him a king), but grieved him very sore and put him to much pain, even so, they that will beautify and honor the sacraments and church of Christ with the ceremonies of his adversary Antichrist do not honor truly Christ and his sacraments, but dishonor them and deface them. [. . .]

The teachers of the gospel in Saxony could scarcely drive away the abuses, no, not after that the foundation of the abuses were taken away; neither at this hour can our auditors be delivered from those abominations and superstitions which they were brought up withal from their tender years until the time of the preaching of the gospel. Wherefore with a little preaching of those old rites and ceremonies that they were brought up withal, they will easily run again to the whole sink and abomination of the whole popedom (a few young persons excepted, that were born since the preaching of the gospel, that never heard neither saw any such abomination). [. . .]

The spouse of Christ is dishonored and put to shame, when she is clothed with the garments of the whore of Babylon. [. . .]

What conformity is this whenas the spouse of Christ is made like the whore of Babylon in ceremonies? God, who is jealous, will not suffer that the church, his spouse, should be clothed with the garments appointed by a wicked man. [. . .]

1. These are the incommodities that rise and spring of the receiving of some of the pope's ceremonies. They bring home the popedom again. [. . .]

2. They open the windows to all the superstitions of Antichrist. [. . .]

3. They darken the gospel and hinder the light of it so throughly to shine as it did before. [. . .]

4. They receive again wolves into the sheepfold, and drive away true shepherds. [. . .]

5. They make faint and discourage all godly men, and confirm and strengthen all stubborn and wicked papists in their papistry, etc.[19]

19. Matthias Flacius Illyricus, *Liber de veris et falsis adiaphoris* . . . [ED.] In *Omnia* . . . *Scripta* . . . (1550), a cataena of quotations from fol. X2, X7, Y5, Y7, Y8, Z1, Z4, Aa2, Aa5, Aa8, Bb3-4, Bb5, Cc2, Cc4, Dd3, Dd5, Dd6, Ee3, Y6, Bb1, V6, V8, with some paraphrasing, which adheres to the meaning of the original. The selections are in the German edition of 1550, from fol. Iii to Tii. This work also had been debated by Parker and Crowley.

8. PHILIP MELANCHTHON

8A. There may be also reasons gathered of the difference of powers. God hath given charge unto the magistrates, or rulers, that they should make just laws. Therefore he will also that we should be obedient unto those laws. But he delivered unto the shepherds or pastors the sure word. Neither will he that we shall be lawmakers any further, or to put thereunto any other laws. Therefore he requireth that we should be obedient unto that word, and not unto new laws which men shall further add unto the word. And so the difference between one power and another bringeth more light unto this question. Yet for all that, it is more safe to lean unto another reason (to wit), that the learning of the apostles doth require that we should think that it is deadly sin, and on the contrary part, that the breaking of the ecclesiastical traditions or church ordinances, without the case of offence and contumacy, is no deadly sin.[20]

8B. The error in ceremonies breedeth many great disprofits and hurts. The first is, the doctrine of the gospel of faith and of the benefit of Christ is darkened when the opinion creepeth in that such observances deserve forgiveness of sins, or that by them we are made righteous, as the Jews did imagine of their rites. This opinion doth naturally occupy men's minds except they be taught rightly by the gospel. The second incommodity is, that the doctrine of difference of works is destroyed when ceremonies are preferred before the politic life. But now they are more set by than the inward spiritual exercises are, as are patience, and calling upon the name of God, as monks called their traditions more perfect than others. The third discommodity is, that the opinion of necessity creepeth in, which is a very perilous crucifying of the conscience. The fourth is, that the opinion of necessity (that is) that ceremonies cannot be missed [i.e., omitted] in the church, breedeth uncurable discord and contention, as in time past there was dissension for keeping of the feast of Easter. The fifth is, that there is falsely given to the bishops authority of making new worship-

20. Philip Melanchthon upon Romans 13:1. [ED.] *Commentarii in Epist. Pauli ad Romanos hoc anno 1540 — recogniti* . . . (Wittenberg, 1540), in *Corpus Reformatorum* . . . P. *Melanchthonis Opera* . . . (Halle, 1848), XV, col. 716–17. This quotation, and the two that follow, were used by "J.B." to refute the official pamphlet, *Whether it be mortall sinne to transgresse civil lawes* (S.T.C., 22572), in which Melanchthon's early works had been used to arrive at an affirmative answer to this question.

pings, whenas the true use of ceremonies is not known. And so is the doctrine of the New Testament darkened, and ungodliness is confirmed, and the tyranny of the bishops increased. [. . .] Whenas the opinion of worshipping, or of necessity, cometh unto things indifferent, then such traditions darken the doctrine of the gospel, and the opinion that cometh thereto maketh the traditions made of things indifferent to be ungodly. Therefore it is well done to break such, and to put them away, that that false opinion may be corrected. For it is very necessary and needful that the errors concerning worshipping, merits and necessity should be cast away.[21]

8c. Christ is accused that he hath stirred up sedition throughout all Judea, from Galilee to Jerusalem, and that he forbade tribute to be given unto the emperor. These are great trespasses and accusations, and this kind ofttimes grieveth aforehand the doctors or teachers. We are called seditious because we do not obey the emperor commanding us that we should receive wicked doctrine. [. . .] Christ answereth not unto all the lies that are made against him, but leaveth them that are openly known. But he answereth unto the question of the kingdom, and granteth that he is a king, and maketh an open difference between the kingdom of the world and his own kingdom, whereof he being the son of God is the king. So the church ought clearly to purge herself of the crime of sedition and to say that she would give all lawful obedience in all politic matters unto the magistrate; but concerning doctrine, that she would obey God (as it is commanded) rather than man. And here let all godly men consider the difference between the politic kingdom and the everlasting, wherein the son of God calleth us unto everlasting riches and giveth forgiveness of sins unto us and life everlasting.

And these kingdoms ought not to be confounded and mingled one with another, as the pope, under the pretence of the ministry, will be the king of the world and lord over kings. And after another manner the powers are mingled together, whilst the emperor and princes will set out a new doctrine unto the churches. For they have made the Interim, and will establish in the church the mass and invocation of saints and such other like things. And they will be doctors and pastors, whenas they do not understand the doctrine but are open enemies against it. This is not to

21. Melanchthon upon Romans 14. [ED.] *Commentarii . . . Romanos . . . anno 1540 . . .*, in *Corpus Reform.*, XV, col. 719-20, 721. It is noteworthy that neither the official party nor the radicals made any use of Melanchthon's several equivocal works on the German Interim.

be allowed. But let there be difference made between one office and another, and let every man labor faithfully in his office.

Pilate commandeth Christ to be scourged, and to be crowned with a crown of thorns. Pilate granteth that Jesus is innocent and faultless. And yet for all that he vexeth him with reproaches and punishment, even as some nowadays do, which kill not Jesus and utterly take not away them that preach rightly (because they cannot), yet by many signs they declare their hatred against them, for they despise the poor preachers and suffer them many ways to be troubled. The pope and all his bishops do scourge Christ whenas they set up their kingdom. They crown Christ with thorns and put a purple garment upon him, that is to say, they do work much sorrow to Christ and to his true church by that false and wicked lordship which they arrogantly take unto themselves against the will of God and the health of the Church.

Afterward Pilate is persuaded even to kill Christ when he heard once these words said unto him, "Thou art not the emperor's friend if thou do not crucify him" [Jn. 19:12]. Even such men are they which play with the wicked. For although in the beginning they are not most cruel of all other, yet by little and little they wax worse and worse. Therefore men had need to take heed at the beginning, according unto the saying of the Scripture, what fellowship hath Christ with Belial . . .[22]

[J.B.] Let us think of these horrible examples and let us flee such trifling playing and bearing with our enemies. And let us openly confess that we do differ from them in doctrine. And let us not consent and agree with them whenas they make their compositions. [End J.B.]

JOHN À LASCO (a baron of Poland by birth) in King Edward's days was called into England by the prince at Master Cranmer's, the Archbishop of Canterbury's, commendation and counsel (unknown to the most part of his countrymen), unto whom was committed by the king the charge of the strangers' churches here, which the forenamed worthy King Edward by his letters patents in the fourth year of his reign erected in London; making this John à Lasco superintendent thereof, and appointing thereto such other ministers as the said John à Lasco (who was an earnest suitor on the behalf of the strangers) thought meet for that room [i.e., office]. He, taking this charge upon him, so used himself therein until the death of King Edward that all the godly strangers and sundry others had much

22. Melanchthon upon Matthew 27:12. [ED.] *Conciones explicantes Evangelium Matthaei* (Wittenberg, 1558), in *Corpus Reform.*, XIV, col. 1020–21.

joy and comfort of him, the whole realm had a singular treasure of him, and the enemy had nothing that he could justly charge him withal. Briefly to say, his singular travail in the Lord's harvest in preaching and writing both here and abroad, his profound and deep knowledge of things, his sincere judgment in all points of religion, and hearty affection to the maintenance of Christ's kingdom against open enemies and counterfeit gospellers corrupting the simplicity of Christian religion—besides his uprightness of life, godly conversation and other qualities meet for such a personage—causeth much lamentation for the lack of him in the church of Christ throughout Christendom at these days, and will procure a continual remembrance of him with honor amongst the godly unto the world's end. This testimony hath King Edward of famous memory, under the great seal of England, given of him, which is in print at this day extant in Latin to be seen of all the world:

"John à Lasco, born in Poland, a very famous and notable man both for his honest uprightness and innocency of life and behavior, and also for his rare and singular knowledge in learning . . ." [23]

9. THE JUDGEMENT OF MASTER JOHN à LASCO *of removing the use of singular apparel in the church ministry, written the 20th day of September, in the fifth year of the reign of King Edward VI, which was as followeth:*

First of all I affirm that in the church of Christ there are some things to be observed continually, some things are indifferent and free, other some things are by no means tolerable. Such things as ought continually to remain in the church are the pure doctrine of the prophets and apostles, which for the sustenance of the soul are to be diligently proponed to the sheep of Christ by the ministers of God, whereunto are adjoined the sacraments of baptism and the Lord's supper, ministered according to the apostolic order set forth in the writings of the evangelists and apostles, to the which may very fitly be annexed ecclesiastical discipline.

I call those things free whatsoever they be that serve profitably and commodiously to the ministry of the word and sacraments, so they have their original ground in the Scriptures, have no commandment against

23. [ED.] An excerpt from the royal charter granted to the refugee churches in London. See J. Lindeboom, *Austin Friars, History of the Dutch Reformed Church in London, 1550–1950* (The Hague, 1950), 199, 202.

them, contain a manifest commodity to the church, and be void of tyranny binding men's consciences. Of this sort are these: to assemble together in the church this hour or that hour, this day or that day, to use in
the administration of the sacraments this kind of prayer or that kind, the
several times in the year to celebrate the supper of the Lord—but once or
oftener.

These things that are utterly to be removed from the church are of
two sorts: [A.] Some have so manifest impiety annexed to them that they
cannot deceive those that are but meanly instructed in God's word, as are
worshipping of images, worshipping of bread and wine, profanation of
the Lord's supper through the mass, praying to saints, praying for the
dead, and infinite such other monsters which Antichrist hath brought into
the church of Christ. [B.] There are other things brought in by the same
Antichrist which are much contrary to Christian liberty, obscure Christ,
increase hypocrisy, and bring in pride and swelling into the church, and
yet in the meanwhile have a certain show of profit and comeliness. Of
this sort are the appointed fasting days, choice of meats, much singing in
the church and such as is not understood, organ playing, and use of
church apparel in administration of the sacraments.

Now what great incommodities and hurt have crept into the church
by means of every one of these, and yet may more creep in except they
be removed, I cannot at this present particularly declare. I have here only
to entreat of the use of apparel, and to show cause why by no means
it ought any longer to be borne with of a godly magistrate in a reformed
church of Christ, although many devices invented by witty heads may be
alleged for some defense thereof. But we regard not witty heads, but the
testimony of God's will.

First of all, I conclude that even these garments are utterly to be removed from the church as a device of man, by that ground and reason
which Christ (*cf.* Mt. 15:1–9) and the prophets and apostles (*cf.* Col, ch.
2) use in excluding or thrusting forth of the church, as a pernicious
thing, all men's doctrines, traditions or devices. Polydore Virgil beareth
witness [24] thereof [that] it is a manner taken from the Hebrews that
priestly apparel, with covering of altars, with other things necessary for
the use of the temple, should be consecrated, and the garments appointed
over to the priests and others within orders, who should put them on
when they occupied themselves about holy things. Which Pope Stephen I

___

24. Polydore Vergil, *Li 6 de invent.* [ED.] *An abridgement of the notable woorke
of P. Vergile* . . . (1570; *S.T.C.,* 24658), Bk. VI, chap. VII, fol. cxxv verso.

did first appoint should be done amongst our churchmen. For he saith that in the beginning, when religion began to spring, priests were wont to put nothing more upon them when they went to divine service, standing rather to deck themselves inwardly with virtues of the mind and to cast away affections and vices of the body, than to take on them new attire. Now thus reason I and gather, if they changed not their garment or apparel when they went to God's service, then they used none for them that were admitted into the ministry of the gospel.

Paul and Barnabas were contented with laying on hands, fasting and prayer. Paul, diligently prescribing to Timothy and Titus all the offices of a bishop, maketh no mention of peculiar garments and other ceremonies. And that the use of apparel did not by and by go over all churches, it is evident enough by the decree of Celestine, the first bishop of Rome, whose words are these against such peculiar vesture of bishops: "We are to be discerned," saith he, "from the common people or other in doctrine, not apparel, in conversation, not in habit, in purity of mind, not in attire. For if we begin to give ourselves to novelties, we shall contemn and cast away the order that the fathers have delivered and left us, and shall make a place for superfluous superstitions. We must not therefore draw the simple minds of the faithful to such things. For they must rather be instructed than beguiled and mocked. Neither must we deceive their bodily eyes, but pour in precepts into their minds." Thus far he [i.e., Celestine]. Yet can we not deny but as men bend and incline to superstition of themselves, so some kind of garments, although very simple and plain, had crept into many churches before this man's days. For Sylvester no doubt gave the occasion. But Carolus (called the great) [i.e., Charlemagne] finished the matter, as stories bear witness. Now it is made manifest that the use of peculiar apparel in the church or ecclesiastical persons is a mere device and invention of men, and therefore to be rejected for this cause if there were no more.

They which would keep the use of this apparel in the church, as a thing instituted of God, refer the same to Aaron's priesthood. But they little foresee what they say. For we know by the Scriptures that Christ is not a priest after the order of Aaron, but of Melchizedek, and that Aaron's priesthood was extinguished and took end in Christ, with all the parts thereof, among the which we reckon also the apparel. Therefore Christ, the very wisdom of the Father, used no new or peculiar kind of apparel in holy ministry, neither appointed any other to be used. For that the figurative priesthood as a shadow was perfected and ended in Christ, the one and only Priest. All they therefore that call again Aaron's apparel into the church dishonor Christ's priesthood, as though being the light itself he needed shadows. Neither will that excuse serve, to say that all Aaron's priesthood is not called into use again, but some part thereof only. But he that receiveth a part doth not reject the whole. But all Aaron's priesthood, being a figure and shadow, is no doubt to be rejected, for that it is abrogated. And as many as do restore again those things that the authority of God's word hath destroyed and abrogated, are transgressors of God's law. Paul therefore well teacheth that the bondmaid is to be cast forth, and her son [Gal. 4:30], signifying that all the bondage of the law is to be rejected after the light of the gospel is sprung forth and risen. And he willeth us not to suffer ourselves to be removed from our liberty in Christ. Now it is too plain that the doctrine and commandments of whatsoever kind of apparel peculiar in God's ministry is a transgression of God's laws, for because Aaron's priesthood is [thereby] called into use again.

If any man, by occasion of the first argument, deny that the garments are a portion of Aaron's priesthood, and say that they were by a certain liberty brought in of the bishops of Rome to adorn and set forth priestly order, yet saith he not enough why they may be lawfully retained. We know that the pope of Rome is very Antichrist himself. Wherefore his priesthood also is antichristian, whereby Christ's priesthood wholly is soiled and utterly trodden under foot. But forasmuch as the chiefest part of the priesthood of the pope consisteth in ceremonies, anointing, shaving, miters and garments (for without these they account no man bishop, and they count him bishop whatsoever he be otherwise that is set out with these things), it followeth that if we condemn the popish priesthood for that it is antichristian, we ought to avoid all the parts and notes thereof also. For how can a godly and Christian heart love the mark of the blasphemous popish priesthood wherewith Christ's priesthood is so greatly contaminate and defiled? He therefore that hateth Antichrist's priesthood must hate also all the notes and marks thereof. Again, he that loveth parts thereof cannot hate the whole.

Moreover if we know that the pope's priesthood, with all the notes and signs thereof, be Antichrist's priesthood, and every work of Antichrist be Satan's work, we must not promote and help it forward but overthrow and destroy it, if so be we will be workers together with Christ, who came to destroy the works of the devil as the Scriptures bear record.

And let us not think that it is lawful for any man to institute, reduce
or keep in use by his authority these garments. For all power is given to
edify, and not to destroy (as Paul saith), who in the same place saith we
can do nothing against the truth, but for the truth. And edifying is to
build the faithful upon Christ in faith, hope, charity and innocency of
life, contending always to more perfection. But the garments promote or
help forth none of these things, but rather obscure Christ's face, bring in
a certain agreement with Antichrist's priesthood, or rather a backsliding
to the shadows of Aaron from the body of Christ.

The truth is it for the which apostolic men and Christian magistrates
ought to travail. And Christ is content with the ordinance which he himself hath left, neither doth he any longer require shadows. Wherefore
they must and will labor for it, not against it, by revoking those things
which Christ hath destroyed and abolished.

Furthermore, Paul simply admitteth nothing into the church but that
which may edify (that is to say) increase godliness. Peculiar garments in
the ministry edify not. Therefore are they not to be borne. Those things
that minister a certain counterfeit or fantastical occasion to godliness do
not by and by edify. But they must needs give Christians a necessary provocation unto godliness. But garments, contrariwise, partly increase
haughtiness and pride in them that use them, partly hypocrisy, partly
both twain. And to minister occasion to hypocrisy it is very ready for
them, yea it must needs be. For if that virtue be in thee which thou ima-
ginest to be signified by the apparel, why by showing of it dost thou take
the reward of men? But if it be not, art not thou a plain hypocrite, being
indeed another manner of man than thou pretendest to be? And thou
canst not escape by saying these private garments signify no virtue in us,
but admonish us as it were of our duty and office. What then, I pray you,
admonished the apostles of their duty and office—attire, or the spirit of
the Lord, the love of the church, and Christ? Do they then forget their
duty as often as they put these garments off? Why rather meditate they
not in the word of the Lord day and night, and thereby mend their ways,
for that it pierceth the ground of the heart, when apparel can move only
the outward man? What thing doth Christ three several times require of
Peter to be admonished of his office in feeding his sheep? Surely nothing
but love.

Again it is to be feared lest it breed an opinion of merit or some such
other folly, that the dignity of the minister or sacraments or preaching
the word is diminished, unless these unprofitable and pernicious garments

be used. This fear of man's merit alone should move us that vestments ought to be shut out of the temple with other ceremonies devised by men. It is ungodly to give such occasion of offence or falling to the weak for whom Christ died. How easy a matter it is to put confidence in these things, experience hath taught us. So that he that weigheth these things, and hath no consideration thereof, may seem not to be free from the suspicion of ungodliness. Neither can they excuse themselves that it is known to all men that there lieth no good nor hurt in the garments. For though we grant this, this knowledge was [available also] in those days when they were first brought in of the bishops. We are born not for ourselves only, but we serve the church, and our posterity also, to whom to leave Christ's religion very pure cannot but be very acceptable unto God. No man when he dieth willingly leaveth his children a testament or will unless it be thoroughly perfect, that all occasion of strife may be cut off. Why show we not like diligence and fidelity in God's testament?

I know that some men brag that the holy ministry is adorned and beautified by garments. But it is indeed much obscured and darkened thereby. For the apparel, affecting and occupying men's eyes, do [i.e., does] stay and hinder their minds from the consideration of such spiritual things as are done in the sacraments, and [does] draw them to delights and pleasures of the senses. Holy simplicity commendeth and setteth forth God's ordinances. Examples make of our side, both of Christ and the apostles, and also the primitive church, which it is more safe, more holy and more profitable to follow than to alter and change, or by doing otherwise to condemn Christ. Here further add I that which Paul hath noted of men's doctrines, that outwardly they have a spice and show of wisdom, through superstition and humbleness of the mind and hurting of the body, and not by any honor thereof to the satisfying or filling of the flesh (*cf.* Col. 2:23). At the length tyranny is brought in, and the garment is put upon men will they nill they. And this tyranny surely maketh that if a thing be of his own nature free and indifferent, it now ceaseth to be indifferent. Paul in flat and plain words forbiddeth Christians to submit themselves to such superstitious tyranny: If therefore ye be dead from the ordinances of the world, etc. (*cf.* Col. 2:20), and again, become not the servants of men (*cf.* 1 Cor. 7:23), is it not a very hard bondage, and mere slavery, to be driven to a certain kind of garment in the church that savoreth either gentility or heathenishness, or Aaron's priesthood, or else antichristianism and popery, that is so many ways hurtful and no way profitable?

But what maketh us to delight so to defile ourselves with popish filthiness? Why give we not that honor to Jesus Christ's priesthood which popish priests give to Antichrist's priesthood? There is nothing so small or light by him prescribed, although it dissent or vary from Christ, which his [priests] observe not very superstitiously and precisely to the uttermost. Why do not we again likewise in all things obey Christ, contenting ourselves with his naked and simple truth?

To conclude, seeing that Paul judgeth it meet to abstain from all show and appearance of evil (1 Thess. 5:22), and we have showed that to prescribe garments in the administration of holy things is indeed evil (for that it is a device of men, they be parts or members of the Aaronical or popish priesthood, they edify nothing at all, they breed haughtiness and pride, hypocrisy and opinion of merit or deserving), what Christian is he that will not judge them meet to be eschewed and shunned?

There are objected some things of the favorers and patrons of these garments, which it shall suffice briefly and in few words to note and touch, for that they overthrow not our reasons before alleged.

First objection: In indifferent things we must have regard to the weakness of our brethren after the example of the apostles.

Answer: A man may deny those things to be indifferent which obscure Christ's priesthood, and of themselves engender, stir up, and cause nothing else but hypocrisy, sects and pride in the church, having no original or ground in the Scriptures, and yet are commanded with tyranny unseemly for Christians. The apostles are never read to have done such things as these are (that we falsely pretend not, or vainly cloak ourselves with the godly industry of the apostles to plant the church of Christ). Again, seeing that they themselves think meet to have respect to the weak herein, why grant they not free use hereof to the strong and those that are stayed? And when shall the weak more better learn that those things are vain, foolish and hurtful than when they see them abrogated? How can the simple and ignorant think otherwise with themselves than that some godliness consisteth in those things that yet remain, when they see so many other things which were used in times past done away? Wherefore weakness is not relieved and helped, but hindered and hurt, if garments and such like ceremonies be retained and kept, because they be kept in the opinion of the mind, and by them men measure the dignity and worthiness of the sacraments.

Second objection: Again they object the magistrate's law and decree in retaining garments.

Answer: But I know our magistrate's [i.e., King Edward's] godliness, wisdom and forwardness to be such, that when he shall deeply weigh and well consider the danger and inconvenience of these ceremonies, he will rejoice that there be some that desire to run before in the law of the Lord and to prepare and make the way ready for others, that he may revoke, and bring all things to the sincerity and perfection of the apostles' order. They know that power and authority is given them in the church to edification, not to destruction, to stand on the truth's side to defend it, not to oppress it. Seeing this godliness in our Magistrate is known to be willing and ready, I wot not whether he can be blameless, whatsoever he be, that will under cloak of his [i.e., Edward's] defense tyrannously defend men's traditions or thrust them on other men against their wills, contrary to the Lord's commandment. But those things commonly delight and please much better which we ourselves have chosen than those which God's laws prescribe. Neither again have we here to fear any tumult if men's precepts and rules, especially being superstitious, whereby we kindle and provoke the wrath of God, be removed out of the church. But rather, the nearer we shall come to Christ's institution and orders, and the farther we shall depart or go from Antichrist's institutions and orders, the more quiet peace and rest of the realm have we to look for.

That policy and wisdom of man's reason (which seeketh and promiseth itself peace by unlawful means) is fickle, slippery and deceitful. Saul, seeking God's favor by the sacrifices of the Amalekites, which were forbidden, cast away himself unadvisedly. There is one way and means to attain safety and health by. If we altogether turn to repentance, believe the gospel, walk in innocency of life, and retain nothing into the church which either hath not the express word of God for it (or else [doth] draw and take thence, as out of a fountain, his infallible and sure ground of beginning), and then, that true pastors, and such as be painful and diligent in teaching, be placed and set over churches (dumb and evil shepherds being excluded and thrust forth), so shall the King and his people flourish, according to the promises of God often repeated in the prophets.[25]

25. [ED.] This letter is otherwise unknown, and was not found by A. Kuyper, ed., *Johannis à Lasco, Opera tam edita quam inedita* (2 vols., Amsterdam, 1866).

10. Heinrich Bullinger

10A. It is openly known that our Lord in his first supper, and that the apostles also in the celebration of the supper, used a common and honest garment. Therefore it is not contrary to the first institution if the minister go to the Lord's table arrayed with his own garment, so that it be comely and honest. Surely they that are communicants use no other garments than their common garments. Here had men need to take heed that superstition creep not in. It seemeth that the old fathers used a cloak or an overmost garment above their common garment. But they did not that by any example they had of Christ or his apostles, but after the tradition of man. At the length, this stuff that we see at this time was gathered by following of the sacerdotal apparel of the old law, and was cast upon the ministers that would minister the communion. And Innocent, the third of that name, doth not conceal that. But we have learned a great while ago that the levitical rites and ceremonies are not only abrogated, but that they ought not to be brought again into the church by any man. Therefore, when as we live in the light of the gospel and not in the shadow of the law, by good right we cast away that massly and levitical apparel.[26]

10B. The fathers of old time had used a plain garment, and not greatly costly, which they used in celebrating of the sacraments and other God's service. For the most part they were covered with an overmost garment while the minister went about to serve the church at the table of the Lord. For of old time the priest was covered with that garment which seemed to every country most honest whilst he did consecrate and divide the body and blood of the Lord. [. . .] But the stuff that is used nowadays was set from the Jewish priesthood, as Rabanus is the witness, which, in the first book of his *Institutiones* and the fourteenth chapter

26. Heinrich Bullinger in his *Decades*. [ED.] *Sermonum decades . . .* (5 parts in 3 vols., Zurich, 1549–52). Parts 3 and 4 were dedicated to Edward VI, and Part 5 to Lord Grey. On the controversy over this part of the *Decades*, see the editor's introduction to this document, 81. The *Decades* were widely used by the bishops for instructing the lower clergy who were non-graduates. After Whitgift became archbishop, a special note referring the reader to the letters of Bullinger and Gualter in support of the bishops' policy was inserted at this point in all editions of the work. From 1587 onward, the letters themselves were printed as an appendix. The passage occurs in the Parker Society edition of the *Decades* (Cambridge, 1849–52), V, 420–21.

and in those that follow, doth diligently declare how that this attire in all points is like unto the apparel of Aaron. And Innocent the Pope (for this attire utterly womanish and like unto maids' plays) was so bold as openly to pronounce and give sentence that not all the customs of the law are not abolished or put down. And these doth he write in the fourth book and fourth chapter of the mystical sacrament of the altar.[27]

11. WOLFGANG MUSCULUS

11A. In this our age there are some that earnestly go about that the parties that are at debate should be brought unto unity. But they err, in that whereas they go about to seek it not in Christ which maketh them one that are at debate. But think not that unity may be gotten after this manner, that we should go back over unto them, and return and be made papists again. But by this way true unity cannot be gotten, which cannot consist but in him that maketh of both one.[28]

11B. Is it not the office of a shepherd to bring home again into the way sheep that stray abroad, whether they will or no, lest they should perish? I answer that we do not twitch or speak against the lawful office of true pastors, whose office is to bring again into the way, but against lordship, which first Christ himself spake against and reproved (Luke, chap. 22), and afterward the apostle Peter in the fifth chapter of his former epistle, and God himself in the Old Testament reproved in false shepherds which played the lords too cruelly over his flock. A true shepherd seeketh his sheep that strayeth away. When he hath found it he layeth it upon his shoulders lest it should perish. But a false shepherd killeth and destroyeth. So our lords of churches do not instruct and teach those that they judge to err in the church, because they cannot, nay because they care not. But with commandment [they] constrain them to deny the truth, that with

27. Bullinger in *De origine erroris* [ED.] Part 1, Basel, 1528, Part 2, Basel, 1529; thereafter several reprints. "J.B." perhaps used the widely circulated edition of 1539. In the 1568 edition, where it is reprinted with *De Conciliis* . . . , this passage occurs on fol. 110A. In 1568 Bullinger sent copies of this edition as gifts to Coxe and Grindal. The latter wrote Bullinger on February 8, 1567, that "twenty years ago" (Henry VIII died January 28, 1547) he had forsaken "Lutheran" views on the Lord's Supper after reading *De origine* . . . ; *Zurich Letters*, I, 182, 207 f, 215.

28. Wolfgang Musculus upon Ephesians 2. [ED.] *In epistolas Apostoli Pauli ad Galatos et Ephesios, commentarii* . . . (Basel, 1561), fol. 61 (separate foliation for each book).

their violence they may bring to pass what they will, and with torments
compel them to recant, and cruelly kill them that will not. Is not this to
be lords over our faith in the church of Christ? For what other thing is it
to play the lords, than not by the law and lawful power, not for the
profit of the subjects, to command those things that are right and lawful;
but even at their commandment, for their own lust and pleasure, to exercise lordship over their subjects, and to show the preeminence of their superiority to appoint whatsoever they list to be believed and done, and
that with high looks and great pride, and with cruel threatenings, to exhort in all things obedience of all men, even most servile and fullest of
slavery, and require the same to be performed against the consciences of
the faithful people. If the lords of the churches be free from this kind of
lordship, let them restore the free consciences of faithful men again from
the yoke of man's authority, and let them abide in the Christian liberty
whereby they are not the bondmen of men, but his [bondmen] of whom
they were bought again with a great price or ransom.[29]

11C. We see here how men should obey magistrates, and what difference they ought to put between God and the emperor. For although he
be the officer of God, there is one thing that is due unto him and another
that is due unto God. Therefore we are taught here two things. The first
is that the servants of God not only may, but ought, to obey the magistrate. The apostles did teach this, Romans 13 and 1 Peter 2. The second
thing is that there is one thing due to the emperor, and another due to
God. It that is earthly is due to the emperor, and it that belongeth unto
religion is due unto God. In earthly things we have the image of the emperor in a coin, which teacheth what we owe unto the emperor. Again,
we bear in our soul (by the sealing of Christ and his Holy Spirit, being
signed or coined through baptism and have thereby) the inscription of
the name of Christ, whereby we are taught what we owe unto God. God
forbiddeth not us to give unto the emperor it that is due unto him. Then
were it not great wickedness and ungodliness if that the emperor would
not suffer it that is due unto God to be given unto him, but will take it
unto his own self? [30]

11D. By considering of these things it appeareth plainly [that] although
the care and charge of Christian religion belong unto Christian magis-

29. Musculus upon 2 Corinthians 2. [ED.] *In ambas Apostoli Pauli ad Corinthios
epistolas, commentarii* (Basel, 1559), cols. 58, 59.
    30. Musculus upon Matthew 22:21. [ED.] *Commentarii in Matthaeum evangelistam
. . .* (Basel, 1544), fol. 461.

trates, yet for all that it belongeth not unto them, without the word of God, to ordain anything.[31]

11E. It is therefore out of all doubt that it was ordained by the apostles in the first and apostolic church that the elders of the church, *episcopountes* (that is to say, they that have the charge of the Lord's flock), should exercise the ministry of teaching and governing by their common labor, and that they should be as a man would say, *akephaloi* [headless] (that is to say, subject to no head and president), of which sort even at this time some ministers of the word are found in some churches, amongst whom none is found superior or higher than are other in office and in power, although one be more excellent than another in learning, in the gift of eloquence, or wisdom. But after the times of the apostles (as Saint Jerome saith), when there rose amongst the elders of the church dissensions and schisms or sects (and as I do judge whenas that temptation of superiority or higher authority entered into the minds of the elders, shepherds and teachers), little by little some one of the number of the elders began to be chosen which was made president above the rest, and he, being set in a higher degree, was named a bishop. And so he alone took that name unto him which before, others had common with him. But whether that counsel did profit the church of Christ or no, that such bishops should be made which, rather by the custom than by the truth of God's ordinance, should be brought in and be of greater authority than elders, it was better declared in times following than it was since, when this custom at the first was brought in. For we may blame that custom for all the high pride, riches, tyranny and corruption of all churches of Christ which these princely and knightly bishops have and do now exercise. Which thing if Jerome had seen, doubtless he would have acknowledged this counsel to have been not of the Holy Ghost, to take away division as was pretended, but Satan's counsel, to destroy and to waste the old ministers of feeding of Christ's flock, whereby it might be also brought to pass that the church should not have true pastors, doctors, elders and

31. Musculus, "Of Magistrates." [ED.] In *Loci communes sacrae theologicae* (Basel, 1560). English translation, 1563, by John Man, at the suggestion of Archbishop Parker, to whom Man was chaplain. English translation dedicated to Parker. Two appendices, on oaths and on usury, from Musculus, *In Psalterium commentarii . . .* , *Etiam de iuramento et usura* (Basel, 1551), were added at the end of the book. An "Admonition to the Reader" noted that Musculus' views on some matters were not agreeable to those of the English church. The *Loci* of Musculus had been debated in the exchanges between Parker and Crowley. The passage here quoted by "J.B." occurs in *Commonplaces of Christian Religion* (London, 1563), fol. 569 verso. "J.B." did not use Man's translation.

bishops, but underneath the visors [i.e., masks] of those names idle bellies and mighty princes which not only will not preach themselves and feed the people of the Lord with wholesome doctrine, but will not suffer the flock to be fed by any other, which thing they do by great violence.[32]

I IF. This matter hath been wonderfully tossed with a continual contention through them which hath more aspired for preeminence and gaped for the supreme power than have gone about the lawful exercising of the ministry. For they desired rather to be lords in the church than to serve it. And at this present time the most part of them which, casting away the tyranny of the bishop of Rome, will seem to have brought the churches again into the liberty which was purchased by Christ, are assaulted with this temptation. These, being otherwise good men and exercising faithfully and diligently the office of teaching, suppose that by this means they shall profit the churches, if they deliver the ministry of the word from contempt and despising (which it suffereth now in all places), and would restore it to the old honor again.[33] But on the other side, there are other not evil men, but also well learned and workers in the word of God, that stand up against these, being afraid lest through the study and zeal of these men (not being sufficiently circumspect and wary) the door should be opened by little and little to bring into the church again the old lordship; that is, lest they by their authority which they have of the ministry of the word, might open the way to false and unfaithful ministers to abuse the power that is defended and brought in again by them to the contrary.[34] And they suppose that this fear is not in vain while they, considering the beginning of the popish lordship, call to remembrance under how beauteous a pretence, and by the zeal of great and holy men, by and by, after the time of the apostles, it was brought into the churches. [. . .] It is plainly to be granted that at the beginning some power was given unto the ministry of the word and to the dispensation of the mysteries of God, which is [i.e., are] profitable and mighty to edification, yea and necessary for our salvation which is through Christ. And that is meant by the way of a similitude of Christ himself when, as in Matthew 24:45 he saith, "Who thinkest thou is a faithful servant and a wise, whom the lord hath made ruler over his household, to give them meat in time?" He meaneth that he would give unto his disciples such

32. Musculus, "Of ministers of the Word." [ED.] *Commonplaces* . . . , fol. 165b-166a.

33. O postillick B. that wold be woth proud Lords and humble. Apolie. [ED.] ? Apostolic bishops that would be both proud lords and humble apostles.

34. Some men mark, and some try the lordship, what it is.

power over his church as they have to whom the whole household is committed of the good man of the house, that they should give them sufficient meat. And Mark 13:34–5: Even as a man that goeth into a far country leaveth his house, and hath given power unto his servants, and hath appointed every man his office, and hath given charge unto the porter that he should watch. "Watch ye therefore . . ." Doubtless he spake these things unto his disciples to show what should be their condition in the house of God after that he had departed from them to heaven. [. . .]

[J.B.] Amongst three powers there is one that is called *potestas juris* [end J.B.], that is, the power of right, whereby a man hath lordship over his own substance which is not subject unto another man's right. This power of right is given of God the father unto his son Christ. For he saith, "All power is given unto me in heaven and in earth" [Mt. 28:18]. Peter taketh away this power from the ministers of Christ when he saith "exercising lordship" (1 Peter 5:3). And the apostle Paul refuseth it, saying, "We are no lords of your faith" [2 Cor. 1:24]. And he exhorteth faithful men that they submit not themselves unto them which will exercise lordship over them when he saith, "Be ye not made the servants or bondmen of men" [1 Cor. 7:23]. Wherefore they that challenge unto themselves this power in the house of God, for that end that they shall not be servants of Christ, but lords of the church, are injurious and do wrong to the majesty of Christ and also to the liberty of the church.

As many as do this utterly pertain unto the kingdom of Antichrist, which occupying the place of Christ in the church and challenging all his authority (not only for this cause that he is contrary to Christ, but also for that he thrust himself into the church instead of Christ) is justly called Antichrist, that is the adversary, and also the vicar of Christ, for even as he is called *Antistrategos* [i.e., interloper] not only that is against the chief Captain, but he also that thrust himself by usurpation unto the soldiers to be their chief captain and braggeth of his office.[35]

12. RODOLPH GUALTER

12A. There is no stronger or greater hindrance unto salvation and to faith than is the counterfeit authority of false prelates, confirmed by the

35. Musculus, "Of the power of ministers." [ED.] *Commonplaces* . . . , fol. 170b–171a.

prescription of long time. For by the reverence that men have unto them, it is brought to pass that men dare not depart from them, even for the errors that all men spy in them, because that the common people doth know that so many hundred years amongst all men, of every order and place, have had them in such honor and so greatly regarded. [. . .]

The papists do say that they [i.e., papists] are not rashly to be provoked to anger which are defended by the public authority of kings, whose anger to stir up against any man is very jeopardous. But I answer that such men whom God hath appointed for to be keepers and defenders of the public health or salvation ought not to be afraid of any perils. And we do know that the false prophets have ever had this good luck, that they have had kings and princes to be their defenders and protectors. And yet for all that, neither the prophets nor the apostles gave any place unto them, because the commandment of God drove them unto this, that they should with jeopardy of their lives stoutly both withstand them and their patrons or defenders. And these words of God which he spake unto Jeremiah are well known: "Be not thou afraid when thou seest them, lest I destroy thee whilst they look upon thee. For behold I make thee this day a well defended city, a pillar of iron, and a brazen wall against the kings of Judah, against the princes and the priests of the same" [Jer. 1:18]. Therefore there is no cause why they that are God's officers should fear the tyranny of the world. [. . .]

"Beware," saith he, "of the scribes." Indeed it is but a short sentence. But such a one as many men doubtless thought intolerable. For he speaketh of them which for the space of many hundred years occupied the chief place in the church, to whom God had committed his law and the key of knowledge (as it is said in another place), which also, sitting in the preaching stool of Moses, gloried much that they did succeed the old priests and prophets and occupied their places. Yet for all that, Christ moveth his disciples that they should beware of them, that is to say, that they should not acknowledge them to be their pastors, but rather that they should depart from them. For so Saint Peter the apostle seemeth afterwards to expound these words, whenas he saith to them of Jerusalem that asked counsel of him, "Separate, or depart, yourselves from this crooked and froward generation" [Acts 2:40]. But what other thing was this than to make a schism or sedition, unto them which until that time seemed to be knit together by agreeable consent amongst themselves? But as every concord and agreement is not good, so every division or dissent is not evil. And as they offend which agree together in it that is evil, so they deserve no small praise which disturb and break up such concord and agreement, that they may learn to consent unto the truth which before did conspire and agree together in lies. [. . .]

The pope calleth home again from banishment not only the Jewish ceremonies, but also the ceremonies of the Gentiles. And he putteth them to death that desire to enjoy the Christian liberty. [. . .] In religion all use of images is forbidden by the gospel, whose use also is condemned without all doubt in the law and the prophets.[36]

12B. There ought nothing to be preached or taught in the church saving only such doctrine as was delivered by the Holy Ghost. For the church or congregation is the house of God, in the which the voice of the good man of the house ought only to be heard. And all things ought to be ordered according to his appointment.[37] [. . .] We do gather that the kingdom of God ought to be set abroad and defended neither with carnal weapons, neither by the strength of the princes of this world, but with the preaching of the word wherewith the Spirit of Christ useth for to work strongly in men's minds. If that the apostles durst not take upon them such authority as to go away from Christ's commandment and to thrust new traditions unto the churches, doubtless their rashness and presumption cannot in any wise be accused [i.e., excused] who at this time, under their name and pretence, dare so unshamefastly do it.[38]

36. Rodolf Gualter upon Mark 22. [ED.] I.e., 12. *D. Marcus evangelista, Rodolphi Gualteri Tigurini in evangeli Jesu Christi secundum Marcum homiliae cccxxxix. Accessit operi praefatio authoris, qua docetur, quid hominem Christianum inter nostri seculi diversas de religio ne controversias et graves persecutionum motus facere conveniat* (Zurich, Anno LXI [i.e., 1561]), fol. 152 verso, 152 verso (in paraphrase), 153 recto, 153 verso. This volume of 339 homilies was completed during the final months of the English exile in Zurich. The preface, dated January 31, 1559, refers to the English scene (fol. aa6 verso, aa7 recto).

37. Reformers of religion must not bring in superfluous rites abolished.

38. Gualter upon Acts 1. [ED.] *In Acta apostolorum homiliae CLXXIIII* (Zurich, 1557). This series of sermons was delivered while the exiles were in Zurich. In his dedication to the Magistrates of that city, Gualter asserted that the Book of Acts had set forth a perfect and an absolute pattern of a church, "whereunto all written anywhere else in the Scriptures touching the church" might be referred. By the action of the Magistrates, he wrote, Zurich followed that pattern. On the role of Gualter in the vestment controversy, see the editor's preface, 79. John Bridges, who later figured in the anti-Puritan campaign and in the Marprelate controversy, translated this work into English, *An hundred, threescore and fifteen homeleyes . . . upon the Actes* . . . (1572; *S.T.C.*, 25013); the passage used by "J.B." occurs on 20, 30, 580.

12C. This is also to be marked, that man's traditions can neither be joined, neither be made to agree, with the gospel. And they that go about that purpose do nothing else but by little endeavor to overthrow all religion. For amongst these there is great discord. But whereas Christ is allowed, who is made unto us of God the right wisdom, all the wisdom of man must needs give place, with all his traditions. [. . .]

As in husbandry it is convenient that the thorns and brambles shall be first plucked up by the roots, if thou wilt have any seed to grow and to bring forth fruit, so except all things be taken away even at once it can never bring forth worthy fruits. For of small remnants that abide behind we shall see great heaps of errors to spring up. Wherefore those commandments that were given for the pulling down of altars and breaking of idols in pieces, appear yet still. Which God would so earnestly to be kept, that he would that the very gold which was sometime consecrated unto idols should be cast away and be burnt. And in divers places certain kings are reproved and blamed, which have bestowed no evil or small labor in reforming of doctrine and religion, because they left unput down or not destroyed the high places (which some called chapels) which before their times were the shops or workhouses of false worshipping. And would to God there were not now examples in this our time which sufficiently teach us how jeopardous a thing it is that there do remain some remnants of instruments of old superstition. For they which under pretence of the gospel seek their own profit fetch from hence occasion to sin. Furthermore there is given hope to men that are superstitious, that their superstition shall be restored again, which [therefore] withstand the reformation of the church.[39] Therefore all ministers and magistrates ought diligently to take heed and mark this sentence of Christ, that we go not about to sew the new or raw cloth of the gospel to superstitions, which indeed are an old and a rent garment. But let us use great diligence and unceasable zeal to overthrow them.[40]

12D. The primitive church as we see here had her diseases. Neither are they light trespasses, neither small faults, which are here rehearsed, but horrible faults. They put difference between nation and nation. They are divided with factions. They occupy contention, and that not privately. They betray the bitterness of their minds most wickedly by their murmuring. Therefore we see that the primitive church was infected with

39. Keeping of old rites maketh Bonner and the wicked hope well.
40. Gualter upon Mark 2. [ED.] Gualter, D. Marcus . . . homiliae . . . , fol. 31.

that sin for the which many thousands under Moses were overthrown in the wilderness.[41]

12E. Therefore it is an ungodly and a tyrannical rashness of them which think that they may make new articles of the faith and to thrust into the church traditions by the advice of man's reason.[42]

FINIS

41. Gualter upon Acts 6:1. [ED.] *An hundred . . . Actes*, 274.
42. Gualter upon Acts 1. [ED.] *An hundred . . . Actes*, 21.

PART TWO

❖

The Passive-Resistance Party

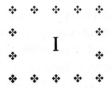

EDWARD DERING

Editor's Introduction

Insofar as Puritanism was a preachers' movement guided by men who were primarily "physicians of the soul" (as William Haller has argued),[1] Edward Dering was certainly the prototype. Born under Henry VIII in 1540, Dering was a university student during Mary's reign. At the age of twenty he became a Bachelor of Arts, and then a fellow of Christ's College, at a Cambridge not much changed by the new Elizabethan Settlement. Over the next decade his activities included those of a successful don, an expert in Greek, a learned defender against Harding of Jewel's *Apology* for Anglicanism, chaplain to the Duke of Norfolk, chaplain at the Tower of London, and rector of his native parish in Kent.[2] Christ's College had not been involved in the conflicts over vestments at Cambridge between 1565 and 1567. As a result, Dering was in generally high favor with officialdom when he was chosen to preach before the Queen on February 25, 1570, even though his patron, Norfolk, was then in the Tower because of his intended marriage with Mary Queen of Scots, and his complicity in the Northern Rebellion of 1569. His remarkably outspoken sermon brought no immediate retort from the Queen. The corruptions in the church of which Dering spoke were also deplored by Parker and other high churchmen, who, however, considered them beyond remedy.

Behind Dering's sermon Patrick Collinson has seen a turning point, "a crisis of conscience," and has suggested that illness, or the lectures of Thomas Cartwright, may have been responsible. Dering's doctrinal views

1. William Haller, *The Rise of Puritanism* (New York, 1938), chap. 1.
2. Patrick Collinson, *A Mirror of Elizabethan Puritanism; The Life and Letters of "Godly Master Dering"* (Dr. Williams' Trust, 1964). On Cecil's situation in 1569, see Conyers Read, *Mr. Secretary Cecil and Queen Elizabeth* (London, 1961), 437 f; on the criticism by the Privy Council of the bishops, in 1569, for the bad state of religion, see Matthew Parker, *Correspondence*, 355, 362.

prior to early 1570 are known only from two anti-Catholic publications, which contain no evidence for any great doctrinal shift during the year 1569–70. What had happened was rather that on the controversial subject of practical reform Dering changed at about this time from a reluctant conformist to a passive resister. Dering may also have undergone a crisis of conscience as a result of the discovery of Norfolk's treason and of his having been in league with the Catholics in the Northern Rebellion. A further shock would have come with the emergence of Gregory Martin, tutor to the duke's children, as a Catholic, and his flight in 1570 to the Continent, where he was eventually to edit the Douay Bible.

Dering's chief fame was acquired during the years 1569 to 1575, when he preached and lectured in London. He gave up his rectory in Kent early in 1570, and that same year he also resigned his fellowship at Cambridge. He continued to preach at the Tower, and was chaplain to the Duke of Norfolk until the latter's execution on June 2, 1572. At some time not later than 1572, under circumstances that are now unclear, Bishop Sandys appointed Dering divinity lecturer at St. Paul's Cathedral, where he became the first of the popular preachers in the Puritan hagiology.

In 1572, when John Field and Thomas Wilcox launched an open attack in their *Admonition to the Parliament* and were imprisoned for it, Dering told his hearers at St. Paul's that he was taking no part in the controversy. But he went privately to visit the men in prison, and finally lost his post at St. Paul's on the grounds that he was a Puritan sympathizer. Brought before the Ecclesiastical Commission, he was able to show that in his official capacity he had never violated even the vestment requirements (which were the concern of the original protest), although he confessed freely he shared the views — though not the actions — of the "Presbyterian" Puritans.[3]

During the 1560s and 1570s the English authorities were in a difficult situation. Every political consideration, domestic and foreign, compelled the civil rulers to an ever-increasing polemic against Rome, whereas throughout the country, among the clergy and the officials of the courts, both civil and ecclesiastical, a very high proportion were not Protestant. Yet the effect of the government's propaganda was to create an antithesis between "English" and "Catholic" for the younger generation without

---

3. Edward Dering, "Lectures . . . upon . . . Epistle to the Hebrews," in *M. Dering's works* . . . (1597; *S.T.C.,* 6677), fol. X8 recto; and the examination of Dering quoted in *Parte of a Register* . . . ([1593]; *S.T.C.,* 10400), 73–85.

offering any sort of religious grounds that a layman could understand. Loyalty to England and to the Crown were the usual explanations. Preaching, and the books that grew out of it, became a serious threat to the government's attempt to "walk the wire." Preaching and books meant discussion, debate and conflict concerning the meaning, the function, the truth of the religious authority which the government felt driven to claim for its actions. As a result, Parker's *Advertisements* of 1566 had been followed by severe restrictions on preaching and publication. The official clergy were in the thankless position of having to prove that it was the will of God for the civil authorities to do many things, but not necessarily for the government to be subject to the criteria (i.e., the Bible and the primitive church) by which it condemned its Catholic opposition. A chronological study of the publications of the 1560s and 1570s makes clear what happened. In a nation of three million people, a church with twenty-two bishops and some eight thousand clergy, plus two universities, a silence reigned greater than in any other nation of western Europe, whether Catholic or Protestant. It became the religious task of the English clergy to control the people. The preaching of the Puritans and the propaganda of the Catholic exiles from abroad, constituted for the official English clergy a threat that all but immobilized them. English bishops and university men wrote a few anti-Catholic works intended mainly for reading by the professional clergy. But almost to a man they were unable or afraid to speak in popular language addressed to the people. To do so would have forced a restatement of the whole issue. So, from a position of superior authority they spoke to the people about loyalty, order and due subjection to their superiors, at a time when England had begun to seethe with new ideas of every kind.

Dering's preaching is perhaps best characterized by its sense of purpose. He was determined to reach the ears of the public, and to interpret Christianity in terms which carried meaning for the people. He saw the institutional, and the purely academic or intellectual, aspects of Christianity as means, not ends. He was convinced that the people needed to understand what was at stake in the violent and continual religious struggles in England and on the Continent. To this situation, Dering believed, frequent, regular, popular (i.e., relevant) preaching was essential. He saw the use of the prayer book ritual and of standard homilies, without real preaching, as at best an evasion of the religious crisis of Europe, and at worst a device by which the needs and views of ordinary people were kept subordinate to the needs of the civil power.

This pastoral concern also made Dering a physician of souls, one whose concern began with the people's own views of their needs. Through long-standing abuse and neglect, this pastoral role of the priesthood in England had passed under the control of an ecclesiastical court system that concerned itself solely with punishing (usually by money fines) various infractions of canon law. Moreover, as a result of the succession of enforced changes in religion between 1534 and 1559, most of the English clergy had become so demoralized that only a few ardent Catholics and a few equally ardent Protestants had a religious basis adequate for a genuine pastoral ministry to a propaganda-bewildered populace. The official clergy, especially the bishops, were forced to bear the brunt both of anticlericalism among the anti-Catholic laity, and of the feeling against heretics among the Catholic laity. A majority of the parochial clergy were in a paralysis of demoralization. Only a few of the Protestant clergy were able to break out of this stasis to reach the people in new ways. To the preaching of these men, even minimally religious people, especially in London, responded out of motives ranging from patriotism to curiosity. As a preacher at St. Paul's, Dering filled a role somewhat like that of Latimer and Hooper during the reign of Edward.

Dering's preaching was much more dependent on the early church fathers than on the Continental Protestant reformers. Following the classical patristic view that man and his world had been created good, and that sin had crippled and ravaged what God had made, rather than destroying it, Dering preached that redemption in Christ was designed to heal it. The much-controverted slogan "Man's Disorder and God's Design," used by the World Council of Churches in 1948, would not have seemed odd to Dering and his colleagues. The sin of man had disordered this world. Nevertheless, God's design for it could even now be seen in the structures of society, in man's reason, in his long historical experience, and most of all in the Bible and in the idealized life of the early church. Salvation was the process of bringing man and his society into conformity with God's design through preaching, teaching and discipline. This "Augustinian synthesis" had been the theology of most of the earlier English reformers under Henry and Edward, and it was to remain characteristic of the majority of Puritan preachers throughout the Tudor-Stuart era. What is so often called "Puritan legalism," supposedly gotten from the Old Testament, is in fact an inheritance handed down by Augustine from the Greco-Roman ethic of becoming good by exercising oneself in that pattern which is truly good, rational and natural.

Because of the multiplying controversies of the day, Dering insisted that neither church nor state could set the pattern according to which the Christian man was to be redeemed. Erasmus and the official Anglican clergy would have agreed on this against Rome, but if the state had intervened they would have fallen back on the doctrine of *adiaphora*. With Dering there emerges a growing emphasis on the person as opposed to the institutions that would make of him a mere instrument or subject. For Dering the evil judges, priests and magistrates were those who forced upon men patterns of life and meaning that were neither of God nor of nature, but represented the arbitrary will and interests of those in power. What Dering thus asserted, as the authorities realized, was the essentially revolutionary doctrine that individuals must have a part in defining those patterns — or, at the very least, be persuaded that they were true and valid. Either way, the Tudor claims that when God instituted the monarchy he gave such power to the monarch alone, were negated. Dering struck deliberately against the caesaro-papal claims of Henry VIII, but criticized the exercise of rather than the theory behind Elizabeth's claims.[4] In the 1570s such views were extremely radical, as were Dering's clear insistence on the priesthood of all believers, and his intention of placing the laity as well as the clergy in a position to know the meaning of the faith. One reason, perhaps, why Dering refused to carry these views further, along with men like Field, Wilcox and Cartwright, was that in the end — like Luther, Latimer and even Erasmus — he remained so committed to the Neo-Platonism of the time as to believe that very little could or would occur toward redeeming the material world.[5]

The personal or individual emphasis in Dering's preaching stressed that it was in man's spirit, in his person, that he was restored to the divine pattern, even though the world as a whole was not. This change or conversion (a term commonly used in this sense even by Erasmus) was a gradual process. The so-called "mystical" or psychological experiences of conversion were seldom mentioned by Dering.[6] As Erasmus and the Protestant reformers had done, he concerned himself with the man who was already Christian, engaged in the warfare of flesh against spirit, against temptation and his own human frailties. Conversion in the sense of an entrance upon the Christian life was not stressed. Faith was understanding, and the religion of the heart was that of man's inner spirit — the equiva-

4. Dering, "Hebrews," *Works*, fol. D3 recto.
5. "Hebrews," *Works*, fol. M1 verso, M6 recto, verso, N3 recto.
6. There were occasional references, e.g. in *Works*, fol. Q1 recto.

lent of obedience to a quality of life. "Godliness is not made of words, as a wood is made of trees, but it is an earnest love proceeding from a pure heart, and a good conscience, and an unfeigned faith, in which we may glorify God, and do good to his people." [7] Because of all this, preaching, as the divine method of illumination of the understanding, was utterly essential, and the neglect of true, popular preaching had led to the failure of religion in England.[8]

Dering's use of the Bible in his preaching is a good illustration of the pattern of preaching which was to become typical of the Puritans. It was not novel with him, though he undoubtedly contributed to its development. From the common Protestant emphasis upon the church as a people rather than as an institution, there had grown up a new appreciation of its history. On the Continent during the Marian exile, this conception had its flowering in the first Latin draft of John Foxe's celebrated martyrology, which by 1570 had been issued in a massive second English edition, combining the whole of biblical history with the history of Christendom and of England down to Elizabeth's reign. Dering's preaching was centered upon the story of the biblical people, people who were like his auditors. He made frequent shifts from ancient to contemporary history, with little emphasis on theology or on learned authorities, but rather on the doings of intensely human people. Even the atonement through Christ became something worked out in history. This emphasis made comprehensible to lay people (as theology could not) why the clergy and the church had failed, why kings were evil, why problems arose; in short, it became in vivid pictorial fashion the so-called "providential interpretation of history," which could later be "authenticated" by reading the Bible at home. Now the lay people, many of whom wrote down Dering's sermons as they were preached, could understand where things stood as well as — or better than — the clergy.

To say that Dering became the prototype of the Puritan popular preacher and physician of souls is not to imply that he was the originator of all that is meant by either phrase. But thanks to his gifts—he was an excellent scholar and persuasive speaker, with a rare capacity for transcending the defensive professionalism so characteristic of the Protestant clergy at the time — combined with his position during the years of crisis, he became both a leader and an exemplar. Of his career as a don little is known. He came to prominence between 1569 and 1575, when, with the

7. *Works*, fol. D5 recto.
8. On illumination, see *Works*, fol. O6 recto, T3 verso.

Scottish queen a prisoner in England, to the threat upon the life of Elizabeth, the rebellion in the North, the papal bull against the Queen, the involvement of England in the Huguenot and Dutch rebellions, the tense parliaments of 1571 and 1572, the execution of Norfolk as a traitor, and the frontal attack made by the Puritans in the *Admonition to the Parliament,* were added the questions of the Queen's marriage, of the royal succession, and the fears that England could not remain Protestant very long. As chaplain at the Tower, and during his brief appointment as lecturer at St. Paul's, Dering was placed, as it were by accident, in a position where he could be heard. That position was reinforced by the efforts of John Field and others in publishing his sermons, with frequent reprintings as the years went on.

It may be noted that Dering did not employ the rhetoric and logic of Peter Ramus (1515–72), which Perry Miller has found so characteristic of those later Puritans who were followers of William Perkins.[9] Nor did John Knewstub, whose addresses are represented in Part Three of this volume. Ramus' influence may be seen in the published works of Perkins, Dudley Fenner, and many other Puritans. It even appears, surprisingly, in Archbishop Parker's *A Brief Examination for the Time* . . . attacking Crowley's *A Brief Discourse against the* . . . *Apparel of the Popish Church.* But in Elizabethan times Ramus had not yet become "standard" among Puritans.[10]

Dering's letter to "Mistress B." — i.e., Mrs. Barret of Bray (Berks.), is undated, but in its language it is close to his second, fifth and eighth lectures on the Epistle to the Hebrews, which were given in 1572.[11]

The text of Dering's preface, sermon and letter are from *M. Dering's Works: More at Large than Ever Hath Heretofore Been Printed in Any One Volume* (1597; S.T.C., 6677). I am indebted to the Library of the University of Chicago for permission to use the copy in its possession. Dering's biblical quotations cannot be traced to any English version. He was reputed to be a superior scholar in Greek, and no doubt made his own translations. A few marginal notes of no importance were added by Dering's editor. These have been eliminated from the text that follows.

9. Perry Miller, *The New England Mind: The Seventeenth Century* (New York, 1939), Bk. II, also Appendix A.

10. W. S. Howell, *Logic and Rhetoric in England, 1500–1700* (Princeton, 1956), chap. 4.

11. Dering, *Works,* fol. B2 verso, E1 recto, H1 verso.

A Sermon Preached Before the Queen's Majesty the 25th Day of February by Master Edward Dering
1569/70

To the High and Mighty Princess, His Dread Sovereign and Most Gracious Lady Elizabeth, by the Grace of God, Queen of England, France and Ireland, etc.

If it had been sufficient charge of every man's duty for necessary causes to attempt a good work, then (most gracious Princess) have I double boldness and safety to present this my labor unto your Highness. For to pretermit the value of this work, which yet must commend it, as I will not strive therein lest I should seem foolish, so I leave it to every man's conscience beseeching all men for truth's sake to give no word of praise unto it above the weight of profit which he shall find in it. But touching my most humble duty in offering it to your Highness, if the causes be not such as constrain me before God and man, let this also be imputed unto me that I know not my duty, nor what becometh my calling.

Of long time and by many means your Highness hath been provoked against me to high displeasure, so that at the last I am henceforth forbidden to preach any more openly within your Majesty's dominions. In this case have I long stood, which how grievous it hath been unto me, or how gladly I would be delivered from it, if I be a good man I cannot easily show. Solomon saith, "The anger of the king is like the messengers of death, but a wise man will pacify it" [Prov. 16:14]. Which word of truth if it do move the affections of our heart, it cannot be but in the disfavor of the prince we must feel a great overthrow of the happiness of our life. And we cannot nor ought not but continually to labor to turn it from us.

For, what though some be despisers, unworthy of a king's protection, who being freed from care have no care of love? Is therefore the bond between prince and subject broken? Or is the word of God of less truth because the wicked do disobey it? Or is this to honor the king in our soul, not to care a whit for his gracious favor? But, what if our displeasure be for a good cause, and we suffer for righteousness? Yet our fear and grief is the same it was. For faith doth overcome affliction, but it taketh not away the sense and feeling of the sorrow. Seeing therefore this case is mine, if your Highness' disfavor and disliking be unto me as it ought to be to every true subject, like as the fear is exceedingly great, so the sorrow of it is not willingly to be admitted if possibly any good remedy can be sought. This is then one case of my boldness, for which I crave my lawful pardon, most humbly beseeching your Majesty favorably to accept it which duty and necessity have compelled me unto.

The other is the cause itself, and the punishment which I do sustain, being now long time forbidden to preach; wherein if I could rob myself of my righteousness and finally by silence acknowledge the faults which never were, should I not be injurious to the graces of God? Should I not pull down whatsoever I have built? Should I not betray the truth of God to the slanderous tongues of many envious men? Should I not sin against the Lord before whom there is no man can plead my cause? And are not all these evils confuted and scattered with this one dutiful and faithful doing, to offer these my Lectures printed unto your Highness, the printing of which shall confute the slanderous, justify the doctrine for which they were preached, discharge my conscience before God, and being offered unto your Highness be a perpetual supplication till your gracious favor be reconciled. And this is the second cause of my doing, which so much constrained me as the love of God did dwell within me. For under that covenant hath he committed unto us his truth and hath bound our care, travail, counsel, ability and all our life to the furtherance of it. Of which the same God, for his Christ's sake, make your Highness a long defender.

But I think it will be here objected, other means might have been made to pacify your Majesty and to justify my cause. Surely whatsoever I had done, this might still be objected, although I have not pretermitted any way which hath seemed unto me good and dutiful, and therefore all other means being frustrate, and the thing necessary to be followed, who but the Lord alone hath led me unto this? Neither do I speak this unadvisedly or without ground, for both I have committed this matter unto the Lord, and I do nothing but what I have heard and seen in his saints. For was it not common in all the primitive church when the saints of God suffered so many slanders, that the emperors' minds were now alienated from them and they had no helpers, that they became suitors for themselves, and offered up to the princes the confession of their faith and their humble supplications to be received to favor? Did not Aristides so to Trajan, Justinus and Melito to Antonius, Miltiades to Maximinus, Quadratus to Adrianus, Apolloninus to Commodus, Zerubbabel to Darius, and finally, Paul himself, a poor prisoner, when all other refuge failed him, did he not boldly call upon Caesar to have his cause tried before him? If this refuge had not been given of God, such men, such an apostle, would never have used it. Why then should it be reproved in me, that hath so good a warrant of such a cloud of witnesses? Wherefore again, with all fear and duty, I most humbly beseech your Highness of your gracious clemency accept it favorably, which by so great necessity is offered unto you. And thus far of the cause of my doing.

Now having this confidence, because yet I speak to your Highness, I must beseech you that no want in my words may be imputed unto me. For the Lord is witness how heartily I do seal them with all humility, though according to my rudeness in titles and terms and phrases of speech, I may often fail. I remember once (when I hearkened to such things) that this I have heard, "He that will speak safely to a king must speak with silken words." But I think the meaning was of silken men. For ignorant people, unacquainted in the Court, never show more folly than when they would be finest in talk.

And Saint Paul, whose counsel was better, hath showed us another example. For being before the king, indeed he gave him his due title of honor, but greater humility of heart than gorgeousness of words. He reposed the hope of his good cause not in his own speech but in the king's wisdom, and rejoiced to be judged before him because he was skillful of the Jews' orders [cf. Acts 26:1–2]. So I before your Highness, with true obedience, will gladly also speak as well as I can. But the hope I have of your gracious favor, I let it rest in the wisdom which the Lord shall give you in the true knowledge and earnest zeal of his gospel. To which good graces of God in your royal personage I appeal, and most willingly put my judgment into your hands.

It is now a great many years as I account them, and they have passed exceeding slowly, even as the years of a ward or apprentice, since first I heard how much your Highness misliked of me.[1] The cause, much more grievous than the time, hath been my preaching, not for any evil which was in it (I must needs protest it, for how should I lay blame upon the word of God?), but for a great deal of envy which followed after it, and kindled flattering tongues to slander and speak evil; who also at last have brought to pass whilst your Highness believed them, and thinketh none to be so evil as to lie before their prince and sovereign, that at their pleasure I am forbidden to preach, whom yet God had called and whose labor he

1. [ED.] Presumably because of his sermon before her on February 25, 1570. But the next paragraph places the cause of displeasure in his *Lectures on Hebrews*, which began at St. Paul's in 1572.

had blessed; which being an injury to him that can recompense it and hurt without good, I shall be the more faithful to God in the good defense of a righteous cause and the more dutiful unto your Highness, in all humble suit to seek your gracious redress of such an injury.

And first of all, for mine own discharge, I offer up these my Lectures printed,[2] for which I have had so much blame, unto which I neither crave any favor nor credit, but as they shall testify for themselves, so let them have their reward. And for my part, I wish nothing but just punishment for all that is done amiss, or favorable release, if I be indeed innocent and unblamable. Then most humbly I beseech your Highness, even for the Lord's sake, whose cause it is, that according to your wisdom and faith toward God, you would well think of what author it is, for a preacher so well known to be so evil reported.

More than this I have nothing to crave, but will daily pray as I am most bound, that your Highness, your most honorable councillors, your whole estate, may have long and blessed prosperity to the rooting out of all idolatries, and perfecting of that pure and true religion which God of his mercy hath planted by your hands, so that the fruits of your Majesty's most gracious labor may most plentifully abound upon yourself. Amen. Amen.

Your Highness' most humble, faithful and obedient subject,

EDWARD DERING

O Lord, open thou my lips, and my mouth shall show forth thy praise [Ps. 51:15].

Psalms 78:70–72: He chose David his servant also, and took him from the sheepfolds, even from behind the ewes great with young took he him, to feed his people in Jacob and his inheritance in Israel. So he fed them according to the simplicity of his heart, and guided them by the discretion of his hands.

The prophet declareth in this Psalm how God of his justice, for the great sin of Ephraim, took from that tribe both the tabernacle and the scepter, and gave them to the tribe of Judah, whom then according to his mercy he had purposed to bless with all perfect happiness. In which we learn not to abuse God's mercies, lest they be taken away from us as from the tribe of Ephraim they were. And then what helpeth it us, that in

2. [ED.] This preface (which was not published in his lifetime) must therefore have been intended for his *Lectures on Hebrews*.

times past we have been happy? And lest this should happen also unto the tribe of Judah, to fall from God's mercies into his displeasure, the prophet in this place stirreth them up to thankfulness, that they may be found worthy to have continued toward them so great blessings. And this he doeth by the example of David, in showing both how mercifully God hath dealt with him, and how obediently David walked before the Lord.

And herein he useth, as it were, three reasons to move them withal. The first is of God's mercy whence he had called David. The second is of God's intent and purpose whereunto he called him. The third of David's own person, how faithfully and how truly he did execute that whereunto he was called. The first argument or reason he comprehendeth in these words: "He chose David his servant and took him from the sheepfold." The second in these words: "He chose him to feed his people in Jacob and his inheritance in Israel." The third in these words: "So he fed them according to the simplicity of his heart and guided them with the discretion of his hands." These arguments will I speak of, as God shall give me utterance. And if they shall be now more effectual to move us than they were then to move the people of Israel, then be we profitable and happy hearers. If not, it is good right and reason that as we have been in the fellowship of the same sin and iniquity, so we should be partakers of the same reward and punishment. That if God shall so deal with us that we lose again both the tabernacle and scepter, as they have done before us, we can say no other but the Lord is righteous, and behold we have eaten the fruit of our own labors. Let us therefore consider of these arguments and stir up as we may the gift of God that is in us, that at length we may learn by them more holy obedience.

The first argument is the good consideration of God's mercies whence he called David. Which argument alone is so effectual and strong to stir us up to the obedience of our calling, that it is able enough to raise us up again though we were never so deep sunken in rebellion. A sure proof of the efficacy of it may be unto us the oft and continual use of it in the sacred Scriptures. For seeing that God's Spirit in his holy word doth so oft apply it both as a help to confirm the godly and as a present remedy to turn again the most obdurate and willful sinner from his obstinate purpose, surely, except all the dews of God's mercies be marvellously dried up in our barren hearts, the same argument, if we can well think of it, will be effectual in us to work our regeneration in the newness of life.

When God would have Abraham to forget his country and his father's house to go that long and weary journey into the land of promise where he and his posterity should dwell after him, he confirmed him with this saying, "I am the Lord thy God which brought thee out of Ur of the Chaldeans" (Gen. 15:7). By this remembrance of his former benefits, he persuaded Abraham to adventure all that he presently enjoyed upon hope of a better promise which yet he had not seen, but which should be fulfilled. When God would move the children of Abraham, that is the children of Israel, to turn again from their great iniquities that they had so long practiced in the hardness of their heart, he useth but this argument to tell them of all the miseries that they were born in: their country to be a cursed country, their fathers idolators (*cf.* Josh. 24:2), themselves given over to all voluptuousness and pleasure not regarding God nor seeking his religion. In which woeful estate when the Lord God did behold them, he pitied their misery and said even then unto them, "You shall live" [*cf.* Ezek. 16:6]. By which promise their former woe vanished away, and instead of nakedness they were clothed with [em]broidered work, they were covered with fine silk, decked with many ornaments, and had a crown of beauty upon their heads. Now therefore, that they should not walk in their own ways or commit idolatry (*cf.* Josh. 23:16) as other Gentiles did, nor tread such benefits under their feet, this argument, as a strong medicine, the prophet repeated often and with many words.

Thus God dealt oft with the kings of Israel and Judah, when they began to fall away and walk as other nations walked that were round about them. He called them back by putting them oft in mind how his mercy had been with them, and from what low estate he had raised them up. Thus the prophets of God dealt often with the people (*cf.* 2 Sam. 12:7–8; 1 Kings 14:7, 16:2–3). Joshua, when he had brought them into the land of Canaan, to the end they might fear God and so make their dwelling sure, he made unto them a long repetition of God's benefits that by remembrance of them their dull spirits might be stirred up the more obediently to follow God. Samuel, when he was afraid of God's heavy displeasure towards the people of Israel because they had asked a king for them, to the end they might turn away God's anger from them by their speedy repentance, he told them what God had before done for them as a ready way to make them beware afterward how they did willingly offend so loving a Father (*cf.* 1 Sam. 10:18–20). Stephen, when he would have persuaded those whose iniquity was now grown to full measure that they had crucified Christ, as though in this alone were the greatest hope of their amendment, he chose no other way to convert them but this, to show in long exhortation what God had done for them and for their fathers (*cf.* Acts 7). And this, as in the beginning it was given by the Holy

Ghost to man as a sovereign medicine to keep him far from unthankfulness, so it hath been continued by the same Spirit from time to time to stir us up not to forget the Lord.

Our savior Christ, to make his disciples sure and that they should never shrink for adversity, he told them often this, that they had not chosen him but he had chosen them (cf. Jn. 15:16). St. Paul, when he would move the Corinthians for to avoid the false apostles and to follow Christ, he persuadeth them thus, that in times past they were Gentiles and were willingly led away to dumb idols (cf. 1 Cor. 12:2). And again to the Ephesians, "You were in times past dead in trespasses and sins, you walked after the prince that ruleth in the air, after the spirit that now worketh in the children of disobedience. . . . But God who is rich in mercies, through the great love wherewith he loved us, even when we were dead . . . , hath quickened us in his son Christ" (Eph. 2:1–2, 4–5).

This argument, dearly beloved, seeing it is so strong, let us apply it unto ourselves, for our disease cleaveth fast unto our bones with long continuance and we have need of sharp medicine to heal it again. Let us therefore use it (I beseech you) and if God's spirit hath not forsaken us that we be uncurable, no doubt we shall recover and grow to amendment. Let us see our own estate and what God hath done for us, what cloudy days have gone over our heads, and in how fair sunshine we be set again, and no doubt when sin hereafter shall allure us as before, it will make us afraid of his deceitful bait, and we will never be bought with the beauty of the golden cup to drink of the spiritual whoredoms that are within. We were in times past Gentiles and uncircumcised people. Now Christ hath pulled down the wall of separation and made us all one, even his children of adoption (cf. Eph. 2:11–14). We were aliens from the commonwealth of Israel. Now we are received as citizens in the company of his faithful. We were strangers from the covenant and promise. Now Christ hath delivered a new testament in which we also are written heirs of mercy. We lived sometime in ignorance and had no hope. Now we have received knowledge and are comforted. We were without God in the world and could nowhere lay down the terrors of our sins. But now we have received the spirit of adoption, by which we cry, Abba, Father (cf. Rom. 8:15). And what should I say more? We were subject unto sin, hell, death and condemnation. Now Christ hath spoiled the principalities and powers (cf. Col. 2:15), delivered us out of the power of darkness, translated us into a kingdom of immortality and grace (cf. Col. 1:13).

Except we have set our hearts as an adamant stone or, as the prophet saith, made our hearts and faces like the flint (*cf.* Ezek. 3:9), it is impossible but that this cogitation should move us. Or if it do not, surely, surely, though the Lord had not spoken it thus often unto us, or if the Scripture were not written for our instruction, yet the law of nature would condemn us for most unthankful men. Day and night we should bear a witness in our own conscience, how fearful judgment God hath reserved for so great iniquity. Who amongst us could bear it, to be rewarded with unthankfulness where we have well deserved? To be contemned of those whom we have raised up to honor? To be spoiled of those whom before we had clothed? To be betrayed of those whom we have especially trusted? And how then are we blind and understand nothing? How shall the Lord bear it at our hands if we be unthankful unto him, if we contemn him, and rob him of his honor, who alone hath made us glorious when we were covered with our own shame and confusion? The Lord grant us his Holy Spirit that we deceive not ourselves.

There is nothing more effectual to move a son to obedience than to know he hath a loving father. Nothing maketh so trusty the bond-servant as to remember he hath a gentle master. Nothing maketh the subject more faithful unto his prince than to feel by good experience his prince's clemency. Nothing joineth man faster in the bond of friendship than to consider well what his friend hath done for him. And let nothing bind our obedience more carefully to the word and will of God than that he hath so long continued merciful unto us. As sure as the Lord doth live, this is his holy truth. He that cannot be moved with this, he hath not God's holy spirit. Poor or rich, bond or free, high or low, noble or low degree, prince or subject, all is one. The remembrance of God's mercy must make us all thankful, were we never so mighty.[3]

This cogitation must banish far from us the pride of a kingdom, to think how God hath raised us from the sheepfolds. Whosoever can say thus, "I have been bond, but I am free"; "I have been in danger, but I am in safety"; "I have been fearful and trembling, I am careless"; "I have been full of sorrow, now my soul is at rest"; "I have been in misery, I am in dignity"; "I have been a prisoner, I am a princess"; believe me, believe me, if the great and goodly cities which he builded not, if the houses full of all manner of gold which he filled not, if the vineyards and olive trees which he planted not, did not make him forget the Lord which brought him out of the land of Egypt, out of the house of bondage, if prosperity

3. [ED.] An allusion to the propaganda concerning Elizabeth's "miraculous" preservation in Queen Mary's reign.

hath not made him drunken so that he hath banished far from him all sense and understanding, the remembrance of this thing will make him thankful unto him that hath been the worker.

Yea, even you that are now a Princess of majesty, if you have felt any such alteration, take heed, fly far away from all unthankfulness. If you have seen the days in which you have said, "O Lord, I have no friend but thee alone," now that prosperity hath brought unto you a great many of fair countenances, forget not that God, who was your only friend in trouble. If in times past you have prayed that you might not build upon the sand (*cf.* Mt. 7:26) to have your house shaken with every blast of wind, now that you have choice of your own ground, take heed, I beseech you, where ye lay your foundation. Now that the stern and helm is in your own hand, guide your ship so that the waves do not overrun it. If you have prayed in times past unto God to mollify your enemies' hearts and to bring their cruel practices to nothing, now that you yourself are set in safety, be not cruel unto God's anointed and do his prophets no harm (*cf.* Ps. 105:15).[4]

I need not seek far for offences whereat God's people are grieved, even round about this chapel I see a great many, and God in his good time shall root them out.[5] If you have said sometime of yourself, "As a sheep appointed to be slain" (Ps. 44:22), take heed you hear not now of the prophet, "As an untamed and unruly heifer" (Jer. 31:18). I will not with many words admonish your Majesty that are wise enough. Only I will say this, return unto your own heart, and search your reins. And here I set before you the tribunal seat of Christ. If you know these things to be true, discharge the faith you owe. Grieve not your quiet conscience lest it begin to accuse you, and the burden of it be greater than you shall be able to bear. If God hath defended you mightily as ever he did David the prophet, discharge your faith with the prophet and cry in spirit, "What shall I give unto the Lord for all those benefits that he hath bestowed upon me?" (Ps. 116:12).

And thus much as God hath given me utterance I have noted unto you out of the first part of this Scripture, how God did choose David from the sheepfold. The Lord give you grace to confess his goodness and show yourself more thankful for all his benefits. One other thing we may note here: that all that we have of God, it is of his free mercy. It is not of our

---

4. [ED.] Possibly a reference to the authors of the *Admonition.*

5. [ED.] Possibly a reference to the much-controverted ornaments in the royal chapel. See *Zurich Letters*, I, 55, 64–7, 74, 122, 129; also Archbishop Parker, *Correspondence*, 79, 97, 105.

deserving. Even as he gave both the tabernacle and the scepter unto the tribe of Judah because he loved it.[6] So God gave unto his people a land that flowed with milk and honey. But he gave it not for their righteousness, for they were a froward people, but because he loved them (cf. Josh. 5:6). So God dealt favorably with Zion, that is, with the children of Israel, not because of their obedience, for they were a rebellious nation, but because he remembered his oath which he swore unto their forefathers [cf. Deut. 7:6–8]. So God fulfilled the prophecy of Jacob and he blessed Judah, but he fulfilled it in David, whom he took from the sheepfolds. So Christ made his kingdom everlasting in the house of Jacob, but he laid first the foundation of it. And now he hath builded it up, neither by the wisdom of the wise nor by the understanding of the prudent, but to testify unto us his free grace and mercy. He hath chosen the foolish things of this world to confound the wise, and the weak things of this world to confound the mighty, and vile things of the world which are despised, to bring to naught the things that are esteemed and had in reputation, for this cause alone (as the Scripture witnesseth) that no flesh should rejoice in his presence (cf. 1 Cor. 1:27–29).

But what need we so far to seek for examples? Let us behold ourselves how plentifully at this day are God's mercies and benefits poured out upon us, both upon our Queen and upon her people. How mightily doth he defend us in so many dangers? How sit we here in safety, when all the world is on an uproar? [7] And is this, think you, of our deserving, or rather of God's mercy? Now surely, surely, we are very blind if we will not all confess with the prophet Jeremiah that it is God's mercy that we be not consumed (cf. Lam. 3:22). So much disobedience both in prince and subject, so little care of duty, so deep forgetfulness of God, what doth it else deserve but heavy judgment? And what can it testify else, but that these good blessings of God are signs of his great mercy?

Well, well, the wisest way is to take heed in time. Let not our sins separate between God and us. If there be nowhere examples that we can look upon, let us beware by the tribe of Ephraim, that we abuse not God's mercies, for fear we lose them. Because we are now out of danger and there is no peril that is present, let us not therefore say as proud Babylon said, "I sit like a queen and shall see no evil, I shall be a lady forever and shall see no loss of children" (Rev. 18:7). "He that thinketh he stands," saith Paul, "let him take heed he fall not" (1 Cor. 10:12).

It is no good argument that our estate is sure because God hath deliv-

6. [ED.] Success was not regarded as a reward for godliness.
7. [ED.] See note 6.

ered us out of a great many troubles.[8] Nay, let us the rather fear, and be the more circumspect. God's arm that hath been stretched out for our safeguard in times past is not now drawn in that he cannot again grieve us. God delivered the people of Israel out of the hands of many and grievous enemies. But yet, when the people of Israel would in no wise amend, God could raise up Shalmanezer to lead them away to perpetual captivity (*cf.* 2 Kings 17:6, 18:9–11). Nay, we have a great many more fearful examples than this. We have fearful examples before our eyes to take heed of God's judgments when we abuse his graces. God defended Sennacherib in the conquest of a great many of countries, in all which he escaped harmless. Yet when he knew not himself, but blasphemed the God of Israel, even before the walls of Jerusalem, God could find him out at home in his own country. And in the temple of his idols his own sons slew him [2 Kings 18:13–19:37].

Agamemnon, ten years together in mortal and bloody wars, could never be hurt. Yet after, at home in his own house, by his own wife he was killed. Bibulus, a noble Roman, got many victories and still escaped peril. Yet afterward, in the city of Rome when he should have had the glory of all his valiant acts and rode through the streets in the pride of his triumph, a tile falling from the house struck so deep into his head that it killed him presently. Julius Caesar, in winning the western part of the world in fifty-one set battles, never received dangerous stroke. Yet after all his dangers so happily escaped, at home in the Senate house in the midst of his nobility and in his parliament robes, he received twenty-four wounds, and all of them deadly. Many such examples are before our eyes to make us beware, and take heed of security, when any danger is past, and to take heed of forgetfulness, when we have received mercy. The Lord enrich us with the graces of his Spirit, that when we often behold from whence we have been delivered, we may seek diligently and be always careful how to be found thankful.

The second argument which I said the prophet used to make the people thankful, was taken of God's intent and purpose, to what end he chose David, and that he showeth in these words, "to feed his people in Jacob, and his inheritance in Israel" (*cf.* Ps. 78:71). These words are very plain and contain so expressly what is the duty of any prince or magistrate, that none can be ignorant but he that will not know. For this purpose they are chosen, "to feed God's people in Jacob, and his inheritance in Israel." Whether he be prince or emperor, duke, earl, lord, counsellor,

8, [ED.] See note 6.

magistrate, whatsoever, for this purpose he is called, discharge it as well as he will. He must feed God's people in Jacob, and his inheritance in Israel. O if God had called them for some other purpose, how gladly would they have executed it? If God had called them to dicing and carding, to swearing and lying, to pride and vanity, the mighty men of our days, how busily had they done their duty? But alas, this is not to feed God's people in Jacob, nor his inheritance in Israel. This is to feed ourselves. Even as the ox is fed to the slaughterhouse, so we do feed ourselves to everlasting confusion. "They that have ears to hear, let them hear" (Mt. 11:15). God hath chosen his rulers "to feed his people in Jacob, and his inheritance in Israel." These are the plain and express words of God's Spirit, and then what outrageous spirit is that, or what Fury rather, that crieth thus with an impudent face, that the prince hath not to do with Jacob and may not meddle with Israel. But these are the steps that the man of sin should tread, to speak against the Lord, and yet say that he cannot err. These are the lively marks of Antichrist, thus to fight against Christ, and yet say he is his vicar.

Such is all the religion of papistry; examine the same if you will, even from point to point. Where God saith one thing, it saith still contrary, and yet crieth with shame enough, "There is no error in it." God, in his holy word, saith it is the doctrine of devils to forbid marriage and the lawful use of meats (cf. 1 Tim. 4:1–3). The pope very presumptuously forbiddeth both, and yet saith still that he hath the Holy Ghost. Saint Paul the apostle saith, "If you observe days and times, I am afraid that the gospel is preached unto you in vain" (Gal. 4:10–11). The pope saith, "You shall observe both, I can dispense with the apostle." And yet he saith he is apostolical. Saint Peter saith, "Be you subject to the prince as to the chiefest" (1 Pet. 2:13). The pope saith the king is not highest, but he is above both king and caesar. And yet he saith still he is the successor of Peter. And what should I say more? It grieveth me to reckon up all that monstrous abominations. It would make a Christian heart to bleed to see how he hath deceived the simple. With his paper walls and painted fires, he made them so afraid that they believed all things whatsoever he had spoken. But he is filthy, and let him be filthy still (Rev. 22:11).

We will return to our purpose, and learn of a princely prophet what is a prince's duty. "He must feed Jacob and Israel," that is, kings must be nurse-fathers, and queens must be nurses (cf. Is. 49:23) unto the church of God. Unto this end they must use their authority, that God's children may learn virtue and knowledge. For to seek only wordly peace and security, or to make us live at ease here in this wayfaring city, that is, rather to feed flesh and blood than to feed Jacob, rather to make happy this worldly fellowship than to instruct Israel. The true Israelite is strong against the Lord and cometh with violence to claim the kingdom of heaven [cf. Mt. 11:12]. What helpeth it in this respect to be rich or honorable? "If I had all the riches in the world, yet could I not pay the price of my brother's soul" (Ps. 49:7–8). Or if I had never so much rule and authority, I am not therefore the nearer to make intercession unto God. They are other weapons that must prevail against Satan (cf. Eph. 6:13), and it is another attire that will be accepted for the marriage garment. If we will feed Jacob and Israel, let us lead them to the house of wisdom, and train them up in the fear of God. The Lord open the Queen's Majesty's eyes, that she may look to this charge. Otherwise, if we lived never so peaceably under her, yet when the Lord shall come to ask account of her stewardship, how she hath fed her fellow servants with the meat appointed them (cf. Lk. 12:42), then she will be found eating and drinking with sinners.

But because we are so dull of hearing that a little teaching of our duty is not sufficient for us, I will show out of the Scriptures somewhat more plainly, if ought may be plainer what is the duty of a prince. The prophet Isaiah very effectually setteth it out in the person of our savior Christ, saying, "Righteousness shall be the girdle of his loins, and faithfulness the buckler of his reins" (Is. 11:5). It is true that the prince must defend the fatherless and widow, relieve the oppressed, and have no respect of persons in judgment, seek peace unto his people, and gird himself with righteousness. But this is also his duty, and his greatest duty: to be careful for religion, to maintain the gospel, to teach the people knowledge, and build his whole government with faithfulness.

For this cause King Solomon, both the mightiest and the wisest king that ever was, called himself a preacher. And the holy King David, to make manifest how he [ac]knowledgeth his duty, spake openly to his people saying, "I will instruct thee and teach thee in the way that thou shalt go, and I will guide thee with mine eye" (Ps. 32:8). This general rule King Solomon gave unto other, "Be diligent to know the estate of thy flock and take heed unto thy herds. For riches remain not always, neither the crown from generation to generation" (Prov. 27:23–4). Hereby expressly showing, that to increase riches or to set forth the glory of a kingdom, that is not the greatest duty of a magistrate. Thus the prophet

Hosea, crying out against the people of Israel, he reckoneth up this as their greatest disorder, that lying and swearing and ignorance of God was not punished amongst them (*cf.* Hos. 4:1–2).

And alas (dearly beloved) if this be the saying of the prophet, let us look unto it. I dare not but speak the truth, seeing God of his goodness hath called me hither. He hath raised me up so high when I was cast down, that I cannot forget his benefits. If this will not serve, I will surely speak it more plainly when the Lord shall open my mouth again. Surely if this be the saying of the prophet (as it is indeed) that lying, that swearing, that blind and willful ignorance shall be punished, let not the Princess deceive herself. The Spirit of God doth not possess her heart, if she hear daily lying and blasphemous swearing and see the people's ignorance, and yet leave all unpunished. Look unto these things better, if you will look well unto yourself; you cannot pretend ignorance; this is plain enough, if anything be enough. And yet lest you should seek too busily to be deceived, I will rehearse the plain law of the Lord. That this doctrine may be warranted with the surer witnesses, God saith of a king in the seventeenth of Deuteronomy (vs. 18–20), "When he shall sit upon the throne of his kingdom, then shall he write him this law repeated in a book by the priests of the Levites. And it shall be with him and he shall read therein all the days of his life, that he may learn to fear the Lord his God and keep all the words of his law and these covenants for to do them. That his heart be not lifted up above his brethren. That he turn not aside from these commandments neither to the right hand nor to the left. But that he may prolong his days in his kingdom, he and his sons in the midst of Israel."

This law I know not how your Majesty shall interpret, because I know not your spirit. But of this I am sure, it made David that he would not suffer a wicked man in his house (*cf.* Ps. 101:7). It made Asa drive away the Sodomites out of Israel, put down the idols, depose his own mother from her dignity (*cf.* 1 Kings 15:11–13).[9] It made Jehoshaphat (*cf.* 1 Kings 22:41–3), Hezekiah (*cf.* 2 Kings 18:1,4), Josiah (*cf.* 2 Kings 22–23), even in the beginning of their reign[s], to make godly and zealous reformations in religion, and never consulted further with the high priest. Nay, it made Solomon to put down Abiathar that was the high priest, and to put Sadoc, a better, in his room (*cf.* 1 Kings 2:26–7, 35). This made many godly emperors in the primitive church to call general

9. [ED.] Elizabeth's mother, Anne Boleyn, had been deposed and beheaded.

councils, to reform many misorders crept into the church, to depose many ambitious and proud popes and place better in their room. And he that denieth this, denieth the sun to shine at noondays.[10]

And as this law hath thus wrought heretofore, so when it lighteth in a good spirit, I am sure it will do the like hereafter. It will move a godly magistrate to have his chiefest care to maintain religion and to suppress superstition. And such is God's righteous judgment, that whosoever shall do the contrary, I am sure his own conscience will condemn himself. It is the law of nature, and it maketh the most wicked magistrate to sigh and say in his heart in remembrance of his sin, "Sure this doing will not last always, God hath appointed me for some other purpose." This was the greatest fault that proud Agamemnon could find in all the glory of his kingdom. "When God's cause goeth not upright it layeth the glory of my kingdom in the dust, it turneth upside down all my life and happiness." [11]

Thus it happeneth with the wicked, whosoever they are. They condemn their own doing when they seek not to set out the glory of God. The law of God hath thus commanded it. The godly kings of Judah and Jerusalem have evermore practiced it. The faithful emperors in the primitive church made it their chiefest study. The law of nature hath engraved it in the heart of man, and what godly prince can now sleep in security if he have no care unto it? Especially seeing God is God of all magistrates, and they are his creatures. This is their greatest study, to show obedience unto him, to feed his people, and set forth his religion.

But here I think some will easily say, If this be so as you teach it, then the case is clear, the prince is a spiritual magistrate. It belongeth unto him to reform religion. He is the highest judge in the church of God to establish that by law which the law of God hath appointed. How is it then that the pope seeth not this? Why do not others see it that read and know the Scriptures? The emperors themselves, why have not they seen it? How grew the pope up to such unbridled authority?

How the pope should come to so great authority, I know no cause but this, that it was the will of God, and such was the depth of his secret judgments. The purple whore should make all the princes of the earth to drink of the cups of her fornications (cf. Rev. 17:2, 4). But for the pope's seeing or not seeing of his own abominations, I know not his eye-

---

10. [ED.] Pope Pius IV's bull against Elizabeth was issued on February 25, 1570, the day the sermon was delivered.

11. [ED.] The source of this quotation was not found.

sight. I cannot tell whether he doth see them or see them not, but I think he seeth them. For I see in all ages how God hath raised up some that have inveighed bitterly against his intolerable pride. If he seeth it not, his eyes are very sick, and himself is a verier beast than ever was Nebuchadnezzar. And the Lord be praised that hath hardened his proud heart and revealed better knowledge unto little ones (*cf.* Mt. 11:25). Why others should not see it that read the Scriptures as well as we and are as well learned as we, I can assign no other cause, but say with the prophet, God's judgments are like to a great depth (Ps. 36:6). They are as they are, and what they are it skilleth nothing unto us. I came not hither to compare with learning, who be Hebrews and who be none. I am sure if they did seek him in the simplicity of their heart, and call after him in the truth, not in their own inventions, that they should find him. Now they seek the living springs (*cf.* Jer. 2:13) in vain, because they seek them in the puddles that they have digged themselves. And they seek for the gospel of salvation in vain, because they follow the doctrine that is but precepts of men (*cf.* Mt. 15:9). But what if many learned see it not? Is it not therefore the truth of God that is so plain in the Scriptures?

Let me ask again, I beseech you, this question: Why did not Pharaoh see that Moses and Aaron were sent of God? They turned all his waters into blood, they brought upon him frogs that covered all his land, they plagued him with great swarms of lice and flies, they feared him with thunder and lightnings and with great tempests, they made darkness thick and sensible upon the face of the earth, they slew the first born of all that was in the land. Why knew not Pharaoh that they were sent of God? They divided the Red Sea and went through on dry land. What madness made him venture to go so desperately after? Why would he not be taught, till the water covered him and all his host (*cf.* Ex. 7–14)? Should the age that came after him reason thus against Israel: If your God be the Lord of heaven and earth, why did not our fathers know him, why did not the scribes and Pharisees know Christ to be the Messiah? They heard John Baptist give him plain testimony. Why did they not believe him? The same Christ fulfilled all that was spoken by the prophets. Why could they not see that he was the savior of the world? He made the blind to see, the deaf to hear, the dumb to speak, the lame to go. He made the sick and diseased whole. He raised up the dead (Mt. 11:5). He told unto them even their thoughts and cogitations (*cf.* Mt. 9:4). How were they so dull of understanding that yet they could not know him? If this may be sufficient to reprove a truth (why do not others see it) then the Pharisees reason well against Christ when they said unto the people, "Why do none of the princes and rulers believe in him?" (*cf.* Jn. 7:48).

But see, I beseech you, how great is our madness, that thus reason of other men why they see or see not. Why have we ourselves so great beams in our eyes that we cannot see our own estate and condition (*cf.* Mt. 7:5)? Why do we not see the shortness of our life, but thus live in the world as though we should live ever (*cf.* Heb. 13:14)? Seeing we have a righteous God that will be a revenger of his own cause and punish our transgressions (*cf.* Rom. 3:5), why do we sin yet daily more and more? Seeing our life is but a vapor (*cf.* Jas. 4:14), and all our glory is but as the flower in the field, why be we so bewitched with love of so great vanity? Seeing our estate shall be before God everlasting, and these accounted days come so fast to an end that we shall be speedily called, why be we still so careless in what sort we shall appear? Seeing God's threatenings are so near unto us, and the dangers that hang over our heads are so many, seeing God's judgments are so fearful, and his wrath burning forever [*cf.* Rom. 2:5], why are we so careless? And why is it yet true that was spoken so long agone, "Why do we live as though we should never die and as though hell fire were an old wives' fable?" [12]

Believe me, believe me, this is intolerable blindness. Seeing we be so bleareyed ourselves that we cannot see before us neither heaven nor hell, yet that we will reason against God's truth, by any man's eyesight whether he see or not see. If we list to marvel at the dullness of man's eyes, we cannot well marvel at any thing so much as at our own foolishness that cannot see ourselves (*cf.* Jn. 10:24). Let us look at the last to our own estate, and as for other men, let us leave them unto the Lord. He doth know most assuredly who be his (*cf.* Jn. 10:27; 2 Tim. 2:19). They are not the wise and prudent of this world that he hath chosen [*cf.* Lk. 10:21]. There are not many princes and noblemen in the face of his church. If princes and magistrates will be still rebellious, what is that to us? If the pope and his hirelings will be blind still, yet the Scripture is the Scripture.

The unthankful steward never liveth more riotously than when his lord is even at hand to call him to his accounts (*cf.* Lk. 16:1). The foolish virgins are never faster asleep than when the bridegroom is ready to enter into his wedding chamber (*cf.* Mt. 25:6). The children of this world are never busier occupied than the night before their souls shall be taken from them (*cf.* Lk. 12:20). The son of perdition shall never be more lofty

12. [ED.] Source not found.

than in these latter days when he shall be revealed (*cf.* 2 Thess. 2:3-4).
But for these that are so blind, let them be blind still. Let us approach
unto the throne of grace with faith (*cf.* Heb. 4:16), that the secrets of
the Lord may be revealed unto us.

As for kings and emperors, if you will ask why could they not see it,
but commit themselves unto so great slavery, alas, poor creatures, how
could they see in the midst of so great darkness? How could they read,
when the Book was fast sealed (*cf.* Rev. 5:2)? How could they discern
the voice, when they heard no sound but of tinkling cymbals? But this
was the great subtilty and craft of Satan. He knoweth how willingly we
be carried to worldly studies, and whither we did incline, thither he
thrust us headlong. He knoweth what corruption he hath sown in our nature and how unwillingly we meddle with the things of God. And therefore it was an easy practice for the pope, his minister, to pull away heavenly cares from all princes' governments. They are grievous unto flesh
and blood, and such as kings love not to meddle withal. This was one
mean why princes did not their duty. Another was as great as this. They
heard the pope so magnified that they thought him half a god. When
they were once persuaded the pope's pardons should be no small discharge, who would not willingly submit himself with all humility to receive it? If we may live all our life in riot, and yet after, through the
pope's blessing, rest in the peace of the church, who would refuse any
popish subjection? Make men once drunk with this opinion, and they are
at your commandment to do what you will. Barefoot and bareleg they
will wait at your gate. Set your foot (if you will) in the emperor's neck,
he will refuse no villainy.[13] Well, now that God hath delivered us out of
that kingdom of darkness, now we know the pope to be Antichrist, his
prayers to be evil, his pardons to be worse than the sin of witchcraft, let
us look at the last to our own duty and trust no more to such a broken
staff. If God hath made us princes and magistrates, let us feed his people
in Jacob and his inheritance in Israel.

This is our duty. Let us hearken unto it. And that we may do it the
better, let us inquire how it may be best discharged. And I beseech your
Majesty to hearken. I will speak nothing according to man, which may
easily be contemned, but that which I will speak shall be out of the
mouth of the Lord, in obeying whereof shall consist your safeguard and
the health of your kingdom. Especially, and above all things, look unto

13. [ED.] John Foxe, *Acts and Monuments*, II, 189-96, on Henry IV, the emperor
whom Pope Gregory VII subdued.

your ministry. There is no commandment given oftener in the Old Testament, none given oftener in the New.

When God would specially bless the people of Israel, he scattered the Levites among the other tribes, that the law might be taught in all the coasts of Jewry. When Christ would bring into the world the light of the gospel, he sent forth his apostles to preach unto every creature. In the old law God signified by many outward tokens how necessary the priesthood was for the instruction of his people and what priests he required. The staves were always in the rings of the Ark (*cf.* Ex. 25:15), the lamp ever burning (*cf.* Ex. 27:20), to show that the priests should always declare the will of God unto his people, and offer up the sweet incense of continual prayer. On the nether end of the robe of the ephod were bells always sounding, to teach that the priests should be ever heard wheresoever he did go, and show himself a messenger of the Lord of Hosts. In the breastplate he had Urim and Thummim, two lively representations of God's presence, to be witnesses unto the priest of his knowledge and righteousness. In the plate of gold upon his forehead was engraven in great golden letters, "Holiness unto the Lord" (*cf.* Ex. 28). To testify his upright life and conversation, God forbade any stranger to enter in among them except he were circumcised in heart. And of the children of Aaron, if any had faulted in the ministry, he should by no repentance be received again to the priesthood, that he might keep in holiness all the children of Israel.

This is the care that we must have of our ministry, if we will have the gospel of Christ to grow. This care was greatest unto the godly rulers and princes of Israel, to the end they might keep the sanctuary undefiled. This care must be greatest in those that are Christian magistrates, if they love God's glory and the increase of his gospel. Thus did King Solomon in the beginning of his reign, when he put down Abiathar (*cf.* 1 Kings 2:26, 35) and made Sadoc high priest. Thus did Jehoshaphat, when to reform religion he sent forth Levites into the coasts of Israel (*cf.* 2 Chron. 17:9). Thus did Hezekiah at the entrance of his kingdom, when this was his first care, how the Levites might be provided for (*cf.* 2 Chron. 29:4). But of all other, Moses, who had received the commandment from God himself, as appeareth, did especially see what was the necessity of the minister. In the thirty-third [chapter] of Deuteronomy (vs. 8–11), a little before his death, thus he maketh his prayer: "Let thy Urim and Thummim be with thy holy one whom thou didst prove in Massah and didst cause to serve at the waters of Meribah, who said unto his father and to his mother, I have not seen them neither knoweth he his brethren nor yet his own children, but they observed thy word and kept thy covenant. They shall teach Jacob thy judgments and Israel thy law. They shall put incense before thy face, and burnt offering upon thine altar. Bless, O Lord, his substance and accept the work of his hands. Smite through the loins of them that rise up against him, and of them that hate him, that they rise not up again."

Mark (I beseech you) both his great care how the Levites might prosper, and his notable describing of them, what manner of men they shall be. First, he prayeth that true knowledge and understanding might never be removed from them, their affection towards God's holy sanctuary might be such that neither father nor mother, wife nor children do keep them back from obedience to the law and covenant. Oh that our ministers were such as Moses prayed for. Then no doubt God would bless them according to their request, and confound their adversaries that rise up against them. And here also mark his great zeal for their prosperity. He was the most patient man and had the mildest nature of all the people of Israel. Yet could he not suppress his good and great affection, but broke out into these words, "Smite through the loins of them that rise up against him and of them that hate him, that they rise not up again." Oh Lord, if Moses had lived in our days and seen this adulterous generation that so spoileth the Levites, how would his zeal have been inflamed against them? [14] He would have cried out as good Nehemiah cried, "Plague them, O Lord, that defile thy priesthood" (Neh. 13:29). And good were it for these sinful men, that God would send his plagues upon them while yet they have time to repent. Now we want a Moses to pray for their punishment, for they sleep in their sins, and God (I fear) hath reserved them to a greater punishment. The Lord grant us grace to remember the latter end, and now look while it is yet time to the good order of the ministry.

When God promised to establish his mercies with his church, he promised this as the greatest token of his love, "I will give you pastors according to my heart, that shall feed you with knowledge and understanding" (Jer. 3:15). When he would have them have sure hope that he was their God and they were his people, he said he would give them Levites that should teach his people the difference between the holy and profane, between the unclean and the clean. He promised them this as a perpetual convenant, "The lips of the priest shall keep knowledge, and they shall

14. [ED.] The reference is to the plundering of church property by the English government.

seek the law from his mouth. For he is the messenger of the Lord of hosts" (Mal. 2:7). And this was the charge that God gave straitly unto the priesthood, "That they should tell his people of their sins, and the house of Jacob their offences" (Is. 58:1). A miserable commonwealth it must needs be, and far separated from God and his mercies, that hath blind leaders who cannot lead themselves. Who so feareth the Lord, will surely look unto it that he maintain no such offences within his kingdom, nor nourish any such sores within the body of his country. If a man be once called to the ministry, let him attend upon his flock and feed them (1 Pet. 5:2), as his duty bindeth him, with the food of life, or let him be removed. Christ said, "Feed, Feed, Feed" (Jn. 21:15–17). This charge he hath given even, as we love him, so to see it executed. Say what we will say, and the more we say it the more impudently we shall lie, if we say we love him while we keep not his commandments. Would to God we were wise to understand it. Christ said, "They are the salt of the earth" (Mt. 5:13). And what shall be done with them if they can season nothing? Christ said, "They are the light of the world." And what heap of miseries shall they bring with them if they themselves be dark? Christ said, "They be the watchmen." And what case shall the city be in if they do nothing but sleep and delight in sleeping? Who seeth not these incurable sicknesses that can see anything? They are the pastors, and how hungry must the flock be when they have no food to give them? They are the teachers, and how great is the ignorance where they themselves know nothing? They are the evangelists or messengers of glad tidings. How little hope have they, and what slender faith, whose messengers cannot tell what the Lord saith.

The Lord enlarge within your Majesty the bowels of mercy, that you may once have pity upon your poor subjects. This cogitation made Paul the apostle say to Timothy (a painful father unto a careful child), "I charge thee before God and before the Lord Jesus Christ, that shall judge the quick and dead at his appearance, and in his kingdom. Preach the word, be instant in season and out of season, reprove, rebuke, exhort . . ." (2 Tim. 4:2). Of all miseries wherewith the church is grieved, none is greater than this, that her ministers be ignorant and can say nothing. What could Jeroboam do more than this to strengthen all his idolatry, than to make his priests of the lowest of the people (cf. 1 Kings 13:33)? What could have made Asa (being otherwise religious) so soon to have turned away from the service of God saving only he suffered his people to be without a priest which could teach them the word of God (cf. 2

Chron. 14–16)? What plague did God threaten greater against a rebellious people, than that he would take from them their true prophets? When were the people's sins so ripe to procure vengeance, as when their preachers were dumb dogs and could not bark (*cf.* Is. 56:10)?

And what, I beseech you, is our condition better? Or what be many ministers of our time and country, other than dumb dogs? Surely, as Abijah said of the people of Israel, so we may say of our ministers, Have we not made us priests like the people of our country? Whosoever cometh to consecrate with a young bullock and seven rams, the same may be a priest for them that are no gods (*cf.* 2 Chron. 13:9). And so surely, if we served Baal, a great number of our priests at this day were tolerable. But if we serve the Lord, what do they with that function they cannot skill of? Let them return again to their old occupation. And yet this is but one evil, and if it were reformed, yet much still were amiss. If I would declare unto your Majesty all the great abuses that are in our ministry, I should lead you along in the spirit as God did the prophet Ezekiel. And after many intolerable evils, yet I shall say still unto you, behold you shall see more abominations than these (*cf.* Ezek. 8).

I would first lead you to your benefices. And behold, some are defiled with impropriations, some with sequestrations, some loaded with pensions, some robbed of their commodities.[15] And yet behold, more abominations than these. Look after this upon your patrons. And lo, some are selling their benefices, some farming them, some keep them for their children, some give them to boys, some to servingmen, a very few seek after learned pastors. And yet you shall see more abominations than these. Look upon your ministry, and there are some of one occupation, some of another, some shake bucklers, some ruffians, some hawkers and hunters, some dicers and carders, some blind guides and cannot see, some dumb dogs and will not bark. And yet a thousand more iniquities have now covered the priesthood. And yet you, in the meanwhile that all these whoredoms are committed, you at whose hands God will require it, you sit still and are careless. Let men do as they list. It toucheth not belike your commonwealth, and therefore you are so well contented to let all alone. The Lord increase the gifts of his Holy Spirit in you, that from faith to faith you may grow continually, till that you be zealous as good King David to work his will. If you know not how to reform this, or have so little counsel (as man's heart is blinded) that you can devise no

15. [ED.] See especially Christopher Hill, *The Economic Problems of the Church* . . . (Oxford, 1956).

way, ask counsel at the mouth of the Lord, and his holy will shall be revealed unto you.

To reform evil patrons, your Majesty must strengthen your laws, that they may rule as well high as low. For as Esdras said once so may I boldly say now: The hands of the princes and rulers are chief in this trespass (Ezra 9:2). If you will have it amended, you must provide so that the highest may be afraid to offend.[16]

To keep back the ignorant from the ministry, whom God of his goodness hath not called to such a function, take away your authority from the bishops. Let them not thus at their pleasure make ministers in their closet, whomsoever it pleaseth them. To stop the inconveniences that grow in the ministry by others, who say they are learned and can preach, and yet do not, that are (as I said) dumb dogs and will not bark, bridle at the least their greedy appetites. Pull out of their mouths those poisoned bones that they so greedily gnaw upon. Take away dispensations, pluralities, *totquots*,[17] non-residences, and such other sins. Pull down the Court of Faculties,[18] the mother and nurse of all abominations. I tell you this before God that quickeneth all things, and before our Lord Jesus Christ that shall judge the quick and the dead in his appearance and in his kingdom, amend these horrible abuses, and the Lord is on your right hand, you shall not be removed forever. Let these things alone, and God is a righteous God, he will one day call you to your reckoning. The God of all glory open your eyes to see his high kingdom, and enflame your heart to desire it.

The third thing that I said in this place was to be noted, was of David himself, how faithfully he executed that whereunto he was called. The prophet saith, "He fed them in the sincerity of his heart and guided them with the discretion of his hands." An excellent virtue, and meet for King David that was a man according to the heart of God. He knew that obedience was better than sacrifice, and that God's people were never better ruled than when their princes brought into captivity their own understanding, and in simplicity of heart were obedient only to the wisdom of almighty God.

He had too good experience of his own wisdom, and had tried it often how it made him to rebel. Therefore to please God effectually, he walked

16. [ED.] The Court itself was the source of the worst of the abuses in church finances and property.

17. [ED.] I.e., "deals."

18. [ED.] The court of the archbishop in which exemptions from church law were to be sought.

in his simplicity. O that our Christian princes had so great measure of God's Holy Spirit. How many and grievous burdens should then be taken from us, that now Christian eyes and ears can hardly behold and hear. How many sins should be extinct and buried, that now vain policy doth maintain and strengthen. The time is past, and I will say no more.[19] The God of all mercy and Father of all consolation inspire our hearts with wisdom, that we may walk before God in our own simplicity. That what his holy word hath spoken we may humbly hear, and not reason against it because of our commonwealth. Then shall we end these short and evil days with gladness. And when Christ shall appear in glory and majesty to judge the quick and the dead, we shall stand on the right hand in the number of his elect, and hear that last and happiest sentence that never shall be called back again, "Come ye blessed of my Father, and possess the kingdom which is prepared for you from the beginning of the world" (Mt. 25:34). The which time the Lord bring hastily upon us, even for his Son's sake, Jesus Christ our savior, to whom with the Holy Ghost, three persons and one God, be all honor and glory, both now and ever. Amen.

A Letter of Edward Dering to Mrs. Barret of Bray (Berks.)

Grace, mercy, and peace from God our Father, etc. I had much rather, good Mistress B., come myself than write unto you. But as other things are far contrary to my desire, so is it in my coming unto you, and I am constrained rather to write than to come. But God appoints our ways, whether I come and be with you, or else be other where and hear from you. I trust, and am persuaded, that both I shall hear from you and you shall have the same constancy in the love of truth, and still increase in the knowledge of it, till the good grace of God have made the work perfect that it hath begun, and you, with all your heart and all your soul, do fear the Lord and delight in all obedience of his holy will. Whereunto though we be sufficiently persuaded by the nature of godliness itself, which all men do praise and the righteous do love; yet a greater provocation is in you, because God hath given you a good estate, in which your example shall do good to many: and because God hath filled you with a hearty affection to testify his religion, that you may accordingly in all well doing surmount the praise of your profession; and especially because he

19. [ED.] Like Foxe and many others, Dering supposed that the world was in its last age.

that hath called you is holy, that you may express his similitude and likeness in all your ways, and this good course through evil days, when God of his mercy shall make straight unto us we shall see then what is the latter end. Our hearts shall be satisfied with it, and our tongue shall speak not as the world doth, "Blessed are the rich men" or "Blessed are the mighty," for all these have wings to fly away and high estates to sit down in the dust, when man must go make his bed in the dark and say to corruption, "Thou art my father," and to the worm, "Thou art my mother and sister" [cf. Job 17:13–14]. But our song shall be in better harmony, and we shall say with the prophet David, "Blessed is the man that feareth the Lord and delights greatly in his commandments" [Ps. 112:1]. For when all hatred shall grow against this and all adversity shall strive to come upon it, yet all is nothing, and shall not move it. For when our heart is strengthened with this grace, we see our portions in all estates and times: in discredit we see praise, in poverty riches, in anger favor, in darkness light, in bondage liberty, and in death life, yea whatsoever in weakness of body, in envy of time, in uncertainty of estate, in danger of life, or in anything else; because nothing can separate us from the love of God. Nothing can turn unto our harm. For we have his promise that is able to perform it, that to those that love God all things happen for the best [cf. Rom. 8:28.]

This purpose of life is soon had, and this course is easily begun. But the fruit of it doth not fade, nor the gladness of it shall never be lost. So that we shall not, nor by the grace of God we will not, for so little labor lose so great a reward. Nor for a little pleasure which vainly we think is in other things, receive the reward of our foolishness, which assuredly we know hath everlasting grief. We have not so unfruitfully learned Christ, nor so unhappily given witness of his truth. But better things belong unto us, in better ways we will run our course, in a better hope lay down our bodies. The children of the world shall make the world their portion; we look for another City of which the Lord is the workman, and we will not build up our unhappiness in the vain desires and concupiscence of this world; neither yet (seeing God is good to us to fill our days with peace) will we deny any comfort that is offered us in this present pilgrimage. But seeing the earth is the Lord's and all that therein is, we have perfect pleasure in friends, riches, authority, honor. If all be his, all are pure. If all be of him, in all is pleasure. For where his kingdom is, there is righteousness and peace, and joy of the Holy Ghost, and sorrow and sin is cast out. Only let us care as all things are good, so we use them; and as they are corrupt, so to let them alone.

Saint Paul teacheth that to the pure all things are pure, but to the impure all things are impure [Tit. 1:15]. And the things of this world are made according to the conscience of man. Hold this to remember it at noondays, and let our reins instruct us in it in the night season, that we feel our hearts inflamed with the love of God, and that it may be acceptable unto us as our own life to set forth his praise. That we acknowledge his glory which shineth in all his works, and then the Lord hath set us in a large room of liberty, where we walk with boldness in good delight of his creatures. And indeed and in truth this it is when this affliction [?affection] hath taken root within me, and I feel the work of it perpetually within my mind, whether I be following my hawk or my bowl[ing ball], I make a more acceptable sacrifice to God than the heart barren of this love of God can do, though the knee bow or the tongue say, "Praised be the Lord." For everyone that saith "Lord, Lord," shall not enter into the kingdom of heaven; but in whomsoever the love of God doth reign and hath driven out the lewd desires of a dissolute mind, him God hath chosen, and the spirit of his son Christ crieth within him, Our Father. Yet I mean not here to justify these worldly-minded men to whom the day is too short for their vain plays, except they reach it out till midnight at cards and dice. Such people as they commonly fill at [*i.e.*, out] their delights with blasphemy. So let them know that the love of the living God they never felt, but the god of this world hath blinded their unbelieving hearts. And in their uncleanness there I leave them then, till the sins of their youth be rotten in their bones, that they may sink deep in their own shame.

My meaning is that the man of God, whose soul doth thirst to see his glory and hath the joy of his life in immortality, in respect of the which he accounteth all the world to be but dung: I say, that man may have true delight in the days of his vanity, the smelling of the [hunting-] dog, the flying of the bird, the qualities of all creatures. They were made for him. And he is injurious to the blood of Christ that thinks he may not use them. But all these things are good for our recreation, to comfort the frailty of weak bodies, and to bring refreshing to a weary spirit; which end, if we forget, and make it our pastime, and so call it, then we turn our pastime into sin. For what is our time that we are weary of it, or what is our life that seemeth so slow to pass? Are we grieved with the light which the Lord hath set in the heavens, or is the feeling of our body burdensome unto us, or our eyelids pained with being open, or are our ears wounded with the sound of the air? Or what grief, what care, what sorrow is it, why we wish our time forgotten and past? Surely Job knew not this when he said his time passed faster than a post [Job 9:25], nor David knew it not when he thought his life but a span long. And surely he hath but a wretched life, and let him not love it, who is fain to run to the birds of the air and the beasts of the field to seek some comfort against it.

And therefore (good Mistress B.) let pastime alone, and be not wearied with your good days. Your times are passed meetly well, and you have seen forty years filled and gone. The residue behind will pass with them; you shall not hold them if you would. But pastime and they will dwell together till our appointed time shall come, and one end shall be unto all. But then you shall see another state, and this enmity between us and it shall be taken away. We shall not be weary of it to wish it gone, and it will not be weary of us to wear us away. But Time and we shall dwell together, and the glory of God shall be eternally before us, and we before his majesty in immortality. A blessed state, a hope of life, a glorious body, a heavenly mind. And woe be to all these time passers of, that know how to delight in this, but have more pleasure in all uncleanness. When the end of their labor shall come upon them, they shall feel more grief in one day than after shall be ended world without end. And in one sentence of an angry judge ("Go, you cursed, into eternal fire") [Mt. 25:41], they shall be wounded with that misery which world without end shall rest upon them, and their old pastime shall never more be found. But this is the portion of them that know not God.

But as for you, good Mistress B., you have already passed the days of your ignorance, and the kingdom of heaven is come unto you with power. You love the truth of the Lord Jesus, and all false ways you do abhor. You do feel the hope of the elect of God, and it hath quenched the desires of ungodliness. Pray still, that you may have increase; and read the Scriptures, in which you shall have comfort. These will lead you in a perfect way, and neither Paul nor Peter have a more blessed end than is for us, in a like precious faith. And I (as I am bound) will beseech the God of mercy and father of our Lord Jesus Christ, that he will look upon you, to fill you with his grace and Holy Spirit, that it may guide you, and all your children before you, and your children committed to your charge, that you may dwell in the new and blessed testament of the forgiveness of sins, through faith in Christ Jesus, who hath destroyed the work of the devil, and is able to keep you forevermore. And to his gracious defense, I heartily leave you and all yours.

Yours in the Lord,
ED. DERING

❖ ❖ ❖ ❖ ❖
❖   ❖
❖   II   ❖
❖   ❖
❖ ❖ ❖ ❖ ❖

PETER WENTWORTH

Editor's Introduction

The Puritan movement was notable for its vigorous lay participation. Fundamental to the entire Protestant Reformation was a concerted effort by the laity to end clerical control of the civil realm, and to compel the clergy to recognize that the laity made up both the church and the body politic, in which the clergy were merely officeholders. Too often the Reformation is treated as having been initiated, guided and carried out by clerics. But in the larger context of the sixteenth century the Reformation emerges rather as an anticlerical movement. It was the large-scale revolt of a newly self-conscious laity against clerical prerogatives that gave to some reform-minded religious leaders an opportunity (greater in some regions, less in others) to work toward the changes they regarded as desirable. The religious reformers could not have succeeded without the decisive changes brought about in the church by the lay anticlerical powers, working through the state.

Anticlericalism in sixteenth-century England (as well as on the Continent) often had a thoroughly religious motivation. This was true, for example, of Erasmus and other Christian Humanists. Many or even most of the Christian Humanists, however, were or had been clerics themselves. Among the actively anticlerical laymen of the time, a considerable number had a discernibly religious motivation, as well as a significant degree of religious knowledge. Typical of them were the Russells and the Hastingses among the older nobility, Francis Knollys and Walter Mildmay among the "new men" in the Privy Council, a significant number of men in the House of Commons, and a number of second-line civil servants including Laurence Tomson, William Davison, Robert Beale and James Morice, to mention only a few. Such men regarded themselves as no less "the church" than the clergy. As they saw things, theories of ordination, apostolic succession, clerical uniqueness and clerical prerogatives had all been exploded by the new theologies of the Christian Humanists and the Protestant reformers. These men believed, moreover, that by the "Submission of the Clergy" in 1532-4, the clergy themselves had acknowledged the invalidity of all their old claims. In the judgment of these laymen, the clergy, as officeholders without special authority, were useful only insofar as they had ability to teach and preach. Their lay critics were thus quite willing to work with, but not under, the officeholders of the church for the reforms they considered desirable, but they resisted as far as possible any initiative by the clergy toward church reform. These laymen were anticlerical, in short, without being in any way hostile to the welfare of the church, or having an interest only in securing valuable church property for themselves.

Typical of such lay thinking are Laurence Tomson's preface to the Geneva New Testament of 1576, the address by Peter Wentworth to the House of Commons on February 8, 1576, concerning freedom of speech and debate, and the spirited attack by James Morice on the *ex officio* oath, which appeared about 1590. The first two are included in this volume as representing the passive-resistance wing of Puritanism, and the third as representing the more aggressive Presbyterian attitude. But it is the documents rather than the men that are to be classified in this way, since Tomson most certainly belonged to the inner clique of the Presbyterians, and Wentworth was associated with the attempt in the Parliament of 1587 to enact a Presbyterian order for the English church. Moreover, Wentworth was to die a prisoner in the Tower. In the documents here presented, however, neither man went further than to demand changes within the Elizabethan established order, nor was either one understood at the time as expressing a "Presbyterian" point of view. Morice's attack on the *ex officio* oath, on the other hand, was a conscious assault on the official order.

John Neale, the historian of the Elizabethan Parliaments whose study of Wentworth is basic to understanding the man, has remarked that "few English parliamentarians before the age of the Stuarts have left behind them any substantial memory of their parliamentary achievements, and of these few Peter Wentworth is probably the first, certainly the most attractive." [1] Born *c.* 1524, he was the eldest son of Sir Nicholas Wentworth, who had been Porter of Calais under Henry VIII and Edward VI. Peter's first wife was a cousin of Queen Catherine Parr. After her death Wentworth married a sister of Sir Francis Walsingham. The mar-

1. John Neale, "Peter Wentworth," *Eng. Hist. Rev.*, XXXIX (1924), 36.

riage of another of Walsingham's sisters to Sir Walter Mildmay linked Wentworth with a second staunch supporter of the Puritans on the Privy Council. A daughter of Wentworth's married a son of William Strickland, a leading Puritan member of the Commons. Wentworth's family seat was in Northamptonshire, where his active support of Puritan meetings led to an investigation by the Privy Council in 1579. He corresponded at times with Thomas Wilcox, Percival Wiburn and other vigorous Puritan ministers.

Paul Wentworth, Peter's younger brother, had been a member of Parliament in 1559, in 1563 and in 1566, and during those sessions had been a vigorous member of the Puritan parliamentary group. Peter was urged by his friends to stand for Parliament, and from 1571 to 1587 he took part in every session except that of 1584. As the Parliament of 1571 opened, Strickland had moved to reintroduce the package of religious reform bills (the so-called "alphabet bills," A to F) that had been shelved in the 1566 Parliament, and had added one more bill to the package. Commons then moved to debate the Thirty-Nine Articles of Religion, which the House of Bishops had passed in 1563 but which the Queen, as a matter of policy, had refused to allow Parliament to act upon. In defiance of the Queen's wishes, Commons not only debated the content of the Articles but also remodeled them, and forced the Queen to accept its action. The form in which they were enacted, moreover, required ministers of the church to subscribe only to the doctrinal portions of the Articles—i.e., they need not subscribe to the articles dealing with the episcopate and with the prayer book.[2] These highly controversial debates led to the clash with Archbishop Parker to which Wentworth referred in his speech of 1576, and were marked by other exchanges in much the same mode. As the debate intensified, Thomas Norton, the son-in-law of Archbishop Cranmer and a co-sponsor of the "alphabet bills," urged the Commons to deal with the Lords as a part of Parliament and not to accept the direction of the bishops against their own consciences. Another M.P. averred that the Commons had learned as well as the bishops had that there was a God to be served. Still another noted in his diary that Strickland, as an M.P., was a public man by whom even bishops were to be ordered. Strickland was then arrested by order of the Queen—the usual Tudor response to such an airing of views—but this time the House became so

2. Neale connects these "alphabet bills" with the efforts towards reform at the 1563 Convocation; "Parliament and the Articles of Religion," *Eng. Hist. Rev.*, LXVII (1952), 510–21.

aroused that the Queen released him with some face-saving expostulations. Even so, one more Puritan M.P., Robert Bell, was later haled before the Privy Council, where he was severely browbeaten. Eventually the Queen and her supporters managed to adjourn Parliament, only two of the alphabet bills for church reform having passed.

Wentworth returned to his home, as he later recorded, thoroughly aroused by all that had happened. The next session of Parliament, 1572, was chiefly occupied with the debate over Mary Queen of Scots and the painfully complicated question of the succession to the English throne. A further effort was made also to revise the prayer book and to encourage the prophesyings. The very notion of total uniformity in ritual and ceremony was assailed by some debaters as illusory and self-defeating, and Robert Bell, now the Speaker, deplored the manner in which numerous Puritan preachers had been ousted from the ministry over "such trifles." When Elizabeth moved to quash the bills before they could be passed, one M.P. commented in his diary that a message from the Queen forbidding any member to bring in a bill on religion "seemed much to impugn the liberty of the House."

When Parliament assembled again in 1576, Wentworth rose as soon as the first bill had been presented to deliver his address asserting that free speech in Parliament was essential to the proper conduct of its business. The impassioned candor and clarity of what he had to say shook the House. He was stopped before he could finish his speech, placed under arrest, and later brought before the Privy Council for questioning. Wentworth's account of what took place there is, of course, *ex parte*, and no other record has survived. It is clear, however, that the government wished to prevent another Strickland affair. Moreover, Wentworth was not alone in his views about Parliament. A significant body of men in both Houses, and even in the Privy Council, were beginning to hold the conviction that Parliament spoke for the country and therefore ought not to be intimidated, coerced or manipulated into merely assenting to royal wishes. Wentworth remained in prison until two days before the close of Parliament, when, having made his submission and asked pardon, he was released. In Commons, meanwhile, a homily was delivered by Mildmay on behalf of the Crown, asserting that there was a distinction between liberty and license.

Wentworth sat again in the Parliament of 1581, which saw further attempts at church reform. The most comprehensive of these were again halted by the Queen, but a set of articles summing up the concerns of the reformers in Parliament over the past ten years were presented to her by two Privy Councillors on behalf of Commons. The articles were in three sections, one dealing with ministers, one with excommunication, and the third with dispensations. After the Parliament ended, the Queen gave the articles to five bishops, including Whitgift, for their comments. The bishops were hostile to the entire notion of reform through Parliament, and nothing came of the Commons' articles.[3]

Wentworth was not a member of the Parliament of 1584, which saw a determined effort to institute a Presbyterian order in the English church. But during the Parliament of 1586-7, to which numerous petitions arrived from many parts of the nation on behalf of church reform and on behalf of the Puritan preachers, Wentworth came once again into conflict with the Crown. When Anthony Cope, a Puritan M.P., proposed a bill to reorder the church according to Presbyterian ideas, Elizabeth countered once again by exerting pressure on members of Parliament. On March 1, 1587, Wentworth delivered a prepared speech on the rights of Parliament. The Queen called the day's session of the Commons to a halt, and Wentworth and several other Puritan M.P.'s were sent to the Tower. The government's excuse for their arrest was not what they had done in Parliament (that would have been to stir up a hornets' nest), but their having conspired in planning their action beforehand. There is no record of how long Wentworth remained in the Tower this time. He did not stand for Parliament again after 1587. But for his writings and agitation concerning the royal succession, he was sent once again to the Tower, where he died in 1597.

A man who set himself against tradition or official policy in the sixteenth century was risking cooperation with the forces of chaos, disorder, ambition and destruction. Fear of what might be unleashed, if he took the risk, could not fail to give pause to any reformer or advocate of change. Erasmus, Luther, Cranmer and many others had quailed in the presence of what their ideas and actions had begotten. In Elizabethan England, until the defeat of the Spanish Armada in 1588 brought a measure of reassurance to the thirty-year-old regime, this fear of change was increased by an acute sense of insecurity both domestic and international. The agonizing question had always been: which was worse, the old wrong to which the passage of time had brought some amelioration (for the more fortunate), or the chaos, disorder and unbridled ambition to which (it seemed to those in "responsible" places) the desired reforms would surely open the gates?

3. Neale, *Elizabeth I and her Parliaments, 1559–81* (London, 1953), 400.

In such circumstances, only an exceptional person could have remained an unyielding opponent of official policy. The role played by religious ideology in producing the Puritan group of which Wentworth was typical was to set up a referent so powerful that the fear of change lost its power, and reform still appeared urgent enough to make its risks worth taking. So, at the age of seventy-three, Wentworth died in the Tower rather than apologize for what he considered no wrong. John Neale, commenting on Wentworth's "questions" of 1587, aptly observes that "had the temper and courage of Elizabethan parliamentarians equalled Wentworth's, [they] might have precipitated the constitutional crisis that came under the Stuarts." [4]

Wentworth's speech and his account of his examination by a committee are given here as they were first published in Simonds D'Ewes (ed.), *A Complete Journal of the Votes, Speeches and Debates . . . throughout the Whole Reign of Queen Elizabeth* (1682), 1693, 236–44, collated with a transcript of Inner Temple Library, MS. Petyt 538/17, fols. 1–6, and with a few variant readings taken from British Museum, MS. Stowe 302; and Public Record Office, State Papers, Domestic, Elizabeth I, 107/30. The variant readings from the Stowe MS. are marked *, those from the S. P. Dom. #. I am grateful to the History of Parliament Trust and to Sir John Neale for permission to use this transcript, and to Professor Patrick Collinson for collating it for me with the D'Ewes text. I am, of course, solely responsible for the form in which the text appears here. The text of Wentworth's ten questions is from Sir John Neale, "Peter Wentworth," *English Historical Review*, XXXIX (1924).

The biblical quotations used by Wentworth are from the Great Bible of 1540, or are slight variants of its text.

❖   ❖   ❖   ❖

A Speech in the House of Commons, 8 February 1576

Mr. Peter Wentworth his speech in the Parliament House Anno 1576 for which he was put into the Tower.

Mr. Speaker, I find written in a little volume these words in effect: Sweet indeed is the name of liberty, but the thing itself a value beyond all inestimable treasure. So much the more it behooveth us to take heed lest we, contenting ourselves with the sweetness of the name only, do not lose

4. Neale, "Wentworth," *Eng. Hist. Rev.*, XXXIX, 48.

and forego the value of the thing and the greatest value that can come unto this noble Realm by the inestimable treasure is the use of it in this House for unto it it is due. And therefore I do think it needful to put you in remembrance that this honourable assembly (to the great charges of the whole Realm) are assembled and come together here in this place for three special causes of most weighty and great importance.

The first and principal is to make and abrogate such laws as may be most for the preservation of our noble Sovereign.

The second is to make or abrogate such laws as may be most for the preservation of our noble Sovereign.

The third is to make or abrogate such laws as may be to the chiefest commodity, surety, safekeeping and enrichment of this noble realm of England. So that I do think that the part of a faithful-hearted subject [is] to do his endeavour to remove all stumbling-blocks out of the way that may impair or any manner of way hinder these good and godly causes of this our coming together. I was never of Parliament but the last and the last session [i.e., 1571 and 1572], at both which times I saw the liberty of free speech, the which is the only salve to heal all the sores of this Commonwealth, so much and so many ways infringed, and so many abuses offered to this honourable Council (whereby the Prince and State are most chiefly maintained) that my mind (when I have many times since thought thereof) hath not been a little aggrieved even of very conscience and love to my Prince and State. Wherefore to avoid the like I do think it expedient to open the commodities that grow to the Prince and whole State by free speech used in this place, at the least so much as my simple wit can gather of it, the which is very little in respect of that that wise heads can say therein, and so it is of the more force.

First, all matters that concern God's honour through free speech shall be propagated here and set forward, and all things that do hinder it removed, repulsed, and taken away.

Next, there is nothing commodious, profitable, or any way beneficial for the Prince or State, but faithful and loving subjects will offer it in this place.

Thirdly, all things discommodious, perilous, or hurtful to the Prince or State shall be prevented, even so much as seemeth good to our merciful God to put into our minds, the which [no] doubt [we need not doubt *] shall be sufficient if we do earnestly call upon him and fear him. For Solomon saith, "The fear of God is the beginning of wisdom" [Prov. 1:7]. "Wisdom," saith he, "breatheth life into her children, receiveth [relieveth *] them that seek her, and will go beside them in the way of righteousness"; so that our minds shall be directed to all good, needful and necessary things, if we call upon God with faithful hearts.

Fourthly, if the envious do offer anything hurtful or perilous to the Prince or State in this place, what incommodity doth grow thereby? Verily I think none, nay will you have me to say my simple opinion therein, much good cometh thereof. How forsooth? for by the darkness of the night the brightness of the sun showeth more excellent and clear, and how can the truth appear and conquer until falsehood and all subleties that should shadow and darken it be found out? For it is offered in this place a piece of fine needlework unto them that are most skillful therein, for there cannot be a false stitch (God aiding us) but will be found out.

Fifthly, this good cometh thereof, a wicked purpose may the easier be prevented when it is known.

Sixthly, an evil man can do the less harm when he is known.

Seventhly, sometime it happeneth that a good man will in this place (for argument sake) prefer an evil cause, both for that he would have a doubtful truth to be opened and manifested, and also the evil prevented; so that to this point I conclude, that in this House which is termed a place of free speech, there is nothing so necessary for the preservation of the Prince and State as free speech, and without it it is a scorn and mockery to call it a Parliament House, for in truth it is none, but a very school of flattery and dissimulation, and so a fit place to serve the Devil and his angels in, and not to glorify God and benefit the Commonwealth.

Now to the impediments thereof which by God's grace and the little experience I have I will utter plainly and faithfully. I will use the words of Elihu, "Behold, I am as the new wine which hath no vent and bursteth the new vessels in sunder, therefore I will speak that I may have a vent, I will open my lips and make answer, I will regard no manner of person, no man will I spare, for if I should go about to please men, I know not how soon my Maker will take me away" [Job 32:19–22]. My text is vehement the which by God's sufferance I mean to observe, hoping therewith to offend none; for that of very justice none ought to be offended for seeking to do good and saying of the truth.

Amongst other, Mr. Speaker, two things do [very #] great hurt in this place of the which I do mean to speak: the one is a rumour which runneth about the House and this it is, "take heed what you do, the Queen's Majesty liketh not of such a matter, whosoever preferreth it, she will be [much #] offended with him"; or the contrary, "her Majesty liketh of such a matter, whosoever speaketh against it she will be much offended with him."

The other [is #]: sometimes a message is brought into the House either of commanding or inhibiting, very injurious unto the freedom of speech and consultation. I would to God, Mr. Speaker, that these two were buried in hell. I mean rumours and messages; for wicked undoubtedly they are. The reason is, the Devil was the first author of them, from whom proceedeth nothing but wickedness.

Now I will set down reasons to prove them wicked. First, if we be in hand with anything for the advancement of God's glory, were it not wicked to say the Queen's Majesty liketh not of it or commanding that we shall not deal in it? Greatly were these speeches to her Majesty's dishonour, and an hard opinion were it, Mr. Speaker, thus to conceive of the Queen's Majesty. And hardest of all were it, Mr. Speaker, that these things should enter into her Majesty's thought. Much more wicked and unnatural were it that her Majesty should like or command anything against God, or hurtful to herself and the State. The Lord grant this thing may be far from her Majesty's heart. Here this may be objected, that if the Queen's Majesty should have intelligence of anything perilous or beneficial to her Majesty's person or the State, would you not have her Majesty give knowledge thereof in this House, whereby her peril may be prevented and her benefit provided for? God forbid, far then were her Majesty in worse case than any of her subjects. And in the beginning of our speech I showed it to be a special cause of our assembly, but my intent is, that nothing should be done to God's dishonour, to her Majesty's peril, or to the peril of the State. And therefore I will show the inconveniences that grow of these two.

First, if we follow not the Prince's mind. Solomon saith the King's displeasure is a messenger of death. This is a terrible thing to [the] weak nature of frail flesh. Why so? For who is able to abide the fierce countenance of his Prince? But if we will discharge our consciences and be true to God, our Prince and State, we must have due consideration of the place and the occasion of our coming together, and especially have regard unto the matter wherein we both shall serve God, and our Prince and State faithfully, and not dissembling as eye pleasers, and so justly avoid all displeasures both to God and our Prince. For Solomon saith in the way of the righteous there is life, as for any other way it is the path to death [? cf. Prov. 12:28]. So that to avoid everlasting death and condemnation with the high and mighty God, we ought to proceed in every cause according to the matter, and not according to the Prince's mind. And now I will show you a reason to prove it perilous always to follow the Prince's mind. Many times it falleth out that the Prince may favour a cause perilous to himself and the whole State. What are we then if we follow the Prince's mind, are we not unfaithful unto God, our Prince and State? Yes truly. For we are chosen of the whole realm of a special trust and confidence by them reposed in us to foresee all such inconveniences. Then I will set down my opinion herein, that is, he that dissembleth to her Majesty's peril is to be counted as an hateful enemy; for that he giveth unto her Majesty a detestable Judas' kiss; and he that contrarieth her mind to her preservation, yea though her Majesty would be much offended with him, is to be adjudged an approved lover, for faithful are the wounds of a lover, saith Solomon, but the kisses of an enemy are deceitful [*cf.* Prov. 27:6]. And it is better, saith Antisthenes, to fall amongst ravens than amongst flatterers, for ravens do but devour the dead corpse, but flatterers do devour the living. And it is both traitorous and hellish through flattery to seek to devour our natural Prince, and that doth flatterers; therefore let them leave it with shame enough.

Now I will show you a precedent of the last Parliament to prove it a perilous rumour and much more perilous to give place unto it. It was foreseen by divers of this House that if the supposed title of the Scottish King or Queen to the Crown of England were not by Act of Parliament overthrown and manifested to the whole Realm that it had possessed such number of traitorous hearts that it would one day break out to the danger of the Prince and State. For of the wicked Isaiah saith, "They weave the spider's web and break [breed] cockatrice's eggs" [*cf.* Is. 59:5]. And what falleth out of it? Truly they long to see their good brood hatched. Even so this wicked brood of Scottish hearts in English bodies, a detestable and unnatural thing, Mr. Speaker: what web did they weave and what brood did they breed? (I may truly say do they weave or breed, for ill brood hath not yet had such so ill hatching as I do wish unto them) forsooth the spider's web and cockatrice egg, even abominable treason: namely, the life of our noble Prince (whom God long preserve) was, and, I do fear, is yet sought for, and the subversion of the whole State, as the one cannot be without the other. But praised be our loving and merciful Father which never deceiveth them that fear and put their trust in him, according to the saying of Jesus the son of Sirach, "Now I see," saith he, "they that fear the Lord have the right spirit, for their hope standeth in him that can help them" [Ecclesiasticus 34:13]. For things as I have heard have been revealed beyond the expectation of man, yea, even when the greatest traitors stood upon their deliverance, who hath since, blessed be our Lord, received condign punishment for his deserts to the terror of all the rest. If this be a true precedent, as it is very well known to be unto many here present, I heartily beseech you all to examine every matter exactly before you give your voices either affirmative or negative; and so shall you discharge your consciences and duties, first towards God, next to our noble Queen, then to the whole Realm who have put us in trust with all matters concerning the advancement of God's honour, the safety of our Prince and the commodity of the whole State.

Now to another great matter that riseth of this grievous rumour, what is it forsooth? Whatsoever thou art that pronounceth it, thou dost pronounce thy own discredit; why so? For that thou dost what lieth in thee to pronounce the Prince to be perjured, the which we neither may nor will believe, for we ought not without too too manifest proof to credit any dishonour to our anointed, no, we ought not without it to think any evil of her Majesty, but rather to hold him a liar what credit soever he be of; for the Queen's Majesty is the head of the law, and must of necessity maintain the law, for by the law her Majesty is made justly our Queen, and by it she is most chiefly maintained. Hereunto agreeth the most excellent words of Bracton, who saith, "The king hath no peer nor equal in his kingdom; he hath no equal, for otherwise he might lose his authority of commanding, sithence that an equal hath no rule of commandment over his equal. The king ought not to be under man but under God and under the law because the law maketh him a king. Let the king therefore attribute that unto the law which the law attributeth unto him, that is, dominion and power; for he is not a king in whom will and not the law doth rule, and therefore he ought to be under the law." [1] I pray you mark the reason why my authority saith, the King ought to be under the law, for saith he, "He is God's vicegerent here upon earth, that is, his lieutenant to execute and do his will, the which is law or justice . . ."; and thereunto was her Majesty sworn at her coronation, as I have heard learned men in this place sundry times affirm; unto the which I doubt not but her Majesty will for her honour and conscience sake have special regard; for free speech and conscience in this place are granted by a special law, as that without the which the Prince and State cannot be preserved or maintained: so that I would wish every man that feareth God, regard-

---

1. Henrici de Bracton. [ED.] *De Legibus et Consuetudinibus Angliae*, edited by T. Twiss (London, 1878), I, 39.

eth the Prince's honour, or esteemeth his own credit, to fear at all times hereafter to pronounce any such horrible [or tirable * (i.e., terrible)] speech[es], so much to the Prince's dishonour; for in so doing he showeth himself an open enemy to her Majesty, and so worthy to be condemned of all faithful hearts.

Yet there is another inconvenience that riseth of this wicked rumour. The utterers thereof seem to put into our heads that the Queen's Majesty hath conceived an evil opinion, diffidence and mistrust in us her faithful and loving subjects; for if she had not, her Majesty would then wish that all [the] things dangerous to herself should be laid open before us, affirming [i.e., assuring] herself that so loving subjects as we are would without schooling and direction, with careful minds, to our powers prevent and withstand all perils that might happen unto her Majesty. And this opinion I doubt not but her Majesty hath conceived of us, for undoubtedly there was never Prince that had faithfuller hearts than her Majesty hath here; and surely there were never subjects had more cause heartily to love their Prince for her quiet government than we have. So that he that raiseth this rumour, still increaseth but this discredit in seeking to sow sedition as much as lieth in him, between our merciful Queen and us her most loving and faithful subjects, the which by God's grace shall never lie in [his] power, let him spit out all his venom and therewithal show out his malicious heart; yet I have collected sundry reasons to prove this a hateful and a detestable rumour, and the utterer thereof to be a very Judas to our noble Queen, therefore let any hereafter take heed how he publish it, for as [a] very Judas unto her Majesty and enemy unto the whole State, we ought to accept him.

Now the other. There was a message, Mr. Speaker, brought the last session[s *] into the House, that we should not deal in any matters of religion, but first to receive [it] from the bishops. Surely, this was a doleful message, for it was as much as to say, "Sirs, you shall not deal in God's causes, no: you shall in no wise seek to advance his glory; and in recompense of your unkindness, God in his wrath will so look upon your doings, that the chief and only cause that you were called together for, the which is the preservation of the [ir *] prince, shall have no good success." If someone of this House had presently made this interpretation of the said message, had he not seemed to have the spirit of prophecy? Yes, truly, I assure you, Mr. Speaker, there were divers of this House that said with grievous hearts, immediately upon the message, that God of his justice could not prosper the session; and let it be holden for a principle, Mr.

Speaker, that counsel that cometh not together in God's name cannot prosper. For God saith, "Where two or three are gathered together in his name, there am I in the midst among them" [Mt. 18:20]. Well, God, even the great and mighty God, whose name is the Lord of Hosts, great in council and infinite in thought, and who is the only good director of all hearts, was the last session shut out of the doors. But what fell out of it? Forsooth, his great indignation was therefore poured upon this House. [How so? #] For he did put into the Queen's Majesty's heart to refuse good and wholesome laws for her own preservation, the which caused many faithful hearts for grief to burst out with sorrowful tears and moved all papists, traitors to God and her Majesty, who envy good Christian government [and every good Christian government #], in their sleeves to laugh all the whole Parliament House to scorn; and shall I pass over this weighty matter [so lightly or #], so slightly? Nay, I will discharge my conscience and duty to God, my Prince and country. [May I discharge my conscience and duties to God, my prince and country so? #] [So] certain it is, Mr. Speaker, that none is without fault, no not our noble Queen. Since then her Majesty hath committed great fault[s #], yea, dangerous faults to herself [and the State #]; love, even perfect love void of dissimulation, will not suffer me to hide them to her Majesty's peril, but to utter them to her Majesty's safety. And these they are. It is a dangerous thing in a Prince unkindly to [intreat and #] abuse his or her nobility and people [as her Majesty did the last Parliament #], and it is a dangerous thing in a Prince to oppose or bend herself against her nobility and people, yea, against most loving and faithful nobility and people. And how could any Prince more unkindly intreat, abuse [and #] oppose herself against her nobility and people, than her Majesty did the last Parliament? Did she not call it of purpose to prevent traitorous perils to her person, and for no other cause? Did not her Majesty send unto us two bills, willing us to make choice of that we liked best for her safety, and thereof to make a law, promising her Majesty's royal consent thereunto? And did we not first choose the one, and her Majesty refused it, yielding no reason, nay yielding great reasons why she ought to have yielded to it? Yet did we nevertheless receive the other, and agreeing to make a law thereof, did not her Majesty in the end refuse all our travails? And did not we, her Majesty's faithful nobility and subjects, plainly and openly decipher ourselves unto her Majesty and our hateful enemy; and hath not her Majesty left us all to her open revenge? Is this a just recompense in our Christian Queen for our faithful dealings? The heathen do requite good for good;

then how much more is it dutiful in a Christian prince? And will not this her Majesty's handling, think you, Mr. Speaker, make cold dealing in many of her Majesty's subjects toward her again? I fear it will. And hath it not caused many already, think you, Mr. Speaker, to seek a salve for the head that they have broken? I fear it hath. And many more will do the like if it be not prevented in time. And hath it not marvellously rejoiced and encouraged the hollow hearts of her Majesty's hateful enemies and traitorous subjects? No doubt but it hath. And I beseech God that her Majesty may do all things that may grieve the hearts of all her enemies, and may joy the hearts that unfeignedly love her Majesty. And I beseech the same God to endue her Majesty with his wisdom, whereby she may discern faithful advice from traitorous sugared speeches, and to send her Majesty a melting, yielding heart unto sound counsel, that will may not stand for a reason: and then her Majesty will stand when her enemies are fallen, for no estate can stand where the Prince will not be governed by advice. And I doubt not but that some of her Majesty's Council have dealt plainly and faithfully with her Majesty herein; if any have, let it be a sure token to her Majesty to know them for approved lovers. And whatsoever they be that did persuade her Majesty so unkindly to intreat, abuse, and to oppose herself against her nobility and people, or commend her Majesty for so doing, let it be a sure token to her Majesty to know them for sure traitors and underminers of her Majesty's life and safety. God remove them even for his mercy's sake out of her Majesty's presence and favour and either to turn their hearts or to send them their just rewards, for the more cunning they are, the more dangerous are they unto her Majesty. But was this all? No, for God would not vouchsafe that his Holy Spirit should all that session descend upon our bishops; so that the session nothing was done to the advancement of his glory. I have heard of old Parliament men that the banishment of the pope and popery and the restoring of true religion had their beginning from this House, and not from the bishops; and I have heard that few laws for religion had their foundation from them. And I do surely think, before God I speak it, that the bishops were the cause of that doleful message. And I will show you what moveth me so to think: I was amongst others the last Parliament sent unto the Bishop of Canterbury for the articles of religion that then passed this house. He asked us why we did put out of the book the articles for the homilies, consecrating of bishops, and such like? "Surely, Sir," said I, "because we were so occupied in other matters, that we had no time to examine them how they agreed with the word of God." "What,"

said he, "surely you mistook the matter, you will refer yourselves wholly
to us therein." "No, by the faith I bear to God," said I, "we will pass
nothing before we understand what it is; for that were but to make you
popes. Make you popes who list," said I, "for we will make you none."
And sure, Mr. Speaker, the speech seemed to me to be a very pope-like
speech, and I fear lest our bishops do attribute this of the Pope's canons
unto themselves, *Papa non potest errare* [the Pope cannot err]; for surely
if they did not, they would reform things amiss, and not to spurn
[spur *] against God's people for writing their mind therein as they do.
But I can tell them news: they do but kick against the prick, for undoubtedly they both have and do err, and God will reveal his truth,
maugre [i.e., in spite of] the hearts of them and all his enemies, for great
is the truth and it will prevail: and to say the truth, it is an error to think
that God's Spirit is tied only to them; for the heavenly Spirit saith, "First
seek the Kingdom of God and the righteousness thereof, and all these
things (meaning temporal) shall be given you" [Mt. 6:33]. These words
were not spoken to the bishops only, but to all; and the writ, Mr.
Speaker, that we are called up by, is chiefly to deal in God's cause: so
that our commission both from God and our Prince is to deal in God's
causes. Therefore the accepting of such messages, and taking them in
good part, doth highly offend God, and is the acceptation of the breach
of the liberties of this honourable Council. For is it not all one thing to
say, "Sirs, you shall deal in such matters only," as to say, "you shall not
deal in such matters"? And so as good to have fools and flatterers in the
House as men of wisdom, grave judgment, faithful hearts and sincere
consciences. For they being taught what they shall do can give their
consents as well as the others. Well, he that hath an office, saith St. Paul,
let him wait on his office, or give diligent attendance upon his office [cf.
Rom. 12:6–8]. It is a great and special part of our duty and office, Mr.
Speaker, to maintain the freedom of consultation and speech, for by this,
good laws that do set forth God's glory and for the preservation of the
Prince and State are made. St. Paul in the same place saith, "Hate that
which is evil and cleave unto that which is good" [Rom. 12:9]: then with
St. Paul, I do advise you all here present, yea and heartily and earnestly
desire you from the bottom of your hearts to hate all messengers, tale-
carriers, or any other thing, whatsoever it be, that any manner of way
infringe[s] the liberties of this honourable Council. Yea, hate it or them
as venomous and poison unto our Commnwealth, for they are venomous
beasts that do use it. Therefore I say, again and again, hate that that is

evil and cleave unto that that is good; and this, loving and faithful hearted, I do wish to be conceived in fear of God, and of love to our Prince and State. For we are incorporated into this place to serve God and all England, and not to be time-servers, as humour-feeders, as cancers that would pierce the bone, or as flatterers that would fain beguile all the world, and so worthy to be condemned both of God and man. But let us show ourselves a people endued with faith, I mean with a lively faith, that bringeth forth good works, and not a dead faith. And these good works I wish to break forth in this sort, not only in hating the enemies before spoken against, but also in open reproving them as enemies to God, our Prince and State that do use them, for they are so. Therefore I would have none spared or forborne that shall from henceforth offend herein, of what calling soever he be, for the higher place he hath, the more harm he may do; therefore if he will not eschew offences, the higher I wish him hanged. I speak this in charity, Mr. Speaker, for it is better that one should be hanged than that this noble State should be subverted. Well, I pray God with all my heart to turn the hearts of all the enemies of our Prince and State, and to forgive them that wherein they have offended, yea and to give them grace to offend therein no more; even so I do heartily beseech God to forgive us for holding our peaces when we have heard any injury offered to this honourable Council. For surely it is no small offence, Mr. Speaker, for we offend therein against God, our Prince and State, and abuse the confidence by them reposed in us. Wherefore God, for his great mercy's sake, grant that we may from henceforth show ourselves neither bastards nor dastards therein, but that as rightly begotten children, we may sharply and boldly reprove God's enemies, our Prince's and State's. And so shall every one of us discharge our duties in this our high office, wherein he hath placed us, and show ourselves haters of evil and cleavers to that that is good, to the setting forth of God's glory and honour, and to the preservation of our noble Queen and Commonwealth: for these are the marks that we ought only in this place to shoot at. I am thus earnest, I take God to witness, for conscience sake, love, love unto my Prince and Commonwealth, and for the advancement of justice. For justice, saith an ancient father, is the prince of all virtues, yea the safe and faithful guard of man's life, for by it emperors, kingdoms, people and cities be governed, the which if it be taken away, the society of man cannot long endure. And a king, saith Solomon, that sitteth in the throne of judgment and looketh well about him, chaseth away all evil [cf. Prov. 20:8]; in the which state and throne God for his great mercy's sake grant that our noble Queen may be heartily vigilant and watchful. For surely there was a great fault committed both in the last Parliament time and since also, that was as faithful hearts as any were unto the Prince and State received most displeasure, the which is but an hard point in policy, to encourage the enemy, to discourage the faithful-hearted, who of fervent love cannot dissemble, but follow the rule of St. Paul, who saith, "Let love be without dissimulation" [Rom. 12:9].

Now to another great fault I found the last Parliament committed by some of this House also, the which I would desire of them all might be left. I have seen right good men in other causes, although I did dislike them in that doing, sit in an evil matter, against which they had most earnestly spoken. I mused at it and asked what it meant, for I do think it a shameful thing to serve God, their Prince or country, with the tongue only and not with the heart and body. I was answered that it was a common policy in this House to mark the best sort of the same and either to sit or arise with them.[2] That same common policy I would gladly have banished this House, and have grafted in the stead thereof, either to rise or sit as the matter giveth cause. For the eyes of the Lord behold all the earth to strengthen all the hearts of them that are whole with him [cf. 2 Chron. 16:9]. These be God's own words, mark them well, I heartily beseech you all; for God will not receive half part, he will have the whole. And again, he misliketh those two-faced gentlemen, and here be many eyes that will to their great shame behold their double dealing that uses it. Thus I have holden you long with my rude speech, the which since it tendeth wholly with pure consciences to seek the advancement of God's glory, our honourable Sovereign's safety, and to the sure defence of this noble isle of England, and all by maintaining of the liberties of this honourable Council, the fountain from whence all these do spring. My humble and hearty suit unto you all is to accept my good will, and that this that I have here spoken, out of conscience and great zeal unto my Prince and State, may not be buried in the pit of oblivion, and so no good come thereof."

FINIS

Upon this speech the House, out of a reverend regard of her Majesty's honour, stopped his further proceeding before he had fully finished his speech. The message he meant and intended was that which was sent by

2. [ED.] The method of voting.

her Majesty to the House of Commons in the said fourteenth year of her reign upon Wednesday the twenty-eighth day of May, by Sir Francis Knollys, knight, treasurer of her Majesty's household, inhibiting them for a certain time to treat or deal in the matter touching the Scottish queen. Now follows the proceeding of the House upon this speech out of the original journal book itself.[3]

Mr. Wentworth being sequestered the House as aforesaid for his said speech, it was agreed and ordered by the House upon the question (after sundry motions and disputations had therein) that he should be presently committed to the sergeants ward as prisoner, and so remaining should be examined upon his said speech for the extenuating of his fault therein, by all the Privy Council being of this House, the Master of the Requests, the Captain of the Guard, the Treasurer of the Chamber, the Master of the Jewel-house, the Master of the Wardrobe, the Lieutenant of the Tower, Sir Thomas Scott, Sir Rowland Hayward, Mr. Attorney of the Duchy, Mr. Henry Knollys the elder, Mr. Sampoole, Mr. Randall, Mr. Birched, Mr. Marsh, who were appointed to meet this afternoon between two and three of the clock at the Star Chamber and to make report at this House tomorrow next. And then the said Peter Wentworth was brought to the bar, and committed thereupon to the said sergeants ward according to the said order.

This afternoon-passages being thus transcribed for the most part out of the original journal book of the House of Commons, now follows the examination of the said Mr. Wentworth before the committees before appointed, which is transcribed out of a memorial or copy thereof set down by the said Mr. Wentworth himself, being as followeth.

Post Meridiem

A true report of that which was laid to my charge in the Star Chamber by the committees of the Parliament House (viz., the House of Commons) that same afternoon (viz., Wednesday, February the eighth) after that I had delivered the speech in the House that forenoon, and my answer to the same.

COMMITTEES: First, where is your tale you promised to deliver in writing?

WENTWORTH: Here is it, and I deliver it upon two conditions. The first is

3. [ED.] This and the two succeeding paragraphs are by D'Ewes.

that you shall peruse it all, and if you can find any want of good will to my Prince and State in any part thereof, let me answer all [. . .] as if I had uttered all. The second is that you shall deliver it unto the Queen's Majesty; if her Majesty or you of her Privy Council can find any want of love to her Majesty or the State therein also, let me answer it.

C.: We will deal with no more than you uttered in the House.

W.: Your Honours cannot refuse to deliver it to her Majesty, for I do send it to her Majesty as my heart and mind, knowing that it will do her Majesty good. It will hurt no man but myself.

C.: Seeing your desire is to have us deliver it to her Majesty, we will deliver it.

W.: I humbly require your Honours so to do.

C.: Then, the speech being read, one said, "Here you have uttered certain rumours of the Queen's Majesty. Where, or of whom, heard you them?"

W.: If your Honours ask me as Councillors to her Majesty, you shall pardon me: I will make you no answer. I will do no such injury to the place from whence I came. For I am now no private person: I am a public, and a counsellor to the whole State, in that place where it is lawful for me to speak my mind freely and not for you, as Councillors to call me to account for anything that I do speak in the House. And therefore if you ask me as Councillors to her Majesty, you shall pardon me, I will make no answer. But if you ask me as committees from the House, I will then willingly make you the best answer I can.

C.: We ask you as committees from the House.

W.: I will then answer you, and the willinger for that mine answer will be in some part so imperfect as of necessity it must be. Your question consisteth of these two points, where and of whom I heard these rumours? The place where I heard them was the Parliament House; but of whom, I assure you I cannot tell.

C.: This is no answer to say you cannot tell of whom, neither will we take it for any.

W.: Truly your Honours must needs take it for an answer, when I can make you no better.

C.: Belike you have heard some speeches in the town of her Majesty's misliking of religion and succession; you are loath to utter of whom and did use speeches thereupon.

W.: I assure your Honours I can show you that speech at my own house, written with my hand two or three years ago. So that you may thereby judge that I did not speak it of anything that I heard since I came to town.

C.: You have answered that. But where heard you it then?

W.: If your Honours do think I speak for excuse's sake, let this satisfy you. I protest before the living God I cannot tell of whom I heard these rumours. Yet I do verily think that I heard them of a hundred or two in the House.

C.: Then of so many, you can name some.

W.: No surely. Because it was so general a speech I marked none; neither do men mark speakers commonly when they be general. And I assure you, if I could tell, I would not, for I will never utter anything told me, to the hurt of any man. when I am not enforced thereunto, as in this case I may choose. Yet I would deal plainly with you, for I would tell your Honours so. And if your Honours do not credit me, I will voluntarily take an oath, if you offer me a Book, that I cannot tell of whom I heard those rumours. But if you offer me an oath of your authorities, I will refuse it, because I will do nothing to infringe the liberties of the House. But what need I to use these speeches? I will give you an instance whereupon I heard these rumours to your satisfying, even such a one as if you will speak the truth you shall confess that you heard the same as well as I.

C.: In so doing we will be satisfied. What is that?

W.: The last Parliament (by which it may be conceived he meant and intended that Parliament in *anno* 13 *Reginae Eliz.* [1571]) he that is now Speaker (*viz.*, Robert Bell, Esquire, who was also Speaker in the first session of this present Parliament in *anno* 14 *Reginae eiusdem* [1572]) uttered a very good speech for the calling in of certain licenses granted to four courtiers, to the utter undoing of six or eight thousand of the Queen's Majesty's subjects. This speech was so disliked of some of the Council that he was sent for and so hardly dealt with that he came into the House with such an amazed countenance that it daunted all the House in such sort, that for ten, twelve, or sixteen days there was not one in the House that durst deal in any matter of importance. And in those simple matters that they dealt in, they spent more words and time in their preamble, requiring that they might not be mistaken, than they did in the matter they spake unto. This inconvenience grew unto the House by the Councillors' hard handling of the said good member, whereupon this rumour grew in the House: "Sirs, you may not speak against licenses, the Queen's Majesty will be angry, the Council will be too too angry." And this rumour I suppose there is not one of you here but heard it as well as I. I beseech your Honours discharge your consciences herein as I do.

C.: We heard it we confess, and you have satisfied us in this; but how say you to the hard interpretation you made of the message that was sent into the House? (The words were recited.) I assure you I have never heard an harder interpretation of a message.

W.: I beseech your Honours, first, was there not such a message sent unto the House?

C.: We grant that there was.

W.: Then I trust you will bear me record that I made it not; and I answer you that so hard a message could not have too hard an interpretation made by the wisest man in England. For can there by any possible means be sent a harder message to a Council gathered together to serve God, than to say, "you shall not seek to advance the glory of God"? I am of this opinion, that there cannot be a more wicked message than it was.

C.: You may not speak against messages, for none sendeth them but the Queen's Majesty.

W.: If the message be against the glory of God, against the Prince's safety, or against the liberty of the Parliament House, whereby the State is maintained, I neither may nor will hold my peace. I cannot in so doing discharge my conscience, whosoever doth send it. And I say that I heartily repent me for that I have hitherto held my peace in these causes, and that I do promise you all (if God forsake me not) that I will never during life hold my tongue, if any [such] message is sent wherein God is dishonoured, the Prince periled, or the liberties of the Parliament impeached; and every one of you here present ought to repent you of these faults and to amend them.

C.: It is no new precedent to have the Prince to send messages. (There were two or three messages recited sent by two or three Princes.)

W.: Said I: You do very evil to allege precedents in this order. You ought to allege good precedents, to comfort and embolden men in good doing, and not evil precedents to discourage and terrify men to do evil.

C.: You called the Scottish Queen Jezebel. What meant you by that?

W.: Did I not publish her openly in the last Parliament to be the most notorious whore in all the world; and wherefore should I then be afraid to call her so now again?

C.: She is a Queen. You ought to speak reverently of her.

W.: Let him take her part that list. I will speak the truth boldly.

C.: But what meant you to make so hard interpretation of messages?

W.: Surely I marvel what you mean by asking this question. Have I not said, so hard a message could not have too hard an interpretation; and have I not set down the reason that moved me in my speech, that is to say, that for the receiving and accepting that message, God has poured so great indignation upon us that he put into the Queen's Majesty's heart to refuse good and wholesome laws for her own preservation; which caused many loving and faithful hearts for grief to burst out with sorrowful tears, and moved all Papists, traitors to God, to her Majesty, and to every good Christian government, in their sleeves to laugh the whole Parliament House to scorn. Have I not thus said, and do not your Honours think it did so?

C.: Yes, truly. But how durst you say that the Queen's Majesty had unkindly abused herself against the nobility and people?

W.: I beseech your Honours tell me how far you can stretch these words of her unkindly abusing and opposing herself against her Majesty's nobility and people? Can you apply them any further than I have applied them, that is to say, in that her Majesty called the Parliament of purpose to prevent traitorous perils to her person, and for no other cause, and in that her Majesty did send unto us two bills, willing us to take our choice of that we liked best for her Majesty's safety and thereof to make a law promising her royal consent thereunto; and did we not first choose the one, and her Majesty refused it? Yet did not we nevertheless receive the other? And agreeing to make a law thereof, did not her Majesty in the end refuse all our travails? And did not the Lord Keeper in her Majesty's presence in the beginning of the Parliament show this to be the occasion that we were called together? And did not her Majesty in the end of the Parliament refuse all our travails? Is not this known to all here present and to all the Parliament House also? I beseech your Honours discharge your consciences herein and utter your knowledge simply as I do, for in truth herein her Majesty did abuse her nobility and subjects, and did oppose herself against them by the way of advice.

C.: Surely we cannot deny it, you say the truth.

W.: Then I beseech your Honours show me if it were not a dangerous doing to her Majesty in these two respects. First in weakening, wounding and discouraging the hearts of her Majesty's loving and faithful subjects, thereby to make them the less able or the more fearful and unwilling to serve her Majesty. Another time, on the other side was it not a raising up and encouraging the hearts of her Majesty's hateful enemies to adventure any desperate enterprise to her Majesty's peril and danger?

C.: We cannot deny but that it was very dangerous to her Majesty in those respects.

W.: And is it not a loving part of a subject to give her Majesty warning to avoid danger?

C.: It is so.

W.: Then why do your Honours ask how I dare tell a truth, to give the Queen's Majesty warning to avoid her danger? I answer you thus. I do thank the Lord my God, that I never found fear in myself to give the Queen's Majesty warning to avoid her danger. Be you all afraid thereof if you will, for I praise God I am not, and I hope never to live to see that day. And yet I will assure your Honours that twenty times and more, when I walked in my grounds revolving this speech to prepare against this day, my own fearful conceit did say unto me that this speech would carry me to the place whither I shall now go, and fear would have moved me to have put it out. Then I weighed whether in good conscience, and the duty of a faithful subject, I might keep myself out of prison, and not to warn my Prince from walking in a dangerous course. My conscience said unto me that I could not be a faithful subject if I did more respect to avoid my own danger than my Prince's danger: herewithal I was made bold and went forward as your Honours heard. Yet when I uttered these words in the House — "that there was none without fault, no, not our noble Queen" — I paused, and beheld all your countenances, and saw plainly that those words did amaze you all. Then I was afraid with you for company, and fear bade me to put out those words that followed; for your countenances did assure me that not one of you would stay me of my journey. Yet the consideration of a good conscience and of a faithful subject did make me bold to utter that, in such sort as your Honours heard. With this heart and mind I spake it, and I praise God for it; and if it were to do again, I would with the same mind speak it again.

C.: Yea: but you might have uttered it in better terms. Why did you not so?

W.: Would you have me to have done as you of her Majesty's Privy Council do, to utter a weighty matter in such terms as she should not have understood to have made a fault? Then it would have done her Majesty no good, and my intent was to do her good.

C.: You have answered us: we are satisfied.

W.: Then I praise God for it.

And as I made a curtsy, another spake these words:

SECKFORD [Master of Requests]: Mr. Wentworth will never acknowledge himself to make a fault, nor say that he is sorry for anything that he doth speak. You shall hear none of these things come out of his mouth.

W.: Mr. Seckford, I will never confess it to be a fault to love the Queen's Majesty, while I live; neither will I be sorry for giving her Majesty warning to avoid her danger, while the breath is in my belly. If you do think it a fault to love her Majesty, or to be sorry that her Majesty should have warning to avoid her danger, say so, for I cannot. Speak for yourself, Mr. Seckford.

Ten Questions Presented to the House of Commons, 1 March 1587

1. First, whether the Prince and State can be maintained without this Court of Parliament.

2. Item, whether there be any Council that can make or abrogate laws but only this Court of Parliament.

3. Item, whether free speech and free doings, or dealings be not granted to everyone of the Parliament House by law.

4. Item, whether that great honour to God and those great benefits may be done unto the Prince and State without free speech and doings in this place, that may be done with them.

5. Item, whether it be not an injury to the whole State, and against the law, that the Prince or Privy Council should send for any member of this House in the Parliament time, or after the end of the Parliament, and to check, blame or punish them for any speech used in this place, except it be for traitorous words.

6. Item, whether this be a place to receive supplications of the griefs and sores of the Commonwealth, and either that we should be humble suitors unto the Queen's Majesty for relief, or else to relieve them here as the case requireth.

7. Item, whether it be not against the orders and liberties of this House to receive messages either of commanding or prohibiting, and whether the messenger be not to be reputed as an enemy to God, the Prince and State.

8. Item, whether it be not against the orders and liberties of this House to make anything known unto the Prince that is here in hand to the hurt of the House, and whether the tale-carrier be not to be punished

by the House and reputed as an enemy unto God, the Prince and State.

9. Item, whether we do show ourselves faithful unto God, the Prince and State in receiving such messages, and in taking such tales in good part, without punishing of the messenger and tale-carrier by the order and discretion of this House.

10. Item, whether he or they may be not to be esteemed reputed and used as enemies unto God, the Prince and State that should do anything to infringe the liberties of this honourable Council.

❖ ❖ ❖ ❖ ❖
❖   ❖
❖   III   ❖
❖   ❖
❖ ❖ ❖ ❖ ❖

THE ORDER OF THE PROPHECY AT NORWICH

Editor's Introduction

The origins of a particular church office, rite or function are not often deducible from its later forms. This is notably true of the so-called "Puritan practice of the prophesyings." The "prophesyings" were a pre-Puritan device for the improvement of preaching which both Puritans and non-Puritans had found extremely adaptable and useful. When in the 1570s the prophesyings came under attack, some opponents of the Puritans defended them no less, if not even more, vigorously than did Puritans. Moreover, in their defense of these prophesyings the Puritans found themselves somewhat confused about their meaning and purpose. A possible justification for calling them Puritan is that those wings of the Puritan movement here called the "original protesters" and the "passive resisters" sought more consistently and over a longer period of time to preserve an old and useful device. It was significantly altered by the so-called "Presbyterian" Puritans as its ambiguities became apparent during the controversy of the 1570s.

No major study has been made of the origins of the prophesyings or of their various forms.[1] However, the two dominant concerns that led to the trouble in England during the 1570s were present in the prophesyings as far back as the 1520s at Zurich, where even then they were the cause of controversy. These concerns, with improving the preaching ministry and with promoting Bible study, were also near the core of Christian Humanism. In both Christian Humanism and the early forms of Protestantism, proper preaching was preaching from the Bible rather than of

---

1. On the Bible-study groups in Erasmus' writings, see Alfons Auer, *Die vollkommene Frömmigkeit des Christen . . . Erasmus . . .* (Düsseldorf, 1954), 149, and many of the *Colloquies* of Erasmus; also Fritz Blanke, "Zwingli's Prophezei und die Anfänge des Puritanismus," *Neue Zürcher Zeitung*, June 29, 1939, and *Der Junge Bullinger* (Zurich, 1942), 64; August Lang, *Puritanismus und Pietismus . . . M. Butzer . . .* (Neukirchen, 1941), 32-5, 78; also Werner Bellardi, *Die Geschichte der "Christlichen Gemeinschaft" in Strassburg, 1546-50* (Leipzig, 1934), 114 f.

dogma as such. Consequently, Bible study and the improvement of preaching were closely linked.

The problem that seems to have been present from the beginning was that both Christian Humanism and early Protestantism had championed vigorously the right of the laity to read, to discuss and even to debate the Scriptures with the clergy. If ministers and laymen studied the Bible together, what would happen? There were ignorant ministers and erudite laymen, just as there were learned preachers and ignorant laymen. Also, as at Zurich, the need to improve the quality of preaching demanded some form of critique which, if made publicly, could have produced great difficulties in a city of 10,000 where the conflict among Catholics, Zwinglians and Anabaptists was already intense. Erasmus had founded no group or movement, but his widely read writings often depicted a debate on the Scriptures among a group of ordinary laymen. Moreover, the "priesthood of all believers" placed further emphasis on the people as the church and the minister as one of the people, and the introduction of Bible study into the schools opened the way for teachers of the Bible, not all of whom were ministers. The weekday public Bible lectures in the church (which often occurred daily) became yet another means of instruction for both ministers and people.

Out of these and other concerns, "prophesyings" arose in numerous Swiss and south German churches. In some places, as at Zurich, the concern with instructing the former Catholic clergy who had come over to Protestantism seems to have been primary. Here the laity very soon secured the right to participate in the prophesyings.[2] At other places, where the concern with Bible study was dominant, the prophesyings became a more or less informal meeting of the congregation to study the Bible under the direction of the pastor. In England under Edward VI, refugee churches of French and Walloons held prophesyings of various kinds, but there is no evidence of the practice in English churches.[3] However, the casual manner in which prophesying was referred to in the Frankfort exile church, and the spontaneous ease with which the practice arose in many parts of England during the early years of Elizabeth's reign, indicate that the custom was rather well known to Englishmen at an early date.[4]

2. Oskar Farner, *Huldrych Zwingli* (Zurich, 1954), III, 560. I am indebted for this reference to Professor George Mosse, who saved me from a blunder at this point.

3. *Original Letters*, I, 587.

4. *A Brief Discourse of the Troubles at Frankfort, 1554–1558 A.D.* (1574; reprint edited by E. Arber, London, 1908), 166; also S. E. Lehmberg, "Archbishop Grindal

There seems to have been little public mention or discussion of the prophesyings during the first fifteen years of Elizabeth's reign.[5] Then, in 1574, because of some unknown irritation Elizabeth demanded that Parker put an end to the prophesyings at Norwich. Parkhurst, the bishop there, who had been an exile at Zurich and was a close friend of Gualter as well as of Bishop Jewel, tried to evade Parker's order, but was eventually forced to obey the Queen and to forbid the practice. By February 1575 Parkhurst was dead, and Parker died in May of the same year. Grindal, the first bishop of London under Elizabeth, had been a protégé of Ridley and Bucer during the reign of Edward, and an exile at Strassburg under Mary. In the "troubles at Frankfort" he allied himself with the Coxe party in opposition to Knox and Geneva, and he had been an adviser also to the group appointed to revise the prayer book in 1558. During the vestment controversy he had at first refused to force the use of vestments on the clergy of London; this had angered Parker, and Grindal was finally forced into line. In 1570 he had been made Archbishop of York. When the Presbyterian party emerged in 1570–72, Grindal vigorously opposed it. After Parker's death he was shifted to the archbishopric of Canterbury (December 1575), to the great satisfaction of officialdom, and even of those Puritans of the two other wings who believed they knew Grindal's inner convictions. He began at once a series of moderate reforms, which are regarded by Patrick Collinson as giving promise of a constructive new order.[6] But at the time these reforms met with such bitter opposition that as in the vestment controversy, the real issues of the conflict were never openly stated, and the issue in the battle that took place was largely symbolic. That issue was the prophesyings, which now became stigmatized as Puritan. Nevertheless, the conflict reveals more than a little concerning the underlying issues.

In the opinion of Collinson, the attack upon the prophesyings was probably intended to exploit the known attitudes of the Queen, so as to discredit Grindal and bring an end to his projected church reforms. Behind the move was conflict within the royal court between Leicester and Christopher Hatton, Elizabeth's newest favorite and the sponsor of John Aylmer, John Whitgift and Richard Bancroft, who were among the ablest opponents of the Puritans. Grindal had held his new office for only

and the Prophesyings," *Hist. Mag. of the Prot. Episc. Church*, XXXIV (June 1965), 87–145.

5. Patrick Collinson, *The Elizabethan Puritan Movement* (London, 1967), 163–7, 174, 193, 210; also G. C. Gorham, *Gleanings . . . during the Period of the Reformation . . . , 1533–88* (London, 1857), 483–92.

6. Collinson, *Elizabethan Puritan Movement*, Part 4.

a few months when friendly courtiers began to warn him of an impending storm. Summoned before the Queen, he was ordered to suppress all the prophesyings in the Southern Province and to reduce the number of preachers in the entire province to no more than three or four to a shire. From this it appeared that Elizabeth's opposition was to preaching as such. Grindal's next moves reveal, however, that more was at stake. He sent a circular letter to each of the bishops in his province, asking whether or not there had been prophesyings in the diocese, and if so, how they had begun, how they were conducted, whether they had been the cause of disorders, and the bishop's own opinion of their value. In addition, Grindal asked whether lay people had been allowed to attend, and if so, whether they had taken part. This final query was to be of great importance as the controversy developed. Fifteen bishops replied; six did not.[7]

Most of the fifteen bishops replied that prophesyings were taking place — although, interestingly enough, there had never been a prophesying at Salisbury, where Jewel, the great admirer of Zurich, had been bishop. In many areas the prophesyings had been in existence since the beginning of Elizabeth's reign, or from a time unknown. But even where they were of recent introduction, the reporting bishops wrote of the phenomenon as a thing well known. The manner in which these meetings were conducted varied considerably, but they all had the common objective of improving the preaching abilities of the clergy. Also, the question of lay participation had arisen in almost every instance. In most places there was strong lay support for these exercises, frequently taking the form of liberal financial contributions for travel and hospitality, but also at times in a sizable lay attendance. In some places the local dignitaries and magistrates (and even wives) attended regularly. In a very few places there had been lay participation in the lectures and discussions. In some places there had been disagreements that exploded into wrangling, for example where lay people had been too forward with opinions the clerics disliked. Some bishops were troubled because ousted Puritan preachers had become the leaders, or the leading spirits, in these exercises. Most of the bishops believed, however, that the prophesyings should continue, and some were genuinely fearful of the reaction of the laity if the exercises were suppressed.

In a vigorous effort to save the prophesyings as a means toward improving the preaching ability of the lower clergy, Grindal drew up a list

7. See Lehmberg (note 4, above) for a full text of these reports.

of "orders for reformation abuses about the learned exercises," in which the current objections are clearly mirrored. There was to be strict episcopal control of these exercises through an appointed official. Only certain approved ministers were to have permission to speak. All others were to be auditors only, and were to be assigned studies on which they were to report in writing. No cleric was to be criticized in the presence of lay people. No lay person was to speak during the exercise. Any minister who in speaking made any criticism, direct or indirect, of any official or any official act in the church or the kingdom was to be silenced and punished. No minister who had been disciplined for any cause could participate in the meetings. No topics were to be discussed except biblical passages that had been assigned by the bishop. Despite all this, Grindal's efforts were unavailing. Elizabeth demanded an absolute end to all the prophesyings in the Southern Province, and a drastic reduction in preaching. Significantly, the order did not apply to the Northern Province, where Catholic sentiment against royal policy was strong and deeply entrenched. There the government was in favor of much preaching (against Rome).

Grindal and Dering are among the small number of persons who had the courage to speak to Elizabeth as a human being. The Catholic bishops had spoken their true minds to her in 1559. But no Protestant bishop save Grindal ever dared fulfill the role of "father in God" to that insecure and imperious woman. In a long letter to the Queen, Grindal defended the prophesyings as necessary to the development of an adequate preaching ministry, asserted that preaching the gospel was the divine method of salvation, refused to be the Queen's instrument in suppressing the prophesyings, and solemnly pointed out to the "Supreme governor of the church" some of the implications of her office. "Remember, Madam, that you are a mortal creature," he wrote, and reminded her of the celebrated incident in which the ancient bishop Ambrose had rebuked the Roman emperor Theodosius. Grindal told the Queen he would rather offend her than God. He closed by asking her, since this was an ecclesiastical matter, to allow the ecclesiastical officials to deal with it.[8]

Elizabeth's response was to place the archbishop under house arrest. Among others, Cecil, now Lord Burghley, urged Grindal to compromise or equivocate. None of the bishops ventured to make common cause with the archbishop. Their efforts were limited to proposals which would have been a retreat for Grindal. He remained under house arrest and out of of-

8. For an accurate text of this much reprinted letter, see Lehmberg.

fice from December 1576 until shortly before his death in July 1583. Whitgift then succeeded him.

On May 8, 1577, after Grindal's refusal to yield had become clear, the Queen in her own name ordered all the bishops of the Southern Province to put down the prophesyings, and to limit preaching. Her letter contained the bitter charge that incompetent persons were introducing novelties and illegal rites, forms and assemblies which drew lay people from great distances, took them from their ordinary labors, induced idleness, promoted schisms and dangerous opinions, etc.[9] The bishops were to imprison any who continued the prophesyings, and would themselves suffer punishment if they failed to obey this order. The bishops obeyed. They could do little else. There was among them no common mind, no common objective, and no leader whom any of them would follow or support. Within their own sees the bishops did not have the loyalty or support of their own clergy. As religious leaders of the English people the bishops were a nullity. They were the Queen's servants who, as Bishop Aylmer put it, wore the Queen's livery.[10]

The real crisis, of which the prophesyings became the symbol, was the total insecurity of these bishops, who were without any following, clerical or lay, or any clear constitutional status, who were subject to the arbitrary whims of the Queen and were used as pawns in one court rivalry after another, who were in constant financial trouble, who had been estranged from the people by the hierarchical structure of the church, and made the scapegoats of the new Puritan-backed anticlericalism. Grindal was no Puritan. But he did realize that if the prophesyings were done away with, the bishops and clergy would be alienated still more from the local leaders of the people, and made still more impotently dependent on the Court. Because the bishops' reports to him showed that in most areas the prophesyings were under the control of completely conformable men, or of relatively non-aggressive Puritans, Grindal had good reason to see in them the basis for developing a genuine church consciousness, and a popular religion which, being neither Catholic nor aggressively Presbyterian, could live in the official church. So he had been willing to put the prophesyings under rigid episcopal control, but not to limit preaching or to

9. The text of the Queen's letter appears in Lehmberg, and in Edmund Grindal, *Remains* (Cambridge, 1843; Parker Society), 373 f, 467 f. See also John Strype, *History of Life . . . Edmund Grindal . . .* (Oxford, 1821), 327 f, 574 f.

10. Quoted in M. Walzer, *The Revolution of the Saints* (Cambridge, Mass., 1965), 118. The English bishops were vague in their comments to the Zurich leaders on the suppression of the prophesyings. See *Zurich Letters*, I, 324, 329, 332.

exclude lay people from attending. Elizabeth and the Court party, lay and clerical alike — ever alert to suppress any move toward "popularity" — saw the crisis no less clearly than Grindal did. And so, with the aid of the other bishops, the Queen destroyed the prophesyings and the archbishop as well. Yet the popular religious impulse remained, and very soon prophesyings in guises old and new were operating once again, and this time they were more anti-episcopal than ever before.[11]

The order of the prophecy at Norwich in 1575 has been included in this volume for several reasons.[12] An earlier prophesying at Norwich had been suppressed by Parkhurst at Parker's command. When both men died shortly thereafter, and the see of Norwich and the archbishopric were both vacant, a new exercise was organized under local initiative. In methodology it differed very little from that approved and defended until 1576 by Thomas Cooper, bishop of Lincoln (whom Puritans knew as the profane T.C.). Only set topics could be discussed, only approved members of the clergy could speak, speech was rigidly controlled, there was to be no pointless wrangling, there was to be a prayer for the Queen and an orderly critique of the speakers, and any disorderly participants were to be disciplined. In all of this, the pattern was fairly standard. Grindal's own orders for the reform of the prophesyings made all of these same requirements. The novelties of the Norwich order, which led Collinson to see in it a transitional stage to the later Presbyterian "conferences," were that control of the prophesying was in the hands of the group as a whole, rather than of some one appointed by the bishop.[13] Also, there was no mention in the order of the less able preachers who might be taught by the prophesying exercise. The group seemed all to have been of equal ability, and all appear to have participated on an equal basis. There was no mention of lay attendance. This prophesying seems to have been a gathering of abler ministers for mutual edification. Nothing was said, however, about not accepting ousted Puritan preachers as members, or about avoiding criticism of the official church.

The new bishop of Norwich, Edmund Freake, liquidated this prophesying in 1576, and soon afterward the nucleus of the group began forming an underground Presbyterian "classis." But the exclusive, secret, ministerial, Presbyterian classis was far removed from the earlier pro-

11. Collinson, *Elizabethan Puritan Movement,* 208 f.
12. The text has been taken from John Browne, *History of Congregationalism . . . Norfolk and Suffolk* (London, 1877), 18-20.
13. Collinson, 213.

phesying, presided over perhaps by an archdeacon, with attendance required of all clerics in the region, and with J.P.'s and other laymen, along with their wives, free to attend, concluded by a dinner provided by the local merchants (who also provided fodder for the horses), and held in the cathedral or else in the largest church available. The prophesying was not a Puritan invention or a Puritan device. But, like so many aspects of the two types of non-aggressive Puritanism, it appealed to the "vulgar sort" and made for "popularity," for open discussion, the airing of differences, and the development of public opinion. Such things always made a Tudor monarch feel insecure — and with good reason.

The prophesyings left behind a brood of surprisingly vigorous stepchildren, namely the Puritan "fast-days." [14] These cannot be said to have grown out of the prophesyings, or to have had the same patterns or objectives. Fast-days were used by officials of the Reformed churches on the Continent, and by English officialdom under Elizabeth, as occasions for special prayer, with perhaps also special sermons or homilies, in times of particular danger or catastrophe. So long as it was they who decided when a fast-day was required, and so long as it was they who provided the appropriate special prayers or homilies, the English authorities found fast-days useful instruments of official policy. But it was difficult to forbid people to decide for themselves that an epidemic, a crop failure, or some other local danger or calamity indicated that the more zealous among them should call for a day of fasting, repentance and prayer, together with a sermon by a preacher of their own choosing.

Thus the popular, lay, community-wide enthusiasm associated with some forms of the prophesyings could find expression in these fast-day observances. By the 1580s, when they were becoming common, they had begun to draw people from several parishes to a centrally located church, and were being used (mainly by Puritans) to focus attention on the ills and problems of the day and upon the Puritan interpretation of those ills and problems. In this manner they may be said to have become the stepchildren of the prophesyings, which had begun as a means of edification for the parochial clergy. Moreover, the custom of bringing together several parishes for a fast-day and of securing excellent preaching for the occasion, gave Puritan pastors a perfect opportunity to gather, as well as to invite some outstanding Puritan leader to serve as the special preacher for the day. It should also be noted that meetings of the clergy for study and practice in preaching continued well into Stuart times in those parts of

14. Collinson, 208–21.

England where the government hoped through preaching to reduce "the Catholic threat," or where a local bishop professed to be improving his clergy.

❖ ❖ ❖ ❖

The Order of the Prophecy at Norwich in Anno *1575*, Begun Sede Vacante

Orders to Be Observed in This Exercise of Prophesying

Imprimis. It is judged meet by the brethren that the Prophecy be kept every Monday in Christ's Church in Norwich, at nine of the clock in the morning till eleven (if there be speakers to fill that time), and not past, so [and] that the first speaker exceed not three quarters of an hour, and [that] all the rest of the time (to) be reserved to those brethren whom God shall move to speak of the same text, who are very earnestly desired to be very short, specially when they see divers others well able to speak after them.

The names of such as shall be judged by the brethren meet to speak in the Prophecy shall be written in a Table.

Let all the speakers be careful to keep them to the text; abstaining from heaping up of many testimonies, annoying allegations of profane histories, or ecclesiastical writers, applications of commonplaces and divisions not aptly growing out of the text; having always a special care to rip up the text, to show the sense of the Holy Ghost, and briefly, pithily and plainly to observe such things as afterward may be well applied, and more at large handled in preaching, concerning either doctrine or manners.

The text may aptly be handled in this sort: if first we show whether it depend of former words or not; how and upon what occasion the words were written or spoken, the act done, and the history [i.e., biblical narrative] rehearsed, so that this be soundly gathered out of the Scriptures; the drift and the scope of the Holy Ghost, and the plain meaning of the place of Scripture is to be opened; the propriety of the words is to be noted, whether a figure or no; the use of the like phrase of Scripture in other places; reconcile such places of Scripture as seem to repugn; lay forth the arguments used in the text; show the virtues and vices mentioned therein, and to the observance and breach of what commandment they belong; how the present text hath been wrested by the adversaries, and how and wherein they have been deceived; what points observed that many [may] serve for confirmation of faith, and exhortation to sanctification of life, against occasion shall be offered by preaching [i.e., all this to be done in order to prepare for preaching on the text].

The rest are to speak of the same text, and in the same order, having a careful respect to add, and not to repeat; to beware, as much as in them lieth, to utter no contradiction to that which was spoken before, nor to glance [i.e., covertly strike] at the former speakers, much less confuting one another, but reserving the examination of their doctrine to the brethren at their private conference, except manifest false doctrine hath been by any deliberately and contentiously propounded, and then the same is to be confuted and handled with great wisdom as [i.e., so that] it may appear to all that truth is defended rather than contention desired, whereby offence may be removed as much as is possible. None of the speakers shall take upon him publicly to object, or raise any questions, unless he be able presently, plainly and pithily to answer the same. As for old heresies that have been dead many years, let them not be mentioned, for that is after a sort to raise them out of their sepulchers, except they be some very pernicious now revived, which must be soundly overthrown by the Scriptures.

Let all that is spoken in the Prophecy be spoken in the English tongue only, unless the force of some Latin, Greek or Hebrew words, for further construction be showed as a thing most necessary to be noted, where knowledge and judgment will serve.

As it shall be free for any godly-learned brother to lay forth any fruitful matter revealed unto him out of the text, so it is most requisite that they do it not hastily, rashly, disorderly, but soberly and reverently as in the presence of God. For the better observing whereof let the first speaker the day before, or in his absence, some other for him sitting next to him that speaketh that day, by some comely gesture, as by putting off his hat, silently as it were call them as they sit in order to speak, and if they mean not to speak to signify it by some like gesture, as by putting on their hat, and so referring it to him that sitteth next, from one to another, and this to be done by the same brother so oft as any new speaker shall rise up till it have passed through all in order as they sit, if there be so much time, for the two hours being expired the first speaker must presently conclude with a short prayer for the whole church and all Estates, for the Queen's Majesty, her Council, with thanksgiving to God for her, and for all his great mercies towards this land.

The Prophecy ended, the learned brethren coming together, and the first speaker for that time put apart, the moderator or prolocutor for that present (who always shall be the same brother that spoke the day before in the first place, or some appointed in his absence) shall inquire of the brethren in order concerning the first speaker: first of the soundness of his doctrine; how he kept and followed his text; wherein he swerved from it; how aptly he alleged his testimonies out of the Scriptures; whether [he] observed the order of the prophecy set down; how plain or obscure his words were; how modest his speech and gestures; how sound, reverent and sober his whole action was, or wherein he failed; how some of his words being doubtfully spoken may be charitably expounded and construed in the better part. This done, the first speaker must be content, in the fear of God, to be informed or admonished (if need require) by the moderator of the action in the name of the rest of the brethren of such things as shall seem to the company worthy admonition, with the reasons and causes alleged by them; the same inquiry shall be made of the rest of the speakers if need require, and they all are with the spirit of modesty to rest in the judgment of the brethren without any show of pride, stiffness, or arrogancy, which, if it shall be found in any of the brethren, or any like disorder — the same after brotherly admonition not reforming himself — his name is to be put out of the Table till he be reformed, and if he shall proceed to the further disquieting of the church, sharper discipline is to be required, all just occasion whereof the Lord remove from us!

In this conference after the admonition of the speakers, if any doubt shall be made by any of the brethren that justly might arise of the text not answered by any of the speakers, therein he is to be resolved by the learned brethren, but if he seem not so fully resolved, and the question of importance, by consent of the brethren it shall be deferred till the next exercise, for the speaker the next prophesying day to handle in the very entrance of his speech; or if he be not judged sufficient, or shall modestly refuse to deal in so weighty a cause, let it be re-examined by the brethren in the conference.

Let none be suffered to speak in the Prophecy except he will submit himself to the orders that are or shall be set down hereafter by the consent of the brethren.

New orders are to be set down by the knowledge and consent of the brethren only, and not by any one man's authority, as occasion shall be ministered from time to time.

❖ ❖ ❖ ❖ ❖
❖   ❖
❖   IV   ❖
❖   ❖
❖ ❖ ❖ ❖ ❖

PREFACES TO THE GENEVA BIBLE

Editor's Introduction

Few things have seemed more obvious to historians over four centuries than the assertion that the Geneva Bible was the Puritan Bible. In fact, some have even supposed the Geneva Bible to be the cause and Puritanism the effect. Consequently, the literature dealing with Puritanism is replete with both wise and unwise references to this Bible. What is all too often overlooked in such references is the simple fact that the traditional reputation (or ill repute) of the Geneva Bible is rooted in James I's detestation of it, and that this aversion has then been projected back upon the Elizaethan era, whose references to it are ambiguous.

The full details concerning the preparation of the Geneva Bible seem never to have been recorded by the participants. In the fall of 1555, the Knox party were forced out of the Frankfort colony of English exiles, and most of them migrated to Geneva. There the idea was conceived of publishing an English version of the Bible similar to those in common use among the Continental Protestant churches. The legally printed versions of the Bible in English from 1535 to 1553 had been large, bulky and expensive. On the Continent, the advances in printing had begun to make possible vernacular Bibles of manageable size, with numerous aids for the reader, at something approaching popular prices. By the mid-sixteenth century Geneva was the center of a highly organized and efficient group of colporteurs, who at the risk of their lives were circulating Bibles and religious books throughout much of Catholic France.[1] The English exiles at Strasburg and Basel were also in touch with a good deal of Continental Protestant propaganda. A number of the Marian exiles had themselves engaged in such work during an earlier exile on the Continent under Henry VIII. Out of this background the Geneva Bible was born. Just

1. See Robert Kingdon, *Geneva and the Coming of the Wars of Religion in France, 1555–63* (Geneva, 1956), 93–105; also G. Berthaud *et al., Aspects de la propagande religieuse* (Geneva, 1957).

what use was envisioned for it is not known. Those who projected it may, like Tyndale, have hoped to circulate it in Catholic England.

According to tradition, the chief editors of this Bible were William Whittingham and Anthony Gilby. Whittingham, a layman, had received an exceptionally good education in England and France, and had served as a foreign diplomat under Edward; Gilby (M.A., Cambridge, 1535) had been associated with radical reform under both Henry and Edward. Other exiles at Geneva no doubt aided in the enterprise. In 1556 several items were issued for the use of the English exile congregation (which like all refugee groups was obligated to conform its worship to that of its host): a translation (slightly modified) of the Geneva order of service; the Geneva catechism; and a metrical psalter. An annotated English New Testament in a new translation (with Calvin's preface to Olivetan's French Bible of 1535) appeared in 1557; the Psalms in English in 1559; and finally, in 1560, a complete Bible, the New Testament portion of which had been redone since 1557.[2]

The "Geneva Bible" of 1560 carried a dedication to Elizabeth and an address to "Our beloved in the Lord the brethren of England, Scotland, Ireland, etc." A preface to the Apocrypha indicated that these books were non-authoritative but that they showed God's providential care for his people in times of persecution. A preface before Matthew summarized with minimal details the gospel narrative and stated that John's gospel was doctrinal whereas the other three were historical. A special preface to the Book of Revelation cautiously stated that the book foretold events in the period since the apostolic age, but gave no elaborate scheme of history. A topical index and glossary of biblical names were also included, along with several maps and charts or diagrams. For each book, most chapters, and many individual verses, there were interpretive aids, prefaces or notes. For the first time an English Bible had each verse numbered for ready reference. The entire work was printed at Geneva.

In 1576 Laurence Tomson, a layman of strong Presbyterian Puritan convictions, who had studied and travelled on the Continent, issued an English translation of Beza's freshly edited text of the New Testament. This version contained notes by Beza as revised by the Huguenot leader Pierre Loiseleur de Villiers, who dedicated his revision to the Puritan

2. I have profited from reading the unpublished doctoral dissertation on the Geneva Bible by a former colleague, David Alexander (Oxford University, 1957). A brief essay by Hardin Craig, Jr., "The Geneva Bible as a Political Document," *Pacific Hist. Rev.*, VII (1938), 40–49, suggests an approach that warrants further exploration.

noble Henry Hastings, the Earl of Huntington. Tomson, a close friend of many Huguenot leaders, was an M.P. from 1575 to 1589 and served as secretary to Francis Walsingham of the Privy Council, a staunch supporter of many Puritan enterprises, to whom he dedicated his translation. Like the editors of the Geneva Bible, Tomson felt obliged to add a special preface before the Book of Revelation. In 1587 a Geneva Bible appeared with Tomson's New Testament in place of the original 1560 version. A further change came in 1599, when Tomson's version of the text and notes on the Book of Revelation was replaced in its turn by an English translation from the Dutch scholar Franciscus Junius. In this latter edition the Book of Revelation had a larger apparatus than any other book in the Bible. (The significance of these changes will be discussed later.)

    After the exiles had left Geneva in 1560, control of the Geneva Bible passed into the hands of its publisher, John Bodley, an exile English merchant, whose son Thomas (a child in Geneva) was later to found the Bodleian Library at Oxford. From Bodley, control of the venture passed to the enterprising printer Christopher Barker, in whose hands it became a financial success. Before the death of Elizabeth, Barker and his son, who inherited the project, issued nearly ninety printings of the Geneva Bible and New Testament. In their effort to attract as many buyers as possible, the Barkers printed numerous variant editions. Some contained Archbishop Parker's "Sum of the Holy Scriptures," others a "Puritanized" prayer book; still others included the Geneva Catechism, or Beza's "Questions and Answers on Predestination," or the metrical psalter (with music), among other aids. These variants were entirely at the initiative of the Barkers, who had no ideological concern in the matter. After 1583 (when Whitgift became Archbishop of Canterbury) the dedication to Elizabeth seems to have been dropped from most versions. Yet for those who wished it, the unaltered 1560 version was still being issued by the Barkers even in the time of the Stuarts.

    An ancient tradition has it that the Geneva Bible was opposed in the time of Elizabeth because of its tendentious and ultra-Calvinistic marginal notes. The only direct evidence that this was in fact the attitude of the authorities is an ambiguous sentence in a letter from Parker to the Queen, dated October 5, 1568, commending his new Bishops' Bible as free of "divers prejudiced notes inspersed in some translations which have not been laboured in your realm." Yet three years earlier, on March 9, 1565, Parker and Grindal, in reply to a formal referral by Cecil, had given their approval to Bodley's request for a twelve-year extension of his right to print the Geneva Bible. "We think so well of the first impression, and review of those which have sithence travailled therein," they wrote, "that we wish . . . [the] privilege granted him . . ." The bishops went on to say that "diversity of translations and readings" were an aid rather than a hindrance.[3] At this time the Geneva notes apparently were not regarded with any concern. Two other pieces of evidence to support the ancient tradition date from the last year of Parker's life. An anonymous parody of Parker's work on the succession of archbishops of Canterbury accused him, in a marginal note, of "staying" the Geneva Bible. That same year, 1574, the anonymous *Troubles Begun at Frankfort* . . . contained the statement, "But if that Bible [i.e., the Geneva] be such, as no enemy of God could justly find fault with, then may men marvel that such a work (being so profitable) should find so small favour as not to be printed again."[4]

Recent scholars have still been unable to fit together the available evidence and the ancient tradition, although numerous solutions to the problem have been offered by historians of the Bible in English. Two things should be noted, however: first, Bodley asked for an extension of his copyright, not for permission to print in England. The work was printed at Geneva in 1560, 1561-2, 1568-70 — i.e., once after Bodley's request, and with the notes unchanged. There is no record that its importation was ever forbidden. Second, in 1575, the year of Parker's death, two editions of the 1560 Geneva New Testament were printed in London, and in the following year there were two printings of the 1560 Geneva Bible and one of Tomson's new version of the New Testament. Thereafter edition followed on edition up to the end of Elizabeth's reign. Parker's death does seem to have been followed by a change of some sort. Censorship was an episcopal power.

Early in June 1575, less than a month after Parker died on May 17, the London printers, working as a group and supported by some members of the Privy Council, broke the monopoly on Bible printing that had been held up until then by Richard Jugge. It is not at all impossible that the Geneva Bible was effectively suppressed by a close cooperation between Parker and Jugge in the interests of their common venture, the Bishops' Bible. On June 9 seven Privy Councillors, who also had censorship rights,

3. Matthew Parker, *Correspondence*, 261, 338.
4. [Anon.] *The life off the 70. archbishopp off Canterbury* (1574; S.T.C., 19292 [A], fol. Cii recto; *A Brief Discourse of the Troubles at Frankfort, 1554-1558* (1574; reprint edited by E. Arber, London, 1908), 228.

granted Barker the right to print the Geneva Bible in England. Barker would therefore have issued his first printings of it before Grindal was translated from York to Canterbury. This printing was made possible by laymen — that is, the Privy Councillors — rather than Grindal or any ecclesiastic. Barker's patent came up for reconsideration in 1589, when Whitgift was at the height of his power and also a member of the Privy Council. Whitgift did not oppose the Geneva Bible. In his long literary controversy with the Puritan Cartwright, Whitgift referred several times without polemic to the notes of the Geneva Bible, and more than once declared that they expressed his own views.[5]

Whitgift distrusted popular reading of the Bible, and Elizabeth could be quite sarcastic about people who got ideas opposed to hers through their reading of the Scriptures. This fact — that allowing people to read the Bible made problems for officialdom — constituted the real objection to the popularly designed and priced Geneva version. The notes themselves set forth no theological ideas at variance with the Thirty-Nine Articles, with Bishop Jewel's *Apology* for the official religion, or with any other official polemic against Rome. For example, the notations on the "proof texts" for various views of the ministry either were noncommittal, or merely paraphrased the text in the 1560 version, and Tomson's version of the New Testament (which did not come into the Geneva Bible until 1587) made polity an issue in only a few passages. Bishop B. F. Westcott wrote of this apparatus, "A marginal commentary also was added, pure and vigorous in style, and if slightly tinged with Calvinistic doctrine, yet on the whole neither unjust nor illiberal." [6] Westcott, of course, meant "unjust nor illiberal" in terms of sixteenth-century England rather than of the Victorian era to which he belonged. When these notes, for instance, are compared with those of Erasmus' Greek and Latin New Testament (1516–18), by comparison they are not only far briefer but even rather anemic as polemics.

It was King James, at the Hampton Court Conference of 1604, who first explicitly attacked the notes of the Geneva version, asserting that this was the worst of all Bibles.[7] As evidence he cited the notes on Exodus 1:19 and 2 Chronicles 15:16, in neither of which was ecclesiastical polity

5. A. F. Pollard, *Records of the English Bible* . . . (Oxford, 1911), 313–29; John Whitgift, *Works* . . . (3 vols., Cambridge, 1851–3; Parker Society), I, 203; II, 13, 410, 524; III, 81, 514–15.

6. B. F. Westcott, *General View of the History of the English Bible*, 3rd ed. revised by W. A. Wright (London, 1922), 229–30.

7. Pollard, *Records of the English Bible*, 46.

involved. The first echoed the biblical text in commending the Hebrew midwives for disobeying their ruler Pharaoh. The second criticized King Asa for merely deposing his idolatrous mother from the regency. The note said the Bible commanded idolators to be put to death. Mary Queen of Scots, James' mother and the "papist" claimant to Elizabeth's throne, had been beheaded in England in 1587 without protest from James, who was then King of Scotland and heir apparent to the English throne. The "King James" version of the Bible (1611) indeed had no notes, but few Bibles have had a longer or more spiteful preface. Not without reason has that preface long since dropped from sight and memory.[8] The Bishops' Bible of 1568 had few notes; but Parker's long preface was an extended polemic against Rome, which placed the Scriptures above all church authority, tradition and teaching, and which reasserted that the primitive church of England had been founded by Joseph of Arimathea, and that the godly King Lucius had been acknowledged by the pope in Rome as God's Vicar in England.[9] No one in that bitterly controversial century supposed that the reader of the Bible should come to it without "proper preparation," whether by way of prefaces, notes, or some other means.

The apparatus of the Geneva Bible, written in full awareness of the mid-sixteenth-century biblical studies and controversies on the Continent, sought to follow a strictly historical and grammatical interpretation. It did not draw upon any one doctrine, such as justification by faith, or the nature of the sacraments, as a theme to hold the Bible in a unity. Rather, the editors sought to portray Jesus Christ as unifying the Scripture in a kind of historical progression from Eden to the Second Coming. Therefore books like the Song of Songs, Daniel and the Revelation had raised problems. Although the editors regarded allegorical interpretation as wrong, they could interpret the Song of Songs in no other way. Daniel and the Revelation were given strictly historical, i.e., "factual" interpretations. They foretold the future. For this reason, in the 1560 and 1576 versions the Revelation had been treated with a certain reserve. The "Junius" version of the Revelation introduced in 1599 expanded this historical interpretation still further, dividing the post-apostolic age into three periods. The eleventh chapter brought events up to the papacy of Boniface VIII. The end of the thousand-year period of chapter 20:3 was equated with the papacy of Gregory VII. The passage in chapter 14:6

8. It is reprinted in Pollard, *Records*, 340–77.
9. It is reprinted in John Strype, *The Life and Acts of Matthew Parker* (Oxford, 1821), III, 236–57; see also II, 212–21.

which told of sending forth angels to preach the gospel, was regarded as fulfilled by Peter Cassiodorus, Occam, Dante, Petrarch, Wycliffe and other preachers and writers who published the gospel anew. There was thus nothing esoteric or allegorical about the Revelation!

This determination to be rigidly factual, grammatical and exact, rather than to propagate "Calvinism," was what spurred the editors of the Geneva Bible, and this same quality commended it to a broad segment of the literate population of England. It was a "modern," not a traditional book. It was factual, not "superstitious." Its apparatus was brief, and useful as a reference. It covered the main points, as Elizabethans understood them. And, as William Haller has so well said, any English layman who had Foxe's Book of Martyrs and the Geneva Bible saw no reason to quail before the learning of a mere bishop whose "learning" was most likely to be in the "popish canon law." The proofs James cited were weak, but from the standpoint of officialdom he was correct in calling this the worst of all Bibles. He was certain that, like Puritanism, it fostered "popularity." It had been designed to do just that.

The text of the prefaces included here has been taken, by permission, from copies at the Henry E. Huntington Library.

Because so much has been written on the Puritans' use of the Geneva Bible, the introduction to each of the documents in this volume that quote any biblical references concludes with a note concerning the version of the Bible used by its author. From these notes it should be clear that among the Puritans the Geneva Bible was regarded as a useful instrument and not as a test of party loyalty.

❖   ❖   ❖   ❖

To the Most Virtuous and Noble Queen Elizabeth, Queen of England, France and Ireland, etc., your humble subjects of the English Church at Geneva, wish grace and peace from God the Father through Christ Jesus our Lord
[1560]

How hard a thing it is and what great impediments let [i.e., hinder], to enterprise any worthy act, not only daily experience sufficiently showeth (most noble and virtuous Queen) but also that notable proverb doth confirm the same, which admonisheth us that all things are hard which are fair and excellent. And what enterprise can there be of greater importance, and more acceptable unto God, or more worthy of singular commendation, than the building of the Lord's temple, the house of God, the church of Christ, whereof the Son of God is the head and perfection?

When Zerubbabel went about to build the material temple according to the commandment of the Lord, what difficulties and stays daily arose to hinder his worthy endeavors the books of Ezra and Esdras plainly witness; how that not only he and the people of God were sore molested with foreign adversaries (whereof some maliciously warred against them and corrupted the king's officers, and others craftily practiced under pretence of religion) but also at home with domestic enemies, as false prophets, crafty worldlings, fainthearted soldiers and oppressors of their brethren, who as well by false doctrine and lies as by subtle counsel, cowardice and extortion, discouraged the hearts almost of all. So that the Lord's work was not only interrupted and left off for a long time, but scarcely at the length with great labor and danger after a sort brought to pass.

Which thing when we weigh aright, and consider earnestly how much greater charge God hath laid upon you in making you a builder of his spiritual temple, we cannot but partly fear, knowing the craft and force of Satan our spiritual enemy and the weakness and inability of this our nature; and partly be fervent in our prayers toward God that he would bring to perfection this noble work which he hath begun by you. And therefore we endeavor ourselves by all means to aid and to bestow our whole force under your Grace's standard, whom God hath made as our Zerubbabel for the erecting of this most excellent temple, and to plant and maintain his holy word to the advancement of his glory, for your own honor and salvation of your soul, and for the singular comfort of that great flock which Christ Jesus the great shepherd hath bought with his precious blood, and committed unto your charge to be fed both in body and soul.

Considering therefore how many enemies there are which by one means or other, as the adversaries of Judah and Benjamin went about to stay the building of that temple (*cf.* Ezra 4:1–2), so labor to hinder the course of this building (whereof some are papists, who under pretence of favoring God's word, traitorously seek to erect idolatry and to destroy your Majesty; some are worldlings, who as Demas have forsaken Christ for the love of this world; others are ambitious prelates, who as Amasiah and Diotrephes can abide none but themselves; and as Demetrius many practice sedition to maintain their errors), we persuaded ourselves that there was no way so expedient and necessary for the preservation of the one and destruction of the other as to present unto your Majesty the holy Scriptures faithfully and plainly translated according to the languages wherein they were first written by the Holy Ghost. For the word of God is an evident token of God's love and our assurance of his defense wheresoever it is obediently received. It is the trial of the spirits; and as the prophet saith, it is as a fire and hammer to break the stony hearts of them that resist God's mercies (*cf.* Jer. 23:29) offered by the preaching of the same. Yea it is sharper than any two-edged sword to examine the very thoughts and to judge the affections of the heart (*cf.* Heb. 4:12), and to discover whatsoever lieth hid under hypocrisy and would be secret from the face of God and his church. So that this must be the first foundation and groundwork according whereunto the good stones of this building must be framed, and the evil tried out and rejected.

Now as he that goeth about to lay a foundation surely first taketh away such impediments as might justly either hurt, let or disform the work, so is it necessary that your Grace's zeal appear herein, that neither the crafty persuasion of man, neither worldly policy or natural fear dissuade you to root out, cut down and destroy these weeds and impediments which do not only deface your building, but utterly endeavor, yea and threaten the ruin thereof. For when the noble Josiah (*cf.* 2 Kings 22:1–23:30; 2 Chron. 34:5) enterprised the like kind of work, among other notable and many things, he destroyed not only with utter confusion the idols with their appurtenances, but also burnt (in sign of detestation) the idolatrous priests' bones upon their altars, and put to death the false prophets and sorcerers, to perform the words of the Law of God. And therefore the Lord gave him good success and blessed him wonderfully, so long as he made God's word his line and rule to follow, and enterprised nothing before he had inquired at the mouth of the Lord.

And if these zealous beginnings seem dangerous and to breed disquietness in your dominions, yet by the story of King Asa [*cf.* 1 Kings 15:9–24] it is manifest that the quietness and peace of kingdoms standeth in the utter abolishing of idolatry, and in advancing of true religion (*cf.* 2 Chron. 14:5). For in his days Judah lived in rest and quietness for the space of five and thirty years, till at length he began to be cold in the zeal of the Lord, feared the power of man, imprisoned the prophet of God, and oppressed the people. Then the Lord sent him wars, and at length took him away by death.

Wherefore great wisdom, not worldly but heavenly, is here required, which your Grace must earnestly crave of the Lord, as did Solomon (*cf.*

1 Kings 3:9), to whom God gave an understanding heart to judge his people aright and to discern between good and bad. For if God for the furnishing of the old temple gave the spirit of wisdom and understanding to them that should be the workmen thereof, as to Bezaleel, Aholiab and Hiram, how much more will he endue your Grace and other godly princes and chief governors with a principal spirit, that you may procure and command things necessary for this most holy temple, foresee and take heed of things that might hinder it, and abolish and destroy whatsoever might impair and overthrow the same?

Moreover the marvellous diligence and zeal of Jehoshaphat, Josiah and Hezekiah are by the singular providence of God left as an example to all godly rulers to reform their countries and to establish the word of God with all speed, lest the wrath of the Lord fall upon them for the neglecting thereof. For these excellent kings did not only embrace the word promptly and joyfully, but also procured earnestly and commanded the same to be taught, preached and maintained through all their countries and dominions, binding them and all their subjects both great and small with solemn protestations and covenants before God to obey the word, and to walk after the ways of the Lord (*cf.* 2 Chron. 34:31). Yea and in the days of King Asa it was enacted that whosoever would not seek the Lord God of Israel should be slain, whether he were small or great, man or woman (*cf.* 2 Chron. 15:13). And for the establishing hereof and performance of this solemn oath, as well priests as judges (*cf.* 2 Chron. 17:7-8, 19:5) were appointed and placed through all the cities of Judah to instruct the people in the true knowledge and fear of God, and to minister justice according to the word, knowing that except God by his word did reign in the hearts and souls, all man's diligence and endeavors were of none effect. For without this word we cannot discern between justice and injury, protection and oppression, wisdom and foolishness, knowledge and ignorance, good and evil. Therefore the Lord, who is the chief governor of his church, willeth that nothing be attempted before we have inquired thereof at his mouth (*cf.* Is. 30:2). For seeing he is our God, of duty we must give him this preeminence, that of ourselves we enterprise nothing but that which he hath appointed, who only knoweth all things, and governeth them as may best serve to his glory and our salvation. We ought not therefore to prevent him, or do anything without his word, but as soon as he hath revealed his will, immediately to put it in execution.

Now as concerning the manner of this building, it is not according to

man, nor after the wisdom of the flesh, but of the Spirit and according to
the word of God, whose ways are diverse from man's ways. For if it was
not lawful for Moses to build the material tabernacle after any other sort
than God had showed him by a pattern (cf. Heb. 8:5), neither to prescribe any other ceremonies and laws than such as the Lord had expressly
commanded (cf. Deut. 5:31–2), how can it be lawful to proceed in this
spiritual building any other ways than Jesus Christ the Son of God, who
is both the foundation, head and chief cornerstone thereof [cf. Eph.
2:20], hath commanded by his word? And forasmuch as he hath established and left an order in his church for the building up of his body, appointing some to be apostles, some prophets, others evangelists, some pastors and teachers (cf. Eph. 4:11), he signifieth that everyone according as
he is placed in this body which is the church, ought to inquire of his
ministers concerning the will of the Lord, which is revealed in his word.
For they are, saith Jeremiah, as the mouth of the Lord (Jer. 15:19); yea
he promiseth to be with their mouth and that their lips shall keep knowledge, and that the truth and the law shall be in their mouth (cf. Mal.
2:7). For it is their office chiefly to understand the Scriptures and teach
them. For this cause the people of Israel in matters of difficulty used to
ask the Lord either by the prophets or by the means of the high priest,
who bore Urim and Thummin (cf. Ex. 28:30), which were tokens of
light and knowledge, of holiness and perfection which should be in the
high priest. Therefore when Jehoshaphat took this order in the church of
Israel, he appointed Amariah to be the chief concerning the word of God
because he was most expert in the law of the Lord, and could give counsel and govern according unto the same. Else there is no degree or office
which may have that authority and privilege to decide concerning God's
word, except withal he hath the Spirit of God, and sufficient knowledge
and judgment to define according thereunto. And as everyone [i.e., any
person] is endued of God with greater gifts, so ought he to be herein
chiefly heard, or at least that without the express word none be heard.
For he that hath not the word speaketh not by the mouth of the Lord.
Again, what danger it is to do anything, seem it never so godly or necessary, without consulting with God's mouth, the examples of the Israelites,
deceived hereby through the Gibeonites (cf. Josh. 9:14), and of Saul
whose intention seemed good and necessary (cf. 1 Sam. 13:11–12), and of
Josiah also, who for great considerations was moved for the defense of
true religion and his people to fight against Pharaoh Necho King of
Egypt (cf. 2 Chron. 35:20), may sufficiently admonish us.

Last of all, most gracious Queen, for the advancement of this building and rearing up of the work, two things are necessary. First, that we have a lively and steadfast faith in Christ Jesus, who must dwell in our hearts (*cf.* Eph. 3:17), as the only means and assurance of our salvation: for he is the ladder that reacheth from the earth to heaven (*cf.* Gen. 28:12); he lifteth up his church and setteth it in the heavenly places [*cf.* Eph. 1:3]; he maketh us lively stones and buildeth us upon himself (*cf.* 1 Pet. 2:5); he joineth us to himself as the members and body to the head; yea he maketh himself and his church one Christ (*cf.* 1 Cor. 12:12). The next is, that our faith bring forth good fruits, so that our godly conversation may serve us as a witness to confirm our election and be an example to all others to walk as appertaineth to the vocation whereunto they are called (*cf.* Eph. 4:1); lest the word of God be evil spoken of, and this building be stayed to grow up to a just height, which cannot be without the great provocation of God's just vengeance and discouraging of many thousands through all the world, if they should see that our life were not holy and agreeable to our profession. For the eyes of all that fear God in all places behold your countries as an example to all that believe, and the prayers of all the godly at all times are directed to God for the preservation of your Majesty. For considering God's wonderful mercies toward you at all seasons, who hath pulled you out of the mouth of the lions, and how that from your youth you have been brought up in the holy Scriptures, the hope of all men is so increased that they cannot but look that God should bring to pass some wonderful work by your Grace to the universal comfort of his church. Therefore even above strength you must show yourself strong and bold in God's matters; and though Satan lay all his power and craft together to hurt and hinder the Lord's building, yet be you assured that God will fight from heaven against this great dragon, the ancient serpent, which is called the devil and Satan (*cf.* Rev. 12:9), till he have accomplished the whole work and made his church glorious to himself, without spot or wrinkle (*cf.* Eph. 5:27). For albeit all other kingdoms and monarchies, as the Babylonians, Persians, Grecians and Romans have fallen and taken end, yet the church of Christ even under the cross hath from the beginning of the world been victorious, and shall be everlastingly. Truth it is that sometime it seemeth to be shadowed with a cloud or driven with a stormy persecution, yet suddenly the beams of Christ the sun of justice shine and bring it to light and liberty. If for a time it lie covered with ashes, yet it is quickly kindled again by the wind of God's Spirit; though it seem drowned in the sea, or parched and pined in the wilderness, yet God giveth ever good success; for he punisheth the enemies, and delivereth his, nourisheth them and still preserveth them under his wings. This Lord of lords and King of kings who hath ever defended his, strengthen, comfort and preserve your Majesty, that you may be able to build up the ruins of God's house to his glory, the discharge of your conscience, and to the comfort of all them that love the coming of Christ Jesus our Lord.

From Geneva, 10 April 1560.

To Our Beloved in the Lord the Brethren of England, Scotland, Ireland, etc., grace, mercy and peace, through Christ Jesus

[1560]

Besides the manifold and continual benefits which Almighty God bestoweth upon us, both corporal and spiritual, we are especially bound, dear brethren, to give him thanks without ceasing for his great grace and unspeakable mercies, in that it hath pleased him to call us unto this marvelous light of his gospel, and mercifully to regard us after so horrible backsliding and falling away from Christ to Antichrist, from light to darkness, from the living God to dumb and dead idols, and that after so cruel murder of God's saints, as, alas, hath been among us, we are not altogether cast off, as were the Israelites and many others for the like, or not so manifest wickedness, but received again to grace with most evident signs and tokens of God's especial love and favor. To the intent therefore that we may not be unmindful of these great mercies, but seek by all means (according to our duty) to be thankful for the same, it behooveth us so to walk in his fear and love, that all the days of our life we may procure the glory of his holy name. Now forasmuch as this thing chiefly is attained by the knowledge and practicing of the word of God (which is the light to our paths, the key of the kingdom of heaven, our comfort in affliction, our shield and sword against Satan, the school of all wisdom, the glass wherein we behold God's face, the testimony of his favor, and the only food and nourishment of our souls) we thought that we could bestow our labors and study in nothing which could be more acceptable to God and comfortable to his church than in the translating of the holy Scriptures into our native tongue: the which thing, albeit that divers

heretofore have endeavored to achieve: yet considering the infancy of
those times and imperfect knowledge of the tongues, in respect of this
ripe age and clear light which God hath now revealed, the translations required greatly to be perused and reformed. Not that we vindicate anything to ourselves above the least of our brethren (for God knoweth with
what fear and trembling we have been now, for the space of two years
and more day and night occupied herein) but being earnestly desired, and
by divers, whose learning and godliness we reverence, exhorted, and also
encouraged by the ready wills of such, whose hearts God likewise
touched, not to spare any charges for the furtherance of such a benefit
and favor of God toward his church (though the time then was most
dangerous and the persecution sharp and furious), we submitted ourselves
at length to their godly judgments, and seeing the great opportunity and
occasions which God presented unto us in this church, by reason of so
many godly and learned men: and such diversities of translations in divers
tongues, we undertook this great and wonderful work (with all reverence, as in the presence of God, as entreating the word of God, whereunto we think ourselves insufficient) which now God according to his
divine providence and mercy hath directed to a most prosperous end.
And this we may with good conscience protest, that we have in every
point and word, according to the measure of that knowledge which it
pleased Almighty God to give us, faithfully rendered the text, and in all
hard places most sincerely expounded the same. For God is our witness
that we have by all means endeavored to set forth the purity of the word
and right sense of the Holy Ghost for the edifying of the brethren in
faith and charity.

Now as we have chiefly observed the sense, and labored always to restore it to all integrity: so have we most reverently kept the propriety of
the words, considering that the apostles who spake and wrote to the Gentiles in the Greek tongue, rather constrained them to the lively phrase of
the Hebrew than enterprised far by mollifying their language to speak as
the Gentiles did. And for this and other causes we have in many places
reserved the Hebrew phrases, notwithstanding that they may seem somewhat hard in their ears that are not well practiced and also delight in the
sweet sounding phrases of the holy Scriptures. Yet lest either the simple
should be discouraged, or the malicious have any occasion of just cavilla-
tion, seeing some translations read after one sort and some after another,
whereas all may serve to good purpose and edification, we have in the
margin noted that diversity of speech or reading which may also seem

agreeable to the mind of the Holy Ghost and proper for our language with this mark '' .

Again whereas the Hebrew speech seemed hardly to agree with ours, we have noted it in the margin after this sort '' , using that which was more intelligible. And albeit that many of the Hebrew names be altered from the old text, and restored to the true writing and first original whereof they have their signification, yet in the usual names little is changed for fear of troubling the simple readers. Moreover whereas the necessity of the sentence required anything to be added (for such is the grace and propriety of the Hebrew and Greek tongues that it cannot but either by circumlocution, or by adding the verb or some words be understood of them that are not well practiced therein) we have put it in the text with another kind of letter, that it may easily be discerned from the common letter. As touching the division of the verses, we have followed the Hebrew examples, which have so even from the beginning distinct [i.e., distinguished] them. Which thing as it is most profitable for memory, so doth it agree with the best translations, and is most easy to find out both by the best concordances, and also by the quotations which we have diligently herein perused and set forth by this star * . Besides this the principal matters are noted and distincted by this mark ¶ . Yea and the arguments both for the book and for the chapters with the number of the verse are added, that by all means the reader might be helped. For the which cause also we have set over the head of every page some notable word or sentence which may greatly further as well for memory as for the chief point of the page. And considering how hard a thing it is to understand the holy Scriptures, and what errors, sects and heresies grow daily for lack of the true knowledge thereof, and how many are discouraged (as they pretend) because they cannot attain to the true and simple meaning of the same, we have also endeavored both by the diligent reading of the best commentaries, and also by the conference with the godly and learned brethren, to gather brief annotations upon all the hard places, as well for the understanding of such words as are obscure and for the declaration of the text, as for the application of the same as may most appertain to God's glory and the edification of his church. Furthermore whereas certain places in the books of Moses, of the Kings and Ezekiel seemed so dark that by no description they could be made easy to the simple reader, we have so set them forth with figures and notes for the full declaration thereof, that they which cannot by judgment, being helped by the annotations noted by the letters a, b, c, etc., attain thereunto, yet by the perspective, and as it were by the eye, may sufficiently know the true meaning of all such places. Whereunto also we have added certain maps of cosmography which necessarily serve for the perfect understanding and memory of divers places and countries, partly described, and partly by occasion touched, both in the Old and New Testament. Finally, that nothing might lack which might be bought by labors for the increase of knowledge and furtherance of God's glory, we have adjoined two most profitable tables, the one serving for the interpretation of the Hebrew names, and the other containing all the chief and principal matters of the whole Bible; so that nothing (as we trust) that any could justly desire, is omitted. Therefore, as brethren that are partakers of the same hope and salvation with us, we beseech you, that this rich pearl and inestimable treasure may not be offered in vain, but as sent from God to the people of God, for the increase of his kingdom, the comfort of his church, and discharge of our conscience, whom it hath pleased him to raise up for this purpose, so you would willingly receive the word of God, earnestly study it and in all your life practice it, that you may now appear indeed to be the people of God, not walking any more according to this world, but in the fruits of the Spirit, that God in us may be fully glorified through Christ Jesus our Lord, who liveth and reigneth forever. Amen. From Geneva, 10 April 1560.

To the Right Honorable M. Francis Walsingham Esquire, One of the principal Secretaries to her excellent Majesty, and of her Highness' Privy Council; and to the Right Worshipful M. Francis Hastings, L. T. wisheth prosperity in this life and life everlasting, in Christ our Savior

[1576]

If I had to render a reason of this my travail in translating into our mother tongue that that hath been fruitfully labored and put forth in the Latin to the great commodity and profit of such to whom our good God hath given understanding therein, I might truly and justly say it was for my poor brethren's sake, which want [i.e., lack] the blessing before said, for the [lack of] understanding of the Latin, and yet have great riches of the Lord in that he hath given them the benefit to understand and read their own [language]. For as the sun which shineth upon the just and unjust was not made for the benefit of our country only but of all the world, nor the Son of God sent into the world for the Jews only but also for the Gentiles, part of whom we are (for he shut us all under unbelief that he might have mercy upon all), so neither were the Scriptures left for the Grecian only but for the barbarian also, both for the wise and unwise, both for the learned and unlearned of what nation and tongue soever they were, that we altogether through patience and comfort of the holy Scripture might have hope. For so far have the Scriptures of duty to go as the apostles had commandment to preach, and in so many tongues should the apostles preach as by their gift from above they might. And as they themselves are in this sort to be applied to our use, through the gift of tongues which God doth still pour upon his church (though not after the same sort as at the first), even so, whatsoever holy men have written upon them through his unspeakable mercies and by the working of his Holy Spirit in our tongue, ought likewise by the same gift be divided to the profit of the brethren elsewhere, which differ in tongue but agree in unity of faith. For so it cometh to pass that we communicate one with another's benefits, and be come to have a fellowship in those things which otherwise seemed to be several [i.e., unique] to some one of us. This benefit of God for his part, and consideration of every one of our duties for our parts, brought the Scriptures themselves first out of Judea and the Hebrew tongue into Greece and the language of that country, though not so happily as might be wished, from thence to the Romans and into the Latin tongue, and so through the loving visitation of our God into Dutch [i.e., German], French, English, Italian and so forth, which no man repineth at (that Antichrist of Rome only except[ed] who hateth the light because he is not of the light but of darkness, as his father the prince of darkness, the devil is) but all that love God and fear God most humbly thank him for, as obedient and dutiful children showing their obedience toward him in studying in his law both day and night.

And as our brethren and saints of God have done for our behoof in this point touching the Scriptures, so have they done for the works of good fathers and prophets, causing them to speak familiarly to us, as home-born children with us which otherwise were plants of Palestine and grafts of Greece and citizens of the Latins. All this I say for our profit, that we might taste and feel how loving and merciful our God is, and what in part that communion of saints is which we so oft recite and so constantly believe at this present, and shall I trust to the end, when belief shall cease and God shall be all in all. For this we confess and believe all, that wheresoever we are and into how many countries of the world soever we are scattered, we are but one church, we make but one body, we have but one Head, and but one Spirit. If God raise up a prophet in our country as he did at the first in Judea, his mind is that the words of this his own prophet shall be profitable to the whole body, as well the foot which is the furthest part as the heart that is the nearer shall receive nourishment and increase of strength by it. And for this end and purpose he divideth divers gifts unto this body, that the nourishment which seemeth to be so far off may be brought nearer, yea, and so near that each member may live thereby. So that the gift received layeth a burden upon him that hath received it, and it is no more in his power to do or not do, but he must of necessity do, for the profit of God's church, according to the measure of that gift which God hath given him, remembering always with himself that our God is a wary and heedie [i.e., careful] giver, and looketh for an account, because he tendreth [i.e., deals tenderly with] his children. He made us not for ourselves but for our brethren, and so long shall we be here as he hath appointed our brethren to reap commodity by us. If we will seem to make a property of that which ought to be common, and keep it to ourselves as our own which is not ours but our brethren's, the Lord is faithful, who will not be slack to punish our unfaithfulness and to render us the recompense of our faithless dealing both towards him and them. This was one reason no doubt, and not the least, which moved the fathers in old time and our good fathers of this our blessed age yet living amongst us, to do as they did and do still, by publishing those things which they have received of God for us and not for themselves. And hereupon was this our godly brother and father [i.e., Beza] whom we think worthy all reverence in the Lord, not only satisfied to put these his notes forth in the Latin tongue, but desired also some of our godly brethren to communicate them with his countrymen in their own language [i.e., French], which as it hath been godly intended so I am sure it will be performed as the Lord will.

Which thing was no small moving to me, considering as great want in mine own countrymen, and as great profit which may I trust rise unto them by it if they can be as content to take pains to read as I have taken the labor to write, only for conscience sake, and in the fear of God, to make them partakers of that commodity which I myself and many more of my learned brethren have felt by this so singular a blessing of our merciful Father and Lord God, through the tender care that this most reverend father and loving brother, Theodore Beza, had of us. This I thought myself of duty bound unto, being no otherways so presently able to help them, not minding to prevent any other men's doing, for I heard not of any that was or would go about it, but tendering only the profit of the more simple and unlearned which are as desirous of instruction as I would instruction were ready for them, and respecting that that I must be called to an account for in the day of our Lord Jesus.

This reason of my doing I say I have to give and testify to all the world, if it be not so much as I might have done, as happily some will say: I stay myself upon the testimony of a good conscience before God, being assured that herein I have not done amiss, craving pardon at the Lord's hands for all my wants, as well of duty, as of other things in what other respects and parts of my life soever. What profit shall come of it, I leave that to the Lord, for neither the planter nor the waterer is anything, but God that giveth the increase [cf. 1 Cor. 3:7], and yet I doubt not but it shall do that good which the Lord hath appointed it for. The enemies will take occasion to stumble at it and that is one profit, for Christ was made for the fall of many [cf. Lk. 2:34]; others I trust shall receive comfort by it, for the same is a savior to his. As all men have not faith, so all men shall not receive it, and therein as no man can marvel. So I cannot be grieved, for they that are such are prepared to destruction. Only my purpose was, and mine earnest prayer to God is, that if not all, yet many may receive comfort of it to their immortality. As for the rest, if the Lord hath so appointed it that I should be a savor of death unto death to them, and this my pains taken should be a furtherance to their hardening, as I go not about to seek out his unspeakable counsels, so all laud and praise be to his name for it. Howbeit, I determine of none, but unto them that have this sign of reprobation, this I say, and I call heaven and earth to witness against them this day, that if they go on forward in this striving against God they shall undoubtedly perish, and this my labor shall be a witness against them in that day. For he that refuseth to hear the word preached and will not read it, if God have given him that gift that he may read it, pronounceth sentence against himself, that he is none of the children of God, that he is none of the sheep of Christ, that he hath no part of inheritance in that kingdom which was prepared for us before the beginning of the world. For doth not Christ say, "My sheep hear my voice" [Jn. 10:27], and doth not Paul say, "Faith is by hearing and hearing by the word of God" [Rom. 10:17]? We are not Christ's then if we will not hear, and we cannot have faith if the word do not sound unto us. And look where faith is not, there is no Christianity, there is no life, there is no salvation; and if no life, if no salvation, then no Christ, no God. For "God is not the God of the dead but of the living" [Mt. 22:32]; and live without faith we cannot, and to have faith without the word it is impossible, as the apostle speaketh of the ordinary way of our salvation. If it otherways fall out by way of revelation, it is rather by way of miracle and of a special grace, which may not cause us to tempt the Lord in forsaking his appointed way.

David, speaking of the blessedness of the happy man (and there is no happy man but the child of God), setteth down this (we know) as a chiefest point of his happiness, that he studieth upon the law of the Lord both day and night [cf. Ps. 1:2]. And this is not left unto us as a point to be ordered at our discretion, as who would say we may be happy with it and we may be blessed without it. No, not so. It is a thing very requisite and necessary for them which have the gift, as without which they shall not be blessed. For how can we receive a gift of the Lord and not give an account for it? And what is he so void of the Spirit of God that knoweth not how he must repent him of his slackness in using any good blessing of God, and call for pardon and mercy that his negligence may not be imputed to him? And is there any repentance without a sin? Can I crave pardon at God's hands for that wherein I have not offended? Thy very calling for mercy (O man) whatsoever thou art, argueth and telleth thy conscience thou hast sinned therein, and if thou see, it must be so at thy latter end if God give thee space and grace to repent, consider it betime with thyself, make thy reckoning now, that if thou wilt be blessed thou must meditate and study in the Scriptures of thy Lord and God both day and night. If thou remember the recreation of thy body with some lawful pleasures, forget not the refreshing of thy soul with this heavenly food. Let not God's goodness towards thee in giving thee some liberty cause thee to become unmindful and ungrate[ful] to him, and deadly enemy to thyself. Our dutifulness herein and how much God requireth at our hands, is set forth herein, that in the law written by Moses all fathers are commanded to teach it [to] their children, to speak of it sitting at home and going abroad, to write it upon the posts of their houses, to make them frontlets of it and hems of their garments [cf. Deut. 6:6–9]. And shall we think that this law perished with them? Because we are not Jews are we not therefore God's people? No doubt it is written for our instruction, for all things that are written, saith the apostle, are written for our learning [cf. Rom. 15:4]. And what then shall we learn hereby, yea what thing must we learn hereby: but as we have heard and read in

David that if we will be blessed we must meditate in it both day and night [cf. Ps. 1:2], both for ourselves and for our children, for our brethren, for our families. Hereupon also the apostle reneweth the commandment and refresheth the charge to all Christians of what estate, order, calling, condition soever they be, saying, "Let the word of God dwell in you plenteously in all wisdom" [Col. 3:16].

Hearken, you loathsome hearts, and give ear, you that will needs bear about with you this open mark of reprobation: think you that this is spoken to you? For if you be not within the compass of this saying of the apostle you are not within the compass of everlasting life. Are you, or do you take yourselves to be, of the number of them in whom the word of God must dwell plenteously: How shall it come to dwell in you? How shall it take possession of you? Can you tell what dwelling meaneth? It is to have full possession, and a mansion house in you, to sit and rest there, to rule and govern there, as you do in your houses and places of your own abode. And how shall this be but by that ordinary means which God hath appointed you, which is by reading and hearing? It cometh not by idleness and worldly vanities, it cometh not by dicing and carding, dancing and dalliance, it cometh not by chambering and wantonness. This is not the way to have the word of God to dwell in you. You must search the Scriptures? Do you think to have eternal life? You must look into them: "Search the Scriptures," saith Christ, "for they bear witness of me" [cf. Jn. 5:39]. But you pass not for him. If you did, you would never be so careless of yourselves and careful to serve the devil.

I say you are careful to serve the devil when you rise up early and go late to bed, when you leave no labor nor pains to seek after the pleasures of the flesh and cannot abide to hear of the Word. You cannot abide, I say, once to look upon it. It is death to you to hear a preacher once in a twelvemonth. And yet you will be called Abraham's children. He that should say otherways of you should have the defiance given him. But the truth is, you are not his children unless you follow his steps. And what saith the Scripture of him? "I know that he will command his sons and his household after him, that they keep the way of the Lord" (Gen. 18:19). Which of you hath a care to that? Or how can you have a care to it if you know them not? And how can you know them without reading or preaching? Cornelius was a true child of Abraham; he feared God and all his household. So was Eunice, Timothy's mother, and Lois his grandmother, and see what her practice was, being but a woman. She nourished up her son in the words of faith and of good doctrine [cf. 2

Tim. 1:5]. Which of you can bring up his child in doctrine and knoweth none himself? Or how wilt thou have thy child follow that which thou hatest thyself? It cannot be. Such grapes cannot be gathered of such thorns, nor such figs of these thistles.

They of Berea were right children of Abraham and famous fellows, so saith the Scripture; and why so? For "they received the word with all readiness and searched the Scriptures daily, whether those things were so" (Acts 17:11). Why then you are but bastards, and no children. Shameful is your name and hateful to all the world. For where is your readiness in receiving the word? Where is your daily searching the Scriptures? "Give attendance to reading" (1 Tim. 4:13), saith Paul to Timothy, and again, continue in learning "for in doing this thou shalt both save thyself and them that hear thee" (1 Tim. 4:16). And this is not a precept for ministers only, but generally for all men. "For thou shalt save thyself," saith he. Others I am sure will be partakers of salvation as well as they [i.e., ministers]. It is not proper to them only to be saved, no more it is to them also to read the Scriptures. So then if it be a commandment to him, it is to us all, because we will all be saved. Wilt thou be saved then? Then must thou read and hear the Scriptures? Thou must have it dwell plenteously in thee. By dwelling plenteously the apostle meaneth thou must be cunning and perfected in it, both for the knowledge of it to instruct thyself and others, and also for the framing of thy life after it. To you it is, to you I say, which are not ministers, whom the apostle speaketh unto, to you that are troubled with worldly affairs, you especially must read the Scriptures and read them with great diligence. The more enemies a man hath the better he ought to be armed. None have more enemies than the worldly men. Which of you goeth forth to battle and putteth not on his armor? The armed commonly overcome and are saved, and not the unarmed. And who needeth the physician more than he that is most wounded? I will not enter into comparison whether [i.e., which] of you is in most danger, the minister, I mean, or the other that is no minister.

I would rather wish you to consider it yourselves, that so by entering into yourselves you might feel what need of armor you have, what need of a physician. But this I will say, because you feel it to your smart, where it pleaseth God to visit you. When any temptation falleth upon you, as if it please the Lord to strike you with sickness, with lameness, to take away your children, your goods and those things which you love best, instead of comforting yourselves and humbly submitting yourselves to the mighty hand of God, you fall to murmuring against him, you fall to desperation, you remain comfortless, you cannot raise up your own hearts nor the hearts of your brethren which are proved with the like temptation. What a lamentable case is it to see one of you haters and despisers of the word of God to come to a sick man to comfort him, yea to your own wives and children, to your friends and acquaintance. Miserable is the comfort, God wot [i.e., knows], that you give him. You stand like blocks and stocks not knowing how to direct him, thus showing forth your condemnation, being nearer to hell than he is to the grave, and to everlasting death than he is to this bodily death. You can pretend no excuse but only that you are not learned, and why are you not learned (I speak to you that can read), seeing you have the Scriptures in your own tongue? Your common pretence in former times hath been because they were hard. Though that excuse be none, for some of you that can read have travailed in harder, I am sure.

And for the rest, this I say, that the harder it is the more pains you ought to have bestowed in it. For if you be resolved as you ought to be that you are bound to know your Father's will, the hardness of it may not cause you to forsake your duty. I will refer you but to your own judgments. What is he amongst you that if, in his father's last will and testament, by the benefit whereof he looketh to enjoy his father's lands, there were some one clause hard, would not you be diligent in searching it out, by reading and reading again, by conferring with other more learned than himself, by having the judgment of the best lawyers? So that in our causes or earthly matters, hardness cannot cause us to slack our duties, but rather cause us to use more diligence. So should it be, yea, so would it be in this will and testament whereby our hope is to come to the inheritance of everlasting life, if any one clause of it should be hard, that should not cause a hardness of heart to cast off the care of the whole and utterly to surcease from looking upon it. But this showeth, as I said, what we are. For if we were children and not bastards we would have as great a care to it for all the hardness as we have to an earthly will.

Well it hath pleased God in this our latter age to remove this cloak, the Scriptures are made plain unto us, and this New Testament, by these notes of Beza, so plain both for the meaning itself of every sentence and for the plain light of every word and kind of speech, that no man can pretend that former excuse. I dare avouch it, and whoso readeth it shall so find it, that there is not one hard sentence nor dark speech nor doubtful word but is so open and hath such light given it that children may go through with it, and the simplest that are may walk without any guide, without wandering and going astray. So that if thou wilt not still harden thine own heart and purchase wrath unto thyself against the day of wrath [*cf.* Rom. 2:5], thou must now come and take better ways and show forth better fruits than thou hast done. But happily, thou wilt pretend corruption and say that the Scriptures are falsified with these corrections and marred with these glosses. Thus indeed Antichrist saith. But thou hast to follow the counsel of the Holy Ghost by the mouth of the apostles: "Try the spirits, whether they be of God or no" [*cf.* 1 Jn. 4:1]. Thou must examine them and confer them first with the Scriptures before thou condemn them, for so did they of Berea, and so did the Samaritans, as we read in John [? 4:39–42?]. For unless thou hear Christ himself speak in his word and confer those things that are laid before thee with the Scripture, thou shalt be deceived. Thou knowest even in worldly affairs, for a man to condemn another before he have heard him is a great point of rashness and disallowed of all men; and he that will give his judgment upon a matter before he have well weighed it carrieth about him the name of a fool. But if according to the hardness of thine heart which cannot repent thou wilt not come to better ways, and meanest to remain still in like loathing of the Scriptures, and for slacking thy duty therein as thou hast done in former times: I pronounce the wrath and vengeance of God against thee and tell thee from the Lord's mouth, thou shalt have no part in the inheritance of the righteous.

And as for you, my poor brethren, which have tasted and felt the loving mercies of our good and gracious Lord and Father, and have entered into a league with him to take him to be your God as he hath taken you to be his people, receive you this benefit of the Lord, as my trust is you will, with joyful hearts; be mindful to give thanks to the Lord for this worthy brother of ours and pray for his continuance amongst us in his church, that we may be further enriched by his means and receive greater comforts of the Lord by the hands of his servant. I will not stand to commend this work unto you, both for the faithfulness of the translation and for the singular profit of the notes; the commodity which I know undoubtedly you shall reap thereby will commend it sufficiently to your godly hearts. The thankfulness that you can show both to God for him, and to him for his pains, is the diligent and painful reading of that which he hath diligently and painfully written. If otherwise it should fall out, which I hope will not, you should fall into the condemnation of the wicked and turn this blessing of the Lord to your hurt and destruction.

And as you shall think yourselves bound to him for thus opening the

Scriptures of God unto you, so be you mindful to pray for them by whose godly means they come to your hands. This door hath been shut up a great while, you know.[1] Be thankful therefore to God, and pray for the long life and happy reign of our most dreadful sovereign, Elizabeth, by God's gracious and loving mercies towards this his church of England, our most lawful and only prince, our true anointed of the Lord and mother of this Israel. As the Lord hath preserved her Majesty mightily these years passed from the traitorous treasons of traitorous and blood-thirsty dissembling hypocrites' hearts, so it may please him to continue his fatherly protection towards her, and discover all counterfeits and pluck away all vizards from their faces, that her Majesty may see indeed who are her enemies, and he through his mighty power confound and bring them to shame that either with heart or hand intend or mean anything against her. And let all such as fear the Lord say with David touching God's enemies and her Majesty's: "Pour out thy wrath, O Lord, upon the people that have not known thee, and upon the kingdoms that have not called upon thy name" (Ps. 79:6).

Be thankful also and pray for the honorable Council, by whose good means under her Majesty you enjoy this benefit,[2] and shall do greater if with thankful hearts you turn unfeignedly to the Lord, and pray for the increasing of his graces in them whom he hath placed as under-shepherds over this his house of Israel. And for mine own part, as I shall, I trust, remain mindful all the days of my life with earnest and hearty prayer, first, for her Majesty and her long and blessed reign over us with all peace and quietness, to the destruction of all her enemies both open and dissembling, which seek their own wealth more than her Majesty's health, and next, for her most honorable Council, that as good fathers they may rule over us as children and not as servants.

So to your Honor, as I am most bound, I present this testimony of mine hearty goodwill and meaning towards you, being ready to perform all the dutifulness to your Honor which the Lord shall give me, both in prayer to him for your health and increase of zeal to the maintenance of his kingdom, which is the only project of your Honor and the mark you have to shoot at. And as in duty I have and am bound to your Worship, for the great courtesies I have received of you not a few years and for the fear of God which I see in you, which the Lord increase to the honor

---

1. [ED.] Tomson seems to assert that the Geneva Bible had been suppressed.

2. [ED.] Seven Privy Councillors had approved the printing of this N. T. while the see of Canterbury was vacant.

of his name and to be a light to the brethren, so I join you herein, in one poor and simple remembrance of my goodwill, being not able by several gifts to show how much I think myself in debt to you. The thing itself I know is great, but my labor but small, for my chiefest respect was to further and help the more simple sort. God grant it may be profitable to them and that his children may reap that commodity by it which my prayer is they shall. Then shall I think myself blessed of the Lord and thank him heartily for his fatherly goodness towards me, with earnest prayer to him for your Honor and Worship, that his peace may remain upon you forever, and upon all the Israel of God.

PART THREE

❖

The Presbyterian Party

WILLIAM FULKE

Editor's Introduction

If indeed it is true that theology is always problem-oriented and problem-solving, seeking to face the challenge of the changing culture within which the church lives and ministers, it is also true that the discussion and elaboration of the church's order or polity never takes place in a vacuum. Those Puritans who wrote on church structure and polity, did so not as exercises in abstract theory, but in the form of tracts proving that reform (i.e. "godly discipline") could be achieved only after the existing "system" had been supplanted by a new one deliberately designed to produce the desired reforms.

In the England of late 1558, when Elizabeth came to the throne, the attitude toward church reform was dominated by three concerns inherited from the three previous reigns: clerical wickedness, clerical failures and social change.

For those who sought to deal with clerical wickedness, the main focus was on the approximately 250 ecclesiastical courts in England, whose jurisdiction covered a vast range — heresy, marriage, morals, penance, censorship of the press, probate of wills, church attendance, and respect for the clergy, among many other things — and which had the power to summon, try, fine, imprison or deliver to the civil power for beheading or burning. Throughout the entire Tudor-Stuart era, nothing in the church aroused more hatred than these church courts, whether the officials in charge were Catholic or Protestant. Nowhere was the demand for reform more insistent — or more futile.[1]

The problem of clerical failure was most evident at the parish level —

1. C. Hill, *Society and Puritanism in Pre-Revolutionary England* (London, 1964), 298–419; R. A. Marchant, *The Puritans and the Church Courts in the Diocese of York, 1560–1642* (London, 1960).

in the poorly trained clergy, non-residence, pluralism, lack of preaching or instruction, and the virtual abdication of the cure of souls to the ecclesiastical bureaucracy of the courts. These nationwide failures, which were defended or ignored by the hierarchy on the grounds of the uniqueness of the clerical order and its sacred prerogatives, provided much of the background for the reformers' attacks upon the wickedness of the clergy.

In Tudor England, social change was seen largely in terms of social ills. The phenomenon of change in itself was difficult to cope with, either intellectually or emotionally. Changes that were found desirable were usually explained away as merely the restoration of some historic good. Changes that worked out badly proved that change was a sign of decay, bringing with it loss and privation, and was thus a thing to be opposed. Reform had accordingly been difficult for the English under Henry, Edward and Mary.

The inadequacy of the old order had been well understood by Thomas Cromwell, who had introduced many changes in the nation. Somerset had attempted others. Likewise Cranmer, with a group of scholars, had worked out a far-reaching revision of the church law. Bucer, in his *De Regno Christi*, had drafted a comprehensive scheme for bringing England under "the reign of Christ." Latimer, Hooper, Lever, Knox and others had preached a wide range of desirable reforms. The writings of Simon Fish, Christopher St. German, Henry Brinkelow and Crowley (to mention only a few) had touched upon most of the problems of the times. However, neither the lay nor the ecclesiastical authorities had wished to risk their interests or positions on behalf of much actual reform. So the lay power, the Crown, the courtiers and Parliament had exploited the popular frustration as a means of depriving the clergy of all power of independent action — and this had been presented to the people as "reform." Such channeling of popular discontent into anticlericalism was to become a habit in English public life, one that would be invoked again and again by groups demanding reform of the church, and one that was also to frustrate most attempts to achieve it. That after 1532-4 the clergy had lost the actual ability to reform the church was used as proof, for more than a century afterward, that they had no wish to reform themselves. Their loss of independent jurisdiction in 1532-4 made the hierarchy so defensive towards the laity, especially those who were vocally anticlerical, that repeated efforts by laymen to initiate reforms were automatically opposed by the hierarchy, simply on the grounds of prerogative.

Reform in England was dogged also by the great diversity of the society — geographic, economic and social. In 1558 the people of Wales and the north of England scarcely belonged to the same world as the vigorous bourgeoisie of London. The hierarchical society of nobles, patrons, clients and suppliants could either hinder or aid reform. Fear of the lower classes dominated reformers as well as opponents of reform.

So in the thirty years from the fall of Wolsey to the accession of Elizabeth (1529–58), religious reform had been in large measure a process of freeing the laity from clerical control or "tyranny." Very little attention had been given to the internal problems of the church, or to the control of the higher clerics over other clergy. The Elizabethan Settlement again increased the freedom of laymen from clerical controls, but again did little or nothing to affect the canon law, church courts, church finances, pluralism, non-residence, or the abuse of hierarchical control over clerics. In short, what was then called "the church" had seen little reform. The attempt, in 1559 and again in 1571, by Thomas Norton — common lawyer, M.P., son-in-law of Archbishop Cranmer and translator of Calvin's *Institutes* — to bring about the adoption of Cranmer's revised canon law, the *Reformatio Legum Ecclesiasticarum*, was rejected.[2] So were Thomas Sampson's efforts towards implementing Bucer's *De Regno Christi*.[3] Such schemes would have reestablished or augmented clerical power. Once Convocation had rejected the very mild proposals for reform made in 1563, church reform by churchmen was a lost cause. Once that loss had occurred, there was little likelihood that "church reform" against lay interests would ever be instituted by Parliament. Thus the movement for reform became even more anticlerical.

It was a misfortune for the church that in 1566 Parker and the English officials chose so dubious an issue as that of clerical vestments on which to stake the church's right to order its own affairs. The radical Protestants, lay and clerical, who might have aided the Protestant bishops in bringing about church reform were thus turned against them. By the same token, the anticlerical opportunists (a far from powerless group) had been given a standard to wave — the hated vestiarian signs of the papal, clerical order with its now useless claims. Parker and his colleagues were assailed for tyrannically insisting upon status symbols while avoiding true reform, by many opponents who themselves had no interest in reform. Yet the very

2. John Neale, *Elizabeth I and Her Parliaments, 1559–81* (London, 1953), 63, 89, 194–7.
3. John Strype, *Annals of the Reformation . . .* (Oxford, 1824), I, ii, 150.

intemperance of the vestment controversy itself made the insignia of clerical office appear a psychological necessity for the hard-pressed clerical
party; and so Parker himself asserted the vestments were a means of improving public esteem of the clergy. But this was not reform of the
church, nor was it a movement towards reform. So, in 1566, following
the vestment controversy, when six bills for church reform were brought
into Commons (the "alphabet bills" A to F, dealing with theology,
preaching, non-residence and finances), the bishops as a body assured
Elizabeth that this was not their doing. The bills lost as a result of action
by the Queen. And in the stormy Parliaments of 1571 and 1572 the same
bills, along with others promoting reforms in the church, were once again
defeated.

None of the attempts at reform made in Convocation or Parliament
between 1559 and 1572 would have altered basically the structure or polity of the church. All the proposals made in these official bodies were for
reforms within the existing structure, along lines laid down in Edward's
reign by Cranmer, Bucer, Ridley or some other by now venerated hero
whose devotion to the English church was unquestioned. Following the
defeat of the Puritan party in the Parliament of 1572, the situation
changed. For the next ninety years (up until 1662), the "parliamentary
interest" was set against the "church interest," and most efforts in Parliament to bring about church reform assumed that radical institutional
change was a prerequisite to actual reform. Moreover, it was increasingly
assumed that "church reform" was being prevented by episcopal self-in-
terest. At the same time, the public image of the bishops was so bad that
for a century to come many a lay politician successfully condemned them
for what they could not, and what the politician would not, have
changed: pluralism, non-residence, appropriations, misuse of church property, etc. Moreover, since the 1530s most English politicians had come to
regard bishops as royal servants rather than as the divinely designated successors of the Apostles towards whom God required laymen to be obedient. Even bishops as able as Whitgift became so intent on upholding clerical prerogatives that they defended abuses that were indefensible rather
than allow laymen in Parliament to mend them — even when these same
bishops knew that the clergy themselves were powerless to do so. Martin
Marprelate in 1588-9 could easily make capital out of bishops who
prized clerical prerogatives more than church reform. This is the miserable context in which the long battles from 1572 to 1643 over church pol-

ity and structure must be studied. Those battles did not break out in a vacuum.

For political and ecclesiastical — as well as theological — reasons, nothing in early Elizabethan religion was quite so sacred as the primitive church. Upon it was hung the entire case of English religion against Rome, whether that case was argued by the Queen, by Bishop Jewel, by John Foxe, or by any other spokesman. It was ironic that early in 1570 Thomas Cartwright, newly appointed Lady Margaret Professor at Cambridge, should have chosen to lecture on the primitive church as described in the Book of Acts. Before he had gotten through the sixth chapter, Whitgift, who was then vice-chancellor, had him removed from office. Cartwright's biblical findings, as such, were not novel. He found in the much idealized primitive church no archbishops, no archdeacons, no episcopal chancellors, no ecclesiastical court system, no clerical order existing apart from some particular office or duty, and no clerical status that could be "sought" by an interested individual and "conferred" by some bishop. The ministry was an office in the church that could be conferred only through election by the people of the church. Not much else could be deduced on church polity from the early chapters of the Acts. But because of the omnipresent argument concerning the primitive church, Cartwright's method of "returning to the sources" was, as Whitgift wrote to Burghley, dangerous and tending towards schism.[4]

In 1572, as officialdom once more ground down all Puritan demands for reform, John Field and Thomas Wilcox, who were both still in their early twenties, published an open letter known as the [First] Admonition to the Parliament. This ably and cleverly written piece of propaganda heralded a significant development in Puritan attitudes and in the history of English religion. A new generation impatient with the entire old order had been coming to the conclusion that the wrongs in church and society were caused by "the system" and that no improvement could be hoped for until the source of the wrong had been removed. Moreover, since the system had to be destroyed, there was no reason to debate learnedly about it. So in racy English the Admonition scornfully compared the church of England with the true primitive church. With a liberal use of "then" and "now," the pomposity of the English prelates was contrasted with the simplicity of the early apostles, the difficult compromises of the

4. A. F. Scott Pearson, *Thomas Cartwright and Elizabethan Puritanism, 1535–1603* (Cambridge, 1925), 26 f.

Elizabethan Settlement with the stark ideology of the early New Testament church, the abuses, foibles and miscarriages of the Elizabethan official church with the rigorous discipline revealed in the Book of Acts; the "venerable and laudable ancient customs of our church" were ridiculed in the light of the rejection by the "truly primitive" church of Jewish and pagan ceremonialism. Almost every wrong and error was laid to the system, and especially to the tyrannical and popish prelates who maintained it as a vested interest.[5]

The *Admonition* was bolstered by inserting two hitherto unpublished letters from the vestiarian controversy of 1566. In one, Gualter had written to Parkhurst protesting the publication by Grindal of his and Bullinger's letters of May 1 and 3 of that year supporting the bishops, and denouncing the tyranny of the bishops over their brethren, and their cowardliness before the Queen and the politicians. The other letter, from Beza to Grindal, courteously but firmly took the Puritan side in the conflict.

The purpose of the *Admonition*, however, was to urge Parliament to lay aside the episcopate, along with such current fiscal methods as that of impropriation, the current ecclesiastical courts, the homilies, the prayer book, vestments and ceremonies — the entire system, in short. In its place the *Admonition* called on Parliament to adopt a very simple plan for instituting ministers, elders and deacons in each parish, with the aim of restoring true discipline and thus paving the way for genuine reform. Although the plan was not given in any detail, a reference to the examples of the reform movements in Scotland and of the Huguenots made clear what was intended. England had given military aid in launching these. If the English authorities thought such a system was good for those countries, the *Admonition* asked, would it not be good for England as well?

The parting of the ways had now come. The *Admonition* caused a major uproar. Many of the original radical opponents of the vestments — Foxe, Humphrey, Sampson, Gilby and Lever, among others—openly rejected the new manifesto. So did such prominent lay supporters of the non-aggressive forms of protest as Thomas Norton. But other men saw it as a way out, now that the hopes of pinning reform on the side issue of

---

5. Patrick Collinson, "John Field and Elizabethan Puritanism," in *Elizabethan Government and Society: Essays Presented to Sir John Neale*, edited by S. T. Bindoff *et al.* (London, 1961), 127–62; *Puritan Manifestoes* . . . , edited by W. H. Frere and C. E. Douglas (London, 1907; new ed., 1954).

the vestments had proved futile. For many laymen, the institution of lay elders and deacons amounted to a constitutional recognition that the laity had a right to participate fully in the life of the church, instead of being merely subjects governed by the clergy. That others looked forward to whatever they could get out of the proposed liquidation of the episcopal sees (with their endowments), soon became no less clear to the new "Presbyterian" Puritans than it was to their opponents.

During the final three decades of Elizabeth's reign the "Puritan problem" centered on this third group, the Presbyterian Puritans. Their revolutionary proposals in fact drove such "Puritans" as Crowley, Humphrey and Foxe to become defenders of the established order. Because those representing the two non-aggressive forms of Puritanism had made their major protest in the first ten or twelve years of Elizabeth's reign and had thereafter contented themselves with passive resistance, whereas the Presbyterian Puritans kept up their attack in one form or another for the remaining three decades, many historians have tended to regard Presbyterianism as the logical development of Puritanism. For these same reasons other historians have concluded that Presbyterianism was no more than an aberration within the Puritan movement, the effect of impatience, frustration and foreign influences.

The appearance of the *Admonition* was the opening shot in a fierce and prolonged literary battle between the Presbyterian Puritans and the defenders of the established order. The Puritans, for their part, very early established what might be called a "central committee," who were responsible for devising propaganda, soliciting manuscripts, collecting funds, financing publication, and giving aid and advice to those of their associates who got into difficulties with the officials. The members of this loosely organized "committee" included Tomson (secretary to Walsingham of the Privy Council), Field, Christopher Goodman, and many others. Their connections gave them access to the Privy Council, to Parliament, to several foreign ambassadors, and to numerous nobles and other leaders in London.[6]

One of the projects undertaken by this committee was to draft a comprehensive statement of its program. The *Admonition* was acknowledged to have been sketchy and hastily done. As early as March 1573, Tomson wrote to Cartwright concerning William Fulke's manuscript, *A Brief and Plain Declaration* . . . (which was then in the hands of Goodman and

6. Collinson, *Elizabethan Puritan Movement* (London, 1967), Part 3.

"the brethren" — i.e., the committee), and certain unnamed aspects of it to which he had objections.[7] Fulke, a Cambridge don, had vigorously supported those at the university who opposed the vestments, and later supported Cartwright's lectures. His manuscript remained unpublished until 1584, and by then Fulke had dissociated himself from the Presbyterian radicals. Whether any essential changes were made by the committee before publishing the work is now impossible to determine. A few minor changes are quite obvious. The book's cumbersome title, which sums up the way in which debate arose over church polity and structure in England, proved troublesome to the printer, who used "A learned discourse" as a running head. Under this title the work soon became regarded among Presbyterian Puritans as one of the best statements of their "desires for discipline and reformation." [8]

But what chiefly characterized the Presbyterian wing of the Puritans was an agressive determination to alter the structure, polity and functioning of the church so as to bring about the practical reforms long desired by all Puritans. The "central committee" in which Field and Tomson were leaders had begun as early as 1571 to try to coordinate the new Presbyterian approach. By the 1580s small groups of Puritan preachers were meeting in groups that were unpublicized, if not secret, for mutual edification, support and guidance in the face of episcopal opposition. Gradually these groups began also to clarify their own views on the issues of the times as seen by their party. These deliberations produced two important developments: first, the groups began to formulate judgments on numerous practical issues which they expected their members to accept; and as a consequence they became aware of an acute need for some commonly accepted practical book of polity on which to ground their judgments. By the early 1580s, these "classes," i.e., groups of from ten to twenty pastors in a county or shire, and a less permanent "synod" of ministers from the classes, who met annually (or less often), formed what is usually termed now "the Presbyterian classical movement." [9]

In 1589–93 Richard Bancroft, an aide to Whitgift and later his succes-

7. Pearson, *Cartwright*, 83.
8. Dudley Fenner, *A defence of the godlie ministers* . . . (1587; *S.T.C.*, 10771), fol. 120, gives as authoritative works on the party's views, "The books of Master Cartwright" (i.e., his *Reply* to Whitgift, in three parts [*S.T.C.*, 4711, 4714, 4715]); Travers, *Full and plaine declaration of ecclesiasticall discipline* (1574; *S.T.C.*, 24184); the work of Fulke, and L. Chaderton, *Fruitful sermon upon* [*Romans 12:3–8*] . . . (1584; *S.T.C.*, 4926). On these various works see Pearson, *Cartwright*.
9. Collinson, *Elizabethan Puritan Movement*, 222 f, 291 f.

sor as archbishop, made a sensational "exposure" of this classical movement. Working through the High Commission, whose procedures made use of the *ex officio* oath, Bancroft brought several Puritan preachers to give information about these classes and synods. He was able also to seize numerous records and letters of the "central committee" and of the classes. This material became the basis for charges of sedition and subversion by which the classical movement was destroyed. More recent research by Patrick Collinson has placed less emphasis on the conspiratorial character of these classes and more on the frustrations with which the Presbyterians met as they tried to transform the Puritan movement from an expression of discontent to a means of concerted action.

The text of the *Brief and Plain Declaration* here reproduced has been taken, by permission, from the copy held by the Folger Shakespeare Library. There is no record of reprintings.

Fulke was a superior biblical scholar, and evidently made his own translations from the New Testament. Three of the longer quotations from the Old Testament seem to be derived from the Geneva Bible. The others follow no published English version.

❖ ❖ ❖ ❖

A Brief and Plain Declaration Concerning the Desires of All Those Faithful Ministers that Have and Do Seek for the Discipline and Reformation of the Church of England:

Which may serve for a just apology against the false accusations and slanders of their adversaries

A Preface to the Christian Reader

The holy prophets, having oftentimes but searched when and at what time the foreseeing Spirit of God declared unto them the manifold afflictions and troubles of the church to come, have thereupon entered into great lamentations for the same, and have not only wept and fasted themselves, but have compiled for the church whole books of lamentations, therein instructing them what way to take for appeasing the fierce wrath of God breaking out against them. Which duty in semblable manner should now long ago have been done of us, did not the hope we conceive in the midst of so many tempests confirm us in such expectations of her Majesty and her most honorable Council as that (according to their clemency towards the poor ministers and their families, but most especially according to their holy and zealous care which ought to abound for the clean driving out of the Canaanites and planting, hedging, pruning and continual preserving of the Lord's vineyard from foxes, yea little foxes) this civil war, as a man may say, of the church wherein so much of that blood (whereof Paul speaketh) is poured to the ground, should by their holy and just authority fully be ended.[1] Now whenas we at this time are subject almost unto all the afflictions which can come unto a church blessed of God with such a Christian and happy regiment [i.e., governorship], as [subject] [a] to the profane scoffing of the Ammonites at the building of the church, as at a wall which a fox should destroy; [b] to the conspiracies of the Arabians and those of Ashdod; [c] to the false charges of sedition, contempt of all good laws and proceedings, like to that of Sanballat; [d] yea to the prophets themselves, undermining, nay reviling, displacing and grievously afflicting the godly and learned ministry, and so consequently plaguing the church with that plague whereby the priests may mourn because there is no offering and the people perish, even the young men, with the famine of hearing the word of God preached — when, I say, we are subject to all these [afflictions], we can think of no way for reconciling the brethren at variance, and after a most sure and holy union of both their forces for a courageous setting upon the common adversary, than the certain, peaceable, and reasonable way following. Which [way] is that, whereas both by books already written and by treatises lately and now published,[2] it may appear we seek that which at the least in the judgment of all true Christians hath no small probability (as we judge *necessity*) of truth out of the Scriptures, it may please her most excellent Majesty and their Honors [i.e., the Privy Council] to appoint on both sides the best learned, most godly and moderate men, to debate all differences of weight between them and us.[3] So that, [a] first upon sufficient consideration, the questions to be debated be without all ambiguity set down, the reasons of both sides without all

1. [ED.] This preface was written, probably by John Field, after Whitgift became archbishop and launched his campaign to crush the Puritan opposition. At Whitgift's appointment, many Puritans had expected him to take a "moderate" course. Burghley also had shared this hope.

2. [ED.] A reference to the work of the "central committee."

3. [ED.] The use of debates to settle religious policy was common during the Reformation. In England the most widely publicized of such debates had been that of March 31, 1559, between Catholics and Protestants, in which the new Elizabethan policies were ruled victorious. The demand for a conference between the bishops and the Puritan spokesmen led to the one held at Hampton Court in 1604.

out-goings shortly and plainly delivered in writing each to other; [b] that after upon sufficient examination the reasons of both be continually confirmed and resolved, till either by the evidence of truth one part yield unto the other, or the folly and madness of those which gainsay it do in equal judgment become manifest in regard of the contradictions and absurdities whereto they shall be driven by the force of God's word. Which way though it should come naked unto us cannot well be refused, but being richly attired with all robes and ornaments which the Scripture giveth unto the synodical assemblies for such conferences, as namely, that there be much searching of the truth by sufficient reasoning without all by-matters, quarrels, evasions and colorings whatsoever, that there be much order, when the spirit of every prophet shall be subject unto the spirits of the other prophets, and the judgment of all shall be sufficiently heard without stopping of free and sufficient answer, without lordly carrying away of the matter (with no substance of reasons) where no authority, pregnancy of wit, plausible persuasion of man's wisdom, shall turn the truth aside, but all shall stand in the evident demonstration of God's Spirit. [c] Lastly, that there be peace without all bitterness, revilings, suspicions, chargings of men dead and alive, whereby affections are moved, judgment blinded, and men driven as with a mighty stream from the love of the truth.

When it cometh thus adorned we think that which we labor to procure to be so honorable, not only before God but also before men, that none can judge otherwise of it than we do. For if any shall object that the grave authority of archbishops and bishops shall receive a check, whilst they are brought to deal with those whom they judge few, young, unlearned and not comparable to themselves; or that it is a challenge not much unlike the papists; or lastly, that it shall be prejudicial to the estate of government established; it may please their wisdoms who are to be judges, to consider what we have to answer unto these things, which, if they have the truth of God's word, contain the safest and best way in such cases, tend to the full quieting of all, and the removing of the plagues which are upon us and are like daily further to come, even from the common adversary, we may boldly yet most humbly upon our knees require them before God and all his elect angels not to cast it away.

Wherefore for the first, let us grant the great difference which they make of years and learning, yet the speech of Elihu giveth them sufficient answer, that this understanding is not tied to such outward respects, but to the revelation of God's Spirit, and to accept in such cases the persons of men or to give titles, is but to provoke God to destroy us. Yea, let the memorable examples of Hezekiah and the priests, of the apostles in their councils, of Paul in his epistles, and even of Peter in yielding to the challenge of some not so well instructed, move them, who [i.e., Hezekiah and the priests] not only not refused the Levites and elders, but accepted the people in some manner to be heard to speak and to authorize their determinations and writings. At least let their [i.e., the bishops'] own opinion that in interpreting the Scriptures and delivery of doctrine we are equal with them, persuade them not to refuse those who, if they could strain their consciences to subscribe to the Archbishop's articles, they would gladly receive them to be the ambassadors of Jesus Christ.[4] As for the fewness [of the Puritans] it may be, if the ignorant ministers [and] the variety of others which subscribe (some doing it with this limitation and some with that, some holding their former judgment as not gainsaid by their subscription, some lamenting their slip in that behalf) were deducted, the number of the one would not so greatly surmount the other.

As for the challenge of the papists knit up with the consideration of the [welfare of] the estate, the difference [between us and the bishops] may be considered in the matter and manner. [a] Concerning the matter, they [i.e., bishops] make it [consist] in the substance of religion which hath in divers assemblies abroad and at home been disputed, resolved, and now publicly maintained for our true and holy faith. We [assert that it consists] in matters concerning the government of Christ of great moment indeed, yet never thus handled. Nor [are we] urging the alteration, but perfection of the estate of the church and further good of the commonwealth. Whilst [i.e., because] by this means amongst many other things of great importance, the ignorant ministry, and by it popery, and by popery rebellion, should be avoided, which by the other [our present procedure] are most manifestly bred and nourished. [b] Concerning the manner, they [i.e., the bishops] call it [i.e., liken our desired conference] to a sudden and tumultuous reasoning, where the readiest wit, the best memory, the most filed [i.e., well-honed] speech, shall carry away the truth, at least marvellously move the ungrounded hearers. We require that where both sides may upon mature and sufficient deliberation be heard without any of these shows, and the matter delivered unto her Majesty, their Highnesses, and whomsoever they shall choose to receive and examine the allegations of both sides. So that it need not be communicated

4. D. Whitgift's book, page 389. [ED.] John Whitgift, *The defence of the Answer to the Admonition* (1574), *Works* (Cambridge, 1851–3; Parker Society), II, 265.

unto the people until the manifest light of truth appear first unto them. And if this so safe and reasonable an offer cannot be liked in the respect of the last objected consideration [i.e., popular disturbance], we think it impossible but the persons which desire a way so sound, peaceable and dutiful shall recover this favor [at least] that with safety of their consciences, they shall [be permitted to] exercise their ministry with that liberty which is meet for those who shall be tied in all things to have especial regard to the peace of the church and public orders [i.e., Christian pastors]. Wherefore, most Christian reader, when thou shalt by these few [i.e., the Puritans] take knowledge of these things, pray unto God for us, and as thy place is, solicit and further so just a cause, to this end only, that Christ's kingdom may be perfectly established, the consciences of all the godly quieted, and the happy regiment of her Majesty honored, with much peace, joy and quietness at home.[5]

A Learned Discourse of Ecclesiastical Government, Proved by the Word of God

THE DEFINITION OF THE CHURCH

The church of God is the house of God, and therefore ought to be directed in all things according to the order prescribed by the Householder himself; which order is not to be learned elsewhere, but in his holy word. The first of these principles or propositions is the very word of the Holy Ghost uttered by Paul (1 Tim. 3:15). The second followeth necessarily of the first. The third is a manifest truth believed of all them that acknowledge the Scripture of God to be a perfect rule of all our life,

5. [ED.] This insistence that the royal supremacy be defined from within the context of a church polity deriving from the nature and function of the church, rather than defining the church's polity from a theory of the royal supremacy, was a sore point all through the Tudor-Stuart era. The non-Presbyterian Puritans, as well as the royalist-episcopal party (Hooker included), looked to the godly monarch to order the church's polity. The complaint of non-Presbyterian Puritans was that Elizabeth did not do her duty. Men like Wentworth and Morice looked to Parliament (or the Crown in Parliament) to order the church's polity. Such men favored Presbyterian schemes insofar as they gave laymen a genuine role in the church's life. But they were intensely opposed to granting any coercive power to clerics. Had matters ever come to a choice under Elizabeth, these "Puritan M.P.s" would no doubt have been as Erastian as their successors proved to be in the 1640s. The moment "Presbyterianism" took on the color of clericalism, these men rejected it in favor of a "parliamentary supremacy" to replace the "royal supremacy."

and able to make the man of God perfect, prepared to all good works (2 Tim. 3:17).

WHAT MINISTERS ARE APPOINTED IN THE CHURCH

This foundation being surely laid, against which the gates of hell cannot prevail, we ought diligently and reverently to search the holy Scriptures, that we may find what order our savior Christ, our only Householder, hath set forth in them, by which he would have his house or church to be directed in all things appertaining to the eternal salvation of us men, his unprofitable servants. Now we find in the Scriptures that our savior Christ ascending into heaven was not unmindful of his church on earth, but ordained a holy ministry of men, to the building up of the body of Christ in unity of faith and knowledge (Eph. 4:11; 1 Cor. 12:28). We find also that as the offices are diverse of this ministry, so they are not general unto all the church. But as order and necessity require, for executing of their office [they are] distributed and limited unto certain places or particular churches, according to the division of regions, cities and towns. For we read that Paul and Barnabas ordained at Derbe, Lystra, Iconium, Antioch, etc., elders by election in every church, with prayer and fasting, and so commended them to the Lord, in whom they believed (Acts 14:23). Also Paul left Titus in the Isle of Crete, that he should ordain elders in every city, as he had appointed (Tit. 1:5). Concerning the divers offices of the ministry, we are taught by Saint Paul, Romans 12:6, also 1 Corinthians 12:28 and Ephesians 4:11, where we read that God hath ordained in the ministry of his church these several offices, namely, apostles, evangelists, prophets, pastors, doctors, governors and deacons, also men endued with the gifts of healing, of powers or miracles, and of divers tongues.

Of these offices, some were temporal [i.e., temporary], serving only for the first planting and foundation of the church among the heathen. Some are perpetual, pertaining to the nourishing and building up the church forever. Of the former sort were apostles, prophets, evangelists, men endued with the graces of powers, of healings and of divers tongues. Of the latter kind are doctors, pastors, governors and deacons. The apostles were ordained by God and sent forth immediately by Christ, having a general commission to spread the gospel over all the world; which work when they had accomplished, that office ceased (Mt. 28:19; Mk. 16:15). Such were the twelve apostles, Paul and Barnabas, etc.

And for this cause the apostles appointed Matthias in the place of Judas, according to the Scriptures (Acts 1:15–26), permitting nevertheless, the election unto God by casting of lots, that the number might be full for the first planting of the church. But when Herod had slain James the brother of John with the sword, they chose no man to succeed in his place because they had no warrant of God's word (Acts 12:2). But the Holy Ghost, as he saw it was expedient for the church, afterward separated Paul and Barnabas which lived at Antioch, as prophets and teachers to the work whereto he had called them (Acts 13:2).

The prophets were such as were endued with a singular gift of revelation in the interpretation of the Scriptures and applying them to the present use of the church, of whom some also did foreshow of things to come, as Agabus. Also there were [some] in every city that prophesied to Saint Paul (as he passed by them) that bonds and afflictions were prepared for him at Jerusalem (Acts 11:28, 21:11; 20:23). This office being in the number of them that were ordained for beautifying the gospel in the first publishing thereof, it ceased, with that singular and extraordinary gift, to be an ordinary function of the church.

The evangelists were such as were stirred up of God to assist the apostles in their ministry of general charge, in planting the gospel, and confirming the same by their preaching, but inferior in dignity to the apostles. Such was Philip that first preached the gospel in Samaria, whither Peter and John were sent by the apostles to confer unto them by prayer and imposition of hands the visible graces of the Holy Ghost, which Philip did not (Acts 8:5, 16). The same Philip in Acts 21:8 is called an evangelist. So is Timothy [in] 2 Timothy 4:5. Such was Titus, Silas and many others. This office also with the order of the apostles is expired and hath no place.

Likewise, as we do plainly see, that the gifts of healing, of powers or miracles, and of divers tongues, have long since ceased to be in the church. So the offices of them which were grounded upon these gifts must also cease and be determined. Therefore the papists do vainly retain the name and office of exorcists when they cannot cast out devils, and extreme unction when they cannot cure diseases, and to speak with strange tongues which they have not by inspiration, and that without any interpretation, which Saint Paul expressly forbiddeth (1 Cor. 14).

WHAT OFFICES REMAIN IN THE CHURCH

There remaineth in the church, therefore, of those before rehearsed only these ecclesiastical offices instituted of God, namely, pastors, doctors, governors, and deacons: by which the church of God may, according to his word, be directed in all matters which are commonly called ecclesiastical. And therefore as it is unlawful, so it is unneedful for men, following the devices of their own brain without the warrant of God's word, to institute and ordain any other offices or kinds of ministry besides these appointed and approved by God himself, exercised in the primitive and pure church (until the mystery of iniquity working a way for Antichrist's pride and presumption, changed God's ordinance and brought in all kinds of false doctrine and confusion) and [which offices are] now again restored in all rightly reformed churches, with such daily increase and glory of the kingdom of Christ and suppression of the tyranny of Satan, that the only experience hereof might be a sufficient persuasion to us to leave this disordered state of ours wherein we have so long labored with so little profit, and to embrace that most beautiful order of ecclesiastical regiment, which God so manifestly doth bless and prosper in our neighbors' hands.

But while we speak of ecclesiastical government, it may be thought of some that we should entreat first of the supreme authority of Christian princes, whereupon it seemeth that all the regiment of the church dependeth. Which [supremacy] is such a mist to dazzle the eyes of ignorant persons, that they think all things in the ecclesiastical state ought to be disposed by that only high authority and absolute power of the civil magistrate.[6] Others there be, with more color of reason, that refer only indifferent matters to the disposition of princes. But in determining indifferent matters, they show themselves not to be indifferent judges. For, whatsoever it shall please the civil magistrate, or themselves, to call or count indifferent, it must be so held of all men, without any further inquiry.[7]

But of the supreme authority of Christian princes in ecclesiastical causes, how far it extendeth by the word of God, we shall have better oc-

6. [ED.] On the difficulties which the doctrine of the royal supremacy in the church caused for the Presbyterian Puritan theorists, see A. F. Scott Pearson, *Church and State, Political Aspects of Sixteenth Century Puritanism* (Cambridge, 1928), 52 ff.

7. [ED.] The vestment controversy.

casion to entreat hereafter, when we have described the ecclesiastical state. And that it is neither needful nor agreeable to good order of teaching to begin first therewith, it may be plain to every man by this reason. The church of God was perfect in all her regiment before there was any Christian prince. Yea, the church of God may stand, and doth stand at this day in most blessed estate, where the civil magistrates are not the greatest favorers. By which it is manifest that the regiment and government thereof dependeth not upon the authority of princes but upon the ordinance of God, who hath most mercifully and wisely so established the same that as with the comfortable aid of Christian magistrates, it may singularly flourish and prosper, so without it, it may continue, and against the adversaries thereof prevail. For the church craveth help and defense of Christian princes to continue and go forward more peaceably and profitably, to the setting up of the kingdom of Christ. But all her authority she receiveth immediately of God.

Let us therefore return to those offices of ecclesiastical regiment which now remain to be exercised in the church of God, being instituted and ordained by Christ himself, which before we have proved out of the Scriptures to be only these: doctors, pastors, governors and deacons, whereof some appertain to doctrine, some to government and discipline.

Doctors

The duty of doctors and pastors is chiefly to teach and instruct the people of God in all things that God hath appointed them to learn. The office of elders and deacons is to provide that good order and discipline be observed in the church.[8] These offices being rightly established and

8. [ED.] This attempt to restrict the clergy's role to teaching, and to place all coercive authority in the hands of laymen, went back to pre-Reformation critiques of the church, and was especially advocated by the Christian Humanists. Every variety of Protestantism in the sixteenth century made some attempt to shift coercive power from clerical to lay hands. The peculiar character that was common to the Geneva, Heidelberg, Huguenot, Dutch, Scottish and Presbyterian-Puritan polities became manifest in their attempt to distinguish not between clerical and lay power but between civil and church power. They were alike in giving "disciplinary" (i.e., coercive as most men saw it) power to mixed ministerial and lay church bodies. The practice raised once again the problem of clericalism, and many "Reformed" churches — those of Zurich, Bern, St. Gallen, Lausanne, Basel and some Huguenots, among others — took what came to be called the "Erastian" position, that all church power save preaching, teaching and administration of the sacraments resided in the state. See further, Walther Köhler, *Zürcher Ehegericht und Genfer Konsistorium* (2 vols., Leipzig, 1932–42); also the literature on the controversy at Heidelberg

exercised in the church, are able to make us meet together in the unity of faith and knowledge of the son of God, unto a perfect man according to doctrine (Eph. 4:13). And both for doctrine and order of government, to make us one body of Christ and members one of another (1 Cor. 12:27). Now what should be desired more than this in the church of God? Or what wisdom of man can espy better than the Spirit of God by what means this should be brought to effect which we do desire? What man's wit can devise better than the wisdom of God hath expressed? Or when God hath established an order for the administration of his own house, what presumption of man dare change it? But what dare not dust and ashes presume to do against his maker, and that with greatest inconvenience, when with best pretences [they set about] of correcting and reforming that which they do think to be imperfect in his [i.e., God's] doings? Examples thereof we have most evident.

That which is alleged as the chief defense of this disordered state which now remaineth in our church, namely, that our fathers of old time were not content with the simple order instituted by Christ and established by his apostles, but for better governing of the church thought good some offices to add thereto, some to take away, some to alter and change; and in effect to pervert and overthrow all Christian and ecclesiastical policy which was built upon the foundation of the prophets and apostles, Jesus Christ being the chief cornerstone (Eph. 2:20).[9] But how unhappy a success this good intent (as they call it) of theirs deserved to have of God, who always abhorreth all good intents of men that are contrary to the good pleasure of his will, expressed in his holy word, the age before us (alas) hath felt, the present time doth plainly see, and we pray God the posterity, warned by examples of their ancestors, may take heed of it. For where there are specially two things propounded in the church of God: doctrine and discipline, as if a man would say, knowledge and practice, by which the glory of God is sought and shineth therein, instead of true doctrine [there] followed all manner of corruptions of the same, both in the whole and in every part thereof, as ignorance, heresies, idolatry, superstition, etc. The discipline degenerated unto intolerable tyranny and external domination, clean contrary to the commandment of Christ, whereof ensued all unbridled license of ungodly living. To be short, the

---

over Erastus, and the opposing reactions to it of Zurich and Geneva, especially R. Wesel-Roth, *Thomas Erastus* . . . (Lahr–Baden, 1954).

9. [ED.] An oblique attack upon the official use of arguments based on the primitive church.

exchange of the ordinance of God and Christ (*cf.* 2 Thess. 2:12) brought in nothing else but the devil and Antichrist.

Wherefore if we mind such a reformation as shall be acceptable to God and profitable unto his church, we must thoroughly be resolved to set up no new kind of ministry of our own invention, neither for teaching nor for discipline in the ecclesiastical state. But [we must] bring all things to that most perfect and absolute order, which God himself hath established by his word. And because all offices of the church are so linked together, as the members of one body whereof Christ is the head, we will so describe one part as the description of them all may be sufficiently comprehended therein. As if a man would set forth the manifold office and uses of the hand, he should declare what it doeth alone and what it doeth with the help of the other hand, or with the arm, with the breast, with the knee, or with the foot, etc.; what it can do with divers kinds of tools, and what without all manner of instruments. This order we thought good to observe, in describing the ministry of the church, as by which both the distinction and communication of all offices and services in the church might most plainly appear. Otherwise we force [i.e., argue] not by what method, so the same truth be plainly set forth by any man. And as we control [i.e., regulate] not other men's methods by ours, so we would not that other men's manner of teaching should be prejudicial to ours. This we say because of them, which either for lack of wit or through too much willfulness, if they see any difference in the form and order of teaching of divers men, though in matter and substance they all agree, they exclaim there is no unity and therefore no truth among them. Let us then proceed in our purpose.

The office of teaching is the chief and principal office that is in the church. By that we be taught to know God, and how to serve him, and what benefits to look for at his hand, without which knowledge there can be no felicity but only destruction looked for, according to the saying of the wise man: "Where prophesying faileth, there the people perish" (Prov. 29:18). The ministry is divided into two functions: they that exercise the first are called pastors. The other are called doctors or teachers.

The Office of a Doctor

The office of a doctor is to teach, as the very name doth declare, but yet every teacher is not meant thereby, for it appertaineth to pastors also to teach. Yet this latter is distinct from the former. Almighty God, being careful that true doctrine should continue in his church, from time to time most wisely provided that certain men (whom he hath endued with gifts meet for the same purpose) should be appointed in every congregation which should employ themselves, either wholly or principally to the study of holy Scriptures, thereby to learn to avouch the principles of true religion, and to repress and beat down all false and strange opinions, of which Satan never ceaseth to sow the seeds, but chiefly where this office is not set up and maintained according to God's ordinance. These men must not content themselves with contemplative knowledge. But, as by the grace of God they excel other men in understanding, so they must diligently instruct other men in the same learning, and openly confute all false doctrine and heresy. And especially they ought to take pains in the instruction of such men as may be made meet to serve in the church as pastors, and to succeed in their place as doctors.

Their institution is set forth, 1 Corinthians 12:28, also Ephesians 4: [8], 11. In the former place the apostle teacheth that they are the ordinance of God. Saith he, "God hath ordained in the church: first, apostles, secondly prophets, thirdly doctors, or teachers." In the latter place he testifieth that our savior Christ ascended on high, led captivity captive, and hath given gifts unto men, amongst which gifts he accounteth the function of teachers. Who should then refuse to embrace the ordinance of God? Who should deprive us of the free gift of Christ? The office of doctors is briefly expressed in Romans 12:7: "Let him that is a teacher, attend upon teaching," where also it is distinguished from other offices, and namely from the office of pastors. For it followeth immediately, "Let him that exhorteth" (Rom. 12:8), (which is a principal part of a pastor's office, not necessarily required in a teacher) "be diligent in his exhortation." For the office of doctors is only to teach true doctrine and to confute all heresies and false opinions by the word of God, concerning all articles and principles of Christian religion, without applying their teaching to any particular state of time, of persons or places.

The example or practice of this office is set forth Acts 13:1, where it is recorded by Saint Luke that Paul and Barnabas (before the Holy Ghost commanded them to be separated for the work whereunto he called them) were in the number of prophets and doctors, with Simeon, Niger, Lucius of Cyrene, and Manahen in the church of Antioch, where they continued in that office a whole year, in which city the disciples were first called by the name of Christians, Acts 11:26. Likewise Apollos which was an eloquent man and mighty in the Scriptures, first at Ephesus but afterward being more perfectly instructed in the way of God by Aquila and Priscilla in the church of Achaia, exercised the office of a teacher with great profit of them which had believed and to the great confusion of the stiffnecked Jews, while he proved plainly by the Scriptures that Jesus was the Christ, Acts 18:28.

Therefore if we purpose to have the church to flourish in true knowledge, we must provide that this office be restored, both in the universities and in as many other places as may be, as well for the better instruction of all men which are desirous to learn, as especially for the information of those which should occupy the rooms of pastors, of which sort there ought to be a great number always in good towardness to take charge of so many several flocks as must of necessity be in so great a church as this is.[10]

Pastors and Their Titles

Besides doctors, there must be pastors ordained in every congregation, which have divers appellations in the Scripture, as Ephesians 4. They are called by the name of pastors because they ought to feed the several flocks of God's sheep committed to their charge. As it appeareth Acts 20:28; 1 Peter 5:2. They are called also elders, not always in respect of their age but of their office and gravity. For Timothy was but a young man and yet had the office of an elder. This name was received of an ancient custom of the people of Israel, who used so to call those that were rulers and officers among them, as it appeareth by many places both of the Old and New Testament, but chiefly in Numbers 11:16, where God ordained seventy ancients to assist Moses in his government, who were also endued at the same time with the spirit of prophecy, from which time it became an ordinary office and name of governors in Israel.

Wherein we have to note against the papists, that the ministers of the church are never called in the New Testament by the name of sacrificing priests, which were under the law, but often are called elders, of the similitude of those ancients that governed the people of God. Whereas, if they had been appointed of God to be sacrificers, the similitude and name of sacrificing priests would a great deal better have agreed unto them. But, whereas both these names were usual amongst the Jews, *iereus* and

10. [ED.] In this Presbyterian scheme, no account seems to have been taken of the Puritan "lecturer," who was classified as a doctor in other Puritan literature; Collinson, *Elizabethan Puritan Movement*, 341–3. See also Paul S. Seaver, *Puritan Lectureships: The Politics of Religious Dissent, 1560–1662* (Stanford, 1970).

presbyteroi, the one signifying sacrificers and the other elders, the Spirit of God doth often call the ministers elders, but evermore precisely avoideth to name them sacrificers or priests (as we use the term), yea, though they succeed them in one principal part of their office, that is to say in teaching, as it is written, "The lips of the priest should preserve knowledge, and men shall seek the law at his mouth" (Mal. 2:7). The cause whereof is evident to be this, that the sacrificing priesthood of Aaron is wholly translated unto Christ, in whom only it resteth, and passeth from him to none other (Heb. 7:11–25).

But by the name of elders the pastors are called, Acts 14:23, where Paul and Barnabas ordained elders by election in every congregation. And, Acts 20:17, Paul sent for the elders of Ephesus to Miletus. Also he affirmeth those elders especially, which labor in preaching and doctrine, to be worthy of double honor (1 Tim. 5:17). Which place also testifieth of another kind of elders, of whom we shall have occasion to speak more hereafter, whose office consisteth only in government and not in public teaching. Moreover, he showeth that he appointed Titus to ordain elders in every city, and afterward describeth what manner of men he would have to be chosen into the office (Tit. 1:5). Also Saint James, in chapter 5:14, willeth that if any be sick they should call for the elders of the church, who being endued with the gift of healing at that time, should pray for the diseased and anoint him with oil, and he should be restored to his health. Finally, Saint Peter, as a fellow elder, exhorteth the elders to employ all their diligence to the feeding of the flock of God (1 Pet. 5:1–2).

Another name they [i.e., the pastors] have in the Scripture, which is superintendents or overseers, because they ought to be vigilant and watchful to oversee the flock and every member thereof. Which name is never used in the Scripture for such bishops as claim and exercise dominion and authority over whole regions, and [over] all the pastors of the same, but only for those that be pastors of every several congregation, having no superiority over their fellow pastors, but be all of equal dignity and authority. So are they named, Acts 20, where Saint Luke in the seventeenth verse calleth them "elders of the church of Ephesus." Saint Paul in the twenty-eighth verse calleth the same overseers, saying, "Take heed to yourselves and to the whole flock, over which the Holy Ghost hath made you overseers, to feed or govern the church of God, which he hath purchased with his own blood." In this place all the three appellations concur: namely, of overseers plainly, and pastors inclusively in the word flock, and in the word *poicainan*, which signifieth to feed or govern, as a pastor doth his sheep. Where is to be noted, that bishops or overseers of one city were many, which plainly argueth that they were none such as nowadays are commonly called bishops, which can be but one in one whole diocese, much less many in one city.

The same thing is to be observed in the name of bishops, used by Saint Paul, Philippians 1:1, where he and Timothy send salutations unto the bishops and deacons of the church which was in the city of Philippi, which bishops were the elders or pastors, else would he not have saluted in special words the deacons which were in inferior office, and omitted the elders, which were of more excellent calling. In the same manner of speaking, he describeth the qualities of those which were to be chosen into the office of the bishops and deacons (1 Tim. 3:2–8). Likewise unto Titus 1:5, he calleth them elders and immediately after, describing the qualities of such as were meet to be ordained elders, he calleth them bishops, saying: "For this cause did I leave thee in Crete, that thou shouldest continue to redress the things that remain; and that thou shouldest ordain elders in every city, if any be unreprovable, the husband of one wife, having faithful children which are not accused of riot, nor are disobedient. For a bishop or overseer must be unreprovable as the steward of God, not froward . . ."

Finally, Saint Peter, chapter 5:1, the place before alleged, comprehendeth all the three names of elders, pastors and bishops: "The elders," saith he, "which are among you, I beseech." The name of pastor is understood by relation of the names of feeding and the flock which he useth, also by the name of *archipoimen*, which signifieth the chief of pastors, which is our savior Christ. The name of bishops or overseers is included in the word *episcopountes*, which signifieth them which do carefully exercise the office of bishops or overseers. His exhortation is this: "The elders which are amongst you I beseech, which am also a fellow elder and a witness of the sufferings of Christ, and also a partaker of the glory that shall be revealed, feed the flock of God which is committed unto you, so much as in you lieth, carefully overseeing, not by constraint but willingly, not for filthy lucre, but of a ready mind, not as exercising lordship over the heritage, but that you may be examples to the flock. And when the chief pastor shall appear, you shall receive an incorruptible crown of glory" (1 Pet. 5:1–4). Saint Peter in this place reproveth three notable vices which do great hurt among the ministers of the church if they be not taken heed of: slothfulness in teaching, covetousness of lucre, and ambitious desire of exercising lordship; exhorting them to painful diligence because they were bishops or overseers; to a ready care because they were pastors, and therefore should labor for love of the flock and not for lucre like hirelings; to modest humility, because their chief dignity in that they were elders was to excel in godliness, that they might be an example to the flock, which cannot be except they submit themselves and their lives to the common rule of other men; which most excellent virtues if they embrace, they should be sure to be plentifully rewarded by him who only deserveth to be called the chief of all elders, pastors and bishops, to whom only these honorable names of *archipresbyter, archiepiscopus, archiepoimen*, and such like, do properly agree. For as the apostle calleth our savior Christ in this place the chief pastor, so in the second chapter, the twenty-fifth verse, he calleth him both the pastor and bishop of our souls. Wherefore as he only is our chief pastor or *archiepoimen*, so is he also our only archbishop. And that the name of *archipresbyter* or chief of elders pertaineth to no mortal man may be seen by this place, where Saint Peter, that excellent and high apostle, who if any man could might as well as any have challenged that name, durst not call himself other than *sunpresbyteros*, a fellow elder, no not when he sought authority to himself by that name to be bold to exhort the elders of the church.

But lest any man should think we stay only in names and terms which are not so greatly material, let him consider that Saint Peter expressly forbiddeth the elders to exercise lordship over their several congregations. How much more over their fellow elders? Which thing also our savior Christ precisely forbiddeth, when there was a contention among his apostles about the primacy: "The kings of the nations have dominion over them, and they that bear rule over them are called gracious lords or beneficial, but you shall not be so" (Lk. 22:25). Also [in] Matthew 20:25 and Mark 10:42, upon the ambitious request of the sons of Zebedee and the disdain of the other against them: "The princes of the Gentiles exercise lordship over them, and they that be great exercise authority over them, but it shall not be so amongst you, but whoso will be great amongst you, let him be your minister, and he that will be first among you, let him be your servant." The same thing he taught by his example when he washed his apostles' feet and commanded them to show the like humility one toward another, which were all brethren, which he their Lord and Master showed towards them (Jn. 13:14). Also, Matthew 23:8, etc., he forbiddeth all ambitious titles of Rabbi, Master, Father, etc., the reason he addeth, "for you are all brethren." For these names agree properly to God and Christ. For the greatest dignity of an ecclesiastical person is a ministry and not a lordship. Saint John also, in his Third Epistle (v. 9), sharply reproveth Diotrephes because he was *philoproteuon*, one that desired the primacy in the church.

Howbeit in this case we must take heed that we spoil not the ministers of the church of all their lawful authority. For, although these testimonies of Scripture directly condemn the authority of one pastor above another, yet neither do they set every pastor at liberty by himself, to do what they list without controlment. Nor yet do [these Scriptures] take away the lawful authority he hath over his flock, but that imperious and pompous dominion which is meet for civil magistrates and great potentates to exercise in worldly affairs. Otherwise in respect of their lawful authority, they [i.e., pastors] are called by the apostle in his Epistle to the Hebrews (13:7) guides, such as are appointed to oversee the flock with authority, and unto them submission and obedience is commanded in the same chapter, verse 17.

Other names are applied to them [i.e., pastors] in the Scripture, but they be for the most part more general, pertaining to all kind of teachers in the church of God, both in the time of the law and of the gospel, as seers, prophets, watchmen, angels, laborers, builders, stewards and suchlike. All which with many others, serve to express some part of their office, as their knowledge, their diligence, their authority, their faithfulness, their discretion, also the necessity of them, the commodity that cometh by them, etc. But concerning the names of pastors, as they are a special office in the church, this may suffice.

But forasmuch as we have undertaken so to describe a pastor and his office, as all other offices of the church may be described therewith, we must not stay only in the name, but set forth also the whole substance of the person. For which intent, it shall be necessary for us to consider a pastor or bishop these two ways: in the proper function of his ministry, and in government with his elders. By which we shall understand how this ministry ought to be reformed and restored amongst us.

As touching his office, something hath been said before generally, under the description of his several names. But now more particularly, we must examine what belongeth to his charge. The pastor must be limited to one only congregation of such competent number as he (if he be but one) or if they be two, may be sufficient to the instruction of all and every member of the same church. And first, he may no more lawfully have charge of two or three churches than he can be possibly in diverse places. No more than a shepherd, of whom he taketh his name, may have the leading of sundry flocks in divers places. Neither may he be absent from his charge with better reason than a shepherd from his flock. As for substitutes or hirelings, [these] will not be allowed in this case. For pastors are substitutes of God and have an office of credit committed unto them. Therefore by no good reason may they make any substitutes in their place, or commit their charge unto another. The law of a man grounded upon good reason, alloweth not substitutes of substitutes, nor committing over of an office of credit in temporal matters. How shall God almighty then take it in good part, when the flock of Christ which he hath purchased with his own blood shall be so greatly neglected, to the endangering of their everlasting salvation? Therefore the ordinance of God is that the pastor should attend unto his peculiar flock. That elders should be ordained in every city, town, and other places, Titus 1:5 and Acts 14:23. The apostles ordained elders in every church of Derbe, Lystra, Iconium and Tichia [i.e., Antioch] and all the congregations about.

[The Office of the Pastor]

[1. *Preaching.*] Secondly, the office of pastors is not only to teach the same truth in their several flocks, but also to apply it to the time and persons of whom they have charge, with exhortation and reprehension, with consolation of the afflicted, and threatening of the obstinate, etc. This in few words is set forth by St. Paul; speaking of the diverse gifts of God in his church, he saith: "Whether it be he that teacheth, in his doctrine, or he that exhorteth, in his exhortation" (Rom. 12:7–8). The doctor therefore teacheth without exhortation. The pastor teacheth and exhorteth withal. More at large he setteth forth the same office in his exhortation unto the pastors of Ephesus, willing them to follow his example who supplied that office, until they were able to succeed in his place (Acts 20). Also very briefly and yet fully, he describeth the same unto Timothy, showing first that all his foundation must be out of the Scriptures, which were sufficient for all parts of his charge, and then most earnestly commandeth him to practice the same with all diligence. His words are these: "All Scripture is inspired of God and profitable for doctrine, for exhortation, for reformation, and for instruction which is in righteousness, that the man of God may be prepared to all good works. Therefore I charge thee before God, and before the Lord Jesus Christ which shall judge the quick and the dead at his appearing and in his kingdom: preach the word, be instant in season and out of season, improve, rebuke, exhort, with all long suffering and doctrine" (2 Tim. 3:16–4:2).

The first part therefore, and the chiefest of a pastor's office or duty is to feed with wholesome doctrine the flock that is committed to his charge, and therefore Saint Paul, describing what manner of men are meet for that charge unto Timothy, requireth that a bishop or pastor be apt or able to teach (1 Tim. 3:2), for if a man have never so much knowledge and be not apt or able to teach, he ought by no means to be admitted unto this vocation. And unto Titus writing, chapter 1, verse 9, he requireth that he be such a one as "holdeth fast the faithful word, according to doctrine, that he also may be able to exhort with wholesome doctrine, and improve them that say against it." Whereupon it followeth necessarily that whosoever is himself ignorant in the knowledge of God's word, and therefore unable either to exhort with wholesome doctrine or to confute them that gainsay it, is altogether unmeet for the office of a pastor or bishop.

Wherefore if ever we mind such a reformation as God shall thereby be glorified and his church edified, we must utterly remove all the unlearned pastors, as men by no means to be tolerated to have any charge over the Lord's flock; and also provide that hereafter none be received into that office but such as are sufficient for their knowledge and ability in teaching to take so weighty a charge in hand.[11] What man having but one hundred sheep would make such a man shepherd or overseer over them as were a natural idiot, or otherwise altogether unskillful or unable to perform those things that belong to a shepherd? If no man have so little care of brute beasts, what brutish negligence is it to commit the people of God, redeemed with the precious blood of Jesus Christ, to such unskillful and insufficient pastors as neither themselves know the way of salvation, neither are able to lead others unto it whereof they are ignorant themselves? If there be no way of salvation but by faith, and none can believe but such as hear the word of God preached (Rom. 10:14), O Lord, how miserable is the state of many flocks in this land who either seldom or never hear the word of God truly preached and therefore know not how to believe that they might be saved.

But here it will be answered that, as it is a thing greatly to be desired, so it is altogether impossible to provide the church of so many learned

11. [ED.] For an account of the various Puritan surveys of the pastorate, see Albert Peel, ed., *The Seconde Parte of a Register* (2 vols.; Cambridge, 1915).

pastors as should take charge of every several congregation.[12] But hereto we reply that it is a thing necessarily required at our hands by God almighty, and therefore we must object no impossibility, especially when our own negligence is the cause of all the difficulty, or if you will so call it, impossibility. We confess it will be hard at the first, but we must do our endeavor, and commit the success unto God, and there is no doubt but in time it will grow to an happy end. But when we shall be altogether careless, as we have been of long time, and that [i.e., what] is worse, not acknowledging any default in this behalf (as there [i.e., some] be that do not); and that is [done] most of all, maintaining such lets and hindrances as be continual nurseries of ignorance and ignorant pastors; [then] we may be ashamed to allege that difficulty, for which none are to be blamed but we ourselves.

We may be ashamed, now that our church hath had rest and peace, with free preaching of the gospel this twenty-five or twenty-six years under the protection of our most gracious Queen, to be so unfurnished of learned pastors as we are.[13] Whereas, if that diligence had been used of all parts, as might and should have been employed of all them that unfeignedly seek the kingdom of God and his righteousness, almost in half the time this necessity might have been well supplied. If we seek [to learn from] experience what diligent and careful provision is able to do with the blessing of God, look to our neighbors and brethren in Christ of France, who although they never enjoyed one day of such peace as we have done so many years, yet how plentifully they are furnished with all kinds of ecclesiastical ministers, and namely with godly and learned pastors, it would rejoice any Christian heart to behold in them, and lament to see the lack in us.[14]

But as for those that acknowledge no defect in our church, through the great multitude of ignorant pastors, we had rather at this time pray to God to lighten their blindness than by any long discourse to discover

12. [ED.] See Christopher Hill, The Economic Problems of the Church (Oxford, 1956), especially Part II.

13. [ED.] Part, if not all, of this section must have been added c. 1584, and thus could not have been written by Fulke.

14. [ED.] On the building up of the Huguenot ministry see Robert M. Kingdon, Geneva and the Coming of the Wars of Religion, 1555–63 (Geneva, 1956). From Geneva alone, in the single year of 1561, a hundred pastors were sent into France. On the fear, in England during the 1580s, that the new dedicated Jesuit missionaries would succeed because the non-preaching, non-resident English clergy could not hold the allegiance of the people, see Christopher Hill, Society and Puritanism in Pre-Revolutionary England (London, 1964), 54 f.

their palpable darkness. Would to God there were not more difficulty in reforming them that maintain such inconveniences, as [i.e., for] except they be taken away, we shall never be disburdened of the cankers of the church, those unlearned ministers. For while non-residents and pluralities be retained, we shall never want unlearned curates, that for small stipends will supply the absence of pluralities and non-residents.[15] Which gross corruptions of pastoral office, as they may have some honest pretence, so can they have no better pretence, neither are they retained with a better conscience, than the priests in our savior Christ's time suffered the exchangers of money, graziers and poulterers to make a burse or shambles [i.e., meat-market] and a poultry [shop], yea, a den of thieves of the temple of God, which was appointed to be a house of prayer to all nations, Matthew 21:12–13; Mark 11:15–18; John 2:14–17.

But especially, while the whole office of a pastor shall be thought to consist in reading only a prescript number of psalms and chapters of the Scriptures, with other appointed forms of prayer; and that he may be allowed as a sufficient pastor which doeth the things which a child of ten years old may do as well as he, so long shall we never lack unlearned pastors, ignorant and ungodly people, simonical and sacrilegious patrons, so long the building of God's church shall go but slowly forward beside other superstitious fantasies maintained in the peoples' hearts, which for shortness we omit to speak of. What though some say formal reading might be borne withal for a time, until the church might be provided of sufficient pastors (which yet is not granted) shall it therefore continue always to the perpetual decay of knowledge and hurt of the church of God?[16] What greater discouragement is there unto students than to see the rewards of learning bestowed as commonly upon the ignorant as upon the learned? What encouragement is it to idleness and slothfulness in them that be already in that vocation, to behold them that take no pains, to live in wealth and ease, without punishment of their negligence?

But here again it will be objected because there are not livings able to maintain all learned pastors, we must be enforced to admit many ignorant ministers. But again we answer, it is our part not only to provide learned pastors, but also livings sufficient to maintain them, upon the necessity of God's commandment. "Let him that is instructed in the word," saith Saint

15. [ED.] See Hill, *Economic Problems*, chaps. VI and IX.
16. [ED.] Because the officials trusted neither the pro-Roman nor the pro-Puritan party among the clergy, severe limitations on preaching were maintained all through the Elizabethan era

Paul, "minister to him that doth instruct him in all good things. Be not deceived for God is not mocked" (Gal. 6:6–7; *cf.* 1 Cor. 9:7–15). By which saying the apostle confuteth all vain excuses, which many are wont to allege, why they would contribute nothing to the maintenance of their pastors; all which he affirmeth to be vain, because they have to do with God, and not with men only. For here is not regarded the living [i.e., the maintenance] of a man, but how much they esteem Christ and the gospel of God. Therefore except we will mock God to his face, let us object nothing to testify such shameful ingratitude that we would doubt how they should be provided of bodily food, of whom we receive the food of our souls, as though we could not afford them an earthly recompense, of whom we receive heavenly benefits.

If nothing had been before time allotted towards the living of the pastors, yet were we bound in pain of damnation to provide sufficient for them. And now there is somewhat towards a living where there is least. And in all places [there would be] sufficient, if it were well disposed. Why should we object necessity through lack of livings to retain idols instead of true pastors? Look once again into France (for examples move much) and behold the churches there impoverished and spoiled with long wars, persecution and unquietness. They have neither bishoprics, deaneries, prebends nor benefices to bestow on their pastors. And yet [they] minister unto them all things necessary for an honest sober life. And shall we that have all this while lived in peace and prosperity under a godly and religious princess, having all these helps, think it is impossible by disposition of godly and wise governors to appoint a sufficient portion for so many learned pastors as are necessary for our churches?

There is none excuse therefore to be admitted, but that we must endeavor to the uttermost of our power that every several congregation, church or parish be provided of a learned pastor. For unskillful shepherds have been too long thrust upon us, to the great dishonor of God and defacing of the gospel of Christ. We have hitherto taken upon us without warrant of God's word to allow such for pastors of men's souls whom no careful owner of cattle would make overseer of his sheep's bodies. Which thing almighty God hath always detested, and signified his misliking by divers testimonies, both of the Old and New Testament. Therefore he saith by the prophet Isaiah, complaining of the unlearned pastors of Israel, which was the only cause of their affliction and miseries, "Their watchmen are all blind, they have no knowledge, they cannot bark, they lie and sleep and delight in sleeping, and these greedy dogs can never have enough, and these shepherds cannot understand, for they all look to their own way, every one for his advantage and for his own purpose. Come, I will bring wine and we will fill ourselves with strong drink, and tomorrow shall be as this day, and much more abundant" (*cf.* Is. 56:10–12). If the prophet had lived in these our days, might he not have spoken the same more truly of many shires in England? We see therefore that blind watchmen and ignorant dumb dogs, and idle greedy curs, and unlearned shepherds that serve for nothing but to fill their own purses or their paunches, by the testimony of God's spirit, are denied to be meet pastors of the people of God.

The prophet Ezekiel also inveigheth at large against the unfeeding shepherds of Israel, saying, "(Woe) be unto the shepherds of Israel which feed themselves: should not the shepherds feed the flocks? Ye eat the fat and you clothe you with the wool; ye kill them that are fed, but ye feed not the sheep. The weak have ye not strengthened, the sick have ye not healed, neither have ye bound up the broken, nor brought again that which was driven away, neither have ye sought that which was lost . . ." (Ezek. 34:2–4), [and thus] throughout the whole chapter. When feeding of God's sheep is a matter of so great importance and consisteth of so many parts, which the prophet hath here described, how should we admit them whom God rejecteth, which being ignorant and unlearned, know nothing at all and therefore nothing can do that appertaineth to this charge, or any part thereof. Undoubtedly the retaining of such is a manifest token of the vengeance of God against us, for so he threatened by the prophet Zechariah. His words are these, "And the Lord said unto me, take to thee yet the instruments of a foolish shepherd, for lo, I will raise up a shepherd in the land which shall not look for the thing that is lost, nor seek the tender lambs, nor heal that is hurt, nor feed that which standeth up, but he shall eat the flesh of the fat and tear their hooves in pieces. O idol shepherd that leaveth the flock, the sword shall be upon his arm and upon his right eye; his arm shall be clean dried up, and his right eye shall be utterly darkened" (Zech. 11:15–17).

Now, seeing we are taught by these words of the Lord God that it is a great and horrible plague to have the church of God encumbered with such foolish and idol shepherds, let us study to remove such plagues from the flock of Christ, whose arms are clean dried up that they have no force, and their eyes utterly darkened that they have no skill, so that they are not able to perform those duties which pertain to a wise and faithful shepherd, except we will betray the sheep of Christ into the mouths of ravenous wolves, and specially into the teeth of that great ramping lion, the Devil, who never ceaseth going about to seek whom he may devour for his prey (1 Pet. 5:8). For what do these reading ministers differ from those idol shepherds, which God in his vengeance threateneth to send for the ingratitude of the people?

It will be answered (no doubt) that to supply their ignorance, there are added to their appointed service many godly and learned homilies, which if they read with their service, there is not so great need of preaching and interpretation of the Scriptures. We will derogate nothing here from the dignity of those homilies. We will not accuse here the unsensible reading of unlearned ministers, neither yet the unreverent contempt of the ignorant hearers. But [that] which all godly and wise men must needs confess [is that] those exhortations [of the homilies] that are not applied to the proper circumstances of times, places, persons and occasions are of small power to persuade any man, and least of all the ignorant people. Let long experience, the mistress of fools, teach us, if knowledge the instructor of wise men cannot move us. How many papists converted? How many ignorant instructed? How many wicked reformed, are ye able to show by this ignorant and unlearned ministry, with all the helps of reading of formal prayers and homilies, without preaching and applying the Scriptures to the proper circumstances before rehearsed?

Again, who seeth not, but he that is so blind that he will see nothing, that these parts of a true pastor's duty, which both the prophets Ezekiel and Zechariah rehearse, namely, to strengthen the weak, to heal the sick, to bind the broken, to seek the lost, to bring home that is carried away, to cherish the young lambs, to feed the strong sheep, etc., cannot be performed of any man by such means as these, but only by such one as is a godly and learned shepherd. Wherefore, these poor helps of prescript form of reading of prayers, of homilies and suchlike, when they are alleged to maintain the ignorance of unskillful pastors, are called no better by the judgment of God, but the instruments of foolish and idol shepherds, which have a certain pretence of pastoral office but in effect are altogether unmeet for the same. Even as idiots and idols are good for nothing but able to do much hurt, concerning whom our savior Christ pronounceth this fearful sentence, "If the blind lead the blind, they shall both fall into the pit" (Mt. 15:14). How long therefore shall we suffer the blind to lead the blind, to the destruction of both? Let us therefore now at the length remove these blind guides, and place in their steads faithful overseers that may lead the flock of Christ into the way of salvation. The ministers of the church are the salt of the earth. "If the salt be unsavory, wherewith shall it be seasoned? It is good for nothing but to be cast out and trodden down of men's feet" (Mt. 5:13). Let us not therefore seek politic shifts to maintain the unsavory salt, which our savior Christ pronounceth to be good for nothing but to be cast out.

By these and many other testimonies of the Scripture, it is as clear as the sun at noondays that it is the office and duty of a pastor both to be able and willing to teach his flock, and that no ignorant and unlearned person is to be admitted to that charge or retained, if he be crept in, no more than a blind man is to be suffered in an office which must be executed only with the sight, or a dumb dog to give warning which cannot bark, or an idol to have the place of a man, or a fool of a wise man, or a wolf of a shepherd, or darkness instead of light, or salt that is unsavory to season withal.

But while we entreat of teaching to be the duty of a pastor, we do not only mean public preaching, when the congregation is assembled, but also private exhortation, reprehension, consolation, of every particular person within his charge, so often as need shall require. And that this also is the duty of a faithful bishop, Saint Paul testifieth, setting before the elders of the church of Ephesus the example of his diligence which he would have them to follow. "You know," saith he, "from the first day that I came into Asia, after what manner I have been with you at all seasons, serving the Lord withal modestly . . . And how I kept back nothing that was profitable, but have showed you and taught you, both openly and throughout every house" (Acts 20:18–20). By which it is manifest that the pastor must not only teach all his flock openly, but also he must instruct every family privately, wheresoever he shall see it to be needful or expedient, which duty cannot be accomplished by a reading minister. Also, in the twenty-sixth verse of the same chapter, he commendeth unto the elders a general care of the whole flock. "Take heed to yourselves," saith he, "and to the whole flock." Which care cannot be well or at all undertaken except they be diligent to teach, both all and every one of their flock, as need shall require. Which thing also he willeth them once again to observe in his example, verse 31, saying: "Therefore watch ye, remembering that by the space of three years, I ceased not night and day, exhorting every one of you."

By these testimonies it is evident to see what diligence the Holy Ghost requireth of pastors in teaching, both publicly and privately, as well gen-

erally all their flock, as particularly every one of them. He therefore that
is unapt to execute this part of a pastor's duty is altogether unmeet [to be
one] to whom governance of the flock of God should be committed. In
temporal affairs, no man will commit the least charge that can be to such
persons as he knoweth to be altogether unmeet, or unable to answer unto
the charge. And shall we continue as we have done hitherto, to put them
in trust with the greatest charge that can be, the salvation of so many
thousand souls redeemed with the blood of Christ, whom we know certainly to be able to do no part of a pastor's duty sufficiently? God forbid
that we should still continue so lightly to esteem so weighty a matter, as
though we accounted the blood of Christ, by which we are sanctified, to
be profane, and would contumeliously withstand the Spirit of God.

But necessity (you will answer) hath no law. This necessity we have
answered before to consist in two points: in lack of livings, and lack of
learned men. The first we have showed ought to be no let [i.e.,
hindrance], no, not of an hour, if the other want could so soon be supplied. And both must of necessity be provided for in time, or else we testify before God and his holy angels, that they which neglect or withstand
this provision shall be guilty of the blood of all them that perish through
the default of teaching in the whole realm.

The lack of livings may be supplied, either by restoring the sacrileges
[i.e., plunderings] of abbeys, [such] as impropriations of benefices, etc., or
by dividing the superfluities of some places that have too much unto them
that have too little, or by any other godly means that may be thought
meet to these godly and wise governors that by duty ought, and by authority may do it.[17]

The lack of learned preachers must be so far forth supplied as it may
presently: [a] by encouraging and exhorting so many as are able to take
that charge in hand, by overseeing the readers and scholars in divinity in
the universities to do their duties, the one in teaching purely, the other in
learning diligently; [b] by thrusting out these unprofitable heads of col-
leges and other drone bees, which either are unable or unwilling to set
forward the study of divinity in their several houses, and placing diligent
and learned governors and students in their places, and by other good
means reforming universities by erecting of doctors and teachers in as
many places as may be;[18] [c] by compelling the unlearned ministers, in

17. [ED.] Some Presbyterians, but not all Puritans, would have recovered for the
church at least some of the endowments plundered under the Tudors.

18. [ED.] Perhaps, by "teachers in as many places as may be," is intended an
acknowledgment of the "lecturers."

whom is any towardness to become scholars in divinity, with some allowance of living if they be willing to study,[19] or else to send them from whence they came, to get their livings with sweat of their brows; [d] and especially considering the greatness of the harvest and fewness of the laborers, by praying earnestly the Lord of the harvest in this great necessity of ours, to thrust forth laborers into his harvest (Mt. 9:37–8). [e] And in the meantime till God shall bless us with a sufficient number of learned pastors, to take some extraordinary and temporal [i.e., temporary] order for overseeing the churches, that although they cannot be all sufficiently instructed and governed, yet so many shall not be altogether destitute of all knowledge and spiritual government as there are now in this most corrupt state of the church in which we have hitherto continued.[20]

If any man think this is overly hard to be brought to pass, let him consider that there was never work of more difficulty than to build up the church of God. So that the necessity and commodity of the work should cause us to stay nothing at the difficulty thereof. For with our faithful endeavor, we shall not want the mighty assistance of God, who will bless our godly labors with greater success than we can look for. If God therefore will grant that these and such like means may take place by the high authority of our dread sovereign the Queen's Majesty, and continue this comfortable peace which we enjoy under her most gracious government, we dare jeopard our lives, that in less than half the time that is already prosperously passed of her Majesty's most honorable and glorious reign, the necessity of learned pastors shall be so well supplied as we shall have no great cause to complain for lack of them, if we may use like diligence to continue them. If not, we will spend the rest of our life in mourning and expectation of the heavy vengeance of God, which must needs fall upon us for this manifest contempt of his express commandment and neglect of increasing the glorious kingdom of our savior Christ. In the meantime, we may boldly say with the apostle, Acts 20:26–7, "We testify unto you this day, that we are clean from the blood of you all, for we have not failed to show you the whole counsel of God . . ." concerning the regiment of his church.[21]

[2. *Administration of the Sacraments.*] Hitherto we have somewhat at large set forth the principal part of a pastor's office, which is to preach

19. [ED.] This scheme would have gone far beyond that of the prophesyings.

20. [ED.] Under Edward VI, "royal preachers" were sent into areas destitute of regular preaching. Also, some attempts had been made to restore the office of "rural dean."

21. [ED.] Once again, the hand of Field is evident.

the word of God and to instruct the people committed to his charge in the same. Here followeth now in the second part of his duty, which consisteth in right administration of the sacraments of God. For seeing it hath pleased God to add such outward signs to be helps of our infirmity, as seals for confirmation of his promises, uttered by his word, Romans 4:11, he hath appointed ministers of the same, to deliver them unto his people, Matthew 28:19; Luke 22:[?]19. For no man may take upon him any office in the church, but he that is called of God, as was Aaron, Hebrews 5:4. Seeing therefore that God hath given some to be pastors in his church, Ephesians 4:11, and it is the duty of pastors to feed the flock of God committed to their charge with all manner of spiritual pasture of their souls, appointed by God. And that the sacraments are a part of this spiritual food, it is manifest that it belongeth to the duty of pastors to administer the holy sacraments; and that the sacraments appertain to the doctrine and word of God, it is evident, that whom God hath instituted to be minister of the word, him also hath he made to be minister of the sacraments; and as the sacraments are compared by the Holy Ghost unto seals, and the word or promise of God unto writings, so it appertaineth to him to deliver the seal which delivereth the writings. For, as the seal hath always relation unto the writings, so have the sacraments unto the word of God.

By this it appeareth that as it is the duty of every pastor to administer the sacraments of Christ, so this office appertaineth to none but to those which are ministers of the word. Our savior Christ authorizing his apostles to baptize all nations, saith: "Go ye forth and teach all nations, baptizing them in the name of the Father, the Son, and the Ghost, teaching them to observe all things that I have commanded you" (Mt. 28:19). Likewise to the same effect, "Go ye forth into the whole world and preach the gospel to every creature; he that shall believe and is baptized shall be saved . . ." (Mk. 16:15–16). Also, instituting his holy supper, he said, "Do this in remembrance of me" (Lk. 22:19). Which remembrance Saint Paul declareth, that it ought to be celebrated by preaching of the Lord's death. "So often," saith he, "as you shall eat of this bread and drink of this cup, you shall show forth the Lord's death until he come" (1 Cor. 11:26).

By these testimonies it is evident that the administration of the sacraments ought to be committed to none but unto such as are preachers of the word, that are able to teach them that they baptize, that are able to preach the mystery of Christ's death to them to whom they do deliver the outward sign thereof. How intolerable an abuse then is it of the sacraments of the Lord, to commit the administration of them to those men that are not able to expound the mystery of them. And seeing the elements of the world, of which the outward part of the sacraments is taken, be dead and beggarly of themselves except they be animated and enriched with the promise and word of God, which is the life of the sacraments, what can it be better than sacrilege to separate the ministration of preaching of the word from the sacraments? And forasmuch as the Spirit of God compareth the sacraments to seals that are added for confirmation of writings, we know well that a word or writing may be available without a seal, but never a seal without a writing.

Therefore in this behalf we have had great default, so long time to commit the administration of the sacraments to those men who not only have been known to be unable, but also have been forbidden to preach the word. And that which is more strange, to be suffered in this clear light of the gospel to permit the ministration of baptism not only to ignorant men, but also to women (which have no voice to speak in the congregation, 1 Cor. 14:34 and 1 Tim. 2:11), and that in private places, but in cases (they say) of necessity. As though there were such necessity of the outward sign [even] when it cannot be ministered according to the institution of Christ. Which is nothing else but to affirm with the papists that sacraments confer grace of the work wrought, and that the sacrament of baptism is a sacrament of such necessity that whosoever is not dipped in water must be eternally condemned. Which heretical opinion, as we have hissed out in our profession and preaching, so is it a great shame for us to maintain [it] by such corrupt usage of Christ's holy sacraments. Let us therefore retain this principle, that the administration of the sacraments is a part of the pastor's duty. For although the office of preaching be more excellent than of ministration of the sacraments, as Saint Paul speaketh comparatively, "Christ sent me not to baptize but to preach," 1 Corinthians 1:17, yet they are of such affinity that the accessory cannot be separated from the principal thereof. For where is no preacher of the word, there ought to be no minister of the sacraments.

[3. *Public Prayer.*] Furthermore, it pertaineth to the duty of the pastor to make prayers, as Acts 16:16, not only private, as all men are bound to do, but also public prayers in the name of the whole church, being the mouth thereof, Acts 6:4, 1 Timothy 2:1. For whereas the Spirit of God commandeth all things to be done in decent and comely order, and forbiddeth all confusion and disorder (*cf.* 1 Cor. 14:40), as it were great confusion and uncomeliness for every man to make his several prayers in the public assemblies, so is it orderly for one to pronounce the prayer in the name of the rest, and the rest to pray with him in silence and to answer, "Amen" (cf. 1 Cor. 14:16). It is also decent that he which is the shepherd should go before the sheep in prayer, and the sheep to follow him in lifting up of their hearts in mutual consent. Moreover, forasmuch as preaching and administration of the sacraments ought not to be used without public prayers, as it is the pastor's office to preach and minister the sacraments, so is it his duty also to go before his flock in public prayers.[22]

But here we have to observe two things: the first, that as it pertaineth to the pastor to conceive public prayers, so it is the duty of the whole church, in the name of the whole church, to join in heart with the pastor in the same prayers, that they knowing and understanding what he hath prayed, may at the end give their consent by answering, "Amen" (1 Cor. 14:16). Wherein there is great abuse in our churches. For, as though it were not enough to keep out preaching by long prescribed forms of prayer, these prayers are so pronounced by the minister that a great number, and some not of the worst disposed people, think it pertaineth not to them to give ear or consent of mind unto them. We speak not here of such insensible readers whose voice either cannot be heard, or else cannot be understood, whereof there be great numbers; nor of the unfit place prescribed for the ministers, standing at prayer in the east end of the house, when the simple people shall stand oftentimes forty or fifty yards off in the west end; or of the confusion of voices whilst all speak at once, besides screens of rood-lofts, organ lofts, idol cages, otherwise called chantry chapels, and high pews between them (which although they do manifestly hinder edification, yet may they not be removed in many places, for defacing the beauty of the material houses, whereas Saint Paul so much esteemeth the building of God's spiritual house that he commandeth the glorious gifts of the Holy Ghost to cease in the congregation when they do not help to edification (cf. 1 Cor. 14:28)).[23] But we

22. [ED.] On the issue of officially required forms of prayer, which has been avoided here, the various Puritan leaders were never in complete agreement. Even so, in 1584, the very year of Fulke's Discourse, the Puritan party in Parliament attempted to make official a slight modification of the Geneva order of service, providing for some fixed and some free prayers.

23. [ED.] The controversies in Tudor England over church architecture, ecclesiastical art, stained-glass windows, etc., arose because in the pre-Reformation church all these things had been a functional expression of Catholic faith and piety. The iconoclasm of 1534, led by Cranmer and Latimer, was directed against the worship of the saints and against the doctrine of purgatory. The very intensive campaign led by Ridley in 1547–9 had been directed against the mass, saints, purgatory and Catholic

speak of this, that a great multitude think they have well served God if they have been present at common prayers, or any part of them, as they were wont to think in popery, although they be never so vainly occupied in the church, some in walking, some in talking, in gathering of money not only for the poor, but for other contributions, etc. And they that think they do best, are occupied in their private prayers, or in reading of books, while their minister pronounceth public prayers.[24]

Thus as preaching is neglected, upon color of public prayers, so public prayers, by private exercises are made altogether unprofitable to a great number. For who knoweth the right use of public prayer but they that are taught by the word of God? Let us therefore establish public preaching, and public prayers will follow of necessity. But if we continue [so] to uphold formal prayers that preaching be neglected, it will come to pass that neither shall be regarded. For what did thrust out preaching from the Romish church but long prescript forms of reading, of singing, of praying; so that their ordinary was enough and too much, to occupy the whole day, though there were no sermon. Whereas [if things were] contrariwise, there would be no ordinary public prayer without preaching.

Which terrible example of the practice of Satan in the man of sin, should make us afraid to give any like occasion of such inconvenience hereafter to come. For is not this opinion already grown into a great many men's heads, that the service may not give place to a sermon, no, though the time be not sufficient for both? And are there not many that had much rather hear a chanted Matins and Evensong than a godly and learned sermon? Yea, they frequent the one and refuse the other. Let cathedral churches, etc., be an example, where you shall see a great number that tarry while the service is sung, but depart so soon as the sermon beginneth. While the organs pipe, some are drawn with the sweetness of music to come up. But while the preacher crieth out, [they] continue beneath, and in laughter or brawling be louder than he oftentimes.[25]

---

piety in general. It did away with all altars, all statuary and pictures, all old service books and manuscripts, all shrines and pyxes, and much ornamentation, including many church windows. Parker and Coxe had both been active in all this. Valuable studies of the Erasmian backgrounds of such attitudes towards ecclesiastical art are Charles Garside, Jr., *Zwingli and the Arts* (New Haven, 1966); E. L. Surtz, *The Praise of Wisdom* (Chicago, 1957).

24. [ED.] A common complaint during Tudor-Stuart times.

25. [ED.] The employment of organs and choirs, and of the newer, more complex musical settings of the mass, were severely criticized by Christian Humanists such as Erasmus and Thomas More. In 1549 Ridley led a campaign to silence the organs or remove them altogether from English churches. On the backgrounds of these

So, that which was wont to be said of the Mass, "The Mass was a gentle beast, and did bite no man," and therefore was so well beloved of many, may rightly be verified of our ordinary service. For therefore a great number can so well away with it, because it doth not sharply reprove them of their sins, nor disclose the secrets of their hearts, but that they may continue still in all kinds of voluptuousness and all other kind of wickedness. Whereas by preaching, their conscience is galled, their wickedness and hypocrisy discovered, their damnation threatened, they are called to repentance and forsaking of their pleasant sins, and to holiness and innocency of life. So that if there be any spark of the fear of God in them, hearing preaching so often as they use to hear service, they will fall down on their faces and worship God, acknowledging the great power of God in his ministers, 1 Corinthians 14:25. But that they cannot away with all, being like unto Felix, the lieutenant of the Romans in Jewry, who when he heard Paul, a poor prisoner that stood before him bound in chains, preaching of righteousness, of temperance, and of the judgment to come [cf. Acts 24:24–5], he was weary of him because he was a great oppressor and an intemperate person. And therefore [he] feared the judgment of God for his sin, which he purposed not to forsake. Such is the majesty of God's word when it is preached, that either it boweth or breaketh the wicked in pieces. God grant therefore that instead of ordinary forms of prayers, we may have preaching in all places.

The second thing that we have to observe is this, that although we make it the duty of the pastor to pray in the name of the whole congregation, yet we do not so mean but that the whole congregation with one heart and with one voice may praise God with singing of psalms all at once (cf. 1 Cor. 14:15, 26). For this custom hath continued in the church from the beginning, that the congregation have praised God with psalms singing altogether.

[4. Ceremonies.] And these three parts of a pastor's duty, to preach, to minister the sacraments, and to pray, are so necessarily required of him in the word of God as no man may rightly execute the office of a pastor but he that performeth all these, each one in their due time.

And to this part of prayer may be referred the blessing of marriages, not of necessity, but of an ancient use of the church.

Furthermore, in those things that are necessary parts of the pastor's of-

attitudes see Garside, *Zwingli and the Arts*, 32 f, 57 f, 61 f; also Percy A. Scholes, *The Puritans and Music* . . . (Oxford, 1934).

fice, the church hath authority to dispose them: [a] as touching the circumstances, for order and comeliness' sake, but chiefly for edification; [b] as the days and times of preaching and administering the sacraments, the places meet for the same, and for public prayers; [c] also the form and manner of using those things so that all things be done comely and agreeably to order, but especially that in all things principal regard be had to edification, which Saint Paul so often and so precisely urgeth in the fourteenth chapter of the 1 Corinthians. For therefore ought our assemblies and comings together to serve, that therefore we may be better, that we may be taught, that we may be edified, 1 Corinthians 11:17, 1 Corinthians 14:23–6, 31.

And therefore we have great marvel that some are so precise in urging ceremonies, as many think much hindering edification, but as most men confess, nothing profiting to edification, having always in their mouth that sentence of Saint Paul, 1 Corinthians 14:40: "Let all things be done decently, and according to an order," and do so little remember that the apostle in that long chapter laboreth altogether to drive all things to edification, or else to drive them out of the church. As he saith of him that hath the gift of tongues, being of itself an excellent and comely gift of the Holy Ghost and being used orderly of one or two by course, with an interpreter, might do much good in the church. But if there be none interpreter (saith he), let him hold his peace in the congregation, 1 Corinthians 14:28.

The uncomeliness that Saint Paul reproveth was that women should preach in the church, as verses 30, 35. The disorder, that those gifts which served least for edifying were preferred before them that served most for edifying, as tongues before prophecy. By which it is evident that Saint Paul's words are wrested of some clean contrary to his meaning, to make him a patron of idle, if not hurtful ceremonies, maintained more upon will than reason, or granted of God's word under the color of order and decency, not only with neglect, but also with great hindrance of God's building, by spoiling the church of so many learned pastors.

There are beside these things certain other matters, as confirmation, churching of women, burial of the dead, [which are] thought to belong to the office of a bishop or pastor, whereof the first two are mere devices of men and ought to have no place in the church of Christ. The other, albeit it be to be retained with a certain honesty, yet it is not to be tied to the proper office of a pastor. And as for confirmation, it ought therefore to be shut out and have no place in the church of God, [a] as well because it displaced catechizing and brought instead thereof vain toys and childish ceremonies to the great hurt of the church; [b] as for that also it derogateth much from the dignity of baptism, the sacrament of the Lord, and is extolled above it, being a device of man, and is pretended to be a sign to certify the children of the favor and gracious goodness of God towards them, falsely grounded upon the example of the apostles, whereas the ministration of baptism is permitted to every hedge-priest, minister and deacon.[26]

And as for churching of women, because it savoreth of the Jewish purification and of popish institution, it ought altogether to be omitted. For it breedeth and nourisheth many superstitious opinions in the simple people's hearts; as, [a] that the woman which hath borne a child is unclean or unholy, whereas the apostle pronounceth that godly women are sanctified and saved by bearing of children, 1 Timothy 2:15; [b] that it is unlawful for her for any necessity to go out of her doors before she be churched; [c] that this churching is a necessary part of the pastor's office; [d] that she must wear a white veil over her head when she goeth to church by the midwife, waited home with [by] the parish clerk, with divers suchlike baubles, which in a well reformed church are not to be suffered.[27]

As for the burial of the dead, because Satan took occasion, upon ceremonies appointed thereunto, to sow the seed of many heresies in the church, as prayers for the dead, oblations for the dead, purgatory, etc.; also many superstitions, as hallowing of churchyards, distinction of burials, as some in the chancel, some in the church, and some in the churchyards; some with more pomp, as singing, ringing, etc., some with less, burying towards the east, lights and holy water bestowed upon the dead, etc., it is thought good to the best and right reformed churches to bury their dead reverently, without any ceremonies of praying or preaching at them, because experience hath taught them what inconvenience may grow thereof, by example of that which hath been before.[28]

And as they are not to be excused, if any for small trifles only, raise up hot contentions; so they have much to answer before God, that suffer the

26. [ED.] For a more recent discussion of baptism *versus* confirmation, see G. W. H. Lampe, *The Seal of the Spirit* (London, 1951).

27. [ED.] See the clever Puritan satire on the notion of "purifying" women, *Certaine questions . . . betwixt a chauncelor and a kinswoman of his concerning churching of women* (1601; *S.T.C.*, 20557).

28. [ED.] Criticism of the Roman doctrine of purgatory, and the saying of masses for the dead, took many forms among Protestants. Fulke does not commit himself here beyond urging simplicity.

people of God to lack the only food of their souls for such human constitutions. But to conclude, it is the duty of every true pastor to observe those things that are concluded by the lawful authority of the church, concerning ceremonial matters, for order and comeliness' sake and for edification, and not to control [i.e., regulate] public order by his private judgment, but [i.e., except] upon great and weighty causes.[29]

[AUTHORITY IN THE CHURCH]

We have hitherto entreated of the proper duty of a pastor himself. Now it followeth that we likewise set forth his authority in common government with the elders. But lest any man should mistake that which we purpose to say of his authority, we have need to express what we mean by this word "authority." For even those things that we have showed before to be the duty of a pastor may also be called his authority, as to preach and teach, wherein is included his authority to forgive and retain sins; also his authority to minister the sacraments, and to do other things in the church which none may do but he. But in this place we understand "authority" for power of government in the church. Whereof the apostle speaketh (1 Cor. 12:28), that it is one of the graces and gifts of God necessary for the building of his church. This authority of regiment [i.e., government] we have declared that it ought not to be a lordly ruling (1 Pet. 5:3) neither over their flock, nor yet over their fellow servants and brethren (cf. Lk. 22:26); and least of all, that they ought to have dominion or lordship over the faith of the church (2 Cor. 1:24). In all these the man of sin hath exalted himself contrary to the word of God, so that he would be head of all the church, bishop of all bishops, and have authority to make new articles of faith,[30] whose intolerable presumption as we have long since banished out of this land, so we wish that no steps of such pride and arrogancy might be left behind him, namely, that no elder or minister of the church should challenge unto himself (or accept it if it were offered unto him) any other authority than that is allowed by the Spirit of God, but chiefly to beware that he usurp no authority which

29. [ED.] The Presbyterian Puritans would contend most for polity, but not so vigorously on ceremonies. Puritans of the two other groups were in contention mainly over ceremonies and preaching, and less, or not at all, over polity. Their differences involved not only strategies, but also different views of the church, of the ministry, and of the role of the civil magistrate in the church.

30. Hierarchia.

is forbidden by the word of God. For wherefore do we detest the pope and his usurped supremacy, but because he arrogateth the same unto himself, not only without the warrant of God's word, but also clean contrary to the same? Now if the same reasons and authorities that have banished the pope do serve to condemn all other usurped authority that is practiced in the church, why should not all such usurped authority be banished as well as the pope? We can allege against the pope and rightly, that which Saint John Baptist did answer to his disciples, "No man can take unto himself anything, except it be given him from heaven," John 3:27, and that saying of the apostle to the Hebrews: "No man may take upon him any honor (in the church of God) but he that is called of God, as was Aaron" (Heb. 5:4). Insomuch that Christ himself did not give himself to be a high priest (*cf.* Phil. 2:6), but he that said unto him: "Thou art my Son, this day I have begotten thee" [Ps. 2:7], he saith in another place, "Thou art a priest forever after the order of Melchizedek" [Heb. 5:6].

Now seeing these rules are so general that the Son of God himself was not exempted from them, but showed forth the decree wherein he was authorized, by what rule can any man retain that authority in the church of God which is not called thereto by the word of God? Likewise we can allege again, against the supremacy of the pope, to prove that Peter was not superior to the other apostles, that which our savior Christ saith to his apostles, Luke 22:26 and Matthew 20:25, Mark 10:42: "It shall not be so among you, but he that is greatest amongst you shall be as the youngest, and he that ruleth as he that serveth"; and Matthew 23:8: "You have but one master, which is Christ, and all you are brethren." If these places prove that the pope ought not to be above other ministers of the church, why do they not likewise prove that the ministers are equal among themselves? And for the most part, all those arguments and authorities of Scripture that are used to confute the usurped authority of the pope, are of as great force against all other usurped authorities of one pastor over another.

Therefore, while we entreat of the authority of the pastors, we must take heed that we open not a window to popish tyranny instead of pastoral authority, and that we enlarge not the bounds of authority without the bounds of the Scripture. Wherefore while we search the Scripture, the only rule whereby the church of God ought to be governed, we find that in regiment and governance of the church, the pastor, bishop or elder hath none authority by himself, separated from other. For in the church there ought to be no monarchy or sole absolute government, but that is referred peculiarly to our savior Christ only, 2 Timothy[?] 6:7; Jude 4. And that regiment which he hath left unto his church is a consent of his household servants to do all things according to his prescription, as he witnesseth, Matthew 18:19: "If two of you consent upon earth upon any matter, whatsoever ye shall ask, it shall be granted to you of my Father, which is in heaven. For wheresoever two or three be gathered together in my name, there am I in the midst of them." Seeing therefore that our savior Christ hath neither authorized nor promised to bless any other form of regiment than that which consisteth of the consent and gathering together of his servants in his name, we hold us content with this simplicity. And therefore we are bold to say that the authority of a pastor in public regiment or discipline, separate from others, is nothing at all.

Let us then see what is his authority joined with others, and first, who are so joined in commission with him, that without their consent he can do nothing. We say therefore, that the authority of Christ is left unto his whole church, and so to every church. That none may challenge episcopal or metropolitan authority (as it is with us at this day) over others without great tyranny and manifest injury. For seeing our savior Christ promised his presence and authority to every church indifferently, Matthew 18:19,20, none may challenge any such prerogative afore other. But as the churches are limited out for order and conveniency, so is every one of them of like authority in itself. But because they make all but one church and one body of Christ, therefore there is but one authority in them to determine of matters concerning them all.

By which there appeareth to be a double authority of the pastor: one with the several [i.e., particular] congregation in which he is pastor, the other with the whole synod or assembly whereof he is a member. And both these authorities we find sufficiently authorized in the Scripture, as shall plainly appear in the several discourses of them.

First therefore, we will speak of his authority in his several church, in which he may do nothing without the consent of the church. And first, let us examine whether this authority be so diffused over the whole church that the hearing, trying and determining of all matters pertaineth to the whole multitude, or to some special chosen persons amongst them, meet for that purpose.

[1. Elders]

The authority is the power of our Lord Jesus Christ granted unto the church. But because the judgment of the multitude is confuse [i.e., diffuse], whereas God is not the author of confusion but of order, and that we find in the word of God certain officers appointed for government; we are bold to affirm that that charge belongeth unto those that are such. And that doth St. Paul plainly declare, where he putteth a difference of the several offices of the church, whereof he nameth governors for one, 1 Corinthians 12:28–9; and Romans 12:8: "Let him that ruleth do it with diligence." Therefore there ought to be in every church a consistory or seignory of elders or governors, which ought to have the hearing, examination and determining of all matters pertaining to discipline and government of that congregation. Which authority of theirs nevertheless ought to be moderated, that their judgment may be rightly accounted the judgment of the holy church. Which thing consisteth in these two points.

[A.] First, that the elders be elected and chosen by consent of the whole congregation, men of godliness and wisdom, in whom the whole church reposeth such confidence that they commit unto them their authority in hearing and determining such matters as without horrible confusion they cannot perform themselves. And hereto also may be referred that which is said of election of pastors, that the apostles Paul and Barnabas did ordain, by election of the congregation, elders unto many churches, Acts 14:23; because the name of elders is common to both, to pastors and governors, and is used in the Scripture to comprehend both at once, as it appeareth manifestly by Saint Paul, 1 Timothy 5:17: "Those elders that govern well are worthy of double honor, especially those that labor in the word and doctrine." Of which testimony, we learn these three things: First, that there be elders in the church which meddle not with teaching, but are occupied altogether in governing. Secondly, that the elders which labor in teaching, otherwise called pastors, are joined also in government with them which teach not. And thirdly, that the name of elder comprehendeth both sorts of elders. And especially in the place before alleged for election, there is great reason to lead us to think that the elders for government are as well understood as the other for doctrine.

Because it is written in the same place, that after they had ordained them elders in every congregation by election (Acts 14:23), as having set the churches in perfect order (which could not be except they had established discipline as well as doctrine) they committed them to the Lord, in whom they believed.

[B.] The second point for moderation of the elders' authority in such sort that their sentence may be the sentence of the church is this, that when the consistory hath travailed in examining of causes pertaining to ecclesiastical discipline, and agreed what judgment ought to pass upon the matters, they propound it to the whole multitude, that it may be confirmed by their consent.[31] Whereof Saint Paul speaketh touching the execution of excommunication (because the fact was manifest), "When you are gathered together with my spirit, in the name of our Lord Jesus Christ, and with the power of our Lord Jesus Christ, to deliver such a one unto Satan . . ." (1 Cor. 5:4–5).

Now therefore, to prove that there ought to be a consistory of elders in every church for governing of the same, it is manifest by the commandment of our savior Christ touching him that despiseth private admonition: "If he hear not them, tell the congregation; if he hear not the congregation, let him be unto thee as a heathen and publican. Verily I say unto you, whatsoever you shall bind upon earth shall be bound in heaven" (Mt. 18:17–18). In which saying of our savior Christ, this word "congregation" is not so largely taken, as in other places, for the whole multitude, but for the chosen assembly of elders. For our savior Christ in that word alludeth unto the assembly of elders that was among the Jews which they called but corruptly of a Greek word *synedrion*, which signifieth a council or consistory, *sanhedrin*, which had the hearing and determining of all difficult and weighty matters among the Jews, the like whereof he willed to be established in his church for administration of government. For, seeing it was first instituted by God for government of his church in the old law, as hath been showed before out of Numbers 11:16, although it was shamefully abused by the wicked Jews, our savior Christ translateth it into his church also in the New Testament. And the name of elders doth most aptly agree unto them that be governors in the church now, even as it did to the ancients of Israel. So that the pastors seem to have borrowed the name of elders, specially in respect of their government.

The name of this consistory also in the New Testament we find to be

31. [ED.] Not all "Reformed" or "Presbyterian" versions of polity conceded this as the right of the whole church. During the civil wars of the 1640s, this was one of the issues over which the clash between Presbyterian and Independent Puritans became catastrophic.

agreeable with that of the Jews, whereof our savior Christ speaketh when he saith: "Tell the congregation or assembly" (*cf.* Mt. 18:17). Saint Paul, 1 Timothy 4:14: "Despise not the gift which was given thee through prophecy, with imposition of hands of the eldership," where the Greek word is *presbyterion,* the assembly or consistory of the elders. Which word is used also by St. Luke in his gospel, speaking of the consistory of the Jewish elders, Luke 22:66: "As soon as it was day, the whole eldership or assembly of elders came together, both chief priests and scribes, and brought him into their council." In which saying, their council *synedrion* is called *presbyterion.* Also Saint Paul, Acts 22:4–5, that he had been a persecutor of Christians, taketh witness of the high priest and of the whole consistory of elders, using the same word *presbyterion.* By which it is evident that our savior Christ by this word *ecclesia* in that place, meaneth a consistory or assembly of elders whose authority he doth ratify with such power that whatsoever is bound or loosed by them on earth, in the fear of God and with hearty prayer, the Lord will bring it to pass, yea he himself will be in the midst of them, as president of their council, to direct their consultations, to the glory of God and the profit of his own church. Therefore in every church there ought to be a consistory of elders or governors, which with the pastor may take charge of ecclesiastical discipline and good order to be observed in the church, to the punishment of vice, and the advancement of true virtue. These, if they govern well, as Saint Paul doth testify, are worthy of double honor, both that honor which is due to godly men and that which is due to good governors.

[2. The End of Discipline]

How necessary it is that discipline should be in the church, to keep men in awe from offending and to bring offenders to repentance, to avoid the infection of sin within the church, and the reproach that groweth by neglecting the punishment of sin among them that are without the church, we think it needless to stand long in proving, the matter of itself is so apparent and hath such plentiful testimonies in the Scripture.[32] And especially, let the reasons of Saint Paul, 1 Corinthians 5:1–6 and 2 Cor-

32. [ED.] The question of whether the church should discipline those outside itself was another on which the Presbyterian and Independent Puritans were to find themselves at issue.

inthians 2, where he purposely entreateth of ecclesiastical discipline, be weighed, "A little leaven soureth a whole lump of dough." For infection, "Ye are puffed up where ye should be sad and ashamed." For ignominy, "We deliver him to Satan, to the destruction of his flesh, that his spirit may be saved in the day of the Lord." For repentance, public reprehension of many, "which being godly refuse to eat with such a one," is profitable both to drive himself to repentance and to keep other in order for fear of like punishment. Where this discipline is not, no marvel if all wickedness overflow, to the dishonor of God and of his gospel, to the destruction of many and corrupting of more, to the grief of the godly, offence of the weak, encouragement of the wicked, and rejoicing of the adversary.

Let us therefore proceed in setting forth the authority of the pastor with the elders, which is, first, to punish offenders and bring them to repentance, or else to cut them clean from the church as rotten and infected members. But here we have to inquire for what offences the church may proceed to so sharp a punishment. For God forbid that the sword of excommunication should be drawn out to cut off the members of our body for every small disease that is in them, but only when the disease is deadly and the member rotted thereby. For we ought as hardly to be brought to excommunicate any of our brethren as we would have a leg or an arm cut off from our body.

Therefore the popish tyranny is detestable which thundereth out their pretended excommunication for every trifle, yea such as are no sins, as nonpayment of a little money where it is not detained of fraud, non-appearance [before the ecclesiastical court] where men otherwise have necessary impediments, as though it were but a small matter to put men out of the protection of Christ and to deliver them unto the tyranny of Satan, to deprive them of eternal salvation and to cast them into everlasting damnation.[33] Lest, therefore, we should use such unreasonable rigor, the Spirit of God teacheth us what manner of sins deserve excommunication, 1 Corinthians 5:11, "If any that is called a brother be a whoremonger, or a covetous person, or an idolator, or a slanderer, or a drunkard, or an extortioner, with such a one see that ye eat not." These offences therefore and such like, are to be punished by excommunication. Also an obstinate heretic that will not repent by admonition, is worthy of this punishment, Titus 3:10, 2 Timothy 2:16, 1 Timothy 1:20, 2 John 10 and 11. And not only these great and notorious sins deserve this correction, but also lesser

33. [ED.] See Hill, *Society and Puritanism*, chaps. 6, 8, 9.

crimes, increased with contumacy and contempt of the church's admonition, become worthy of the same castigation.

Therefore saith our savior Christ of private offences, Matthew 18:15–17: "If thy brother sin against thee, go and reprove him between him and thee alone; if he hear thee thou hast won thy brother; but if he hear thee not, take with thee one or two, that in the mouth of two or three witnesses every word may stand; if he disobey them, then tell the church, if he disobey the church, then let him be to thee as a heathen or publican."

The apostle Saint Paul likewise, 2 Thessalonians 3:6, etc., concerning those that were idle and walked disorderly, will have all gentle means used to bring them to labor and good order. But if they would not be reformed for any admonition, he commandeth them to be separated by excommunication.

But it may be objected that hitherto appeareth not so great use of this consistory, why it should be thought necessary for excommunication. Neither doth St. Paul make mention of it in all places where he speaketh of excommunication. We answer that although the simple institution of Christ and approbation of the Holy Ghost should suffice us to think it necessary, yet there are many necessary uses thereof to be alleged. For whereas our savior Christ commandeth in private offences the matter to be brought before the congregation, except you understand thereby the congregation or assembly of elders, there shall follow horrible confusion and disorder thereby. For, admit a man might accuse his brother unto the whole multitude, yet how should the whole multitude admonish him and exhort him to repentance? Again, of these notorious offences that are worthy of excommunication, some are openly known, so that they need no trial, as the adultery of that Corinthian, 1 Corinthians 5; some are in controversy and are to be examined, concerning which Saint Paul warneth Timothy that he admit not any accusation against an elder but under two or three witnesses, and chargeth him before God and before the Lord Jesus Christ and his elect angels, that he do nothing through rash or over-hasty judgment, and that he do all things without partiality or affection unto parties, 1 Timothy 5:19,21.

We see here manifestly a necessary use of the eldership. For how is it possible for the whole church to examine and discuss such difficult controversies? Therefore it behooveth the church to have such ordinary delegates as may and ought to apply their diligence unto such matters. Moreover, to oversee the church for matters pertaining to order and discipline: how can the multitude oversee themselves, or the pastors only, which have a principal care of doctrine to attend upon? And to the second part of the objection, that Saint Paul doth [not] make mention of the eldership or consistory of elders in all places where he speaketh of excommunication, we answer that it is not necessary he should so do. For whereas our savior Christ hath prescribed a form thereof, that he which obeyeth not the congregation should be excommunicated; and that in other places, he maketh sufficient mention both of the elders and of the assembly; we ought to understand that his purpose is to observe that form to the uttermost. And although he do not always make express mention thereof, yet must we not imagine that he meant to alter or change the same. In the first to the Corinthians, the fifth verse [*cf.* 1 Cor. 5:1–5], it is manifest that albeit he desired nothing more than that the incestuous adulterer should be excommunicated, and therefore determined of him for his own part as absent in body but present in spirit; yet he acknowledgeth that he could not be excommunicated without the consent of the congregation being gathered together in the name of our Lord Jesus Christ, 1 Corinthians 5:4. Likewise when he should be received again, he was to be pardoned not only by him, but by them also, 2 Corinthians 2:10.

And therefore, if so high an apostle could not by his private authority excommunicate that Corinthian, we must not think that by his private authority, but by consent of the church of Ephesus, he excommunicated Hymenaeus and Alexander, although he do not make express mention of the consent of the church in that place, 1 Timothy 1:20. So likewise where he speaketh to Timothy in the singular number, concerning the hearing and determining of matters pertaining to discipline, we ought to acknowledge that he teacheth in Timothy's person the duty of elders, and never meant to give Timothy an absolute or singular authority to be judge in these matters without consent of the eldership, whereof he maketh mention but a little before.

To conclude, therefore, the pastor with advice and consent of the elders, hath authority to hear and examine matters pertaining to ecclesiastical discipline, and, as the cause requireth, to excommunicate offenders, and upon their repentance and amendment, to receive them again into the bosom of the church, approved by the word of God. Instead of which, Antichrist hath set up a tyrannical jurisdiction of one bishop to be judge of excommunication, which is practiced neither for causes sufficient nor by sufficient authority. Insomuch as [i.e., whereas] it hath been already testified by the Scripture that the power of excommunication is in no one man, no not in an apostle, but is common to the whole church, and ought to be executed by lawful delegates of the church also. But so much [doth] that usurped authority presume, that the bishop, as an absolute owner thereof, committeth it over to his chancellor or archdeacon, the archdeacon to his official, and he to his register, and he again to his substitute, and his substitute to his servants, man or boy as it happeneth; insomuch that a learned preacher may be excommunicated by a foolish boy.

If this matter seem not to require speedy reformation, God hath blinded our eyes that we cannot see the clear light of the sun shining in our faces. For if we look to banish the tyranny of the pope out of all men's hearts, we must utterly remove all his detestable enormities out of the realm, as it was wont to be said in the common prayers of the church in the time of King Henry and Edward,[34] whereas now, by retaining still all the detestable enormities of his prerogative [courts] and [courts of] faculties, and [the] whole course of his canon law, the papacy is not so much banished in name as translated indeed from the See of Rome to the See of Canterbury, under the shadow of the prince's supremacy, with as heinous injury and contumely of the lawful authority and godly supremacy of the prince, as joined with the great dishonor of God and the miserable disorder of the church.[35] But we mean not in this place to prosecute our just complaints, nor to inveigh against the abuse of these things with such vehemency of words as the worthiness of the matters deserveth; but only in setting forth the plain truth, to give a glimpse by the way of the contrary falsehood.

[3. Deacons]

We must therefore return to the authority of the pastor, which he hath, joined with the elders of the church whereof he is pastor.[36] The church hath always had great care for provision of the poor, by which compassion they showed that they were lively members of the body of

34. [ED.] The litany in the prayer book of 1552 included this petition, deleted in 1559: "From the tyranny of the Bishop of Rome and all his detestable enormities, — Good Lord, deliver us."

35. [ED.] For a summary of criticisms of these ecclesiastical courts by men such as Richard Hooker, Archbishop Parker, Archbishop Sandys and others, see Hill, *Society and Puritanism,* 316 f.

36. [ED.] This section makes the deacons subsidiary to the elders, a pattern not followed in all Reformed churches.

Christ, and avoided great reproach of them that were without. For what shame is it for them that profess to be all sons of one father and therefore all brethren; yea that be members all of one body, to suffer their brethren and fellow members to lack necessaries to sustain their temporal life, as though they that communicate in all spiritual graces and blessings were not worthy to take part of these worldly benefits, at leastwise so far forth as to supply their necessities? Therefore our savior Christ always commendeth brotherly love among his disciples, to teach us how ready we ought to be to distribute unto the necessities of our brethren, which is a true testimony of our love declared by his own example. For although he were so poor that he lived of the alms and liberality of other men, yet of that which was more than served his own necessity, he used to bestow upon the poor (as John 13:29) to teach them whom he hath blessed with temporal riches (which he refused to enrich us with heavenly treasures) that they of their superfluity would be content to give to the relief of their poor brethren, which he did not neglect in his extreme poverty. To teach also them that have but mean substance that they ought not to be excused, but somewhat to contribute unto the necessity of their poor brethren, when he that had nothing at all but that which was given, even of that bestowed part.[37]

Therefore the apostles in the primitive church thought it to be expedient for the better providing for the poor that certain men should be appointed of approved godliness and diligence, which should take the special charge of the distribution unto the poor, Acts 6. These men were called deacons or ministers, because they did minister and serve the poor in their necessities. And because the occasion of the ordinance continueth always (as our savior Christ hath said, we should always have the poor amongst us, John 12:8), whereby God would exercise our charity, the office of deacons also is perpetual.

Therefore the apostle Saint Paul prescribeth what kind of men are meet for that office, 1 Timothy 3:8. And in every well-constituted church they were ordained accordingly, as Philippians 1:1. Also after the ordaining of the seven deacons, this office was divided into divers parts, as necessity showed divers occasions. For some were appointed for the collection and distribution of alms, as Romans 12:8, and some for attending upon the sick and impotent among the poor, as in the same place:

37. [ED.] See Hill, *Society and Puritanism*, chap. 7, "The Poor and the Parish," and the literature cited there; also W. K. Jordan, *Philanthropy in England 1480–1660* (London, 1959).

"Let him that distributeth do it with simplicity, and let him that showeth mercy do it with cheerfulness." Which kind of deacons, 1 Corinthians 12:28, are called helpers; and for the service of this office were appointed divers old poor widows, who as they were maintained by the church, so they served the church, attending upon the other poor, who being sick and impotent, had need not only of things necessary, but also of service and attending, 1 Timothy 5:5.

These offices being instituted by the spirit of God for the necessary use of the church, which use still continueth, ought also to be retained among us. For we see, for want of these offices, what great inconveniences are among us concerning the poor. For although there be very good politic laws made for provision of the poor, yet small relief cometh thereby to the poor indeed. At leastwise many abuse the relief which they receive, which cometh of this, that there be not in every church or congregation such deacons as the Holy Ghost hath appointed, which should take a special care and employ a great diligence for the provision of the poor. Not only some to gather and distribute, but also to see it well employed on the poor, and to employ the poor that live of the alms of the church to the relief of their fellow poor which are more impotent than they, as it was used in the primitive church. And above all things, to beware of them that walk disorderly and labor not if they be able. Of which kind of people, when there is so great multitudes in this land that they do even overflow the countries and have been known to be practicers of great matters against the state, it is marvel, that neither by political nor by ecclesiastical law, they are brought into order and set to labor, or else (as Saint Paul prescribeth), so that they should not eat until they be willing to labor, 2 Thessalonians 3:10.

But now, to return to the election of deacons. Concerning the form of choosing of deacons, we may read at large, Acts 6, that they were chosen by consent of the whole church and had the approbation of the apostles. And because we may not think there was any confusion in that blessed company, we must needs confess that which hath been before declared, that there were even in that assembly and first church at Jerusalem, certain elders appointed, which in the name and by the consent of the rest, had the disposition of such matters, as appeareth by many places of the Acts of the Apostles where the elders are named with the apostles (as Acts 15:4–12, etc.). But especially concerning this matter of the distribution unto the poor, we read that when the church of Antioch was so well disposed as to make a collection to be sent unto the poor brethren that dwelt in Judea, they sent unto the elders by the hands of Barnabas and Saul, Acts 11:30.

By which it appeareth that the elders had the disposition and appointing of such as should distribute it unto the congregation, which were the deacons. For it is agreeable to reason that he that should do any service in the name of all, should be chosen and approved by the consent of all. For the regiment of the church, as it ought to be furthest off from all tyranny, so ought it to be as far from confusion and disorder. Tyranny is avoided when no one man (contrary to the ordinance of Christ) shall presume to do anything in the church without the advice and consent of others that be godly and wise, and authorized by the consent of the church. Confusion is prevented by the grave counsel and orderly assembly of elders, unto whom the church hath committed her authority.

By this it may easily appear what great default there is in our church, where those that are said to be ordained deacons never purpose in their life to execute any part of a deacon's office, neither are chosen for that end; but only that within a short time after, they may be made priests or ministers, nothing in the world differing from the superstition of popery, where the office of deacon was conferred only as a step unto priesthood. As though it were necessary that everyone which is ordained an elder should first be a deacon, and yet when he is made a deacon he is but an idol, yea scarce an idol of a deacon, having no resemblance at all unto a deacon indeed but that he is a man. This profaning of God's institution God will not always suffer unpunished, especially when it is not maintained of ignorance or infirmity, but defended against knowledge, and upon willfulness.

Therefore, the [present] collectors [for the poor] are more like to deacons a great deal than those that the bishops make deacons. For first they have, after a sort, election of the church, whereas the other have but the approbation of one man. And secondly, they gather and distribute the common alms unto the poor, which the other never think of. But yet we may not allow them for lawful deacons indeed, because they are not always endued with such qualities as the apostle requireth, 1 Timothy 2. For they ought to be men of good estimation in the church, full of the Holy Ghost and of wisdom, that should be chosen, Acts 6. For as it is an office of good credit, so ought the person to be of good reputation. Therefore, saith Saint Paul, that "Those deacons that minister well do get themselves a good degree, and great liberty in the faith, which is in Christ Jesus" (1 Tim. 3:13). Insomuch that Saint Paul himself doth salute in special words the deacons, next to the bishops or overseers in the church of Philippi (Phil. 1:1). We read also what worthy men were chosen to be the first deacons, as Stephen the first martyr, and Philip which afterward was an evangelist when the church was dispersed through the persecution raised about Stephen. So that every ignorant contemptible person is not to be allowed unto this office, but as godly, wise and worshipful as may conveniently be found in the congregation may not think themselves too good to minister unto Christ in his members and in the name of the church. The election also of our collectors is too profane for so holy an office. We may read in the history of the Acts, Acts 6, with what gravity, reverence and religiousness the apostles ordained deacons, with prayer and imposition of hands.

For these and such like causes, although the ordinary collectors have some resemblance with the deaconship of the church, yet we cannot in all points allow them for deacons, whose office truly consisteth only in ministration unto the poor, as we have showed, in that they be deacons.

[The Synod or General Council]

We have declared before that there is a double authority of the pastor, the one joined with the elders of the church whereof he is pastor, the other with the synod or holy assembly whereof he is a member. Of the former we have entreated hitherto. Now it followeth that we speak of the latter. There ariseth oftentimes in the church divers controversies pertaining to the state of the whole church which cannot be otherwise expressed, than by a general assembly of all the pastors of that church, which is called a synod or general council. Also there be divers cases wherein the several churches are driven to pray the aid of the synod, where matters cannot be determined among themselves. For this cause the Holy Ghost hath ordained these holy assemblies, with promise that they being gathered together in the name of Christ, he himself will be among them.

With the synod, the pastor hath authority to determine concerning regiment of the church. Wherefore we have to inquire of what persons a synod doth consist. For which intent we find in the history of Acts 15:6 that when a controversy arose concerning the ceremonies of the law, whether they were to be used by those Christians that were converted of the Gentiles, the apostles and elders came together to consider of this matter. And that the people was not excluded appeareth by the twelfth verse, the whole multitude being persuaded by the arguments alleged by Peter, held their peace and quietly heard Paul and Barnabas declare what signs and wonders God had wrought by them amongst the Gentiles. And lest ye should understand "the multitude" in that place for "the multitude of the apostles," it followeth in the twenty-second verse, "Then it pleased the apostles and elders, with the whole church, to choose certain men. . ."

By which Scripture we learn that the synod consisteth principally of pastors, elders, teachers, and men of wisdom, judgment and gravity, as it were, of necessary regents.[38] For although the whole multitude came together, yet the apostles and elders came together to inquire and consider of the matter in controversy. The multitude heard, and for their better instruction and modesty, submitted their consent unto the determination of the apostles and elders. All men's reasons were heard, for there was great disputation. But the authority of God's word prevailed. Good order was observed. So, after the matter was thoroughly discussed, by the godly arguments alleged by Peter and Barnabas and Paul, the controversy was concluded by the sentence of James, to whom that prerogative was granted, not of singular authority, but for order's sake.

And this place doth admonish us to entreat somewhat of the preeminence of one elder or pastor above the rest. We confess that in every assembly or company, some one of necessity must have this prerogative, to order and dispose the same with reason, or else great confusion is like to follow.[39] But this preeminence is only of order and not of authority, as to propound matters to be decided, to gather the reasons and consent of the rest, and so to conclude, etc. As we see in this place James did, of whom also we read that he had this preeminence, Acts 21:18, etc. And we may gather the same [from] Galatians 2:9,12. Not that James had greater authority in his apostleship than Peter or Paul, or John, or any other of the apostles. But because he was chosen of the rest to have prerogative of order, which someone must have in every assembly. And such was the prerogative at the first which was granted sometime to the bishop of Rome, and sometime to some other bishops, to be president or prolocutor

38. [ED.] This view, that the membership of a synod should include "men of wisdom . . ." as well as pastors, elders and doctors, was not shared by all Presbyterians. Also, according to this *Discourse* "the multitude" were not wholly to be excluded. Later Puritans such as William Bradshaw and Henry Jacob, who stood midway between the English Independents and the rigid Presbyterianism typified by the Scots, rightly claimed succession from the earlier Presbyterian Puritans.

39. [ED.] The moderator could be either elder or pastor. But there is no suggestion here of the long-term leadership held by Calvin in Geneva, Bullinger in Zurich, or Bucer in Strassburg.

in the general councils, being chosen thereto for the time by consent of the rest, as the prolocutor is chosen in our convocations that are called with parliaments. Therefore, as it were an absurd thing for our prolocutor in our convocation to take upon him to be a controller of the whole synod, and to challenge that office to him and to his heirs forever, so unreasonable is the authority that the pope claimeth over general councils. One therefore is to be chosen by consent, to be as it were the prolocutor or moderator of order, but not of authority, in every assembly, whose prerogative must so be tempered that in all things tyranny be avoided. Which we see by experience easily creepeth in upon proud natures, to whom if you grant an inch they will be ready to take an ell, according to the proverb.

But let us return to the authority of the synod, which consisteth in deciding and determining such matters as cannot otherwise in particular churches be concluded, either because they concern the common state of all churches, or because they lack sufficient authority in some one church.

[A.] First therefore, the lawful synod hath to consider, if any controversy of doctrine do arise, that it be determined by the word of God (for in the controversy of binding the Gentiles to the observations of the ceremonial law, [there] was a matter of faith and doctrine).

[B.] Secondly, it hath to determine of the use of the ceremonies, not of will without reason or ground of Scripture, but upon necessary causes of avoiding offence and similitude [i.e., appearance] of superstition, of bearing with the weak, of order and comeliness and edification. So did the synod of the apostles and elders command for a time abstinence from meat offered to idols, otherwise lawful in itself, for offences' sake and for avoiding of all pollution of idolatry, Acts 15:20,29, and forbearing the weakness of the Jews in abstinence from eating of blood and of [animals] strangled, which was forbidden by God before Moses' time, to teach that childish age of God's people to abstain from cruelty, as in Genesis 9:4. Such ceremonial constitutions are but temporal [i.e., temporary], and so long are to be retained as the cause continueth for which they were made. So that if weakness cease or be turned to obstinacy, they are no longer to be retained.

Also for order and comeliness and best edification, the synod hath to determine what shall be observed in particular charges: as of the time, place and form of preaching and praying, and administering of the sacraments. For who should be able to know what order, comeliness and edification requireth according to God's word, but they that be teachers and preachers of the same unto all others? For it is absurd that they should be taught, in these small things, by such as ought to learn the truth of them in all matters.

This authority therefore cannot be granted unto any civil Christian magistrate, that without consent of the learned pastors and elders — yea against their consent (of whom, as in some respect he is a feeling member), he may lawfully make ceremonial constitutions whereby the church must be governed in mere [i.e., wholly] ecclesiastical matters.[40] It is out of [i.e., beyond] all controversy that before there were any Christian magistrates (for we will not speak of Sergius Paulus, Proconsul of Cyprus, because he was but a lieutenant of the Roman emperor [41]) this authority was proper unto the synod. Which authority we know to be granted to the church by our savior Christ; practiced by his apostles; continued by their successors three hundred years before there were any Christian emperors (for we receive not Philip for a Christian emperor [42]); and long time after there were Christian emperors, even as long as any purity continued in religion, until both emperors and synods were thrust out of all lawful authority which they ought to have in the church, by the tyranny of Antichrist.

But we find not in the Scripture this authority granted by Christ to civil magistrates, which in his and his apostles' time were not [in existence], nor [do we find] any promise that when they were the synod should resign it unto them. Therefore it remaineth that it be showed by them that defend that this absolute authority is in the civil magistrate, by what spirit or revelation or scripture [they defend it] (if there be any that we know not). For we would be glad to learn how this authority was translated from the church (in which it was once lawfully vested) unto the civil Christian magistrate.[43]

40. [ED.] The synod was to have the power to decide, and the civil magistrate the power to confirm, support and enforce its decisions. Men such as Wentworth and Morice would have objected that this division of power left too small a role for Parliament.

41. [ED.] On Sergius Paulus, see G. Wissowa, *Paulys Realencyclopädie der classischen Altertumswissenschaft* (Stuttgart, 1923), II, A, 2, 1715–18.

42. [ED.] On M. Julius Severus Phillippus (Philip the Arabian, emperor of Rome A.D. 244–9), see A. Hauck, ed., *Realencyklopädie für protestantische Theologie und Kirche* (Leipzig, 3rd ed., 1904), XV, 331–4. Legend made Philip the first Christian emperor.

43. [ED.] This is one of the more specific Puritan rejections of the current view of the royal supremacy — a rejection not shared by the Puritans of Group I, and never expressed by those of Group II.

Therefore, until this may be showed by sufficient warrant of God's holy word, we hold that the synod of every province hath authority to decree concerning ceremonial orders of the church, whereof some may be general to all congregations, some particular to certain churches. For, as it were to be wished that all places might be brought to one perfection, so it is not always necessary that they be like in all things. The wisdom of the synod therefore ought to have such regard of all churches, that they have special respect to every one. Wherein we of long time in England have been carried away with an untrue principle, that uniformity must be in all places and things alike. As though we would feed old men and sucking infants all with one kind of meat. Or as though we would clothe all ages in a robe of one assize [i.e., regulation]. And that which is more absurd, compel men of ripe age to suck the dug, to wear their biggins [i.e., child's cap], and to carry rattles and other childish baubles. Our land is not yet wholly converted to Christ (so great hath been our negligence hitherto), therefore there cannot be such a uniformity of orders in all places as shall be profitable for all. Therefore it were meet that the overseers and elders of the church should come together to consider of this matter, what orders were most meet for diverse places, to bring them to the obedience of Christ, what for the furtherance of them that are newly come, and what for the continuance and increase of them that are very well come on.

The same doctrine, although not the same parts of doctrine, is to be everywhere. But ceremonies, even as they be ceremonies, do admit variety, as time, persons and occasions serve to be diverse. Yea, Christian liberty in them sometimes is necessary to be testified, because there are many so simple that they know not the difference between those things that are necessary in the church and those that are not of necessity. There be that think a cross or font (as they call it) is as necessary in baptism as water; and that kneeling at the communion is more necessary than preaching of the Lord's death; that a surplice in common prayer is more necessary than a devout mind. And great occasions [are] offered to the ignorant so to think, when they see them that preach most diligently, pray most fervently, and minister the sacraments most reverently, according to Christ's institution, to be displaced of all ministry for a cross or a font, or a surplice, or some such other trifle

The synod, therefore, ought to be careful in ordaining of ceremonies, not only that they be pure and agreeable to the word of God, but also that they be expedient for the time and persons for whose use they are ordained. And as willful contemners of good orders established by public authority are worthy to be corrected, so entangling of men's consciences or tyrannical coaction in these indifferent matters must always be avoided.

[c.] The synod hath further authority concerning discipline, to reform and redress by ecclesiastical censure all such defaults and controversies as cannot be determined in the particular churches; as for example, if the pastor himself have need to be severely punished, where there is but one pastor in a church, or if elders, which should be reformers of others, have notoriously misgoverned themselves, or if they have been led by affection to condemn an innocent or to justify the ungodly. In these and suchlike cases, all contention is to be concluded by the authority of the synod. Some example we have thereof, Acts 15, where those contentious schismatics that withstood Paul and Barnabas at Antioch were constrained to yield by authority of the council, and Paul and Barnabas restored to their credit. For which causes synods ought oftentimes to be assembled, though not general of the whole realm, but particular of every province or shire, as it may be most conveniently, that such things as are to be reformed may be redressed with speed.

[D.] Last of all, forasmuch as the election of pastors is a great and weighty matter which ought not to be permitted to the judgment of any one man, but pertaineth to the church whereunto they should be chosen, it is convenient that it be done by judgment of the particular synod, both for better advice in choosing of a meet man and for authority in causing him to accept their election. That no one man hath authority to ordain pastors and to impose them over churches hath been before declared, by example of the apostles Paul and Barnabas, who although they were apostles, yet would they not challenge that prerogative unto themselves, but by common election they ordained elders in every church, Acts 14:23. Timothy also received his charge, although it were through prophecy, by imposition of hands of the eldership, 1 Timothy 4:14. Therefore as it hath been evidently declared before, the assembly of elders, consisting of grave, wise and godly men, ought to inquire when the pastor's place is void, where they may find a man meet to supply his room, and therein to desire aid of the synod. The man by such godly advice so chosen, ought to be presented to the congregation and of them to be allowed and received, if no man can show any reasonable cause to the contrary.[44] This

44. [ED.] The author moves quickly over questions in dispute concerning ordination, who was to perform it, etc.

is the right election and ordaining of pastors, grounded upon the word of God, and practiced by the primitive church two hundred years after Christ until the mystery of iniquity grew to work more openly to the setting up of the tyrannical kingdom of Antichrist.

By this we may plainly see that our presentation of patrons is both profane and prejudicial; our giving of orders by bishops is presumptuous and full of absurdities.[45] First, because they take upon them to do that which none of the apostles durst do, that is, without election of churches to ordain elders.

Secondly, that they give an office without a charge, to make a pastor and send him to seek a flock where he can find it. Which is as unreasonable a thing as if one were chosen to be a church-warden and had never a church to keep, or made a constable that had never a town or place appointed whereof he should be constable. For the name of a pastor, elder or overseer is the name of an office in "deed and being," because it is a proper relative, and not a potential ability in the clouds.[46] If bishops as they be now were consecrated after the same manner to seek their bishoprics where they could find them, it were no greater absurdity than it is to ordain pastors and let them prowl where they can for their benefices.

Thirdly, by this wandering (we may also say vagabond) ministry, shifting from place to place and in all places to be counted a minister where he hath no charge, it would grieve a man to think what inconveniences doth follow, but principally, how filthily it stinketh of the old popish indelible character, from whence it hath his [i.e., its] ground, and neither [i.e., not] of any reason or of the word of God. And yet forsooth it is so perfect that it may abide no reformation!

Fourthly, if you will see how well the authority which they claim and practice is used of them that only have the choice and admission of ministers, look over the whole realm of England, what a multitude of unfit pastors shall you find in every place? So that Jeroboam never made worse priests of the refuse of the people to serve his golden calves [cf. 1 Kings 12:25–33] than they [i.e., the bishops] have ordained ministers to feed

45. [ED.] To challenge the right of the patron incurred danger even for the Puritan cause, which had its own patrons, including certain nobles.

46. [ED.] "Proper relative": i.e., ministerial titles had meaning only in relation to an office, as did those of chairman, secretary, etc., and did not confer status or rank, as did the designations male, noble, royal, deity, etc. Later, as the Presbyterian Puritans became more and more "clerical," only the Independent-Congregational Puritans held to the view that a minister did not possess any "clerical status" unrelated to his office.

the flock of Christ which he hath purchased with his own blood. This complaint we confess is grievous, but the indignity of the matter enforceth it. We know that vain excuses shall not be wanting, of necessity, etc. But if necessity compelled them to take such at the first, what necessity compelleth them to suffer them to be such still? For if they would needs admit ignorant persons to that charge, yet should they have enforced them to study, as well as to other things they have enforced them unto, that in time they might have grown to be meet for their calling. Which if they had done in ten, twelve or thirteen years' space, a great many might have proved excellently well learned and able to serve in the church with great fruit and profit. And the rest, according to proportion of their time, might have come to some mediocrity in knowledge.[47] Whereas now as ignorant and as unfit as they were the first day, so are they still for the most part, and will so continue to their lives' end, if they may be suffered in idleness as they have been hitherto.

Then it is a torment to think what ambitious suing, what envious laboring, what unseemly flattering, what prodigal bribing, is used to attain to great dignities in the church, too far unmeet for the modesty and gravity that should be in Christian preachers. And as for the inferior benefices, from the fattest parsonage to the poorest vicarage almost, if it be worth forty pounds by the year, what simonical bargains of leases, annuities, reservations, exhibitions, yea, notwithstanding the Act of Parliament, 13 Eliz. cap. 20, by antedates and other subtle conveyances! What Christian heart can think of them without detestation of such horrible abuses?

Shall we speak here anything of the popish priesthood, the greatest blasphemy that ever was, how long was it allowed for a lawful ministry, until by the godly meaning of the said Parliament [i.e., of 1571] some brand-mark of shame was set upon it? But how pitifully that authority was abused which was by the same statute [13 Eliz. cap. 12] committed to the bishops, in allowing of priests that came to do their penance, by negligence of the bishops and bribery of their officers. The country crieth out of it, and the state of the church is little amended by it. Old Sir John Lacklatin, that had not seen some of his benefices a dozen years before, was carried about on his mare and sometimes on a cart, first to the bishop (whom he chose, if he might, for his purpose, such one as had been a priest of his own order and cared least what ministers serve in his diocese), and then from shire to shire, one distant a hundred miles from another, mumbling up his articles in his morrow-mass [i.e., sepulchral] voice

47. [ED.] Possibly a reference to the suppressed prophesyings.

in every church where he had living, and returned as very a beast as he came.[48]

But this and all other inconveniences before rehearsed should utterly be avoided if we might once establish the lawful election of pastors according to the word of God. It were also greatly to be wished that it might be brought to pass that in every congregation there should be two pastors at the least, both because the charge is great, and also for supplying the lack of the one if the other were sick or absent upon necessity, or any suchlike case. Which thing were both agreeable to the example of the apostolic church, and also very profitable for the congregation. We do not mean this in every parish as they be now distinguished, but in every congregation as they may be disposed, both for best edifying and also for sufficient living for the pastors.

It will be objected, when we have all things at our pleasure concerning the election of pastors, yet will there creep in many abuses. We answer, they shall not so soon nor so easily, nor so many abuses creep in, as now at wide windows, yea, great port-gates do throng in. But if as many or

48. [ED.] Parliament in 1571 forced the Queen to accept a religious bill, 13 Eliz. I, cap. 12, compelling all Marian clerics to subscribe to the Thirty-nine Articles of Religion, and limiting subscription to items "which only concern the confession of true Christian faith and the doctrine of the sacraments." This allowed the Puritans freedom in respect to the articles on episcopacy, ceremonies, etc. As a result of the debate in Parliament, the bill used the terms "ministers" and "pastors" rather than "priests." It was on this occasion that Peter Wentworth clashed with Parker in committee. Parker's proposed book of Canons was passed at the time by the bishops in Convocation, but not by Parliament, and it did not receive the Queen's approval. These Canons ignored the law of 1571, and required total subscription to the Thirty-nine Articles. But the pressure exerted by the Queen and the bishops forced total subscription upon the Puritans, despite the illegality of Parker's Canons, and a showdown with the old Marian clergy was avoided. By May 19, 1572, Parker himself was complaining to Burghley that the Queen's "Machiavel government" treated papists better than true Protestants. Under Grindal and Whitgift, the Queen's support made limited subscription to the law a dead letter. Parliament and the Puritans bitterly resented this flouting of the law. In October 1573, as criticism mounted, the Queen issued a royal proclamation denouncing "the bishops and other magistrates" for not enforcing "the good lawes and actes of Parliament made in this behalfe" — i.e., in behalf of the prayer book. But once again Elizabeth worked behind the scenes to frustrate the law of Parliament, and once again its intent was defeated. Parker correctly guessed that a "Machiavel" concern with her royal authority was the Queen's prime motivation. The M.P.s and the Puritans in their turn, however, saw in Parker a will to have his own illegal Canons of 1571 prevail as the chief motive behind his and the bishops' actions and policies. Fulke was writing around 1572, while these controversies were at their height. See John Neale, "Parliament and the Articles of Religion, 1571," *Eng. Hist. Rev.*, LXVII (1952), 510-21; Parker, *Correspondence*, 391; Royal proclamation, October 20, 1573 (*S.T.C.*, 8065).

more abuses (if more could be) were crept in, yet were the case better than it is now. For we should be sure that God approveth our order (though he condemn the abuses) because it is grounded upon God's word. Whereas now he abhorreth both.

But of the authority that pastors have as members of the synod, we have spoken hitherto sufficiently. By which it is evident how all things have been corrupted in popery which had at the first any good institution. Which corruptions we also retain at this day without desiring of any reformation.

For to begin first with our particular synods, good lord what a mockery they are of lawful synods, being held for no other end almost but to gather up fees, both ordinary and extraordinary, with daily new devices to poll the poor priests of their money, which they extort for seeing the letters of orders, for dinners and such like matters. And yet a new invented pillage, whereby they compel men to buy books of them for four pence or six pence, which are too dear of [i.e., overpriced at] a penny or two pence. And not only such small ware, but also great books, being such as every parish is appointed to buy, must be bought of them for two or three shillings in a book dearer than it may be bought in Paul's Churchyard. Yea otherwhiles, though the parish be furnished of them already, they are not authentic except they be bought at Master Chancellor's [nor] official, [unless] at Master Register's hands. As for reformation of anything in the church, there are indeed many presentments and men sworn to present matters, but little or none amendment at all doth follow. So that it is a common saying in the country, when the presentment is once received they shall never hear more of it. Soon after the visitation or synod, the petit-bribing sumner [i.e., summoner] rideth forth laden with excommunications which he scattereth abroad in the country as thick as hailshot, against this parson and that vicar, this church-warden and that side-man, whom he himself (when he came to summon him to the synod) for a cheese or a gammon of bacon had undertaken to excuse for non-appearance. But when he is once excommunicated, there is no remedy. But he must trudge to the chancellor or official for absolution, who after he hath once absolved his purse of a few groats, giveth him his blessing and sendeth him away. And this is the image of our little or particular [diocesan] synod! [49]

Our general convocations have a more show of good order, but in ef-

49. [ED.] On these visitations, see W. P. M. Kennedy, *Elizabethan Episcopal Administration* (London, 1924), I.

fect little better. For first they are stuffed full of popish and profane chancellors and other lawyers, which being mere laymen and unlearned in divinity, by their own law ought to be no members of the synod. And yet these will bear the greatest sway in all things.[50]

The bishops, as though they were greater than the apostles, must have their several [i.e., separate] conventicle. Whereas the apostles and elders came together with the whole multitude, Acts 15. And as they are severed in place, so will they be higher in authority. So that whatsoever is decreed amongst them, that must be called the determination of the whole synod. So that no man must be suffered to speak anything against it, be it never so reasonable or agreeable to the word of God. Yea, whosoever will not subscribe to all such things as they decree must be excluded out of the Convocation, as was practiced and threatened in the Convocation at the foresaid Parliament [i.e., of 1571] unto divers godly and learned preachers that offered to speak against divers gross and palpable errors that had escaped the bishops' decrees: as for the distinction of canonical and apocryphal books, for explication of the clause in the article of predestination where it is said that the elect may fall from grace, and suchlike matters. If this be not to practice lordship over our faith — to set down decrees of religion which must be accepted of all men, without either reason or testimony of the Scripture to prove them, and no man permitted to show any reason or Scripture that enforceth his conscience to the contrary but only to hang upon the authority of bishops — let some other declare what Paul meaneth, 2 Corinthians 1:24, where he denieth that he would exercise any lordship over the faith of the Corinthians.[51] For although their decrees were never so perfect, yet it were an example of tyrannical dominion neither to give reasons to satisfy the ignorant themselves, nor to hear or confute that which might be alleged against them by others. But for a few lord bishops, in comparison of all the Convocation, to sit by themselves and order all things at their pleasures as though the gospel sprang first from them or had come unto them only, it savoreth of nothing so much as of popish tyranny. Whereas otherwise it is well known they are not all of the best learned, nor all of longest study, nor all of soundest judgment, nor all of greatest zeal, nor all of best example, and therefore not meetest to be the only determiners in ecclesiastical matters to the prejudice of the whole synod.[52]

50. Chusing of clearkes of the Convocation house.
51. [ED.] Albert Peel, ed., *The seconde parte of a register* . . . (Cambridge, 1915), I, 74-7.
52. [ED.] See F. O. White, *Lives of the Elizabethan Bishops of the Anglican Church* (London, 1898).

Wherefore it is greatly to be desired that our synods also, which are so far out of order, may be reformed according to the Scripture and the example of the primitive church, that all things may be done with such modesty, gravity and judgment as they were by the apostles and elders, Acts 15.

[The Civil Magistrate]

And now that we have set forth the whole ecclesiastical ministry according to the word of God, with all the duties and authority that pertaineth unto it, the place requireth that we should also entreat of the authority of the civil magistrate in matters ecclesiastical.

Of the title of the prince's supremacy, if it be truly understood, we move no controversy; but [agree] that it doth properly appertain to the civil magistrate to be the highest governor of all persons within his dominion, so that the sovereign empire of God be kept whole. But herein resteth all the doubt how this is truly to be understood. And that shall we best understand by the contrary, namely by the usurped tyranny of Antichrist. For Antichrist did challenge unto himself all authority, both that which is proper to God and that which is common to men. Therefore that the pope claimed to be that only head of the church from which the whole body received direction and was kept in unity of faith, this was blasphemous against Christ and therefore may not be usurped by any civil magistrate, no more than by the pope. Likewise, where he challengeth authority to alter, change and dispense with the commandment of God, to make new articles of faith, to ordain new sacraments, etc., this is also blasphemous, and ought not to be usurped of any civil prince. On the other side, where he challengeth authority over all princes and so over all the clergy, that he did exempt them from the civil jurisdiction, this is contumelious and injurious against all Christian kings. And therefore every prince in his own dominion ought to cast off the yoke of his subjection and to bring all ecclesiastical persons unto his obedience and jurisdiction. Here have we the first part of the title of supreme government over all persons.

In matter or causes ecclesiastical likewise, the pope doth not only presume against God, as we said before, but also against the lawful authority given by God unto men. For he forbiddeth princes to meddle with reformation of ecclesiastical matters, or to make any laws pertaining to causes of religion, answering them that those things do appertain only to him and the general council. But when he cometh to debate anything with his clergy, then all laws and knowledge are enclosed in the closet of his breast. When any general council must be held, all that they do receiveth authority from him. For except he do allow, it is nothing. And he is so wise that neither with the council, nor without the council, he can err or think amiss in matters ecclesiastical. Whereas it is not only lawful but also necessary for princes, if they will do their duty, to look to the reformation of religion and to make laws of matters ecclesiastical, but so [i.e., provided] that we confound not the offices of the prince and the pastor.

For, as it is not lawful for the prince to preach nor administer the sacraments, no more is it lawful for him to make laws in ecclesiastical causes contrary to the knowledge of his learned pastors. For as these three parts of a pastor's duty are granted to him by God — preaching, ministering of sacraments, and ecclesiastical government — he may no more take from a pastor the third than he may the two first.

By this it appeareth how far it is lawful for princes to intermeddle with causes ecclesiastical, namely that it is the chiefest point of their duty to have especial regard that God may be glorified in their dominion. And therefore they ought to make civil laws to bind the people unto the confession of true faith, and the right administering and receiving of the sacraments, and to all ecclesiastical orders, that they [the princes] (being instructed by the word of God through the ministry of the preaching of the same) shall understand to be profitable for edifying of the church of Christ and the advancement of the glory of God. If any shall offend against the laws, whether he be preacher or hearer, beside the ecclesiastical censure which he should not escape, he is also to be punished in body by the civil magistrate.[53]

This we see that all Christian emperors observed, that when any controversy arose, either of doctrine or of order and ceremonies, they commanded the clergy to consult and determine thereof according to the Scripture, who assembling together in council obeyed their commandment. Their conclusion then by authority of the emperor was commanded everywhere to be observed, and those that impugned it, to be punished. The same order we read also to be observed by the Christian kings of France and Spain, yea and of this our Brittany also, in governing their ecclesiastical state, by the advice of the clergy of their dominion.[54]

But it will perhaps be said that for princes to subscribe to the determi-

53. [ED.] See note 40, above.
54. [ED.] On this notion of a royalist, pre-papal, pure, primitive church, see the material on John Foxe in Part One of this volume.

nation of priests (as they call them) is no supremacy but a subjection. We answer, it is no subjection unto men, but to God and his word, to do nothing in these matters but by the faithful advice of them that know his will and are bound to teach it unto all men. No more than it is to be counted a subjection for a prince in civil affairs to follow the advice of wise and faithful counsellors. Whereby we see that if God's ordinance were not plain in the Scriptures, yet reason itself would conclude that if in temporal matters a wise prince will do nothing of weight without the counsel of wise men, how much more in God's business (which is of greatest importance) should they not decree anything without the advice of them that be learned in those matters. And if all princes by heathen wise men's judgments are so rulers that they are servants of the laws and of the commonwealth, why should it be accounted for any dishonor unto princes to be obedient to the laws of God their father, and to serve to the commodity of the church their mother? It is a greater honor to be the son of God and the child of the church than to be a monarch of all the earth.

Of this honorable subjection to God and his church, Isaiah prophesieth, chapter 49:23: "Kings shall be thy nursing fathers and queens shall be thy nurses. They shall worship thee with their faces towards the earth and lick the dust of thy feet, and thou shalt know that I am the Lord." The prophet meaneth that kings and queens shall be so careful for the preservation of the church that they shall think no service too base for them, so they may profit the church of Christ withal. Unto this honorable subjection the Holy Ghost exhorteth princes in the second Psalm, after that they have tried that they prevail nothing in striving against the kingdom of Christ: "Be now therefore wise (O ye kings); be learned that judge the earth. Serve the Lord with fear, and rejoice unto him with trembling" (Ps. 2:10–11), declaring that it is a joyful service to be obedient to Christ, yea to serve God is indeed to reign. And especially it is to be noted where Saint Paul commandeth prayers and supplications to be made for the conversion of kings unto the knowledge of the truth and their own salvation, that he allegeth this reason: "That we may lead a quiet and peaceable life, in all godliness and honesty under their protection" (1 Tim. 2:2).

A godly and honest life we may live, under enemies of the church and persecutors; but a peaceable and quiet life in all godliness and honesty, only under a Christian prince. This thing therefore the church most humbly desireth of the prince; for this end the church continually prayeth to

God for the prince; in this respect the church most obediently submitteth herself unto the prince as a child to his nurse; that both prince and people may honor God in this life, and after this life reign with Christ everlastingly.[55]

[CONCLUSION]

Thus have we briefly set forth a form of reformation touching matters ecclesiastical (as we are thoroughly persuaded) agreeable to the word of God, and as we are able to prove, consenting with the example of the primitive church, building only upon the most sure foundation of the canonical scriptures; but intending more at large, if occasion shall serve, hereafter to set forth the practice and consent of the godly fathers in their acts, counsels and writings, following the same rule and interpretation of the Scripture that we have done.[56] Therefore we protest before the living God and his holy angels, and before the Lord Jesus Christ that shall come to judge the quick and the dead, and before the Queen's Majesty our most gracious sovereign, and the whole assembly of all estates of this realm; that as the whole world may plainly see, we seek hereby not our own profit, ease nor advancement, but only the glory of God and the profit of his church. So by this present writing we discharge our conscience, according to our duty, which is to show unto all men the true way of reformation, and to move them that have authority to put it in practice, and to seek by all lawful and ordinary means that it may take place. That if it may please God to give it good success at this time to be embraced, we may fulfill the rest of our course with joy. But if our sins be the let [i.e., hindrance], that this or the like grounded upon God's word may not now be received, yet the present age may see and judge what is the uttermost of our desire concerning reformation, which hitherto for lack of such a public testimonial [57] hath been subject to infinite slanders devised by the adversaries of God's truth and hindrance of godly

55. [ED.] The *Discourse* nowhere refers to the role of Parliament.
56. [ED.] Field probably added this last section.
57. [ED.] See the subtitle Field placed upon Fulke's work: "Which may serve for a just apology . . ." The "lack of a public testimonial" implied not a lack of statements of Presbyterian polity, but rather the need for a public vindication of the Puritans' intentions. Apparently the "central committee" at last decided to publish this manuscript (which had been in their hands since 1573) after the failure of the Puritan party during the Parliament of 1584. See John Neale, *Elizabeth I and her Parliaments, 1584–1601* (London, 1957), 58–83.

proceedings unto reformation. And that the posterity may know that the truth in this time was not generally unknown nor untestified concerning the right regiment of the church of God, nor this disordered form of ecclesiastical government which we have received for the most part of popery [be] delivered to our children without contradiction, that our example should not be prejudicial unto them as the example of our godly fathers (which in this point neglected their duty) hath been prejudicial unto us. The Lord grant for Christ's sake that we being so far from perfection, God may open all our eyes to see the same, and bend our hearts earnestly to labor to attain thereunto. And in the meantime, so far as we have attained, that we may proceed all by one rule, that we may be like affectioned to seek the glory of God, and to build up the ruins of his temple, that with one heart and with one voice we may praise the Father of our Lord Jesus Christ in his holy temple, which is the congregation of saints in the Holy Ghost, to whom be all honor and dominion for evermore. Amen.

FINIS

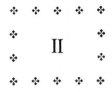

II

JOHN KNEWSTUB

Editor's Introduction

Was there a "Puritan theology"? To a sixteenth-century mind, the question was hardly even legitimate. Every professedly Christian body — Roman Catholic, Lutheran, Zwinglian, Anabaptist, Calvinistic or other; Continental or English — pinned its entire case on the assertion that there was and could be but a single "Christian faith." To say that a man adhered to the Papist, the Lutheran, the Calvinist, or any other denomination of faith amounted, in the sixteenth century, to an accusation of heresy. The furious intolerance, the polemics and persecutions of the era were rooted in this total inability to accept pluralism, intellectually, culturally or in any form whatever. The formula "one Lord, one faith" had to mean that there was only one God, one church, one faith, and the problem was to determine who was or was not a part of that church, who did or did not understand the faith aright. Thus the controversies of the sixteenth century found every group professing to hold the faith of the Bible and of the early church. This meant that the concepts, problems, analyses, doctrines with which the various European Christian bodies wrestled were largely those which had already become fixed in the Western church. The issues were in a general way posed by the Bible, upon which the patristic texts were the somewhat diffuse commentaries; thus every dispute of the day could be reduced to a question of whether or not the medieval church had properly construed this or that commentary by one or another of the fathers. The Protestant reformers took the position that the patristic writings had been misconstrued, and set out to clarify the one, true, biblical faith so as to bring it intact down through the patristic era to the sixteenth century. Those who disagreed with what any reforming group might do were — along with the papists — heretics, schismatics or sectarians who had not grasped and did not follow the one true faith.

It is important to be circumspect, therefore, in looking for the "Puritan theology," just as it is in looking for a "Lutheran," a "Calvinist," an "Anabaptist," an "Anglican" or a "Catholic" theology. What took place in the sixteenth century was a fierce and bitter struggle, conducted on numerous fronts and among several major contending parties, each of which sought to assert the one true faith. But so difficult were the problems, both intellectual and practical, that within each of these parties themselves — Catholic, Lutheran, Anabaptist, Reformed, Anglican, and all others — there were disagreements over everything from controlling assumptions to practical consequences. As the century drew toward its close, all over Europe a certain consolidation of "official opinion" took place within each of these parties — the Catholic Council of Trent, the Lutheran *Formula of Concord*, and the Reformed *Zurich Consensus* and *Harmony of the Confessions*, among others. The three Puritan wings within the English church, and likewise the divisions among their opponents, must be seen in the same light as, for instance, the parties at the Council of Trent, or the conflicts of opinion among Lutherans from 1546 to 1580. What set the English controversy apart was a cultural situation in which these theological controversies gave force to a wider range of social grievances, and to pressures for change. Even after an official consolidation of opinion had taken place, the old contestants, the old issues, the old causes, and above all the old books were still in existence and still an influence. To suppose, however, that within each of these major Continental groups the area of conflict had been the same as within the English church is to ignore the setting within which the disputes occurred. For example, the doctrine of predestination as discussed at Trent, among Lutherans, at Zurich, or at Cambridge, drew upon controlling assumptions and emerged with practical consequences so diverse that the meanings read into Jeremiah, Paul or Augustine had almost nothing in common. To repeat the all too common observation that the Puritans attempted to introduce "Calvinism" into England, whereas the defenders of officialdom championed "patristic theology," is to misunderstand a very great deal.

Each of the three major wings of the Puritan movement during the Elizabethan era denied holding to any theology other than the one true faith as set forth in the Thirty-nine Articles of the Church of England. Until the 1590s, officials of the English church likewise asserted that the various Puritan groups were orthodox except in certain unnecessary conclusions they had drawn from correct doctrine. Yet the situation was not quite so simple. Beginning around the year 1565, it can hardly be denied that a distinct outlook, called "Puritan," existed, and that the Protestant officials of the English church were determined not to accept it. The long struggle that culminated in civil war involved a good deal more than the question of vestments and ceremonies. If the official position itself was something more than mere bigotry, those who held it must have believed that something more than mere "decency and order" was at stake in what the nation was to endure from 1559 to 1714. Even in 1714 the official Anglican position was unrelenting, and force alone restrained its intolerance.

The great religious problem of the sixteenth century concerned the relation between the activity of God and the activity of man. This was no new problem, to be sure. But the Renaissance had brought a new and revolutionary vision of human possibilities in every field, from art to the exploration and conquest of new worlds. This burst of human confidence had come, moreover, at a time when the Western church had lost much of its sense of vocation, and was so mired in corruption that many men feared for the future of religion as such. The situation became explosive when, faced with new currents of thought, the clergy reasserted the old dogma that only men in holy orders were competent to deal with religious matters. This impasse forced open every kind of question — political, educational, fiscal, social and religious. All over Europe the "lay" and the "clerical" came into conflict over the question of how God related himself to men — which was another way of inquiring into the bounds or limits of man's activity, into what was or was not "given once for all," what man could change and what he could not change.

As discussed theologically in the sixteenth century, the relation between the activity of God and the activity of man was dealt with in a variety of ways and categories, such as

redemption	vis à vis	creation
revelation	" "	reason
predestination	" "	freedom
grace	" "	nature
gospel	" "	law
divine purpose of God	" "	human purposes
church	" "	world
ecclesiastical order	" "	civil order
ecclesiastical power	" "	the state
the sacred	" "	the secular

As most theologians realized, these categories dealt with one major problem under a variety of names. The problem was this: Christianity was a religion of redemption instituted by God to deal with a secondary problem; i.e., sin was not part of the original created order but had entered it subsequently. Moreover, sin had infected only the mundane sphere, and could therefore have no ultimate or transcendent meaning. Was it not true, then, that God's original and ultimate purpose concerning man — insofar as men could grasp it — was to be found in creation, reason, nature, law, and all such "given," "natural," "human" categories? Was not sin a disease, a crippling, a handicapping, and a blinding thing? Was not redemption a healing, a restoring thing? Since the patristic era, and especially in the thought of Augustine, the answer had been that God's activity and man's activity were so related that God in his grace and mercy enabled weak and sinful man to do his will — as it was truly natural, reasonable and lawful that a man should do. Man's role was to do what he could, and God through grace would do the rest. Man's reason would be supplemented by the divine teaching of the church — i.e., by revelation. Whatever was natural, reasonable and just was also right. Grace, revelation and the sacraments added what was lacking. So Christianity became the support of the family, of government, property and culture. Thus the church maintained that man's activity, so long as it was in accord with his created nature, would be upheld and fulfilled by God, and thus man would learn the right way to live, to order society, and to serve God.

This "supplementation" theory, correlating God's activity and man's activity, came under widespread attack in the sixteenth century. Many men asserted that the once innocent terms "natural," "reasonable," "divinely established," "created," merely served to prop up ancient wrongs that were by no means natural, reasonable or godly. God had not created such wrongs, and he would not uphold them. For others the entire scheme of "supplementation" amounted to blasphemy — an assertion that through the church God could be "used" to solve any problem, to support the political status quo, to vindicate custom, to crown with success any human design whatever. In the popular religion of the day the indulgence racket, the miracle-mongering, the cult of the shrines, showed how far this "supplementation" theory could be carried. Against such abuses, Erasmus was hardly less vehement than Luther.

It was the intent of Protestant reformers to reaffirm the transcendence and freedom of God. Therefore they stressed redemption above creation, revelation above reason, divine predestination above human freedom (or "needs"), grace above nature, gospel above law, etc. In a polemic against ancient wrongs, against superstition or clericalism, this line of attack could be devastating. But by the same token, every attack on the old order also opened the way to questioning any authority, any doctrine, any religious observance. Men began to ask the new religious leaders perfectly legitimate questions that went further than those leaders had intended. If the pope was not truly the vicar of Christ on earth, could it be said that the king ruled by divine right? Was there any divinely appointed human authority? If the pope was not infallible, if he could be rebuked by the reformers and their followers, could not the people likewise rebuke the king, or any other civil magistrate? If, as the reformers argued, the ways of God were not "reasonable," in the sense of conforming to human expectation, but must remain unpredictable and essentially unknowable, how could men know anything at all about God? If religion was not "natural" if it was not a means of enlisting supernatural aid (with the priest as intermediary) concerning things beyond one's own power, then what use was it? If God's grace came only by predestination (as they understood the reformers to say), then many people declared they would have none of it; better, instead, to go to the shrines and pray to the saints for help as their forefathers had done. The reformers' polemic against the merit of good works left many persons uncertain about the relation between divine holiness and human ethics. To many people the doctrine of merit meant simply that God helped you to be good. Would not the new Protestant attack upon the old order end by destroying everything, without offering anything to take its place?

The various reforming groups dealt with this question in different ways. In regions where the civil government tended to be authoritarian, Protestant leaders generally felt little obligation to deal with the popular reaction as a religious and theological problem. Thus, in parts of Lutheran Germany, in Scandinavia, and in England, civil magistrates were able to impose a new religious order with little or no concern for its implications for the people. The infallibility of the magistrate merely supplanted the infallibility of the pope. Conversely, in those regions in Europe where at least a segment of the population had come to play a major role in government and society, spokesmen for the new official Protestantism found themselves obliged to explain to the population their understanding of how the ways of God and the purposes of men were to be related. In such places it was not enough for the Protestant reformers to persuade a duke or a small group of nobles to accept their views on a few restricted topics. (Luther was protected for a number of years by Frederick the Wise, who remained a Catholic but was proud of his university and jealous of "German" rights against the papacy.)

Very early in the Reformation era, it became customary for Protestant leaders in the free cities of Germany and the Swiss cantons to formulate a theology and a religious policy in which the patrician and middle classes could be acknowledged as having a responsible role. Such theologies had to be formulated in a manner which could be explained to, and adopted by, an enfranchised class. Moreover, once the reformed religion was accepted, its continuance was dependent on a victory at each election for officeholders who were sympathetic to it. The voters had to be kept loyal to the reformation by continued explanation. Inevitably, therefore, the Protestantism of Zurich developed in a way that made it increasingly different from that of Saxon Wittenberg or of England under Henry VIII. In Zurich, Strassburg, Bern and Bremen (for example), the reformers had to offer their proposals to the city fathers, who then voted whether or not to accept them. Under such conditions, the reformers could hardly expect to achieve anything they could not make comprehensible to the laity.

Thus, for reasons that were social and political as well as theological, the Protestant reformers — particularly those in the German free cities and the Swiss cantons — found themselves obliged to develop a new theological language. An idiom had to be found that would convey both the positive ideas and the negative polemics of the new faith, and do so in such a way that those in control of the city or canton could understand them well enough to be persuaded to forsake the old faith for the new. On the other hand, the new language could not be so new as to run afoul of the sixteenth-century abhorrence of change, or come under suspicion of novelty in doctrine, i.e., heresy. Out of the search for usable terms arose the so-called "federal theology" or "covenant theology." The notion of covenant pervaded the Bible, where it was associated with the concept of fundamental law, as well as with oaths of allegiance, promises, testaments, alliances and sacraments. The Christian Humanists, Erasmus especially, had popularized the view of baptism as an oath of allegiance to Jesus Christ, implemented by accepting the *disciplina* of Christ. Many political thinkers now interpreted the coronation oath as a covenant or contract entered into by the king. Likewise, the notion of fundamental law was acquiring greater currency. Here, then, was the possibility of developing a new theological language, and a new orientation within which to discuss the basic problem of God's relation to man. This new language of "covenant," "alliance," "allegiance" and "discipline" emerged during the 1520s, in the earliest years of the Protestant Reformation, so pervasively and so confidently that no explanations of it appeared to be needed, either in Wittenberg or in Zurich.

No statement of Protestant theology has in fact emerged full-blown; rather, each has been hammered out in a period of conflict and experiment. The covenant theology did not reach its full development before the decade of the 1580s, when the consolidation of so many systems took place. But as early as the 1520s it was already an attempt to deal with the relation of God's activity to that of man.[1]

Starting from the common Christian assumption of a redemptive process set in motion by the covenant God made with Abraham (Gen. 15:18), the covenant theologians drew a number of basic conclusions. They asserted that the relationship between God and man was personal — a covenanted one — involving mutual obligations of love and fidelity, a common purpose yet to be achieved, a known and accepted statement of that purpose, with a role for God and a role for man in its achievement. Although that common purpose was inseparable from the personal relationship, in the sixteenth century it was not difficult to accept the idea that God *gave* or *established* the covenant, and that man *accepted* it. Thus the priority and transcendence of God were clearly asserted. The notion of fundamental law (the terms of the covenant) was stated as a common purpose rather than legalistically. Because man could understand the terms of the covenant, and it posited a common purpose, there was full scope for his creative energies within its bounds. Its terms had been stated in the Bible, and were to be accepted by men in an act of faith. Accord-

1. Elsewhere I have traced the history of the covenant theology in England. See "The Origins of Puritanism," *Church History*, XX (1951), 37–57, and "A Reappraisal of William Tyndale's Debt to Martin Luther," *Church History*, XXXI (1962), 3–24. The best treatment of the Continental origins of the covenant theology is Joachim Staedtke, *Die Theologie des jungen Bullinger* (Zurich, 1962). On its later forms, see G. Schrenk, *Gottesreich und Bund im älteren Protestantismus* . . . (Gütersloh, 1923). On seventeenth-century covenant theology, see Perry Miller, "The Marrow of Puritan Divinity," *Publications of the Colonial Society of Massachusetts*, XXXII, 247–300; also *The New England Mind: The Seventeenth Century* (New York, 1939), Book IV and Appendix B. *Reformed Dogmatics*, edited by John W. Beardslee, III, in A Library of Protestant Thought (New York, 1965), is an excellent presentation of the later "double covenant" theology.

ingly, no priest was required to dispense grace; but an interpreter of the terms of the covenant (i.e., a preacher) was deemed necessary. Within the covenant, moreover, the study of the Bible was essential to the life of a Christian.

Because the covenant posited a common purpose yet to be achieved, change — as such — was to be expected. Thus, what had prevailed under the Old Testament or old covenant — the temple, with its ritual and priesthood, the rite of circumcision, the feast of Passover, the Davidic kingship — had given way to the new covenant: the church, with its worship and ministry, the rite of baptism, the feast of the Lord's supper, the nation-states of Europe. But within the covenant, Abraham's relation to God had been one of faith, and so it was for the Christian man. Change therefore did not need to be regarded as ruinous, despite the common fears of change and novelty.

All that the covenant theologians regarded as "given," "fixed," "eternal" and "unchangeable" in the relation between God and man was to be found in this covenant relationship, whose essential character would remain, whatever its institutional expression. The ultimate revolutionary implications of such a view were spelled out, in the sixteenth century, only by a few extreme radicals. What most covenant theologians did instead was to fall back upon the consistency and continuity of God's activity among men. Looked at in this way, the institutions of the past could be seen to contain both an ephemeral and a constant element. For these theologians, the notion of a covenant, contract or alliance came alive when it was combined with the notions of fundamental law and of a purpose yet to be achieved.

The sixteenth century witnessed an extensive debate over the nature of law, a debate whose influence on theologians was profound. By the mid-1520s, one aspect of it was turning away some reformers from the developing covenant theology. For Luther, the concept of law meant power, authority, willful coercion — and thus a thing contrary to love, alien and hostile to man. All this he found both in Pauline theology and in the culture of his part of Germany. It noteworthy that Luther drew on the notion of the covenant mainly during his early career, in connection with a doctrine of baptism. He used it in a paternalistic pattern that avoided those aspects of the covenant implying the consent of the people.

According to another view, rooted in Christian Humanism and in the cultural experience of the Rhineland free cities and the Swiss cantons, law was an expression of man's rational effort to construct an ordered society. Here law had the connotations of reason, conscience, justice, equity, purpose and societal life. In these Rhineland and Swiss communities, society was scarcely "permissive." But for their leaders the coercive aspect of law was shifted to the breaker or the violator of the law, which was itself a benefactor, protector, and promoter of cultural life. This view was also to be found in the Bible, and it had behind it the Greco-Roman classical tradition as well as the historical experience of the Rhinelanders and the Swiss themselves.

In the developing covenant theology, accordingly, the law played an extremely important role. The promises of God were beyond man's fulfillment or even his complete comprehension. Therefore, this fulfillment must be received as a free gift — man did not earn his salvation, his entry into this covenant. But he was *received*, by God's free forgiveness in Christ, into a covenanted relationship which had a purpose still to be achieved. The terms of the covenant, the fundamental law, stated the meaning of man's fidelity and obedience within God's purpose in general ways, and in historical, cultural contexts. The positive laws (i.e., the laws enacted to apply this fundamental law to man's everyday life) would change as time went on. But every good and valid positive law was a "case study" of the fundamental law, a commentary upon it; and in that sense the positive law was a guide to obedience to the covenant, though it was never the actual covenant itself. Man did not earn his salvation (his being in the covenant) by obeying the particular positive laws. But, by his attitude toward these laws he revealed his attitude toward the common purpose within the covenant — and thus his attitude toward God. Also, by obeying the particular positive laws he furthered the achievement of the common purpose for which the covenant stood. A favorite illustration of the covenant, therefore, was human love in the marriage relationship and in family life.

In England, the Christian Humanist roots of this kind of thinking went back to pre-Reformation times. In the biblical works of William Tyndale, and in the writings of the early Protestant reformers, the notion of covenant played a great role. Because England was deeply concerned about the nature of law, and the common law tradition fitted easily into this developing covenant-contract scheme, this way of thinking was very appealing. Among the Marian exiles it received such expressions as John Ponet's *Short Treatise of Politic Power* (1556), and Christopher Goodman's *How Superior Powers Ought to be Obeyed* (1558). Although most English Protestants were aghast at the political implications of these works, they did not question either the covenant schema or the theological orthodoxy of the writers.

The Puritan popular preachers, those most concerned to reach the popular mind, were the chief exponents of the covenant theology. Among them it took the form, initially, of a biblical picture of man covenanting to be a true servant of God. These popular preachers used the covenant imagery to show that in the divine economy there was a significant role for man which took account of him as a person and which allowed him a full expression of himself in love. Such preaching made orthodox Protestant theology comprehensible in terms of the biblical story, human love, the family relationship, the laws of England, and the experiences of everyday life. It explained also the psychological phenomena of religious experience.

The early formulations of this covenant theology, because they were not set against any Protestant creed and because they had roots everywhere, met with no opposition. In fact, a truly systematic covenant theology did not emerge until 1585. By that time, important shifts in thought were occurring all over Europe. In England men such as Bancroft and Hooker were attacking the covenant-contract theology. A polarization of thought was forcing all Englishmen beyond the patterns of earlier years. Officialdom, on the one hand, was becoming more and more royalist, prelatical, priestly, traditionalist, sacramentalist — a movement that would culminate in the later Laudian position — while the Puritan movement, on the other hand, became increasingly anticlerical, biblicist, anti-institutional, and experiential — attitudes which were to prove explosive during the Civil Wars.

From 1585 onward the Puritan leaders labored to produce a comprehensive theological and social ideology grounded upon the covenant-contract schema. These men were all quite conscious of belonging to an international group of scholars in the Rhineland, Switzerland, France, the Lowlands and Scotland, who were likewise concerned to develop a Protestant world-view which would be an answer to the religious, political and social problems of the day. Dudley Fenner's *Theologia Sacra*, published in 1585, showed the system that was soon to become standard among covenant theologians in England and on the Continent. This system posited two covenants, or more exactly, a double covenant. First came the "covenant of works," which God had made with Adam at his creation, and which therefore applied to the entire human family (all nations, all races, pagan, Jew and Christian) from the beginning to the end of the world. Under this covenant God obligated all men to live according to his law, their own nature, and the nature of the world about them. This covenant of works amounted, in short, to a résumé of the Reformed Protestant world-view of the day. After it came the "covenant of grace," entered into by God with Adam after his fall into sin had made redemption a necessity. All matters relating to the doctrines and means of man's redemption were referred to this covenant, which had been renewed to Abraham, then to Moses, then on several occasions to the children of Israel, and finally had its culmination in Jesus Christ.

This post-1585 covenant schema was often referred to as the "double covenant" because it was said that God worked through both covenants towards one common purpose. Christian and non-Christian, secular and sacred, church and state, all came under the covenant of works and were rightfully obligated to obey God's law. But only what was Christian, what was of the church, came under the covenant of grace; only the Christian and the church fully and properly understood the law of God. They alone were regenerate and wholehearted in seeking to know and do the will of God. Therefore, the covenant of grace alone could make the convenant of works operative in a sinful world. But — it was asserted against all "heretics" such as the Anabaptists, the Family of Love and the "spiritualists" — the right way to order society and human life under God had been laid down in the covenant of works (the Christian world-view), whereas the covenant of grace dealt only with forgiveness of sins, love, peace, joy, as experienced by those regenerate persons who lived according to the will of God.

Because of the long, complex history behind this covenant-contract thinking (theological and political), few Englishmen ever regarded it as uniquely or exclusively Puritan. It was looked on, rather, as a means of setting limits to authority, of demanding to know the purpose behind positive laws, of requiring the government to operate for the good of the people as the people understood that good, in short, of making law the guarantor of rational government. Seen in this light, official demands for conformity, for "decency and order," became merely the device of an authoritarian government that recognized no significant role for the citizen. As a religious vindication of contract political thinking, in late Elizabethan and Stuart England, the covenant theology became almost standard for those opposed to the royalist-prelatical trends in English thought. But this by no means made it exclusively Puritan or Presbyterian. One of its ablest exponents was James Ussher, Archbishop of Armagh 1625–56, who supported Charles I and opposed the Westminster Assembly of Divines, but who disliked the policies of Laud.

The document chosen here to show the developing covenant theology is from John Knewstub's *Lectures . . . upon the Twentieth Chapter of Exodus and Certain Other Other Places of Scripture,* which went through at least four printings between 1577 and 1584. Among the Puritans Knewstub (1544–1624) was "a Hebrew of the Hebrews." From his university days (M.A., Cambridge, 1567) onward he was involved in nearly every major Puritan movement. At Cambridge he took part in the vestment controversy. He was a strong supporter of Thomas Cartwright from 1570 onward. When John Field and others gathered a sort of "central committee" to guide the Presbyterian Puritan movement, Knewstub became a very prominent member. He took an active part in the prophesying movement, and later in the secret classical movement. Under James I, Knewstub was one of the four spokesmen sent by the Puritans to the conference at Hampton Court in 1604. Thanks to strong lay support, he managed to remain active in a pastorate in Suffolk for several decades, despite being frequently summoned before the authorities.

Knewstub's lectures are typical of the covenant theology in the form of preaching, which antedated the more systematic treatment first given it by Dudley Fenner in 1585. Knewstub took the covenant pattern so completely for granted that the word itself appears only now and then, quite casually. It receives no more definition or analysis than do "good," "nature," or "conscience" — terms that are essential to the entire covenant theology as well as to these lectures. Even without the word, Knewstub's preface sets forth the theology more fully than almost any other treatise before 1585. Similarly, the range of topics is wider than in any other Puritan document of this time. Although not all of the lectures are reproduced here, the structure of the series is completely represented, and most of Knewstub's ideas are given some kind of statement. It may be added that many of the stereotypes concerning what Puritans thought and taught are refuted by this Puritan among the Puritans.

The text reproduced here is from the second edition, as corrected by Knewstub himself, and published in 1578. At least three printings of this edition were made. Permission has been granted by the Henry E. Huntington Library to use a transcript from the copy in its possession.

Knewstub quoted from the Geneva Bible in the headings of his lectures, but in the lectures themselves he often departed from that version in favor of his own translation.

The influence of the Latin style is all too apparent in Knewstub's English. A few changes in punctuation have been made, and in three or four passages a phrase or clause has been shifted for the sake of clarity.

This second edition included a brief summary of each lecture, which was printed in the margin. The summaries have been omitted here.

❖   ❖   ❖   ❖

The Lectures of John Knewstub upon the Twentieth Chapter of Exodus and Certain Other Places of Scripture

Seen and allowed according to the Queen Majesty's injunctions

Imprinted by Lucas Harrison Anno 1578

The Epistle Dedicatory

. . . The Christian reader shall perceive in perusing this treatise of the law, that my travail [i.e., concern] hath been to let him see that Christ is a savior indeed unto him, that he might perceive the length, breadth and depth of his mercies, and so be brought to embrace them accordingly. And because the greatness of our corruption discovereth the riches of his grace, which is by so much the richer as the poverty is greater which it doth relieve, I have labored therefore to lay out our poverty and want in every particular commandment, and to declare how that our affection standeth naturally not indifferent, but an utter enemy to the obedience required in the same. That in the sight of so much rebellion and sin, bleeding (as it were) in every part of us of some deadly wound, we might slack no time in seeking unto Christ Jesus the only physician of our soul. And considering the number and danger of those wounds that he doth cure and cover in us, we might never forget or smally account of, but always worthily magnify the greatness of his grace and mercy towards us.

Which manner of proceeding (if it be indifferently examined) shall be found to have great fruit and profit in it. For to make us careful in seeking after physic [i.e., medicine], this is not sufficient that we know ourselves to be diseased and sick. But to know a number of diseases to be growing upon us (and those of that quality that every of them threateneth present death) having infected the principal parts of our life: that is it which maketh a man with all speed to take him to the remedy appointed for the same. Many there are who will not deny themselves to be sinners and sick of sin. But because they neither know how many parts are infected nor yet how dangerous their infection is, their care to be relieved is the smaller, and their labor the less to be rid of it. Whereupon also it followeth that he is so much the less regarded who is to work that cure upon them. So that we see this general lapping up of sin, when it is not unfolded to our consciences and laid out in the several branches thereof, is not only hurtful unto us, but also injurious unto the due estimation of the death of Christ.

I cannot more fitly compare those men (who will most willingly confess themselves in general words to be sinners, and yet are very loath to be troubled with any particular knowledge thereof) than unto some notorious offenders against the laws and peace of their prince, who can willingly hear these general words, that they be offenders and have not kept the several statutes and laws of their land, so that they will proceed no further with them. But, to be brought forth and charged with their several felonies, murders or treasons that they have committed, and to have their wickedness particularly laid out in number of deeds and manner of doing that may best set out the heinousness thereof, that in no case may be abidden [i.e., tolerated]. And yet notwithstanding before that time, neither is their own estate greatly feared, nor yet the law so much as thought upon how to be satisfied. It is this particular sight of sin that sendeth us forthwith unto Christ, and maketh him appear both glorious in the multitude of his so great mercies, and most necessary in the consideration of our so many dangerous infirmities.

If it please the reader in the examining of himself in any commandment, forthwith to join to the same that which is written here of the properties of love [i.e., Lecture 12], and that other next lecture [i.e., 13] of the use of the law, he shall find (I hope) some help in them, the sooner to depart from himself, and the more carefully to embrace Christ. And that he may be acquainted the better with my meaning and purpose in this matter, I will give him in few words the reason of the same.

I see in the law of God that we are not only forbidden the works of our own devotion and intent, and bound to that choice of works that God hath appointed in his word; but also that we are strictly charged to do the same, all and every one of them in love, which is an affection that carrieth a man so in delight after the things which he loveth that he oftentimes forgetteth himself in respect thereof. According as it is reported by the Holy Ghost (as a property to know it by) that love seeketh not her own things. This is the cause why after the commandments I have set down the notes and properties to discern love by [Lecture 12], that when we have seen what works they be that we are bound to do, we may also see with what affection we are charged to do them; that we may be as careful to bring the right manner of doing unto the Lord as the very deed that he approveth. For we are as well to perform duty in the manner of doing as in the deed itself. It is one and the same God who hath enjoined both unto us, and therefore may not be denied in either of them.

The use of the law which is in the lecture following [i.e., 13] will declare with what conditions we have wages promised for our work, and whether the covenant be so favorable as that we need not to doubt but that we shall be able to perform it, and therefore to live in it, or otherwise so hard (as the truth is in very deed) that he remaineth under the curse of God, who continueth not in all things that are written in the book of the law to do them. Let us then set these together. First, the number of deeds; then, the manner of doing, which must have in it those properties that be in love; and last of all, the hard condition, which is not to have our good doings to blot out and strike off our evil, but to remain under the curse if we shall not continue in everything that is written in the book of the law to do it. And then we shall be forced to give over this stronghold, even this confidence in ourselves, and betake us wholly to the mercy of our God and magnify the same accordingly.

And lest we should imagine the matter of letting go the opinion of ourselves and our worthiness to be nothing so hard as is supposed, and therefore no such need to have so often before us (in meditation and earnest consideration thereof) the multitudes of deeds to be done, the loving manner of doing, and the hard condition if they shall not be done, let us advisedly consider how that singular instrument of God, Saint Paul, confesseth that he himself was so subject unto this over-great opinion of himself that the messenger of Satan was sent unto him to buffet him lest he should be puffed up with the measure of graces which were given him (*cf.* 2 Cor. 12:7). The danger is greater therefore than we are aware of, when so rare an instrument and chosen servant of God as was Paul, so hardly and with so much ado, is brought to have a humble opinion of himself and his worthiness.

The Romish religion likewise (fighting so stoutly for the desert [i.e., merits] of man) may teach us that this doctrine (of true humbling and submitting of ourselves unto our God) will not so easily enter into flesh and blood as at the first we would imagine; but that we have need often to set before us this looking-glass of the law, in manner as hath been declared, to humble us withal. And all shall be found little enough to bring us truly from ourselves, and to send us, not in part but wholly, unto the mercies of our God, which are declared unto us at large in the next lecture [i.e., 14] after the use of the law.

When we shall have profited in drawing near unto Christ, and making much of his mercy by an often and true sight of ourselves in the law, there is yet remaining another use and fruit to be taken by it of no less profit than the former, which is, that when we shall have taken comfort in the mercies of Christ and decreed to walk in the obedience of his will to declare our thankfulness thereby, the law will stand us in good stead to quicken us thereunto, while we learn by it both the number of things that are to be done, and also the backwardness of our natural disposition and inclination thereunto. Which we could not once (without this admonition from the law) have suspected to have been so great, and therefore our care to suppress it would have been so much the less. But having determined once to walk in the ways of his commandments, and then having warning from the law that there is both in our wit and will enmity thereunto, altogether bent to resist it, it cannot but increase our care, and add unto our pains and travail, for the attaining unto that end of obedience which we have propounded unto us. For the man who hath a desire unto anything, understanding once of any let [i.e., obstacle] in the way, is thereby more provoked and stirred up to bestow cares and pains upon the same, knowing very well that the thing which he desireth cannot otherwise be compassed.

And who is he then, that seeing what duties are to be performed both to the Lord and to his brethren, and in what manner of affection (for it is the end of Christ's death and the purchase of his passion, to have a number not only given, but zealously given unto good works (cf. Tit. 2:14)) remembering withal what an enemy he hath at home of his own nature, if there be any fear of God in him, that shall not be occasioned hereby more plentifully to practice the means of his salvation — especially knowing that those who are ingrafted into the body of Christ must die unto sin and rise up into these fruits of righteousness?

Moreover, the knowledge and meditation of the law and commandments do help us forward unto true and sincere Christianity. For a great number deceive themselves, in a general good meaning which they have to serve the Lord, taking that to be the true service of him; and in the meantime are nothing careful to keep a good conscience in the several duties of the law, nor anything travailing to train up their affections to delight therein. As if in Christianity we were to rove uncertainly about good motions and good meanings, and had no certain marks of several duties set before us to shoot at, that we might so judge of ourselves as we see us come short or wide of them. Whereas the true Christian in very deed profiteth in drawing nearer and nearer unto the Lord, in making his life and conversation more conformable unto the several duties set down in the commandments. Being likewise careful to approve his doings by the laws and statutes made for the same, as in civil dealings and traffic a man will fear to offend against the laws and statutes provided in that behalf.

And as a wise man that hath much dealing in the world will have some abstract of the statutes, that (as occasion requireth) he may turn to them and so deal without danger of law, so it standeth well with the policy of a Christian to be skillful in the statutes of his God, that when he hath to deal with the name of his brother, looking in this abstract he may see the cautions to be observed in the same, that he offend not against the laws and statutes of the Highest. And whensoever he hath to deal with his goods, he may turn in like manner to that statute that hath provided for well dealing therein, and so avoid the dangers that otherwise he should fall into. The like is to be done when there are dealings immediately between us and the Lord, that we should often look into this brief abstract of the stautes of our God, to see always what is the proviso that is made for his glory and the suppressing of our own corruption. Our corrupt nature doth ask all this of us, and the man that feareth God giveth no less unto it. For the blessed man is said to meditate in the law of his God day and night.

Nay, we see that the only wise God (who knoweth better than we ourselves what need we have) hath appointed us yet more means. And therefore we must think that there is more untowardness in us than we could of ourselves suspect. For he hath left it a perpetual order for the education of his children that there should be men of special gifts, both for learning and aptness to teach, and also for good life, who by teaching, exhorting and reproving should (as it were) whet the word to make it enter. It must of necessity be a hard matter that requireth such instruments and such workmen, for both the instrument and the workmen are from above.

The wisdom of the world could not perform this, and therefore the gospel (which is the arm and power of God unto salvation) was sent from the bosom of the Father. And for the workmen we are not at our choice to take where it seemeth good unto us. But they are appointed to our hand by the Holy Ghost, who hath set down such notes of good learning and good life to discern them by who are of his sending and fit for so weighty a work as that they give forth a plain testimony unto us, that they come from heaven, framed and prepared of the Lord himself unto this work. As the goodness of our God could not deny us anything necessary, so his wisdom would not that we should be loaded with anything superfluous and unnecessary. Which must force us to conclude against ourselves, that we are not known unto ourselves unless we see matter within us necessarily requiring to be pricked forward with the lively preaching and sounding ministry of the word. And that we tempt the Lord if we content ourselves with our private readings and meditations, and despise the preaching of the word, which the Lord hath seen to be so necessary that he hath appointed it not for one sort of men, but unto all, of what condition soever, neither unto [one] age alone, but perpetual for all ages and times. The labors therefore of them that do write are not taken in hand that men standing upon them should contemn or less frequent the public ministry of the church, but to bring them into greater love and liking with the same. . . .

The First Lecture, upon the First and Second Verse of the same Chapter

Then God spake all these words, saying: I am the Lord thy God, which have brought thee out of the land of Egypt, out of the house of bondage.

It hath always been and now is a fruitful travail of men to draw arts and sciences plentifully laid out, into brief heads and some few general rules and principles. Not only for memory (which in many and long discourses becometh so entangled as it can hardly with any fruit get out) but also for practice, which of necessity must be so much the later as it shall be longer before we learn the matters to be practiced. And the slower we are in perusing matters to be done, the slacker must we be in the performance thereof. But yet all this notwithstanding, as well reason as the practice of the learned might easily be avoided, because all is but the reason and practice of man, if the only wise God had not left unto us the whole doctrine of Christianity, comprehended in very few words. Examples whereof we have divers, both in the Old and New Testament, which may be a sufficient warrant for enterprising thus briefly to comprehend Christianity (Ex. 20; Deut. 5; Mt. 22:37; Heb. 6:1).

If any shall take exception against the preaching and opening of the law in this clear light of the gospel, calling it (as it is called in the Second Epistle to the Corinthians 3:6–7), the ministry of death and the killing letter, let him understand that the Holy Ghost in the same place speaketh of the law without Christ, what it worketh in our infirmity. Whereas otherwise, of the law (being considered in the covenant that is in Christ) it is truly said by the prophet in the Psalms: "The law of the Lord is perfect, converting the soul; the statutes of the Lord rejoice the heart" (Ps. 19:7,8).

At the publishing of this law of God, there was great terror and fear on every side. For, as appeareth in this former chapter [Ex. 19:18], the mount Sinai was all on smoke, and the Lord came down upon it in fire, and the smoke thereof ascended as the smoke of a furnace, and all the mount trembled exceedingly. The people, hearing the thunders and lightnings and the sound of the trumpet, seeing the mountain smoking, and feeling such terrible trembling and shaking of the earth, fled, and stood afar off, making earnest suit unto Moses that he would speak unto them, and that they might not hear the Lord lest they die. So great was their fear, and so wonderfully were they amazed at the matter. It was very requisite and necessary that this majesty of the Lord should come in with the entrance of his word. For we are given to make small reckoning of it, and lightly to reject the authority thereof. For, do not thousands imagine that they sufficiently reverence the majesty of the Lord, when notwithstanding, they live without all awe, fear and reverence of his word? Needful therefore was it, nay most necessary, that the majesty of the Lord should visibly come forth after a glorious manner at the delivery of the word, that men might understand that the neglect of the word is the contempt of the majesty and honor of the Lord. For the Lord hath coupled his honor and glory to his word, so that they cannot neglect the one but that they must in so doing contemn and despise the other.

Those plentiful testimonies that are recited to the Hebrews to advance the dignity of Christ, proving his divinity and giving him superiority above the angels (Heb., chap. 1), are in the second chapter applied by way of exhortation to the reverencing of his word, telling them that if the word spoken by angels was ratified, and that every disobedience received a just recompense of reward, how could they think once to escape, neglecting so great salvation? Which at the first began to be preached by the Lord, and afterward was confirmed by them that heard him, God bringing testimony and authority thereunto both with signs and wonders, and divers miracles, and gifts of the Holy Ghost [Heb., chap. 2]. Well did the Lord understand that words are but wind with men, and therefore it was the good pleasure of his will that neither his law nor gospel should come naked and bare into the world, but with the credit of his own glory and countenance of his own majesty. For the gospel (as now we have heard) was not only preached by the Lord Jesus, but also confirmed (by the ministry of those that heard him) with signs, wonders and miracles. So that to neglect the government of the word is to tread under feet the majesty of the Lord.

Having made this entrance I do proceed unto the text, where I am enforced to speak a little of the nature of the words, because they bring great light to the true understanding and meaning of the commandment. The word Jehovah, which is here Englished Lord, is a name of God giving unto him his true nature and essence, which is, so to have his beginning and being of himself, as in him and by him all things that are, have their being. And therefore it is usually set before the promises and covenants of the Lord in the Scripture, that we should not doubt of the performance thereof seeing it is the covenant and promise of that God that hath his beginning and being of himself and procureth the being and performance of all things unto them. Insomuch that the Lord denieth in Exodus that he was known to Abraham, Isaac and Jacob by his name Jehovah, because he had not performed in their time the promises made for their deliverance out of Egypt, and for their possession of the land of Canaan [cf. Ex. 6:3–8]. The verb is not usually expressed of the Hebrews in the like phrases where the sense is apparent, and therefore of some is set down before the word Lord and read thus, "I am the Lord thy God"; of other some, next after the word Lord, and then it is read thus, "I the Lord, am thy God." Wherein, although in sense there be no difference, but that both affirm one and the self-same thing, yet because there is more clear understanding of that one and the same thing by placing the verb next after the word Lord. I see no cause why the practice of some should be prejudicial in this matter, but that it may be said, "I the Lord am thy God."

In affirming that he is their God, he assureth them of all mercy and happiness from himself alone, both in this life and in the life to come. Making a league with them, to make himself known to be their God, by the mercies he had to bestow upon them, and that he would have the care and charge of their welfare reserved to himself alone. It remaineth to be proved by the Scripture that this manner of speaking, "to be their God," containeth promises in it for this life, and for the life to come. In the psalm, the prophet having made mention of sundry outward blessings, in children, in increase of corn and cattle, peace and freedom from enemies, concludeth thus, "Blessed are the people that be so; blessed are the people whose God is the Lord" (Ps. 144:15), making these outward blessings to be contained under the benefit of having the Lord to be their God. In Exodus, promising their deliverance from Egypt, he saith that he will be their God, containing that outward deliverance within this mercy of being their God. And as for the spiritual and inward blessings (as writing his law in our hearts, pardoning our sins and not remembering them any more), that they are contained within this covenant of being our God may appear in the Epistle to the Hebrews, "After those days, saith the Lord, I will put my laws in their mind, and in their heart I will write them, and I will be their God and they shall be my people. . . . For I will be merciful unto their unrighteousness, and their sins and their iniquities I will remember no more" (Heb. 8:10,12). And in Ezekiel we may clearly see that the removing of our stony hearts, the receiving of us to mercy after we have transgressed, the causing us to walk in his statutes and laws, are streams that flow from this free fountain of grace that the Lord is become our God. "A new heart," saith the Lord by his prophet, "will I give you, and a new spirit will I put within you, and I will take away the stony heart out of your body, and I will give you a heart of flesh. And I will put my spirit within you, and cause you to walk in my statutes, and ye shall keep my judgments and do them, and ye shall dwell in the land that I gave to your fathers, and ye shall be my people and I will be your God" (Ezek. 36:26–8, where these benefits received are made the fruits that follow of having him to be their God). Which is all done freely and undeservedly, as the Lord plainly professeth in the same chapter (v. 32) in these words: "Be it known unto you that I do not this for your sake, saith the Lord God. Therefore O ye house of Israel, be ashamed and confounded for your own ways." Neither doth this mercy of having the Lord to be our God contain itself within the compass of this life, but reacheth unto the blessings of the life to come. As appeareth in the gospel after Saint Luke, where our savior Christ proveth that it must needs be well with Abraham and that he must rise again, because it is written the Lord is the God of Abraham. For he is not the God of the dead, saith our savior Christ, but of them that live (Lk. 20:37–8).

In the Epistle to the Hebrews, Abraham and others the children of God are reported to have been strangers in the land of promise, and not to have seen the promises fulfilled in their time (*cf.* Heb. 11:13). Which might seem to make against this that I have said concerning the blessing of them to whom the Lord is become God. But it is answered there that he was not ashamed to be called their God for he had prepared for them a city. As if that which seemed to be wanting in this life were so sufficiently recompensed in that joy that did abide for them, as that the Lord needed not to be ashamed to be called their God, so rich was his mercy towards them. By this we learn that the first commandment containeth in it the promises of the gospel (as it is well noted by M[aster] Peter Martyr), contrary to that damnable opinion of certain who hold that the fathers of the Old Testament had no promises, saving of the land of Canaan and temporal things. We see that the Lord made promise to be their God, which (as we have heard) hath promises both of this life and of the life to come. And (as it appeareth in Genesis 17:7) all the mercies that Abraham received were contained under these words which are the words of the covenant: "I will be God to thee and to thy seed after thee."

The benefit that here is set down (of bringing them out of the land of Egypt and from the house of bondage), is an experience which they had of this goodness of God wherein he did apparently declare himself to be their God. And so likewise it is in other places brought in as a confirmation of the covenant, "Because the Lord loved you," saith the Holy Ghost, "and because he would keep the oath which he had sworn unto your fathers, the Lord hath brought you out by a mighty hand, and delivered you out of the house of bondage, from the hand of Pharaoh king of Egypt, that thou mayst know that the Lord thy God he is God, the faithful God, which keepeth covenant and mercy unto them that love him and keep his commandments" (Deut. 7:8-9). This experience of God's goodness towards them, and the trial [i.e., proof] that he is become their God, maketh much to bring on obedience, and therefore is placed with the covenant. For when we have trial indeed that the Lord hath special goodwill towards us, it hath great force in it to bring us willingly under his obedience. Therefore we are taught by this always to have in memory those benefits of God that have in them the note and mark of special goodwill and liking such as he beareth unto his children. For the remembrance of those will draw duties from us that shall proceed from a frank and free heart. Let us therefore have a register of his greatest benefits done unto us. Let us call to mind what a special benefit this is, if we had none other, that when we were (as is the disposition of all Adam's children) following the lusts and affections of our own heart in that broad way that leadeth unto death which so many follow, it hath pleased him to pick us out of so many, to give us misliking of that course of life which by nature we are so addicted and inclined unto and the earnest hungering and thirsting after that righteousness that is approved by his word. His benefits may not be overpassed without consideration. They carry with them strong persuasion unto obedience, and the faithful do use this help to further obedience unto God. In the last chapter of Joshua, there is mention made of the several benefits of God bestowed upon his people, and all for this end, to reclaim them from sin and to stir them to the free and willing service of the Lord. And the people (in the same chapter) allege his benefits received as a reason why they neither may nor will refuse obedience unto him. "God forbid," say the people, "that we should forsake the Lord to serve other gods. For the Lord our God, he brought us and our fathers out of the land of Egypt, from the house of bondage, and he did those great miracles in our sight, and preserved us in all the way that we went, and among all the people through whom we came, and the Lord did cast out before us all the people, even the Amorites which dwelt in the land; therefore will we also serve the Lord, for he is our God" (Josh. 24:16–18). They gather by these benefits that he is their God, and conclude therefore that they will serve the Lord because he is their God and hath been so singularly good and beneficial unto them.

And in very deed, this persuasion that he is our God and so tenderly affected towards us is the mother of all true obedience, the fountain from whence floweth all true worship and service of God. It is the note that discerneth between the works of a true Christian and the deeds of an infidel or heathen man. The Christian worketh his obedience having this persuasion, that God is already his God. The infidel and unbeliever hath no such persuasion, and therefore his doings come not frankly and freely from him to honor the Lord, but slavishly and servilely to serve himself and after that manner, as it were, to get within the Lord and to earn his salvation of himself. It is this faith which made the difference between the sacrifice of Abel and the sacrifice of Cain, as the Scripture doth declare. It is this faith that maketh the difference between the continency that we have read to have been in infidels and pagans, and that which is in Christians; between the mercy and alms that proceedeth oftentimes from civil men, and that merciful relief that cometh from them that serve the Lord in spirit and truth. It is this persuasion of his goodness that justifieth the one, whereas the other, wanting this, is odious and hateful in his sight. It is this persuasion that God is so rich in goodness as to accept of us, which sendeth us to the true service of him. The Lord is not only contented to say that he is their God, but also to bring good evidence for the same, in putting them in mind of that singular benefit of their deliverance from Egypt which he had bestowed upon them.

We learn then in this commandment, which chargeth us that we take the Lord for our God, that he hath taken upon himself the provision to store us with graces and blessings, both for this life and for the life to come. And he will have the honor and glory of it himself alone, because he will declare the riches of his grace towards his faithful people, and by his dealing with them be known to be their God. Therefore he bindeth us to seek for all good things at his hands alone. And in like manner, when we have received anything, by humble thanksgiving to return the whole praise thereof unto him again.

Now that we know the meaning of this commandment, it behooveth us to apply it to our profit. Wherein we must first understand that by the means of sin (which is in every man by nature) man's wit and understanding hath received such a blindness as it cannot conceive the truth of this commandment, and also his will and affection is so poisoned as it cannot take any joy or liking in it. The trial whereof, may be had in this manner, when the man that is not born again and received unto mercy (whom the Scripture calleth the natural man, because all are such by nature), when he (I say) is in any strait or necessity, either because he wanteth necessary food for this life, or for that he is in danger to lose wealth, credit or life, and seeth not the ordinary means by the which it is likely he should escape the danger — let it then be told him that God is his God, and hath a love towards him and a care over him, and will in his time by lawful means provide for him; yet notwithstanding his wit neither conceiveth this persuasion, nor his will and affection is anything made joyful or comforted thereby, as one that desirously inclineth after the hope thereof. Which is declared [i.e., made evident] by this, that some fall to stealing, or seeking unto witches, wisemen or wisewomen (as they call them) to have their griefs remedied and their wants supplied. Others, not using the same, yet by one unlawful means or other, wind themselves out of danger, not waiting by faith upon the Lord until by lawful means he procure their deliverance.

This corruption also of the natural man is no less evident when he is out of danger, and hath ordinary means to maintain him by. For when a natural man hath credit, wealth or friends to compass matters by, either not at all doth he seek to God by prayer to prosper those means which he useth, either else if he pray unto him, it is so coldly as that every man may perceive, but especially his own conscience may tell him, that his hope ariseth rather from the means he hath than from the goodness of God without whose blessing all helps are nothing. And yet for all that, he findeth no fault with himself for want of faith, but will protest that he taketh God to be his God and looketh for all things from him, believing as assuredly in him as the best of them all. Neither is it to be marvelled at if the natural man give so much unto the means, for it cometh oftentimes to pass that the Lord is constrained in dealing with his children, to withdraw something from the number or strength even of his lawful and ordinary means, that the glory may be wholly his. A notable example whereof we have in the book of the Judges, where the Lord caused Gideon to send away the greatest part of his men when he should go to battle, giving the reason of his doing in these words: "The people that are with thee are too many for me to give the Midianites into their hands, lest Israel make their vaunt against me and say, Mine hand hath saved me" (Judg. 7:2). Thus corrupt is the estate that all men are born in.

And in this estate do all men continue, finding no fault nor misliking of the same, save that little flock of Christ's that by the benefit of his death are exempted from it. Whom when it pleaseth God to call unto the hope of everlasting life by the means of his word, he cleareth their wit and understanding to conceive the goodness of their God to themward, he purgeth their will and affection to take comfort in it. And therefore when means want, they are not (as the wicked) altogether without hope, running after unlawful means, but wait better upon their God. And when they have the ordinary means whereby God usually bringeth matters to pass, they are careful in craving the success of them, yea, with inward persuasion of heart, to find no fruit but by his blessing.

The man that will truly examine himself in this commandment must well consider with himself what evil and unlawful shifts he hath made throughout his life, in his distress and necessity; or what doubts and fears, of not being well and in due time provided for, have arisen at any such time in his heart, and how tickle [sic] his nature is thereunto. Likewise, when he hath had the usual means of God's mercies, he must consider well how sparing and how cold he hath been in prayer to God for the success of them. Which declareth that his trust was rather in them than in

God the giver of them. Thus may he easily perceive in what a miserable condition he should have been had not the mediator and redeemer, Christ Jesus, answered the matter for him. It is therefore required that after this manner he thoroughly examine his infirmity and disobedience, until he be truly humbled and brought to Christ, to see the benefit of his death and passion, how great it is, and how needful for him.

When by due examining of himself, he doth well understand that he is wholly beholden unto God for the benefit of his salvation, because by the law they are accursed that continue not in all things which are written in the book of the law to do them. Then is he forced to acknowledge that it is good right and reason that his life should be ordered after the pleasure and will of him that by his death hath brought deliverance unto him from everlasting death and destruction (*cf.* 2 Cor. 5:[14–15?]), and the hope also of a blessed estate to continue forever. Whereupon he proceedeth not only to the misliking of this corrupt nature of his, but also to the suppressing of it, that it deal not as it was accustomed, neither when it wanteth means, nor yet when it enjoyeth them, calling earnestly unto God by prayer that he may so increase in faith that he may glorify him in the obedience of this commandment. His profiting in this obedience (how great soever) is always joined with true humility. Because he well understandeth, by the sight that he hath of himself, that he standeth by the mercies of God in Christ alone. Because also he plainly perceiveth that his obedience is not without frailty and manifold infirmities cleaving unto it. As his obedience is not without humility, so his falls and infirmities are not without grief and vexation of heart. For he seeth in them the dishonor and disobedience of that God of whose free goodness he holdeth all that he hath or hopeth for.

A great number persuade themselves that their faith is perfect enough, and no want in it at all, when notwithstanding in their necessities and distresses they are as ready to doubt and distrust of comfort as if they had never heard of the gospel, nor learned anything of the promises made unto the faithful. Nay, which more is, they shall no sooner be in any distress but they are as far from hope in God and as ready to help themselves by one evil shift or other, as those civil men which have no religion in them at all. And all this notwithstanding, they cannot see nor be brought to acknowledge any want in their faith. Let a man be brought something behind hand (as we say) either by loss that he hath had in his sheep or cattle, or by means of evil creditors with whom he hath had dealings, and by and by he will be ready to imagine that he shall not be able to live, unless he utter his commodities at a greater price than before he hath done. When notwithstanding he hath gone as far before as conscience could in any respect give him leave. He thinketh that his former decay doth privilege and make lawful this kind of dealing. And understand by the way, that in all this purpose and practice he receiveth not any suspicion that there should be any want of faith or weakness in that behalf. When as in very deed then is there true trial of our faith if in our necessity we shall thereby stay us from evil means in hope to have us provided for according to his promise, albeit we see not any likelihood thereof so far as our reason can reach. For in faith there is hope beyond hope.

The children of God by the eyes of faith see a secret blessing promised which they apprehend by hope; when as the common sort, wanting this eye, cast away all hope unless by a sensible manner they perceive and presently may grope [i.e., seize] the goodness and help of God. The man that will take no knowledge that there is want of faith in him, but doth profess (as the most will do) that he trusteth in God with all his heart, and that there is no mistrust in God in any part or corner thereof, is to be sent back to his doings and thoughts that are and have been in him in the time of his troubles, dangers, poverty or decay, to consider if there have been then in his heart no more doubting, fearing or suspecting to be provided for from the Lord than hath been in other times. By this means (if there be any sense or judgment in him) he shall be constrained to confess the weakness of his faith, and so seek his comfort in Christ, being convicted within himself of such mistrust and unbelief as the law doth accurse and condemn. For if a man will not willingly be wise in the beguiling of himself, he may soon see and perceive a great diversity in himself between those times. That where so long as he had helps and holds to go by, he was comfortable, bold and confident; those being taken away, he is become without all courage, comfort or hope. If there were no want of faith, how could there be any lack of comfort or hope? If his confidence were not in the means, how could he be as a man without all heart or hope so soon as the means are either utterly taken away or else diminished? Especially, seeing the goodness of the Lord, which is the ground of faith, endureth forever.

And that the man which will take no knowledge of the want of his faith may be brought to the sight of himself, let him well consider with himself what should be the cause, that when he hath abundance and wanteth no necessary help, he is so exceeding sparing and careless in his manner of serving and seeking of the Lord; in respect of [i.e., as contrasted with] the fear and care that he is in so soon as he shall be any way distressed, and the pains also that then he taketh in his manner of serving the Lord. If his faith be at both times one, why should his care, which doth betray his fear, be almost none at one time and so plentiful at another? But only that there was want of faith before, albeit he could not espy it, the means standing as a mist or a cloud between him and the light that would teach him truly to discern. The man, therefore, that boasteth of the perfection of his faith, not feeling any want therein, denying that he trusteth in his riches, friendship, authority or wealth, must be willed to set them a while aside in his thoughts and considerations imagining seriously and in good earnest, that he had them not. Then let him ask his conscience and truly search out his spirits, whether he could be as confident, comfortable and hopeful in his heart in the wanting as in the having thereof. His heart will then tell him the contrary, if he search truly and thoroughly, and his deeds will declare no less. For we shall see such as courageous, and as confident as may be in their wealth, credit and health; and when they are taken away, as faint and feeble as men that neither have heart nor hope.

Thus must a man be sifted both in abundance and want, that in the true sight of his poverty he may be forced carefully and thankfully to lay hold upon the mercies brought by Jesus Christ. As for us that profess we know Christ, and are led to magnify his mercies by the experience of sin that we have within ourselves, let us remember that it is our part to declare that we are his, and in him, by dying unto sin and living unto righteousness. Let us therefore be ashamed to bear the name of Christ and to carry the countenance of them that love his gospel, and yet in our necessities to be as mistrustful and as ready to help them by one unlawful shift or other, as ever we were; or as they are, that neither profess nor know the gospel. Let us be ashamed to profess the gospel, and in the meantime to be at no more misliking nor war with our mistrustful thoughts than we have been when we had no knowledge of the same.

Hath not the Lord therefore died, that by his power we might die unto sin (*cf.* Rom. 6)? Hath he not appeared to weaken the power and strength of sin in those that be his that although they cannot drive sin from being at all in the flesh, yet they might drive it from reigning and ruling in them, abating the power and force thereof? How can men think then, that there is any truth of Christianity begun in them, being in the same manner affected toward their mistrustful thoughts and evil shifts that proceed thereof, as they were from the beginning ere ever they knew the word and gospel of their God, having no more hatred of them nor greater war and strife with them? It is true that the Lord in mercy for Christ covereth the sins of his; but it is as true that the Lord cureth the sins of his. It cannot be denied but that for Christ he doth pardon the sins of his servants; neither may we deny but that in Christ he doth also purge the sins of his servants.

Let us therefore, brethren, resort unto God by faithful prayer, that as he hath taken away the condemnation of sin, so he would more and more abolish the rule and kingdom thereof. Our hope is great, for our promises are many. Our Captain is strong. Our enemy hath often been foiled, even in frail flesh as feeble as we be; but the conquerors have ever been careful, much given to use the means of the word and prayer, often in the field with their own affections, having upon them the complete harness of a Christian.

Now let us pray unto our heavenly Father that we may so see our want of faith, that we may truly magnify the grace and mercy of God in Christ, which covereth the imperfection thereof; and also that we may have such strength from the power of his death that by the means thereof, we may more and more prevail both over our mistrustful nature in want, and also over our careless and secure estate in plenty and abundance.

The Sixth Lecture, upon the Thirteenth Verse

Thou shalt not kill.

The former commandment hath given forth instruction for particular callings, from the which (by reason of more particular employing of benefits mutually one upon another) there ariseth more particular duty of the one unto the other, than that which every common man may claim unto himself. Now we are to be instructed in those duties that generally we do owe unto all men, amongst which this commandment of not killing hath the first place. Wherein we are forbidden to do any violence, injury or wrong to the body and life of our neighbor, and commanded to defend, maintain and cherish the same. It is to be observed that the Lord, bidding us show forth love unto our neighbors, hath not left it unto us to devise wherein to pleasure them but hath set down what things are most dear unto them, that by our help given for the preservation of those things

safe unto them, and in benefiting them therein, they may have true trial
of the love and affection that we bear them. Our neighbor therefore in
this consideration is not shut up in the alone flesh and blood of the man,
but the duties of neighborhood reach unto the life and body, wife, goods
and good name of the man. Neither is love the not hating or not hurting
of a man, but the helping and furthering of him to receive more comfort
in those things above recited, over the which every man is so tender, that
being in any of those annoyed he can no longer account himself as a man
loved or regarded of the authors thereof. For he himself is upheld in life
and liking by the comfort of them. The Lord, in forbidding murder, forbiddeth also all violence, cruelty and wrath towards our neighbor, laboring in the detestation of this greatest evil to work in us a hatred towards
all [things] that be of any affinity with it, and therefore not letting us see
them [i.e., these things] but in that form which may most fear us from
them, putting upon them all that fearful form of murder. For this is the
name whereby the Holy Ghost will have them [i.e., those things] all
known that be of that kind.

The punishment of the offences against this commandment will help us
to judge the greatness of the same. Touching the murderer, it is said in
Leviticus 24:17, "He that killeth any man, he shall be put to death." Violence bursting forth into extremities of dealing, in the old law was punished with the like of that that was done, what kind soever it was. According as it is written in Leviticus 24:19–20, "If a man cause any
blemish in his neighbor, as he hath done so shall it be done to him, breach
for breach, eye for eye, tooth for tooth; such a blemish as he hath made
in any, such shall be repaid to him." Hereby the offender was drawn to
the better consideration of that grief which he had brought upon another,
in feeling the displeasure thereof within himself, and also feared the more
from offending, being well assured before that he could offer no great
wrong unto his neighbor which self-same in so doing he should not bring
upon his own head. This punishment doth not only declare the unlawful-
ness of violence which here is forbidden, but also by that punishment
which the just Lord did appoint for it, we see how great the offence is
which hath had such a punishment appointed for it from the justice of
God, that more account may be made of such injuries than commonly
there is in any place.

In this commandment is forbidden all cruelty. And therefore in the
punishment of certain offences, there was a number of stripes appointed
which in punishing they might not pass, as we read in Deuteronomy

25:2–3. So doth the Lord abhor cruelty that he would not have it covered, no, not under the cloak of justice and zeal against sin. Which under that pretence might be shadowed if in any respect at all it were to be maintained. This law was so religiously observed amongst the Jews that they would always give one stripe less unto the offender whosoever. And therefore forty being the number of stripes which they might not pass, the usual punishment was to give forty save one, which number they did not exceed, no not in punishing of Paul towards whom they bore so deadly hatred, as he testifieth of himself to the Corinthians, "Of the Jews," saith he in that place "five times received I forty stripes save one" (2 Cor. 11:24). Thus would the Jews give out some signification how they did abhor cruelty, being very unwilling to be publicly noted of that crime, how bloody soever their hearts were, no not at that time whenas they might have had some shadow in pretending the zeal of justice for their fact.

But Christians must abhor that in deed, which these in show would be thought to be far from. Cruelty was restrained in that which we read of in Leviticus 19:14 (of not putting a stumbling block before the blind nor reviling the deaf), for such wants get compassion amongst all those in whom there is any humanity of pitiful inclination. Those therefore must of necessity be cruel and savage that are so far from any touch therewith as that they can abide to increase it by insulting upon them and adding more torment unto them.

To repress cruel dealing it was forbidden them to withhold the hire of the poor and needy hired servant, as it is written in Deuteronomy 24:15, "Thou shalt give him his hire for his day, neither shall the sun go down upon it; for he is poor and therewith sustaineth his life; lest he cry against thee to the Lord, and it be sin unto thee." To the same end was the commandment given in Exodus 22:23–4 (for not vexing nor oppressing the strangers, widows and fatherless children) with this threat, "If thou vex or trouble such, and so he call and cry unto me, I will surely hear his cry. Then shall my wrath be kindled, and I will kill you with the sword, and your wives shall be widows and your children fatherless." For that cause, in the same chapter they are commanded to restore the garment taken to pledge before the sun goes down. "This is his garment for his skin," saith the Lord, "wherein shall be sleep? Therefore when he crieth unto me I will hear him, for I am merciful" (Ex. 22:26–7). The commandment that was given in Leviticus 25:35 (concerning those that were impoverished and fallen into decay) to relieve them but in no case to take usury or advantage of them, had in it the same purpose and end to meet with cruelty and unmercifulness. For every such condition hath in it matter to move us to pity and compassion, which occasion is taken of the good as offered them from the Lord to declare whose children they are, by being merciful even as their heavenly father is merciful [cf. Lk. 6:36].

But when men are so far from compassion and mercy, as being provoked by present and visible occasion offered, they do not only shut up the bowels of compassion against them, but even make a prey and spoil of them, most cruelly increasing their misery, it is a plain proof that there is no drop of humanity and much less of Christianity within them. To conclude this speech of cruelty, that which is written in Deuteronomy 25:4 of not muzzling the mouth of the ox that treadeth out the corn, and is applied by Saint Paul to the Corinthians to prove that the laborer may not be denied his hire and wages for his pains (1 Cor. 9:9-10), maketh plainly against cruelty and battereth down all the walls of unmercifulness that are so strongly upheld by the general practice of so many nowadays. For what man almost is there of any worship or wealth, who thinketh not that he may lawfully use his tenant or poor neighbor without any wages? Yet the prophet Jeremiah pronounceth woe against this kind of cruelty in these words, "Woe unto him that buildeth his house by unrighteousness, and his chambers without equity; he useth his neighbor without wages, and giveth him not for his work" (Jer. 22:13). It is nothing so cruel a fact to rob a stranger, whom thou knowest not, as to suck out (by his labor) the blood of thy friend and neighbor, and after to send him away without wages. If such buildings stand upon unrighteousness (as saith the prophet), it is to be feared that many a fair house in this land hath such a ruinous foundation as threateneth the destruction of the owner. This kind of cruelty, how heinous it was in the sight of God, and what plague it might bring in justice upon the things that were in such unrighteousness accomplished, did Job very well understand, and therefore saith, "If I have eaten the fruits of my land without silver, or have grieved the souls of the masters thereof, let thistles grow instead of wheat, and cockle instead of barley" (Job 31:39-40). "A righteous man," saith the Holy Ghost, "regardeth the life of his beast, but the mercies of the wicked are cruel" (Prov. 12:10). If he neglect not his beasts, but giveth them food in due time, much less will he neglect his family or servants, in defrauding them of that, either in meat or wages, that is convenient.

These examples that now I have alleged, as they spring from an unmerciful heart and tend to the unjust grief and molestation of the body and life of our brother, so are they directly against this commandment. Notwithstanding, as they bring damage unto him by detaining that which is his due, they are against this commandment also, "Thou shalt not steal," so that it is not impossible for one kind of action to be guilty both of murder and theft. The negligence of man, whereby his neighbor receiveth either loss of life or hurt of body, is forbidden in this commandment. The reason is very good. For if the Lord hath lawfully and in equity laid upon us the care of our neighbor's life, by good right may he require at our hands the willful neglect thereof. The punishment of such willful negligence toward the life or body of their brethren was most sharp and severe in the old law, as we may see in Exodus, where the man's own life must answer for the life of his brother, who perished by his negligence, according as the example is set down there, of a man not keeping up his ox which he knew was wont to push [i.e., gore]. "If the ox were wont to push in times past," saith the Holy Ghost, "and it hath been told his master and he hath not kept him [in], and after, he killeth a man or woman, the ox shall be stoned, and the owner shall die also" (Ex. 21:29).

In this offence of negligence are all those transgressors against this commandment who by delaying to take up matters in controversy or suits of law with all possible speed that may be, do by their negligence give occasion to the frail nature of man to commit murder, or some other mischief against him with whom he is in controversy. And if careless negligence be thus dangerous, how hard a matter will it be to reckon with the Lord for deliberate purpose to keep men at variance and debate, that their gain may grow thereby. It will be a hard matter to answer before the Almighty, if we have given occasion whereby our neighbor hath received loss of life. David's carefulness herein is worthily commended to all posterity, who when his men (breaking through the host of the Philistines with the danger of their lives) had brought him water to drink which he so greatly thirsted after and wished for, immediately poured it out for an oblation unto the Lord, and said, " 'Let not my God suffer me to do this. Should I drink the blood of these men's lives? For they have brought it with the jeopardy of their lives.' Therefore he would not drink it" (1 Chron. 11:19). A notable example to fear us for being occasion to any (though servant or inferior) rashly to hazard his life either for our profit or pleasure.

In this commandment the Lord is not only careful to have obedience from our hands, but also from our hearts and tongues. So that both thoughts and words must come under subjection unto him, that neither of them be infected with malice which the Lord so hateth and abhorreth. For we must interpret the law according to the nature of the Lord who is the lawgiver.

Man, by reason that he only seeth the deed and cannot discern of the heart, maketh laws for the outward doings, and punisheth them alone without proceeding further. But the Lord, who searcheth the heart and reins [i.e., affections], maketh laws for it [i.e., the heart] and punisheth even the consent of the heart going against his law. For inasmuch as the Lord hateth the evil itself, he cannot but abhor it wheresoever he shall find it, whether in heart, hand or tongue. It is written in the First Epistle of Saint John 3:15 that "whosoever hateth his brother is a manslayer." We see then that not only gross evils come into reckoning before the Lord, but even hatred settled in the heart, although the hand hath never been stretched forth to execute the same. Neither cometh it before him as some trifling thing which doth not greatly displease him, but appeareth monstrous, having none other shape upon it, nor other account made of it than of murder. Thus must we think of hatred consented unto in the heart, that it hath a bloody face in the sight of the Lord, and therefore is to be abhorred and loathed as the cruelty of murder. This was the cause why the Lord, forbidding hateful and malicious thoughts in this commandment, would give it none other name than murder, teaching us that howsoever we nourish such thoughts and make small account of them, yet his judgment is plain that they be no better than murder when the heart is settled in them.

In the gospel after Saint Matthew we see how the Lord hateth words proceeding from malice and anger. "Whosoever shall say, Fool! unto his brother," saith our savior Christ, "shall be worthy to be punished in hell fire" (Mt. 5:22). Hatred towards our brethren is so grievous in his sight that it staineth and defileth whatsoever it toucheth, be it word or thought, and maketh it so heavy that the Lord can no longer bear it. And because words betray that which lurketh in the heart, and bringeth it to light that otherwise would not so easily be espied, we must keep some good watch over them [i.e., words], that from thence we may be led to the privy chamber of the heart to see how all things go there. For of the abundance of the heart the mouth speaketh. So that there is no outward thing that can bring us sooner to the sight and speech of the heart, than can the tongue itself, which if it be infected with hatred or disdain, sure it is that all things are not well at home in the heart. And therefore all men must observe the inclination of the heart by the usage of the tongue, that when it cometh abroad casting forth hatred, wrath and debate, we may with speed return to the fountain, that is the heart, to purge and cleanse the same, because we are sure that from thence the tongue receiveth all poison.

If we shall prevail much in suppressing hatred both in our heart, tongue and hand, yet is not that all which is here commanded. For the Lord in forbidding murder, meant not to stay there, but in removing hatred his purpose was to make way and passage for merciful dealing towards the life of others. And necessary it was that he should give us warning of the stumbling block which lieth in the way; lest we suspecting no such matter, should have imagined that there would have been true care for the life of our brother where there was no victory before over our own disposition, which is altogether otherwise given and inclined. The true proof whereof we shall then have when our affections shall be stirred up by any dealing which shall mislike us. For then we shall well perceive wrath to be mightily working in us, which before (because it had peradventure no great matter to work upon) we thought that we had been altogether void of, or at the least not greatly infected therewith.

But now in this manner of speaking used by the Holy Ghost (who battereth down hatred, when his purpose is to build up love) we see that there will be no passage to any loving dealing in truth but by treading down of our contrary affections, which are noted to be in us by the form of speaking. For to what end should the Holy Ghost will us to do no murder if there were no disposition in us thereunto? This is the cause why the Holy Ghost dealeth so plainly with us, in telling us what we are, that our care may be great to reform it. And when we shall have profited anything herein, it may be acknowledged from whence we had that which we are assured was not to be found in our nature. The Holy Ghost therefore in this place detecteth our nature of want of love, nay, of hatred and cruelty, which otherwise we should not have marked, no, nor suspected ourselves of it, if we had not had warning from the Almighty that our nature is poisoned therewithal.

For if a man (not fearing God, yet otherwise of good understanding to conceive the truth of things) be demanded what his opinion is of himself, whether he be prone and bent to hatred, and whether he findeth his nature greatly inclining thereto or no, he will with great protestation constantly affirm that in him (he thanketh God) there is no such matter, abjuring it with admiration [i.e., amazement], and wondering how any man should be brought to think so of him. And thus not perceiving his own corruption, he seeth not what need he hath of a savior and redeemer. And therefore whatsoever he saith, he is in deed and truth unthankful for that benefit, while in finding no great thing amiss in himself, he cannot see what way he should so greatly be beholding to a savior that would answer for his transgressions (which in his own opinion is no great matter to do, they being either few, and so borne out in the number of those good things which he hath done, or else none at all).

Moreover, if we shall have done something, or divers things that may be thought loving and friendly, yet if the inclination to wrath (which is by nature in us) be either not known, or being known, the strength thereof shall not be subdued, and the sting pulled out that it reign no more within us, we shall never be provoked by any evil dealing of others, but that forthwith (letting the rein go to our heat) we shall dishonor his name in following the rage of our mind contrary to the law of our God. So might it come to pass that a man (having some good opinion of himself for some outward things, but never tried with any injurious dealing of another) might take it to go well with him, when notwithstanding this corrupt nature of his standeth whole in her full force and strength, being never a whit subdued unto the Spirit, as he well perceiveth when that any great occasion shall be offered to try him withal. We see then how just cause there is, that the Lord should admonish us of this corruption of hatred which is within us. Not only that we should see the benefit of our savior and mediator, but also that subduing it and treading down the strength of it, we might find free passage to do, and not to be removed from doing, the works of mercy and love which are here commanded, even the contrary of those that (as we have heard) were forbidden us. We are commanded to have care of the body and life of our brother, to maintain it as his necessity shall require and our ability can perform, remembering that the Lord hath committed that care unto us. The Jews were commanded to make places of refuge and defense (*cf.* Deut. 4:41–3), where the guiltless persons might have protection against the rage of them who pursued them unto death, that (as it is written in Deuteronomy 19:10) innocent blood be not shed within their land, and lest blood should be upon them. For these are the very words of the text in that place, signifying that the not regarding and providing for the safety of their life were matter sufficient enough to make them and their land guilty of their blood, that thereby they might well understand that the care of their brethren's life was commended unto them, not without great danger if there were to be found any negligence therein. Merciful dealing is here commanded towards all, but especially towards inferiors, widows, fatherless children and those that be in any great extremity. A notable practice we have of this in the person of Job suffering his servants to plead their right and to maintain their good cause before him, not using his authority to oppress them, and cruelty to execute his rage, without regarding the equity of their cause, only standing upon his own authority over them. "If I did contemn the judgment of my servant and of my maid," saith Job, "when they did contend with me, what then shall I do when God standeth up? And when he shall visit me, what shall I answer? He that hath made me in the womb, hath he not made him?" (Job 31:13–15) Here is the true trial of a merciful man. For it is no commendation not to offer wrong unto those who are our equals and able to match us. But then have we true trial of our affections that there is some mercy in truth within us, when we shall show pity and compassion towards those whom (for our authority or place that we be in) we might easily oppress, when we shall be kept from fleshing our affections upon those that lay open unto us having no sense of power or credit that is sufficiently able to hold us. His example of compassion is no less commendable towards all of them that were in any great want or extremity, as the Holy Ghost (under his person) witnesseth in these words: "I delivered the poor that cried, and the fatherless; and him that had none to help him. The blessing of him that was ready to perish came upon me, and I caused the widow's heart to rejoice" (Job 29:12–13). The Jews were bound to declare their compassion towards their brethren by that law which commanded them to lend their brother that was needy amongst them sufficient for his need, taking for assurance a pledge which he might forbear, as appeareth in Deuteronomy 15:7–10, where they have a strait charge that when the year of Jubilee should approach (at what time all men were charged to release their debts), they should not at that time shut up their compassion from him that would borrow for his need, but frankly give unto him, notwithstanding the year when all debts must be released be even at hand. There is a promise added to encourage them, that for so doing the Lord would bless them in all that they should put their hand unto.

They were charged also to relieve their brother or the stranger that dwelt with them who was fallen into decay, and forbidden in express words to take any usury or increase of such, either of money or meat, as appeareth in Leviticus 25:35–6, but to use their goods to such comfort of their brethren as might well witness the love that they had unto them.

The law and commandment that was given to this people at the time when they had made an end of the tithing of their increase, doth declare that they had in charge from the Lord to relieve with their goods the Levite, stranger, fatherless and widow. For in Deuteronomy 26:13, before the people should crave of God that he would bless their land, they must protest in set words that they had given unto the Levites, stranger, fatherless and widow accordingly as he had commanded them, and so proceed after declaration of this their obedience to his will, to crave his blessing for the people and the land. Thus using their goods to the commodity of their brethren, in lending and giving according to God's appointment, they did give apparent tokens of love toward their neighbors. The apostle Paul will not acquit him that hath stolen if he shall steal no more, but chargeth him that he shall labor that he may have something to give to him that needeth, that way to practice love and the works thereof upon his needy brethren [cf. Eph. 4:28]. It is not only therefore the duty of rich men to give something towards the relief of the needy, but even the poor must spare somewhat of their poverty to the comfort of Christ in his needy members. Which, be it never so little that they offer of their poverty (if there go a willing and a faithful mind withal) is much more acceptable to God than great sums given from some wealthy men of their superfluity, only without like faith or love unto the Lord. As we are taught in the parable of the widow casting in her two mites into the treasury, which are justified by our savior Christ to be more than all that the rich had cast in, because theirs was of their superfluity, but hers of her poverty (cf. Mk. 12:41-4). If any ought to be dispensed withal from declaring their love in this part, it is very reasonable that he (who by reason of his long loitering and acquaintance with stealing and idleness was become through custom, which is another nature, unapt for labor) should be discharged upon the maintenance of himself by some honest trade; yet notwithstanding, even he standeth charged from the Lord to reserve something for the provision of his needy members.

To encourage us to duty in this part of merciful dealing and giving to the needy, the Lord doth promise that it shall be paid us again in our greatest need. For thus saith the prophet Isaiah, "If thou refresh the hungry and troubled soul, then shall thy light spring out in darkness. The Lord shall satisfy thy soul in drought, and make fat thy bones, and thou shalt be like a spring of water whose waters fail not (cf. Is. 58:10-11). A great blessing of God to be provided for in drought. A goodly forecast to lay up in prosperity that which we may be assured will not only come again, but also will be sure to watch that time when for our need it shall be most welcome unto us. Who would not be content to give, if he might be sure to have it again at his most need? And behold we have letters patents from the Lord under the broad seal of his blood for the finding of that we have laid out for him, even in our greatest need. How can we then be slack in the liberal laying out of something for an evil day? According to the counsel of the Holy Ghost in Ecclesiastes 11:2, "Give a portion," saith he, "to seven and to eight, for thou knowest not what evil shall be upon the earth."

Moreover, the sentence of that great day proceedeth against the damned persons in this form: "Depart from me, ye cursed, into everlasting fire which is prepared for the devil and his angels; for I was an hungered and ye gave me no meat, I thirsted and ye gave me no drink, I was a stranger and ye lodged me not, I was naked and ye clothed me not, sick and in prison and ye visited me not. [. . .] Verily, I say unto you, inasmuch as ye did it not to one of the least of these, ye did it not to me" (Mt. 25:41–5). And if the promise cannot draw us, the form of sentence must necessarily provoke us to obedience herein. We learned before that negligent delaying, whereby our neighbor is endangered in his body or life, was forbidden in this commandment; and then is speedy help and diligent using of the present occasion that is offered to do our neighbor good given us here in commandment. We have a singular example of this in Esther 4:14, where Mordecai telleth the Queen that if she should let slip that present occasion then offered her to do good unto the Jews, she and her father's house should perish, and yet deliverance would appear unto the Jews from some other place. In like manner Job professeth that he had not caused the eyes of the widow to fail in long looking and waiting before their request were granted, but had with all speed satisfied her desire (cf. Job 31:16). Acknowledging it for a great offence if he had been but slack therein, even such [an offence] as if he should have been guilty thereof might justly have brought a curse upon him.

Our natural inclination goeth wholly amiss in this commandment as in the rest. Which notwithstanding it lie hid in some more closely than in other, for all that it is not so cunningly covered in any, but that it is disclosed and discerned when occasion is offered. The man that is born again unto the hope of everlasting life doth so clearly perceive his infection herein, that both in heart and word he acknowledgeth the great necessity and benefit of a savior and redeemer. Being privy unto himself not only of many evil fruits that have appeared in his life contrary to this com-

mandment, but also of disposition within that is naturally prone and inclined to offend herein. The hope that he hath in his mediator and savior
Christ Jesus, doth not make him secure and careless in his sin, following
the inclination of his own heart; but leadeth him to a continual strife and
debate with it, because it is against the honor of his God and savior, to
whom he well perceiveth that he is only beholding for his salvation, and
quickeneth him to all loving dealing which is so often commended and
commanded of his good and merciful Father. The natural man seeth not
any such inclination in himself to wrath or dullness unto loving dealing
with his neighbors, as through the grief therewith [i.e., grief over which]
driveth him to make much of the alone savior and redeemer Christ. But
when he is charged with his offences that burst forth contrary to this
commandment, he maketh light of them, and putteth them up in a common bag, saying, "All men have infirmities," never so touched with them
as [that] he can be compelled to magnify the grace brought by the alone
mediator Christ. And much less is he driven to any earnest war with
them, or great care to profit in the works of love that are contrary to
them.

To conclude, this commandment, if we shall do some outward things
commanded here, which shall obtain great commendation of many men,
and for all that the Lord want his glory, which consisteth in the four
points which were spoken of in the former commandment, it shall avail us
nothing. Those things that appertain unto God must of necessity go with
those duties unto men that shall be accepted. Neither indeed can we hold
out in these, except we have life and encouragement from the other. For
the love that God is our God, tenderly favoring and plentifully reward-
ing us that be his, must make us to persevere in those duties which otherwise would not abide the reproaches and injuries of men, but would burst
forth to requite them. And much less would we labor to overcome them
and their evil, with our good done unto them. But this persuasion of his
good favor towards his, and plentiful mercy which is to be showed upon
them, maketh men willingly to forbear the ensuing and satisfying of their
own corrupt affections, not envying the wicked their transitory delights,
but prosecuting their course in his obedience, through all their reproaches, while they do well perceive what a plentiful recompense of reward abideth for them by the free gift of their God.

The man that cannot be persuaded but that he loveth his neighbor as
himself, performing all that is required of him in that behalf, must be sent
to examine himself, if there have at no time appeared in him any cruel

dealing towards his inferiors, any neglect or delay in helping and relieving the distressed, if compassion hath always, as occasion served, drawn him to speedy relieving by lending or giving, so shall he easily see into the error of his opinion.

Now let us pray unto our heavenly Father, that we may so see into our cruel and careless disposition, that we may magnify the free mercies of our God in the forgiveness thereof, and also have power more and more to subdue it, that we abounding in all merciful dealing, may glorify him in this life, and be glorified of him in the life to come.

The Eighth Lecture, upon the Fifteenth Verse

Thou shalt not steal.

It hath been showed before, that our neighbor is not to be considered in his person alone, but in whatsoever thing is dear unto him: as goods, good name and such like. And therefore the love which we must bear towards him, may not be towards his body alone, but also towards his goods, providing always that our dealing with them be so upright as may declare in deed that we do love the man. For if any thing of his, passing through our hands, shall not find fidelity and faithful dealing, but deceitful conveyance of it or some part thereof to ourselves, can it be truly said we love the man? There is no man that can so judge of it, that can (I say) persuade himself that he is beloved of those men, when nothing of his goods cometh to their hands but it is sure to be fleeced and to pay toll before it shall depart. The Lord therefore (commanding safe passage and loving dealing towards our neighbor's goods), whensoever (according to the manifold necessities of every man, to deal and communicate with another in buying and selling, or otherwise) they have occasion to pass through our hands, hath forbidden stealing, and all unfaithfulness in their goods, condemning it of want of charity and love towards themselves, whose goods are diminished by us, whensoever we shall have dealing with them.

And because we go so closely to work and are so cunning to deceive ourselves, imagining that we love our neighbors when indeed there is no such affection in us, the Holy Ghost is compelled as it were to trace us, and by such unfaithful footsteps as these be, to descry [i.e., expose] us. For when we are so often taken with untrusty dealing and unfaithfulness in our neighbor's goods, good name and such like, is there not just cause to arrest us for not discharging this duty of love, which is so due unto them? This unfaithful dealing with the goods of our neighbor, how greatly it did displease the Lord and with what laws he did restrain his people of Israel from the same, the statutes and orders of that government can best declare. From whence it shall not be amiss to take some help in the interpretation of this commandment. In Exodus 22:1,4 we do read that if any man should steal a sheep, and kill it, or sell it, he should restore for that one sheep, four. But if any man should steal an ox, and after kill it, or sell it, he should restore five oxen for that ox. The reason why he must pay more for the ox than for the sheep was for that his neighbor's loss was greater in the want of the one than of the other, as bringing more profit to the owner thereof. But if they were found with the thief alive, not sold nor killed, then must he restore but the double of the ox, ass or sheep, for that his obstinacy in this evil did not appear so great as when he should make sale of them, and turn them into gain. For it might be, while they were alive, that he being touched with repentance, would restore them again. But when they were sold or killed, the thief gave a greater token of his impudency and confirmed obstinacy, and the owner also was one degree further from any likelihood to come by them again. If the thief be nothing worth, and so not able to make restitution, then (as it is there declared) he must be sold for his theft, and so make restitution thereof.

Thus did the just God in the Old Testament, by laws made for that purpose, and punishments appointed accordingly, declare his hatred of the evil, and in what reckoning it cometh before his judgment seat, that we might take light at his judgment, how to discern of theft, and how to judge of this kind of hatred towards our neighbor, that betrayeth itself in so unjust dealing with his goods.

The love that we must show forth towards our neighbor by dealing well with his goods, may not only be seen in this law (so sharply punishing the thief for his want of love evidently appearing in his theft and injury committed) but also in the law made for him that should borrow any of his neighbor's goods. Which law did very well provide for faithful dealing with it, in punishing the contrary so sharply, as his unfaithfulness (how great soever) should gain him nothing at all. For thus it is written in Exodus 22:14,15: "If a man borrow aught of his neighbor, and it be hurt, or else die (the owner thereof not being by) he shall surely make it good. [. . .] If it be a hired thing, he shall not make it good, it came for his hire."

It appeareth here plainly that the owner must have his loss made good of the borrower, unless his own eyes could testify that the hurt or loss thereof came not through any default of the borrower. But he that shall lend for hire must stand to the adventure [i.e., risk] of the principal if it decay. The reason is rendered, because it came for hire, and not of love alone, as did the thing borrowed. And therefore the reason is good why he should not be charged in this case, as the borrower, to make good that which he hath hired being hurt or dead. Mark well, I pray you, this law of God for lending and hiring: that the borrower must make good things borrowed if they decay, but not the hirer. Mark it well, I say, for this is the ground of many things that are to be spoken of hereafter.

The equity of this law bringeth great light to discern of the usuries that are so common at these days.[1] In things borrowed, it appeareth (by this law) that only the hurt or death of the goods was provided for. Here is then no help for money that is borrowed or lent, which perisheth not with use, but is still of the same value and worth that it was at the first delivery of the same. Besides that, if it were worse for the use, there is no more required but to make the decay of it good. How then can those who lend their money to usury (which decayeth not with use) claim anything above that which was delivered? By this law of lending, their recompense was commanded only in this title, that the thing by lending was certainly known to be impaired. How dare then the usurers claim a right of recompense under no other title but that it was likely with the use thereof that they might in that time, thus and so greatly have gained? It is the equity of God to require no recompense for the use of things borrowed, that are the worse with using, so long as there appeareth no casual hurt (as we call it) of the whole. What equity then must it be, that for things not worse with use contenteth not itself, no not with the whole? Here, in this law of God, goodwill is no better recompensed, but that it be no loser. Shall a covetous desire then so richly be requited as that it shall be sure always to come home a gainer? By this equity of God, when it is certainly known that by the use of the thing borrowed, the borrower hath good gain, yet doth the Almighty allow no return of commodity to the lender for that gain. By what equity then can the usurer claim gain for the use, yea oftentimes when it is certain there is no gain gotten at all? By this law of God, the lender could never gain. For there is no other proviso made but for his principal. By our practice, he is ever assured of gain.

1. [ED.] See the introduction by R. H. Tawney to the reprint (London, 1925) of Thomas Wilson, *A Discourse upon Usury* (1572).

By that law the borrower was assured of the gain that was to return to him. By this [our] practice the lender is oftentimes the whole gainer. If it be granted that this law of God in borrowing and lending have in it any equity, this practice in borrowing and lending of money must be condemned of plain wrong and injury, as directly standing against the same.

If this dealing shall fear the strict justice of borrowing and lending, and seek cover under the liberty of things let out to hire, it is also shut out there, and findeth worse entertainment. For hired things, because they go for hire, have not the ordinary allowance of the principal, if they shall decay, which borrowed things justly claim because they come freely and without hire. Therefore the law that we heard of hired things, handleth the usurer more hardly, than that law of borrowing and lending. For here because of his hire, he hath no hold of the principal if it do decay.

Thus if it should be granted that money may be hired, which I think never can be proved, yet must it be with hazard of the principal, according to the equity of this law. That by the equity of this law (which is the equity of God), it can have no better allowance (if it shall be proved lawful to let it out for hire) than to stand to the danger and decay of the principal, these reasons will plainly prove. The goods which naturally yield commodities in the use of them to him that possesseth them, as sheep and such other, must stand to the adventure of decay if they be hired. Therefore much more must they do so, which naturally and of themselves yield no commodities.

The goods that in yielding their commodities do spend and wear away themselves are contented with their hire, and lay no claim to have the whole repaired. By what justice then may goods that are never a whit the worse for wearing, besides their hire, bind a man to uphold the whole? If it be equity, that those goods which naturally of themselves yield by use a certain gain should not be charged with the danger of decay, it is against all equity that those things which neither of themselves, nor yet with like certainty yield their commodity, should beside their hire, have the whole upheld.

To conclude, if those goods which (by all men's judgment) may most lawfully have consideration for their use, be not better considered, it seemeth to me good reason why those goods (which the most think are not at all to have hire for their use, and all men think, they may not so justly require it as the other) should hold themselves well contented when their allowance is as good as theirs is, which best do deserve it.

If any man shall reply, and say that some of great deserving in the

church of God, men of singular learning and judgment, have thought and
taught otherwise, let them understand that there is no usury that is now
in use with us that can be upheld by their doctrine. For proof whereof I
refer myself unto that which is written by that worthy instrument of
God, Master Calvin, upon this matter in his commentaries upon the eight-
eenth chapter of Ezekiel, a man that hath said the most for the allowance
of usury in some special cases. His words are these: "Now we must consider when, and of whom, we may take usury. And here that common
saying taketh place, not everywhere, not always, not all things, not of all
men. This was spoken of gifts, and this law was made for the rulers of
provinces; but it agreeth very fitly unto this cause. A man may not therefore take all gain, for if it exceed measure (because that is against charity)
it is to be refused. And we have said already that often to use it, and to
make a common and usual practice of it, cannot be without fault. Neither
is it to be allowed everywhere, because the usurer (as I have said) ought
to have no place, nor once to be suffered in the church of God. Moreover, it is not to be taken of all men, because it shall always be extreme
wickedness to take usury of a poor man."

This is the opinion of that man, who of all other giveth most liberty,
and is thought to be most favorable in this cause. As for him that liveth
upon usury, as the husbandman doth upon his husbandry, his judgment is
that he ought to be thrust out of the society of men. Thus much for his
judgment, whom some usurers in this matter pretend to build upon.[2]

We see in this commandment what hedges and fences the Lord hath
made for the safety of our goods, to reserve the propriety and benefit
thereof unto ourselves, and to keep us also from witnessing any want of
love, by breaking in upon any other men's goods unlawfully. This want
of love, witnessed by evil dealing with our neighbor's goods, was likewise
provided for by laws made for their faithful dealing, that had anything
given them to keep. We read in Exodus 22:7–13, that if a man deliver his
neighbor money or stuff to keep, and it be stolen out of his house, if the
thief be found, he shall pay the double; if the thief be not found, then the
master of the house must be brought unto the judges to swear whether he
hath put his hand unto his neighbor's goods to defraud him of it or no
(not being acquitted of the suspicion, before he shall have purged himself

2. [ED.] John Calvin, *Commentaries on the First Twenty Chapters of the Book
of the Prophet Ezekiel*, English translation (Edinburgh, 1850), II, 225–8, especially
227; also André Biéler, *La Pensée économique et sociale de Calvin* (Geneva, 1959),
453–76, in part correcting Tawney as noted above.

by an oath). If a man shall deliver unto his neighbor to keep, ass, ox or sheep, or any beast, and it die or be hurt, or taken away by enemies, and no man see it, the owner (hearing him testify by an oath that there was no deceit of his part in the matter) must hold himself contented therewith. But if it were stolen from him to whom it was given to keep, he must make restitution to the owner thereof, because therein appeared his negligence. If it were torn in pieces (which might be, notwithstanding his diligence were never so good) he must bring some part of it, and show that it was devoured, and in so doing he is not bound to make it good.

These testimonies are here brought in, to testify how careful the Lord is of faithful and loving dealing with our neighbors in their goods, and to let us see and understand that we are not so free from duties in that behalf as commonly we are wont to esteem ourselves to be; but that we stand bound before the Lord, to leave records behind us of our loving affection towards them, whensoever by any occasion we shall have to deal with their goods.

What natural man can be persuaded that there is any conscience binding to restore goods that were put in trust unto him, if they should be stolen? What natural man would not fret and fume at this, that when his neighbor maketh request unto him to keep it, he should notwithstanding be bound to answer [for] it if it were stolen, or be troubled for his goodwill, to purge himself before a magistrate by an oath, that there was no unfaithful dealing on his part with those goods? Would not flesh and blood storm at this, as an unlawful and unjust thing? But the just Lord, by these laws letteth us see that we stand more bound unto loving dealing with our neighbors in their goods, than our corrupt nature would willingly yield unto. And those laws are good glasses for us thus far to look into them, that we may learn that we are bound to show more fidelity and love towards our neighbors in their goods, than our corrupt nature can be brought with any goodwill to acknowledge.

The negligence whereby another man suffered loss or damage in his goods, was accounted as a kind of deceit and injury before the Lord. And he was bound to make it good, through whose negligence it did perish. According as it is written in Exodus 21:33, "When a man shall open a well or dig a pit, and cover it not, and an ox or an ass fall therein, the owner of the pit shall make it good, and give money to the owner thereof, but the dead beast shall be his."

What shall we then think of them that of deliberate purpose, wittingly and willingly shall bring damage or loss to their neighbors, when careless negligence (not being joined with any purpose to hurt or impoverish) is bound to make good the hurt and damage of his negligence? And yet nothing is so common nowadays (even among Christians and gospellers) as upon the least grief or displeasure conceived, to force a man to spend his money and goods in suit of law. These men are far from fearing the punishment of negligence, while their deliberate purpose (without any lawful cause) to impair his wealth is accounted as no fault with them, no, not half the price of their displeasure, be it never so unjustly or without cause conceived.

We have heard how careful the Lord is to make safe passage for our goods, whether they come within the coasts of the borrower, receiver or careless passenger. The same care hath he also of them, when they must pass by the buyer or seller. For even the buyers and sellers have charge to deal well with them, that there appear not lack of love towards the owners in their doings and dealings with their goods. And therefore our own greedy affection must not make the market, nor set the price upon the things that are to be sold. But the worthiness of the thing itself that is to be bought or sold, and the benefit that it is likely to yield to him that shall enjoy it, must strike the stroke.

A law was given unto the people of Israel for fidelity and faithful dealing in buying and selling, as appeareth in Leviticus 25:14-17, "When thou sellest aught to thy neighbor or buyest at thy neighbor's hand, ye shall not deceive one another. But according to the number of years after the Jubilee thou shalt buy of thy neighbor, also according to the number of the years of the revenues he shall sell unto thee. According to the multitude of years thou shalt increase the price thereof, and according to the fewness of years thou shalt abate the price of it, for the number of fruits doth he sell unto thee. Oppress not ye therefore any man his neighbor, but thou shalt fear thy God; for I am the Lord your God."

These are the very words of the text. At the year of Jubilee every man returned again to his lands and possessions that he had sold and made away. Therefore as that year was further off or nearer, so they bought or sold things dear or better cheap. And the reason and equity of this law is added. For (saith the Holy Ghost) the number of fruits doth he sell unto thee, and those canst thou not have after the year of Jubilee. And therefore if he should sell otherwise than after that rate, he should take in some money of thee, not giving anything out for it. For the number of fruits doth he sell unto thee. As if he should say, he hath not right to take but in regard of that fruit and commodity that doth come unto thee by that which he doth sell thee. For he maketh this the reason (why he must abate according to the near approaching of Jubilee), because the other after that time could receive no benefit of that which he bought. As if it were an undoubted truth that there must be some equality of mutual benefit between the buyer and the seller, that a man may not take money for nothing of his neighbor, but must give him a penny worth for his penny. The year of Jubilee is gone, with other the like laws made for the government of that people. But the reason and equity of this law standeth, and bindeth us to have conscience in our buying and selling, and not to let our covetous affection set the price upon that we have to sell.

Out of the equity of this law, which yet remaineth (being the equity of that God which cannot be contrary to himself), it appeareth that the seller must in selling, look what commodity and benefit it is likely that the buyer shall enjoy by that which he selleth unto him, making conjecture thereof, according unto the usual rate of those wares as they go at that time; and to increase or abate the price of his wares, or that he hath to sell whatsoever accordingly. For they must buy and sell according as the year of Jubilee (which being once come they might no longer enjoy it) was sooner or later, increasing the price, if it were longer to that year, because the buyer's commodity should increase; and abating the price, if the time were shorter, because the buyer's commodity must be so much the less.

By the equity and reason of this law, we may learn two rules which will teach us to discern well of true buying and selling, and learn [i.e., teach] us to buy and sell in the fear of God and with a good conscience. The first is, that our covetous affection must not set the price of that we utter [i.e., offer for sale]. For here we see he must have an eye to that time when the other's commodity must cease, and take his rule from thence; so that he is sent from himself in making of the price, and must look at another [i.e., the advantage of the other man]. This is the first rule given us to buy and sell by, and is drawn from the equity of this law, which is the equity of our God.

A marvellous good rule, savoring of love to our neighbor, and bridling self-love, which without regard of others looketh to itself alone. If this rule were observed, then should these speeches cease in Christian mouths and not be heard: "I may and will sell thus, because I have had losses heretofore." Or, "I will sell as I can get for my wares howsoever, because I may have losses hereafter, and this must help to bear when that cometh." As if we had commission from the Lord to take up upon the buyer our shipwrecks, or the recompense of our losses whatsoever. Or as if we had authority to lay those strokes upon his shoulders that should first deal with us, which we have justly borne from the hand of the Lord. It were very requisite, if any do so, that his commission were seen why he should so do. For sure it is, the Lord giveth not out any such large commission as by virtue whereof any may challenge a recompense in another man's goods whensoever the Lord for just causes hath thought it good to diminish his.

The second rule is, that in buying and selling, we drive the commodities given and received as near equality as possibly we can; that so far forth as we can gather (by the present value, rate and account that is made of those things exchanged) there be equal commodities coming to both the parties by that exchange, and that neither party be a deceiver, or oppressor of his brother, for such hath the Lord threatened that he will be revenged of (1 Thess. 4:6). Therefore this reason is given (why he must take less if the time be nearer when the buyer shall forego his commodity), for (saith the text), "Thou sellest him the fruits, and the fruits he can no longer enjoy," as if he should say, he can no more have the commodity of that which he bought of thee, and therefore must thy price be abated accordingly, that there may be mutual benefit and neither part be found oppressing another. For thou art not licensed to take any penny from thy brother for nothing.

Thou must (as nigh as thou canst discern) give him as good as thou takest. Thou art bound to give him a penny worth for his penny, and a penny for his penny worth. Thou mayest not do that to him which thou wouldst be loath that he should do to thee. Thou wouldst not that he should take any commodity from thee unless he gave thee the worth of it again.

I perceive the time passeth, and I have much yet to speak of this matter. I will therefore here make an end, reserving the rest until the next day. Now let us call upon our heavenly Father in the name of his Son, that we may witness the love which we bear unto our brethren, by all faithful and loving dealing with their goods, etc.

The Ninth Lecture, Continued upon the Fifteenth Verse

We learned the last day, that a man might not take any commodity from another unless he gave him the worth of it again.

This rule saith sore to the usual buyings and sellings of these days, when commonly all men regard themselves alone, to make the most they can of their commodities, without any regard had what his commodity is like to be that dealeth with them, by that which he receiveth from them. Yet it is no other rule but that common one which we have received by the light of nature, that we may not do that unto another we would not have done unto ourselves. And who (I pray you) would have the worse at another man's hand? Who would have willingly less given him than he had delivered unto another? Or who could bear that another man should have no regard how well or ill he had dealt with him? Then may we not do so unto others. We must therefore think that when we come to buying and selling, we come to witness our love towards our neighbor by our well dealing with him in his goods, and to leave some testimony of the fear of God and a good conscience behind us. We come to make trial of our faith to God, that we depend upon his blessing for our provision to live well and happily, inasmuch as we follow the rule of love and upright dealing which he hath left us, and not the desire of our own ravenous affection.

But in very deed, if a man should look into the dealings that now are common in the world in all buyings, sellings and exchanges, he must be forced to confess that men come to buying and selling as it were to the razing and spoiling of some enemy's city or hold [i.e., stronghold], where every man catcheth, snatcheth and carrieth away whatsoever he can come by. And he is thought the best that carrieth away the most. His booty is taken to be the warmest that hath made the most naked in the streets. He cometh home the merriest that hath caused the most [people] weeping and wailing, sighing and sobbing to utter the heaviness of their heart. Yet in all this oppression, every such offender persuadeth himself that he is not out of charity with his neighbor, but that he loveth him entirely, and showeth it well enough. For he giveth him good words in buying and selling, and he intendeth no hurt unto his person. But the Holy Ghost will bring us to another trial of our love. He will not be bound to that alone, and therefore doth send us to see how loving we are by our loving and friendly dealing with him [i.e., the neighbor] in his goods.

Therefore doth the apostle say very well to the Romans that this commandment, "Thou shalt not steal," is as the rest, fulfilled no otherwise than by love (cf. Rom. 13:8-9). These oppressions therefore, these frauds and deceits to pull another man's goods into their hands that are so rife everywhere, do no less declare their want of love (by the testimony of the apostle) than do murders, slaughters and bloodshed.

Now to come to the matter more particularly, by this rule is condemned all uttering of naughty [i.e., of no value] and counterfeit coin or ware. For how can there be equality of commodities where the one is not commodious or profitable at all?

Secondly, here is condemned all that uttering of money or wares (though good in themselves) which have some things closely joined with them, to utter them withal, and to increase their price above that which they are worth (and without those additions do usually go for) which things are no commodities nor merchandise at all of themselves, neither will they always abide with the use of the things, and departing, they cannot but bring loss unto him that must have the use of them, and leave him (as we say) in the lash.

In this number are all those that sell their commodities whatsoever dearer than otherwise they are sold for in those times, because they give day [i.e., credit] with them, and longer time before they be paid, taking money for time, and making it to increase and add to the value of their commodities.

First understand, that time is no merchandise. For who dare be so bold as to say that he hath brought time into the market to sell? Or who hath given thee leave to sell days and months? There must also be equality of commodities. The man hath given out [i.e., paid] for time, but when he cometh to the using or wearing of that thing, he findeth no benefit by reason of that time which he hath paid for. Indeed if a coat or cloak cloth sold dearer for time, would be longer time in wearing than another coat of the same or like piece sold for present money, there were some reason in it, because the buyer should have the same commodity of time in the using of it, that the other had in the sale of it.

Or if the corn sold dearer for time would feed a man's family longer than so much bought for ready money, there were something to be said for it. And if it be answered that he who receiveth it of us maketh a commodity of time as we do, for he selleth it thereafter, the matter is not yet answered, unless it be first proved that thou mayest lawfully take money for that which though peradventure one do not lose by (through his as unjust dealing as thine own), yet thou art sure another cannot but smart of it. For it cometh so much the dearer to him that must use it, who reapeth no commodity for time, but rather loss and hindrance, notwithstanding it hath increased thy gain. And who hath given thee leave to take something the more for thy commodity, in consideration of that which will be gone when thy commodities shall come to be taken commodity of, and to be put to the use for the which they were bought and sold, that is, to occupy, spend or use them as their nature doth require? There is no equality in that exchange, when a man must give out something for that which he is never a whit the more, but rather so much the less benefited by, whensoever it shall be put unto that use for the which it was made and in respect whereof we do take money for it. For we have no authority to take money for it, but in respect of that commodity which it will yield when it shall be put to that use and end which the nature of the thing requireth.

Moreover, if there be anything of good report (*cf.* Phil. 4:8), we Christians must seek after it. And surely it can purchase no commendation of brotherly dealing and good speech that way, when our dealings shall be harder than the usual dealings of those times are, even among those men that have no other thing to get their living by besides the commodity and profit that cometh unto them by that their trade.

Hereunto may be added that it is often prejudicial to the reasonable sale of that man who must sell his wares for present money, his necessity so constraining him. The like is to be said of other things which (notwithstanding they be good and sufficient for the most part thereof) yet have something mingled among to increase the quantity, and so the price, which in the use thereof, bringeth no benefit, but hurt, hindrance and deceit unto him that occupieth the same. One example may be, when cloths are stretched five, six or seven yards in a cloth above that which the cloth doth of necessity require. It is well known unto the seller who taketh money for the same, that all of them will shrink in again so soon as ever they shall be wet, and that the wearer shall have no good by them. And how then can these men take money for nothing? They cannot be privileged to take in some part of money for that which hath no piece of commodity in it, when it shall come to the trial and use that should be of it.

There is no equality to take a commodity for that which in his hands or house if it lie by him, will vanish into nothing. It is no otherwise than if some juggler had closed in our fist (as we thought) some piece of coin, but when we open our hand there is no such thing to be found there. As for their desire to have it so which do buy it of us, that cannot maintain anything in us not lawful of itself. For no man's appetite can warrant our wrong dealing in deceitful wares.

If the commodity which we do utter be neither altogether nor yet in part deceitful, but wholly good and sufficient, yet if we shall oversell it, we trespass against this rule of equity and reason which forbiddeth the commodity of one to arise of the loss of another, and laboreth for equal commodity in exchange, as nigh as may be. Neither can we be truly entitled unto any other their commodity, but by departing from some other thing of ours unto them again as commodious as that is, and the same either in weight, measure or value. Those men therefore that in buying and selling do always lay in wait for them who, for some one necessity or other, must necessarily utter their commodity, thinking to make a prey of their necessity, and to make the price after their own lust and desire, are not simple thieves (for it skilleth not to make it theft, whether it be much or little that we take from another, which we have no right unto, neither yet whether it be done under some color, or without any show of right), but also this kind of dealing hath in it a spice and smack of cruelty and murder. Because it is towards those men whose necessity (if there were any Christian bowels in us) were rather to be pitied as it already is than further to be increased by us, as if their affliction were not yet enough to be under our feet unless we trampled upon them, and did our good will that they might never arise again.

It is no more lawful to leave testimony that there is want of love towards our neighbor by our dealing with his goods in buying and selling, than it is in our borrowing, keeping or lending, as was before declared. For the Lord hath forbidden us to show any lack of love towards our neighbor. And for trial of our obedience herein, he followeth our footing to the gate of his goods, as well as to the door of his person, to espy whether we return from thence both merciful and helpful, or cruel and hurtful. For thus doth he trace us and try out our heart towards our brethren, leading us to see the secrets of it by the outgoings that it hath to the things that be especially necessary and commodious for them, and also best beloved and most dear unto them.

As the Lord hath bound the borrower, lender, keeper, buyer or seller to good a-bearing towards our goods, so hath he granted the peace for him that shall find anything of ours.[3] (No exception admitted to the contrary, no not in the finding of the goods of his enemy.) For the man that shall find his enemy's ox or ass going astray is charged to bring him again. And if he shall see his enemy's ox or ass lying under his burden, he must help him up with it, according as it is written in Exodus 23:4-5. He is also charged with all the lost things of his brothers that he shall find, to restore them again. And if he know not whose ox or sheep they be that

3. [ED.] I.e., bound him to keep the peace who finds anything of ours.

he findeth going astray, they must remain with him at his house until his brother seek after them (*cf.* Deut. 22:1–3). If any man should deal deceitfully (and therefore uncharitably) with his neighbor's goods, then were they bound to restore that whatsoever it were, which their conscience did charge them withal, adding the fifth part more thereunto, and giving it unto him that was so wronged, injured or deceived by them, the same day which they should offer for that their trespass to the Lord so that the Lord would not be appeased until their brethren were satisfied. Thus must they do when their conscience should prick them in anything, according as it is written in Leviticus 6:1–5. The wrongs that are there set down to be restored again are: to deny his neighbor that which was taken him to keep, or that which was put to him of trust; oppression, either by fraud or violence; finding that which was lost and denying it; and whatsoever one hath hindered his neighbor in by a false oath (Deut. 22:2–3, Lev. 6:1–5).

These things are expressly set down in that place, to be restored in the whole, and the fifth part thereof added thereunto, at the summon of their conscience whensoever. It appeareth in the book of Numbers 5:8 that the offenders in this part must pay this damage unto his next kinsman, if he were dead whom thus they had wronged; neither was he so acquitted if he [i.e., the wronged man] had no kinsman, but [the offender] must give it to the Lord, for the priests' use. If so be it shall please the Lord to call any man and let him see a universal oppression and hard dealing in all his doings, not grieving him with the alone remembrance of one, or some few, then the counsel of Daniel 4:27 is to be followed: "To break off his sins by righteousness, and iniquities by mercy toward the poor"; that plenty of merciful dealing may follow there, where there hath gone before great store and plenty of the contrary. "Is not this the fasting," saith the prophet Isaiah, "that I have chosen: to loose the bands of wickedness, to take off the heavy burdens, and to let the oppressed go free, and that ye break every yoke? Is it not to deal thy bread to the hungry, and that thou bring the poor that wander unto thine house? When thou seest the naked, that thou cover him?" (Is. 58:6–7). Thus must he not only leave oppressing, but also take up merciful dealing with the needy. We see how by this which hitherto hath been said, the Lord hath fenced our neighbor's goods; and how contrary it is to the love of our neighbor to hurt or hinder him any way in them, and how agreeable to the will of the Lord, that we should be means that he might enjoy the commodities thereof.

Therefore was there a law among the children of Israel made, to show their love towards their neighbor who had planted a vineyard but not tasted of the fruit thereof, wherein it was provided that the officer should make proclamation at their going to warfare against their enemies, that if there were any who had not eaten of the fruit of their labors, they should return home and take comfort and use of their own (*cf.* Deut. 20:6).

This law of love might not be dispensed withal, no not in the heat and urgent necessity of wars. A notable testimony to show how well it liketh the Lord that men should take comfort of their own. As doth that law also which was given in Deuteronomy 19:14 of not removing the landmark which they of old time have set. And therefore we are commanded to show them this kindness and love, to reserve unto them the comfort of their commodities without impairing of them, whensoever we shall either borrow, keep or find anything of theirs, or in buying and selling exchange with them. For we please God and show love unto them whensoever we shall deal truly with their goods, according as we heard before, that God maketh trial of our heart toward our neighbors by our hands, as they are wont to deal with them in their commodities.

It is an undoubted truth therefore, that God is greatly pleased when for obedience unto him, we deal thus faithfully and lovingly with them in that which is theirs. It is a true fruit of love, and faithful obedience unto this commandment. And because of that, whensoever it is done for obedience sake unto God (who doth command it), and of goodwill unto them who receive the fruit of it (even this fidelity in his goods that we borrow, find, or be trusted withal, either else receive by way of exchange in buying and selling), is a good work indeed, and a humble obedience to the charge of God given us in this commandment. There are two things, without the which we shall never be able to perform any acceptable obedience to God in this commandment.

The first is an assured faith in God's promises that he will provide for us things necessary, as well for the body as the soul, and that he hath charged himself as well with the care and provision for the one as for the other. This faith (if it were true) would consume many fears and cares of our mind for wordly matters. So might we employ ourselves upon the care of better things. This did the Holy Ghost know very well, and therefore meaning to cure covetousness, he maketh the plaster of faith, saying, "Let your conversation be without covetousness, for he hath said, I will not fail thee, nor forsake thee" (Heb. 13:5).

When our hearts shall be fully persuaded that the Lord will not leave us, nor forsake us, we cannot be so greatly tormented with the care to live and obtain necessary things for us, having so strong assurance for it, as is his promise who hath made all things of nothing with his word. And therefore in the former place, exhorting them to conscience in buying and selling, he sendeth them to the covenant, saying, "I am thy God." Which words (as we have learned in the first commandment) contain promises for all things needful for this present life. If this be steadfastly believed, that the Lord will not leave us nor forsake us, there will be no doubt of evil dealings with the goods of our neighbor, whether we buy or sell, borrow or keep the things that be his.

The second thing is, to find a contented mind with that which we have already. And therefore to stay in it, as in a rich portion, with great thankfulness of heart to our God for it, bearing our port and countenance in all our doings accordingly, without any exceeding whatsoever. For if once our affections shall overflow the banks of our own condition, so that in mind we burn with the desire of a better, our doings can never be persuaded that they must so nearly be looked at, but that they may borrow a little of conscience and equity, to make the provision according as their desire directeth. This doth the apostle confirm in plain speech to Timothy, where after persuasion to be content with that we have (because the gain of godliness is great), he telleth us plainly that they who will be rich fall into many temptations, snares, and many noisome lusts (cf. 1 Tim. 6:9). This is the danger of them that are fallen so far into friendship and love with a better estate that they will be rich. This being once set down and determined, not only conscience is constrained to depart, but also thankfulness to God for our present estate doth in like manner forsake us.

Let us learn by this commandment to know our corrupt inclination towards the goods of our neighbors, and so to view our deceits that have been in us at any time, either in buying or selling, borrowing or keeping anything of theirs, together with our corrupt inclination thereunto, that the remedy of redemption (brought us by Jesus Christ) may truly be taken hold of; and that we being made comfortable in his mercy, may with courage go about the obedience of his will in this commandment, so that still we may be more and more freed of all manner of deceit, and more and more enabled to glorify him in all loving and faithful dealing with the goods of others.

Which that it may be performed, let us call upon our heavenly Father in the name of his Son, that it would please him in the multitude of his mercy, to hold us up by the hope of his promises, that we standing assured of his help, may not be drawn by any necessity to do contrary to his blessed will, and also that we having a contented mind, may not be tormented with the hungry desire of a better estate, which being once entered, unjust dealing cannot long be kept out.

The Twelfth Lecture, upon the First to the Corinthians, Chapter 13

Love suffereth long; it is bountiful; love envieth not; love doth not boast itself; it is not puffed up. It disdaineth not; it seeketh not her own things; it is not provoked to anger; it thinketh not evil. It rejoiceth not in iniquity, but rejoiceth in the truth. It suffereth all things; it believeth all things; it hopeth all things; it endureth all things.

We have learned out of the law, what several duties they be that we owe unto God, and also unto man. But in the law we are not only charged to do those duties there appointed to be done, and to forbear the contrary, but also of love to do them, and of love to keep us from the other. Therefore it shall be expedient to examine what properties be in love, necessarily adjoining unto the same, whereby we must judge of ourselves, how it fareth with us, whether that affection (without the which all doing of good or ceasing to do evil is to no purpose) ruleth in us both in our doings and also when we shall abstain from doing. The properties and fruits of love are in no place better set forth than in the First Epistle to the Corinthians, from whence I mean to give you some light, thereby the better to see into love, the nature of it, and how great things are contained in it. Where the first note given to know it by is that "it suffereth long," (1 Cor. 13:4) or is patient, a property that moderateth the heat and hastiness of a man's mind, that he follow it not in the boiling appetite and desire thereof. . . .

When we shall have tried truly our dealings towards God, our dealings towards our neighbors, and our dealings in our several callings by these affections which are reported by the Holy Ghost to be in love, it will appear that to be a Christian is a rare matter, a mighty, rare and especial work of God. Now let us pray, etc.

The Thirteenth Lecture, upon the Third Chapter to the Galatians, and Tenth Verse

As many as are the works of the law are under the curse, for it is written, "Cursed is every man that continueth not in all things which are written in the book of the law, to do them."

Having learned what things are to be done of us, and in what manner they are to be done, it remaineth to consider whether any man can do all these good deeds that are commanded by the law of God in that form and manner that he hath commanded, that is, from the ground of a loving heart. Which must be discerned to have the tender affection of love in it by these properties which never are wanting where love is to be found, according as of late it was proved unto us. The Scripture is plain in this matter, that no man can fulfill the law. . . .

This mischief is redressed by the law, by the light whereof we clearly perceive where the force of the adversary lieth sorest upon us, that we may turn our prayers and all spiritual armor to that part especially. So shall our prayers not be cast off without care at adventure and by custom, but being both warned of great danger (which without the alarm of the law we would not have feared), and also having warning to what place the adversary directeth his power, our prayers may carefully and directly stand against it. Now let us pray unto our heavenly Father, that we may learn by the law both to be humbled under his mercies, and also to be directed unto his own good pleasure and will to the praise of his name, and our own everlasting comfort, etc. . . .

The Fourteenth Lecture, upon the Third Chapter of Saint John, Verse 16

God so loved the world that he hath given his only begotten Son, that whosoever believeth in him should not perish, but have everlasting life.

After the knowledge of the law and the use thereof, it is necessary to speak of Christ (who is the end of the law), how by faith he is received both to justify us from the curse and rigor of the law, and also to sanctify our hearts to such a liking of those duties that there are appointed to be done, as bringeth with it a careful attending upon the doing thereof. This doctrine hath been somewhat touched in the law, but a more plentiful discourse thereof is yet required, where the matter may be laid open more at large than hitherto we have heard of. For the performance whereof, this portion of Scripture that now I have read unto you promiseth very much.

Wherein we may understand that the first spring and fountain of our salvation is the love of God. That is the first cause, the principal ground, and chief beginning of all our happiness, and therefore it is set down here as the cause why Christ was given for our sins. "God so loved the world," saith the text, "that he gave his only begotten Son."

The tender affection and love of God towards us is placed before that great gift, to commend the goodness of it. For not so much the gift as the mind of the giver is wont to be considered. This is noted by the Holy Ghost with a special note of commendation in these words: "Herein is love, not that we loved God, but that he loved us, and sent his Son to be a reconciliation for our sins" (1 John 4:10). Likewise in the Epistle to the Romans 5:17–21, there is set against the single transgression of Adam, as an over-match, the grace of God, and the gift in grace or by grace. The benefit and medicine of Christ's obedience was sufficient for the wound of Adam's transgression, to make it whole withal. Then remaineth, as an advantage or over-plus, the grace and goodwill of the Father, wherein this medicine was lapped and closed up, which is the cause why he maketh a special note of the grace of God, and of the gift in grace, or by grace. These things are diligently to be observed, for they are the grounds of much good doctrine that is established strongly hereby.

When we consider what that was that first turned the favor of God towards us, we may not begin at ourselves (as if it had come of our works preparing ourselves for him, and addressing ourselves towards his obedience). We may not begin at our merits. Nay, we may not begin at the work of our redemption, and the merit of Christ, to make that the first thing that ever turned his heart towards us. For here it is affirmed by the Holy Ghost that he loved us, and therefore gave his only begotten Son for us. When we come to the meriting of Christ, we must not look upon the virtue of it without the goodwill and favor of God wherein it was founded, and from whence it hath the worthiness and merit that it hath. So far off then are our own works from bringing their desert with them and opening by themselves the gates of his goodness, that the goodwill of God the father prepared the way even for the merit of Christ's passion. Our own works come short of being the first that have commended us unto God, when both the goodwill of God the father and the merit also of Jesus Christ have been there before them in our behalf. Let men therefore cease to say or imagine that their own works were the first that ever spake one good word for them, when it is so assured by the word of God that they have had friends in that court that have done for them, when all the credit of their own doings was utterly rejected and could not be heard. Whensoever therefore we seek out the chief cause and the first spring of our blessedness, let us come to the love of God.

For it is said that "God so loved the world that he gave his only begotten Son, . . . " Let us take heed of beginning at ourselves and our own doings. For (as hath been said) it was the love of God that did begin all our blessedness, yea and that even then, when we were enemies unto him, and therefore far from deserving any good thing at his hands. Which thing commendeth his love above all the love and affection that is to be found in the world. For who hath ever been known (the Son of God excepted) to give his life for his enemies? Therefore doth the Holy Ghost upon just cause affirm that the love of God towards us is herein set out and commended above all love and affection that we have heard of, because while we were yet sinners and enemies unto him, Christ died for us (*cf.* Rom. 5:8).

The Scripture beareth record that Christ died for the ungodly. But (as it is there affirmed) he is scarce to be found that will die for a good man. What good man hath ever been found that would have such compassion as to offer himself to die for a godless person? The Son of God giveth his life for ungodly men. Marvel not at these words, neither think there is anything too much spoken in this matter. For in that chapter it is said plainly that Christ died for the ungodly, for sinners, for his enemies, and all to commend the greatness of his love. It will be granted of all men, that indeed before the death and passion of Christ we were godless, ungodly, enemies to God, without any hope of a better life. But all men are not persuaded that we do now come such men into the world and continue so, until by the special grace of God working with his word, we be reclaimed and reformed, which (for that change) is called regeneration or new birth.

All men are not persuaded that when Christ beginneth Christianity in any, he doth begin with his enemy. Yet doth the apostle Saint Paul affirm that he, as others, was by nature the child of wrath, that before his calling he, as other men, was dead in trespasses and sins; walking after the course of this world, after the spirit that worketh in the children of disobedience. "But God," saith he, "which is rich in mercy, through his great love wherewith he loved us, even when we were dead by sins, hath quickened us . . . " (Eph. 2:4,5).

There is no doubt of it, but that he who liveth the most blameless life of all men in the world is an enemy unto God, and without all hope of any better life, before this especial working and calling of God. I do call Christianity a special work of God, because it is not to be found in the nature of any man, how great good things soever it seem to have in it, but is a peculiar work of God. This is a matter needful to stand upon, because it giveth unto God the commendation of that love which is not to be matched in the world. And in denying this greatest kind of loving dealing, we darken and diminish the glory of his mercy, appearing so clearly and so abundantly herein. We deal unthankfully with God, not giving unto him all the praise that of duty belongeth unto him. If two servants had received equal commodities and benefits of one master, the one having been a very profitable servant to his master, the other a very unthrift, and not only not profitable but also a waster of his goods, should the unthrift sufficiently acknowledge the liberality of his master, if he should confess that he had received as much of him as his fellow servant, making no mention in the meantime of his unworthiness in respect of his fellow?

Every man seeth the goodwill of the master to appear more in the one than in the other, and therefore he should justly be accounted unthankful if he would not both think and confess that he were more beholding to his master than the other. For true thankfulness causeth the benefits received after a certain manner to remain still in the benefactor, by thankful remembrance not only of the gift, but also of the manner and quality of the gift, especially when it addeth anything to the worthiness and desert of the giver.

The cause therefore is great, and a part of our thankfulness unto God is in it, to stand with [i.e., withstand] the church of Rome herein, that not only we have had these benefits that we have from God, but also that we have had them contrary to our deserving; which utterly overthroweth those works of preparation, and setting ourselves in a towardness for the Lord, and maketh the benefit to remain in God, by his just praise, not only for the deed doing, but also for the merciful manner of dealing with unworthy men, wherein his love is tried to have more in it than any affection that hath been heard of amongst men, that we may truly say with the Holy Ghost, not only that God hath loved the world, but as it is said in this place, "So God loved the world," noting in that word "so" no common affection, but the highest and greatest degree of love.

By this that hath been said before, we do learn that God did bear tender affection towards his, not only before any deserving had gone before to procure the same, but also when as yet they were enemies unto him. And therefore the apostle in the Epistle to the Ephesians 1:3,4,7, bringeth the benefits of God to be considered in his free good purpose and gracious goodwill towards us, being the head and spring thereof, which addeth greatly even to the greatest of his benefits. And if the consideration thereof be omitted, the whole deserving of the benefactor is not acknowledged, nor deserved praise rendered thereunto.

When the apostle had given praises unto God the father of our Lord Jesus Christ, for that he had blessed us with all spiritual blessings in heavenly things in Christ [Eph. 1:3]; immediately in the verse following (which is the fourth in number) he hath these words: "As he hath chosen us in him before the foundation of the world, etc." As if his love towards us had not begun then first, when those benefits were bestowed upon us, but that his goodwill (whereof those were testimonies and fruits) was bent towards us, before the beginning of the world; which is the cause why he letteth us see those fruits not barely in themselves alone, but in that goodwill which so long before was inclined towards us. And goodwill the longer it hath continued, the more it is to be esteemed; and the benefits of an old friend and well-willer of long time have just occasion in them to be the more accounted of. It is not to be marvelled then, why with the gift he bringeth in also the goodwill of the giver. For the gift is made thereby the greater, both for that the goodwill hath been of long time continued, and also for that it is his goodwill only, and not any thing either had already, or else hoped for from us, that hath brought all these benefits unto us, as it followeth in the next verse in express words: "That he hath predestinated us to be adopted through Jesus Christ, according to the good pleasure of his will, by whom" (as it is there in like manner affirmed) "we have redemption through his blood, even the forgiveness of sins, according to his rich grace."

In all these places we are let to understand that all our benefits, even the forgiveness of sins, came from the good pleasure of his will and the riches of his grace, and not (as hath been said before) from anything of ours, either had already or else hoped for. Let us learn therefore to set his love before all his benefits as the only cause and spring thereof. For if we shall begin at ourselves, to say that either that which already we had, as a towardness and preparation to goodness, or that which God did foresee would be in us, was the cause why the Lord hath appointed everlasting life for us, and given us the graces that appertain thereunto, we darken and diminish the greatness and the goodness of the gift, which cannot be so commendable if it come for the desert of benefits, either had already or else hoped for, as if it had been sent from the frank and free goodwill of the giver, without any such respect of anything that should proceed from us.

This is the reason why the love of God is here set before the gift of the mediator and redeemer Jesus Christ; and also why the benefit of election and all other, in the first chapter to the Ephesians, are always coupled to the goodwill of God. For we are given to imagine that the good things which are supposed to be in us, do turn his heart and purchase his favor towards us; when in very deed his goodwill towards us brought all those graces, and all the goodness that we have, unto us. Insomuch that both our election and redemption are recited to the Ephesians to have proceeded from the free goodwill of God, and are made not as matters purchasing it, but as matters purchased of it. When this free goodwill of God is not acknowledged to be the beginning of all his gifts, his gifts must of all men that are so persuaded be less esteemed. For it is the mind and goodwill of the giver that doth commend the gift and maketh it to be always the better accepted. Men are wont not to esteem the gift so much as the mind of the giver. Therefore the doctrine of the church of Rome hath and doth marvellously pull away from the benefits of God and the deservings thereof; because it doth not esteem of them as fruits of a well-willing mind towards us, and of such a one as already liketh well of us. For that doctrine professeth that those gifts of his in us, by our use thereof do first turn his favorable countenance to usward. Moreover, because that love was bent towards us when we were bent as enemies against him, which maketh his love so great that it may justly be said of it: "So, God loved the world," as being a rare kind of love, the like whereof we have not known.

Therefore that doctrine of the church of Rome that giveth unto man works of preparation and making of himself fit to meet God and to join with him in the purchase of his happiness, darkeneth greatly this great degree of his love that was showed unto us when we were so far from preparing ourselves to meet with him for our salvation, that we were utter enemies both unto him and unto it. Which is so comfortable unto those that are truly turned unto him that it is the ground of their hope (in their affliction and distress) that their end will be happy, because that if when they were enemies they were reconciled by his blood, much more being now made friends, they shall by his life be saved from wrath.

It hath been declared at large why the great love of God is set before the benefit of our redemption, and the great gift of Jesus Christ given unto us. Now it remaineth after the sight had of his goodwill, to see into the gift, what it is that cometh from so great goodwill. The text saith that this gift is "his only begotten Son." "For so God loved the world, that he gave his only begotten Son." Now we know the gift. It is his only begotten Son, which at the first sight doth witness great goodwill, the gift being so great as to pleasure us with his only begotten Son. But yet it is needful that we unfold this gift, that we may understand of every commodity that lieth hid within it. It is written in 1 Corinthians 1:30 that Christ of God the father is "made unto us wisdom, righteousness, sanctification and redemption." Behold the several commodities that come with this gift of Jesus Christ, given unto us from God the father, which every one of them are of that dignity and worthiness that I cannot join them altogether and in few words dispatch them, but am enforced severally (and yet as briefly as I can) to stand upon them.

First it is said here, that "he is made of God unto us wisdom." Christ is become the wisdom of his servants, he teacheth his chosen children true wisdom, he is appointed of his Father to be their schoolmaster, as it is written in the gospel after Saint Matthew: "This is that my beloved son, in whom I am well pleased, hear him" (Matt. 17:5). And to the Colossians it is written, "That all the treasures of wisdom and knowledge are hidden in Christ" (Col. 2:3). If it shall be demanded how it cometh to pass that so many men in the governing of their lives and dealings do follow their own wisdom and their own wit, going no further, but holding themselves well content with that, never suspecting any want in it; and yet another sort shall so suspect their own wisdom and the devices of their own head, and see such want in it, that letting it alone, they betake them to the wisdom of God, revealed in his word, become painful travailers therein, and careful framers of their lives accordingly: the answer is ready, that Christ (who is made of God the father wisdom unto his) hath laid claim unto the one sort and taken possession of them as upon his own, but not upon the other. This is the cause of this diversity, and none other thing. And therefore the apostle proveth that the testimony of Jesus Christ was confirmed amongst the Corinthians, because they abounded in all knowledge (1 Cor. 1:5–6).

And here by the way, it is manifest that ignorance is not mother, but stepmother unto devotion and true Christianity. For Christ is made unto Christians of God the father wisdom, teaching them the knowledge of his word and will. In like manner, if it should be demanded why in their religion and serving of God, some follow the invention of man (which hath in it great show of holiness in humbleness of mind, not sparing the body, but laying much affliction upon it in doing many things unto God voluntarily, not being bound unto them by him, but frankly and freely of their own accord); and another sort (contenting themselves with the bare and naked simplicity of God's word in the worshipping and serving of him) do condemn and utterly reject all those inventions of men and shows of holiness and humbleness of mind which stand so strongly upon the wisdom and reason of man; the matter is plain and the answer soon made, "Christ is made of God the father wisdom unto his."

This is the cause why his servants find no wisdom but in him. This is the reason why it seemeth madness and extreme folly unto his servants whatsoever is not approved by his word, have it never so strong reasons of man's wit to uphold it withal. It is not their wisdom; they can see no wit in it. For Christ is become wisdom unto them, and they have learned no such thing of him in his word. Therefore it is their wisdom to reject such wisdom.

It is a marvellous thing, that any man who hath wit and reason should mislike that religion which hath nothing else in it but force of wit and strength of reason. But let us cease to marvel, and begin to magnify the goodness of that God who vouchsafeth to become wisdom unto his, teaching them in his word another manner of wisdom than that which is taught them of their own wit and reason.

Here ye see then the first benefit that cometh with Christ unto his, even wisdom in his word. Do ye mean to approve it before God and man, that we are called unto the fellowship of Christ and become Christians indeed? Let us then become wise after his word. Let us give over our own wit and reason in the governing of our lives either towards God or man, and betake us to his word, who is become our wisdom. Let the word of God dwell richly in us in all wisdom, teaching and admonishing ourselves as we are commanded by the apostle (Col. 3:16). For if in our dealing with God or man, we like well enough of the counsel had from our own wit, in vain is this boast made, that Christ is become wisdom unto us. For he pulleth his from the devices of their own wit in the ordering of their conversation, unto the government of his word; letting them understand and feel the want and wretchedness of the one, and the sufficiency and blessedness of the other.

Christ (as you see) at his first coming changeth our wisdom. This is his work. Where is then our frank and free will unto that which is good, when it is manifest we cannot see what is good before Christ, who is become our wisdom, lighten us? We have no will unto anything but that which our wit approveth and our judgment doth embrace; and good things can we not in judgment embrace and like, before Christ (who is our wisdom) shall have changed our judgments. If Christ must open our hearts and change our minds before we can have true wisdom and understanding of good things (which we must approve in judgment before we have a desire and will unto them in our affection), it followeth necessarily that not from our selves, but from Christ, cometh all the free will which we have unto that which is indeed good. For we have no will unto anything but that which we approve and like in our judgment. We can approve and like in our judgment no good thing, before our judgment be good. Good judgment and wisdom we have not of ourselves, but are taught it of Christ, and have it with him who is made our wisdom. Therefore the desire and will unto good things we have not from ourselves but from Christ, amongst whose gifts the very foremost is that he giveth himself unto us, when he giveth us the knowledge of himself in his word.

The second benefit that we receive from God the father by Christ, is "righteousness." For it is written (as we have heard before) that he is made wisdom unto us and righteousness, etc. This righteousness consisteth in two points. The first is in discharging us of our sins. The second is in presenting us blameless before his father, in such perfect obedience as the law cannot reprove nor justly charge with any want.

This is performed to us in Christ, who hath satisfied in his suffering for our sins, and wrought our full discharge; and also perfectly kept the whole law and every commandment thereof in the behalf of us that be his. For he being God (and therefore above the law as Lord and giver thereof) needed not to have become a subject thereunto for himself. Whereby it appeareth plainly that he went under that obedience in our name and for us, and that the same obedience of his is available for us that be his, according as it is written to the Romans in these words: "As by one man's disobedience many were made sinners; so by the obedience of one shall many also be made righteous" (Rom. 5:19).

The tree must be good before the fruit be good; and therefore we ourselves must be righteous before any good fruit of righteousness proceed and come from us. The gift is never welcome when we cannot abide the giver. Neither will the Lord have good liking of anything that is ours before he shall think well of us. We are therefore first to be settled by faith as righteous in Christ, before the Lord will take in good part anything that shall proceed from us. Our root was rotten in Adam and therefore brought forth fruit accordingly.

We must therefore be grafted into Christ, and then draw power from him to bring forth fruit that shall be pleasing unto him and acceptable in his sight, according as our savior Christ saith in John 15:4: "As the branch cannot bear fruit of itself, except it abide in the vine; no more can ye, except ye abide in me." His servants find want of righteousness in themselves, and therefore flee unto him for righteousness. They see so much in themselves, that they well understand that they cannot be accepted for themselves, and therefore stick unto the righteousness of another, which is Christ.

When the question is then, whereupon ariseth this diversity of judgments in men, that one persuadeth himself that the cause why he is acceptable to God first springeth of himself, and another denieth anything that is in himself to have been the cause to make him accepted unto God and doth attribute the whole cause why he is acceptable unto God unto the righteousness of Jesus Christ, which is become his by faith? From hence we have an answer that may satisfy us, which is that Christ is made righteousness unto his. It is the work of Christ in them, to assure them to be accepted for the righteousness of another, and to give over all the hold that they have by reason of anything that they shall have done themselves. Our natural wit and reason cannot allow of that. It is apparent therefore that we have another schoolmaster that doth teach us this doctrine. Can one man for his good works that he hath done, stand so strongly assured in his opinion of salvation, and to be accepted for them, that he shall offer his over-plus to help other withal; and another man (that is not inferior unto this [first man], neither in wit, reason, nor good deeds) so give over all the hope of them that in flat denial and utter renouncing thereof, he should lay claim only to the righteousness that another hath done, and boast of that none otherwise than if he should have done it in his own person? Can this, I say, be thought reasonable unto any that hath not had another schoolmaster than wit and reason to persuade him therein? Can the natural man be persuaded that he must first be righteous and then do righteous things, and not rather that in doing of many righteous deeds at length he becometh to be accepted for righteous himself thereby? Or can a natural man be persuaded that his favor with God cometh wholly in respect of another's doings (who hath done him all this good), and not rather that his own doings have done the most for him and that he is especially beholden unto them? This cometh from another teacher than any that we have at home. It savoreth not of the earth, it is from above.

Cease therefore to marvel at such diversity of doctrine, when the schoolmasters that teach are so far differing one from another as heaven is from earth. The servants of God give over their own righteousness. They find nothing in it. They do clearly see it will not go for payment, and therefore do betake themselves to the merits of another. Neither do they only say that they be unrighteous in themselves, but with grief do find and feel it to be so. But howsoever they stand rotten in their own root, they are notwithstanding strongly stayed in Jesus Christ, whose obedience they do make so great an account of as if it were their own performed by themselves.

The third thing that we do receive with Christ is "sanctification" or holiness of life. This sanctification followeth immediately after righteousness, in the place which before I have alleged. For it is not only requisite that we should remain righteous by the obedience of one man once performed, but that our whole life should continue consecrated unto the service of him, in bringing forth such fruit as he hath appointed. That righteousness which before we have heard of, is as the tree and this holiness is the fruit thereof. The nature of our savior Christ was free from all infection, not having in it any remnant or relic of sin, and therefore he was sanctification itself, and perfectly sanctified. When we begin to separate ourselves from the common corruption of the world and bend ourselves to pureness of life approved before God, this is the work of Christ, sanctifying and working true holiness in us. For of ourselves we are profane and unholy, void of these fruits of righteousness which are wrought in us by Christ.

The cause why a number do mislike such deeds and conversation, both in themselves and also in others, which another sort of men do approve and delight in, following after them with all greediness of desire, is for that Christ is become sanctification unto the one sort of people, and not unto the other, who continue in their profane and corrupt ways, not finding any want therein, when the other sort are vexed and grieved to see such doings abound in others, and tormented in themselves if at any time they shall of infirmity slip into the like, not ceasing to apply the means whereby they may get victory over them.

Here ariseth a question necessary to be discussed, whether righteousness be in the children of God before sanctification and holiness of life, or good works and holy life do go before justification being in his, before they be acceptable unto God.

Wherein notwithstanding that which hath been said already may be thought sufficient unto any indifferent man, yet it shall not be amiss to add some more force and strength unto it. It is proved that righteousness goeth before good works [in] Romans 4:6, where the testimony of David is alleged, pronouncing him blessed and happy to whom the Lord imputeth righteousness without works.

And lest any man should think this to be meant of the ceremonial works, the very words of the prophet are cited in the next verse following [Ps. 32:1–2], affirming blessedness to be in the remitting of sins unto us, and not in the admitting of good works for us. If the apostle do join with the prophet in this, that God imputeth righteousness without works, then must I demand of the adversaries whether this righteousness imputed without works, doth exclude all works, or but some works? If it be answered that all [i.e., every] kind of working is not severed from this justification and righteousness, the question is again, whether those works that stand with justification and righteousness go before it, or spring of it and so come after it.

Here their answer is, we are justified without works going before, but not without works following it, making this justification that is said to be without works to shut out only those works that are before a man be justified, but not the other. For their opinion is that we are justified by them, whereupon it followeth necessarily that righteousness goeth before holiness of life, that good works do flow from a man justified already, and are not sent before to justify him therewith that was not accepted of God as righteous until those were performed. The apostle is plain in this matter to the Ephesians: "God, which is rich in mercy, even when we were dead by sins, hath quickened us . . . " (Eph. 2:4,5). There were no works then that went before to quicken us, seeing it is said that when we were dead in sins (not only sinners but also dead in sins), God hath quickened us.

This proveth plainly that our good works and holiness of life did not procure righteousness unto us, when the matter is clear that we were dead in sins when he in mercy quickened us. In like manner, the apostle proveth that that holiness of life is a fruit of them that be already the servants of God. But now, saith the apostle, "being freed from sin and made servants unto God, you have your fruits in holiness, and the end everlasting life" (Rom. 6:22). There is no work acceptable unto God without faith and persuasion of his goodwill towards us, whether it be done at the desire of vain glory or at the motion and instinct of nature, judging that work to be lawful and honest. For it is faith that doth purify the heart (cf. 1 Tim. 1:5) and the end of the commandment is love, but so that it be of a faith unfeigned. The tree must be good before the fruit can be good. For an evil tree cannot bring forth good fruit (*cf.* Mt. 7:17,18).

Against this it will be excepted that Abraham in offering of his son Isaac upon the altar, as saith the apostle James (James 2:21), was justified; and therefore that the works of men either unrighteous before or else but in part acceptable, do justify them and make them rightly to be accepted of God. It appeareth in Genesis 15:6 that Abraham was justified before Isaac was born, for offering of whom upon the altar the apostle James saith Abraham was justified. For in that chapter [Gen. 15] it is written that the word of the Lord came unto Abraham in a vision, saying, "Fear not, Abraham, I am thine exceeding great reward." And Abraham said, "Oh Lord God, what wilt thou give me, seeing I go childless? Behold to me thou hast given no seed, wherefore a servant of mine house shall be mine heir." Then the word of the Lord came unto him, saying, "One that shall come out of thine own bowels, he shall be thine heir." Moreover, he brought him forth and said, " 'Look up now unto heaven and tell the stars, so shall thy seed be.' And Abraham believed the Lord, and he accounted that to him for righteousness" [Gen. 15:5–6]. By this testimony we see that Abraham was accounted righteous, and not in part righteous or half righteous; but without any addition it was said of him that he was accounted righteous (before he had any son, and therefore before he could offer up his son in sacrifice; even then, when he made complaint unto God for that he had no son, and therefore a servant must be his heir), believing the promise that then was made unto him for a seed and posterity that should come out of his own loins, that faith was reckoned unto him for righteousness, and be himself accepted of, as righteous before the Lord. James saith that he was justified when his own son Isaac was offered upon the altar, and that this deed of his, in not refusing to kill his only son for a sacrifice at the commandment of God, did so please the Lord that he was justified for it. In the other place alleged [Gen. 15:6] the Holy Ghost affirmeth that he was justified before his son Isaac was born, even at that time when the promise was given forth that he should have a son, and that the believing of this goodwill of God towards him herein did so please the Lord that he accounted of him as righteous for it.

How then? Doth the Holy Ghost differ from himself? God forbid. But the apostle Saint James attributeth that to the effect for being joined with his cause, which the Holy Ghost in that other place giveth unto the true and original cause alone. As if one man would justify a workman and commend him above others for works that he hath seen him do, and another would in like manner justify the same, but for the inward skill, knowledge and conceiving that he hath of the rules and principles of that trade or occupation whatsoever, which skill he may discern by his speech, albeit he never saw him work. And albeit a man may say that he is a good workman because his work is good; yet if a man will speak properly, he must say he is a good workman because his skill is good. For his good skill in that trade is the cause of his good workmanship, and the goodness thereof cometh from thence, as from the proper fountain and cause.

Now every man knoweth that when any man is commended for his work, it is because of the skill and knowledge that appeareth therein and is joined therewith, as the only cause and occasion thereof. Even so, because our faith appeareth in our good works, as our skillful knowledge doth in our skillful workmanship, that is given unto good works, which is peculiar unto faith, as the proper cause thereof; and a man shall be called a skillful workman for his skillful workmanship, when notwithstanding it is most assured that his skillful knowledge is before his skillful work, as also the cause thereof, and he justly may be called skillful for it, notwithstanding he should be kept from uttering [i.e., expressing] that his skill in work, many years after the perfect knowledge thereof.

The Holy Ghost therefore in Genesis, justifieth Abraham as skillful for his skill alone; and in that Epistle of James he justifieth him as skillful for that work wherein so much skill appeared. For it may be lawful unto me for the better understanding hereof, to resemble faith by skill and good deeds by skillful workmanship; because as good workmanship hath all the commendation for the good skill that appeareth in it, so have good works all their praise from the faith that hath begotten them and is necessarily joined with them.

This is also to be added, that because there is not in our works that perfection that is required, we are constrained to stand to the mercy of God, and to seek refuge there by a true faith; and this is the cause why we magnify faith (which otherwise is imperfect as be all things that are in us) because it applieth the mercy of God unto us, whereby our sins are pardoned and the want that is in our work not imputed.

And for proof that the apostle Saint James giveth not that title unto works to justify (but because of the faith which hath begot those works and which is joined with them and covereth the imperfections that are in them), in the same place where he ascribeth righteousness unto Abraham for offering up his son, he saith that this Scripture was fulfilled:

" 'Abraham believed, and it was reckoned unto him for righteousness,' and he was called the friend of God" [Jas. 2:23]. So that all the commendation of this work is included in faith, and given unto it for the faith of the doer. For otherwise he should have said: Abraham wrought, and that was received because it was righteous, seeing he had stood upon the commendation of his works so much immediately before, and was even yet in the same matter. But he saith, "Abraham believed, and that was reckoned unto him for righteousness."

They would match works with faith in justification. And the apostle when he speaketh most of works doth shroud them under faith, saying (after mention of his best work) that this Scripture was fulfilled in it: "Abraham believed, and that was imputed to him for righteousness," and not received in the righteousness and deserving of itself, and, "He was called the friend of God." And in the eleventh chapter to the Hebrews, all the works of the godly fathers are ascribed unto faith, and by name in the seventeenth verse of that chapter, this deed of Abraham is fathered upon his faith. For works are so far from justifying us that the cause why they themselves are justified, is in faith. "For without faith it is impossible to please God" [Heb. 11:6]. And in this chief work of Abraham that now we have heard of, that Scripture of imputing righteousness unto him was fulfilled.

Therefore the work did not stand in any account for the worthiness thereof, but only because the Lord did impute it unto him for righteousness. Which thing also it did not attain unto of itself, but because of faith which was joined with it. It is to be noted that the apostle Saint James speaketh here but of one work (as the offering up of his son) and that work also not done, but only purposed to be done. If therefore his meaning had been to debate the worthiness of works and what place they have in the purchase of our salvation, he would have taken works not only purposed but also practiced; not some one work alone, but many works long continued. Neither would he have said of that or those works that they were imputed unto him for righteousness, but that they wrought his righteousness, either wholly or at the least in part. But the apostle's purpose is to signify that a true faith is fruitful in good works and is witnessed by them, and that it is impossible that a true faith should not be rich in good works, or that righteousness should be without holiness of life. For it is impossible that we receiving comfort in his mercies by faith, should not witness the same by a life framed to the liking of him of whom we have those comforts.

The last of these benefits that we receive by Christ is redemption, that is, the delivery from all danger, affliction and corruption. It is the fruit of his resurrection to raise us out of all extremities even from death and the grave, and to place us with his saints in that glory that he hath purchased for us. Thus is redemption taken for our freedom and delivery from our wretchedness. For we hold not with the adversaries of God's grace that our good deeds do redeeem us from the danger of our evil doings; neither yet that by prayers or satisfaction whatsoever, we can deliver either ourselves or other from danger in this life, and much less in the life to come. We confess that howsoever we humble ourselves by repentance, prayers and fruits of good living, when his rod of correction is upon us, that it is only the free benefit of Christ to deliver us from the danger thereof and to put a happy end unto it. We do not thank our deeds for it when we come forth of trouble, albeit that we have plentifully brought forth the fruits of good life. We acknowledge it to be only the work of Christ, who is made of God the father unto us "redemption," to deliver us from sin and all those punishments that come unto man for it. In this benefit of Christ there appeareth a great difference between the children of God and the children of this world. For the children of God glory in trouble, knowing that it will bring upon them experience, and trial of God's goodness in the end, as the apostle teacheth us (*cf.* Rom 5:3). For Christ is made unto them redemption from sin and all the punishments thereof. Whereas the ungodly, howsoever in prosperity they fleshly brag of their hope in God, yet when affliction cometh, they are without all heart, comfort or courage. For why? In truth they know not that Christ is made redemption unto them, to deliver them from all that danger that cometh for sin, as well as for sin itself. This persuasion causeth the godly in all their afflictions and necessities whatsoever, to stay themselves in godly conversation, both toward God and man, with patience and assured hope of a happy end; whenas the ungodly either murmur against God, either else fall into some one evil dealing or other, thereby [seeking] to purchase their deliverance, which is an assured testimony that they do not look to have it from the Lord.

Now we have heard what several benefits do come with Christ, and that we do not receive him naked and alone, but according as he is given unto us from God the father, clothed with wisdom, righteousness, holiness and redemption. Thus is he given unto the believers, and thus is he received of the believers. And hereby we may clearly understand what faith is, even that which findeth all want in itself, and all plenty in Christ; that is poor at home and rich abroad; that in her necessity boasteth, and is comfortable in another man's plenty; that never resteth in herself nor anything of her own (have she never so great plenty in respect of others) and yet is joyful, comfortable and well appaid and satisfied with Christ in her greatest want. For faith is not so highly commended as it is a work of ours, for so it is imperfect as all others be that come from us; but because it giveth all glory from us unto God, therefore hath it so just commendation in the word of God. We give the most unto it because it giveth nothing unto us, that God may have all glory, and that he that will glory, may glory in the Lord. We do not exalt it above other things that proceed from us, because it doth exalt us, but because it doth abase us; that Christ may be exalted, therefore do we magnify it. For faith findeth perfection in God and imperfection in us. Faith findeth true wisdom to be in Christ, charging all the world with folly in their wit (be they never so wise in the opinion of men) before they be lightened with the understanding of his wisdom set forth in his word. Faith findeth true righteousness in Christ alone, and chargeth all men with unrighteousness in themselves, as withered branches proceeding out of the rotten stock of Adam their first father, until we be grafted into Christ, the root of all righteousness.

Faith findeth true sanctification and holiness of life in Christ, and chargeth all men how civilly and honestly soever they live in the judgment of men, to be of a profane and unholy nature and disposition, except they have it reformed by special grace from Christ. Faith findeth deliverance from all danger in Christ, and chargeth the deeds of all men with want of ability in that behalf. Thus we learn that faith doth find all those things in Christ, and the want of every one of them in the nature of man; nay, which worse is, a counterfeit of every one of them deeply imprinted in us; a counterfeit wisdom of man's wit and invention for the true wisdom of his word; counterfeit righteousness of our corrupt works for the true righteousness brought and wrought by Christ alone; a feigned devotion grounded by our own good intent, for holiness and sanctification of life and well doing, guided and directed by his word; a false persuasion to avoid dangers by our own satisfactions, instead of an assured standing to his redemption, and delivery in all our necessities and wants. These are the withered branches of that rotten root, our old Adam, and the nature and disposition of all men goeth this way, except they be reclaimed by Christ; as all those be (in his appointed time) that shall inherit with him in his kingdom. Inasmuch as we do clearly understand what is in us, before that Christ shall call us, it shall be profitable to consider whether (after that Christ hath laid claim unto his and given them that in truth which before they had in show) faith doth yet find any such want and lack, that (notwithstanding such a change) it resteth only in Christ and refuseth to stand to any desert which this new obedience can claim. The Scripture is plain, that faith findeth lack and want in man, notwithstanding that he be changed and renewed by Christ, from that he was before, and come to that perfection that ever any man hath attained unto. This will appear most plainly in the consideration of those several commodities which (as we learned before) are brought with Christ. We that be Christ's do receive wisdom from Christ, yet is there want of wisdom in the child of God that hath received the greatest portion thereof, according as it is written to the Corinthians: "Now we see in a glass darkly, but then shall we see face to face. Now I know in part, but then shall I know even as I am known" (1 Cor. 13:12).

We that be Christ's do receive righteousness from him by faith, but we have such wants in our faith while we be here that this is the prayer of the church and every member thereof, so long as they live: "Lord, increase our faith" [Lk. 17:5]; "I believe, Lord, help mine unbelief" [Mk. 9:24]. We receive sanctification and holiness of life from Christ, but in that measure: that it is the continual prayer of the church unto the end, "Forgive us our trespasses, as we do forgive them that trespass against us" [Mt. 6:12].

The faithful that have been delivered from many dangers already by Christ who is their redemption, have yet for all that many dangers and troubles abiding for them, insomuch that it is thus written of the estate of them: "For thy sake are we killed all the day long, we are accounted as sheep for the slaughter" (Rom. 8:36). And if they should escape all other, yet death will surely have to do with them all at the last, and will not resign her right unto any. These are plain proofs that the faithful never stand satisfied with anything in themselves as being perfect in it, but always return unto their mediator and redeemer Christ, where is the perfection of that which in small measure abideth in themselves, who hath these things perfect in himself, not for himself, but for us.

And therefore the Holy Ghost doth not say (which notwithstanding in truth he might) that Christ hath made us wise, righteous and holy; but he saith that Christ is made unto us wisdom, righteousness and holiness, adding the cause thereof in these words following: "That he that will glory, may glory in the Lord" [2 Cor. 10:17]. For faith refuseth to glory of anything in itself, finding want in all things, that it may glory in the Lord alone. For it is no praise worthy of him if he be but fellow with us in the work; but when we are truly taken (as we are indeed) for nothing, and that that cometh from us as no sufficient payment, then receiveth the Lord the whole right of his glory, which otherwise is clean darkened when it is made to patch up that which we had begun. Let us therefore never forget this, that we do magnify faith above all that which doth come from us, not simply because it fasteneth hard upon Christ; but because it so taketh hold upon him, that it letteth go all the hold that it hath of anything in itself. We may not therefore only consider whether we have any stay in Christ, but whether we have such a stay that acknowledgeth us unstayed in ourselves, and therefore to be upheld by him alone. For faith joineth riches to poverty, and bringeth plenty unto the empty man.

Now let us pray unto our heavenly Father, that his true faith may be increased in us, etc. Amen.

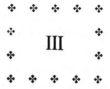

III

EUSEBIUS PAGET

Editor's Introduction

From the start, the Christian world had witnessed conflict between the law of the state and the law of the church. Emperors and popes, civilians and canonists, courts civil and ecclesiastical had known dispute for centuries before the Protestant Reformation. But in England, once Henry VIII had taken for himself the title of Supreme Head of the Church, the dispute became crucial, as between the English statute and common law and the ecclesiastical or canon law, and as between the jurisdictions of numerous civil courts and of ecclesiastical courts, numbering approximately 250. Matters were rendered still worse because the promise Henry had made, to revise the canon law so as to bring it into harmony with the statute and common law, was never carried out by any of the Tudors. What happened, instead, was that Henry, and after him Edward VI and Elizabeth I, exercised control over ecclesiastical policy without the curb of any explicit and acknowledged body of ecclesiastical law. This left the whim or will of the soveriegn as the final authority in the church, placing all administrators of the ecclesiastical law, as well as all those subject to it, in the unhappy position of never being sure of what rights the subject had, or of the limits upon those in authority. The increase in the exercise of royal power as a result of this supremacy over the church was enormous, with little danger of successful challenge.

Under Mary, of course, the traditional Roman Catholic canon law was restored, to be repealed by the first two acts of Parliament in 1559. That Elizabeth intended to reinstitute the policy of controlling the church without reference to any ecclesiastical constitution became apparent during that same Parliament of 1559. But there were several new developments. Parliament was now much more self-conscious than it had been under the earlier Tudors. Similarly, the common lawyers and the courts of common law had begun to resist the arbitrary character of the prerogative claims of the Crown. The statute law and the common law were now bastions of the parliamentary party and of the common law party alike. To both these parties the ecclesiastical law and the ecclesiastical courts, administered by the Crown-appointed bishops and their officials and subject ultimately to the royal will alone, constituted a threat that must be withstood. It was soon clear to those on both sides that in both civil and ecclesiastical affairs one or the other must finally prevail: either the naked royal will, or the statute as determined by Parliament and the courts of common law.

The first concerted resistance by the Puritan preachers against the Elizabethan Settlement took the form of the so-called vestment controversy, which in fact involved more than vestments, and was vigorously taken up by the advocates of the "alphabet bills" in the Parliaments of 1566 and 1571. Most of the M.P.s who led these efforts were common lawyers by profession. After the limited subscription law passed in 1571 (13 Eliz. I, cap. 12) had been flouted by the bishops, and Parker's Canons of 1571 had been put into effect by the bishops and church courts without the sanction of Parliament or the signature of the Queen, the threat to the future of the parliamentary party and of the common law party was evident. The members of both parties thus came out openly in support of the Puritan preachers. When Whitgift, in 1583, opened up a campaign against the Puritans that employed the methods of the old medieval Inquisition, the Puritans in turn used every possible means of obstructing the bishops. Their attitudes and arguments are well stated by James Morice in the *Treatise of Ecclesiastical Oaths* (see 384–439, below). The methods they used are suggested by the testimony of Eusebius Paget reproduced here.

Paget (1547?–1617) was a leader in the Presbyterian Puritan party. He was deprived of his ecclesiastical post in 1574, when Parker, ignoring Parliament's limitations on subscription, was urging all the bishops to require unlimited subscription according to his Canons of 1571. During the period when Grindal was under house arrest, and enforcement of ecclesiastical policy was less thorough, Paget managed to secure another post. In 1585 he was deprived once more, under Whitgift's intensified campaign for total conformity, and he never again held church employment. Many less thorough-going Puritans were tolerated, shielded or permitted some office during these years. Paget was one of those for whom there was to be no toleration.

The text of this report on Paget's case is from *The Seconde Parte of a Register*, . . ., edited by Albert Peel (Cambridge, 1915), I, 176.

❖　❖　❖　❖

The Answer Exhibited 11th January 1584/5, Anno Regni Reginae Elizabeth 27, to the Archbishop and Other High Commissioners: Question Made to Eusebius Paget, Minister, Whether He Would Observe the Book of Common Prayer

I. Paget's Statement

I, Eusebius Paget, minister of the parish church of Kilkehampton in the diocese of Exeter, do acknowledge that by the statute made in the parliament held in the first year of our most gracious Sovereign . . . [I] am bound to use the administration of each of the sacraments and the common and open prayer in such order and form as is mentioned in the book authorized by the said statute, or else to abide such pains as by the law are imposed upon me. And I have not contrary to the said statute refused to use the said common prayer or to minister the sacraments in the said parish church in such order and form as they be mentioned and set forth in the said book. For the said book hath not been showed me in the said parish. And when that book is showed me, I either will use the same, or else otherwise as a dutiful and obedient subject behave myself and humbly submit myself to the laws in that behalf. I have very willingly and with all humble obedience in the administration of the sacraments and other open prayers in the said parish use[d] rites, ceremonies and orders set forth in the said book, although I have not used all rites, ceremonies and orders . . . as is [there] mentioned.

1. Partly for that to my knowledge, there is not in the said church the said book.

2. Partly for that I am given to understand that you before whom I stand, and mine Ordinary [i.e., bishop], and the most part of the BBs [i.e., bishops] and ministers do use greater liberty in omitting and altering the said rites, ceremonies and orders.

3. And especially for that I am not fully resolved in conscience that I may use divers of them.

4. And for that when I took the charge of that church, I was promised by mine Ordinary that I should not be urged to such ceremonies, which I am informed he might do by the law.

In those things which I have omitted, I have done nothing obstinately, neither have I used any other rite, ceremony, order, form or manner of administration of the sacraments, or other open prayers than is mentioned in the said book.

I have not preached, declared or spoken anything in the derogation or depraving of the said book. Although there be some things in the said book which I doubt whether I may use or practice.

Whereof I humbly pray I may have the liberty allowed by the said book, that I may have in some convenient time favorable conference either with mine Ordinary or with some other by you to be assigned. Which I seek, not for any desire I have to keep the said living, but only for the better resolution and satisfaction of mine own conscience, as God knoweth.

Subscribed by me thus, by me, Lame Eusebius Paget.

II. The Common Lawyer's Case

1. The prayer book provided in the church, although printed "With Privilege," is not the one authorized in 1559.

2. The minister was promised by both Ordinary and patron that he would not be required to use such ceremonies as troubled his conscience, nor "urged to the precise observation of the things in the established book."

3. Nevertheless he read the greater part of the book, omitting only things against his conscience or not commanded by the Act of 1559.

4. His Ordinary then commanded him to use the book in every point, but no proper book was provided, and so he behaved as before. At this both Ordinary and patron were enraged, and the latter secured his presentment by means of church-wardens and sidesmen nominated by himself, and not properly elected.

5. Called before the High Commission, the minister made the above statement.

On this evidence "the general question is, whether the said High Commissioners may, for or upon these premises, deprive the said minister?"

This resolves itself into thirteen particular questions, viz.,

1. Ought the minister to provide the book?

2. Does the statute command "the whole use of the said book"? Is it illegal to omit a part of it?

3. Does the statute authorize deprivation for such omission?

4. Does the presentment — which does not mention willful and obstinate omission — afford sufficient basis for deprivation?

5. Can deprivation, the second degree of punishment according to the statute, be lawfully inflicted on a minister not previously convicted?

6. Can the minister be said to "refuse contrary to the statute" when "he was not lawfully required"?

7. Is the request of the parish that he should use the same book as before lawful?

8. If he accede to this request, is he liable to deprivation?

9. Can deprivation be inflicted for an offence not punishable by deprivation, according to the Act?

10. If the minister is irregularly "convented," presented and charged to observe the book, can this reckon as one of the three canonical admonitions which must precede deprivation?

11. If he use the "most material, substantial and essential parts" of the book, can he be legally deprived?

12. Can the Ordinary license a minister to omit immaterial parts of the book?

13. If the Ordinary did this, can the minister be rightly deprived?

III. The principal causes set down in the deprivation are two: the first is the omission of part of the public prayers, the cross in baptism and the surplice; the second, irregularity incurred by dealing in the ministry after suspension.

1. It should be remembered that the book allows liberty to preachers. The minister's infirmity and the distance of his house and his parishioners from the church make it unreasonable to ask that he should read the whole of the prayers as well as preach two sermons.

The permission granted by the Ordinary, and the fact that Paget acted as he did through conscience and not through obstinacy, should have secured him against deprivation. Indeed the deprivation is illegal, for the canon law says that only great offences, and those expressly cited, are so punishable. A non-resident may never come near his charge in twenty years, and yet he will not be deprived, and his is a much greater crime than Paget's. Even the papists would not give so severe a punishment for such a breach of law, and in England no one has ever been deprived for disobeying the Injunctions or not preaching quarter sermons. Mr. Paget

ANSWER TO THE ARCHBISHOP

asked for conference according to law, but he did not receive the three legal admonitions; throughout he has been badly treated.

2. (*a*) The suspension was illegal, and therefore void. There is no legal power to demand any subscription other than that authorized in the Act of 1571.

(*b*) If the suspension were valid, it had long since been cancelled by the Queen's pardon.

(*c*) Mr. Paget did not "deal in the ministry before he had procured from the Archbishop of Canterbury a release of that suspension, as the Earl of Huntingdon can testify."

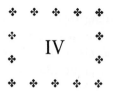

IV

JAMES MORICE

Editor's Introduction

The year 1583, which marked the twenty-fifth year of Elizabeth's reign and saw the death of Archbishop Grindal, brought to an end the era in which the major offices of the church were held by men who had seen some kind of service under Henry or Edward. Matthew Parker (1504–75), who had been among the early reformers at Cambridge, had witnessed the burning of Thomas Bilney in 1531, had been associated with the Cranmer party under both Henry and Edward, and had been chaplain to Anne Boleyn and later to Henry. Although he became archbishop at the age of fifty, he had been among the older of Elizabeth's first bishops. By 1583 even most of the younger bishops of 1559 had passed from the scene. A few, such as Aylmer and Sandys, were to continue for a short time longer. But control of the major offices in the church had passed to new men who had not been deeply stirred by the successive upheavals under Henry, Edward, Mary and Elizabeth.

John Whitgift and his episcopal colleagues saw the Elizabethan establishment in a very different way from the bishops who first accepted office under it. In 1559, for Jewel, Grindal, Parkhurst, Pilkington, Coxe, Sandys, Horne and Parker too, the compromises arrived at by the Establishment were unavoidably necessary although deplorable. They hoped for future progress once they were firmly in control of the church, and once the Catholics no longer held major office. But beginning in 1564 came the devastating recognition that the Queen opposed any further change. Yet Parker declared even then that he would have preferred further reformation, and opposed it only because his first obligation was to obey the Queen. By 1583 the group about Whitgift, the new Archbishop of Canterbury, were defending and enforcing conformity to the established religion with no sign of the inner uncertainties and reservations that had troubled the first Elizabethan bishops. In the eyes of these newer bishops, the English church had been rightly ordered in 1559, and all that remained was to secure total conformity to the established order by a thorough enforcement of the law.

In every battle for a quarter of a century, the official church had won out against both the Catholics and the Puritans. But it had not won the allegiance of either the people or the Parliament, nor had any of the many ills within the church been rectified. Fearful of driving the English Catholics to cooperate with Catholic Spain or France in a major rebellion, the government had found itself obliged to grant a certain toleration, not only to Catholics but also to all but the most extreme of the Puritans. Using the opportunity thus afforded them, the Puritans had managed to build up a popular following by their preaching and their literature. By 1583 the newer bishops, led by Whitgift, were coming to see that the policies of the past twenty-five years had been too hesitant to achieve the total victory they desired.

John Whitgift was the first Protestant Archbishop of Canterbury who was in any way a leader of the English bishops. Because of his whole-hearted devotion to Elizabeth, he also enjoyed her support to a degree never achieved by Parker or Grindal. And in Christopher Hatton of the Privy Council, who was Elizabeth's latest favorite, he had an unswerving patron. Under Whitgift's leadership the old Ecclesiastical Commission became the Court of High Commission, an instrument that was soon to wreak devastation on the Presbyterian Puritan movement. In a new apologetic, developed by men such as Richard Hooker, Hadrian Saravia, Matthew Sutcliffe, Thomas Bilson, Richard Bancroft, John Bridges, Thomas Cooper and Richard Cosin, the Elizabethan church order, based solidly upon the royal will and the royal prerogatives, was set forth as complete and wholly admirable. Any show of discontent with that order, any looking to other countries for guidance in improving it, was reprehensible and a possible evidence of disloyalty. So headlong a defense of the royal will in the church would have been impossible for men who had been directly affected by the Marian years.

At the heart of Whitgift's policy was "law and order," strictly enforced without quibbling or debate. If and when changes were to be made, it would be as the free act of royal authority, guided by the bishops. Parliament could act in religious matters only by permission of the Queen and on the advice of the bishops. It was, however, entirely unnecessary for Parliament to act, and authorization by the Queen was not required for every action by the bishops.

Whitgift's policy was not uniquely his own, but expressed the mood of the times. The first half of Elizabeth's reign had been dominated by concern over the Queen's marrying and producing an heir; by fears of a Spanish intervention and of trouble in Scotland and France; by a serious financial crisis, stagnation of trade, and the uncertain loyalty of English Catholics. Under these circumstances a Queen who was only twenty-five at her accession had been obliged to grant her Privy Council and principal executives a good deal of authority. Most of these men had served under Henry, and they acted as that king would have done. At critical times during his reign, Henry had worked with great finesse through Parliament, and especially through Commons, to carry out the more difficult decisions of the Crown. But Elizabeth was not Henry, and England was no longer what it had been in the 1530s. Privy Councillors, Parliament and strong-minded Englishmen acted and spoke in the 1560s and '70s as no Englishman, whatever his position, would have dared to do under Henry.

The latter half of Elizabeth's reign was notable for two trends — one towards a resolution of England's political and financial problems, the other towards a recovery by the Crown of concessions made in the earlier years. In short, when the last great crisis had ended with the defeat of the Spanish Armada in 1588, no one was to suppose that as the clouds of danger dispersed, the limited concessions would be followed by greater ones. Rather, England was to learn that circumstances no longer compelled the Crown to grant such concessions. In the Privy Council, the Parliament, the courts of law, and the church, the final decades of the century witnessed a strong reassertion of the royal will.

The effect in England of the conflicts that raged on the Continent — religious, dynastic, imperial and national — and led eventually to the Thirty Years' War (1618–48), was an increasing defensiveness. Since the death of Mary Tudor (1558), the nationalism of the English, their hatred of Spain and of the papacy, and their rivalry with France, coupled with the steady drumbeat of the official and unofficial propaganda for national unity and the Protestant faith, had produced, by the later years of Elizabeth's reign, a national self-consciousness which bordered on the messianic and xenophobic. Although the messianism was little concerned with conquest, it emphasized England's uniqueness to a degree that made other nations, cultures and religions of little significance. Therefore, any person, idea or movement which would seem any challenge to English values was vigorously opposed by a wide variety of persuasive reasonings. England, after all, was the bearer of a unique destiny, and nothing must be allowed to hinder its fulfillment. The strong authoritarian trend during the later years of Elizabeth's reign was in fact much more deeply rooted than is sometimes supposed.

Whitgift's policy of exacting total conformity was notable on three counts. It marked out the Puritan rather than the Catholic as the chief threat to unity in religion. It deliberately set aside acts of Parliament where these conflicted with his policies. And it reinstated the methods of the Inquisition for enforcing religious policy — the very methods that had been abolished by Henry after the "Supplication of the Commons" (1532) had singled them out as among the most vicious examples of clerical tyranny. Restored by Mary, they had become a stock exhibit in the "Bloody Mary" legend, and one of the first acts of Parliament under Elizabeth had been their repeal.

In the early years of her reign, any return to such a policy would have been disastrous for both Elizabeth and her Archbishop. Even in his reactionary "Act of Six Articles" of 1539, Henry had not dared to restore the old inquisitorial process for heresy. Nor had he failed to make Parliament responsible for enacting those Articles. Even so, in the outcry that followed, Henry was soon obliged to restrain the heresy hunters. Beyond doubt, Henry had manipulated and browbeaten Parliament (and "packed" it as well). But once it had passed (or been used to pass) an act, he was careful not to flout it. Mary herself had been astute enough to deal with Parliament as the agency for reconciling the kingdom to the papacy. And except under Mary, not since the dubious campaign against the papacy, begun in 1533, had politically loyal Protestants been regarded as a greater danger to national unity than the Catholics. It is true that Henry put Protestants to death. It is also true that Latimer and Cranmer lived, whereas More and Fisher died.

The changing mood of the country, as an older generation that could remember the former times gradually died out, allowed Elizabeth and Whitgift to carry out the new policy of enforcement without making any concessions to those who clamored for further reform. Bancroft made his sensational exposure of the Presbyterian Puritan classical movement; Martin Marprelate published his lampoons; the fanatical Copinger-Hacket conspiracy was brought to light. Yet none of these in themselves could have produced the new generation of men in the Privy Council, in Parliament and the courts of law, who by the 1590s were ready to acquiesce in an exercise of royal authority that, earlier in the reign of Elizabeth, would not have gone unchallenged. It is true that Burghley protested (briefly, and only in private correspondence). But although Knollys fumed and roared, he was old, and not taken seriously. In 1588 Leicester was dead; in 1589, Mildmay; in 1590, Walsingham.

The Parliament of 1584 had seen the defeat of a major effort on behalf of the Puritans. Another effort had been made in 1586–7. But by 1590 the High Commission, under Whitgift's guidance, had begun to take action against leading Puritan preachers with a severity unmatched since Henry's "Reformation Parliament" had stripped the clergy of much of their power. Puritan preachers who had not been found guilty of any specific offence were nevertheless being convicted on vague charges under the Act of Uniformity, or for refusing to answer questions under the inquisitorial procedure Whitgift had restored. Many were being degraded from the clerical order and subjected to prison. This was rougher handling than had been dealt out in 1559 to the Catholic bishops responsible for the Marian persecutions, even though they had pronounced Elizabeth illegitimate, unfit to rule as Queen or as supreme governor of the church. None of these Catholic bishops, and none of the lesser Catholic clergy who refused the Act of Uniformity, had been degraded from the ministry. The Act of Uniformity itself contained no provision for the penalties that were now inflicted, ostensibly on its behalf.

What is most notable, however, in the inquisitorial procedure Whitgift had restored, was that he used it to defend ecclesiastical polity, whereas the Catholic inquisition had been designed to protect the faith. The "procedure by inquisition" had been devised during the twelfth and thirteenth centuries, as a means of combating the Albigensian and Catharist heresies. Because it was difficult to secure evidence against suspected heretics, Innocent III, at the Fourth Lateran Council of 1215, ordered the ecclesiastical courts to make free use of the "procedure by inquisition" derived from Roman law.[1] It provided that a suspect against whom no witnesses could be found, but who had been "defamed" by rumor or by secret informers, could be deemed accused by *clamosa insinuatio* (scandal or public fame). The ecclesiastical judge (the "Ordinary") could then take action against him *ex officio mero* — i.e., by virtue of his office as a judge. The suspect would be asked to take an oath (which therefore came to be called the *ex officio* oath) that he would answer truthfully whatever

1. H. C. Lea, *History of the Inquisition of the Middle Ages* (New York, 1908), I, 399–458; P. Landau, *Die Entstehung des kanonischen Infamiebegriffs von Gratian bis sur Glossa ordinaria* (Cologne, 1966).

questions the judge — who now became the prosecutor as well — might choose to ask him. The suspect was given no bill of charges, and was allowed no legal advice or counsel. Unless he was exceptionally well versed in theology, a suspect who took the oath could expect to be convicted on his own testimony. He would then be asked to abjure his errors and be reconciled to the church. Accordingly, the ecclesiastical authorities insisted that the procedure was not tyrannical but fatherly, that it was "medicinal" rather than penal, because it was "intended for the good of souls," and terminated in reconciliation to the church. If the suspect refused to take the oath, he was adjudged guilty *pro confesso* or *fictione juris* — i.e., a refusal became an acknowledgment of guilt. For centuries the common assumption of Europeans was that when an ecclesiastical judge proceeded by way of inquisition the suspect was never found innocent. The words "inquisition" and "*ex officio* oath" were among the most potent rallying cries in the revolt of the laity against the papacy, the clergy and the ecclesiastical courts.

It was this hated inquisitional procedure that Whitgift, empowered only by the Queen's letters patent, had reinstated — for the sake of vestments, liturgical observances, and the doctrine of the episcopate, as a means of silencing criticism of such things as non-residence and non-preaching. Thus alerted, the anticlerical group were quick to resume their old war.

The conflict that broke out mainly concerned the *ex officio* oath. Under Whitgift the ecclesiastical courts, and notably the High Commission, declared that ecclesiastical judges, when proceeding by way of inquisition, were not limited by any law of the kingdom. The questioning, it was argued, did not constitute a trial, but merely investigated persons publicly reputed to be offenders. Accordingly, the authorities asserted, a person under questioning need not hear the charges against him, the witnesses against him need not be named or produced, and he needed no legal counsel or attorney. One who refused to take the oath was at once imprisoned for contempt, to be held without any charge and without bail, until he relented. One who had taken the oath, but who refused to answer a particular question, was assumed by the court to have done so as a means of concealing his guilt, and was adjudged to have confessed by his silence on that particular. Once the questioning had been completed, the court drew up a bill of charges based wholly on his own sworn testimony, and proceeded to try him on that basis. At this trial he was allowed to have a lawyer for his defense. But by now any trial amounted to a mere formality. Once the court had rendered its decision, there was no appeal to any other court.[2]

Whitgift conceded no less frankly than his enemies that the key to his entire policy of enforcement was the *ex officio* oath, which alone could compel a person to answer the judge or judges who were prosecutors as well. But the entire policy was effective. It was the means Bancroft used to break up the Puritan Presbyterian classical movement, by placing in prison (either for refusing the oath, or as a result of a conviction after taking it) the leaders among the Puritans who were known to be still opposed to official policy, and by unearthing the underground presses, along with some of the participants in the Martin Marprelate tract campaign. Whitgift's victory was complete in 1591, when during the Caudry case, the Court of Queen's Bench declared the Court of High Commission to be a creature of the royal prerogative alone and bound by no law. After that decision, no Puritan — or suspected Puritan — had much reason to hope for a New Jerusalem. Throughout the kingdom, there were various forms of accommodation. Some moderate bishops discreetly ignored Puritans who were likewise moderate. In other dioceses, Puritan teachers who had the support of powerful lords or city officials were tolerated by the bishop. Some prominent Puritans filled the precarious role of lecturer, tutor or chaplain. Some who were forced out of the ministry migrated to Scotland or to the Lowlands. But for all who took any sort of shelter from Whitgift's inquisition, the future remained uncertain. Legally they had no grounds to stand on. They depended on the sufferance of kindly bishops, or the support of laymen whom political prudence might compel to alter their views. The Puritans of Groups I and II were better able to bear the decade between 1593 and 1603 than the Presbyterians of Group III, or than the newly emerging Separatist Puritans.

Those who fought openly against the Whitgift inquisition and the *ex officio* oath included several members of the Privy Council, among them Sir Francis Knollys, Robert Beale and James Morice. The latter two both wrote tracts against it, although Beale's may have circulated only in manuscript. Morice (d. 1597) was Attorney for the Court of Wards and a long-time associate of Burghley, who was Master of that Court. About 1590 he published abroad, anonymously, the tract here reproduced. In

2. Mary Hume Maguire, "Attack of the Common Lawyers on the Oath *Ex Officio* as Administered in the Ecclesiastical Courts in England," in *Essays in Honor of C. H. McIlwain* (Cambridge, Mass., 1936), 199–229; R. G. Usher, *The Rise and Fall of the High Commission* (Oxford, 1913); *Cartwrightiana*, edited by Albert Peel (London, 1951), 21–46.

1591 Richard Cosin of the High Commission published a counterattack (likewise anonymous) against both Beale and Morice, the *Apology* . . . *for* . . . *Jurisdiction Ecclesiastical.* To this Morice in turn produced a reply, which Whitgift was able to suppress. In the Parliament of 1593 Morice, supported by Beale and Knollys, led an attempt to outlaw the *ex officio* oath. Morice and Beale were briefly imprisoned for their audacity, and the Queen suppressed the bill before it could be passed.[3] Cosin's *Apology* was twice reprinted in that same year, 1593, which saw the last major effort by the Puritan party under Elizabeth to deal in Parliament with strictly ecclesiastical matters. Cosin, incidentally, complained that all the hatred and invective of earlier campaigns against the papacy were now being vented on the English bishops. Puritan members of Parliament such as Morice and Beale, on the other hand, openly spoke of the Henrician era as a time in which episcopal arrogance and tyranny had been held in check rather than used by the Crown against the people. This view of the Reformation Parliament under Henry would be carried into the Stuart era by the opponents of Laud.

During this brief and futile contest, Whitgift's ablest defender, Richard Hooker, inadvertently set down what may now be regarded as the inquisition's epitaph. In great gratitude over the course of events Hooker wrote, "By the goodness of Almighty God and his servant Elizabeth, we are."[4] Concealed, even from himself, in the innocent words, "we are," was the tragedy of the entire Elizabethan "reformation." The effort to force upon a vigorous, rapidly changing nation of more three million people a religious order founded merely on official "uniformity" (and to make this attempt while the whole of Europe was torn by religious controversy), could not be accomplished without also changing the very meaning of "religion." All through his *Laws of Ecclesiastical Polity,* Hooker drove a distinction between the visible and the invisible church, between church polity and salvation, between the law of the monarch and the law of God. He asserted that what he called "polity" — administering the sacraments, preaching, the ministry, ceremonies, rites and church laws — was not in itself necessary to salvation but was merely for the furthering of obedience to an authority that was grounded in right reason. This assertion, coupled with the virtual identification under Whit-

3. John Neale, *Elizabeth I and Her Parliaments, 1584–1601* (London, 1957), 267–79.
4. Quoted in P. M. Dawley, *John Whitgift and the English Reformation* (New York, 1954), 191.

gift of the episcopate with the Crown, constituted the seemingly impregnable fortress from within which the ecclesiastical authorities — Hooker's "we" — held out against all criticism and opposition. A few decades later, under Charles I and Archbishop Laud, men convinced that they belonged to the invisible church, who avowed their overriding concern with salvation, and for whom the law of God alone was immutable, were to assert not only that ecclesiastical polity had no necessary connection with salvation, but also that the episcopate in truth existed only by royal will. They therefore saw no loss to religion in whatever sweeping alterations of the visible church Parliament, acting in the name of the people, might see fit to make. One of the first acts of Parliament in this revolt against the power of the bishops and the Crown was the liquidation, in 1641, of the Court of High Commission, along with the method of inquisition and the *ex officio* oath.

The text of Morice's *Brief Treatise* has been taken from the presumed first edition, printed about 1590 (*S.T.C.*, 18106, folios A to Hi). The *S.T.C.* lists a presumed second printing (*S.T.C.*, 18107, folios A — G 4). However, a photographic copy of *S.T.C.*, 18107 shows that it has folios A to Hi, and that the ascription to it of a foliation A — G 4 is a misreading of a manuscript note on the flyleaf. There is, therefore, no known second printing. Permission has been given by the Folger Shakespeare Library to use the copy from which the text in this volume is taken.

Morice made his own translations of biblical passages, evidently from the Latin version of Tremellius and Junius.

An attempt has been made to trace the court decisions cited by Morice to reports and yearbooks extant in his time rather than to later editions or compilations.

❖ ❖ ❖ ❖

A Brief Treatise of Oaths Exacted by Ordinaries and Ecclesiastical Judges,

To Answer generally to all such articles or interrogatories as pleaseth them to propound; and of their forced and constrained oaths ex officio, *wherein is proved that the same are unlawful*

Forasmuch as the matter whereof we mean to entreat is concerning oaths, it will be very necessary for the better understanding thereof first to consider what an oath is and the nature thereof; by whom it was instituted, and to what use, end and purpose; how many kinds of lawful oaths there are, and how they ought to behave themselves that either require or receive an oath.

An oath therefore (as learned divines have defined) is a calling or taking to record or witness of the sacred name of God, or of God himself by the use of his holy name, for the confirmation of the truth of such things which we speak, or for the true performance of our promise. Or more briefly: an oath is a confirmation of the will of man by the testimony of God.

The same of his own nature (inasmuch as it proceedeth from a right faith), is very good, for thereby we acknowledge all things to be thoroughly known unto God, and that he is a lover of truth and a revenger of perjury. It serveth also to the honor of almighty God, because thereby we extol and magnify his most holy name and confess the excellency of his great majesty, for that men swear by him that is greater (*cf.* Heb. 6:16). It is a part of his divine service, and commanded by him (*cf.* Deut. 6:13). And the same is to be used only for the setting forth of the glory of God, and for the profit and benefit of men.

The institution thereof was from and by God himself for the help and relief of our necessity, either for the assurance of such duties, covenants, contracts and promises as we owe or make; or to procure faith or credit (certainty of proof failing) to the truth which we affirm, that an end of controversies may be had. For (as it is written in the same chapter of the Epistle to the Hebrews [6:16]) an oath for confirmation is amongst men "an end of all strife."

Oaths Are of Two Sorts, that Is to Say, Private and Public

Private oaths are made between private persons concerning their particular affairs, as for the assurance of duties, covenants, agreements or promises, or to procure faith and credit to be given to that which is meant to be persuaded. Of which kind of oaths we have many examples in the sacred histories, as in the book of Genesis 24:2-3, and 31:44-53; 1 Samuel 20:1-17,42; 1 Kings 18:10; Jeremiah 38:16; and many other which for brevity's sake I omit.

Public oaths are of divers and sundry sorts, as where kings and princes swear for the establishment of their leagues and conclusions of peace. Or where the prince and people swear to each other: the prince to rule and reign justly, the people in due allegiance to obey faithfully. This kind of oath was used, 2 Samuel 5:3, between David the king and the elders of Israel. In the book of Judges [11:5–10] we read also how the elders of Gilead swore subjection unto Jephthah.

Another kind of public oath we see, 2 Chronicles 15:8–15, where King Asa made the people of Israel to take an oath for the true worship and service of almighty God, and the observation of his law. An oath not much different was that in Ezra 10:1–5.

That is also a public oath which the magistrates, judges and officers of justice take for the true and sincere administration of the law. So is also the oath of soldiers and men of war, swearing obedience to their generals, captains and commanders.

Another kind of public oath is that likewise which the judge or magistrate ministereth unto such as are called to depose and testify the truth in causes of suit and controversy, depending in courts or places of justice.

And that also which either of the adversaries take in the same suits, or the defendant for the final ending and determination of the controversy, which of some is termed a judicial oath, and being offered by the defendant, it is of necessity to the plaintiff, for that he cannot refuse to accept of the same.

Of this last sort, among the laws judicial it is written thus: "If any man deliver to his neighbor to keep, ass or ox or sheep, or any beast, and it die or be hurt, or be taken by force, and no man see it, an oath of the Lord shall be the mean between them twain, that he put not his hand unto his neighbor's goods. And the owner of it shall accept the oath, and the other shall not make it good" (Ex. 22:10–11).

Concerning him that is to take an oath, he is taught by the Holy Ghost first to swear in truth (*cf.* Jer. 4:2), that is to say, truly, without falsehood, deceit or dissimulation, the heart and mouth agreeing in one. For since God is the author and lover of truth, and the devil is a liar and the father of lies, there cannot be a greater dishonor or indignity offered to the sacred majesty of God than to make his most fearful and reverend name a witness of falsehood or deceit. Neither let any man think that by crafty or subtle swearing he can avoid the detestable sin of perjury. For "*Fraus distringit non dissoluit perjurium* (Fraud straineth harder, it dissolveth not the perjury)," as the learned Cicero very well said.[1]

---

1. Cicero. [ED.] *De officiis*, 3:113: ". . . For deceit does not remove the guilt of perjury, it merely aggravates it" (English translation by W. Miller, Loeb Classics, 1913).

Secondly, he that taketh an oath ought to swear in judgment (*cf.* Jer. 4:2), that is to say, with good discretion, soberly, well advised, and assured of that he will affirm or deny upon his oath. Not ignorantly, rashly, vainly, or in causes of no moment or necessity, for such vain and foolish swearing is expressly forbidden by the commandment, wherein also God threateneth that he will not hold him guiltless that taketh his name in vain, that is, will surely punish him that so abuseth his name. The same also in the New Testament is by Christ himself condemned. Moreover, the Holy Ghost by the preacher well adviseth every man not to be rash with his mouth, nor to suffer his heart to be hasty to utter anything before God, for that (saith he) God is in the heavens, and thou art on the earth [*cf.* Eccles. 5:2].

In justice or righteousness also ought an oath to be taken, that is, in things just and lawful, not repugnant to the will or commandment of God. For althought it be true that is said, "*Non est obligatorium contra bonos mores praestitum iuramentum* [An oath made against good manners is not binding]," [2] yet by swearing to do the thing that is unjust or unlawful, the glorious name of God is dishonored. And such a speech, saith Ecclesiasticus [23:12], is compassed about with death. Briefly, the respect of every deponent should be that God by his oath may be magnified, the truth in question confirmed, justice maintained, and that innocents (by fraudulent practices circumvented) may be freed and delivered from peril and danger.

Touching such as have power and authority to require or command an oath, they ought also to be very careful and circumspect that they impose not the same but in causes of weight and necessity, which is never to be intended but when the honor and glory of God is to maintained, or the good of the commonwealth or of our neighbor furthered. For if it be a principle, "*De minimis non curat lex* [The law does not concern itself with trifles]," by good reason the magistrates and ministers of law should spare to use that which is most holy and precious in causes of less price or moment, for daily experience showeth that the frequent use of things reverend (such is the corruption of our nature) causeth them to be of none account. Furthermore, they ought to be well advised that they require it not of men of suspected faith or credit, or of persons defamed in life and conversation. For an oath offered to such (without greater necessity) argueth a lightness and want of good discretion in the magistrate, who thereby wittingly doth minister an occasion of perjury, which if it

2. [ED.] *Corpus juris civilis*, Inst., 3, 27, 7.

follow, how great is the fault? Moreover, that they charge no man by oath to do the thing impossible or beyond his power. For *"impossibilium nulla est obligatio* [the obligation of things impossible is null]," [3] nor anything that is unlawful, inconvenient or ungodly. Neither force any man to swear rashly or unadvisedly. For if the vain and inconsiderate swearer shall not be unpunished, how shall the procurer escape God's vengeance? That they abuse not the simplicity of the deponent by intricate, captious or subtle questions. For let no man (saith the holy apostle Saint Paul) beguile or craftily circumvent his brother, for the Lord is an avenger of all such things (*cf.* 1 Thess. 4:6). Finally, in the ministering of an oath the magistrate ought to respect all those things which the party deposing ought to have before his eyes, that is, the glory of God, the maintenance of truth, and the good of our brethren.

These things granted, which cannot be denied, it consequently followeth that the forcing of oaths by Ordinaries and judges ecclesiastical generally to answer unto all such questions or interrogatories as they shall demand or minister touching either the thoughts, words or deeds of him that is to depose, is contrary to the honorable institution, lawful use and true end of an oath. And that whosoever by color of authority, threatening speeches, duress of imprisonment or other pain, constraineth any man to swear in such manner, doth highly offend against the inviolable rules before remembered.

For first, as it hath been said, the ordaining and institution of an oath was to help and relieve the necessity of men in the causes before rehearsed. But there is no necessity or urgent cause why such a general oath should either be required or taken, since the same is neither for assurance of duty, covenant, contract or promise, neither yet for confirmation of truth in any cause or matter of controversy. If it be alleged that the same is requisite for the inquiring and finding out of suspected faults whereof there is no proof, and to search and try the evil minds and corrupt consciences of dangerous dissemblers, and so necessary for the government both of the church and commonwealth, by this allegation, first all such are justly reproved who having practiced and put in use this general oath where otherwise there was sufficiency of proof. And yet thereby nothing is said for the maintenance of their doings in that behalf, since by the like reason there should be erected a court of inquisition more than Spanish to sift and ransack by oath the most secret thoughts and consciences of all men in general, enforcing them either to accuse themselves (not as in the

3. [ED.] *Corpus juris civilis*, Dig. 50, 17, 185.

papistical shrift [i.e., confessional], where secrecy was enjoined) to their public shame, reproach and condemnation, or else for the avoiding of such mischief and inconvenience, to commit most willful and damnable perjury. But as this, I suppose, in all good men's opinions were intolerable, so of the other I assure myself there can be no sound rule, sufficient precedent or example alleged. Except peradventure the proceeding of the high priest, the scribes and elders of the Jews in their consistory against our savior Christ, shall be vouched and maintained for a sufficient precedent in that behalf, who maliciously apposing [i.e., posing questions to] and examining him concerning his doctrine (although not by oath) would gladly have picked out and drawn from himself some matter of accusation whereby to have condemned him. But the answer and authority of Christ (I doubt not) will be allowed among Christians, both for sound and sufficient [reasons] to refell [i.e., refute] and condemn the practice of those malignant priests who, knowing their subtle purpose and intent, referred them to his auditors, and being unjustly stricken, replied, "If I have evil spoken, bear witness of the evil, but if I have well spoken, why smitest thou me?" [Jn. 18:23], justifying hereby his former answer and forcing therewithal his adversaries to seek for witnesses to testify against him.

The true use and end of an oath is, as aforesaid, that due honor may be given unto God, the truth confirmed, justice maintained, innocency protected, and an end had of strife and contention. But how is God glorified hereby, or not rather dishonored, whenas his sacred institution is so greatly perverted, and an oath forced to another course and purpose than he in his divine wisdom hath appointed, as by that which hath and shall be spoken, doth and shall manifestly appear. The truth in controversy is not thereby confirmed, since there is no issue joined in this case between parties affirming and denying, and how can justice by such an oath be maintained whenas the cause for which the oath is urged, standeth not in lawful course of judgment? For as it is well said of a learned man: *"Iudicium est in qualibet actione trinus actus trium personarum: Iudicis, actoris, et rei, secundum quod large accipi possunt huiusmodi personae, quod duae sunt ad minus inter quos vertatur contentio, et tertia persona ad minus qui iudicet, alioquin non erit iudicium, cum istae personae sunt partes principales in iudicio, sine quibus iudicium consistere non potest* [And it is to be known, that a judgment is in each action a threefold act of three persons, namely, the judge, the plaintiff and the defendant, according to what may be loosely said of such persons, namely, that there are two persons at least between whom the contention turns, and a third person at least who is to judge, otherwise there will not be a judgment, since these persons are the principal parties in a judgment, without whom a judgment cannot take place]." [4]

Then whensoever any fault or matter of offence by means of this kind of compulsory oath happeneth to be disclosed, either we must say that the judge who imposeth the oath is himself, against all order of justice, the party accuser, and so both judge and promoter, which all good laws forbid; [5] or else the deponent must of necessity sustain two principal parts in judgment, that is to be both *actor et reus* (accuser and accused), whereby the three principal parties by the rule aforesaid, failing true judgment, by no means may consist. Furthermore, by this kind of oath it cannot be truly said that innocents circumvented by fraud or practice are cleared, since there is no complaint or accusation judicially exhibited. Except we shall affirm that the judge or magistrate, by enforcing such an oath, doth himself play the part of a subtle circumventor and accuser, which as it is a most wicked sin in any man, so in the person of a public magistrate (whose actions should be sincere) the same is most detestable. And finally, how can an end of controversy ensue by such an oath, whereas no quarrel or complaint is any way depending? Nay, rather the same is oftentimes the cause of stirring up of debate and contention instead of former quietness, being principally used not to make an end of controversies, but to procure some accusation, and that by the secret malice of some undermining or malignant adversary or calumniator.

Again, since an oath is to be taken in judgment, that is with good advisement and consideration of the matter, wherein the deponent is to call the name of God to witness, and that whosoever otherwise taketh an oath doth therein vainly and indiscreetly abuse the name of God. How can this general oath be either rightly urged or received without great offence to his divine majesty, forasmuch as the party deposing is not before he swears made acquainted nor understandeth what questions or interrogatories shall be demanded, but by his oath hath fast bound and subjected himself to the discretion or indiscretion of another, that is the judge ecclesiastical, who having straitly tied and snared this silly [i.e., defenseless] subject, may now use or abuse him at his will and pleasure, either against law enforcing him by the bond of his oath to accuse

4. Henrici de Bracton. [ED.] *De legibus et consuetudinibus Angliae* . . . , edited with English translation by T. Twiss (London, 1879), II, 164–5.

5. 8 Hen. 6 [ED.: *Cf.* Y.B., (*S.T.C.*, 9644), fol. LVI]; 5 Eliz. [ED.: Not found.]

himself even of his most secret and inward thoughts, or contrary to Christian charity, yea humanity itself, constraining him to inform against his natural parents, dearest friends and nearest neighbors, or to betray with grief of heart such matters of secrecy as otherwise were inconvenient and peradventure not honest to be revealed. In which hard proceeding, besides the great hazard and peril of willful perjury without all necessity of an oath, great trouble of mind and scruple of conscience must needs ensue, whenas the deponent on the one side, considering the weight and heavy burden of his oath, feareth to conceal anything, and on the other side, finding himself thereby entrapped, shrinketh to make answer to the questions propounded.

Whereof you may behold a most miserable and lamentable spectacle in the book of *Acts and Monuments*, where in a large table is set forth the great iniquity and rigorous dealing of Longland, Bishop of Lincoln in the time of the late prince of famous memory, King Henry VIII, which bloody bishop, by forced and violent oaths and captious interrogatories, constrained the children to accuse their parents, the parents their natural children, the wife her husband, the husband his wife, one brother and sister another, some of these silly souls of sworn becoming forsworn, while they made dainty to accuse [i.e., were chary of accusing] such as they dearly affected. Of which blind ignorance (or rather, murderous minds) and intolerable iniquity of Romish bishops and barbarous abuse of an oath, that godly man of worthy memory, Master John Foxe, justly complaineth.[6] For what might be added more to extreme cruelty, save only this one point of detestable inhumanity (which also was pursuant as a part of that tragical church government), to compel the children to set fire to their condemned parents. Which example of cruelty, saith that good man, as it is contrary both to God and nature so hath it not been seen or heard of in the memory of the heathen.

That wicked King Herod (as it is recorded by the holy evangelists Matthew [14:7] and Mark [6:23]) voluntarily promised, and that with an oath, to give the dancing daughter of Herodias, his harlot, whatsoever she should demand. As this unadvised oath proceeding of vain pleasure and delight upon the wicked demand of that damsel wrought much grief of mind in the king, so was it the cause of the sudden dispatch and murder of that just man, John the Baptist. And although it may truly be said that Herod was not bound by his oath to have accomplished so foul and wicked a deed, yet can it not be denied but that the same was a rash and

6. John Foxe, *Acts and Monuments* . . . [ED.] IV, 219 f.

inconsiderate oath, and so an offence against the majesty of almighty God. And what difference is there, I pray you, between the oath of Herod and that which now we have in question, the one being to perform or grant whatsoever should be required, and the other to answer to all questions that shall be demanded, since there may be as unlawful and as unhonest questions ministered, as ungodly requests made or desired.

Again, it would not be forgotten that in all the volume of the sacred Scriptures (to my remembrance) there is no one precedent or example to be showed of any such general oath taken by any godly man in private, or exacted by any magistrate in public, neither yet any rule, law or commandment for the same.

But against this our last assertion may happily be alleged by some favorer of this foul abuse: the manner of trial by adjuration of the suspected wife, that is the law of jealousy [cf. Num. 5:14–30]; the inquisition and expiation of manslaughter where the author is unknown [cf. Deut. 21:1–9]; and the examination of Achan [cf. Josh. 7:16–19]; all which nevertheless make nothing for these general oaths or those enjoined ex officio, as by the consideration of the laws and history itself shall easily appear.

For as concerning the law of jealousy, although the wife were to be tried by oath and adjuration in that manner and with those circumstances as is there prescribed, either to satisfy the restless head of her jealous husband, if she were guiltless, or to receive by the wonderful working of that accursed water, if she were faulty, condign punishment for her heinous offence, both of perjury and adultery, yet is it very manifest in this case that the wife is not summoned or cited by the priest or magistrate ex officio, but brought unto him by her accusing husband, who upon offence conceived offering up his complaint, and thereupon the woman is called for and put to her purgation, well knowing her accuser, and having perfect notice before she swear of the crime objected. Moreover, who is so simple that seeth not how weak an argument or conclusion this were. God hath appointed an oath to be taken by the wife in this especial and singular case of jealousy for the satisfaction of the suspicious mind of the husband, ergo every judge ecclesiastical, to satisfy his jealous suspicion or imagination of any crime, may appose [i.e., pose] by oath and compel men to their purgation. For by as good reason the Ordinary or judge ecclesiastical may also upon every such oath denounce a curse of consumption and rotting to the party deposing in such and the same manner as there is prescribed.

And as touching the inquisition for murder or manslaughter before remembered, it is ordained that the elders of that city, which upon measure taken falleth out to be next unto the slain man, should wash their hands over a beheaded heifer, protesting and saying in the presence of the priests, "Our hands have not shed this blood, neither have our eyes seen the slayer. O Lord, be merciful unto thy people Israel, whom thou hast redeemed, and lay no innocent blood to the charge of this people . . . " [cf. Deut. 21:1–8]. How anything here may prove the exacting of oaths to be lawful, I see not. A man is slain, the offender unknown, the elders by this especial law of expiation do protest as aforesaid. But where is an oath in this case given to any particular person? If this protestation shall be thought in some sort to countervail [i.e., equal] an oath of purgation, yet where is there any protestation or oath required or taken to answer generally to such interrogatories as shall be propounded upon unknown, secret, or barely suspected matter? Nay, we see evidently, the fact and felony (to the offence both of God and man) to be public and apparent; the offender only lieth hidden and unknown. On the contrary, those inquisitors *ex officio* have the man before them whom they will examine, but the matter for the most part is secret and concealed which they inquire after, and many times there is no matter at all but bare and naked suspicion or fame [i.e., rumor] of a crime never committed.

Concerning Achan and the proceeding against him, we see by the sacred history how the offence in general is by God himself made manifest unto Joshua, the prince of the people (*viz.*): that an excommunicate or cursed thing was taken and concealed, etc.; the offender was only to be found out. Inquisition being had by lot or otherwise (God assisting), Achan is deprehended as guilty. What followed? He is by Joshua examined of the particular, using these words: "My son, I beseech thee, give glory to the Lord God of Israel and make confession unto him, and show me now what thou hast done; hide it not from me." Hereupon the detected Achan confesseth the truth in particular. But where doth it appear that he was deposed, or by what conceived words or form of oath doth he swear? Except we shall say there is no difference between the entreaty or charge of the magistrate, remembering the glory of God, and an oath taken and pronounced by the offender to confess the truth. Which granted, it must consequently follow that whosoever is in that manner charged and confesseth not the truth, although he have no will to swear, is both a liar and a person perjured, which were a hard conclusion. Nay, rather such kind of charge as "*Adiuro te* [I adjure you]," as a learned man saith, *"Non est alium ad iurandum inducere, sed per similitudinem juramenti alium ad aliud agendum inducere* [To adjure is not to induce a man to swear, but to employ terms resembling an oath in order to provoke another to do a certain thing.]." [7] And such speeches are also used for commandments in the name of the divine majesty, as we read done by the exorcists (*cf.* Acts 19:13–19) and by Saint Paul, who chargeth the Thessalonians in the Lord that his epistle be read unto all the brethren the saints (*cf.* 1 Thess. 5:27). Otherwise, if every such kind of speech should straightway make an oath, then would it follow (which were absurd) that the devil made our Savior to swear at such time as he said, "I charge thee by God, that thou torment me not" [*cf.* Mk. 5:17].

I know very well what that learned and excellent light of God's church, Master Calvin, saith in his book of *Institution of Christian Religion* [2.8.24], that is, how Joshua minding to drive Achan to confess the truth said: "My son, give glory to the Lord God of Israel," meaning thereby that the Lord is grievously dishonored if a man swear falsely by him. And this manner of speech, saith he, was used among the Jews so oft as any was called to take an oath, as appeareth by the like protestation that the Pharisees use in the gospel of Saint John [9:24]. In the book also of Ezra [10:11] we read the same phrase, "Give praise unto the Lord," as some in English have translated it, but according to the Latin translation of the learned Tremellius and Junius, the words are *"Aedite confessionem Jehoua Deo* [Offer confession to Jehovah God]." So that although it be granted that where an oath was given for the confession of the truth, there the magistrate used those words ("Give glory unto God," putting the party in mind thereby of the majesty of almighty God), yet followeth it not that in every place where we find the same speech, there the party to whom it was spoken had taken an oath to confess the matter whereof he was demanded. But be it granted that Achan made his confession by oath, yet nothing will ensue thereof to justify the dealings of those inquisitors *ex officio.* For if those rough and rigorous exactors of an oath following only this legal course of inquisition set forth in this sacred history, that is, after an offence committed so grievous and dangerous to the public estate, and the same made known and notorious, would then only seek out the party offending, and that by due and lawful course of trial; and having found him, then after so mild and courteous a manner, and in the name of God entreat, or (if they think good) depose him to

7. Thomas of Aquinas. [ED.] *The Summa Theologica,* English translation, Dominican Fathers (London, 1922), II, II, 90, 1, 3 co.

reveal the truth in particular: no man (I suppose) would find himself grieved with their proceedings. But this their unjust dealing in this great abuse of an oath, cannot by authority of the holy Scriptures be any way defended or maintained.

Wisely, therefore, and with good discretion did that godly man William Thorp, in the time of King Henry IV, being willed by that bloody persecutor of the true Christians, Archbishop Arundell, to lay his hand upon the book and swear faithfully to submit himself to his correction and to stand unto and fulfill his ordinance, desired first to know wherefore he should be corrected and unto what ordinance he was to be obliged; which being declared to this effect, that he should forsake all the opinions of the sects of Lollards (indeed the true Christians), that he should preach no more unto the people, and that he should from thenceforth become an accuser of such as himself was, he utterly refused to take any such oath, lest thereby he should have fallen into many foul and heinous sins and offences against God, as the abjuring of true religion, the forsaking of his lawful calling against his conscience, and to his public reproach to become a bloody accuser, or (as he himself saith) an appealer of his brethren, every bishop's spy, and the summoner of all England, deeply detesting such a bad office as unmeet for a minister of the word, nay, altogether unbeseeming a faithful Christian.[8] If any man will say, as this archbishop, that a subject ought not to suppose that his prelate will command him any unlawful thing, but should repose himself in the good discretion and upright dealing of his Ordinary, without further answer, let the subtle practice of this one prelate, and the cruel and the accursed dealings of that barbarous Bishop Longland, stand at this present for a sufficient caveat to every man that shall depose, to take heed how he give overmuch credit to such glossing and deceivable speeches, lest too late he find it true that "fair words make fools fain." Neither is this any sufficient allegation to say that the party deponent is no further bound to answer than the law requireth, how general soever his oath be; since it is false for the conscience of such a deponent to stand upon terms and questions, how far by law, and by what law he is bound to answer.

Will you hear also what that godly and blessed martyr, Master John Lambert, saith concerning the exacting of such kind of oaths, after he had acknowledged it lawful at the commandment of a judge to take an oath to say the truth, wishing the magistrates nevertheless to minister oaths with great discretion and good advisement, and exhorting them to forbear

8. Foxe. [ED.] *A. & M.*, III, 252–5.

and spare them in trifling causes and matters of no necessity, lest by too much haunt [i.e., use], first contempt, then perjury, do creep in. He proceedeth further to this effect. "This have I showed," saith he, "because it pitieth me to hear and see the contrary used in some of our nation, and such also as name themselves spiritual men, and should be head ministers of the church; who incontinently as any man cometh before them, anon they call for a book, and do move him to swear without any further respite, yea, and they will charge him by virtue of the contents of the evangely [i.e., gospel], to make true relation of all they shall demand him, he not knowing what they will demand, neither whether it be lawful to show them the truth of their demand, or no; for such things there be that are not lawful to be showed. As if I were accused of fornication and none could be found in me; or if they should require me to swear to betray another that I have known to offend in that vice, I suppose it were expedient to hold me still and not to follow their will; for it should be contrary to charity if I should so assent to betray them that I need not, and to whom, perhaps (though I have known them to offend, yet, trusting of their amendment) I have promised afore to keep their fault secret. Yea, moreover such judges sometimes not knowing by any due proof that such as have to do before them are culpable, will enforce them by an oath to detect themselves in opening before them their hearts. In this so doing, I cannot see that men need to condescend in their requests, for as it is in the law, 'Nemo tenetur prodere seipsum [No man is bound to betray himself].' And in another place of the law it is written, 'Cogitationis poenam nemo patiatur [No man should be punished for his thoughts].' To this agreeth the common proverb, 'Cogitationes libera sunt a vectigalibus (Thoughts be free from toll).' " [9]

By which wise speech of this good man we may see condemned, and that for just cause and upon sound reasons, the indiscreet and unlawful enforcing of this kind of oath, serving to no good, nay rather to bad ends and purposes. We read also how Bonner, that infamous bloodsucker unworthy the name of a bishop, hunting (as the wolf for his prey) after matter of accusation, among many other his mischievous and detestable facts, offered also this oath ex officio unto the fellow prisoners of that holy and worthy martyr Master Philpot, saying after the rash and indiscreet manner before remembered, "Hold them a book. You shall swear by the contents of that book that you shall (all manner of affection laid apart) say the truth of all such articles as you shall be demanded concern-

9. [ED.] Foxe, A. & M., V, 184, 221, 817.

ing this man here present" (meaning Master Philpot).[10] But those wise and godly prisoners, well knowing and considering how they ought to take an oath, answered to this unjust request that they would not swear except they first knew whereunto. And being thereupon offered an oath, and that with threats of excommunication, to answer the articles propounded against themselves, refused it also, saying that they would not accuse themselves.

So that we see plainly by these examples, as also by that ancient and godly writing entitled *The Prayer and Complaint of the Ploughman*,[11] that this kind of general oath and examinations *ex officio mero* were not the first misliked by Jesuits and seminary priests, and from them derived to others that mislike government and would bring the church to an anarchy, as the world hath been borne in hand, but by true Christians, holy, learned and religious men, and that for good causes and considerations why they should so do.

And I should much marvel were it not that the world hath ever been set in wickedness, how any that profess the holy name and title of Christianity durst at any time put in practice within this realm or elsewhere, so profane and more than heathenish manner of inquisition, not only repugnant to God and Christian religion, but contrary also to the rules and canons of the antichristian church of Rome. Which laws (if I be not deceived) are more just and less unjust a great deal, than such as have taken upon them to judge by color of the same. So that in a sort it may be verified of them which was sometimes spoken of the people of Athens, that having just and good laws, they nevertheless behaved themselves as bad and dishonest men. For it is said by some of their canonists, "*Procedere ex officio mero*, [. . .] *est quando iudex a seipso et ex* [*suo*] *officio assumit informationes contra delinquentem, et contra eum procedit, et hoc est, quod dicitur procedere per viam inquisitionis:* [. . .] *Et* [*sic*] *recte loquendo, inquirere contra aliquem, non est ei transferre* [*tranmittere*] *Inquisitionem, sed* [*est*] *recipere testes, seu informationes contra eum* [To proceed *ex officio mero* is when the judge, by himself, and by virtue of his office, receives information against an offender, and takes action against him, and this it is that is called 'to proceed by way of inquisition': . . . And thus, correctly speaking, to make an inquisition against anyone is not to transfer the inquisition to him, but it is to receive witnesses, or

10. [ED.] Foxe, *A. & M.*, VII, 646.
11. [ED.] Foxe, *A. & M.*, II, 737; the passage referred to is "maken us accusen our selfe."

information, against him]." And moreover, *"Formare inquisitionem contra aliquem,* [. . .] *est facere processum informativum assumendo informationes et indicia contra eum super aliquo delicto* [To form an inquisition against anyone . . . is to institute an informative action by receiving information and accusations against him concerning some crime]." [12] So that to proceed by inquisition is not to make the party by oath or examination to be his own accuser, but to accept and receive information and witnesses against him.

And in what sort and manner the proceeding ought to be is also declared to this effect: "[. . .] *Iudex nunquam debet* [. . .] *procedere ex officio, et sic per viam inquisitionis, nisi aliquod praecedat quod aperiat viam inquisitioni scilicet, vel diffamatio, vel querela partis, vel denunciatio, vel huiusmodi, aliter processus erit* [*esset*] *ipso jure nullus* [. . .] *neque in hoc intenduntur* [*attenduntur*] *notificationes factae extrajudicialiter, neque illae quae fiunt incerto autore, et suppresso nomino notificantis* [. . . The judge ought never . . . to proceed *ex officio*, and thus by way of inquisition, unless something precedes which clearly points to [i.e., calls for] the way of inquisition, such as either defamation, or complaint of parties, or accusation, or suchlike, otherwise the action would be null by this very law, . . . neither in that which is threatened by notifications made extra-judicially, nor by those made by an author uncertain and with the name of the informer concealed]." [13] By which words manifestly appeareth that no judge ecclesiastical ought to proceed by way of inquisition, except there precede a defamation of the party complaint, or information against him. Intelligence of faults and offences out of course of judgment, or by uncertain author or suppressed name, is wholly by the law rejected, but by the [present] executors thereof altogether admitted.

Another also thereunto agreeing, saith: That the inquisition is not orderly done but where *"infamia praecedat, vel talia* [*alia*] *judicia sufficientia quae probentur per testes idoneos* [ill fame precedes, or such sufficient considerations which are proved by competent witnesses]." [14] And to prove the fame or infamy, there is required *"testes multi* [many witnesses]," the reason, *"quia dicta paucorum non infamant* [because the statements of a few do not constitute ill fame]." Secondly, they must be *"graves et honesti, non malevoli, nec inimici partis* [credible and honor-

12. Julius Clarus. [ED.] *Sententiarum receptarum, Lib. V, in quo judicii criminalis tractatus* . . . (Venice, 1595), fol. 62 verso col. A, 63 recto col. A.

13. Clarus. [ED.] *Sententiarum,* fol. 68 recto.

14. Joannes Petrus de Ferrariis. [ED.] *Practica judicialis* (Venice, 1492): "Forma inquisitionis et fama publica," fol. V2 recto, V5.

able, not spiteful, nor enemies to the party]." Thirdly, they must be such as are conversant in the place where the party hath lived, whereby they may be acquainted with the order and manner of his life and conversation, whereupon chiefly riseth the true judgment of his good or evil fame. Fourthly, those witnesses ought to be received judicially. Fifthly, they must be deposed. And sixthly, they are to render a wise and sufficient cause of their knowledge of the infamy. The judge in no cause (if he would of his own knowledge say the party is infamous) is to be received or believed; the reason is, for that the law will "*quod secundum acta et probata justitia ministrerur* [that justice be rendered according to things done and proved]." And the ground and foundation of the inquisition must not be extorted or wrested from the party, but lawfully proved as aforesaid by sufficient witnesses. Notwithstanding all which laws, what contrary courses have been practiced by Ordinaries and clergymen, many have felt, and every man knoweth too well. So that concerning their judicial courts and consistories, the saying of the poet is verified, "Piety lay vanquished, and the maiden Astraea, last of the immortals, abandoned the blood-soaked earth." [15]

But since that more than two quaternions of learned canonists have of late taken the pains to set down the undoubted grounds of the law ecclesiastical (as they say) according to which the proceedings have been used time out of mind in all the courts ecclesiastical of this realm, and all other proceedings have been at all times reformable by appellations, let us hear also what they say concerning this matter.[16]

These doctors first grant it to be good and sound law that no man may be urged to betray himself in hidden and secret crimes, or simply therein to accuse himself. They confess further that if any man besides the Ordinary will prosecute in their courts, making himself party to prove a crime whereof there is suspicion, the party convented in that case, albeit he must answer on his oath to other articles not principally touching the very crime objected, is not bound by law to answer upon oath any articles of the very crime itself. Nevertheless, say they, when by circumstances once known abroad secret crimes are become vehemently to be suspected and offensive to the well-disposed and dangerous to be suffered, then are they meet by inquiry and all good means to be discovered, to the

---

15. [ED.] Ovid, *Metamorphoses*, 1:150 (English translation by F. J. Miller, Loeb Classics, 1916).

16. [ED.] For the report of nine canonists in support of Whitgift's policy, see John Strype, *Life and Acts of John Whitgift . . .* (Oxford, 1822), III, 232–5.

end they may be reformed and the party delinquent brought to penitency and others discouraged to commit the like.

The ways and means how suspicion and fame of crimes come to the Ordinary's ears, they say are these: many bruits of credible persons called in the law *clamosa insinuatio* [i.e., scandal], and presentments of church-wardens and sidemen: which presentments if they be not direct, through ignorance of the presenters, or insufficient in the law to prove a fame (yet some scandal thereupon growing) how little by like [i.e., probably] is not respected, the Ordinary by law ecclesiastical and good discretion, may examine other witnesses, being neighbors, warning the party suspected to be present. The fame once proved (say they) or the first presentment sufficient, then the Ordinary, of duty and for the public trust reposed in him, is to proceed against the infamed although no other man will, which by law is termed proceeding by inquiry, especially *ex officio*. They add a reason for confirmation, "*Ne maleficia remaneant impunita, utque provincia purgetur malis hominibus* [Lest evildoers remain unpunished, and in order to purge the provinces of evil men]."

And in this sort, if the Ordinary proceed *ex officio* and the party deny the crime objected, then by law he is enjoined his purgation. At which time of purgation (say they) he must directly answer in clearing or convincing himself "*de veritate vel falsitate ipsius criminis objecti* [of the truth or falsity of the very crime itself of which he is accused]," and his compurgators are to swear *de credulitate* [according to their belief], (weighing his fear of God and conversation of former times) that they believe he hath taken a true oath, which if they all do, then he is held clear or dismissed. But if he fail in his purgation, then *fictione juris* [the law assumes], he is taken to be guilty and to be reformed.

They show likewise a reason of diversity between the proceeding in the case *ex officio*, and that which is by suit of the party, that is, "*Licet nemo tenetur seipsum prodere, tamen proditus per famam tenetur seipsum ostendere utrum possit suam innocentiam ostendere, et seipsum purgare* [Although no one is bound to betray himself, nevertheless, when he has been accused by common fame he is bound to show whether he is able to prove his innocence and to purge himself]." And a reason of that reason is added, because penances enjoined by the Ordinary are not taken in law to be *poenae* [penalties] but *medicinae* [medicines], or tending to the reformation of the delinquent, the example of others, and satisfaction of the church offended. And so they conclude upon all their reasons that the suspected are not to make scruple to discover themselves after fame [i.e., are not to quibble when accused by common fame].

This being the true and only course of proceeding by Ordinaries and ecclesiastical judges in causes criminal, where is then become [i.e., whence has come] the exacting of those general oaths so often used to answer all interrogatories that shall be ministered, and that before notice or understanding (for the most part) of the crime objected, and the extorting by oath of the ground and foundation of the inquisition from the party convented. Doth it not appear by the resolution of these learned men that the same have no good or sufficient warrant by the law, how long or much soever by color and pretence of law and justice they have been practiced or imposed?

And as concerning their proceedings *ex officio* to forced purgations approved (as they seem to affirm) both by the law ecclesiastical and title of prescription, if we look well thereto and take good view thereof, what other thing shall we find than hard and unjust dealing towards men, and great abuse of the name and majesty of almighty God, cloaked and shadowed nevertheless under the glorious and painted glosses of beautiful shows and feigned pretences of purging of provinces, reformation of delinquents, necessary examples, discharge of public trust and satisfaction of the offended church — honest and honorable terms indeed but ill applied to this purpose.

For first, as concerning the injustice offered unto men, if it be a true and sound principle or maxim in law, not denied by themselves, that "*nemo tenetur seipsum prodere* [no one is bound to betray himself]," where should the benefit thereof be had or taken but in their courts and consistories? But if it should be granted that this rule faileth where a man is "*proditus per famam* [accused by common fame]," doth not that (as a gloss [i.e., commentary] confounding the text) wholly and altogether destroy that rule or principle, except for some relief this narrow shift may be used, [namely,] that the fame nevertheless standeth in force where any other than the Ordinary assumeth to prove that crime?

But in this case also they have so weakened this maxim that scarcely will it stand for a minima, affirming (if I mistake them not) that the infamed must answer on his oath to other articles, not principally touching the very crimes objected. For what should be meant by other articles, but such as concern circumstances and inducements to the crime? And is not this to go like the crab obliquely, and to proceed the same way, although not to tread the direct steps? But why there should be any distance between the suit or instance of the party, and the proceeding *ex officio*, I know not the reason. Alleged, therefore, is this: penances enjoined by Ordinaries are not taken to be *poenae* [penalties] but *medicinae* [medicines]. What their law presumeth is not sufficient reason to prove their law reasonable, but what they are in deed, is to be weighed. And shall they be medicines only where proceeding is *ex officio?* Or tend they in that case alone to the reformation of the delinquent, the example of others, and satisfaction of the church? May not all this as well be verified where the crime is complained of, and punished at the instance of the party? And shall not penance although it be but the standing in a sheet, as well as the standing on the pillory, respect of public shame and reproach (grievous and odious unto all men) be accounted for a punishment? True it is, all corrections are, or should be medicines for the amendment of manners. But doth it therefore follow that the same be no pains or punishments?

As concerning the offence to God by the abuse of his name and majesty, have we not learned before that to offer an oath unto persons defamed in life and conversation, and especially concerning the matter of his own corrupt life, argueth a lightness and want to good discretion in the magistrate who thereby wittingly doth minister an occasion of perjury? And are not all those on whom these purgations are imposed, men greatly defamed and vehemently suspected of the crimes objected? For as these doctors affirm the law, when secret crimes by circumstances known abroad are become vehemently suspected, offensive and dangerous, then are they first inquired of. The proceeding also by inquisition beginning upon fame, proved not slenderly, but by presentment upon oath, or by deposed witnesses, being many, honest, void of malice, neighbors to the party, and rendering a wise and sufficient reason of their knowledge concerning the same. And how then may a judge in such a case with any good conscience to Godward or to the satisfaction of his church, force an oath upon such a one for the final end of the cause? Is not the peril and presumption of perjury very great and pregnant? Know we not that all, or the most part of men, liking the counsel, "The shame is greater than the danger of vice," will rather hazard their souls than put their bodies to shame and reproach, presume the law never so much that after fame they should not make scruple to discover themselves. If the like course of purgation should be used at the common law upon indictments of felony or other criminal causes, what doubt were to be made but that perjury in short time would overflow the whole land? And shall we not think that the same is not frequent in these kinds of purgations? But, say they, the party is not trusted alone, he bringeth with him his many compurgators who depose also *de credulitate* [according to their belief], weighing his fear of God and former conversation. Be it so, the matter thereby is no whit amended but rather made worse and impaired. For what do those compurgators but, by lending their oaths, justify in effect him to be honest whom fame and the former deponents have proved to be dishonest, and very near (the circumstances considered) convinced [i.e., convicted] of the crime objected. Why rather do not these Ordinaries which challenge and assume to themselves the goodly name and title of spiritual men, if they respect the honor of God and regard the souls of men, free the people from these pernicious oaths and deadly purgations, and proceed to their sentence of condemnation, not by feigned offices and fictions of law, but by good proof and lawful witnesses, and again, absolve the party defamed where such sufficient proof doth fail them? Why should they think much [i.e., hesitate] to offer to the laity in their ecclesiastical courts, the like good measure and upright and sincere justice that they themselves find and obtain in the courts temporal of this realm, where neither they, nor any other, are forced *ex officio judicis* [by virtue of the judge's office], by straining oaths and strong purgations not healthful, but hurtful, to betray or accuse themselves? Perhaps this counsel would be received if it were as profitable, as [it is] good and honest. But according to the proverb, "when gold speaks, it is well to be silent." For it is no small gain and lucre that daily riseth and accrueth to the clergy and courts ecclesiastical, by slander, fame, rumor and false report; in respect whereof these fair names of "office" and "discharge of public duty" are so cunningly pretexted, and these poisoning purgations so dangerously given for preservatives.

A matter being since well known unto the world, and by the princes of Germany in the Council of Nuremberg, among many other abuses and corruptions most monstrous, complained of to this effect: "It happeneth oftentimes," say they, "that men and women through sinister and false reports and slanders are brought before the official or ecclesiastical judge as men guilty, and shall not be declared innocent before they have cleared themselves by an oath, which purgation so made they are restored to their former estimation. And albeit the damages and costs ought to be repaid unto such as be so falsely accused, yet are the innocents themselves forced to pay two gilders and a quarter for their letters of absolution. And this is the cause why the officials and other ecclesiastical judges do so greatly [i.e., ? greedily?] follow the action of such unlawful, false and slanderous accusations, challenging the hearing thereof only to themselves. Which thing no doubt," say they, "redowndeth to the great and most singular hurt and detriment of all men. For oftentimes it happeneth that women falling together in contention, through anger, hatred or some other affection, do speak evil of or slander one another, and outrage so much, that the one oftentimes accuseth the other, either of adultery or witchery; which being brought before the official, she which through anger had so slandered the other is forced by an oath to excuse and purge herself, that whatsoever injurious or slanderous words she had spoken came not of any deliberate purpose or intent but through wrath and displeasure. In like manner, the other which is accused either of adultery or sorcery is commanded by an oath to declare her innocency; so that it is evident unto all men, that in such cases, whether they be guilty or not guilty, they must swear if they will keep their good name and fame. Whereby not only the unlawful lucre of gain and money is sought, but also willful perjury forced, etc." [17] Thus these honorable persons, you see, have made it clear what is chiefly intended by these canonical purgations, pretend the clergy whatsoever they will, and how such forced oaths are not only offensive unto God but injurious also unto men. Therefore, leaving these men to whom the favor of gain is so sweet, together with their famous law, the matter which we endeavor to prove is that those general oaths, and oaths *ex officio*, publicly heretofore much practiced by Ordinaries and ecclesiastical judges, are altogether unlawful (whether by the canonical sanctions or law canon, I care not) but by the laws of God and of this realm. And therefore since we have sufficiently spoken of the law of God, now lest peradventure it may be said that such Catholic oaths are warranted by the common laws or statutes of this realm, or by the use and practice of some courts of justice, therein let us consider hereof also, and deliver both our laws and the justice of our land from so foul a slander.

Concerning the common laws of this realm, we may find an oath diversely allowed of and used in causes of suit judicially depending. But such a general oath, or suchlike *ex officio*, at any time either offered by magistrate, or taken or made by subject of this land by authority of the common law, can never be proved, I am sure, either by good record or sound report of the same. Long it were and tedious, to remember the particular cases when and where an oath is required by the laws and statutes of this realm. But this may be said in general, and that truly, to the great

17. [ED.] Foxe, *A. & M.*, IV, 311-12, from the "Gravamina" of 1522.

honor and high commendations of our government, that the same common laws have not imposed or appointed an oath to be used otherwise than according to the right institution thereof and the godly rules before remembered. Yea, moreover this may truly be affirmed, that the common law of this kingdom, yea the commonwealth itself, hath ever rejected and impugned as a thing unlawful and injurious, this manner of swearing whereof we now entreat, as by that we shall hereafter say, may evidently appear.

Touching the oaths imposed or admitted at the common law by judges or magistrates (for of them only we are to speak), first, it is used as by good reason in all courts of justice established for determination of causes in suit or controversy, either between the prince and subject, or the subjects themselves, to require an oath of all such as are called or produced to testify their knowledge concerning the matter or point in issue, whereby the truth may appear and the cause receive an end.

The defendant also in divers personal actions voluntarily offering an oath for his clear discharge, is admitted by course of the law thereunto, which manner of proceeding is termed "the doing of his law," and seemeth to have been grounded upon the judicials before rehearsed, given by God unto his people the Irsaelites, as by the observation of the cases hereafter mentioned may be gathered. For in an action of debt brought for money due by reason of some simple contract, or in an action of detinue of goods and chattels, the oath of the defendant in the one case, that he oweth not the money, and in the other, that he detaineth not the things required, is allowed for a final end and bar unto the pleadant. For in the former case the repayment of the money may be private and in secret, and so in the other the delivery of the goods. And although the bailment and delivery of the pleadant's goods to the defendant were by the hands of a third person or testified by writing, yet these are no causes to put the defendant from his oath or wager of his law, forasmuch as the answer is not to the bailment or delivery, but to the detainer or withholding. And in the action of debt, although the defendant either hanging the action or otherwise, had confessed the contract, yet is he to be admitted to his law or oath, insomuch as the point in suit is not the contract but the debt.[18]

But in an action of accompt [i.e., account], supposing the receipt by the hands of a stranger or third person, the law is otherwise. For here the

18. 7 Hen. 4, fol. 7. [ED.: Mich. Y.B. (*S.T.C.*, 9608), fol. 7 no. 38]; 9 Edw. 4, fol. 24. [ED.: ? No. 89, fol. 276a, A. Fitzherbert, *La graunde abridgement* (1565; *S.T.C.*, 10956), Part I].

thing delivered is not precisely in demand, but an accompt only thereof required. And the receipt being the cause of action to which a third person is privy as a witness the oath of the defendant (as a thing not of necessity) is rejected. For that reason was the defendant put from his wager of law. Anno 31 Edw. I, where the case was this: An action of detinue was brought for a chalice, the defendant pleaded how the pleadant delivered the same in gage [i.e., in pawn] for six marks, and that upon the repayment thereof he was ready to deliver the chalice. The pleadant replying that he had repaid the money by the hands of one such [i.e., a third party]. The defendant offering his oath to the contrary, was not admitted thereunto, inasmuch as there was a witness of the repayment [i.e., the third party] by whose testimony the truth might be known.[19]

And as the common law is thus on the part of the defendant, so is it likewise for the pleadant, coming as it were in place of a defendant. Therefore Anno 21 Edw. III, fol. 49,[20] the case was that the defendant upon his accompt would have discharged himself by certain tallies, and so by his oath continued the charge against the defendant. But Anno 29 Edw. III, the defendant in accompt alleged before the auditors payment to the pleadant by the hands of another, and the pleadant offering his oath that he had not received the money was in respect of the third person denied to wage his law.[21] And the good discretion and consideration which the law useth in the allowing and admitting of wager of law is not to be forgotten. Which law (lest men of light credit or doubtful faith should take an oath) suffereth no man to do his law, but such only as is able to bring with him eleven other persons of ripe years and of good name to depose with him, that they think he sweareth truly.

Neither are the one parties or the other in any personal action by the courses of the common law suffered to clear themselves by their oaths where they are charged, either by their lawful writing or matter of record, for that these are testimonies and proofs sufficient whereunto faith and credit ought to be given. Much more might be said in such particulars. But these may suffice to show how in suits for goods, chattels, debts or personal duties, the common laws of this realm admit no idle, vain, suspicious or unnecessary oaths, neither compel any man to swear concerning them, but upon cause allow of the pl. [?] and deserts [i.e., ?the pleadant's?] voluntary and necessary oath for an end of the controversy.

19. 31 Edw. 1. [ED.] Not verified.
20. 21 Edw. 3, fol. 49. [ED.] Y.B. (S.T.C., 9564), fol. 49a–b.
21. 29 Edw. 3. [ED.] Y.B. (S.T.C., 9572), fol. xx.

As touching the causes and controversies for lands and inheritances depending in suit, either in admitting or requiring of oaths, some few cases there be. Nevertheless where an oath for them is used, as if a *Praecipe quod reddat* [22] be brought of land wherein the tenant was not lawfully summoned, he may upon return of the process of *grand cape* [23] wage his law for non-summons, and thereby (as not well executed) abate the demandant's writ. In which case an oath seemeth rightly to be admitted, since the cause is both of weight and necessity to the tenant, this being the only way to relieve him against the untrue return of the sheriff whereby his land, for want of appearance was to be recovered against him. For as the law seemeth [i.e., as it seemeth to the law] to weigh a trial of this summons by twelve men, is not allowable. And although it may be said that the tenant upon his loss by default might have a writ of deceit, and recover again his land, yet that oftentimes falleth out to be a faint remedy, the death of such as were returned summoners depriving [i.e., could deprive] him of that advantage.[24]

In the case also of deceit upon a recovery by default, the summoners, viewers and purveyors are judicially examined by oath, whether they have duly, according to the laws of the land, executed and performed that which appertaineth unto them, who in this case are used but as witnesses, to search and sift out by them the good or evil dealing of the sheriff, by whom the execution of writ and process was committed. In like manner, if the plaint[iff] in a *scire facias*,[25] recover by default, and the defendant bring this action of deceit against the sheriff, the bailiff and the party that sued execution of the land, process shall be awarded against the supposed garnishers; and upon their appearance they shall be examined (and that by oath) concerning the manner of the garnishment, and the same being found insufficient, the plaintiff shall be restored to his land with the profits mean [i.e., the usual or average profits].

We may find also in such real actions an oath required in another manner, but yet to good purpose, that is, to take away unnecessary delays of justice. For if the tenant in a *praecipe* of land [26] will cast an "essoyne of

---

22. [ED.] An action to regain land after end of a lease, or other contract for its use by others.

23. [ED.] Legal writ relative to lands and tenements.

24. 33 Hen. 6. [ED.: Not found]; 41 Edw. 3. [ED.: No. 2, fol. 232b, R. Brook, *La graunde abridgement* (1576; S.T.C., 3828); or, better, Fitzherbert (S.T.C., 10956), Part I, fol. 293a, no. 32].

25. [ED.] Judicial writ to call a man to show cause.

26. [ED.] See note 22, above.

the king's service," [27] the essoygner shall swear, and that directly, the same to be no feigned excuse, otherwise the essoyne shall not be allowed. Some few other particular cases of like nature may peradventure be showed where an oath is admitted or required in these real actions, but none I am sure, tending to any such purpose as these oaths commanded and enforced *ex officio*.

In criminal causes and suits, whereby either the loss of life, liberty, member of the body, or good name may ensue (which among worldly things are most dear and precious unto men), the common laws of this land have wholly forborne (and that for just respects) to urge or impose an oath upon the accused. For in wisdom it was foreseen that the frailty of man for the safety of life, the preservation of liberty, credit and estimation would not spare to profane even that which is most holy, and by committing sinful perjury cast both soul and body into eternal perdition.

This knew the subtle serpent, our adversary, full well in general, although he were deceived in the particular, whenas he said unto God concerning the holy man Job: "Skin for skin, and whatsoever a man hath, will he give for himself and for his life, but stretch out thy hand," saith Satan, "and touch his bones and his flesh, and see if he will not then blaspheme thee to thy face" (Job 2:4–5).

Moreover, every wise magistrate may well conceive upon how weak and feeble a foundation he shall ground his sentence, trusting to such an oath, when beforehand the suspicion and presumption of perjury is so pregnant. Therefore in causes capital or otherwise criminal, these our laws neither urge by oath, nor force by torment, any man to accuse or excuse himself. But [they] reject the oath as unbeseeming a well governed state or commonwealth. And [they] condemn the torture as a thing most cruel and barbarous, whereof although they need no other proof than the daily practice and proceedings against parties suspected of such offences, yet concerning the inquisitions by torture, we may see the same affirmed by that learned judge Master Fortescue in his commentaries of the policy of this kingdom.[28] And for the other there are sufficient authorities in the reports of the laws themselves. Therefore in the Book of Assizes it appeareth that divers jurors were challenged as less indifferent, some for matters that sounded to their reproach and dishonesty, as that corruptly

27. [ED.] An excuse for non-appearance in court because one is necessarily absent in the service of the king.

28. John Fortescue. [ED.] *De laudibus legum Angliae*, edited with English translation, by S. B. Chrimes (London, 1942), chap. XXII.

they had taken money of one of the parties in the suit. Whereupon it was ordered by the justices that such as were challenged for causes not dishonest should be sworn to declare the truth, the other[s] for the reason aforesaid not to be examined at all, but the challenge to be tried without their oath. The same law is again reported unto us, Anno 49 Edw. III, fol. 1.[29] Upon the like reason is the resolution of the Chief Justices, and of the Judges Saunders and Whiddon, that if a bill of perjury committed in the Chancery, against the form of the statute made in the fifth year of her Majesty's reign, were exhibited in the same court, that the defendant should not be compelled to make answer upon his oath either to bill or interrogatories, but that the parties ought to descend to issue, and the trial to be had by jury in the King's Bench.[30]

I shall not need to spend time in declaring [how], after the parties in suit have joined issue [in] trial by jury, how many ways an oath is used about the trial of such matters of fact, as the oath of jurors themselves, and of their triers upon challenge, or to speak anything of the oath to be ministered unto such as require the surety of peace, neither to discourse of the doing of homage or fealty by the tenant to the lord, since these and such like are well known to every one, although but of mean judgment, to be necessarily used for the better administration of justice and assurance of duties, making nothing at all for those fantastical and officious oaths and examinations proceeding rather *ab officio*,[31] the verb, than *ex officio*, the noun.

Neither is it necessary to set forth at large where and in what particular cases oaths are appointed by acts of Parliament of this realm, as to remember the divers oaths of bishops, counsellors, judges, magistrates, officers and ministers of law and justice, the oath ordained for the maintenance of the supremacy royal, and abolishing of foreign jurisdiction, the power of examination by oath by the statute of Anno 5 Hen. IV, cap. 3, 6, 8, and many others, for that by perusal of the statutes the same may (unto him that will search) easily appear. Upon consideration of all which acts of Parliament being in force, it may truly be affirmed that

29. 49 Edw. 3, fol. 1. [ED.] *Le liver des assises* (1580; S.T.C., 9601), no. A, fol. ccxvi recto.

30. 12 Eliz. [ED.] J. Dyer, *Cy ensuont ascuns novel cases* (1585; S.T.C., 7388), fol. 288 recto.

31. [ED.] The verb "officio" = "to come between"; in classical Latin, usually = "to obstruct," but in later, ecclesiastical Latin, = "to come between God and man," and so, "to minister as a priest": i.e., "to officiate." The preposition "ab" = "away from." Morice's pun meant, "To pervert his religious office, rather than to function by virtue of it."

there is not so much as a bare show or shadow of matter to give credit or allowance to these infinite wrested and extorted oaths *ex officio.*

But it may be that some man in the defense of the cause, and for allowance of those oaths will allege the twice damned and repealed statute made upon the sinister suggestion of the clergy, Anno 2 Hen. IV, cap. 15, which bloody and broiling law gave authority to diocesans to cause the persons defamed, or evidently suspected of supposed heresy, to be arrested, and under safe custody to be detained in their prisons till they of the articles laid to their charge did canonically purge themselves, or else abjure it according to the laws of the church, and did appoint the proceeding and determination of the cause against the arrested to be according to the effect of the law and canonical decrees.[32] For answer whereunto I say that although the sword by that statute law was committed into the hands of mad men and the silly [i.e., defenseless] lambs delivered over to the greedy and devouring wolves, yet doth it not appear by any apparent or express words of that law that any authority was thereby given or meant to be given to Ordinaries or judges ecclesiastical to impose any such general oath, or otherwise to compel by oath the prisoner to become his own accuser, for that (and especially in cases of life and death) had been directly against the laws and justice of this land. But if it be alleged that the same was *tacite* [i.e., tacitly] and *inclusive* [i.e., by inference] allowed by those words of "canonical sanctions" or "decrees," and that there be any such, yet the same decree, being against the laws and decrees of God as before is proved, that statute was therein no binding law, neither gave sufficient warrant to put in execution any such corrupt course of proceeding, since all laws and ordinances of man whatsoever, being repugnant to the laws of God, are merely void and of none effect, as the learned Saint German in his book of *Doctor and Student* hath well observed, where he saith "that every man's law must be consonant to the law of God."[33] And therefore the laws of princes, the commandments of prelates, the statutes of communalties, nay, yet the ordinances of the church, is [i.e., are] not righteous or obligatory except it [i.e., they] be consonant and agreeable to the law of God.

But as concerning that statute, will you hear what is declared by Parliament, Anno 23 Hen. VIII, cap. 14. The subjects of this realm at that

32. [ED.] 2 Hen. 4, cap. 15, *De haeretico comburendo,* for the burning of heretics, A.D. 1401, against the Lollards.

33. Christopher St. German. [ED.] *Dialogue between a doctor . . . and a student . . .* (1593; *S.T.C.,* 21575), fol. 7 verso.

time lamentably show unto their sovereign lord and king how that statute was impetrate and obtained (I use the words of the law) by the suggestion of the clergy of this realm, not declaring or defining any certain cases of heresy; that those words "canonical sanctions" or "decrees" were so general, that uneath [i.e., with difficulty] the most expert and best learned men of the realm (diligently lying in wait upon himself) could eschew and avoid the penalty and danger of that Act. And "canonical sanctions," if he should be examined upon such captious interrogatories (note, I pray you) as is, and hath been accustomed to be, ministered by the Ordinaries of the realm in cases where they will suspect any person of heresy, they [i.e., Parliament] moreover affirm that it standeth not with the right order of justice nor good equity, that any person should be convicted and put to the loss of his life, good name or goods, unless it were by due accusation and witness, or by presentment, verdict, confession or process of outlawry; declaring moreover that by the laws of the realm for treasons committed to the peril of the king's most royal majesty, upon whose surety dependeth the wealth of the whole realm, no person can, nay may, be put to death but by presentment, verdict or process of outlawry; and therefore [the Commons affirm it is] not reasonable that any Ordinary, by any suspicion conceived of his own fantasy, without due accusation or presentment, should put any subject of this realm in the infamy or slander of heresy, to the peril of life, loss of name and goods. They further show that there may be heresies, and pains and punishments declared and ordained, in and by the canonical sanctions, and by the laws and ordinances made by the popes and bishops of Rome and by their authorities, for holding, doing, preaching or speaking of things contrary to the said canonical sanctions, laws and ordinances which be but human, mere [i.e., wholly] repugnant and contrarious to the prerogative of the king's imperial crown, regal jurisdiction, laws, statutes and ordinances of the realm; by reason whereof the people of the same, for observing, maintaining, defending and due executing of the king's laws, statutes and prerogative royal, by authority of that Act, may be brought into slander of heresy to their great infamy and danger and peril of their lives.

So we see first how the crafty and subtle clergymen were the procurers of that statute law [2 Hen. IV, cap. 15 against heresy], to the end that they might execute their cruelty, and how under cloaked and covert terms of "canonical sanctions" they unjustly usurped jurisdiction over the people, ministering unto them captious and snarling interrogatories, and (as it should seem by the histories) upon oath, contrary to the true meaning of the law and lawmakers, and against the right order of justice and all good equity; impugning thereby the royal prerogative, the imperial crown, the princely scepter, laws and policy of this kingdom. In consideration whereof and to take from them all color of law positive of this realm, that statute was then repealed, and a new form of inquiry of heresy by indictment, presentment or due accusation by two lawful witnesses at the least, was established [by 25 Hen. VIII, cap. 14].

And it is further to be noted, that although the statute made Anno 31 Hen. VIII, cap. 14, commonly called the statute of Six Articles, was a very strait, sore, extreme and terrible act, as the statute of the repeal thereof [1 Edw. VI, cap. 12] speaketh, yet find we not by that law or any other, these general oaths or examinations by oath *ex officio* of persons suspected or accused for heresy or other crime ecclesiastical to be enacted or allowed of. But rather [we find that] by the courses and forms of inquiry and trial otherwise prescribed in this and other statutes, the same is rejected and disallowed wholly, as unjust and full of iniquity. For by this statute of Six Articles, commissions are appointed to be directed to the archbishop or bishop of the diocese and to his chancellor or commissary and such other as the king should appoint, giving them power to take information and accusation (not by oath of the party convented) but by the oaths and depositions of two able and lawful persons at the least, or to inquire by the oaths of twelve men; giving also to the ordinaries power and authority to inquire in their visitations and synods, and to take accusations and informations as in form aforesaid, and not otherwise. The manner also of process against the persons indicted, accused or presented is there prescribed. And the form of proceeding upon appearance of the party [is] appointed to be not according to those unjust examinations by oath *ex officio*, but according to the laws of the realm and the effect of that Act.

And although at that time this statute law [i.e., the Six Articles] seemed just and equal as concerning the manner of inquiry and trial, yet time (disclosing all things) made it appear that the same was not false [?was not safe?], in respect that divers secret and untrue accusations and presentments might be, and by all likelihood were, maliciously conspired; and therefore it was enacted, Anno 35 Hen. VIII, cap. 5, that no person should be arraigned or put to trial for or upon any accusation, information or presentment concerning any of the offences mentioned in the statute of Six Articles, but only upon such presentments and indictments as should be found and made by the oaths of twelve men or more, etc.

These things standing thus, how may any man justify or defend (much less practice) those general oaths or examinations by oath *ex officio* by any statute law of this realm, being by them not only rejected but utterly condemned as not standing with the right order of justice nor good equity, especially the statute made Anno 25 Hen. VIII, cap. 14 being in force, and limiting unto archbishops and bishops none other jurisdiction than such as they may use without offence to the prerogative royal and the laws and customs of this realm,[34] of which laws and customs the common law [?they assume?] is no part or portion? And as a well-willer, I would advise all Ordinaries and such as exercise ecclesiastical jurisdiction, especially having taken the oath ordained for the maintenance of the supremacy royal (wherein they swear to assist to their power and defend all jurisdictions, privileges, preeminences and authorities granted or belonging to the Queen's highness, her heirs and successors, or united and annexed to the imperial crown of this realm) to take heed that they attempt not to put in practice or exercise any such oaths or examinations *ex officio*, lest happily they be not only found thereby to be impugners of the royal prerogatives, but discredited farther by the breach of their oath.

If it be said (for what will not be moved for a defense) that the king heretofore gave in those commissions, besides the letter and meaning of the statute of Six Articles, power and authority by express words unto the commissioners ecclesiastical to examine by oath the persons accused or presented, as that is not likely, neither as I suppose can [it] be proved, so (admitting it were true, and that such kind of oaths were consonant to the law of God) yet were the same no sufficient or lawful justification; inasmuch as we have proved, and further shall prove, such examinations and inquiries upon oath to be injurious both to the prince and people of this realm, and to impugn our government and form of justice. In which cases the king's grant or commission is of no force in law. For as Bracton well hath written, "*Potestas principis juris est non injuriae, et cum ipse sit author juris non debet inde injuriarum nasci occasio unde jura nascuntur* [His power therefore is the power of justice, not of injustice; and since he himself is the author of justice, an occasion of injustice ought not to arise from the source whence justice originates]."[35]

That the king by his commission or grant, or otherwise than by Parlia-

---

34. [ED.] I.e., the "reactionary" Six Articles act did not throw out the repeal of the heresy laws.

35. Bracton. [ED.] *De legibus*, II, 174–5.

ment, may not change or alter the laws of this realm, nor the order, manner, or form of administration of justice, is rightly also noted unto us by that grave and learned judge, Master Fortescue, saying, *"Non potest rex angliae ad libitum suum leges mutare regni sui principatu, namque nedum regali sed et politico ipse suo populo dominatur* [For the king of England is not able to change the laws of his kingdom at pleasure, for he rules his people with a government not only regal but also political]."[36] And by the book also of Anno 11 Hen. IV, where it is agreed that neither the king by his grant nor the pope by his bulls (for all his triple crown) can change or alter the laws of the land. Whereunto concur divers other books of the report of the law.[37] Worthy also of remembrance is that saying of Justice Scroope, Anno 1 Edw. III, fol. 26. "If the king," saith he, "command anything impossible, that which the law will in the case must be done; if he command anything contrary to law, his justices ought not to do it."[38] Anno 42 Edw. III, there was a commission awarded out of the chancery to apprehend a certain subject of this realm and to seize his goods and chattels; no indictment, suit of party or other due process of law precedent; and the same was by the justices held to be altogether void, as a matter against the policy of the realm and manner of execution of justice.[39] Likewise it appeareth, in the same year, that a writ proceeding from the chancery to inquire of champerties, conspiracies, etc., whereby one of the king's subjects stood indicted, was by Justice Knevet upon the resolution of the rest of the judges damned and adjudged void in respect that such matters are not inquirable by writ, but by commission.[40]

But it will be said of some (I verily suppose) that although neither the common laws nor statutes of this realm nor the king's commission, do or can warrant such manner of oath and examinations *ex officio*, yet the public practice and use of the honorable Courts of Star Chamber and Chancery, the one in causes criminal, the other in suits civil of equity and conscience, concurring in one form of taking answers and examinations by oath, do fortify and confirm the thing which we impugn. Which

36. Fortescue. [ED.] *De laudibus*, IX.

37. 11 Hen. 4 [ED.] Y. B. (*S.T.C.*, 9608), fol. xxxvi verso, no. 67.

38. 1 Edw. 3, fol. 26. [ED.: Y.B. (*S.T.C.*, 9551), fol. 26b, no. 24]; 49 Edw. 3. [ED.: Y.B. (*S.T.C.*, 9601), fol. cccxxi verso no. 8?]; 36 Hen. 6. [ED.: Y.B. (*S.T.C.*, 9752), fol. ?xxvi recto, or ?xxix].

39. 42 Edw. 3. [ED.] Cap. 3: "No man shall be put to answer without presentment before justices, or matter of record, or by due process and writ original, according to the old law of the land."

40. Knevet. [ED.] Y.B. (*S.T.C.*, 9601), fol. cclviii recto.

speech, as it may seem at the first to give some color and show of credit to their cause, so upon consideration had and due comparing the one with the other, it will soon appear to be but a vanishing smoke and shadow void of substance. For first, if it should be granted that such kind of oaths and examinations were used in the Courts of Star Chamber and Chancery, yet would it not follow that the same might be practiced in the courts and consistories ecclesiastical, unless the like allowance thereto and consent of the whole realm might be proved also. And who knoweth not how weak a proof examples and precedents are where an express law or certain policy is to the contrary. Therefore it is well said in the civil law, "*Jus non ex regula sumatur, sed ex jure regula fiat* [The law arises not out of rules, but rules are formed out of the law]." [41] By better logic might they conclude thus: "All answers are made upon oath in the king's Courts of Star Chamber and Chancery, *ergo* the same course may be used in the courts of the King's Bench and Common Pleas," which nevertheless were an absurd conclusion.

It is very true indeed that these honorable Courts of Star Chamber and Chancery proceed not to the trial of causes by jury after the manner of the common laws of this realm, but give their judgments and definitive sentence upon the answer and examination of the defendant, affirmed by his corporal oath, and upon the depositions of witnesses. But who hath ever seen in these courts any subject of this land in a cause concerning himself, brought forth and compelled to depose or make answer upon his oath, no bill of complaint or information formerly exhibited against him? Nay, on the contrary, these courts, observing the due form of justice, enforce no man to answer but where he hath a known accuser and perfect understanding of the cause or crime objected, and therewithall is permitted to have a copy of the bill of complaint or information (being not *ore tenus* [by word of mouth merely]). And allowed, moreover, both time convenient and counsel learned, well to consider and advise of his oath and answer. And if his adversaries' complaint be either insufficient in form or matter, or such as the court hath no jurisdiction to determine, the defendant upon demurrer, without oath, is dismissed, and that with costs. And admit the accusation, such as every way is answerable, yet if the interrogatories ministered be impertinent to the matter of complaint, the defendant without offence to the court may refuse to make answer to the same.

What similitude or likeness then is there between the oaths and exami-

41. [ED.] *Corpus iuris civilis*, Dig. L, 17, #1.

nations used in these honorable Courts [of Star Chamber and Chancery] and those constrainers *ex officio*, since the former sort be orderly taken in courts of justice, the other without all course of judgment; the one where pl[ea] and complaint are manifest, the other where neither accuser nor matter of accusation do appear; the one oath made upon certain knowledge and good advisement, the other suddenly without all discretion upon uncertain demands; the one wisely restrained to certain limits and bounds, the other foolishly wandering at the doubtful will of a sly and subtle apposer [i.e., poser]? Upon the one, the deponent answereth to the accusation of his adversary; by the other, he is compelled oftentimes to be his own accuser and condemner. The one inquireth an answer to matter in fact, done either to the injury of some private person or hurt of the public state; the other constraineth the revealing of words, deeds and thoughts, though never offensive to any.

Then since it is apparent that these manner of oaths are altogether mere strangers to our policy, and not so much as once countenanced by any law, custom, statute or court of this realm, how then, and by whose means, hath this alien heretofore intruded as a troublesome guest into the house of the commonwealth? This partly as before hath been declared, with some grief of mind, by that godly servant of Christ, John Lambert, who noteth the papistical clergy and religious men of his time most irreligiously to have practiced the same.[42] And no doubt the prelates of former ages, feigning and pretending such oaths to be necessary for "the government of the church" and "to purge the province of evil men," as aforesaid, but in truth, finding it a fit instrument to maintain the Romish hierarchy and to tyrannize over the consciences of good men, most impiously violating the laws both of God and man, imposed this manner of corrupt oath upon the people; and no marvel, since there was no evil or mischief that could be devised, either against the prince, people or policy of this land, which these kind of our prelates have not attempted and put in practice. For first, disguising themselves under the visor and mask of hypocrisy and feigned holiness, and making merchandise of all things (even of heaven and hell), purchased and acquired in short time (such was the blind devotion of the superstitious laity) great and large seigniories, lands and possessions (the very mother and nurse of pride, presumption and vain pomp of this world), and not so satisfied, but insatiably and most ambitiously lusting after rule and dominion, spared not against their due allegiance to infest even the kings and princes of the land.

Let the contention and strife of Anselm, Archbishop of Canterbury

42. [ED.] See note 9, above.

with King Rufus, the manifold practices of Thomas Becket against King Henry II, the tragical life and pitiful end of King John (occasioned chiefly by the malicious means of the Archbishop Stephen Langton), the treason of Archbishop Arundell against his sovereign lord and king, Richard II, and the pride and insolency of Cardinal Wolsey against that renowned prince King Henry VIII, among others, be sufficient testimonies in this behalf.[43] And as these pontifical prelates with others more, puffed up in swelling pride and ambition, struck at the head, so the crew of that antichristian clergy ceased not from time to time to wrestle and make war even with the sinews and strength of the body politic of this realm (the laws, I mean, and customs of this kingdom, being the principal stay and stop to their insolent and ambitious attempts), endeavoring themselves to writhe out and exempt themselves from their due subjection to the same, sometimes again encroaching and usurping the right and jurisdiction of the king's courts, coveting to draw all causes into their costly and lingering consistories. And oftentimes bringing in (to the prejudice both of the prince and the people) foreign decrees and constitutions, with the corrupt canons and ceremonies of the accursed See of Rome. For proof whereof, let the particular examples hereafter mentioned serve as a few amongst many.

The pope (saith Polydore Virgil) made a law in the Council of Lyons that the clergy should not be taxed without his leave or commandment,[44] which law of immunity, although it were of no force to bind within this realm for that the same is not subject to any foreign made laws or constitutions not suffered by the king and voluntarily accepted and used by his people, as is expressly declared by the statute made Anno 25 Hen. VIII, cap. 21. Yet see the good disposition and obedience of the clergymen of this realm in the time of King Edward I, which churchmen with great obstinacy refused to pay the subsidy granted to the king. Robert, then Archbishop of Canterbury (head and primate of that faction), wickedly abusing this text of holy Scripture to serve his rebellious intent, "It is necessary to obey God rather than men" [Acts 5:29], the pope and his purse being his best beloved gods;[45] how much better and more bishoplike might he have remembered, "Render to Caesar the things which are Caesar's and to God that which is God's" [Mt. 22:21].

That holy Saint Hugh, sometime Bishop of Lincoln, related amongst

43. [ED.] Foxe, *A. & M.,* II, 145f, 205f, 327f; III, 215f; IV, 589f.
44. [ED.] Cited, it seems, from Foxe, *A. & M.,* II, 368f, 432f, quoting Matthew Paris, not Polydore Virgil.
45. [ED.] Foxe, *A. & M.,* II, 580f.

the Romish gods, puffed up with the like arrogancy in the time of the several reigns of King Henry II and Richard I and of King John, denied the payment of tribute and subsidy, blustering and puffing out moreover, like Cacus [46] in his den, his smoky blasts of curse and excommunication against the king's collectors.[47] A notable example of humility and obedience in a pope-holy bishop.

It is said also by Master Frowick, Anno 10 Hen. VII, that the clergy had a constitution that no priest should be impleaded by the common law of this realm for any cause whatsoever.[48] Whether he said truly therein, let the canonists judge. But certain I am the whole rabble of that Romish clergy did from time to time their best endeavor to make themselves lawless altogether, as by the grievances exhibited by the princes of Germany at the Council of Nuremberg in the time of the Emperor Charles V, may well appear.[49] And this our haughty Hugh of Lincoln, either emboldened by such a canon or of his own free courage as a lusty champion of that irregular confederacy, drew out his wooden dagger of excommunication against the kings, judges and magistrates, secluding them as far as his folly might from the fellowship and company of Christians because they had by course of law imposed a fine upon a proselyte of theirs, newly crept into their unholy orders, for his trespass committed in the king's forests.[50]

So likewise the reverend judge Master Fitzherbert declared that in the time of King Henry VI a bishop of Winchester, being outlawed for no less fault than willful murder and his temporalities therefore seized into the king's hands, refused the judgment of law and sued to the court of Rome, the pope writing to the king in his behalf. Answer was made that the laws of this realm were such, whereupon as vanquished and driven from his shifts, the bishop submitted himself to the grace of the king (and though unworthy) obtained pardon.[51] We heard also in the second year of King Henry IV how the pope's publication, or collector, took upon him by usurpation of authority to take both oath and obligation of a certain vicar, to hold himself contented with such endowment as the collector had appointed, the parsonage being appropriate to the deanery of

---

46. [ED.] Son of Vulcan, brigand living in a cave, slain by Hercules.
47. [ED.] See D.N.B., "Hugh, 1246?-55," X, 169f.
48. 10 Hen. 7. [ED.] Y.B. (S.T.C., 9922), Hilary, fol. xvii.
49. [ED.] Foxe, A. & M., IV, 307–14.
50. [ED.] See note 47, above.
51. 27 Hen. 8. [ED.] Y.B. (S.T.C., 9963), fol. xiiii recto, reporting on case of Bishop of Winchester, temp. Hen. 6.

Windsor, and how the dean drew the vicar into plea before this new-found judge the collector, for the breach both of his oath and bond. Upon which wrong done to the royal jurisdiction, the vicar complaining, had a prohibition.[52] In which case are principally to be noted the unlawful imposing of an oath by one that was no magistrate (but *quid domini facient audent cum talia fures* [what are masters like to do, if their knaves are so bold? [53]]) and the injurious prosecuting and drawing into plea of the king's subject before an incompetent judge by this dean, a clergyman of the realm.

In like sort the Hospitallers and Templars, assuming to themselves jurisdiction in prejudice of the king and of his crown, drew the subjects of this realm into suit before the conservators of their privileges for causes pertaining to the jurisdiction of the king's courts, for reformation whereof the Statute of Westminster the 2, cap. 43,[54] was ordained.

How rigorous, injurious and intolerable the dealings *ex officio* by those prelates and Ordinaries were (whereof these examinations by extorted oath were a principal part), the grievous complaint of the whole communalty of this realm in the twenty-third year of the reign of King Henry VIII doth sufficiently declare.[55] Whereby the king was informed how these merciless Ordinaries by their extraordinary and lawless power, cited and summoned his subjects, feigned and framed strange accusations against them, no accusers appearing, examined them upon articles captiously devised for their purpose, and in the end admitting no defense and disallowing all purgation, forced them to abjure, or condemned them to the fire, a most fearful and barbarous course of inquisition. Unto which complaint those pharisaical clergymen (who will not enter Pilate's common hall lest they should be defiled, and yet cry out with loud voice "Crucify, crucify,") made (as to the king himself there it seemed) a very weak and slender defense.[56] And no marvel, since wickedness may more easily be committed than well defended.

But will you see more fully and clearly, behold as in a glass the manifold usurpations, encroachments, injuries and oppressions committed and done from time to time by the pope, prince of that cursing and accursed

52. 2 Hen. 4. [ED.] Brook (*S.T.C.*, 3828), Part II, fol. 50, no. 20.
53. [ED.] Vergil, *Eclogues*, 3:16 (English translation by H. R. Fairclough, Loeb Classics, 1953).
54. [ED.] 13 Edw. 1, cap. 43.
55. [ED.] "Petition of the Commons": see H. Gee and W. J. Hardy, *Documents Illustrative of English Church History* (London, 1910), 145–53.
56. [ED.] "The answer of the Ordinaries": see Gee & Hardy, 154–76.

clergy, and by his sworn and devoted baalamites and shavelings, against the rights and prerogatives of this imperial crown, the laws of this monarchy, and the liberties of the subjects thereof, then read and consider the grievances of the Commons exhibited against the clergy Anno 21 Hen. VIII,[57] the several statutes of Provision and *Praemunire*, the statutes of Mortmain, with the divers kinds of prohibitions to the courts and consistories ecclesiastical. Among which you may find an especial prohibition with an attachment thereupon devised against these injurious oaths and examinations, as against abuses greatly offensive to the crown and dignity royal. Which the better shall appear by the writs themselves, which are in this form set down in the Register, "*Rex vicecomiti salutem. Praecipimus tibi quod non permittas quod aliqui laici ad citationem talis episcopi, aliquo loco conveniant de caetero ad aliquas recognitiones faciendas, vel sacramentum praestandum, nisi in casibus matrimonialibus & testamentariis, teste, etc.* [The King to the Sheriff, Greetings. We command that henceforth you not permit that any lay persons appear in any place at the citation of such and such a bishop to answer upon examination, or to take an oath, except in causes matrimonial and testamentary, witness, etc.]."[58] And the Attachment is in this manner: "*Rex vic., salutem. Pone per vados, [vadium] etc. talem episcopum quod sit coram Justiciariis nostris, etc. ostensurus, quare fecit summoneri, et per censuras ecclesiasticas distringi laicos personas, vel laicos homines & foeminas, ad comparendum coram eo, ad praestandum juramentum pro voluntate sua ipsis invitis, in grave praejudicium coronae et dignitatis nostrae regiae, necnon contra consuetudinem regni nostra, etc.* [The King to the Sheriff, Greetings. Take bond of such and such a bishop that he show before our judges why he has summoned, and by ecclesiastical censures constrained lay people, either lay men or lay women, to appear before him merely by his own will, and against their wills to take an oath, in grave prejudice to the crown and the dignity of our regality, as well as contrary to the custom of our kingdom]."[59]

By the consideration of which writs, and especially of these words "*recognitiones et sacramentum pro voluntate sua* [examinations and oaths at their own will]" and "*ipsis invitis* [themselves unwilling]," we may plainly perceive how all these inquiries, examinations and sifting out of matters by oath and by way of inquisition in the courts ecclesiastical are

---

57. [ED.] See note 55, above.
58. [ED.] *Registrum omnium brevium* . . . (S.T.C., 20838), fol. 36 verso.
59. [ED.] *Registrum* (S.T.C., 20838), fol. 36 verso.

by the regal authority impugned, and that as prejudicial to the crown and dignity royal and the laws and customs of this realm [60] — these words *"pro voluntate sua"* expressly denoting unto us the usurped officious power and licentious pleasure, whereby contrary to all due course of justice they constrain an oath. And these words *ipsis invitis* manifestly painting out the rigorous, injurious and compulsory exacting of the same. Moreover, we see it declared by the Statute of Marlebridge, cap. 23, that no man may compel any freeholder of this realm to swear against his will, without the king's precept or commandment,[61] that is, according to the law and justice of this realm; for so are we taught to understand the same by the book of Anno 2 Rich. III [62] whereby it is evident that unless these Ordinaries could prove their forcing of oaths *ex officio* to be warranted by authority of the laws and justice of this land (as in truth they cannot), all their dealings in such cases are by the same laws utterly disallowed and condemned.

But here (methinks) some reckless or inconsiderate reader steppeth forth and saith, "What is your meaning, to circumscribe and include all authority of ministering oaths in the courts ecclesiastical within the strait limits and bounds of causes testamentary and matrimonial? How then shall all other matter subject to their jurisdiction (being in number many and in nature divers) receive due examination?" For answer thereunto this shortly may suffice, that the state of the question which at this present we have in hand, is not in what cases those courts may give or impose an oath. But the matter whereof we now entreat is concerning forced and constrained oaths *ex officio,* and especially in that general manner before remembered.

And as touching the trial of causes by examination of witnesses judicially depending between party and party in the ecclesiastical courts, it standeth firm and for sound law, according to the said prohibition; and the opinion of Master Justice Fitzherbert (in his book of *Justice of Peace*) is that those judges ecclesiastical have no lawful power or authority to force or constrain, by censures of the church or otherwise, any subject of this realm against his will to testify upon his oath, other than in the foresaid causes of marriage and testaments; although coming before

60. Hind's case and 18 R. Eliz. proveth no less. [ED.] "Hind's case," known only from margin of Dyer (*S.T.C.,* 7388), fol. 175 verso; "18 Eliz.," (?) case on usury in Dyer, fol. 346 verso.

61. [ED.] 52 Hen. 3, cap. 22.

62. 2 Rich. 3. [ED.] Y.B. (*S.T.C.,* 9911), Mich. nos. 1, 8, 9, 10, 24, 45, 47, 51, all involved this issue, especially the last three.

them, as produced by the parties in the suit, they may lawfully (as unto men voluntarily accepting the same) minister an oath; otherwise it is plain extortion and wrong unto the party.[63] And admit they would deny to depose, what prejudice were that to the court Christian, but rather a failing in proof in the party suing? And in this state and sort standeth the proof of causes by witnesses at the common law. Nevertheless, since the statute made against willful perjury, the witness served with process and having his charges tendered, making default incurreth a pain pecuniary.

And why should the clergy and judges ecclesiastical think it much to be ruled and restrained concerning their jurisdiction by the king's prerogative and the common laws of this realm, since what jurisdiction or authority soever they have or enjoy (matters of the divine law excepted) yea, even in those especial causes of testaments, marriages, divorces and tithes, is no otherwise theirs than by the goodness of the princes of this realm and by the laws and customs of the same, as the statute of Anno 24 Hen. VIII, cap. 12 [64] well declareth, and may be taken from them and restored to the temporal judges (especially the abuses of the clergy well deserving it) at the will and pleasure of the prince and people.

But to return again to our prohibition and attachment, it is evident thereby that all the summons and citations which those ecclesiastical judges send forth under these general terms *"propter salute animarum* [for the good of souls]" or *"ex officio mero* [merely by virtue of office]," and all their arrests, distresses, impeachments, excommunications and imprisonments thereupon ensuing, are altogether injurious both to the prince and people. And of this opinion seemeth to be that learned Judge Master Fitzherbert, who in his book *De natura brevium,* saith upon these writs in this manner: "By this appeareth, that these general citations which bishops make to cite men to appear before them *pro salute animae* [for the good of a soul], without expressing any cause especial, are against the law.[65] And true it is, for by the statute of Magna Charta (containing many excellent laws of the liberties and free customs of this kingdom) it is ordained that no free man be apprehended, imprisoned, distrained or impeached, but by the law of the land.[66] And by the statute made Anno 5 Edw. III, cap. 9, it is enacted that no man shall be attached upon any accusation contrary to the form of the great Charter [Magna Charta] and

---

63. Fitzherbert. [ED.] *La novel natura brevium* (S.T.C., 10963), fol. 41A.

64. [ED.] Restraint of appeals.   65. [ED.] See note 63, above.

66. [ED.] *Statutes of the Realm,* edited by A. Luders *et al.* (London, 1810–28), I, "Magna Charta," 11, line 24.

the law of the realm.[67] Moreover it is accorded by Parliament, Anno 43 Edw. III, cap. 9, for the good government of the communalty, that no man be put to answer without presentment before justices, or matter of record, or by due process, or by writ original, after the ancient law of this land.[68] And how then shall that kind of proceeding *ex officio* by forced oaths, and the urging of this general oath and strait imprisoning of such as refuse to swear, be justifiable?

If these things were not, yet a man would have thought that at least the sharp and severe statutes of Provision and *Praemunire*, so offensive to popish Polydore [Virgil] and such like should have stayed and stopped the violent course of those injurious inquisitions, examinations, and wrested oaths *ex officio*. For, no doubt, the Ordinaries and clergymen practicing the same are all offenders, and do incur the forfeitures of those penal laws. For proof whereof, let us consider the words of the statute of *Praemunire*, made Anno 16 Rich. II, cap. 5, and the judgments and expositions thereupon had. That statute (reciting first the grievous complaint of the whole realm against the pope of Rome, who impeached many patrons in the presentations to their ecclesiastical benefices, excommunicated the bishops of this realm for executing the king's writs *de clerico admittendo*,[69] sought to translate some of them against their and the king's will, and divers other inconveniences in derogation of the king's crown and regality) provideth remedy for those and suchlike mischiefs in this manner: That if any purchase, or pursue, or do to be purchased or pursued in the court of Rome, or elsewhere, any such translations, process and sentences of excommunications, bulls, instruments or any other things which touch the king, against him, his crown and his regality, or his realm, or them receive, or make thereof notification, or any other execution within the same realm or without, that they, their notaries, procurators, maintainers, abetters, favorers and counsellors shall be put out of the king's protection, and their lands and tenements, goods and chattels forfeit to the king, etc.

Since the making of which statute, it hath been held and adjudged for clear law in the king's courts, that if any subject of the king's sue or implead another in any ecclesiastical court of this realm, for any cause or matter appertaining to the examination and judgment of the courts of the common law, or any judge ecclesiastical presume to hold plea thereof, or

---

67. [ED.] I.e., "due process."   68. [ED.] Almost a direct quotation of the law.
69. [ED.] Writ to the bishop for admitting a cleric whose title to his benefice has been cleared.

deal in any causes not belonging to his jurisdiction, that they incur the danger and penalty of *Praemunire*, as by the book of 5 Edw. IV, fol. 6,[70] and by the opinion of the court Anno 11 Hen. VII, remembered by Master Fitzherbert,[71] plainly doth appear. According also thereunto is the case of Master Barlow, late Bishop of Bath, reported by Master Justice Brooke,[72] which bishop, in the time of King Edward VI, depriving the dean of Welles whose deanery was a donative, passing therein beyond the limits of his jurisdiction, fell into the danger of *Praemunire*, and being called into question and having no just defense, was fain to appeal to the king's mercy, and obtained a pardon. And that book of 5 Edw. IV [73] before remembered, setteth down the reason, noting these words of this statute "*in curia Romana vel alibi* [in the court of Rome or elsewhere]," in which words "*alibi*," saith that book, is intended the courts of bishops. So that if a man be excommunicate in any of their courts for a thing which appertaineth to the royal majesty, that is to say (saith that book) in a matter of the common law, the party excommunicate shall have a *Praemunire facias*,[74] and so was it adjudged.

In which words among other, is especially to be noted that whensoever a wrong or injury is offered to the common law of this land, there the king is said to be touched, and his royal majesty impeached. For according to the princely speech of that most noble King Edward III, in the Statute of Provision made in the thirty-eighth year of his reign, the king's regality chiefly consisteth in this, "To sustain his people in peace and tranquillity, and to govern them according to the laws, usages and franchises of this land, whereunto he is bound by his sacred oath made at his coronation." [75] If then by usurping cognizance of plea [i.e., jurisdiction] in causes concerning the common law and the jurisdiction of the king's courts, the ecclesiastical judges touch the king in *capite* [i.e., in his regality], do against him, his crown, regality and realm, and so consequently incur the forfeiture and penalties of *Praemunire*. How much more do they touch the king, nay rather lay violent hands on him, and impugn his royal throne and scepter, who contrary to the policy, justice, laws, customs and freedoms of this kingdom, yea the law of God itself,

---

70. 5 Edw. 4, fol. 6. [ED.] Fitzherbert (*S.T.C.*, 10956), Part II, fol. 17a, no. 5.
71. 11 Hen. 7, Fitzherbert. [ED.] Subsidiary to note 70, above.
72. Brooke. [ED.] See note 70, above.   73. [ED.] See note 70, above.
74. *Praemunire facias*. [ED.] A warning, and demand for rectification, that a matter has been taken into ecclesiastical court in violation of the king's law which defines that matter as triable only in the king's (civil) courts.
75. [ED.] 38 Edw. 3, cap. 1.

enforce and constrain by censure of excommunication and otherwise, the king's people to appear before them, and extort from them an oath to accuse themselves.

And for more plain demonstration (if plainer may be) put the case that a judge, justice or commissioner, authorized by the king to execute justice according to the laws of this realm, should take upon him by color of his office and authority to convent the king's people before him, and upon their appearance to offer unto them this general oath to answer unto all such questions as himself should propound, playing in causes criminal the part both of accuser and judge, or seeking by oath and captious interrogatories matter of accusation whereupon to proceed to condemnation, and to commit the party refusing such oath to strait prison without bail or mainprize, could any man justify this his doing to stand with law or justice? Nay rather, might not every man justly cry out against him, as against a subverter of law and judgment and a hateful enemy to our policy and commonwealth? Yea should not that be verified of him which is recorded in the judgment against Sir William Thorp, sometime chief justice of England, for his corrupt dealing, which is, that as much as in him lay, he had broken the oath which the king is bound to keep towards his people?[76] If all this may truly be affirmed of such a one, how then shall the ecclesiastical judges, practicing in their courts and tribunal seats the self-same unjust and unlawful manner of proceeding against the king's people, escape the severe sentence of law, pronouncing them offensive touchers, and violators of the king, and injurious dealers against his regality, crown and kingdom, and so consequently worthy to suffer the pains and penalties declared in this statute of *Praemunire?*

That this is no new opinion or construction, we find the resolution of that learned man Saint German, in his book of *Doctor and Student* well agreeing, where he writeth in this manner: "If any man be excommunicate in the spiritual court for debt, trespass or such other thing as belongeth to the king's crown and to his royal dignity, there he ought to be assoiled [i.e., absolved] without making any satisfaction, [. . .] for they not only offended the party, in calling him to answer before them of such things as belong to the law of the realm, but also the king, who by reason of such suits, loseth a great advantage, which he might have of the writs, originals, judicials, fines, amerciamentes and such other things [. . .] if the suits had been in his courts according to his laws." He showeth further that if the ecclesiastical judges will not make the party his letters of abso-

76. [ED.] See *D.N.B.*, XIX, 804, "William Thorpe, *fl.* 1350."

lution where he ought, the party shall have his action against him. He affirmeth also, "the law to be according where a man is accursed" (he meaneth excommunicate) "for a thing that the judge had no power to accurse him in, notwithstanding that he may have his suit of *Praemunire facias*." [77]

Again we read how the late Cardinal Wolsey, the pope's legate here in England, erected a new court or consistory called "The Court of the Legate," in which he took upon him to prove testaments, and to hear and determine causes in prejudice of the jurisdiction ecclesiastical of this realm. And how by his usurped power legative, he gave and bestowed benefices by prevention, to the disinheritance of the king's subjects, and visiting the state ecclesiastical under color of reformation, gained to himself exceeding great treasure.[78] But this lofty height of unlawful authority, weak and feeble in foundation, could not long continue. For in the one and twentieth year of the reign of King Henry VIII, this proud priest with all his glorious pomp and glittering show of all his crosses, silver pillars, gilt axes, embroidered cloakbags and purple hats, was attainted by his own confession in a *Praemunire*. And the next year following, all the lords spiritual, having deserved the same pains and punishments for their unjust maintenance and supportation, were called to answer in the King's Bench, and knowing themselves guilty, before their day of appearance, exhibited to the king their humble submission, joining thereunto an offer of a 100,000 pounds to purchase their peace, which after much suit, the king accepted, and by Parliament gave them a pardon.[79]

If then this Romish legate, for assuming to himself jurisdiction by authority papal, in prejudice not of the king's courts, but of the courts ecclesiastical (nevertheless to the hurt of the royal majesty), and for disturbance of the rights and inheritance of the king's subjects, fell into the danger and penalty of *Praemunire*, and all the bishops and Ordinaries of this realm likewise, through their maintaining only and supporting the same — may we not safely conclude that the bishops and Ordinaries in these days, usurping power and jurisdiction in like sort and manner (although not in the same particulars), by color of antichristian decrees, or practicing those popish canons, the very head of that hellish Cerberus of

---

77. St. German, *Doctor and Student*. [ED.] Fol. 118 recto.

78. [ED.] Foxe, *A. & M.*, IV, 589.

79. [ED.] See the first "Submission of the clergy," March 22, 1531, in D. Wilkins, *Concilia Magnae Britaniae et Hiberniae* (London, 1737), III, 742–4; also Jeremy Collier, *Ecclesiastical History of Great Britain*, edited by T. Lathbury (London, 1852), IX, 94–7.

Rome (as a learned man well termed them), and the sinews of his tyrannical authority, repugnant to the royal majesty and policy of this realm, that is to say, forcing unjustly the people of this land to such unlawful oaths and examinations as are before remembered (injuriously touching thereby the prince in her regality, and her people in their lawful liberty whereunto they are inheritable, matters of more weight and moment than the hindrance of the bishop's jurisdiction or loss of a presentment to a benefice) — do incur the penalties and forfeitures limited by the foresaid statute of *Praemunire?*

If any man nevertheless urge and contend that these things are justifiable by force of the pope's testament (the canon and pontifical law I mean) of long time practiced and continually used within this realm, giving a new probate and allowance thereto (after so public and just condemnation and firing [i.e., burning] of them by that famous clerk and doctor of the church, Martin Luther, and by the great number of godly and learned men his associates, as laws and ordinances contumelious against God, injurious to magistrates, and especially established to maintain antichristian tyranny),[80] let him know that this kingdom is not bound or subject to any foreign made laws or constitutions not suffered by the king, and voluntarily accepted and of long time used by his people, as it is well declared by the said statute of Anno 25 Hen. VIII, cap. 19, whose words are these: "For where this your Grace's realm, recognizing no superior under God but only your Grace, hath been and is free from subjection to any man's laws, but only to such as have been devised, made and ordained within this realm for the wealth of the same, or to such other as by sufferance of your grace and your progenitors, the people of this your realm have taken at their free liberty, by their own consent, to be used among them, and have bound themselves by long use and custom to the observance of the same, not as to the observance of the laws of any foreign prince, potentate or prelate, but as to the accustomed and ancient laws of this realm, originally established as laws of the same, by the said sufferance, consents and custom, and not otherwise, etc." [81]

So to prove any foreign made law allowable within this realm, there must concur toleration by the king, voluntary acceptance of his people, and a long and a large time of usage, none of which can be averred in

---

80. Sleidanus. [ED.] Joannes Philippson, *A famouse cronicle of our time* (London, 1560; *S.T.C.,* 19848), fol. xxvii recto.

81. [ED.] The definitive "Submission of the clergy," May 16, 1532; see Gee & Hardy, *Documents,* 195–200.

these manner of oaths and examinations. For first it may not be said that the king suffereth that which he expressly forbiddeth by his writs and process as offensive to his crown and regality. Neither can his people be said to have given voluntary consent thereto, having always repined and often complained and cried out against it as a thing intolerable and injurious to their lawful liberty. The custom pretended, being ever impugned (and that justly), can create no lawful prescription, nor stand for an ancient law of this realm, but being against both law and reason, it is nothing else but an inveterate error or disorder.

If defense be sought by any canon or constitution (these oaths being so apparently against this our state, commonwealth and government), I see not how any Ordinary, but to his reproach, may once open his mouth therein, considering that in the Parliament held Anno 25 Hen. VIII, the whole clergy of England not only for them then living, but for their successors also, submitting themselves to the king's majesty, promised *in verbo sacerdotii* [82] if that be ought worth, that they would never from thenceforth presume to attempt, allege, claim or put in use, or enact, promulgate or execute any new canons, constitutions, ordinances provincial or other, or by whatsoever name they should be called in their convocation, without the king's most royal assent or license. And considering also that in the same Parliament, by their full consent, it is enacted and provided that no canons, constitutions or ordinances should be made or put in execution within this realm by the authority of the convocation of the clergy, which should be contrariant or repugnant to the king's prerogative royal, or the customs, laws or statutes of this realm, nor to the damage or hurt of the king's prerogative royal, should still be used and executed until, etc. [83]

But [84] notwithstanding [A] all those provident and politic laws and statutes thus for the good of the commonwealth wisely established in the great assembly of the realm, and notwithstanding [B] also those solemn promises and protestations made as aforesaid, and although [C] in the twelfth year of the reign of King Henry III, there was a most severe sentence of curse and anathematization denounced in the presence of the king and the nobles of this kingdom by Boniface, then Archbishop of Canterbury, and many other bishops, apparelled in their pontifical

82. [ED.] Speaking in their capacity as priests rather than merely as subjects.
83. [ED.] See note 81, above.
84. [ED.] A very involved sentence. Read: "Despite A, B and C, which make "against all such as hereafter. . . ," ". . . yet the unbridled clergymen . . ."

[regalia],[85] against all such as thereafter should willingly and maliciously, by any craft or engine, violate, infringe, diminish or change secretly or publicly by deed, word or counsel, any of the free customs of this kingdom, and especially those contained in the said great Charter [i.e., Magna Charta]; yet the unbridled clergymen in the papistical time, nothing regarding the good estate of this our policy, neither yet terrified by their own cursing censures and execrations, nor by the severe laws of *Praemunire*, most impudently (to satisfy their own licentious and lordly lusts) have from time to time cited and summoned by their lawless process, and arrested and attached by their malapert apparitors, messengers and pursuivants, the free people of this realm, by violence drawing them not only into their public courts and consistories, but privately also into secret corners and privy chambers, forcing them there with rough and rigorous terms of disgrace and reproach, upon every bare surmise and uncertain rumor, to take a corporal oath to be examined upon articles captious and deceitful, seeking thereby most uncharitably for matters of accusation. Against whom if any man durst (standing upon terms of his lawful liberty) but a little repine and refuse to swear, straightway he must be committed to prison, without bail or mainprize, there to abide pain *forte et dure* [i.e., severe and hard] depriving men of that which is more precious than life itself, and as it is said in the civil law, a jewel inestimable, liberty I mean, more to be favored than anything, as the same law speaketh, tyrannizing in such cruel manner over the poor and miserable people, in their vile and filthy coalhouses, murdering towers and turrets, and in their dark and deadly dungeons, as no tongue or pen is sufficient to express.

And whereas the prisons of this realm were ordained either for the punishment of such as are by due course of law condemned, or for restraint of persons suspected, not bailable for a time convenient of examination and judicial proceeding, those merciless magistrates void of all pity and compassion, after their sudden and raging commitments, for the most part proceeded not to full examination and sentence but after long and miserable imprisonment, insomuch as it was thought a great favor if after one year's grievous and strait imprisonment, the poor distressed party were called forth to answer. At the time of which sitting in their tribunal seat (how gloriously soever they paint out their sentences, to have God and justice in their sight) these men, or rather monsters, coveting more the destruction of mankind than any amendment or reformation of manners, fed with delight their fierce and cruel minds with the pitiful sight of

85. [ED.] Foxe, *A. & M.*, II, 424f.

pined, sickly and wretched creatures, they themselves in the meantime being fat and well fed. And although the heathen emperors Claudius, Caligula, etc. who took delight to be present at the bloody tortures and executions of their subjects, and to hear their pitiful groans and grievous sighs (commanding the executioners so to strike as the condemned might feel himself to die) [86] may worthily be termed fierce, cruel and barbarous according to that saying: "He is a savage who delights in punishment," [87] yet the extreme cruelty of those men which termed themselves Catholics, and would be accounted true Christians, was more horrible and detestable a great deal. Insomuch as they, by lingering torments of long and painful imprisonment, exceeded the leisure used by the other in the time of execution, taking from Death his due title of "king of terrors," and making him a welcome friend that ends so many miseries. Add hereunto that the tyranny of those heathen men [Claudius and Caligula], as fully satisfied, ceased with the life of the tormented; but the cruelty and fury of those Catholics, as never wearied, condemned and put to fire the dead bodies of those whom they before most treacherously had slain and murdered.

But as these good pastors, or rather devouring wolves, were in this inexcusable manner most cruel against Christ's dear servants, so again in some other things they were as vain and ridiculous. For in this matter of an oath, they have devised (according to their toying fantasy) a certain foolish figurative ceremony in the ministering thereof. For the deponent forsooth, must lay his three middle fingers stretched outright upon the book, in signification of the holy Trinity and Catholic faith, and his thumb and little finger he must put downwards under the book, in token of damnation both of body and soul if he say not the truth: the thumb belike, as the greater, representing the heavy mass of the body, and the little finger, the light and incorporeal substance of the soul. How superstitious also they were concerning this ceremony of the book (little regarding the true use and end of an oath) as appeareth by the allegorical exposition curiously set forth by one of their parsonate and counterfeit prelates, who saith that the circumstances in the act of an oath are very great and weighty, inasmuch as he that sweareth by a book doeth three things. First, as though he should say, "Let that which is written in the book never do me good, neither the new nor the old law, if I lie in this mine oath." Secondly, he putteth his hand upon the book, as though he

---

86. [ED.] Foxe, *A. & M.*, I, 90.

87. [ED.] Claudius Claudianus, "On the consulship of Manlius," *Carmina*, XVII, 224 (English translation by M. Platnauer, Loeb Classics, 1922).

should say: "Nor the good work[s] which I have done profit me aught before the face of Christ, except I say the truth which is founded in Christ." Thirdly, he kisseth the book, as though he should say, "Let never the prayers and petitions which by my mouth I have uttered avail me anything to my soul's health, if I say not truly in this mine oath." Yet you must take this, I suppose, as meant only by this reverend father, where lay men, or the baser sort of the clergy, take an oath. For that blessed Bonner not long since hath taught, as this trick of their law, as he termed it, that a bishop may swear (such is his privilege) "bare sight of the book without touch or kiss," will well enough serve his Lordship's turn.[88] Again, the imposing of oaths upon the rotten bones, rags and relics of their canonized and counterfeit saints, and upon the image of the crucifix, is both foolish and idolatrous.

But to conclude, leaving these unjust and lawless men with their bad practices and fond inventions, I doubt not, by these few yet effectual proofs and authorities it doth manifestly appear unto all men of upright and sound judgment, that as well the imposing as the taking of these general oaths is a profane abusing of the holy name of God. That the exacting of oaths *ex officio*, is a great indignity to the crown and scepter of this kingdom, and a wrong and injury to the freedom and liberty of the subjects thereof. That the same is not necessary or profitable to the church and commonwealth, but hurtful to them both, brought in only by the practice of the popish clergy, to the prejudice of the public peace and tranquillity of this realm, and that the same never had any good allowance by any law, custom, ordinance or statute of this kingdom, neither yet put in ure [i.e., practice] or use by any civil magistrate of this land, but as it corruptly crept in among many other abuses, by the sinister practice and pretences of the Romish prelates and clergymen, so this their unlawful dealing hath been from time to time by lawful and just authority impugned and restrained.

FINIS

88. [ED.] Not found.

Selected Bibliography

From the very large literature on Puritanism the following titles have been selected to provide a base for further study. Most of these works themselves include bibliographies and comments on the literature.

A. BIBLIOGRAPHIES

A Short-Title Catalogue of Books Printed in England, Scotland, and Ireland, and of English Books Printed Abroad, 1475–1640, edited by Alfred W. Pollard, Gilbert R. Redgrave *et al.* (London, 1926). Abbreviated as *S.T.C.* Reprinted several times. A revised edition is now in preparation. This work lists 26,143 items by author and abbreviated title, and provides some aid in locating copies. Since its publication great changes have occurred in library resources and aids. The Folger Library in Washington, D.C., now owns about three-fourths of the items in the *S.T.C.* The Huntington Library in San Marino, California, has a large collection also. Most university libraries today have sets of microfilm copies issued by University Microfilms Inc., which reproduce nearly all the items in the *S.T.C.* From these films, Xerox copy-flow reproductions are also available. Almost every surviving publication of any Elizabethan Puritan, together with a very complete coverage of the printed literature of his times, is thus made readily available for the student.

READ, CONYERS, ed. *Bibliography of British History: Tudor Period, 1485–1603* (Oxford, 2nd ed., 1959). The standard work of its kind. Very comprehensive, critical, and well classified; lists works published through 1956.

LEVINE, MORTIMER, ed. *Tudor England, 1485–1603* (Cambridge, 1968; Bibliographical Handbooks of the Conference on British Studies). More recent than the work listed above, but much briefer. Very usable.

WALCOTT, ROBERT. *The Tudor-Stuart Period of English History (1485–1714): A Review of Changing Interpretations* (New York, 1964; Service Center for Teachers of History, No. 58).

ZAGORIN, PEREZ. "English History, 1558–1640: A Bibliographical Survey," in Elizabeth C. Furber, ed., *Changing Views on British History: Essays on Historical Writing since 1939* (Cambridge, Mass., 1966), 119–40.

B. THE SETTING OF THE PURITAN MOVEMENT

BINDOFF, STANLEY T. *Tudor England* (Harmondsworth, 1950).

BLACK, JOHN B. *The Reign of Elizabeth, 1558–1603* (Oxford, 2nd ed., 1959; The Oxford History of England).

DICKENS, ARTHUR G. *The English Reformation* (London, 1964).

ELTON, GEOFFREY R. *England under the Tudors* (London, 1955; reprinted with a new bibliography, 1962).

FRERE, WALTER H. *The English Church in the Reigns of Elizabeth and James I* (London, 1904; A History of the English Church, Vol. V).

HUGHES, PHILIP. *The Reformation in England* (3 vols., London, 1951–4).

HURSTFIELD, JOEL. *Elizabeth I and the Unity of England* (London, 1960).

———, ed. *The Reformation Crisis* (London, 1965).

KOCHER, PAUL H. *Science and Religion in Elizabethan England* (San Marino, 1953).

MEYER, ARNOLD O. *England and the Catholic Church under Queen Elizabeth*, translated by John R. McKee (London, 1916).

Original Letters Relative to the English Reformation, 1531–58, Chiefly from the Archives of Zurich, edited by Hastings Robinson (Cambridge, 1846–7; Parker Society).

USHER, ROLAND G. *The Reconstruction of the English Church* (2 vols., New York, 1910).

WRIGHT, LOUIS B., and VIRGINIA A. LaMAR, eds. *Life and Letters in Tudor and Stuart England* (Ithaca, N.Y., 1962).

C. GENERAL STUDIES OF PURITANISM

COLLINSON, PATRICK. *The Elizabethan Puritan Movement* (London, 1967).

HALLER, WILLIAM. *The Rise of Puritanism: or, The Way to the New Jerusalem as Set Forth in Pulpit and Press from Thomas Cartwright to John Lilburne and John Milton* (New York, 1938).

HILL, CHRISTOPHER. *Society and Puritanism in Pre-Revolutionary England* (London, 1964).

KNAPPEN, MARSHALL M. *Tudor Puritanism* (Chicago, 1939).

MARCHANT, RONALD A. *The Puritans and the Church Courts in the Diocese of York, 1560–1642* (London, 1960).

D. FURTHER READINGS ON PART ONE

A Brief Discourse of the Troubles at Frankfort, 1554–1558 A.D., edited by Edward Arber (London, 1908). Formerly attributed to William Whittingham. Thomas Wood is now believed to be the author.

BURRAGE, CHAMPLIN. *The Early English Dissenters in the Light of Recent Research (1550–1641)* (2 vols., Cambridge, 1912).

GARRETT, CHRISTINA H. *The Marian Exiles: A Study in the Origins of Elizabethan Puritanism* (Cambridge, 1938).

HALLER, WILLIAM. *Foxe's "Book of Martyrs" and the Elect Nation* (London, 1963).

HAUGAARD, WILLIAM P. *Elizabeth and the English Reformation* (Cambridge, 1969).

HUDSON, WINTHROP S. *John Ponet (1516?–1556), Advocate of Limited Monarchy* (Chicago, 1942).

HUIZINGA, JOHAN. *Erasmus and the Age of the Reformation* (New York, 1957).

KNOX, JOHN. "A Narrative of the Proceedings and Troubles of the English Congregation at Frankfort on the Main, 1554–5," in David Laing, ed., *Works of John Knox* (6 vols., Edinburgh, 1846–64), IV, 41–9.

MACCAFFREY, WALLACE. *The Shaping of the Elizabethan Regime* (Princeton, 1968).

McCONICA, JAMES K. *English Humanists and Reformation Politics under Henry VIII and Edward VI* (Oxford, 1965).

MOZLEY, JAMES F. *John Foxe and His Book* (London, 1940).

OLIN, JOHN C., ed. *Christian Humanism and the Reformation: Selected Writings* (New York, 1965).

PHILLIPS, MARGARET M. *Erasmus and the Northern Renaissance* (London, 1949).

PRIMUS, JOHN H. *The Vestments Controversy: An Historical Study of the Earliest Tensions within the Church in England in the Reigns of Edward VI and Elizabeth* (Kampen, 1960).

The Zurich Letters, Comprising the Correspondence of Several English Bishops and Others during the Early Part of the Reign of Queen Elizabeth, translated and edited by Hastings Robinson (Cambridge, 1842–5; Parker Society).

E. FURTHER READINGS ON PART TWO

GREEN, ROBERT W. *Protestantism and Capitalism: The Weber Thesis and Its Critics* (Boston, 1959).

HILL, CHRISTOPHER. *Economic Problems of the Church, from Archbishop Whitgift to the Long Parliament* (Oxford, 1956).

LEHMBERG, STANFORD E., ed., "Archbishop Grindal and the Prophesyings," *Historical Magazine of the Protestant Episcopal Church*, XXXIV (June, 1965), 87–145.

MERRILL, THOMAS F., ed. *William Perkins, 1558–1602, English Puritanist* (Nieuwkoop, 1966). Contains Perkins' "A Discourse of Conscience" and "The Whole Treatise of Cases of Conscience."

MORGAN, IRVONWY. *The Godly Preachers of the Elizabethan Church* (London, 1965).

NEALE, JOHN E. *Elizabeth I and Her Parliaments, 1559–1601* (2 vols., London, 1953–7).

——— *The Elizabethan House of Commons* (London, 1949).

PORTER, HARRY C. *Reformation and Reaction in Tudor Cambridge* (Cambridge, 1958).

SAMUELSSON, KURT. *Religion and Economic Action,* translated by E. Geoffrey French and edited by Donald C. Coleman (New York, 1961).

WRIGHT, LOUIS B. *Middle-Class Culture in Elizabethan England* (Chapel Hill, 1935).

F. FURTHER READINGS ON PART THREE

AINSLEE, J. L. *The Doctrines of Ministerial Order in the Reformed Churches of the Sixteenth and Seventeenth Centuries* (Edinburgh, 1940).

FRERE, WALTER H., and CHARLES E. DOUGLAS, eds. *Puritan Manifestoes* (London, 1954). Important documents, including *An Admonition to the Parliament.*

KNOX, SAMUEL J. *Walter Travers: Paragon of Elizabethan Puritanism* (London, 1962).

PEARSON, A. F. SCOTT. *Thomas Cartwright and Elizabethan Puritanism* (Cambridge, 1925).

PEEL, ALBERT, ed. *The Seconde Parte of a Register, Being a Calendar of Manuscripts under that Title Intended for Publication by the Puritans about 1593* . . . (2 vols., Cambridge, 1915).

SALMON, JOHN H. M. *The French Religious Wars in English Political Thought* (Oxford, 1959).

SEAVER, PAUL S. *Puritan Lectureships: The Politics of Religious Dissent, 1560–1662* (Stanford, 1970).

SYKES, NORMAN. *Old Priest and New Presbyter* (Cambridge, 1956).

—— *The Church of England and Non-episcopal Churches in the Sixteenth and Seventeenth Centuries* (London, 1948).

USHER, ROLAND G. *The Rise and Fall of the High Commission* (Oxford, 1913).

Index